AUTOCRACY AT WORK

*A Study of
the Yung-cheng Period,
1723-1735*

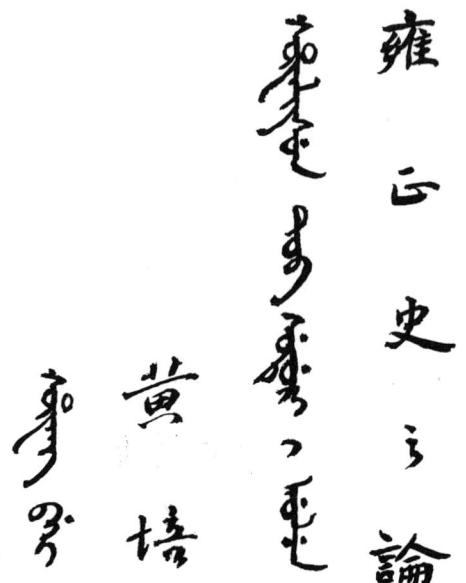

EAST ASIAN STUDIES

INDIANA UNIVERSITY

AUTOCRACY
AT WORK

A Study of

the Yung-cheng Period,

1723–1735

PEI HUANG

Indiana University Press   Bloomington & London
for the International Affairs Center

This book was brought to publication with support from Ford Foundation funds made available through the Office of Research and Advanced Studies, Indiana University.

The portraits are taken from *Ch'ing-tai ti-hou hsiang* (Portraits of Ch'ing Emperors and Imperial Consorts), compiled and published by the Palace Museum, (2nd ed., 4 vols., Peiping, 1934-1935), v. 1.

Copyright © 1974 by Indiana University Press

All Rights Reserved

No part of this book may be reproduced or utilized in any form or by any means, electronic or mechanical, including photocopying and recording, or by any information storage and retrieval system; with permission in writing from the publisher. The Association of American University Presses Resolution on Permissions constitutes the only exception to this prohibition.

Published in Canada by Fitzhenry & Whiteside Limited,
Don Mills, Ontario

Library of Congress catalog card number: 73-16678 | ISBN: 0-253-39103

Manufactured in the United States of America

Library of Congress Cataloging in Publication Data

Huang, Pei, 1928-
    Autocracy at work.

(Indiana University East Asian series)
  1. China—History—Yung-chong, 1723-1735. I. Title. II. Series: Indiana University. East Asian series. DS754.2.H78 320.9'51'03 73-16678
ISBN 0-253-39103-2

Contents

Preface ix

Part One. Introduction

I. Aspects of Autocracy in the Yung-cheng Period 3

Part Two. The Making of an Autocrat

II. The Person of the Yung-cheng Emperor 27

    1. Boyhood 27
    2. Personality 29
    3. Ideology 35

III. The Road to the Throne 51

    1. The Issue of Legitimacy 51
    2. The Struggle for Heirdom 60
    3. A Lucky Successor 75

IV. Consolidation of Power 81

    1. The Nature and Role of the Clique 81
    2. Suppression of Cliques 88
    3. Three Case Studies 94

Part Three. Machineries for Autocracy

V. The Weakening of the Censorial System 113

    1. Merging of the Censorate and the Offices of Scrutiny 113
    2. Enforcement of the Palace-Memorial System 119
    3. Political Significance of the Palace-Memorial System 130

VI. A New Instrument of Autocratic Rule—The Grand Council 136

	1. Formation of the Grand Council	136
	2. Problems Concerning the Grand Council	144
	3. Political and Cultural Role of the Grand Council	151
VII.	Bureaucratization of the Banner System	162
	1. The Banner System under the Early Ch'ing	162
	2. The Process of Bureaucratization	168
	3. Political Importance of the Bureaucratization of the Banner System	180

Part Four. Effects of Autocratic Rule

VIII.	The Literati	187
	1. Promotion of Orthodox Ideology	187
	2. Literary Inquisition	204
	3. Summary	221
IX.	The Populace of the Period	226
	1. Emancipation of the People of "Mean" Occupations	226
	2. Measures for the Welfare of the Common People	236
	3. Tax Reform	245
	4. Summary	266
X.	Non-Han Ethnic Minorities: The Miao, Yao, and Lolo Tribes	273
	1. The Tribes and Their Geographic Distribution	273
	2. The Tribal Headman System	280
	3. Bureaucratization of the Tribal Headman System	285
XI.	Conclusion	302
	Notes	309
	List of Chinese Characters	383
	Bibliography	409
	Index	493

List of Tables

1	Statistics of Trips by Princes during the K'ang-hsi Period	72
2	Statistics of Services Assigned to Princes during the K'ang-hsi Period	73
3	Procedure for Transmission of Palace Memorials	128
4	Proportion of Chinese and Manchu Grand Councillors during the Yung-cheng period	159
5	Dates for Legalization of the Meltage Fee	255
6	Percentage of the Meltage Fee before and after Its Legalization	256
7	Annual Customary Gratuities Received by Some High Provincial Officials	257
8	Extra Stipends for Officers in the Provincial Army	260
9	Starting Dates of the Merger of the Land and Labor-Service Taxes	264

Preface

Since my reasons for undertaking this study are presented in Chapter I, this Preface simply serves two purposes: an explanatory note on the special usages in this work and an expression of my appreciation to those who have helped me in different stages of the study. I have used throughout the work the Wade-Giles system of romanization for Chinese words and names except for a few long-established practices and some spellings preferred by the individuals concerned. Neither the circumflex nor the breve is used because they tend to clutter up the page. With respect to the Manchu personal names, I have followed Arthur W. Hummel's *Eminent Chinese of the Ch'ing Period (1644-1912)* and the *Hakki tsūshi retsuden sakuin* ('Index to the Biographical Sections of Pa Ch'i T'ung Chih') compiled by Kanda Nobuo, Matsumura Jun, and Okada Hidehira. Most place names follow the spelling used by the Post Office of the country, according to internationally accepted practice. I render Chinese and Japanese names in their traditional order, with the surname first and the personal name last. Ch'ing emperors except Nurhaci and Hongtaiji are generally mentioned by their reign titles, with their temple names indicated in the first citation. Whenever available, dates of birth and death are given after personal names.

In citing Chinese and Japanese sources I use the full names of the authors, in their original order, for identification. For European sources by Chinese authors, I cite authors' names according to the Western practice, with personal name first and family name last. After its first appearance a source will be cited by its shortened title—if the title is long—together with the author's full name if the material is in Chinese or Japanese and only his last name if the work is in a Western language. Many Chinese and Japanese journals provide English translations for their articles. In some cases the translated titles retain a few Chinese words for terminological clarity. I enclose the original translations in single quotation marks and keep the entire citation reference in the bibliography; but, to facilitate the typesetting, I omit the Chinese words from the notes.

Throughout this study, in citations of the *Chu-p'i yü-chih*, a voluminous collection of memorials in the Yung-cheng period, the volume number is given first, then the author of the memorial, the page number, and the date if any. For some large collections of Yung-cheng Emperor's decrees, such as the *Shang-yü ch'i-wu i-fu*, the *Shang-yü nei-ko*, the *Shang-yü pa-ch'i*, and the *Yü-hsing ch'i-wu tsou-i*, the volume number is cited first, then the page number, and finally the date. In citing the *Kung-chung tang*—the Ch'ing archives housed in the National Palace Museum, Taiwan, China—I give, in order, the author of the document, the page number, and the date, if any. Although the documents in these archives have been coded, in microfilming my material the technicians left out, with a few exceptions, the code numbers. As a result, these numbers are omitted in most of my citations. For the *Veritable Records* the period is noted first, then the chapter (*chüan* in Chinese) instead of the volume, the page, and finally the date. All dates are transpositions from the old Chinese to the Western calendar.

I also want to take this opportunity to thank those individuals whose assistance has been helpful to this study. Two scholars were of great importance to my initial interest in Ch'ing studies. The late Professor Li Tsung-t'ung of National Taiwan University introduced me to the sources of the Ch'ing dynasty and directed my M.A. thesis; Professor Wu Hsiang-hsiang, then at the same institution, inspired me to study the Yung-cheng period and frequently provided valuable suggestions. My special thanks go to Professor Robert H. Ferrell of Indiana University, a distinguished scholar and a stimulating teacher. He has never failed to help and inspire his students. Since 1959 I have greatly benefited from his advice and encouragement, which were important to the completion of this book. Dr. Ssu-yü Teng, University Professor at Indiana University, was my major adviser and directed my course work and dissertation with inspiration and great patience. He too is always eager to help and encourage his students, and it is to him that I gratefully dedicate this work.

My cordial thanks also go to Professor and Mrs. Chaoying Fang, both of the Ming Biographical Project, for some very useful suggestions. Equal appreciation should be expressed to Professor Wu-chi Liu, Director of the Indiana University East Asian Series, for his support of the publication of this book. In preparing the present study I am indebted to many scholars of social science, especially of Ch'ing history, in this country and abroad for some revealing ideas. Because it would make for tedious reading to mention each of them by name in this Preface, I acknowledge my debt by citing their names and works in the relevant notes.

Special thanks are due to the late Professor Clyde F. Lytle of Kutztown, Pennsylvania, for reading my manuscript and for his editorial help. I am very grateful to Dr. T. K. Tong, formerly of the East Asian Library, Columbia University, and his friendly staff for their cooperation; I spent several fruitful summers doing research in that library. Dr. K. C. Wu, head of the Chinese and Korean Section, Library of Congress, and Mr. P. K. Tseng of the same section generously made their facilities available to me. Professor Stanley J. Granat of Trenton State College and Mrs. Granat of the University of Pennsylvania were good enough to reproduce for me three useful Japanese articles when they were doing research in Japan. My gratitude is also due to Dr. Chiang Fu-ts'ung, Director of the National Palace Museum, Taiwan, China, and to two of his senior staff members: Professor Liu Chia-chü and Mr. Shen Ching-hung. They granted me permission to use material from the Ch'ing archives and helped microfilm it. Last but not least, my gratitude goes to my wife, Hetty, who typed the draft of the manuscript and its revised pages.

I wish to express my thanks to the following publishers for their permission to use the following copyrighted material: the Arthur Probsthain Publishing Co., London, England, for a passage quoted from the *Complete Works of Han Fei Tzu: A Classic of Chinese Legalism* (vol. 1, p.151), translated by W.K. Liao and published in 1939; the Harvard University Press, for sentences from pages 5 and 170 of *Totalitarian Dictatorship and Autocracy* by Carl J. Friedrich and Zbigniew K. Brzezinski (2nd ed.,

1965); the John Murray Publishing Co., London, England, for passages from pages 83 and 119 of *Memoirs of Father Ripa during Thirteen Years Residence at the Court of Peking* by Matteo Ripa, translated into English by Fortunato Prandi (1885 ed.); and the University of Chicago Press, for a translated passage from Ping-ti Ho, "Salient Aspects of China's Heritage" in *China in Crisis*, Vol. I, Book I: *China's Heritage and the Communist Political System* (pp.12-13), ed. by Ping-ti Ho and Tang Tsou. The three pictures of the Yung-cheng Emperor were taken from the *Ch'ing-tai ti-hou hsiang*, 2nd ed., Peiping, Palace Museum, 1934-1935.

Youngstown, Ohio   PH

PART ONE

Introduction

I

Aspects of Autocracy in the Yung-cheng Period

This work is a case study of autocracy in the Yung-cheng period (1723-1735), an unusual era in Chinese dynastic history in which autocratic rule functioned with great success and brought about prosperity and order. Such a study must explore the various aspects of the autocratic system of government—its background, basic structure, operational features, and effects on the lives of different status groups in Chinese society. This introductory chapter summarizes problems addressed in detail in subsequent chapters.

In its Greek origin, the word autocracy suggests a form of rule by absolute power. Historians and political scientists have applied it to political systems of an absolute, arbitrary, despotic, or tyrannical nature. Because the term is related to the theory and operation of the supreme power in the state, definitions of it tend to stress its legal implications. Carl J. Friedrich's statement is particularly apt:

> From this [legal] viewpoint, an autocracy is any political system in which the rulers are insufficiently, or not at all, subject to antecedent and enforceable rules of law— enforceable, that is, by other authorities who share in the government and who have sufficient power to compel the lawbreaking rulers to submit to the law.[1]

Autocracy has been a form of government throughout most of recorded history. In early Egypt the pharaohs were autocratic rulers, while in the West autocracy may be traced back to ancient Greece. In China it had successfully made headway since the formation of the imperial system in 221 B.C.; the Yung-cheng period was an important phase of its long history.

It will be easier to understand its fundamental character if Yung-cheng autocracy is examined in the light of the traditional political system of China before the Ch'ing dynasty (1644-1911). Since the very inception of the imperial system the emperor had enjoyed power without any effective checks.[2] In traditional China, the popular belief was that the emperor's power derived from the Mandate of Heaven.[3] His power was, therefore, intrinsic in such a mandate *per se*. Although he was accountable for the well-being of his subjects, he was not responsible to them. The Mandate of Heaven seems to have exercised a kind of religious check on imperial power because it related the cosmic order to human affairs. When severe natural calamities occurred, it was the practice for the emperor to reproach himself publicly, to proclaim amnesty, and to invite open criticism. Nevertheless, such acts had no effect on the basic nature of his power; he remained infallible.

Nor did Confucianism, which provided the theoretical basis of the traditional Chinese state, furnish an effective restraint to the emperor's power. Although the moral teachings of Confucianism humanized the imperial system, they also legitimated the emperor's claim to possess the Mandate of Heaven. Short of power obtained by usurpation of the throne by regicide, Confucius justified any kind of governing authority and conceded it the supreme power in the state.[4] After centuries of evolution Confucianism syncretized elements from Taoism and Legalism and became more flexible and amenable to the imperial system.

Confucianism was made an orthodoxy in the second century B.C. by a famous autocrat, Emperor Wu of the Former Han dynasty (206 B.C.-A.D. 9); it defended the imperial institutions and was protected by the state. The Confucian school and the traditional Chinese state thus became interdependent. From the decline of the imperial system at the end of the Later Han dynasty (25-220) until the rise of the Sung (960-1279), Confucianism could not contend with Buddhism and Taoism. However, the genius of Sung philosophers allowed it to reemerge under the name of Neo-Confucianism, which proved even more serviceable to the imperial system than had its predecessor. As one scholar has put it, in Neo-Confucianism the subject's loyalty, the son's filiality, and the wife's obedience became "almost one-sided moral imperatives."[5] It is not surprising that the School of Principle or Reason (*Ch'eng-Chu li-hsüeh*)—a Neo-Confucian school more rigid and formalistic than its counterpart, the School of the Mind or Intuition (*Hsin-hsüeh*)—served as the state philosophy of imperial China for nearly 600 years, from the fourteenth century onward.

The political institutions of traditional China were too weak to restrain the emperor's power. Of these institutions, the premiership (*tsai-hsiang chih-tu*) and the censorial system (*yü-shih chih-tu*) might impose checks on the emperor to some extent. At the height of his power, for instance, the premier was the policy-maker of state affairs and served almost as the "vice-emperor" on a nonhereditary basis,[6] but the institution was progressively weakened by autocratic rulers. Emperor Wu of the Former Han dynasty was the first of such rulers who weakened the premier's power through a small, informal, and controllable group known as the Inner Court, usually comprising several imperial favorites of different backgrounds and titles.[7] Later autocrats in Chinese history followed this practice or invented new means—such as fragmentation of the premier's functions—for the same purpose. Continuously weakened by the emperors, the office of premier underwent changes in function and basic structure. It practically became an imperial secretariat in the Sung dynasty and was finally abolished in 1380 by the Emperor T'ai-tsu (Chu Yüan-chang, r.1368-1398), founder of the Ming dynasty (1368-1644).

In the face of autocratic rulers the censorial system met with the same fate as the premiership. Under the chief censor (who served as the vice-premier) the censors kept an eye on palace, central, and local government activities and, during the early stages of the institution, had the right to remonstrate and impeach. The autocratic ruler meanwhile attempted to reduce the power of the censorate: his favorites intruded into its functions. The censorial apparatus was gradually taken out of palace affairs, and in the Sung period the ruler was, in fact, above its restraints or remonstrance, which was now directed solely at officials.[8] By Ming times, fearless censors and supervising secretaries (*chi-shih chung*) were frequently threatened and punished by the ruler or powerful eunuchs.[9] It is no exaggeration to say that the censorial institution now exercised no constraint over the emperor's power and virtually became a tool of imperial control over bureaucrats.

In their quest for unlimited imperial power, autocratic rulers also attempted to weaken the local administration. After the introduction of the Chinese imperial system the local administrative structure had two levels headed by the commandery (*chün*). As the highest local official, the grand administrator (*chün-shou* or *t'ai-shou*) was allowed to select various subordinates as well as take initiatives and make decisions pertaining to local administration. His salary and rank were the same as those of the Nine Ministers (*Chiu-ch'ing*) in the central government, and he was subject only to the supervision of the prime minister and to the surveillance of circuit inspectors (*tz'u-shih*) sent from the capital at intervals.[10] Consequently the grand administrator was hardly a tool of the central government. As long as he retained the initiative and decision-making powers in local affairs, he effectively limited the emperor's power in the commandery. In other words, the local administrative structure indirectly checked the imperial power.

Beginning with the reign of Emperor Wu of the Former Han, the local administrative structure had undergone a series of changes. As soon as he had weakened the premiership in the central government, he tightened his control of local administration by dividing the country into 13 circuits, each of which covered several commanderies and was supervised by a circuit inspector. These divisions originally were made for the convenience of central supervision, but in time they became superadministrative units over the commanderies; their supervising personnel—circuit inspectors—were appointed permanent administrators. The central government had to send additional personnel to watch over these new administrators whenever necessary. After lowering the administrative status of the commandery, the autocratic ruler further prohibited the grand administrator from selecting his own subordinates.[11] Nor was the administrator of the superunit allowed to appoint officials below him: instead, all local officials were appointees of the central government. By the Ming dynasty the office of grand administrator had been reduced to an inferior status in the local administrative hierarchy, which now consisted of four levels—province, circuit, prefecture, and district. The top two levels were apparently the superstructure for the purpose of central control over the local administration. The more divisions in the local administrative hierarchy, the less power held by the administration.[12] At each level the administrator was directed and supervised by his superior. As a result, no one except the emperor could make final decisions.

In the long history of the Chinese imperial system the bureaucracy failed to curb the growth of imperial power. The Confucian scholars who had gradually become dominant in central and local officialdom contributed to the molding of China's political character. Because they decried force, despised the military, and revered education and the literary arts, they laid the foundation for the civilian ideal of traditional Chinese government.[13] However, for at least three reasons the scholar-officials did not provide an effective bureaucratic check on the growth of autocracy. First, they were a group ideologically and culturally committed to Confucianism. They worked for their rulers within the confines of Confucian norms, mores, and values—which were, however, fully exploited by ingenious emperors for autocratic purposes. On occasion they raised opposition to the actions of autocratic rulers, as reflected in many remonstrances and impeachments of censors, but their protests were far from effective in constraining their imperial masters, who monopolized the means of reward and punishment to bring officials into compliance.

Secondly, the Chinese bureaucrats were incapable of making a concerted effort to check imperial power. Chiefly Confucian scholars, they were a loosely organized group of individuals from various social levels. Although a large number of them were from the gentry, they owed their official careers to their personal academic achievements. As individual officials they were not strongly motivated by any specific social sense to unite in a body to check the emperor's power in the interest of a certain class; as Confucian scholars they were ideologically oriented to work for the imperial system, which drew moral support from Confucianism. In Chinese dynastic histories there were many cases in which upright administrators defended the rights of people against the imperial will, but these were rather individual actions. At times bureaucratic factions—such as those that existed during the T'ang (618-906) and Ming periods—did weaken the imperial system, but what they struggled for had nothing to do with the nature of the emperor's ultimate power.

Lastly, in the traditional Chinese state the bureaucrats and the autocratic rulers had interests in common. Both were beneficiaries of the Confucian system. Confucianism legitimated a differentiated political and social order, in which the bureaucrats were second only to the ruler; both were far above the common people. While Confucian scholars constantly looked for opportunities to fulfill their alleged missions—country-governing and world-pacification (*chih-kuo p'ing t'ien-hsia*)—the rulers needed bureaucrats to carry out their will. Whatever their channels to officialdom, examination, purchase, or others, the bureaucrats were individuals of social and legal privileges protected by the state.[14] As long as they had common interests with the rulers, both were closely associated. Their alliance dethroned the aristocracy, suppressed the peasant revolts, and most important of all, perpetuated the emperor system. Even though in the course of their alliance there were factors that strained their relations, the rulers were always able to mobilize support from various sources to relax the tension in the imperial favor.

All in all, in the traditional Chinese state there were some potential checks to the emperor's power, but none was effective. Being unable to restrain effectively the autocratic system of government, philosophical schools, popular beliefs, political institutions, and bureaucrats proved to be the sources of imperial authority. The first two provided the autocrats with moral force; the last two pushed the autocratic system of government into actual operation, reinforced the emperor's power, and contributed to its perpetuation. Hence, autocracy was a persistent characteristic of Chinese dynastic history. Although there were periods of relaxation in its development, they were followed by eras of reassertion and intensification.

Of all the dynastic periods in Chinese history, the Former Han was perhaps the crucial formative era of China's autocracy, and the reign of Emperor Wu was its peak.[15] The early rulers of the period rescued the imperial system when it was on the brink of destruction following the collapse of the Ch'in dynasty (256-206 B.C.). Emperor Wu enlisted Confucianism for imperial service, enfeebled the premiership, subdued the aristocrats, and strengthened the supervision over the grand administrator. He set a model for his successors and later autocrats. However, during the last half century of the Former Han, the emperor's authority was partially eclipsed owing to the imperial affinals; during the later years of the Later Han and the three post-Han centuries, autocracy suffered further setbacks because of the power of eunuchs and important families who established hereditary strengths in central and local administration. Yet these failed to change the historical course of China's autocracy, which was reasserted after the empire was reunified in 589.

The Sui (581-618) and T'ang dynasties witnessed another crucial period in the development of autocracy. They added the symbolic and ritual prescriptions of two popular religions—Taoism and Buddhism—to the Han amalgam of Taoist, Legalist, and Confucian philosophies that had been in imperial service. This new combination was meant to unify diverse social groups and geographical areas, after several centuries of political chaos and disunity, in a common faith and allegiance to a ruler.[16] The same period also saw the institutionalization of the civil service examination, through which the rulers drew from South China more nonaristocratic bureaucrats to sweep away the remaining patrician influence from officialdom.[17] Without the opposition of the aristocracy, imperial authority made substantial progress. Thus, the revival of the Chinese empire in the Sui and T'ang periods was also a reassertion of autocracy.

Changes in ruling houses did not break off the working of autocracy in China. Imperial authority continued to grow during the Sung and Yüan (1279-1368) dynasties. Although the Sung was frequently threatened and finally conquered by outside contenders, it was more concerned about possible internal rivals. Combining delicate statecraft and elaborate political institutions, its founder, Chao K'uang-yin (reigned 960-976), reduced the power of the premier and the censorial system and cast aside the aristocrats, eunuchs, and regional commanders, the latter two having plagued imperial power during the late T'ang and the Five Dynasties (906-960). Free from impediments, the Sung rulers enjoyed absolute power. On the Sung ruins the Yüan dynasty added nomadic elements to the traditional Chinese state. Its rulers were notoriously autocratic, strengthening their power through the use of military control, ethnic hierarchy, corrupt lamas, feudal practice, and various brutal means.[18] Although the aristocrats confronted the rulers throughout the dynasty, their conflicts did not change the autocratic nature of Mongol rule.

The founder of the Ming dynasty, Chu Yüan-chang, may well have been the most autocratic ruler in Chinese dynastic history. When he restored the traditional Chinese state in 1368, he also remodeled its political institutions. The changes he imposed on the political system were meant to do away with potential institutional and procedural checks on imperial authority. After his abolishment of the premiership, he and his successors ran the government personally. On important matters they often consulted with high officials individually or in a group, but they retained the ultimate authority to accept, modify, reject, or reverse the advice resulting from such consultations.[19] What made Ming autocracy unprecedented in Chinese history was the unbelievable harshness of its penal code, especially as applied to bureaucrats. Because of his wrath or suspicion the founder of the dynasty flogged or executed many officials and their families. His administration was indeed a "Reign of Terror." His successors arrested and tortured officials and common people on alleged or substantiated charges through a eunuch-run secret service.[20] These ruthless measures frightened political critics even though Confucian scholar-officials fearlessly but helplessly remonstrated with the Ming rulers.

Ming emperors were noted for their sponsorship of education; but all education has a political function,[21] and in Ming schools students were inculcated with the concept of loyalty to the emperor which, according to the Neo-Confucianism of that period, "ranked more highly in the scale of obligations than had been the case in prior times."[22] From every viewpoint the Ming dynasty was the period of intensification of autocracy in Chinese history.

Autocracy had persisted in the Chinese political system since at least 221 B.C. A tradition of more than eighteen centuries could not fail to make an imprint on the Ch'ing dynasty, whose political system was largely copied from that of the Ming.

The environment in the early years of the Ch'ing dynasty laid the groundwork for the autocracy of the Yung-cheng period. As a regime of alien conquerors, the Ch'ing dynasty was born in violence, which is frequently a precursor of autocracy.[23] Many Chinese dynasties emerged from bloody intrigues, brutal struggles, or other kinds of violence; the Ch'ing was a typical example. While still a frontier power in Manchuria, it ruthlessly exploited many Chinese under its rule. After its conquest of China in 1644, the Ch'ing dynasty continued to be confronted by challenges, especially the Revolt of the Three Feudatories (*San-fan*, 1673-1681) and the anti-Manchu movement under Cheng Ch'eng-kung (1624-1662) and his successors.

In addition to challenges from Ming loyalists or pretenders, rulers of the early Ch'ing also needed more power to deal with Manchu aristocrats entrenched in the banner system, the core organization of the dynasty. Although they were the key supporters of the dynasty, the banner aristocrats nevertheless tended to encroach on the power of the throne. For example, Dorgon (1612-1650) was prince regent and actual ruler in the first seven years of the Shun-chih period (1644-1661), while Oboi (d.1669) dominated the central government during the first eight years of the K'ang-hsi period (1662-1722). Although the deaths of Dorgon and Oboi allowed the two rulers, the Shun-chih Emperor (Shih-tsu, 1638-1661) and the K'ang-hsi Emperor (Sheng-tsu, 1654-1722), to exercise more imperial authority, still other Manchu nobles had a strong voice in state affairs and contributed even more to the autocracy of the Yung-cheng period.[24] For during the second half of the K'ang-hsi period, the first, third, fourth, eighth, ninth, and fourteenth sons of the K'ang-hsi Emperor contended for the heirdom. The contest was violent with each participant rallying a following mainly from the banners. Thus, the Manchu aristocracy was seriously divided. As a result of this conflict, the fourth son became the Yung-cheng Emperor (Shih-tsung, 1678-1735). Since his former competitors refused to recognize his authority after his accession to the throne, his primary concern was to consolidate his power.

Yung-cheng was hindered in attaining this goal because of administrative laxity during the second half of the K'ang-hsi period. The transgression of Ch'ing aristocrats, the struggle between members of the imperial family, and factionalism weakened the ruler's control over his subordinates and impaired the government's efficiency. Furthermore, local administration was plagued by political corruption.[25] If autocracy is a cyclical phenomenon,[26] the latter half of the K'ang-hsi period was a time of relaxation of early Ch'ing autocracy. Because these forms of deterioration weakened not only the imperial power but also the foundation of the Ch'ing dynasty, the K'ang-hsi Emperor in his last years made unsuccessful attempts to halt them. After his succession to the throne Yung-cheng attempted to change the situation.

The personal character of the Yung-cheng Emperor undoubtedly played a decisive role in his autocratic rule. He was a dauntless, persistent, and active ruler, and, in some ways, can be identified as an unusual monarch in the Ch'ing dynasty. When he took over the throne, he was already forty-four years old, older than any other Manchu emperor at the time of accession, and also ideologically and behaviorally mature. This maturity was greatly responsible for the successful working of his autocracy. One may also compare him with the K'ang-hsi Emperor and the Ch'ien-lung Emperor (Kao-tsung, 1711-1799, reigned 1736-1795), two Manchu rulers more familiar to Western historians. The K'ang-hsi Emperor was famous for leniency, and the Ch'ien-lung Emperor was vain. Both were interested in scholarship and literary activity, which resulted in their appointment of renowned Neo-Confucian scholars and men of literary fame to key positions. To be sure, these appointments were political tactics, but to some extent they also suggested the emperors' personal taste. They and the scholar-officials influenced one another and in consequence these two rulers were Confucian-minded to a certain degree. The Yung-cheng Emperor, however, was inclined to Buddhism and Taoism, both of which were rebuffed by Confucian scholars.

His state policy showed him to be a practical-minded ruler. He laid stress on practical administration; his subordinates were men of administrative ability and docility, not of high literary accomplishments. To promote a practical manner of dealing with state affairs, he discouraged officials from the use of empty compliments and literary expressions in memorials.[27] What he pursued was administrative efficiency. For practical purposes he paid more attention to domestic politics than to military conquest. This emphasis can be seen in his policy toward the Dzungars, a Mongol tribe. When he found it necessary to defend the northwestern frontiers, he fought them only after careful preparations.

Furthermore, when he realized the difficulty of defeating his enemies completely, he agreed to a truce with them after winning a battle in 1732.[28] Clearly, he was a political realist, not a military expansionist like his successor, the Ch'ien-lung Emperor.

His political conduct showed Yung-cheng to be the most diligent and responsible of the Manchu rulers. He personally examined state papers, read memorials, wrote comments on them, and even corrected their errors. The *Chu-p'i yü-chih* (Vermilion endorsements and edicts), a selected collection of memorials submitted primarily by the provincial officials in the Yung-cheng period, may serve as an example of his labors and responsibility. His diligence and dutifulness even won the applause of his philosophical opponents. Father Contancin, for example, wrote of him from Canton in 1725: "This prince is untiring in his work; he thinks day and night to establish a sage government and work for the welfare of his subjects."[29] Under his influence officials adopted the same pattern of conduct, or tried to; consequently, the most powerful officials of the Yung-cheng period were dutiful and hard-working bureaucrats. In short, diligence and responsibility brought about administrative efficiency, an attribute of sovereign authority.

To sum up, the political heritage of the traditional Chinese state, the special problems of the Manchu dynasty, and the personal character of the Yung-cheng Emperor were conducive to autocracy. Their repercussions were evident. From the long dynastic political tradition he drew philosophical arguments and political techniques for his autocratic rule. During his reign, for instance, he emphasized political loyalty, filial piety, and chaste behavior, all being important for maintenance of imperial authority. Because these were included in the Confucian value system, it is not strange that he strenuously promoted the Neo-Confucian School of Principle, even though he was personally less Confucian-oriented than his father or his son. Since Confucianism also embraced some elements unfavorable to the imperial interest and was frequently exploited by, for example, bureaucrats for their personal purposes, he deliberately diluted it with Buddhism and Taoism and harshly punished its devout adherents.

He identified the roots of the Ch'ing perennial problems and tried to remove them. Thus, since the banner system was a feudal institution from which the Manchu aristocrats at large and members of the imperial house recruited supporters in their struggle for power, it became his first target. He forced undesirable elements out of it by whatever means he saw fit, and after painstaking work for most of his reign, he successfully changed it in his favor.

In all likelihood, Yung-cheng's personal character was the factor which made his autocratic rule a success. Ideologically and technically he did not differ substantially from preceding autocratic rulers in Chinese dynastic history, but his persistence, consistency, and energy enabled him to mobilize all traditional forces, Chinese and Manchu, and revitalize them for his cause. His success can also be examined from an institutional viewpoint.

The main institutional characteristics of Yung-cheng autocracy were embodied in two instruments, the palace-memorial system (*tsou-che chih-tu*)[30] and the Grand Council (*Chün-chi ch'u*). Although they had their bases in previous administrative practices, Yung-cheng gave them new life, charged them with important missions, and institutionalized them on a permanent basis. They enhanced his autocratic power; moreover, they became the effective tools of autocracy for the remainder of the Ch'ing dynasty.

The palace-memorial system recruited members mainly from provincial officials. Their memorials contained information about local, or sometimes state, affairs, suggestions, requests, and evaluations of other officials' personal or administrative conduct. Since palace memorials went directly to the imperial desk as confidential reports, the ruler personally read and commented on them. After imperial endorsement they were returned to their authors. From the imperial comments the reporters received instructions directly from the ruler. Through the palace memorials the monarch learned what was going on in his empire, especially about the personal and administrative aspects of officials. Local governments were thus brought under direct imperial control.

The palace-memorial system operated at the cost of the censorial system. The suggestions and expositions in the palace memorials were largely traditional functions of the censorial system, which was mainly in charge of remonstrance and impeachment. However imperfect, the censorial institution served as at least a partial check on autocracy and corrupt officials. Autocratic rulers or arbitrary bureaucrats made every effort to reduce the power of the censors. The Ch'ing censorial system, patterned after the Ming model, was composed of the Censorate (*Tu-ch'a yüan*) and the Six Offices of Scrutiny (*Liu-k'o chi-shih chung*). Its functions were broad, but it had limited power to carry them out. Besides the inherited weaknesses of the system itself, the Ch'ing censorial organs were further enfeebled by ethnic tension. Manchu rulers had no confidence in Chinese censorial officials, and more particularly, they were aware of their alien origin. Censors and supervising secretaries suffered different kinds of punishment in the Shun-chih and K'ang-hsi periods. In 1723 the Yung-cheng Emperor rendered a deadly blow to the censorial system by putting the Six Offices of Scrutiny under the administrative authority of the Censorate. Although at the beginning this change was administrative in nature, it affected the functions of both organs. Supervising secretaries, originally document inspectors, could put "a kind of editorial veto" on various state papers.[31] During the Yung-cheng period, they were not allowed to interfere with imperial decrees and palace memorials. Hence, they were no longer document inspectors. In the meantime, the censor's surveillance functions were greatly weakened by the palace-memorial system. Thus, during most of the Ch'ing period, the censorial system played a minor and passive role in state administration.

Like the palace-memorial system, the Grand Council was also a tool of autocracy. In Chinese history, rulers generally needed the services of a small, informal, and carefully selected coterie of officials. This office formally appeared at a time of military necessity in the Yung-cheng period, but it was actually a repetition of previous dynastic administrative practices and a result of the political motivations of the autocratic ruler. Grand Councillors (*Chün-chi ta-ch'en*) were men of ability, credibility, and loyalty, and were the ruler's most trusted assistants in dealing with important affairs. The Grand Council handled affairs in a highly secret and speedy manner. The office admitted no outsiders; its work allowed no surveillance or inspection from the censorial officials. Grand Councillors were constantly on the alert for imperial summons at any time. They put imperial orders in the form of court letters (*t'ing-chi*) dispatched by the postal system straight to the provincial addressees, many of whom had the privilege of presenting palace memorials directly to the throne.

This direct communication between ruler and provincial officials helped make autocratic rule effective throughout the empire.

Since its formation the Grand Council had developed into the most important tool of Ch'ing autocracy. As Grand Councillors were at the apex of the bureaucracy, the Grand Council became the highest institution in the Manchu bureaucratic structure. After the rise of the Grand Council, the Grand Secretariat (*Nei-ko*), originally the highest office of state, was reduced to an organ for routine affairs. Because Grand Councillors were always in charge of the reception and transmission of palace memorials for the ruler, they gradually acquired some authority over the palace-memorial system after the Yung-cheng period. After the establishment of the Grand Council, it also overshadowed the Office for Administrative Deliberations (*I-cheng ch'u*), the last stronghold of Manchu nobles. Grand Councillors were chosen for their personal qualifications rather than for their ethnic origin; their appointments, unlike those in other central governmental offices, were not made on the basis of numerical equality between Chinese and Manchu. This reduced the negative influence of ethnic tension that had plagued the Ch'ing administration before the Yung-cheng period. Both Chinese and Manchu officials were the obedient servants of the ruler. The Grand Council was the main tool for the realization and institutionalization of the Yung-cheng Emperor's autocratic ideas.

While the palace-memorial system and the Grand Council played an active part in Yung-cheng autocracy, the banner system played a passive role. In discussing feudalism, Max Weber saw the struggle for power between a lord and his vassals as chronic.[32] This was true of the banner system. In the early Ch'ing period, the banner system was the stronghold of the Manchu aristocrats who contended among themselves or challenged the ruler. The first two Manchu rulers had changed the banner system in many ways; Yung-cheng completed the transformation by introducing the process of bureaucratization. The banner aristocrats were prevented from having too many retainers and were prohibited from maintaining feudal practices. Concurrently, he removed many influential princes, such as his former competitors for the heirdom, as an example for others. The banner aristocrats were allowed a limited number of retainers. When the banner nobles lost their political and social sources of power, their sons had to be indoctrinated in schools founded specifically for this purpose. As a result, the emperor succeeded in putting the aristocrats under strict control.

During the Yung-cheng period the administrative structure and procedure in the banners underwent a great change. In the Shun-chih and K'ang-hsi periods the Manchu rulers wrested the banner commandership from the princes and appointed it on the basis of personal merit, but they did not change the captaincy, which was largely based on heredity. The Yung-cheng Emperor gradually and tactfully replaced many hereditary captains with people appointed on the basis of merit. Additionally, he appointed one or two new administrative staff members to each level of the banners. While these new appointees helped their unit chiefs deal with administrative work, they also checked the latter. Prior to the Yung-cheng period, the banners had followed their individual administrative procedures, a feudal vestige. Yung-cheng set uniform rules and published them as a guide to banner administration. These rules were enforced by newly appointed banner censors, who also supervised the personal conduct of banner officers. After these changes the banner system became a part of the state bureaucratic structure. Although it did not play an active role in the emperor's autocratic rule, it passively followed his will. Beginning with the Yung-cheng period, it remained in that position until the end of the Manchu regime.

The autocracy of the Yung-cheng period had an effect on every status group of the time. The upper classes felt it first. Since they suffered more restrictions than other groups under autocratic rule, they responded to it unfavorably. Thus, they regarded the Yung-cheng Emperor as a notorious autocrat. The effect of autocracy on the bannermen varied with their individual status within the banner system. While the emperor made efforts to deprive the banner aristocrats of their sources of power, he tried to improve the fighting spirit and economic life of the common bannermen. After their conquest of China, the majority of the Manchus gradually gave up their warrior virtues and sank into poverty because of corrupt life, increasing population, and insufficient incomes. The emperor encouraged them to practice archery, riding, and the Manchu language in order to maintain their warrior status. He provided more economic opportunities for the bannermen to serve the state, reduced the population pressure on them, and appealed to the time-honored well-field (*ching-t'ien*) system.[33] At the same time he rigorously prohibited their extravagant life and lawless acts.

    The Chinese literati were another group of the upper classes influenced by the autocratic rule of the Yung-cheng period. They were under tighter imperial control than during the K'ang-hsi period, for example. Although the Yung-cheng Emperor permitted more Chinese scholars to enter public service than were admitted in either the K'ang-hsi or the Ch'ien-lung period (1736-1795), he had more trust in those who obtained appointments by purchase. In the conflict between the scholar-officials and those who had purchased their offices, he was always on the side of the latter. Officials received higher pay through the system of extra stipends for cultivation of incorruptibility (*yang-lien*), but were strictly prohibited from carrying on factional activities, seizing illegal incomes, or engaging in any activities against the imperial interest. They became careful, diligent, and docile. The local gentry felt the same autocratic influence as their counterparts in officialdom. In the Shun-chih and K'ang-hsi periods they were relatively free, seeking and extending their privileges beyond the legal limits, whereas the Yung-cheng Emperor put them under discipline. Under tough provincial administration many of them, especially those in Kiangsu, were impoverished and unable to pay off debts owed the central government.

    Ideological control of intellectuals was perhaps the most successful imperial restriction imposed during the Yung-cheng period. Such an unprecedented thought regimentation resulted from two factors. First, the intellectual climate of the early Ch'ing favored a return to the School of Principle after the height of the School of the Mind. In spite of its humanistic accentuation, Neo-Confucianism, especially the School of Principle, reinforced the traditional imperatives of political and ideological conformity as contained in early Confucianism.[34] Second, autocratic rulers always encouraged conformity to facilitate rule. In addition to other means, they were ready to patronize or exploit any philosophy for their political satisfaction. It was in these circumstances that Ch'ing rulers supported the School of Principle, and given Yung-cheng's unusual devotion, ideological regulation became very strict.

During the Yung-cheng period ideological control was imposed throughout the empire. Whatever their status—officials, students, or private individuals—intellectuals had to familiarize themselves with special works championing the imperial cause written by the Yung-cheng Emperor or sponsored by him. These works were distributed among officials, put on the reference shelves of schools, and read before soldiers and common people twice a month. Whenever necessary, the emperor dispatched special commissioners to watch over the literati in the provinces. Moreover, he strengthened the local education administration, which became a regular instrument for enforcing the imperial requirements in schools. All these were designed for ideological control. The ruler favored those whose thought and behavior complied with the required pattern; he punished those who deviated from it. Through coercive and consensual means the literati of the time conformed to the imperial will. Conformity, voluntary or involuntary, provided a source of strength for the autocrat.

The common people of the Yung-cheng period shared with the ruler the benefits of autocracy. They enjoyed a better life than in the Shun-chih or K'ang-hsi era or even in some other periods under the Ch'ing. After his succession to the throne, Yung-cheng took various measures to improve the well-being of the broad masses of people. He carried out a river conservation program broader in scope than that of his father or his grandfather. He completed an irrigation system in the metropolitan area as well as in the southwestern, southeastern, and northwestern regions. Under his encouragement provincial governments engaged in reclamation works. The river conservation, irrigation, and reclamation programs facilitated and increased agricultural production. His tax reform was, however, the most important of all measures. During the early years of the Ch'ing dynasty, male adults had to pay land tax and perform labor service. Besides, corrupt local officials exacted from them charges in excess of the regular taxes. Tax reform during the Yung-cheng period reduced the common people's extra burden on the one hand, and combined labor services into land tax on the other. The reform in fact released the landless people from the labor-service tax.

Among the populace two more groups were also affected by autocratic rule in the Yung-cheng period. First was the so-called "people of mean occupations," a group of outcasts scattered in different localities and discriminated against legally as well as socially. They told different stories about their obscure origins and had different names varying from place to place. Their number was small, but they did not escape the attention of the Yung-cheng Emperor even at the beginning of his reign. He issued orders of emancipation between 1723 and 1730. Since these people were always preyed upon by influential individuals and corrupt officials, their emancipation suggests an autocrat's effort to remove status barriers against effective central control.[35] After emancipation these pariahs did not substantially change their status because of the influence of tradition. At any rate, the emancipation orders were epoch-making, politically and socially.

The second group to benefit from Yung-cheng policies was the non-Han ethnic minorities—Miao, Yao, and Lolo—in the provinces of Hunan, Kwangtung, Kwangsi, Kweichow, and Yunnan. They were also neglected and discriminated against by successive dynasties, which isolated them from the regular Chinese administrative system. They were governed by the headmen (*t'u-ssu*) selected by local Chinese authorities and approved by the central government. In this situation these ethnic minorities formed another social and legal barrier within the universal empire. While claiming absolute power in China, the Yung-cheng Emperor introduced a positive policy toward them. In the years 1726-1735 he first vigorously put them under regular local administration through armed interference and then tried to eliminate cultural barriers through education and intermarriage. Although his work was frustrated by large-scale uprisings of the Miao in the years 1733-1735, his reign was a hallmark of Ch'ing minority policy.

From the foregoing discussion one may draw several general conclusions concerning the character of the autocracy of the Yung-cheng period. In every respect the Yung-cheng Emperor was a successful autocrat. His success depended on his ability to balance various forces—ideological, institutional, social, and ethnic. If any of these forces were left uncontrolled, it would be against his interest. Confucianism was the only state philosophy, from which all interest groups recruited moral support. As a matter of fact, Confucianism was not always on the ruler's side, and in some situations it opposed the emperor. Therefore, the Yung-cheng Emperor counterbalanced it with Buddhism and Taoism, which, although they checked Confucianism, did not replace it. In terms of institutional balance, he founded new institutions to take over important functions from the old ones, but retained the latter. Just as the Grand Secretariat and the Grand Council coexisted, the censorial institution and the palace-memorial system were charged with similar duties. Such functional fragmentation kept these offices under his control.

The emperor also maintained a social balance. Since he had no confidence in those bureaucrats who obtained appointments through the regular examination system, he balanced them with officials who purchased their positions. As a group enjoying high status, the gentry frequently abused its privileges. Whereas tough local administrators controlled the gentry, the ruler strictly supervised its counterpart, the imperial officials. At the same time, the emperor emancipated the people of mean occupations and improved the conditions of commoners, thereby breaking status barriers. Furthermore, he refused to differentiate between Manchu and Chinese. Instead, he emphasized personal merit rather than ethnic background. He punished Manchus or Chinese without discrimination; he trusted officials of docility, loyalty, and ability regardless of their ethnic derivations. Thus, both groups were under his effective control. As long as non-Han Chinese were under the headman system, a feudal structure was preserved, a decentralized force in conflict with the imperial desire for centralization. The emperor's attempt to change the traditional headman system was not fundamentally different from his effort to bureaucratize the banners. In both cases he meant to increase his authority.

During the Yung-cheng reign no single individual or group was allowed to acquire power beyond the emperor's control. His leadership transcended all forces and he held the lever of balance. No group was strong enough to challenge him; hence, all competed for his favor. By converting power-seekers to power-followers, his rule was absolute and universal within the empire.

The Yung-cheng Emperor died in October 1735, the greatest centralizer and stabilizer of the Ch'ing dynasty. In his short reign he amassed more power than any other Manchu emperor, revitalized the state administration, and fostered a time of economic prosperity. In Chinese history, then, he may be considered one of the most successful autocrats. For while many dynastic rulers were autocratic, they were not successful. The Yung-cheng Emperor was both autocratic and successful. His will was followed by all bureaucrats, central and local, and his authority penetrated all barriers in the empire. Whereas many autocrats worked for themselves and their dynasties, he worked for the common people as well. After reading his edicts and personal comments on various memorials one cannot fail to be impressed by his sincere concern about the common people. Many of his measures were directed toward improving the well-being of the populace. He was a rare dynastic ruler who worked painstakingly for their interest. Jean Baptiste du Halde wrote of the emperor: "He applies himself to the Affairs of his Empire, in which he is indefatigable, and is always employ'd for the Good of his People."[36]

Although it may be argued that he attempted to help the common people because of "operational necessity,"[37] his conservancy, irrigation, and reclamation projects were beneficial to his subjects, even as they also increased the acreage of taxable land. His tax reform raised the number of taxable people in a similar way. However, the term "operational necessity" is not a proper criterion for political judgment. The achievements of a government should be evaluated according to their effect on the majority of the people. During the Yung-cheng period the life of the people was much better than that of their counterparts in many other countries. In short, the Yung-cheng Emperor was a paternal and conscientious autocrat. Consequently, his regime was the culmination of Chinese benevolent despotism.

There are two major reasons for studying Yung-cheng autocracy. The first reason is its importance to the general study of Ch'ing history. Although every era had made its own contribution to history, the Yung-cheng period was a particularly significant one in Ch'ing history. For example, the K'ang-hsi and Ch'ien-lung periods—each of which covered more than half a century—are generally considered two glorious epochs. By comparison, the Yung-cheng era was equally, if not more, glorious. It was marked by peace and order. During the T'ung-chih period (1862-1874)—an era of domestic and foreign troubles—Manchu power was successfully maintained despite the Taiping, Nien, and Moslem rebellions. In retrospect, the Yung-cheng period peacefully arrested the dynastic cycle which had begun in the last half of the K'ang-hsi reign. The Yung-cheng period, a time of stability and prosperity, laid the foundation for the splendor of the Ch'ien-lung age. If K'ang-hsi was a power-holder, Yung-cheng was a power-maker, and Ch'ien-lung, a power-spender. Each of the four reigns accomplished more than any other period of the Manchu regime, and each can be treated as a major topic in Ch'ing studies. Yet, of the four, the Yung-cheng period has enjoyed the least attention from Sinologists, with the exception of a few Japanese historians, notably Miyazaki Ichisada, formerly of Kyoto University.

The second reason for studying Yung-cheng autocracy is the importance of the period to the study of Chinese autocracy. The Yung-cheng Emperor's autocratic rule was so effective that it was a climax in Chinese dynastic history. Thus, an understanding of it may shed light on Chinese autocracy in general. Moreover, an understanding of Yung-cheng's benevolent despotism may contribute insights to the comparative study of autocracy in world history.

PART TWO

The Making of an Autocrat

1. Yung-cheng as Scholar: He is in official dress and concentrates on reading.

II

The Person of the Yung-cheng Emperor

1. *Boyhood*

The Yung-cheng Emperor was born in 1678, the same year that the anti-Manchu Revolt of the Three Feudatories, led by Wu San-kuei (1612-1678), was declining. The future emperor was named Yin-chen (lit., "inheritor of good omen") and was the eleventh son born to the family. He became the fourth after the death of seven of his elder brothers. His father was Sheng-tsu, the K'ang-hsi Emperor, to whom Louis XIV of France and Peter the Great of Russia sent envoys and about whom Catholic missionaries in China would write many laudatory accounts.[1]

The imperial family in the time of K'ang-hsi was a large one, consisting of twenty sons and eight daughters.[2] In addition, there were a few dozen imperial consorts and concubines. Sons and daughters were brought up by their mothers, by ladies-in-waiting, or even by eunuchs and relatives. Large as it was, the imperial family constituted a special group, whose members enjoyed both social and political relations. The K'ang-hsi Emperor's paternal love went first to Yin-jeng (1674-1725), his second son and heir apparent, and then to others of his sons. Although it is said that Yung-cheng was reared by his imperial father personally,[3] he could not compete, in terms of paternal love, either with Yin-jeng or with Yin-shih (1672-1734), his eldest brother whom some Jesuits called the first "Regulo" (prince) and applauded for his kindness.[4] He was no match for Yin-chih (1677-1732), his third elder brother, who was later entrusted by their father with the compilation of the *Ku-chin t'u-shu chi-ch'eng* (Synthesis of books and illustrations of ancient and modern times) and the *Lü-li yüan-yüan* (Compendium on calendar, mathematics, and music).[5] In their accounts the Jesuits said almost nothing about the Yung-cheng Emperor before his accession to the throne. He seems to have had a melancholy boyhood, which had an important impact on the development of his personality.

In Chinese dynastic history the Manchu ruling house is credited with strict education of princes. As they grew up, most of them acquired a profound knowledge of China. Every Manchu prince had to attend the Palace School (*Shang shu-fang*), which was located in the Inner Court. Yung-cheng began his education with his brothers, their curriculum covering mental and physical training.[6]

To preserve their own language the princes had to study Manchu. During the Ch'ing dynasty Manchu and Chinese were official languages, although Mongolian, to a certain extent, was also used as an official language. Documents in Chinese had to be translated into Manchu and vice versa. For instance, the *Veritable Records* (*Shih-lu*) of the Ch'ing had two separate versions, Chinese and Manchu. Nevertheless, to understand the great majority of the Chinese people, Manchu princes learned the Chinese language, classics, and history. As a way of political management, these educational practices were continued until the end of the dynasty.

The schooling of the prince was rigorous. Teachers were Chinese and Manchu scholar-officials, chosen mostly from members of the Hanlin Academy, grand secretaries, and presidents of the Six Boards (*liu-pu*); they were classified in two categories, senior and junior.[7] While the junior ones were responsible for teaching individual students, senior professors supervised both students and instructors. For example, Chang T'ing-yü (1672-1755), a famous scholar-official, was once a senior professor of the Palace School in the Yung-cheng period. The Yung-cheng Emperor studied with Gubadai (d.1709), a Manchu scholar-official, Hsü Yüan-meng (1655-1741), a famous translator of both Manchu and Chinese literature, and Father Theodore Pedrini (1670-1746), a member of the Congregation for the Propagation of the Faith, a Christian missionary order.[8] From morning until evening the young princes were in their classroom.[9] During his service at the court, Father Joachim Bouvet (1656-1730) every day saw Yin-jeng on his way to the Palace School and confirmed that the K'ang-hsi Emperor frequently visited there to test his sons.[10] Students had to show respect to their teachers and were not allowed to be absent without imperial permission. Students were warned or disciplined if they failed to do their work, while teachers would receive punishment if they neglected their teaching or supervisory duties.[11]

In the Palace School physical training covered riding and archery. The Manchus were a warlike people, and their conquest of China was partly due to their high fighting spirit. To maintain this spirit all Manchu youths, of common or royal blood, had to be versed in riding and archery. These two skills were considered a guarantee of their control over their Chinese subjects. In due time princes participated in archery and riding contests witnessed by their imperial fathers.

While it is generally impossible to give any more specific information about the Yung-cheng Emperor's education, he seems to have been attracted more to the mental training of the curriculum than to physical education. No source indicates that he displayed or boasted of his archery or riding as did some other Manchu rulers, notably his father. Nor do any documents show his interest in hunting, which was a hobby and military drill of many other Manchu monarchs. Before his rise to power, he had never taken charge of any military post. On the contrary, Chinese classics, language, and history had a great influence on him. His essays and penmanship show him to be an excellent student of these subjects. He learned from Pedrini, but the Father's tutoring left no imprint on him. Unlike the K'ang-hsi and Ch'ien-lung Emperors, who liked some Western subjects such as astronomy, mathematics, and painting, he had no curiosity about any of these.

2. *Personality*

If one accepts Carl Friedrich's analysis of the impact of a founder's personal characteristics upon an organization,[12] the Yung-cheng Emperor's personality was a main factor in shaping the autocracy of the Yung-cheng period. Sources are inadequate to present his personality in its entirety, but fragments of information reveal some of his distinctive personal traits. The following pages suggest some of these traits although they make no claim to be a psychological study.

The family background was naturally important in the formation of the Yung-cheng Emperor's personality. His mother was from a family without aristocratic forebears. As she was only an imperial consort, she could not compare with the empress in status and dignity, and the future Yung-cheng Emperor could not compete with the heir apparent or several other half-brothers whose mothers were of noble blood. His was a melancholy boyhood. He was different from several of the other young princes, such as Yin-shih, Yin-ssu (1681-1726), and Yin-t'i, who were active, outspoken, and somewhat rough. He lived in quiet, had little association with his brothers, and quarrelled with no one. However, a strong undercurrent flowed beneath calm water, for he was, at heart, ambitious and dissatisfied, anxiety-ridden and jealous. He craved respect and anxiously tried to match his peers.

This environment undoubtedly developed a sense of inferiority in him,[13] which found expression in some aspects of his early conduct. The special politico-social environment of the imperial family contributed to his emotional disturbance, which in turn may have been connected to his sense of inferiority. As a melancholy boy he responded to events irregularly. Even his closest relatives found it difficult to comprehend his emotions and his father considered him a moody boy.[14] A melancholy man tends to irascibility. The Yung-cheng Emperor had been impetuous from his boyhood, and more than once his father advised him to be moderate.[15] After ascending to the throne, he placed on his desk a small tablet inscribed with his father's admonitions, and sometimes he advised officials not to be irascible.[16] His own irascibility made him impatient with officials who were not quick to correct their errors. He also could not tolerate dissent. He punished more high officials than had his father, whose reign was about five times longer than his own. Antonio Sisto Rosso described him as a "quiet and petulant despot."[17]

In his early manhood, Yung-cheng continued to be overshadowed by some of his brothers, and the contrast became even more striking than before. For example, Yin-chih, only one year older than he, was first entrusted with military affairs and then with important literary work.[18] When Yin-chih was made a prince of the second degree in 1698, the young Yung-cheng was a prince of the third degree.[19] Yin-ssu, one of his juniors by three years, was made a prince of the third degree the same year, and acquired a reputation in the court. In 1708 many high officials supported Yin-ssu openly and unanimously as a candidate for heir apparent.[20] Yin-t'ang (1683-1726), the ninth imperial son, had a large amount of wealth and was active in recruiting followers and making alliances with other princes. Yin-t'i, ten years younger than Yung-cheng, emerged as a prominent prince and was appointed commander-in-chief of the Manchu troops against the Eleuths, a Mongol tribe, in 1718.[21] Under these unfavorable circumstance the young Yung-cheng's sense of inferiority persisted. He confined himself to his home, found relief in alcohol,[22] and turned to philosophical studies.

This sense of inferiority put the future emperor in a defensive position. Some of his adult actions substantiated this. After succession he issued long edicts frivolously stating that he was favored by the late emperor for his ability, sincerity, and filial piety.[23] His sense of inferiority also moved him to take the offensive against political dissenters, especially against his former competitors for the throne. Princes who had had advantageous positions in the struggle were the first targets of his attack. During the first four years of his reign, he repeatedly exposed their years of improper conduct. Yin-ssu, the most prominent of the competitors who had overshadowed Yung-cheng, was attacked more frequently than the others. The imperial edicts during these years were made up in large part of rebukes and reproaches. Although these attacks were a strategy to ward off criticism of fratricide, they also served to compensate for his sense of inferiority. In contrast, after his accession he treated three princes—Yin-hsiang (1686-1730), Yin-lu (1695-1767), and Yin-li (1697-1738)—in a very friendly manner. They probably had supported him against his opponents.

The Yung-cheng Emperor took the same measures to prevent officials' contempt for him. For example, after reading a memorial submitted by Li Fu (1675-1750), a famous scholar and governor-general of Chihli, his comment on it was a blunt warning to the official:

> If you are proud of your ability for having memorialized a number of ancient essays and selected a few sentences from history books and thus cherished a contemptuous attitude toward me, I am afraid that it will be too late for you to regret [your attitude].[24]

During his reign many other officials—among them the powerful and arrogant Nien Keng-yao (d.1726) and Lungkodo (d.1728)—were charged with being either followers of his political enemies or simply disloyal to him.[25]

His sense of inferiority made Yung-cheng suspicious of the intentions and conduct of others. His accusations against some officials were based merely on suspicion. Yin-ssu, for instance, was charged with constructing the K'ang-hsi Emperor's mausoleum. As the prince knew that the new ruler was frugal, he built a less expensive tomb. Yung-cheng, however, chose to interpret this as evidence of the prince's evil intentions.[26] Except for a few officials the Emperor trusted no one, not even the subordinates of the men he himself trusted.[27] Hence, he frequently warned those officials not to place too much trust in their aides and servants.[28] He did not value public opinion because he felt certain officials would not report it accurately.[29]

Even in unfavorable circumstances the young Yung-cheng developed a realistic mind. He was never a Don Quixote. His practical nature expressed itself in frugality. In adversity he accustomed himself to a thrifty life; hence, after coming to power, he made frugality one of the main economic policies of the Ch'ing state,[30] and imposed frugality on himself as well as on officials. It is said that at meals, he wasted not even one grain of rice.[31] He repeatedly forbade imperial cooks to throw away leftover food which, he thought, if dried in the sun, could be eaten at least by domestic animals and birds.[32] He was also frugal in selecting consorts: he had fewer than his predecessors and than many of his successors.[33] In sum, his emphasis on frugality greatly contributed to the economic prosperity of the Yung-cheng period.

Practical-mindedness made the Yung-cheng Emperor a political realist. In competition with his brothers for the throne, he avoided open acts which would undoubtedly have invited counteractions by his opponents. Instead, he tried quietly to win his father's favor, which was naturally of vital importance to the contest. After his rise to power he viewed state affairs realistically. His primary concerns were peace and order instead of military glory. For this reason, he dispersed factions, punished lawbreaking individuals, Manchu and Chinese, protected law-abiding people, and concentrated power in his own hands.

A sense of inferiority is not entirely hurtful; it may become one of the greatest assets an individual possesses: it may impel him forward. Yung-cheng was exceptionally diligent and responsible. Immediately after his rise to power he issued eleven decrees to provincial and local officials from governor-general to prefect,[34] in which he advised, encouraged, and even threatened officials to work hard. He himself worked tirelessly, day and night, receiving or interviewing officials, reading memorials thoroughly, and making comments on them with vermilion ink. Privately, he revealed that since boyhood he had been advised by his father to work honestly.[35] Such advice added force to his propensities toward diligence and responsibility. The officials he favored were able, docile, diligent, and honest. He successfully injected a new spirit into his administration, which was marked by competency and justice.

By circumstance or by nature the Yung-cheng Emperor developed a personality of introversion.[36] Melancholy attracted him to philosophical studies, which laid the foundation for his ideology. The Palace School provided orthodox philosophy for him; his self-education supplied him with other schools of thought. In Chinese dynastic history he was a rare ruler, well equipped with profound philosophical knowledge of Confucianism, Legalism, Taoism, and Ch'an Buddhism. He was the first Ch'ing emperor to use philosophical teachings to defend the Manchu regime against Chinese nationalist feeling.[37] He was also the only Manchu ruler to master Ch'an Buddhism, learning and practicing it with a Mongol Lama and other Ch'an monks.[38] He was also author of several Ch'an books, notably the *Yü-hsüan yü-lu* (A collection of selected Buddhist and Taoist sayings) and *Chien-mu pien-i lu* (Criticisms of Buddhist heresies). Ch'an Buddhism's emphasis on meditation led him to examine his situation and that of the Manchu empire introspectively.

By the time of his succession the Manchu empire was in need of new guidance. After the conquest of Taiwan in 1683 the Ch'ing regime consolidated its position in China, but the Chinese intelligentsia and the Manchu aristocracy were still two unfriendly forces. Some Chinese intellectuals considered the Ch'ing conquerors alien and barbarian, and the Manchu aristocrats preserved a feudal tradition that ran counter to the regime. Both groups required guidance and discipline. While the broad masses of Chinese subjects were suffering under an unjust administration, the majority of the bannermen lost their fighting spirit and were severely impoverished. These were potential dangers to the security of the Manchu dynasty, which was in urgent need of sound direction. The Yung-cheng Emperor's introspective nature encouraged the reflection and self-examination necessary to the regime, which found practical expression in the emphasis of the Yung-cheng state administration on domestic peace and order.

In terms of his personal character, ideology (see below), and political behavior after succession, the Yung-cheng Emperor was a strong person, with a sense of being "called" to the throne.[39] He claimed personal superiority to his competitors, legitimacy to succession, and absolute authority. To be sure, the position of the Chinese ruler depended philosophically on his special quality as the Son of Heaven,[40] but Yung-cheng particularly emphasized this in several ways. He made inspirational and emotional appeals to reorient his officials and subjects. He also applied coercive measures to remove opponents and command obedience from bureaucrats. Since he carried on his policies vigorously, his administration was marked by religious zeal. He changed the governmental structure handed down from his grandfather and father to fit his ideal and improved the general condition of the people to fulfill his imperial duty. Besides, he published works to promote Ch'an Buddhism and even claimed attainment of sudden enlightenment,[41] the final stage pursued by Ch'an monks. In the last years of the Yung-cheng period, he organized a seminar group to study Ch'an Buddhism.[42] He concentrated not only political but religious authority in his person.

In sum, Yung-cheng's sense of inferiority largely contributed to the shaping of his personality, but this was by no means a handicap to him. His conduct was normal. As early as 1736 du Halde wrote: "He is witty, and speaks well but too fast...."[43] As a ruler he devoted himself to autocracy, but his state policy was not dogmatic. He was always realistic. Since he removed political opponents, suppressed factional leaders, and punished self-seeking gentry with harsh measures, he was hated by the upper classes. They felt relieved when he died. Under their influence his successor returned to a policy that favored the rich and powerful. Yung-cheng emphasized domestic peace and prosperity and did not seek military glory.

As a result, subsequent generations have not given him proper credit for his achievements. Instead, he has been remembered as a harsh ruler. He became a tragic character. A careful study of his reign, however, shows that earlier judgments of him were inaccurate. Although his autocracy satisfied his desire for power, it also protected the common people from exploitation by oppressive local officials and selfish gentry. Perhaps one of his Western contemporaries has summed him up best:

> As little a Favour of Religion as this Prince [the Yung-cheng Emperor] appear'd, it is impossible not to praise his unwearied Application to Business, for he applied his Thoughts night and day to the reforming of Errors in the Government, and to procure Happiness to his subjects: You cannot do him a greater Pleasure than to present him a Plan which tends to promote the publick Welfare, and the Ease of the People; he immediately enters therein, and puts it in Execution without any regard to Expence: He hath settled a great many excellent Rules to dignify Merit, and reward Virtue, to cause a worthy Emulation among Artificers, and to assist his Subjects in Years of Famine: These Qualities have gained him in a short time the Respect and Love of all his Subjects.[44]

His reign was short, his contribution to the Ch'ing empire was practical, and he substantially strengthened Manchu rule.

3. *Ideology*

If the Yung-cheng Emperor's personal character constituted an important factor in the autocracy of his reign, his ideology played an even more vital role. Ideology served not only to remove obstructions to increasing political centralization but also to direct his statecraft. It shaped his political behavior and influenced the bureaucrats under him.

Personal character may have a strong impact on one's thought, but ideology is largely an outcome of philosophizing. Yung-cheng's ideology was drawn from traditional sources of Chinese philosophy. He was a student of Confucianism, a disciple of Legalism, a patron of Ch'an Buddhism, and an admirer of Taoism but he did not unequivocally commit himself to any of the four. He selected points and applied them to special cases as he saw fit. His ideology was a restatement of traditional Chinese ideas, on the one hand, and the modification or distortion of them, on the other. He was a traditionalist and at the same time a nontraditionalist.

Confucianism had long been associated with the traditional Chinese state. While rulers relied upon it for moral justification of their qualifications, scholars depended on it for official appointments. Naturally it was a source of the Yung-cheng Emperor's ideology. He began to study Confucian classics in boyhood; although he was also attracted by other philosophical schools, he could not help respecting Confucianism, which was accepted by the majority of his subjects. As soon as he ascended the throne, he showed his allegiance to Confucianism. In 1724 he repaired the Confucian temple at Ch'üeh-li, the birth place of Confucius, and added Yen Hui (514-483 B.C.), Tseng Ts'an (505-437 B.C.), two disciples of Confucius, as well as Mencius (c.372-c.289 B.C.) and some other famous Confucian scholars to the Confucian temple for worship.[45] He also promoted Confucian doctrines through other means. As early as 1723 he restored the *Hsiao-ching* (Canon of filial piety), dropped during the K'ang-hsi period, to the list of requirements for the provincial and metropolitan examinations, and later published the book in Chinese and Manchu.[46] In the second year of his reign he expanded the Sacred Edict (*Sheng-yü*), a group of sixteen maxims largely based on Neo-Confucianism and published in 1671, into a long essay.[47] On many occasions he declared that Confucianism should be the foundation of statecraft.[48] Since he concentrated on domestic affairs, his administration was characterized by pacifism. If pacifism is a characteristic of Confucianism,[49] he was qualified to be a Confucian.

Despite all these measures, Yung-cheng's Confucian fidelity is open to question. There were many factors that drew him away from close attachment to Confucianism. First, because Confucianism stressed man's virtues in state administration, it permitted no separation of politics and ethics. When confronted with complicated state affairs, its moral principles were impotent. As a consequence, Confucianism began to embrace other philosophical viewpoints, and many rulers departed from their initial Confucian course.[50] As a realistic monarch, Yung-cheng was certainly not satisfied with pure Confucian ethical guidance.

Second, Yung-cheng's divergence was also due to the development of Neo-Confucianism itself. After a long period of philosophical domination, Neo-Confucianism had lost its vitality as a leading ideology toward the end of the Ming dynasty. Because of its scholastic methods and rigid pattern of thought, the School of Principle, though state-supported, was nearly surpassed in the middle of the Ming by the School of the Mind led by Wang Shou-jen (best known as Wang Yang-ming, 1472-1529), who emphasized an intuitional approach and encouraged free speculation. But the School of the Mind gradually lost its philosophical appeal in the second half of the sixteenth century since its intuitionalism drifted into pedantry and disorderliness.[51] When coupled with the political situation of the time, this intellectual development facilitated the rise of the scholars from the Tung-lin Academy, and led to a political movement against the evil eunuchs in the early seventeenth century.[52] While opposing political evils, the movement was philosophically a crusade tending to mediate the differences between the two Neo-Confucian branches but inclining toward the School of Principle.[53] Although the movement reflected the true spirit of the Sung Neo-Confucians who struggled for political and philosophical innovations, its influence declined along with that of the Ming dynasty, which collapsed in 1644. As a whole, the development of these two schools clearly demonstrated the decline of Neo-Confucianism. With the patronage of the K'ang-hsi Emperor, the School of Principle returned to its orthodox position, but what the Manchu sponsorship amounted to was political support rather than philosophical reinforcement. As a result, what the Ch'ing restored was a mere shadow of Sung and Ming Neo-Confucianism. Small wonder that except for its political usefulness, it lost its appeal for the Yung-cheng Emperor, who was attracted to other schools of thought.

Lastly, in the early Ch'ing, Confucianism did not sufficiently serve the imperial interest as expected by the ruler. This can be seen in the political process of the time. As soon as the Ch'ing adopted the Confucian pattern of government in its early years, many Chinese Confucian scholars entered into its service and some were even put in the imperial coterie, notably the Southern Imperial Study (*Nan Shu-fang*). If Confucianism provided ruler and Confucian scholar with a common front, it also furnished a background for their conflict.[54] The tension between monarch and bureaucrat was not new, but it was further strained by the struggle among the Manchu aristocrats, especially the contest between the princes for succession.[55] During the second half of the K'ang-hsi period this aristocratic struggle almost endangered the central power structure of the Ch'ing. Many Chinese scholar-officials were engulfed in the strife for one reason or another. However closely or loosely this political process was related to Confucianism, it moved forward within the Confucian order, on which the imperial authority was based. Suffice it to say that Yung-cheng, a true autocratic ruler, could not cling to Confucianism.

From the ruler's standpoint, the best situation was to have the service of Confucianism but avoid its undesirable effects. This was the course Yung-cheng pursued. To approach this goal he modified and distorted Confucianism, declaring, as had many Chinese dynastic rulers, his affiliation with it. During his reign Confucianism was merely the equal of Buddhism and Taoism. In response to a palace memorial, he privately ordered the memorialist to protect Buddhism and Taoism on the ground that they were as important as Confucianism to the governing of the people.[56] Humanitarianism (*jen*), a central point of Confucianism, with emphasis on kindness, considerateness, and leniency, was substantially reduced to an insignificant position. In his comments on a memorial submitted by O-er-t'ai (1680-1745) he wrote: "In general, with humanitarianism as theory and righteousness as practice, there certainly will be no serious mistakes."[57] Officials who acted against his wishes, even if motivated by humanitarianism, would be severely punished, no matter how much loved by the people. The case of Yang Ming-shih (1661-1736) provides a typical example. As a true Confucian, he extended leniency to people and officials in his governing of Yunnan, but he was finally humiliated and dismissed because he failed to follow imperial directives completely. Thus humanitarianism underwent a qualitative change.

Sincerity (*ch'eng*), a relatively minor Confucian virtue, took the place of humanitarianism as a leading ethical principle in Yung-cheng's mind. He stressed it for effective control over bureaucrats under the Confucian guise because he believed that officials had become more pretentious since the Han and T'ang dynasties.[58] In his reasoning, sincerity meant not only honesty but unselfishness. Since false and selfish conduct of officials was undoubtedly in conflict with the sovereign's interest, he also treated sincerity as a problem in state administration and advocated it through different means. His first effort was to promote it by his personal example, trying to convince officials that he had observed the cause of sincerity even before his rise to power.[59] He then encouraged officials to get rid of nepotism and to decline the requests of powerful individuals for privileges, and warned or threatened them against making dishonest reports.[60] As a last resort he enhanced sincerity by associating it with the cosmic order. In 1725, for example, he pointed out in a decree that his sincere prayer had resulted in relieving some places of drought (he believed that an insincere prayer would bring nothing).[61] When a lucky omen was reported in Yunnan province in 1729, he attributed it to the sincere work of the chief provincial administrator and asked other bureaucrats to follow the official's example.[62]

In Yung-cheng's ideology, Legalism, another major Chinese philosophy, played a greater part than Confucianism. His approach to Legalism was quite natural since his mental state provided him with a background for adoption of it. Moreover, the political situation—such as factional activities and administrative evils extant on the eve of his succession—pushed him to adopt Legalist principles, which were undoubtedly more effective than Confucianism for removal of these ills. While Confucianism regards virtue as the common asset of man, stresses people's capability of self-cultivation, and believes that ethics, not law, should rule, Legalism considers selfishness man's common nature, questions the ability of moral instruction to stop human evils, and insists that only punishments and rewards can force people into compliance with desired behavior. Inasmuch as both sets of ideals are dogmatic, neither can be institucionalized in its pure form. Nevertheless, they are complementary at the operational level. The imperial system and the Yung-cheng Emperor needed aspects of both Confucianism and Legalism for political guidance.

The Legalist influence on Yung-cheng can be seen in both his words and deeds. He interpreted several major Confucian points from a Legalist perspective. Among other Confucian doctrines, he showed a particular interest in righteousness (i), which was also given a strong Legalist connotation. In Confucian vocabulary righteousness was regarded as a principle of conduct, by which man knew what he should or should not do. Legalists gave it a more concrete meaning and considered it the standard of justice. The Yung-cheng Emperor followed this Legalist interpretation and further explained it in terms of justice, equality, and the mean (in Chinese, *kung*, *p'ing*, and *chung*, respectively).

"Justice" and "equality" have legal implications. Since Confucianism placed scholars above the common people, these two principles received little or no emphasis in the Confucian value system. Scholars and common people belonged to two different status groups and were treated differently—which may be a reason for Confucian scholars' aversion to law, the efficiency of which depends upon the universal application of justice and equality. Any breach of law will inevitably make justice and equality impossible and ultimately have repercussions on the authority and legitimacy of the ruler.[63] Because Yung-cheng came to power through a court struggle, authority and legitimacy were his chief concerns. Hence, justice and equality became the central points of his administration. For instance, he told one of his officials that, although they varied, statecrafts were based on these two principles.[64] On another occasion, he cautioned a provincial governor against a series of temptations: disregarding official duties for vain reputation, maintaining one's prestige at the expense of the law, acting in a perfunctory manner for the sake of tranquillity, causing disturbance for the purpose of stirring up oneself or others, seeming gentle and kind so as to appear benevolent, compromising in the hope of inviting subordinates' gratitude, and cheating the ruler for the benefit of friends or influential officials.[65] He was urging that justice and equality be promoted in the public, not the personal, interest.

To the Yung-cheng Emperor, the principle of the mean was as important as justice and equality. All three were necessary for the maintenance of law. Time after time he taught officials to apply rewards and punishments properly and to take lenient or strict measures as appropriate.[66] His respect for the principle of the mean led him to order the compilation of the *Ch'in-ting chih-chung ch'eng-hsien* (Historical examples of the mean), in which he highly commended Yao and Shun, two sage-rulers in Confucian tradition, because they were believed to have followed the principle of the mean in dealing with state affairs and maintaining justice and equality.[67] On the same principle, he avoided issuing orders that could not be executed. In 1725, for instance, commanders of the Eight Banners suggested that he prohibit officials, soldiers, and civilians from wearing dress and ornaments that were not consistent with their status. He refused on the grounds that such an edict could not be enforced, arguing that regulations that could not be enforced should not be made.[68]

In the final analysis, justice, equality, and the mean were necessary to the fair application of law, another major Legalist point which Yung-cheng attempted to achieve. According to him, there were two requirements for the fair application of law: first, the innocent should not be made to suffer; and second, thieves, robbers, covetous officials, local bullies, and bad gentry should be punished without compassion.[69] He further explained to officials that compassion for the convicted was itself cruel because it would encourage lawbreakers and therefore lead to more punishments.[70] His explanation echoed the points of Han Fei (d.233 B.C.) and Machiavelli (1469-1527), both of whom abhorred compassion and warned the ruler to make punishment definite so as to maintain the authority of the law.[71] As long as the authority of the law was closely related to the ruler's interest, it became the chief concern of all monarchs. With this point in mind, Yung-cheng did not spare anyone, including his brothers and favorites, from punishment when he found it necessary. For the same reason he even forgave the officials who maintained the authority of the law with excessive severity.[72] However, punishment was only his means, not a goal. As he revealed in a decree of 1733, his real aim was to establish, through punishment, a country without punishment,[73] a Legalist ideal based on the principles of justice, equality, and the mean.

In evaluating the influence of Legalism on Yung-cheng's ideology, the fact that he never openly mentioned the name of the Legalist School in his public decrees or private works may seem strange. This omission can be explained through an understanding of the historical and political context in which he lived. First, many Legalist principles were absorbed into Confucianism when the latter was made an orthodoxy in the Han dynasty. Provided he could draw on these principles from this orthodoxy, he did not have to name the Legalist School specifically. Second, as an alien ruler, he was afraid of inviting the aversion of the Chinese Confucian scholars by publicly recognizing Legalism. In Chinese history dynastic rulers leaned toward Legalism, but they always cloaked this tendency in Confucianism. This was also the case with Yung-cheng.

In comparison, even Buddhism—Ch'an Buddhism in particular—and Taoism played a more important role than Confucian and Legalist components in the formation of the Yung-cheng Emperor's ideology. He studied and practiced these two religions in his early life and maintained this interest until his death. Buddhism and Taoism differed in origin, doctrine, and practice, but they adapted to each other and functioned side by side as two religions of salvation with a great appeal to the general Chinese public.

Some of the Yung-cheng Emperor's religious beliefs were part of Manchu tradition. The Manchu Imperial House practiced Shamanism, a popular religion of the people in Siberia, Mongolia, and the far northeast of China.[74] Shamanism involves a belief in heaven and hell, gods and demons, and its priests are regarded as magicians able to invoke blessings from deities and alleviate misfortunes through spirits. In dogma and practice it is close to religious Taoism. At the same time the Manchu court had a strong attachment to Buddhism, especially Lamaism. While Tibetan and Mongol Lamas received imperial favor for religious and political reasons, some Ch'an monks seemed to be imperial spiritual guides during the Shun-chih period.[75] Under imperial sponsorship Buddhism acquired new strength. In 1668, for example, there were 79,622 Buddhist temples in the Manchu empire, among which 12,482 were founded by imperial order and the rest by the people.[76] In these circumstances Yung-cheng developed his interest in traditional Chinese religions.

The Yung-cheng Emperor's connection with Buddhism and Taoism was also a result of the religious movement of the time. Since the middle of the Ming dynasty, Buddhism, Taoism, and Confucianism had developed closer relations. Buddhists adopted the Taoist schedule of merits and demerits, and a number of Confucians were attracted to Buddhism.[77] These developments tended to minimize the philosophical disparities between the three schools, and Yung-cheng continued to search for their common elements. Since he preferred the School of the Mind, he emphasized the importance of the mind, which he identified as that which linked the three. According to him, the mind was fundamental to knowledge and action, and the cultivation of it was equally important to Confucians and Buddhists.[78] As he moved a further step from Confucian interpretation to Buddhist and Taoist versions, he held that the mind was identical with Buddha and the universe.[79] He felt that the three schools provided moral education for the people and were complementary in their purposes.[80] His religious beliefs had a relativistic aspect. He placed Confucianism, Buddhism, and Taoism on the same plane, selected ideas from any one of them to interpret the two others, and treated the three as equals. For instance, he compiled the *Yü-hsüan yü-lu*, a selection of sayings from the three schools and ordered the repair and construction of Confucian halls, Buddhist temples, and Taoist shrines.[81] This same relativistic approach to philosophical studies also found expression in his compilation of the *Ch'in-ting chih-chung ch'eng-hsien*, in which he used Legalism and other schools of thought to interpret Confucianism.

Of the three schools, he showed the greatest interest in Ch'an Buddhism. He studied Buddhist philosophy, discussed it with monks, and practiced meditation with a Lamaist Living Buddha. He revealed that in 1713 he achieved sudden enlightenment,[82] the final goal pursued by Ch'an monks. The main feature of his Ch'an belief lay in the emphasis on Buddhist scriptures and discipline. Although these two points had already been advanced by two monks, Yen-shou (904-975) and Chu-hung (1535-1615), in their movement toward unity of Ch'an and Pure Land Buddhism,[83] Yung-cheng transformed them into political action to rectify the Ch'an Buddhism of his time. His stress on Buddhist scriptures and discipline largely resulted from three factors. First, his commitment to the School of the Mind made him an advocate of the unity of knowledge and action, which respectively can be regarded, from the Buddhist viewpoint, as the equivalents of scriptures and discipline. During his time, many Ch'an monks read no scriptures and followed no discipline. Second, like other autocrats, he had a passion for ideological and behavioral conformity, which he deemed important to imperial authority. Third, as a Ch'an believer, he felt obliged to save Ch'an Buddhism, which, according to him, was endangered by the Ch'an monks who gave up scriptures, cast aside Buddhist discipline, or engaged in worldly interests.[84]

In the last few years of his life Yung-cheng pushed forward a movement to reorient Ch'an monks. His rectification program had two parts. One was his promotion of what he considered the proper pattern for Ch'an monks to observe. To achieve this, he compiled and reprinted, in addition to the *Yü hsüan yü-lu*, several other Buddhist works and sutras.[85] In line with this goal he bestowed posthumous honors on a few Taoist priests and Buddhist monks, especially Yen-shou, a monk who probably authored the *Tsung-ching lu* (Mirror for Ch'an Buddhists) published in the eleventh century. In 1734 Yung-cheng reprinted the monk's work, with two imperial prefaces and an edict attached to it. Besides, he outlined and annotated it as a separate book entitled *Tsung-ching lu ta-kang* (An outline of the Mirror for Ch'an Buddhists); it was published the following year. This outline was distributed among Ch'an monasteries as a required reading. The thesis of these two publications argued three points: that Ch'an monks should read scriptures for true Buddhist teachings; that they follow strict Buddhist discipline; and that there was a unity between Ch'an and Pure Land. To reinforce these points, he insisted that calling on the name of Buddha was no obstruction to practicing meditation and that Ch'an and Pure Land were not incompatible.[86]

Another part of the Yung-cheng Emperor's rectification program was to denounce undesirable Ch'an monks by issuing decrees and publishing works. The exemplar of such works was the *Chien-mu pien-i lu*, which centers posthumous attack on Fa-tsang (1573-1635) and his disciple, Hung-jen, and their followers. The two monks advocated freedom from established Ch'an practices and criticized the two authoritative Ch'an schools, Ts'ao-tung and Lin-chi. In the perspective of Ch'an history, their liberal approach was not extraordinary, but Yung-cheng's anger at them caused him in 1733 to order their works burned and their followers excluded from Ch'an monasteries.[87] In the hope of reorienting Ch'an Buddhism along stricter lines, he dispatched favorite monks from the court to take charge of famous monasteries in the country, and he held examinations for learned monks in 1733.[88]

In the last three years of his reign the Yung-cheng Emperor took further action to unify Confucianism, Buddhism, and Taoism into one school as the philosophical basis of his administration. In 1733, he sponsored a special seminar group in Ch'an Buddhism. It was a small assemblage of only fifteen people high in political and social status. Besides the Emperor, five of the members were princes: his two favorite brothers, Yin-lu and Yin-li, two sons, Hung-li (later the Ch'ien-lung Emperor), Hung-chou (1712-1770), and Fu-p'eng (designated Prince P'ing, d.1748). Three members were high officials—Chang T'ing-yü, O-er-t'ai, and Chang Chao (1691-1745), who was then president of the Censorate. The others were five leading Buddhist monks and one Taoist priest.[89] Each of the fifteen members had a religious essay included in the *Yü-hsüan yü-lu*. This group also served as a political advisory committee. For instance, Wen-chüeh (sometimes known as Yüan-hsin) was a member of the group and is said to have been the emperor's advisor in the suppression of Yin-ssu and Yin-t'ang and in the liquidation of Nien Keng-yao and Lungkodo.[90]

Political and religious systems in China, like Confucianism and monarchy, attracted and at the same time repulsed each other; this was also the case in other centralized empires.[91] For example, Taoism and Buddhism emphasized other-worldliness, developed relatively autonomous organizations, managed their economic resources, attracted followings, and operated at a society-wide level. Their interest was mainly religious, but in a concrete sense they intruded into the political sphere. Under certain circumstances they supplied a unifying force among the elements of the lowest social stratum and became organizers of popular revolts. Even in its early phase, religious Taoism was able to provide an organizational force for the Yellow Turbans (*Huang-ching*), who devastated the Later Han dynasty. Inasmuch as Chinese secret societies always had religious affiliations with Taoism, Buddhism, or a combination of both, these two schools were in competition with political institutions and were a potential threat within the Chinese empire.

In spite of their competition and conflict, Taoism and Buddhism continuously existed as popular Chinese belief-systems. Meanwhile, they and the political system developed side by side and were interdependent. The coeval relations of the political and the religious were not incidental. They carried on activities within the same social framework in which the political institutions operated. Religious activities needed support and protection from the political authorities. Such dependence was further strengthened by the fact that some ambitious religious leaders looked for official opportunities within the political sphere to enhance their religious or worldly influence.

The rulers, for their part, tried to enlist support from the religious domain, because religious symbols and values were helpful for enhancing their moral qualifications. In addition, since Taoism and Buddhism were contenders with Confucianism in the philosophical sphere, they could be used to mitigate the Confucian influence. The rulers largely maintained their dominant position by balancing off different influences. In ruling a centralized empire like China, it was difficult to extend direct political control over the villagers who made up the largest percentage of the population. Since Taoism and Buddhism kept in close touch with the broad masses of people, the rulers needed their service to maintain the necessary balance between political passivity and activity among the majority of people. For these practical considerations, religious and political systems were intertwined. The problem facing the rulers was how simultaneously to eliminate the latent threat from Taoism and Buddhism but increase their political serviceability.

The Yung-cheng Emperor's religious inclinations and his efforts to unify the three schools—Confucianism, Taoism, and Buddhism—were directed toward serving his political purposes. He established affiliations with the three schools in order to control, unify, and exploit them. Their independent development meant a plurality, which was contrary to the interests of autocracy. The autocrat always tried,

if at all possible, to command the greatest amount
of power resources, to exercise his jurisdiction
over the greatest amount of territory, and to regulate the greatest number of subjects by a norm
applied to his whole domain.[92] These considerations
may also explain Yung-cheng's relativistic approach
to the three schools: he had affiliations with all
of them and treated them impartially. Partiality to
one would make it disproportionately influential,
and thus a potential threat to the ruler's interests.

Political necessity was a factor in Yung-cheng's
impartiality toward the three schools; it was also
a reason for his strong affinity to a particular
school when the situation required it. Before his
succession to the throne, for example, he was more
interested in Ch'an Buddhism and Taoism than in
Confucianism. After his rise to power, he openly
professed his affiliation with Confucianism and
covertly attached himself to Legalism, for he identified his best interest with these two schools in
the face of his political rivals and factionalism.
As soon as he had solved his major problems, he
returned to Taoism and Buddhism. He never forgot
political considerations even when he found it
necessary to show a special interest in a certain
school. While preferring Confucianism, he tried to
do away with certain aspects of the school which
he deemed undesirable to his interests. During the
first half of his reign, for example, he repeatedly
attacked those Confucian values that he considered
to be sources of factional differences.

Political considerations led him to condemn
some Taoist and Buddhist practices. For instance,
he called a Taoist priest from Honan province for
medication when he fell ill in 1730. In the course
of medication the Taoist is said to have used magical
means to call on deities and spirits. The practice
is a typical Taoist superstition, but it implied a
challenge to the authority of the ruler. As a result,
the Taoist priest was charged with a political crime
and sentenced to death.[93] The case demonstrates the
ruler's effort to regulate the use of religious
symbols that were related to the imperial authority.
In another instance, Yung-cheng attacked relentlessly
the iconoclastic practice of a Ch'an monk. In his
writings he bluntly pointed out that if Buddhist
monks were allowed to destroy the Buddha's image,
ordinary people might wreck their ancestral tablets
without fear, and officials could also cast away the

deceased ruler's slab.[94] His resentment is understandable, for these images and tablets had religious and political significance.

The Yung-cheng Emperor's relativistic approach to Confucianism, Taoism, and Buddhism had a great impact on the religious policy of the state. He had no aversion to any religion. To him all religions were helpful for social morality, provided they did not go against the political order. During the Yung-cheng period some officials repeatedly petitioned for the prohibition of Islam on the grounds that Moslems dressed differently, used a different calendar, worshipped a different deity, and formed a different group.[95] In a long decree the emperor denied one such petition with an argument that was political, cultural, and utilitarian. He pointed out that (1) the Moslems had lived for a long time in China and were not different from other people in the country; (2) they had not violated state regulations; and (3) Islam was merely a form of local religion in China.[96]

He looked upon Christianity in the same way. He privately revealed that he felt no disgust at Christianity, and in a public decree he explained that Chinese and Western religions, though different from each other, shared the same feature of revering heaven.[97] In short, the religious activities that he tried to prohibit were not folk beliefs or any heterodox worship *per se*,[98] but those which had political involvements or intentions.

Given the above discussion, the reasons for exclusion of Christian missionaries from China during the Yung-cheng period can be explored. Since early missionaries and recent scholars have provided detailed descriptions and studies of the subject,[99] this discussion will analyze their conclusions and emphasize a few points. The studies of Arnold H. Rowbotham and A. Thomas, for example, stress political motivations for Yung-cheng's exclusion of Christianity.[100] Although there is no strong evidence to indicate the missionary involvement in the court struggle for succession during the last years of the K'ang-hsi period, the relationship between Father João Mourão (1681-1726), a Portuguese Jesuit in Peking, and Yin-t'ang, one of the emperor's competitors for the heirdom, caused the Yung-cheng Emperor to be suspicious of Christian missionaries.[101] That suspicion was strengthened by the association between Sunu (c.1648-1725), a Manchu prince who was a pious Christian, and the missionary.[102] Sunu's conversion to Christianity was not necessarily political in nature, but he and his family were nonetheless supporters of Yin-t'ang. To a ruler of the eighteenth century, especially an autocrat, suspicion was in itself evidence enough to justify his actions. When Yung-cheng started to suppress his political rivals, he also ordered the exclusion of Christianity. This move revealed the political nature of his action against the missionaries—which he indicated in private conversations with the Catholic priests, in a letter to the Pope, and in a public decree before and after the exclusion.[103]

Some authors attribute the exclusion of Christianity to Yung-cheng's personal intellectual preference, or to his affiliation with Buddhism and Taoism, or to both.[104] Some recent scholars, however, find answers in the broad cultural sphere.[105] Father Maurus Fang (orig. Hao Fang) points out that the Japanese persecution of Catholicism had an important influence on the prohibition of Christianity in China.[106]

All of these points help to shed light on the question, but political considerations were the first and most important factor in the Yung-cheng Emperor's suppression of Christianity. During the K'ang-hsi period the "Rites Controversy" between China and Rome, though largely cultural in nature, also involved political considerations.[107] Since the papal court required Chinese converts to give up their traditional native practices, such as ancestor worship, to pay reverence only to God, and to take orders from Rome, it unavoidably challenged the Manchu ruler's authority—a conflict no less significant than that between the Pope and the Holy Roman Emperor during the Middle Ages. This controversy naturally became a political struggle when the Yung-cheng Emperor was consolidating his power.

In discussing the prohibition of Christianity in the Yung-cheng period one should note two facts. First, the early missionary work in China depended chiefly on the imperial favor, which could be withheld by the ruler whenever necessary. With the "Rites Controversy" deadlocked in the last few years of his reign, the K'ang-hsi Emperor denounced the requests of Rome, allowed no Chinese converts to follow the papal order, and decreed that without an imperial patent no missionary could preach.[108] It can be reasonably inferred, therefore, that he might have completely forbidden the preaching of Christianity in China had he lived longer. His death left the full resolution of this problem to his successor. Logically, Yung-cheng enforced his predecessor's restriction on the spread of Christianity, and, owing to such additional factors as his suspicion of the association between his political rivals and the missionaries, he moved a little further.

Second, Yung-cheng did not take harsh measures against missionaries, with the exception of Father João Mourão, a supporter of Yin-t'ang. Compared with the persecution of Christians by the Tokugawa Shogunate in Japan, his acts were moderate and reasonable. After his expulsion order in 1724, missionaries in Peking still served in the Manchu government as technicians and were permitted to use their chapels. In the provinces missionaries with scientific and technological knowledge were allowed to go to Peking or to leave for Macao.[109] After 1724 many missionaries actually shifted from urban to rural areas. The emperor advised local officials that the missionaries should be leniently and reasonably treated because they were not criminals.[110] After the exclusion order many local churches were confiscated by local officials to serve as schools or places for other public functions, but Yung-cheng did not encourage the confiscation. In 1729 when a local official discovered some missionary property that had not been seized by the local government, he petitioned the emperor for the right to confiscate it. In reply, the ruler told the memorialist that the missionary had not committed any crime justifying the outright confiscation of property; instead, he issued instructions that the property be sold, with the proceeds to be given to its owner in Peking.[111] These cases provide further evidence that Yung'cheng's purpose was to remove the potential political influence of the missionaries and their religion.

III

The Road to the Throne

1. *The Issue of Legitimacy*

In the first decade of the eighteenth century the Manchu court had a succession crisis. The K'ang-hsi Emperor established, deposed, reestablished, and redeposed his heir apparent. This crisis involved many high officials, Chinese and Manchu, threw the court into confusion, and lasted until the emperor's death. From this chaotic situation the Yung-cheng Emperor came to power. In discussing his succession, one is confronted with the problem of its legitimacy, which has long been a question among historians. Even in his lifetime there were at least three stories alleging that his succession was illegitimate. One of these stories claims that on his deathbed K'ang-hsi designated the fourteenth prince, Yin-t'i, as successor, but that the will was changed by Yung-cheng. According to another story, K'ang-hsi's will appointing Yin-t'i his successor was concealed and changed by Lungkodo, then General Commandant of the Gendarmerie (*Pu-chün t'ung-ling*), in Peking, in favor of Yung-cheng. The last story alleges that Yung-cheng poisoned his ill father, succeeded to the throne, and then recalled and imprisoned Yin-t'i, who was believed to have been made a successor.

It is in general impossible to trace the origins of the three stories,[1] but in all likelihood they were the work of the Yung-cheng Emperor's political opponents. The stories were privately circulated from capital to provinces without his knowledge, but they were at last brought to the imperial attention in 1729 when Tseng Ching (1679-1736),[2] a Chinese scholar arrested for his nationalistic activities, revealed them. Upon hearing the stories the emperor carried on a thorough investigation and is said finally to have identified their circulators, who were eunuchs banished by him for their support of his opponents. In order to defend himself the emperor in 1730 published the related testimonies and his detailed refutations in a book entitled *Ta-i chüeh-mi lu* (A record of great tenor for the deluded). As far as the sources are concerned, this publication was the first account of the three stories and the origin of all later unofficial works on Yung-cheng's disputed succession. Scholars, Chinese and Western, are convinced by the stories and have concluded that he was an illegal successor.[3]

Other factors support this verdict against the emperor. A scrutiny of his edicts and other documents on his succession reveal certain discrepancies. These are evident from comparing different sources—such as the *Tung-hua lu* (Tung-hua records), the *Shang-yü nei-ko* (Edicts and decrees to the Grand Secretariat), the *Shang-yü pa-ch'i* (Edicts and decrees for the Eight Banners), the *Ta-Ch'ing li-ch'ao shih-lu* (Veritable records of successive reigns of the Ch'ing dynasty) for the K'ang-hsi and Yung-cheng periods. Discrepancies are also found in the edicts included in the same source, and in the same edict. The discrepancies extend to the identity of the persons who witnessed the dying ruler's will or were present when the Yung-cheng Emperor was told of his designation. These discrepancies are the basis for the penetrating article written by Meng Sen (1868-1937), a renowned Ch'ing historian.[4]

Some scholars also examine the illegitimacy of the succession from another viewpoint. For instance, Lungkodo and Nien Keng-yao, once two favored and influential officials, were important to Yung-cheng's victory in the struggle for accession but were later harshly punished by him, presumably because he was afraid that they might disclose the secrets about his illegal succession.[5] A few historians, notably Wang Chung-han, provide another approach to the problem. They have collected detailed facts about Yin-t'i, who in 1718 was appointed by K'ang-hsi as Generalissimo for the Pacification of Distant Lands (*Fu-yüan ta chiang-chün*) to command the armies against the Eleuth Mongols; these historians regard the prince as the most likely successor to the throne.[6] To all the approaches mentioned above, another scholar adds a new perspective. After comparing the average number of volumes of the *Veritable Records* for each of the Manchu reign periods, he finds that the K'ang-hsi period had the smallest number, 1.1 volumes per year. He thus concludes that Yung-cheng, who ordered the composition of the *Veritable Records* for the K'ang-hsi period, suppressed or altered any records that he disliked.[7]

The case is not completely against Yung-cheng, however. A careful study of the controversies yields arguments in favor of the defendant. The three stories concerning his succession are exciting, but they originated with the unsuccessful competitors and their partisans, who were easily moved by emotion and tended to be slanderers. For example, Yin-jeng was the target of many slanders and rumors before his final deposal in 1712. They may have influenced K'ang-hsi's decision to remove him from the heirdom. Since the struggle was long and bitter, especially after the first deposal of Yin-jeng in 1708, hostility between the competitors was deeply rooted. Words from the unsuccessful aspirants may not necessarily represent the truth.

One may also disagree with the interpretation that Yin-t'i's appointment as Generalissimo for the Pacification of Distant Lands suggested K'ang-hsi's desire to make him successor. It is true that such an appointment, made in a critical time of competition, might well cause conjectures among contemporaries and later historians. Their conjectures seem further to have been reinforced by the fact that even while in custody Yin-jeng dreamed of the same position, in the hope of obtaining freedom and influence and a step toward the throne.[8] It should be noted, however, that such an appointment carried no specific significance in connection with the heirdom.[9] When the Eleuths invaded Tibet in 1717, the previous appointees to that post having died, the emperor quite naturally selected the next Generalissimo from among his sons. In essence Yin-t'i's command was no different from those commissions assigned to his brothers by K'ang-hsi, who wanted the imperial sons to acquire experience in state or military affairs.

In 1724 Yung-cheng pointed out to princes and high officials that it had been impossible for his father, aged and ill, to send a desirable successor to the distant frontier. He sent Yin-t'i, Yung-cheng continued, simply in an attempt to prevent any possible trouble-making by that prince, who allied himself with others in the succession struggle. Although it is difficult to substantiate these words, they are logically related to the situation of the time. First, according to Jesuit reports, the K'ang-hsi Emperor had suffered from serious palpitations, since the displacement of Yin-jeng in 1708.[10] Fully aware of his poor health, he was worried about the succession problem; this concern was a major reason for his dramatic restoration of the deposed crown prince to the heirdom by the same year.[11] Instead of ending the succession struggle, his action heightened it. He finally redeposed Yin-jeng in 1712, and, despite the requests of officials, refused to designate another heir apparent. Because the competition between his sons could not be stopped, his health continued to deteriorate. It is impossible that in this situation he would send out to a distant place a qualified candidate for the throne; none would believe that he would let such a desirable prince return to the frontier after being called back to the capital for a meeting a few months before his death.[12]

Second, it is highly unlikely that K'ang-hsi would select as a candidate from among his sons one backed by factional support in view of the fact that he made efforts to stop the succession struggle. After 1708 he was almost hysterical toward factional activity and punished many people. A severe punishment of some high officials and the imperial sons even frightened the missionaries.[13] Inasmuch as Yin-t'i was supported by a strong faction in the succession struggle, he was unlikely to be selected as a candidate for heir apparent. Furthermore, it is improbable that, while trying to stop the struggle, K'ang-hsi would choose a candidate with military power, a situation that might lead to a war of succession. On the contrary, he probably meant to paralyze the factions by sending away one of the aspirant princes, after having openly discouraged or punished some others.

Discrepancies in the sources concerning Yung-cheng's accession provide no definite evidence against the defendant. It is generally true that editors of official historical compilations were always subject to political influence, especially with the growth of autocracy in the Ming and Ch'ing dynasties, or concerned with the Confucian ethical requirement for appropriate concealment.[14] These factors affected the reliability of official historical publications in one way or another. However, discrepancies in the sources for the succession disputes might result from other factors. One was the span of time between Yung-cheng's enthronement and the issuing of his defensive edicts. Although he moved to attack the rival princes almost as soon as he ascended the throne, most of the edicts of defense came out after September 1724, a period of more than one year after his succession and of nearly three decades from the beginning of the struggle. In such edicts the statements were evidently based on his recollections, which allow, as always happens, differences or errors, and some details necessarily slipped from his memory while others lost their original sequence. This may explain some of the discrepancies.

Another reason for discrepancies was the literary skill of official editors, whose techniques and standards varied with the individual. Although many documents in official compilations for the Yung-cheng and other periods of the Ch'ing were based on the same sources, after editing by their compilers they were no longer identical with the originals. When cited in several official works, they frequently differ in wording. This is particularly true of the *Veritable Records* of the Ch'ing, a general reference work for the Manchu rulers who often read it. Editors of these records were, as a rule, eminent scholar-officials of high editing skills, who presented the material in the most summarized and literary form. An edict of January 13, 1723, for example, requiring 173 words in the *Yü-chih lu* (Record of imperial edicts of the Yung-cheng period) and 112 in the *Shang-yü nei-ko*, uses only 37 in the *Veritable Records*.[15] Moreover, Manchu names in the *Veritable Records* were usually transliterated into meaningful Chinese names.[16] In their summarized and readable form, the documents remain almost the same in content, but some details are left out. These omissions are evidently a result of literary style rather than of political involvement.

Some of the discrepancies in official publications can be explained in the light of their functional differences. Since each official record was compiled for a special purpose, it covered materials different from other works. Some documents are included in one compilation but left out of others. The *Veritable Records* has the broadest coverage in comparison with other official sources for the Yung-cheng period, but there are omissions, some of which happen to be related to the succession controversies. In a long edict, for example, Yung-cheng traced his relations with Yin-li, one of his loyal brothers, and revealed something about his succession. The edict appears in the *Shang-yü pa-ch'i* but not in the *Veritable Records*.[17] Meng Sen regarded this omission in the latter as a deliberate attempt to conceal and thus considered it as evidence of the emperor's illegal succession.[18] A careful comparison suggests a different reason for this omission. The *Veritable Records* contains only about fifty percent of the total data that are in the *Shang-yü pa-ch'i*, which was compiled specifically for the banners. Yung-cheng meant to make Yin-li a model for the Manchu bannermen. Thus, the edict in question was naturally placed in the *Shang-yü pa-ch'i* but was beyond the coverage of the *Veritable Records*, which needed space to include other matters of a more general nature.

Avoidance of duplication seems to have been another reason for the discrepancies. Major official works for the Yung-cheng period were edited and published at different times. In the *Shang-yü nei-ko*, documents for the years 1723-1729 were compiled and published in 1731, while material for the rest of the period was added to the 1731 compilation and incorporated into one work in 1741. The *Shang-yü pa-ch'i* is a ten-volume work compiled in possibly two or even three periods. The first five volumes for the years 1722-1727 were compiled in 1732. Covering the period 1728-1732, volumes 6-9 seem to have been completed around 1733, while the last volume for the years 1733-1735 might have been published about 1735. The *Veritable Records* was edited in 1741. A comparison of the three works indicates a practice that seems to have been followed by their editors[19]— while working on the later compilations, they avoided duplicating some material that had been covered by the earlier ones. This can explain at least some discrepancies. For example, in 1729 the Yung-cheng Emperor issued an edict in reply to some officials' petition for executing Tseng Ching. This edict appears in the *Shang-yü nei-ko* but not in the *Veritable Records*,[20] perhaps for the same reason that the edict concerning Yin-li is retained in the *Shang-yü pa-ch'i* but left out of the *Veritable Records*.

The above explanations are also applicable to some major unofficial publications on the Yung-cheng period such as the *Tung-hua lu* of Chiang Liang-chi (1722-1789) and of Wang Hsien-ch'ien (1842-1918). Because of different editorial philosophies and skills there are discrepancies between the *Tung-hua Records* and some official works, notably the *Veritable Records*. As private works intended for personal reference, the Chiang and Wang editions were free from the considerations that had limited the official publications. Chiang and Wang obtained material largely from the *Veritable Records*, but they omitted, summarized, and combined some data to accommodate the limited space of their works. As a result, in some cases there are differences in dates and wording of the same documents published in the two private compilations and the *Veritable Records*.

Another reason for some discrepancies between the two editions of the *Tung-hua lu* and the *Veritable Records* lies in the fact that the former did not rely solely on the latter as a source. Chiang and Wang collected information from other official works, and when omitted in the *Veritable Records* for the reasons discussed above, such information produces an apparent discrepancy. Wang's edition, for example, contains some edicts issued between July and November 1729, in relation to Yung-cheng's succession, but the same documents are not included in the *Veritable Records*, the *Shang-yü nei-ko*, and the *Shang-yü pa-ch'i*.[21] It would be interesting to know where Wang obtained the edicts and why they were omitted in the three official works. In fact, the edicts are also resumes of the documents in the *Ta-i chüeh-mi lu*.[22] All of the three official publications were compiled, as stated earlier, for special aims and came out later than the *Ta-i chüeh-mi lu*. These are probably the reasons why they excluded the edicts that are retained in the *Ta-i chüeh-mi lu*, a work that Yung-cheng specifically ordered so as to defend himself.

Some scholars also believe that the destruction of all copies of the *Ta-i chüeh-mi lu* by the Ch'ien-lung Emperor in 1736 is related to the succession issue.[23] Its destruction, however, does not necessarily prove the illegitimacy of Yung-cheng's succession. The case can be made that Ch'ien-lung differed from his father in personality and in attitude toward state affairs. Immediately after his succession he changed many of his father's policies. For example, he expelled from the court the Taoist priests his father had trusted, and removed the pressure of reclamation and collection of taxes in arrears that were seriously carried on during the Yung-cheng period. Thus, the destruction of the *Ta-i chüeh-mi lu* can be seen as part of the changes in general state policies that Ch'ien-lung carried out in the early years of his reign.

As far as the material on the accession disputes is concerned, the *Veritable Records* claims the largest coverage of all sources, official and unofficial. If the *Veritable Records* represents the percentage figure of 100 for the subject in question, Chiang's and Wang's compilations of the *Tung-hua Records* are 20 and 98 respectively. In comparison, the *Shang-yü nei-ko* covers more than ninety-five percent of the data while the *Shang-yü pa-ch'i* less than twenty.[24] On the same subject the *Ta-i chüeh-mi lu* is also below the coverage of the *Veritable Records*. However different, the five sources together suggest another fact: the documentary disparity is far from being strong evidence of the illegal accession of the Yung-cheng Emperor. If an edict was altered in or omitted from one source for political or ethical reasons, as some scholars suggest, why should the same document be allowed to appear in another? If this discrepancy resulted from the negligence of the Yung-cheng Emperor and his successor, how could their loyal compilers, who were not allowed to include or exclude a document without imperial permission, neglect it too?

The case of Nien Keng-yao and Lungkodo is also an exciting issue related to the same disputes. As their punishments were in connection with factionalism, a detailed discussion will be presented in the next chapter.

The last point of examination is the problem about the quantity of the *Veritable Records* for the K'ang-hsi period, which totaled only 300 *chüan*. In light of its long span (sixty-one years) the period should have had four times more records than those for the Yung-cheng era, which had 159 *chüan*, or at least half of those for the reign of Ch'ien-lung, whose records cover 1,500 *chüan*. The scantiness of the *Veritable Records* for K'ang-hsi's reign invites suspicion that material on the succession issue was suppressed or changed by his successor. In explanation of this suspicion, however, Yung-cheng's personality should be considered. Unlike his father or son, both of whom patronized literary activities, Yung-cheng was a practical-minded ruler who did not sponsor any large literary enterprises. His various writings, literary and philosophical, make up about 100 *chüan*, a number much smaller than those of his father or his son. If his introverted disposition made him uninterested in physical training during his boyhood, his practicality made him inattentive to literary activities after his succession to the throne. This propensity affected the quantity of the *Veritable Records* for the K'ang-hsi period that was compiled under his order.

There is another fact also worthy of discussion. During the Manchu dynasty the *Veritable Records* for the first few rulers, in particular Nurhaci (1559-1626), was rewritten. If Yung-cheng had altered or suppressed some documents in the records of his father's reign, that act may not necessarily have been connected with the legal aspects of his succession. He simply followed the practice of his predecessors if he did so. Naturally, in the process of rewriting, there were changes and omissions. Furthermore, a close check of the *Veritable Records* for the years 1708-1722, a period that saw the climax of the succession crisis, discloses that the heirdom issue occupies the largest percentage of the total material. Some data about Yin-jeng, Yin-shih, and Yin-ssu can be identified as reliable material by the account of the contemporary Jesuits at the Manchu court and also by the Korean dynastic records.[25]

The discussion in the preceding pages is an attempt to provide some new perspectives on the succession issue. It does not represent an effort to justify the legitimacy of Yung-cheng's accession. The question is perhaps an insolvable puzzle of Ch'ing history. Any interpretation will inevitably invite disagreement. The term legitimacy questions the rightfulness of rulership, but this is not the main purpose of the present study, which emphasizes Yung-cheng's political control after his succession. One should not overlook the fact that the problem of legitimacy was derived from court struggles rather than the reverse. Yin-jeng, twice given legitimate status as heir apparent, found himself a victim of such struggles. It is clear that after his redeposal whoever succeeded to the throne would be considered illegitimate by his competitors. The legitimacy issue became a cheap political means used by unsuccessful contestants and their partisans.

2. *The Struggle for Heirdom*

A discussion of the struggle for the throne should start with Yin-jeng, the first heir apparent of the Manchu dynasty designated through formal ceremonies according to China's dynastic tradition. The Manchus, from Nurhaci to the Shun-chih Emperor, had never had a well-established heir-apparent system. Successors to the throne were not necessarily the eldest sons by empresses. They were selected from among princes by elder members of the imperial clan according to their ability and talent or by the influence of powerful princes. The former practice accounts for the rise to power of Hong-taiji (1592-1643, r. 1627-1643), generally known as Abahai in many Western books, while the latter explains the selection of Shun-chih. These practices, especially when connected with the feudal tradition of the banners, became a reason for the succession trouble of the early Ch'ing.[26] The succession of K'ang-hsi to the throne was the result of the dying words of his father. He was the first Manchu ruler to try to follow the Chinese tradition by starting an heir-apparent system, but all his efforts were of no avail.

Yin-jeng was born in 1674 of Empress Hsiao-ch'eng, the Benevolent (1654-1674), who was from a noble family. Her uncle, Songgotu (d.1703), was one of the envoys and signers of the Treaty of Nerchinsk in 1689 and had been appointed to many important positions. When the war against the Three Feudatories came to a critical point in 1676, Yin-jeng was publicly designated as heir apparent. Considered together with the adherence of the Manchu regime to Confucianism, which also took place during the same crucial period, this designation seems to have been another political stratagem to inspire the loyalty of Chinese to the alien regime by showing its attachment to their tradition. The designation was accompanied by a gracious imperial proclamation of nine articles.[27] In early boyhood Yin-jeng was taught to read and write by the emperor himself and by distinguished Chinese scholar-officials such as Chang Ying (1638-1708), Hsiung Tz'u-li (1635-1709), and T'ang Pin (1627-1687).[28] As a result the young prince knew both Manchu and Chinese. His personality and talent for riding, archery, speech, and literature earned praise not only from his father but from

many officials and even the Catholic missionaries.[29]
A brilliant future seemed in store for him.

Before 1708 Yin-jeng enjoyed a status unchallengeable but envied by other princes. The emperor showered favors and honors on him. He was always at the head of the imperial suite on trips. For example, when he fell ill while accompanying the emperor on an inspection of river conservation in 1702, the emperor, concerned with his son's health, abandoned the journey.[30] Although the throne was unhappy with the crown prince first for his indifference to his majesty's illness in 1690 and again for his "immoral" practices in 1697, he was still the recipient of the imperial paternal love.[31] When K'ang-hsi led campaigns against the belligerent Eleuths in the years 1696-1697, the prince was twice regent in charge of the central government.

Yin-jeng proved to be an unfortunate crown prince. When he was designated, most of the Manchu nobles were still under the strong influence of feudal practices centering in the banners. They were high officials of the state and also loyal servants of their individual lords. To them the heir-apparent system was completely new. In addition, Yin-jeng had many ambitious brothers who envied his special status, and he was finally brought down by their jealousy. The first prince who struggled with him for the heirdom was Yin-shih. Although sources are insufficient, a general picture of this struggle can be drawn.

Yin-shih's ambition was closely connected with his status. As eldest son of the imperial family he had many advantages. First, he had more opportunities than his younger brothers to receive important appointments. In 1690, for instance, he was the chief associate of Fu-ch'üan (1653-1703), one of K'ang-hsi's brothers, leading the expedition against the Eleuths. He was recalled from his vice-commandership the next year because of his disputes with the commander, but was again dispatched with Songgotu to command the advance guards of the banners in the campaign against the Eleuths in 1696.[32] These assignments enhanced his prestige and made him influential over others. Secondly, he had more opportunities to recruit followers. An analysis of the political background of his supporters shows that quite a few of them were from the Three Superior Banners (*Shang san-ch'i*)—the Plain Yellow,

Bordered Yellow, and Plain White—all belonging to the imperial family and commanded by the Office of the Imperial Household (*Nei-wu fu*).

Yin-shih recruited many important supporters with key posts.[33] Maci (d.1739), a powerful official from the Manchu Bordered Yellow Banner who had helped Yin-jeng conduct the government in 1696 and 1697 while K'ang-hsi was away on campaigns against the Eleuths, was one of Yin-shih's supporters. T'ung Kuo-wei (d.1719), an influential official from the same banner as Maci and a maternal uncle of K'ang-hsi, kept close relations with Yin-shih. In fact, the whole family of T'ung Kuo-wei supported the same prince. Lungkodo, his third son, Sunggayan, his grandson and husband of the emperor's ninth daughter, and Olondai (d.1726), his nephew, were accused by the throne of supporting Yin-shih's struggle for the heirdom. Examination of their activities indicates that the above officials were also connected with other princes. Whomever they worked for, they aimed to bring down Yin-jeng. As Maci and T'ung Kuo-wei were two powerful nobles of the Manchu Bordered Yellow Banner, Yin-shih was in a strong position. Besides these followers, he recruited many others from the Five Inferior Banners (*Hsia wu-ch'i*)[34]—the Bordered White, Plain and Bordered Blue, and Plain and Bordered Red Banners.

The activities of Yin-shih were directed against Yin-jeng. With the support of his followers Yin-shih collected information about the monarch and the heir apparent, spread rumors, and threatened those who did not go along with him. When the struggle became intense, he locked every door of his house at night in fear of other competitors.[35] After Yin-jeng was first put into custody in 1708, Yin-shih secretly offered the throne a scheme to kill the degraded crown prince without leaving any trace of complicity on the emperor's part, and he waited, according to the Jesuits, for his designation to the heirdom.[36] A few days after Yin-jeng's first confinement, he informed the throne of the activities of Yin-ssu, probably once his collaborator, against the heir apparent.[37] He seems to have expected to win the throne's trust through this report, but to his disappointment it only caused Yin-ssu's confinement and deprivation of rank as a prince of the third degree. As a last resort Yin-shih sought magic power by using Lama sorcerers to cast a spell on Yin-jeng.[38] Despite his efforts, he was not successful; finally, for his reliance on magic, he was sentenced to life imprisonment, during which he died in 1734. His activities, however, contributed to the displacement of the crown prince.

Yin-jeng was deposed in a dramatic way. When K'ang-hsi was in Inner Mongolia on a hunting trip in October 1708, he suddenly summoned the heir apparent and, before the high officials, declared the latter's imprisonment. A few days later he formally dismissed Yin-jeng from the heirdom with a gracious imperial proclamation of thirty-two articles, five of which were in direct connection with the prince.[39] The alleged crimes charged against him can be grouped into three categories: (1) immorality, extravagance, and harsh treatment of princes and high officials; (2) factional activities and usurpation of power; and (3) plots against the throne.[40] The imperial action threw the whole court into confusion, but it failed to solve the problem. Only a few months later the throne determined to release the prince and restored him to the heirdom.

There were three reasons that moved K'ang-hsi to restore the crown prince. The first was psychological. As Yin-jeng was the only son born of the empress and a prince of talents, the throne still bore him in mind after his dismissal and regretted its haste. Added to this uneasiness was sorrow for the death of Yin-chiai, the eighteenth son. The dismissal and the death exercised a great psychological influence on the emperor. Second, a serious palpitation seized him, and he thought that his days were numbered. In this situation he believed that he must name a successor to prevent any possible disturbance caused by his death. Third, the court struggle did not stop with the displacement of Yin-jeng. On the contrary, aspirant imperial sons exhausted their devices and employed extreme measures in an attempt to take up the position of the heir apparent, and they brought the struggle to a new phase. The emperor tended to believe that the deposed heir apparent was a victim of the succession struggle. This belief was strengthened when Yin-shih and Yin-ssu were discovered to have used illegal and magical means against the crown prince. While all these three factors were at work, the monarch took another dramatic measure. He took Yin-jeng from imprisonment to the court, and made him confess to faults before the officials, and redesignated him crown prince.[41] Restoration of Yin-jeng proved to be a temporary solution, for it lasted only three years. In the intensity of the court struggle, the emperor again declared the immorality and incapability of Yin-jeng—actually a repetition of his previous accusations—and deposed the latter forever.[42]

In a brief span of four years (1708-1712) Yin-jeng experienced displacement, restoration, and redeposal. These events were without historical precedent, and they had a great impact on the Manchu regime. They brought the last fifteen years of the K'ang-hsi period to such confusion that the Manchu court almost split into factions. Each supported a candidate for the heirdom. This chaotic situation finally ushered in the Yung-cheng period. How does one then reasonably explain the underlying factors for this dramatic occurrence? Some students of Ch'ing history provide no explanation or accept at face value the charges against Yin-jeng.[43] Another group of scholars believe the charges of "crimes" against the one-time heir apparent and feel that the emperor should have corrected Yin-jeng by strict supervision at an earlier time. Thus they place on the emperor a moral responsibility for his son's "lawless" acts.[44] A few scholars regard Yin-jeng's conduct as rebellion against his rigorous Confucian education and this reaction as a partial reason for his fall.[45] It is clear that the three groups all have neglected the influence of the court struggle on Yin-jeng. At this point Yin-jeng's "crimes" are worthy of study.

The court succession struggle was a major factor responsible for Yin-jeng's "crimes." Discussion of these may start with his "immoral" practices, one of the charges against him. According to the official accounts, his immoral conduct involved sex and alcohol.[46] As a matter of fact, these were not unique to Yin-jeng. Many Manchu princes, for example, Dorgon, were more addicted to sex and alcohol than he. Private accounts, for example, provide information which runs counter to the official images of K'ang-hsi and Ch'ien-lung.[47] The official charge against Yin-jeng does not necessarily carry its full weight. The contemporary private records such as the literary works of high officials and the Jesuits' letters did not mention his immorality. Nor after succession did Yung-cheng repeat the same charges against him. Furthermore, if his life was really immoral, why did K'ang-hsi re-establish him as heir apparent? At the risk of their official careers or lives, some courtiers such as Wang Shan (1645-1728), a Grand Secretary, Chu T'ien-pao (d.1718), a corrector of the Hanlin Academy, and a few censors petitioned at different times after 1712 for the restoration of Yin-jeng to the heirdom.[48] Obviously, their petitions would be in part based on the ability and character of Yin-jeng. Immorality and the other charges against him were greatly, if not solely, forged, and were exaggerated by the partisan propaganda of Yin-shih and Yin-ssu. On different occasions the K'ang-hsi and Yung-cheng Emperors revealed this truth.[49]

In the final analysis, other charges against Yin-jeng were related to the court struggle for the heirdom. His extravagance, for example, was not a meaningless outlay but rather a deliberate effort, largely resulting from the advice of Songgotu, to show his status as heir apparent.[50] His harsh treatment of princes and high officials was a practice also adopted by other competitors for the purpose of frightening rivals and recruiting followers. It was no wonder that in the struggle Yin-jeng organized a faction and engaged in activities against the challenge of his contenders. As a legally instituted heir apparent, he enjoyed more opportunity than other princes and even improperly exercised his influence with the hope of consolidating his rights.

In the same light his "plots" against the throne can be regarded as an expression of psychological insecurity due to the drastic struggle. True, in consideration of Yin-jeng's special status, one may deem his participation in the contest an inadvisable action. However, the situation of the time made his involvement inevitable. When confronted with challenges, he was forced to take defensive action. He drew supporters from influential bannermen—presidents of Boards, minister of the Office of the Imperial Household, General Commandant of the Gendarmerie of Peking, lieutenant-generals of the banners, and so forth—all of whom were severely punished after his deposals. As a whole, they formed a clique so loyal to him that some of them planned to release him from imprisonment when K'ang-hsi fell ill in 1718.[51] After rallying a defense, Yin-jeng moved farther and farther with the development of the situation.

Although it is difficult to give a date for the beginning of the struggle, the middle of the

1690s seems to have been a turning point in the contest. Competitors became alarmed at two new developments. One was the regency of Yin-jeng in the absence of the emperor. His regency was short, but it brought the struggle to an open battle. The partisans spread slanderous words about the prince regent that proved to be an effective weapon in removing him from the heirdom. At the end of 1708 the K'ang-hsi Emperor revealed that sometime around 1697, he heard about the "crimes" committed by Yin-jeng and since then he had lost confidence in the crown prince.[52]

The other important development that affected the struggle was the emperor's declining health. Since 1690 he had frequently fallen ill. This physical condition probably led him to entertain the idea of retirement in favor of the crown prince.[53] This situation clearly indicated that a showdown was near. Both Yin-jeng and his contenders felt a sense of emergency, and thus the struggle increased in intensity. Challenge and counterchallenge caused a sort of chain reaction. Under the constant pressure of his competitors, Yin-jeng needed security; he was ready to take any measure which would help to consolidate his position. Added to this was the advice of an astrologer who is said to have foretold that he would lose the throne if he failed to mount it by a certain year.[54] Naturally this advice made it seem that the best way for him was to seize the throne before it was lost to someone else. This may explain why he participated in "usurpation of power" activities and "plots" against the throne. He had to rely upon these activities as long as his contestants defied him. As the wrestling became more drastic after his reestablishment, he went back to his old activities and was finally removed from the heirdom forever. He was a victim of the succession struggle, according to a private scholar of the Ch'ien-lung period.[55]

The above discussion indicates the relationship between the court struggle and the alleged "crimes" of Yin-jeng. His "crimes" were to a great extent his tactics for self-defense. It would be a mistake to regard them as the manifestation of his revolt against rigorous Confucian education. It would be equally wrong to accuse K'ang-hsi of failure to correct him at the proper time. If the emperor had any responsibility for this heirdom problem, his fault lay in the fact that he did not firmly support his crown prince. He should have stopped the contests, but he did not take positive and consistent action. He imprisoned Yin-shih but tolerated other contenders to a great extent. Although he did stand firm in restoring Yin-jeng to the heirdom, his susceptibility to partisan propaganda encouraged further competition. When encircled by rumors, he could not identify the chief competitors and their followers, but he had no difficulty discovering the activities of his heir apparent, who was the common target of contestants. In these circumstances, Yin-jeng was accused of "lawless" acts, deposed, and redismissed.

If the deposal of Yin-jeng ended the first phase of struggle, his restoration marked the beginning of another stage of strife. Yin-ssu was a prominent figure in both phases and contributed, no less than Yin-shih, to the first confinement of the crown prince. Like other aspirant princes, Yin-ssu had dreamed of the heirdom for a long time. Born of a mother of obscure origin, he was designated a prince of the third degree in 1698 and began to be prominent among his brothers. It should be noted that most information about his personality and activities is based on the *Veritable Records* for the K'ang-hsi and Yung-cheng periods, but these sources are not necessarily records of detraction. Their major points about the competitors proved to be authentic by related facts and the Jesuits' accounts. For example, Yin-ssu's ability and intelligence won the admiration of his life-and-death opponent, Yung-cheng.[56]

In the course of the struggle, Yin-ssu tried by every means to increase his prestige, which was vital to the recruiting of followers. For the purpose of winning compliments from literary and academic circles he associated closely with Chinese scholars such as Ho Ch'o (1661-1722) and Ch'in Tao-jan (1658-1747).[57] They served as his political and literary advisers. His followers included imperial bodyguards, eunuchs, Chinese and Manchu officials, astrologers, physiognomists, magicians, and adventurers.[58] Yin-t'ang, Yin-e (1683-1741)—the tenth son of K'ang-hsi—and Yin-t'i were aspirant princes, but they cooperated with him closely. As a result he enjoyed high popularity; almost the whole court was under his influence. Many officials praised and supported him. When the emperor asked the high officials to suggest a candidate for the heirdom in

1709, they unanimously recommended Yin-ssu as a proper choice to succeed Yin-jeng.[59]

Yin-ssu was more responsible than Yin-shih for the deposal of the heir apparent in 1708. As a prince of ability and popularity, Yin-ssu was a contender of great weight. He was so active that Yin-jeng felt the pressure and reported his illegal act to the throne.[60] This led to open antagonism between them. While Yin-ssu is believed to have attempted the assassination of the heir apparent, his supporters, Alingga (d.1716), K'uei-hsü (1674?-1717), and Mawu (d.1727), all Manchu nobles, contributed to the downfall of Yin-jeng.[61] When Yin-ssu undertook activities with the hope of taking the place of his ill-fated brother, Yin-shih responded with strong moves for the same purpose. With a view to terminating these activities, the emperor punished them and declared that he would never give them the heirdom.[62] This ended the first phase of struggle and paved the way for the reinstatement of Yin-jeng.

The second phase of the struggle started almost immediately after Yin-jeng's restoration and moved with ferocity. The compromising attitude of the throne was the major reason for the resumption of the struggle. Although he punished Yin-shih, Yin-ssu, and their factions, he failed to carry out his orders. Probably because of appreciation of Yin-ssu's ability, the throne did not put him under strict custody. Yin-ssu was sometimes released from imprisonment for special assignments, and some of his chief supporters, such as Maci, were restored to official positions.[63] It is also possible that the emperor was unable to enforce his orders in the face of strong factionalism. For example, he punished two Manchu officials for their part in the struggle, but they were freed by their respective patrons, Yin-jeng and Yin-ssu.[64] Because Yin-shih remained under custody until his death, Yin-ssu became the principal contender against Yin-jeng in this second phase. Both sides strengthened their factions and prepared for a decisive campaign. While Yin-ssu formed a united front with Yin-t'ang and Yin-t'i and took over Yin-shih's followers, the crown prince cooperated with the police chief of the capital and dispatched agents to watch the persons under suspicion.[65]

The struggle was intensified with the participation of two new contenders—Yin-chih and Yin-chen who later succeeded to the throne. They tried to win their father's good feeling by showing filial piety and followed this approach until the end of the K'ang-hsi period.[66] Although their tactics were less violent than those of their rivals, their participation made the strife more complicated. The atmosphere at the court was tense. In 1712 in a great fury the emperor deposed Yin-jeng and punished other princes. As a witness Father Matteo Ripa (1682-1745) left a vivid description of Yin-jeng's redismissal. He wrote:

> When we arrived at Chan-choon-yuan [Ch'ang-ch'un yüan], the imperial residence near Peking, to our great terror we saw in the garden of that great palace eight or ten mandarins, and two eunuchs upon their knees, bare-headed, and with their hands tied behind them. At a small distance from them the sons of the Emperor were standing in a row, also with their hands bound upon their breasts. Shortly after, the Emperor came out of his apartments in an open sedan, and proceeded to the place where the princes were undergoing punishment. On reaching the spot he broke out with the fury of a tiger, loading the heir apparent with reproaches, and confined him to his own palace, together with his family and court. In a public manifesto he subsequently deposed the unfortunate prince as suspected of treason.[67]

Thus the unfortunate crown prince was permanently removed from the scene, but his archrival, Yin-ssu, did not succeed either. The emperor never appointed another heir apparent. As days passed, the last phase of the struggle became public.

The last phase covered last decade of the K'ang-hsi era. It was distinguished by the final effort of Yin-jeng for another restoration, petitions of officials for a new heir apparent or the old one's reestablishment, and the participation of new competitors. The situation became intricate. Yin-jeng was not willing to bow to fate, and before long he resumed activities even in his confinement. Through secret letters he maintained close contact with his clique and requested a Manchu noble to recommend him to the throne for the post of Generalissimo for the Pacification of Distant Lands to command the armies on the northwestern frontier.[68] Apparently he meant to reestablish himself. Although his plan came to naught, his name did not sink into oblivion. He found hope in the petitions of some officials in later years.

The vacancy of the heirdom created great confusion in the court. It provided reasons for a great many officials to petition the throne for reappointment of an heir apparent. Many if not most of the officials had factional affiliations and were loyal in support of their candidates. At the same time they stubbornly worked against those who were not the ones they desired. If one prince gained power, he would reward his followers and punish those who supported others. This consideration hardened factional lines. From a different viewpoint the nonfactional officials also petitioned the throne to take action in selecting an heir apparent, for they were anxious to curb the competition and in the meantime were concerned about the declining physical conditions of their imperial master. In either case, they deemed it necessary to fill the vacancy by appointing a new person or restoring Yin-jeng.

During the last ten years of his reign K'ang-hsi refused to appoint a successor. He needed to settle the problem of a successor, but he was afraid of the factional struggle that had rooted itself deeply among his sons. In consequence he suspected the motives of petitioners and turned down their proposals. In 1713, for example, Chao Shen-ch'iao (1644-1720), president of the Censorate and without factional attachment, took the lead in urging the monarch to designate a successor. In response, the emperor pointed out that his inaction did not mean his lack of attention to the problem but that, on the contrary, he had to take serious consideration of the choice so as to avoid any recurrence of a case like Yin-jeng's.[69] Four years later Wang Shan and eight censors memorialized the throne on the necessity of nominating an heir apparent, and they were accused by him of attempting to form a coalition for their own benefit.[70] In 1721 Wang Shan made another petition to the same effect, after one presented by twelve censors.[71] Suspicious of their self-seeking motives, the emperor punished them severely.[72]

The case of Chu T'ien-pao perhaps represented a high point in the petitioning for Yin-jeng's restoration after his redeposal. With the support

of his father and some others, Chu T'ien-pao, then
a junior scholar in the Hanlin Academy, in 1716
petitioned for the reappointment of Yin-jeng as heir
apparent on the ground of the latter's superior talent
and character.[73] The emperor is said first to have
been moved upon reading the memorial, but then at
the instigation of Alingga, one of Yin-ssu's
supporters, to have been enraged at this memorial.
The throne examined the petitioner in the presence
of high officials, accused him of unfaithfulness
and factional motivation, and sentenced him and his
principal followers to death. The others involved in
the case were also punished.[74] By the same year
high officials of the central government made collective efforts to memorialize the emperor twice on
the importance of appointing an heir apparent, and
their proposals were also suppressed.[75] As the tide
ebbed, Yin-jeng was past hope of a second reinstal-
lation.

   The last phase of struggle saw the contest of
three princes in the wake of Yin-shih, Yin-jeng,
and Yin-ssu. The three contenders were Yin-chih,
the Yung-cheng Emperor—known then as Prince Yung—
and Yin-t'i. The first two came to the scene a
little earlier than the last, who had become prominent since 1718.

   Many students of Ch'ing history have neglected
the fact that Yin-chih played an important role in
the struggle for the heirdom. In 1698 he was made
a prince of the second degree. The next year he
suffered a demotion because of violation of the
mourning practice concerning an imperial concubine,[76]
but as a whole he was a learned prince and one of the
monarch's favorite sons. Together with a few imperial
sons, he was mentioned by K'ang-hsi in 1709 as one of
the filial princes.[77] During the K'ang-hsi period he
was the prince chiefly responsible for compiling two
encyclopedias and regulating imperial musical instruments.[78] In the early phase of the struggle for the
heirdom he seems to have been on the side of Yin-
jeng. His report of Yin-shih's recourse to magic
power contributed greatly to the latter's imprisonment, and the same report helped the restoration of
Yin-jeng.[79] However, Yin-chih plunged into the
struggle after the redeposal of the crown prince in
1712.

   The situation after 1712 favored Yin-chih. The
three earlier contestants, Yin-shih, Yin-jeng, and
Yin-ssu, were publicly reprimanded by the throne and

their cause therefore became hopeless. This encouraged other aspirant princes, of whom Yin-chih was one. On one occasion in 1713 K'ang-hsi declared that a new crown prince, if appointed, should possess the same personality as his own.[80] He did not go into further detail, but it can be discerned from his various decrees that he meant an able, frugal, lenient, and nonfactional successor. It seems that Yin-chih's character was close to the imperial *sine qua non*. In the early phase of struggle, he was a peace-minded person without a faction and was one of the few princes with the imperial commendation. Before 1712 he was probably the prince next only to Yin-jeng in the emperor's thoughts. Some statistics, particularly those on imperial trips, support this point. In the K'ang-hsi period the emperor took many trips for private and administrative reasons, and from 1682 on he brought sons into his suite each time. During the years 1682-1722 he made 117 trips. Table 1 indicates the participation of his sons in the imperial tours:

Table 1*

Statistics of Trips by Princes during the K'ang-hsi Period

Name of the Participant	Date of Birth	No. of Trips Taken	Date of the First Trip
Yin-shih	1672	49	July 6, 1683
Yin-jeng	1674	52	March 3, 1682
Yin-chih	1677	64	July 16, 1683
Yin-chen	1678	46	Sept. 16, 1686
Yin-ch'i	1680	28	Sept. 9, 1687
Yin-yu	1680	26	Sept. 9, 1687
Yin-ssu	1681	39	Sept. 9, 1687
Yin-t'ang	1683	19	Sept. 10, 1695
Yin-e	1683	9	Sept. 10, 1695
Yin-t'ao	1686	9	May 28, 1710
Yin-hsiang	1686	39	Sept. 3, 1698
Yin-t'i	1688	20	March 4, 1699
Yin-wu	1693	55	Sept. 9, 1700
Yin-lu	1695	59	Sept. 9, 1700
Yin-li	1697	15	July 14, 1705
Yin-chiai	1701	4	July 5, 1707
Yin-i	1706	16	June 3, 1716
Yin-hsi	1711	4	May 18, 1720
Yin-hu	1711	4	May 18, 1720

*This table is based on the *CSL*, KH, chs. 13-294.

The Making of an Autocrat 73

The table suggests the father-son relationship in the imperial family. Yin-chih was in the imperial suite sixty-four times, more than any other prince. It is safe to say that he was a prince with the special favor of the emperor. In a decree K'ang-hsi implied that a father's love for his sons was not all the same.[81] This implication lent additional force to the validity of the table. If the number of trips sheds light on the relations between the emperor and his sons, that of assignments may imply the ability of the princes. It is generally true that the ablest were given the largest number of assignments. In the K'ang-hsi period the princes were commissioned with various assignments—some were routine work while others were special performances on behalf of the monarch. Table 2 covers all kinds of services charged to the princes during the K'ang-hsi period:

Table 2*

Statistics of Services Assigned to Princes during the K'ang-hsi Period

Name of Prince	Number of Services Assigned	Beginning Date of the First Service
Yin-shih	12	March 15, 1688
Yin-jeng	14	Jan. 31, 1690
Yin-chih	18	Jan. 31, 1690
Yin-chen	15	Jan. 31, 1690
Yin-yu	3	Nov. 14, 1699
Yin-ch'i	9	June 15, 1702
Yin-ssu	2	March 8, 1709
Yin-t'ang	2	Nov. 7, 1709
Yin-t'ao	9	Dec. 15, 1717
Yin-hsiang	2	Nov. 25, 1702
Yin-t'i	1	Dec. 3, 1718
Yin-lu	1	March 13, 1721
Yin-li	2	Jan. 14, 1720

*Source: *CSL*, KH, chs. 133-300.

Again Yin-chih was ranked first of the thirteen princes in the table. Like the figures from the first table, these are also limited by the age of the princes involved. Those who had the smaller figures may not necessarily be the recipients of less favor from the monarch, but the individuals who made larger figures were the princes of importance. Furthermore, Yin-chih's assignments of editing encyclopedias and regulating musical instruments started just one year after the redismissal of Yin-jeng. His commission was perhaps not ordinary in nature. Simply because of its significance, Yung-cheng after his succession deliberately omitted Yin-chih's name from the *Ku-chin t'u-shu chi-ch'eng*, one of the two encyclopedias.[82] During the Yung-cheng period, Yin-chih was also among the princes condemned as disobedient and punished by the emperor. These facts should serve as evidence of the important role played by Yin-chih in the struggle for the heirdom.

Since the situation after 1712 was encouraging, Yin-chih thought, and many officials believed, that he would be the logical choice to fill the heirdom vacancy.[83] To achieve his goal he took a rather single-handed but direct approach. As the K'ang-hsi Emperor fell into a decline, physically and psychologically, Yin-chih invited him to feast away his trouble, a total of nineteen times.[84] These frequent feasts should not be interpreted simply as an expression of filial piety because in a ruling family the relationship between parents and sons was always politically oriented. When examined in terms of chronology, these feasts present an interesting distribution. The first banquet was given as early as 1707, while the rest were in and after 1712. Such a pattern of distribution also suggests the political implications of the feast.

The approach which Yin-chih adopted was effective. After 1712 he always found himself in the suite of imperial trips and received more assignments. At the same time his successful strategy attracted the attention of his rivals. Yung-cheng, one of his competitors, vied with him in inviting the throne to feasts. His rivals also spread word that he illegally left the capital for visits to various places.[85] Although these rumors proved unfounded, they reflected his successful activity that caused others' jealousy. However, the effect of his tactics was reduced by the fact that he lacked strong supporters. If he had any, they were literary men like Ch'en Meng-lei (b.1651), Wang Mou-hung (1668-1741), and some others.[86] As he realized the importance of powerful supporters, he began to recruit men of influence in the last few years of the K'ang-hsi era. He seems to have tried to cultivate friendly relations with Lungkodo, who was then in charge of the security of Peking, and Nien Keng-yao, then governor of Szechwan.[87] It was too late, for they had been recruited by Yung-cheng. Without powerful supporters his failure was inevitable.

3. *A Lucky Successor*

If it is impossible to prove that Yung-cheng's succession was illegal, it is safe to say that he won the throne through competition. Like some of his brothers, he had for a long time dreamt of the throne, but he appeared in the arena relatively late. He possibly started in the last phase of struggle. His accession to the throne surprised not only his rivals but also his mother, Empress Hsiao-kung, the Benevolent (1660-1723). According to his testimony, immediately after the death of K'ang-hsi and the proclamation of his succession, Yin-ssu was at a loss how to face the reality and in the meantime Yin-t'ang felt regret that the crown was taken by a rival.[88] Even the new emperor's mother also was bewildered, telling some officials:

> I had been a concubine of the late emperor since I was young. I did not do anything for him, but he appointed my son his successor. This I did not dare to expect and even dream of.[89]

Why was Yung-cheng's succession so surprising? It was largely an outcome of his successful strategy.

Yung-cheng, who was familiar with Chinese philosophical schools and combined their strengths for his own ideology, derived his strategy from his philosophical studies, especially the dialectical Taoist principle about action and nonaction. He knew how to protect himself from the confusion of struggle and how to act under the cover of nonaction. When some of his aspirant brothers were busy organizing cliques, he lived quietly and prepared silently. As soon as the powerful competitors, Yin-shih, Yin-jeng, and Yin-ssu, fell, he emerged on the scene. His strategy centered on two objectives. The first was to win the imperial favor by showing filial respect for his father. When the emperor fell ill, he attended the patient very carefully.[90] He made every effort to please the monarch. He was perhaps the first of the princes who treated his imperial father with feasts in 1707.[91] Yin-chih immediately followed suit. Subsequently the two brothers competed with each other for their father's favor by numerous invitations and feasts. During the years 1707-1722 Yung-cheng invited and feasted his father twelve times. The chronological distribution of his feasts followed the same pattern as that of his opponent, Yin-chih. It is interesting to note that just eight months before the death of the monarch, Yung-cheng gave two birthday feasts within two weeks.[92] This frequency unmistakably showed the tension of the struggle. Compared with Yin-chih's eighteen banquets, Yung-cheng fell behind, but he exerted himself to compensate in other ways. When his father went to the summer resort in Jehol, he hurried there four times to pay his respects.[93] As a result he was praised by the throne as a filial son.[94] He also cultivated the friendship of his brothers, interceding with his father on behalf of Yin-jeng and other princes. Thus he won the deep appreciation of his father and was considered a "great man."[95]

The second objective of his strategy, like that of other competitors', was to win supporters, civilian and military. Early in 1707 he extended his favor to Yen Jo-chü (1636-1704), a famous classicist, mathematician, and geographer. He invited this scholar to Peking and treated him with exceptional honor.[96] By this he won not only the gratitude of the Yen family, but the applause of literary men of later generations.[97] Also, he tried unsuccessfully to win over Ho Ch'o from Yin-ssu.[98]

Yung-cheng did manage to recruit powerful supporters among the bannermen. The most distinguished of all was Nien Keng-yao, whom Yin-chih had futilely tried to enlist. The second eminent bannerman was Lungkodo, the third son of T'ung Kuo-wei, who supported first Yin-shih and then Yin-ssu. The third was Maci, originally a henchman of Yin-shih and then of Yin-ssu. His connection with Yung-cheng probably resulted from the introduction of his brother, Mawu, who had been an imperial bodyguard in the K'ang-hsi period and taken care of the K'ang-hsi Emperor when the monarch was a child.[99] Another important follower was Ts'ai T'ing (d.1743), a Chinese bannerman, who was then a member of the Hanlin Academy and later governor of Szechwan.[100] Yen-hsin, a member of the Imperial Clan, who had served first on the staff of Yin-t'i in the campaign against the Eleuths and later was made commander of the first army, was also a very significant follower of Yung-cheng. In 1722 Yung-cheng, Yen-hsin, and some others including Lungkodo were sent by K'ang-hsi to inspect the granary in Hopei.[101] This was perhaps the beginning of their relationship.

Yung-cheng's secretiveness was a very important factor that contributed to his success in the struggle for the throne. His activities were secret to such an extent that even his followers could not identify each other. Lungkodo and Nien Keng-yao, for example, both worked for his cause, and yet Lungkodo suspected Nien's political affiliation.[102] Supported by so many potent followers and armed with so shrewd a strategy, Yung-cheng was ready to meet any situation.

In the last stage of struggle Yin-t'i, the youngest of the three competitors, became the center of attention. Although he and Yung-cheng shared the same mother, he enlisted under the banner of Yin-ssu and Yin-t'ang. The redismissal of Yin-jeng in 1712 turned out to be the beginning of his good fortune. Yin-ssu found himself unable to realize his dream, and he tended to support Yin-t'i. However, Yin-t'i had not been, as it seems, influential enough to form his own clique before his appointment as Generalissimo for the Pacification of Distant Lands in 1718, a landmark in his life. As this was an important appointment, he, then only a prince of the fourth degree, was given the retinue and honors due a prince of the first degree.[103] When he left for his post early in 1719, the whole court, including his brothers and many other princes, were ordered to see him off.[104] Actually the appointment itself does not necessarily imply an imperial decision about the heirdom. The honors that Yin-t'i enjoyed after his appointment were but a dynastic tradition, according to which the commander-in-chief of expeditionary forces was given special deference on the occasion of his installment. The only difference lay in the fact that as an imperial son Yin-t'i received some extra deferences, over and above those accorded other princes.

Yin-t'i himself believed that his appointment was a step toward the throne, his followers had the same confidence, and "the whole nation," as Mailla recorded, thought the same.[105] This situation cemented the relations between him and his supporters. Yin-ssu became his strategist, while Yin-t'ang extended his generous financial help in addition to other forms of support.[106] After his departure for the front, these two princes were his chief agents in the capital. Yin-t'ang dispatched his intimate eunuch as courier to inform him of the situation in the capital.[107] His faction also included such high-ranking courtiers as Hsiao Yung-tsao (d.1729), a Grand Secretary, and Fahai (1671-1737), the second son of T'ung Kuo-kang (d.1690) who was his maternal granduncle.[108] With these important supporters at the capital, Yin-t'i is said to have been provided with all the money he requested by the central government.[109]

Yin-t'i did not forget to promote his reputation, even at the front. He twice sent messengers to invite a famous philosopher of the pragmatic school of the Ch'ing dynasty, Li Kung (1659-1733), whom Yin-chih had attempted to enlist before.[110] Yin-t'i's frugal life in the army won his father's great appreciation, and his good commandership moved the throne to order an inscription of his merit on a monument.[111] All in all, he was an active and powerful competitor in the last phase of struggle. He overshadowed Yin-chih and thus became the archopponent to his fourth elder brother, Yung-cheng. The struggle was in fact a competition between two royal brothers of the same father and mother.

At the last minute, however, Yin-t'i lost the contest to his rival. To understand the reasons these two competitors must be compared in terms of their tactics and strength. The first consideration is their political awareness. After Yin-t'i's designation as commander-in-chief, he was considered by himself and many other people a logical successor to the throne. This anticipation undermined his and his supporters' political sensitivity to their rival's strategy, and Yung-cheng was happy to find an open target and prepared counteractions. The second consideration is their strength. Yin-t'i did not lack followers in the court, but he needed men of military power at the capital. In spite of his armies on the front, he had no military strength in Peking.

The last, and probably the most important, factor is Yin-t'i's absence from Peking in the critical months of 1722, when the K'ang-hsi Emperor's health was declining. Late in 1721 he requested an audience in order to discuss strategy vis-à-vis the Eleuths, and he returned to the capital in early

1722.[112] The motive behind this request was perhaps to observe personally the political climate at the court, especially the physical condition of his father. When he left again for the front, he asked Yin-t'ang to report to him on the health of the aged ruler.[113] At such a critical time he should have stayed in Peking, but he did not. It is difficult to understand the reason for this. It may be asked, if K'ang-hsi meant to make Yin-t'i his successor why he did not ask the prince to stay with him when his health was worsening? As a matter of fact, he let Yin-t'i leave the capital. Was he also blinded to the activities of his fourth son? Whatever the reasons, the absence of Yin-t'i from Peking was a dominant factor in his defeat in the struggle. Had he remained there, the outcome of the competition might have been different. For example, Lungkodo—then a man in control of the metropolitan police and whose cousins were the irreconcilable opponents of Yung-cheng—was a possible supporter of Yin-t'i. He seems to have been recruited by Yung-cheng when they were assigned to inspect the granary in Hopei just one month before the death of the emperor.[114]

By contrast, Yung-cheng avoided his rival's errors. Yin-t'i's disadvantages became his advantages. He kept his activities covert and was well prepared for the showdown. Of his supporters, Lungkodo and Nien Keng-yao were the most important, both being men of military power—one in Peking and the other at the front. With their support from within and without, the future emperor became invincible. Besides, he stayed in the capital and watched the political situation there. When the emperor suddenly took ill in the Pleasant Spring Villa (*Ch'ang-ch'un yüan*) outside Peking in 1722, Yin-t'i with his troops was far in the northwest and under the surveillance of Nien Keng-yao.[115] Without military support, Yin-ssu and Yin-t'ang were unable to do anything for their younger brother, while Yin-chih had no powerful supporters and was equally ineffective. Yung-cheng now became the only prince who could control the situation. Only a few days before the death of his father, he was sent to perform the Winter Solstice Sacrifices at the Temple of Heaven on behalf of the throne. While fulfilling his assignment, he sent his agents frequently to watch the ailing monarch so as to meet any emergency caused by the latter's death.[116] When the emperor's illness turned out to be terminal, he himself appeared at the side of his dying father, and finally declared his designation as successor.[117] Under the protection of metropolitan police commanded by Lungkodo, he succeeded to the throne. Again, Father Ripa witnessed the situation at the moment of Yung-cheng's accession and wrote in his memoirs:

> On the twentieth of December, 1722, I [Father Ripa] was talking after supper with Father Angelo in the house of His Majesty's uncle, where we resided, when I heard an unusual noise, as if arising from a number of voices within the palace. I instantly caused the doors to be locked, and remarked to my companion that either the Emperor was dead, or else that a rebellion had broken out at Peking. In order to satisfy myself as to the cause of the disturbance, I climbed up on the wall of our dwelling, which skirted the public road, and saw with astonishment an innumerable multitude of horsemen, riding furiously in every direction, without speaking to each other.
>
> After watching their movement for some time, I at last heard some persons on foot say that Emperor Sheng-tsu [K'ang-hsi] was dead....One of the first cares of the new Emperor was to have the corpse of his father clothed, and conveyed the same night to the palace at Peking, attending it himself on horseback, followed by his brothers, children, and relatives, and escorted by his countless host of soldiers with drawn swords.[118]

In view of the confusion in which Yung-cheng succeeded to the throne there is reason to doubt the legitimacy of his accession. Nevertheless, such confusion resulted from the competition which in turn gave rise to the problem of legitimacy. If it is hard to prove the legitimacy of his accession, it is equally difficult to judge him an illegitimate ruler. Whoever ascended the throne would be considered illegitimate by unsuccessful competitors. At any rate, Yung-cheng was the lucky competitor. On the basis of his contributions to the Manchu regime, the Ch'ing dynasty was fortunate to have such a ruler.

IV

Consolidation of Power

1. *The Nature and Role of the Clique*

Yung-cheng's determination to consolidate his power dominated his political conduct and found expression in many aspects of the political life of the era. Historically, consolidation of power is a long-standing problem, occurring in all political groups. It always involves competition created by the power situation, particularly on the occasion of political transition between dynasties or reigns. To put it more specifically, it usually appears in the form of a power struggle within the ruling group. The present discussion will focus on the struggle between the ruler and the elites: the aristocrats and the bureaucrats. The basic issue of this struggle is power itself. The ruler and the elites belong to the same ruling group, but they are not at the same level. Their goals are not always identical. The ruler is primarily concerned with maintaining his position—unchallenged—at the top of the political hierarchy, while the elites are frequently inclined to try to further their personal interests at the expense of the sovereign. The difference between these two goals is, in effect, that between centripetal and centrifugal forces. The constant factional tensions resulting within the ruling group necessitate consolidation of power by the ruler.[1] Fundamentally, it is the process of political centralization. History has provided numerous examples. Consolidation of power in the Yung-cheng period was a repetition of this historical pattern.

Yung-cheng's struggle to consolidate power can also be understood in the general context of autocracy. Since autocracy has a centralist tendency, the autocrat is always prone "to concentrate the greatest possible number of powers" in his own hands.[2] With the support of power he is able to claim absolute and universal rule, the basic requirement for autocracy. Absolute rule makes the ruler independent of the will of any other individual or group. The elites are the instruments to carry out his will, but they are not the men to share his authority. If the ruler is the power-holder, the elites can be called power-followers. As a matter of fact, elites, whatever their social background, are disposed to be acquisitive and thus create a situation that moves the ruler to consolidate his power. In this sense, absolute rule is the stereotyped relationship between power-holder and power-follower.

Universal rule implies the authority of the ruler to make rules such as law valid for the whole territory under him.[3] The universal validity of such rules relies upon their authority over other values, interests, and beliefs. In other words, these rules should be the central norms. The effectiveness of the rules also depends upon their faithful enforcement, which involves personal and legal considerations. With reference to the first, the elites must carry out the rules faithfully according to the will of the ruler. Any disobedience or deviation on the part of the elites will weaken the effectiveness of the rules. As to the legal aspect, the rules must be carried out with justice. Any breach of them is an attack on the ruler's authority. In the political realm, authority is largely based on power and justice. During the Yung-cheng period, consolidation of power was directed toward the realization of absolute and universal rule.

During the Yung-cheng period, the emperor's consolidation of power sprang from the special background of the succession struggle. Yung-cheng won the throne, but his former rivals, Yin-chih, Yin-ssu, Yin-t'ang, and Yin-t'i, were not obedient. They and their partisans retained relations as coherent as before. The emperor repeatedly reprimanded them for factional activities and accused them of disobedience or even disloyalty. Although some of his accusations may have been exaggerated, these charges clearly revealed the deep enmity that the struggle for succession had engendered. The situation was still competitive. While the competition provided the background for his rise to power, it also created a situation requiring consolidation of power. To achieve his goal he had to punish the former contenders and their supporters, whose influence and activity were inimical to imperial authority. His moves to consolidate power were a continuation of the old struggle.

It would be an error to regard the removal of these princes by Yung-cheng as retaliation for their having participated in the struggle for succession. Their castigation should be examined in connection with the problem of legitimacy—a problem that was, in the minds of his rivals and of some students of Ch'ing history, related to the emperor's succession to the throne. Whatever the nature of his succession, legitimacy was important to him, for the question of legitimacy involves not only the rightfulness of the ruler's succession, but also his qualifications to administer and to demand political obedience. Naturally, legitimate rule makes "the ruled feel obliged or bound to render obedience."[4] As has already been pointed out in Chapter 3, the problem of Yung-cheng's succession was derived from the competition. The continuing factional activities of the old competitors lent further flavor to the question of the legitimacy of his succession. Unless he removed them, he could not expect to rule effectively. If his removal of them did not completely solve the problem, it did do away with the source of new agitation. Furthermore, since the effectiveness of his authority was based on his ability to remove whoever was in his way, he punished them as an example to others. His action was meant to consolidate power and thus to facilitate rule.

To consolidate his power, Yung-cheng had to remove another group of influential individuals also related to the succession struggle. Lungkodo and Nien Keng-yao, for instance, belonged to this group. They were Yung-cheng's supporters, to whom he owed his successful competition. For their support, he rewarded them with high titles and positions, and they became the elites of the new reign. Their strategic positions in the officialdom and their special relations with the throne were sources of power and influence. For personal considerations, individual bureaucrats gradually rallied around them, and they became factional leaders. Their factions differed in nature from those of the princes, but both developed at the cost of the sovereign power. As followers of Yung-cheng in his struggle for the throne, Lungkodo and Nien Keng-yao were power-supporters indispensable to him. As heads of their own factions, they became power-seekers, obstacles in the way of the new ruler. If their rise to power is seen as a consequence of the succession problem, they may be treated as a case in the same category as the princes.

Yung-cheng's consolidation of power was also a timely action to meet the needs of the Ch'ing dynasty. Since Hong-taiji, the Manchu regime had been plagued by various kinds of factions, most of whom recruited members from the banners. As the banner system was an establishment unique to the Ch'ing, the factions from it were a special problem to the dynasty. Their activities were needlessly associated with the succession issue, but they were in general oriented against the sovereign power. Because of their banner background, they presented a particularly strong challenge to the sovereign. If connected with the succession problem, they intensified the struggle. Early Ch'ing history included a long list of such factions.

In one way or another the early Manchu rulers all suffered from factional activities. During the period 1627-1643, Hong-taiji had trouble in dealing with powerful factions led by princes, notably Daisan (1583-1648), Amin (d.1640), and Manggultai (1587-1633)—each of whom was in charge of a banner. These three princes were actually equals of Hong-taiji, and the four ruled jointly. It was not until 1632 that Hong-taiji was able to rule alone,[5] but the abolition of four-man rule did not mean the elimination of factionalism. New factions took the place of the old. Dorgon was in all likelihood the most powerful factional leader of the early Ch'ing period. He was a prince during the three reigns from Nurhaci to Shun-chih and at last acquired the title of Imperial Father Regent in the Shun-chih period. The actual ruler of China in the years 1644-1650, he placed his cohorts in important positions, and his will was followed throughout the empire.[6] He died in 1650, but it took a few more years to root out his clique. After his death Jirgalang (1599-1655), another prince, immediately took over.[7] Because his reign was short and marked by factional struggle, the Shun-chih Emperor enjoyed little sovereign power.

If the K'ang-hsi period was marked by its long duration, it was also characterized by its factional strife. Oboi, the most powerful of the four regents of the Kang-hsi Emperor, practically took charge of state affairs in the first eight years of the period.[8] In furthering the interests of his faction, he came into conflict with other officials. He died in humiliation, and many members of his clique were executed.

When influential Manchu nobles founded cliques, a few high-ranking Chinese officials emerged as leaders of their own factions. Hsü Ch'ien-hsüeh (1631-1694), a scholar-official and also a famous bibliophile, was an example.[9] In the last years of the K'ang-hsi period, factionalism merged with the succession struggle and was strengthened. The above brief examination may serve as evidence that factions were a serious political problem of the early Ch'ing. Since they handicapped the exercise of imperial power, they were targets of strong rulers. After accession to the throne, Yung-cheng was ready to clear the way for consolidation of his power.

Factions in the Yung-cheng period deserve detailed exploration. In general, they fell into three groups. The first group included imperial clansmen; Yin-chih, Yin-ssu, Yin-t'ang, and Yin-t'i were representatives. As members of the ruling house, they were powerful individuals in their own right. True, in dynastic history, Chinese or Western, imperial princes were influential by virtue of birth. What made the early Manchu princes different from many of their predecessors was that besides having dignified titles, they occupied offices of importance. At the very beginning of the dynasty Nurhaci made his elder sons banner commanders with the title of prince. Hong-taiji not only followed this practice but also assigned experienced princes to take care of political affairs. Thus, their social status was embodied in political prerogatives, that were in turn supported by military privileges. It is no wonder that they were the major threat to the sovereign power. In the Shun-chih and K'ang-hsi periods, their influence was gradually diluted by bureaucrats, but they still enjoyed political and military privileges sufficient to sustain factional activities against the sovereign interests.

The second category consisted of imperial affinals, whose strength rested upon the marriage relationship with the ruling house. When their daughters, sisters, or granddaughters were made empresses or imperial consorts, they naturally achieved prominence. This group had been serious contenders for the throne in Chinese dynastic history. Although they never formed the major menace to the Manchu sovereigns, they were earnest participants in factional activities. The K'ang-hsi period supplied a significant example. Songgotu was the maternal granduncle of Yin-jeng and a powerful factional leader.[10] T'ung Kuo-wei was K'ang-hsi's father-in-law. While his nephews, Olondai and Fahai, supported Yin-ssu, Yin-t'ang, and Yin-t'i, his son—Lungkodo—was an important adherent of Yung-cheng. In the early years of the Yung-cheng period Lungkodo led a powerful faction.

The last group comprised ordinary officials. They were an indispensable part of the imperial system, but they were, on the other hand, prone to self-seeking. Bureaucratic factions had been a dynastic problem of long standing. Nien Keng-yao's faction, active during the first three years of the Yung-cheng period, is illustrative. In view of Nien's status as a bannerman, and the fact that he was born a member of a privileged group, one may question the validity of equating his clique with those cliques of ordinary officials who came to power mainly from the open-examination system. Also, Nien's sister is said to have been a concubine of Yung-cheng.[11] However, two factors put his clique in the category of ordinary officials. First, Nien Keng-yao owed his prominence largely to the regular examination channel; this gave him the credentials of a typical bureaucrat. Secondly, members of his clique were predominantly bureaucrats. In consequence, his faction stood distinct from the first two categories.

In terms of social background the three factional groupings of the Yung-cheng period fitted in two classes, aristocratic and bureaucratic. Imperial clansmen and affinals were aristocrats who acquired social and political strength through their special attachment to the ruling house, and they were always holders of hereditary titles and important offices. In contrast to their predecessors, the Manchu aristocrats during Yung-cheng's time were consolidated into the banner system. If they gained importance through their unusual relationship to the throne, they obtained more of it through their status in the banner system. From the beginning, the banners were organized in a feudal way for the purpose of conquest. Leadership of various units was hereditary and with it came a continuing relationship with subordinates, because their standing was also hereditary. While the banners performed social, economic, and political functions for their members, they operated as a group of hereditary cohorts of the Manchu ruling house. Manchu aristocrats were invariably banner dignitaries. As long as they maintained their special status in the banner system, they had political and military influence. High status in the banner and special connections with the throne gave the Manchu aristocratic faction double strength with which to challenge the sovereign power.

The bureaucratic faction, such as the Nien clique, was far weaker than its aristocratic competitors. Inasmuch as they were recruited from various social groups by the examination system on the basis of personal academic achievement, the members of the bureaucratic faction were a nonhereditary status group. Their knowledge was essential in bureaucratic work; their nonhereditary standing helped the rulers cut out the aristocracy. They contributed to the growth of sovereign power, and were the foundation of the imperial system. As a group of administrative functionaries, however, they had the acquisitive inclinations that inspired them to organize cliques against the ruler's interest.

Since the three factional groups had different characteristics, they exercised different influences on the Yung-cheng Emperor, and his reactions to them were different. The clique of the imperial princes was the strongest of the three. Its strength was derived from the capacity of its leaders, imperial princes who had blood ties to the throne and the feudal support of their men in the banners. During the struggle for the heirdom they cooperated, and after defeat they were again united, psychologically and politically, in their efforts to confront the new situation. With such a cohesive *esprit de corps*, their clique presented the strongest challenge to the emperor's right to succession and his sovereign power. In response, he made the most cautious and persistent effort against it.

The faction under Lungkodo was different. Its purpose was to gain personal profit through corrupt means but not to accede to the throne. After the succession of Yung-cheng, the faction was loosely organized by self-seeking individuals. Its members depended on the patronage of their leader, Lungkodo, who in turn relied upon imperial favor and trust. Compared with the factions under the princes, it had only limited influence on the ruler. Because imperial favor and trust were fundamental to Lungkodo's rise to power, his removal was relatively easier than that of the princes. As soon as the ruler was able to get a grip on his arch-opponents and discovered the factional activities of Lungkodo, he began to get rid of the clique.

In many ways the Nien clique was similar to that of Lungkodo. Members of these two factions worked for self-interest and were bound together by the personal influence of their respective leaders. Both were removed in a similar way. As for their influence on the sovereign, there was a difference between the Nien clique and the factions of the princes and Lungkodo. The latter two cliques consisted predominantly of Manchus, were active in the capital, and had a greater aversion to sovereign power than the Nien clique. In comparison, Nien Keng-yao was a provincial administrator and commander-in-chief on the frontier. He recruited faction members from Chinese bureaucrats in local governments and officers in the army under him. The activities of his faction centered around certain localities over which he had jurisdiction or influence. But these differences did not sharply distinguish the Nien clique from the other two. While the factions of the princes and Lungkodo handicapped the sovereign power at a high level, the Nien clique tended to undermine imperial rule from below. All three formed a counterforce which the Yung-cheng Emperor tried to eliminate.

2. *Suppression of Cliques*

Suppression of the clique was a significant political achievement of the Yung-cheng period and greatly contributed to the consolidation of the sovereign power. Of the early Manchu rulers, Yung-cheng was the most powerful. It was factional activities that undermined the power of the Manchu rulers who preceded him. Why, then, did they fail to suppress the cliques? This question may be answered in terms of the political climate of the time.

Before 1644 the Manchu regime was essentially a confederation of banners with emphasis on military conquest. There was, in a strict sense, no concept of sovereign power. The princes were almost the equal of the ruler. If the factions, which were actually identified with the individual banners, intruded into the ruler's power, they also united members under their leaders—banner commanders—for more conquests. Hong-taiji took action against the factions only when he found good excuses and was strong enough to do so.

Hong-taiji's successor, the Shun-chih Emperor, was aware of the factional activities, but he died without taking a positive stand against them. His legacy was a few maxims and short essays about official conduct. In 1652 he set out eight maxims for all local schools.[12] Two of these admonish scholars against forming cliques and literary societies. In 1655 he published a short work entitled *Yü-chih jen-ch'en ching-hsin lu* (Imperial admonitions on the conduct of officials and subjects), a booklet of eight essays, the first of which discusses factional activities. In this essay he briefly analyzed the origins and evils of factionalism and warned the people not to practice factional activities.[13]

K'ang-hsi defended his sovereign power with word and deed. He denounced the evils of factionalism,[14] and on some occasions punished factional leaders with resolution. For instance, he castigated Oboi, penalized Songgotu, and even disciplined his sons, Yin-shih and Yin-jeng, for factional activities. If the Three Feudatories can be defined as factions, his removal of them should be mentioned as a typical antifaction campaign. But his efforts to thwart factionalism were not systematic; rather he removed factions only when they seriously threatened the Manchu regime. With the exception of these cases, he was reluctant to take positive measures. Courtiers were dismissed for factional activities, but were reinstated after a few years.[15] Consequently, factions remained active throughout the K'ang-hsi period and were strengthened by the succession crisis.

Several reasons would appear to account for K'ang-hsi's less-than-determined attempts to curb factionalism. One was his personal character—he tended to tolerate factions provided they did not go beyond a certain point. His limited efforts were, from another viewpoint, a stratagem to maintain a balance between different official groups. When factions rapaciously struggled for personal interests, he let them fight and check each other; thus, he profited from the divide-and-rule principle. Also, his restraint may have been a technique to maintain sovereign power. When officials, Manchu and Chinese, had enjoyed some private gain from factional activities, they were more likely to support the throne. His attitude toward the Chinese scholar-officials was particularly in line with this policy.

In contrast, Yung-cheng was implacably opposed to factional practices. Immediately after his succession, he took strong measures to root out the factions, and he carried out his policy with religious fervor. In all of Chinese history few rulers had made efforts as systematic and persistent as he made to eliminate factionalism. Remarkable in this regard were his philosophical arguments about sovereign power and the factions. In his campaign against the factions, these arguments served him both as principle and as method. His arguments appeared in many decrees and while it is impossible to discuss all of them in this study, two typical ones should be elaborated.

The first decree was issued before the high-ranking courtiers a few months after his succession. In it he started from the premise that factionalism was an extremely evil practice with pernicious results in politics.[16] He expressed regret that his officials continued this practice and stated that, as a prince, he had stayed away from factionalism and that for this reason he was made successor by the late ruler. Thus, he offered his personal conduct as a model. The practice of criticizing the ruler behind his back was, he pointed out, evil conduct of unworthy people. He seemed to identify this practice with factionalism. If officials disagreed with the ruler, they should speak their minds to him. Finally, he concluded that officials should act in conformity with the likes and dislikes of the ruler. In fact, the entire decree centered on the issue of conformity, which was also the central idea of all his decrees concerning factionalism. For example, he explained in another decree that conformity to the likes and dislikes of the ruler brought about a uniformity in judgments.[17] Such uniformity, he considered, would encourage good conduct and make factionalism impossible.

His most authoritative arguments were contained in the essay "On Factions" (*P'eng-tang lun*), published in 1724. Although he frequently quoted from the Confucian Classics to support his argument, this essay was a typically Legalist exposition of the subject. It covered all the points that an autocrat might use to defend his autocracy. To begin with, he claimed that the distinction between ruler and minister was as fixed as that between heaven and earth—one was exalted while the other was low.[18] He implied that officials should always have their ruler in mind and conform to his likes and dislikes. Otherwise, they subverted this distinction, and according to him, such subversion always resulted from factional practices. To expose the pernicious effect of factionalism, he gave as an example the matter of official appointments. When the ruler pondered an appointment, he needed advice to make a sound decision. If he was misadvised by factional-minded officials, he unintentionally deviated from impartiality. Thus it would have been better if the ruler had depended on his own judgment. As for other evil aspects of factionalism, he went on:

> When the ruler employs a man, factional-minded people discuss the matter and say: "This man was recommended by so-and-so"; and with this they stay away from him as though he were unclean, saying: "We avoid suspicion; we depart from sycophancy"; and with envy, one after another they slander and revile him, and will not be happy unless they get rid of him. When the ruler dismisses a man, they talk: "This man was denounced by so-and-so." His intimate friends express regret for it; his distant friends condole with him on his misfortune; and even his former opponents sympathize with him and try to make up with him. On the contrary, nobody urges him to rectify his faults and reform himself; and so the man ceases to be aware of his defections and is increasingly moved to express feelings of resentment against the sovereign.[19]

These factional practices confused impartial standards of right and wrong, the emperor complained in the same essay. He again emphasized that the officials should tell their disagreements directly to the ruler instead of talking about them behind his back. Also, he stressed that his nonfactional disposition and righteous conduct were the reason for his being made successor to the late monarch. He once more asked the officials to follow his model.

The last part of the essay is a refutation of the treatise with the same title written by Ou-yang Hsiu (1007-1072), a famous scholar-official of the Sung dynasty. Ou-yang Hsiu's treatise, a memorial presented to the throne at a time of bitter factional struggles, emphasized the importance of factions formed by righteous scholars. He distinguished a good faction from a bad one in terms of the motivation and personality of its members.[20] Men of integrity, according to him, were united in common ideals and thus formed a faction for the public interest. This faction was a good and permanent association, he further stated, while inferior men were attracted by material interests, temporarily bound together by mutual advantage, and formed a group for personal profit. Because they shared no common ideals, he insisted, their clique was bad and temporary, and they had no real faction. This treatise naturally ran counter to that of the Yung-cheng Emperor. He denounced Ou-yang Hsiu's argument as a perverse theory for the protection of factionalism.

As a whole, the emperor's arguments manifested his personality, ideology, and the political situation of his reign, and they may be condensed into two points—legitimacy and conformity. During the Yung-cheng period the question of legitimacy carried double weight. In a special sense it was the chief weapon used by the partisans under the princes to challenge his succession. It served to bind them together and was even exploited by Chinese nationalists for their anti-Manchu movement. Since sheer force could not solve the problem, the emperor had to legitimize his succession through other means. While attacking factional activities, he stressed the reasons for his being selected by the K'ang-hsi emperor as the successor, and the same reason was repeatedly presented on many other occasions, especially when he repudiated the princes who formerly participated in the competition for the throne. Obviously, he meant to acquire legitimacy for his succession.

In a general sense the problem of legitimacy was connected with the quality of rule and was therefore a primary concern of Chinese rulers. They legitimized their rule in Confucian terms, for

Confucianism was the orthodox philosophy of the traditional Chinese state. But in reality they ruled by Legalist doctrine, which better served their desire for political centralization. In this the Yung-cheng Emperor was no exception. What he employed in denouncing factionalism was Legalist ideas beneath the veneer of Confucianism. He thus exploited both schools in his efforts to eliminate factionalism.

Legitimacy and conformity were related to each other in that legitimate rule makes the governed feel obliged to give obedience, and that, in quantitative terms, there is a proportional connection between them.[21] When the faction of princes raised the problem of Yung-cheng's legitimacy, other factions challenged his interests in different ways. In the final analysis, both were a problem of conformity, which required political obedience without personal considerations. This best explains why Yung-cheng stressed both legitimacy and conformity at the same time. He meant to combine them to serve his purpose of suppressing factions. To achieve conformity he asked officials to share his likes and dislikes and to use his personal conduct as a model. It is clear that only in a situation of conformity could he root out factionalism and consolidate his power. As a matter of fact, autocrats greatly encourage conformity.

In Chinese political history, autocratic rulers always looked with suspicion on any political or even personal grouping between officials. Such groupings were likely to be regarded as factions that would ultimately encroach on the sovereign power. Consequently, all factions were considered in a political light and regarded as bad even though they were morally motivated. The Yung-cheng Emperor also interpreted them in this way.

The above discussion indicates that Chinese autocrats tended to define the term factionalism loosely. As a result, the conformity that they stressed was more than political obedience, and its application was not solely limited to suppression of factions. In the same light Yung-cheng's "likes" and "dislikes" extended over political boundaries, and were not merely applied to the stopping of factionalism. Conformity to his likes and dislikes rather suggests compliance with the autocrat's central norms, political and nonpolitical. Any values at variance with these norms were seemingly to be considered violations by him. In his personal instructions he once asked a provincial governor to give up considerations of private fame and friendship for public duty.[22] In his treatise, "On Factions," he insisted that after a man took office "he gives himself to his ruler, and can no longer consider himself as belonging to his father and mother."[23] True, in Chinese history dynastic rulers were inclined to cherish the same ideas, but Yung-cheng was the rare one who bluntly brought them out and tried to put them into practice. Since his requirements were opposed to the traditional Chinese bureaucratic behavior,[24] which could not be transformed overnight, he frequently had to remove officials in the name of factionalism and issue decrees as instructions. He was not only a ruler but a devoted teacher working for consolidation of power.

If the Yung-cheng Emperor's publication of decrees and special treatises to denounce factionalism were consensual in nature, his punishments of violators were coercive. He gave priority to the consensual means, but when they did not serve his purpose, he did not hesitate to employ the other method. His punishments included physical and economic aspects. The death sentence was reserved for a few serious offenders such as Nien Keng-yao and Olondai. The princes and their chief supporters received life imprisonment. Banishment and flogging were applied in some relatively light cases. When men received the death sentence or life imprisonment, their property was confiscated. Dismissal and degradation were the rule for common cases. Besides punishments, new coercive means were devised. In dealing with strong factions such as those of the princes and Nien Keng-yao, he usually picked out a member and forced him to denounce, or propose a punishment for, another one of the same group.[25]

In short, Yung-cheng applied every possible means to transform the officialdom to his ideal— "an autocracy in which officials fanned out from a single point of concentration, the emperor, with no individual connections between official and official."[26]

3. *Three Case Studies*

The following pages relate three case studies corresponding to the three categories of factions. Since there are no other first-hand sources for Yung-cheng factions, the three case studies are necessarily based on the official works of the time. As a result, the studies are not made to confirm the "crimes" with which the emperor charged the factional leaders. Instead, they are designed to indicate an autocrat's desires, behavior, and steps taken to remove opponents, actual or possible, to consolidate his power.

During the first four years of the Yung-cheng period, the emperor concentrated his whole attention on suppression of cliques. The princes—Yin-chih, Yin-ssu, Yin-t'ang, and Yin-t'i—were his first targets. Two Western writers, Herbert A. Giles and John Ross, believe that they plotted the ruin of the Yung-cheng Emperor.[27] However, this is very unlikely—even the Ch'ien-lung Emperor, son and successor of Yung-cheng, denied it.[28] They were, it can be ascertained, still powerful after losing the struggle for the throne. They drew force mainly from their status as princes and from their supporters who had high positions in the court and banners. Evidently they could not all be removed at one time, and the emperor needed time to build up his strength. This situation determined his strategy, which was to tarnish their reputations, isolate them, and limit their wealth. The work was painstaking and time-consuming.

First, in the second half of 1723, the year he acceded to the throne, Yung-cheng enlisted three unswerving supporters from among his brothers—Yin-hsiang, who besides serving in the Council of Supervisors (*Tsung-li shih-wu wang ta-ch'en*), took charge of the Board of Revenue; Yin-lu, who was appointed acting director of the Office of the Imperial Household at the end of 1722 and was responsible for the security of imperial villas in Peking; and Yin-li, who since 1723 had frequently been made banner commander.[29] When Lungkodo controlled the security forces in the capital, Nien Keng-yao commanded the army at the front. Among provincial administrators and army commanders the emperor planted his personal memorialists, who had the obligation of sending reports directly to him.

His next step was the introduction in September 1723 of a new succession system,[30] according to which the ruler personally selected an heir from any of his sons and put the candidate's name in a sealed box, not revealing the selection to anyone, including the candidate himself. This system departed slightly from both Chinese and Manchu traditions of imperial inheritance. In most cases the Chinese ruler picked the eldest son born by the empress and publicly designated him heir apparent. Giving the right exclusively to the eldest legitimate son, this practice minimized the possibility of succession disputes, but the heir apparent thus selected was not, in practice, a man of ability in many cases. In Manchu practice before the K'ang-hsi period, the successor, not so strictly limited to the eldest son from the legal imperial wife, might be any one of the princes selected by influential members of the imperial family. Although this early Manchu practice made it possible to choose a prince of personal merit, it was susceptible to outside influence and led to the struggle for inheritance. The K'ang-hsi Emperor was the first Manchu ruler who seriously attempted to follow the Chinese pattern. Because this adoption led to factional strife and was never institutionalized, the Yung-cheng Emperor's innovation was a measure that deserves elaboration.

The significance of the new succession system lay in the fact that it had the advantages of the Chinese and Manchu usages of imperial succession and yet limited their disadvantages. When all the imperial sons were on the list of candidates, the ruler had more opportunity to make a better choice. Because, according to the new system, the ruler selected a successor from among his sons at his discretion in complete secrecy, succession became simply a matter for the imperial family. It thus prohibited the Manchu aristocrats from participating in the decision—which was of vital interest to the sovereign power—and prevented a possible court struggle for succession. Since the Yung-cheng period, factional fighting between princes for the throne has never been repeated. In short, the selection system that Yung-cheng introduced was fundamentally related to his suppression of cliques and conformed to his autocratic practice in that he designated a successor consistent with his likes and dislikes.

Of the princes, the most influential was Yin-ssu, who enjoyed great popularity among the aristocrats. He won the unanimous support of the courtiers when they were asked to recommend a candidate for the throne in 1709, and even admiration for his ability from the Yung-cheng Emperor, his arch-opponent. His popularity and ability were the sources of power and also the factor that kept Yung-cheng on the alert. In his suppression of cliques the emperor turned his eye first on Yin-ssu. Immediately after his succession to the throne, he appointed the prince a member of the Council of Supervisors in charge of central administration while he observed the mourning period, soon made him president of the Board of Colonial Affairs, and a few months later promoted him to a prince of the first degree.[31] These distinctions upon Yin-ssu were but a tactic of the emperor, whose real intention was to keep the prince under his surveillance. For instance, when Yin-ssu was made a member of the Council, three of the emperor's chief supporters, Yin-hsiang, Lungkodo, and Maci, were assigned to the same office. That made a ratio of 1:3 in favor of the emperor, and naturally Yin-ssu was a member of no importance in the Council. When the three others were rewarded in 1725, he received blame.[32] Certainly, from the very beginning he was aware of his situation and seems to have cherished no illusion of a lasting reconciliation. When congratulated on the princely title the ruler granted him, his wife is said to have remarked that the monarch meant to have her husband's head.[33]

At the same time the emperor tried to isolate Yin-ssu from his supporters. No sooner had the K'ang-hsi Emperor died than Yin-t'i was recalled from the frontier.[34] Since Yin-t'i had the army under his command and maintained close contact with his collaborators in Peking, his recall was not only an act against him, but a measure to cut off Yin-ssu's outside support. Yin-e, another follower of Yin-ssu, was sent on a mission to Mongolia in early 1723.[35] Yin-t'ang, also a collaborator and supporter of the same prince, was dispatched to Kokonor—in effect, banishment.[36] Now Yin-ssu was at the mercy of the emperor.

Imperial decrees loaded reprimands upon the prince to weaken his reputation and win a general concensus among the officials in the ruler's favor.[37] When Yin-e was accused of disobedience, the Yung-cheng Emperor forced Yin-ssu to consider a punishment for the prince, who was finally imprisoned permanently.[38] Many of Yin-ssu's supporters were degraded, banished, or executed during the years 1724-1726.[39] In early 1726 the emperor put him informally in custody, forced his wife to commit suicide, and expelled him from the imperial clan.[40] To conform with the emperor's wishes, all the high courtiers immediately submitted a memorial, charging Yin-ssu with disloyalty, treason, and a lack of filial piety, and imploring the throne to execute him. In response, the emperor happily sentenced the prince to life imprisonment and severely punished the official who did not actively make the same request.[41]

Yung-cheng reserved more punishment for Yin-ssu even while the prince was in custody. By imperial order he altered his name to *acina* ("dog" in Manchu).[42] Again, all of the courtiers submitted a long memorial, accusing him of forty "crimes," most of which had to do with his coveting the heirdom, factional activities, undermining state affairs, immoral conduct, and disobedience; they also requested the emperor to put him to death.[43] The emperor did not sentence him to death, but approved the accusations. Yin-ssu died in prison in October 1726. Some scholars suspect that he was murdered according to the imperial will,[44] but there is insufficient evidence of this. In any case, the most influential leader of the aristocratic faction was successfully removed.

Yin-t'ang's fate was similar. In personal ability and influence he was no match for Yin-ssu, but he possessed enormous wealth, which became an important source of power. He was virtually the financier of the clique of the ambitious princes. To suppress him the emperor took measures to reduce his wealth. As soon as he was sent to Kokonor, his property was probably confiscated, and even before that he had been forced to pay large sums of money.[45] Some of his rich supporters, too, suffered confiscation of property.[46] The monarch also separated Yin-t'ang from his followers, the most important of whom were the Sunu family and the Portuguese Jesuit Father João Mourão.

The Sunu family was from the line of Cuyen (1580-1615), Nurhaci's eldest son. Because Cuyen was condemned by his father to confinement for various offenses, his descendents were less favored by the Manchu rulers. In the competition for the heirdom Sunu and his sons took sides with Yin-ssu and became partisans of Yin-t'ang out of the common purpose they shared. Besides, Sunu also had a close relationship with Yin-t'ang's father-in-law—Ch'i-shih, another prince. His relations with Yin-ssu and Yin-t'ang were so unshakable that the emperor felt it necessary to do away with him and his family, and the Catholic missionaries recorded in detail the persecution of the family. Since many members of the family were Christians, in their accounts the

Jesuits interpreted the persecution from a religious viewpoint.[47] Although A. Thomas has provided a good analysis which emphasizes the political factor, he favors the emperor unduly.[48] In light of the emperor's ideology, the basic reason for his punishment of the Sunu family lies simply in his determination to suppress factionalism.

Father Mourão had long been associated with Yin-t'ang. He supplied the prince with Western luxuries and seems to have worked with him to win over Nien Keng-yao.[49] His affiliation with Yin-t'ang was probably mainly religious and without political motivation. When Yung-cheng succeeded to the throne, the priest was in Macao. Against the advice of his friends he returned to Peking and presented the sovereign with European curiosities.[50] But the emperor considered his connection with Yin-t'ang from a political viewpoint and banished both of them to Kokonor, where they were imprisoned in two apartments but still had contact. In 1726 he was brought back to Peking for examination. The examiners recommended death for him, but the emperor sent him back to the frontier. Because this case caused fear among the other Jesuits in the capital, they begged the throne to have mercy on him and asked the King of Portugal to intercede with the emperor for Mourão. The priest was, however, executed in exile.[51]

Yin-t'ang apparently did not realize Yung-cheng's determination to get rid of him. Shortly after his arrival in Kokonor, he petitioned to return to the capital.[52] But in answer to this request, the emperor sent his family, except for one son, to join him in 1724. Nien Keng-yao kept close watch over the prince and reported his activities to the throne.[53] In confinement he won the affection of his attendants, who followed him into exile, and the sympathy of some of the people in the region where he was imprisoned.[54] When the emperor suspected the loyalty of Nien Keng-yao, he sent another henchman to watch his brother.[55] Side by side with his increasing pressure on Yin-ssu and other partisans, Yung-cheng tightened his grip on Yin-t'ang. Under strict surveillance and without money, the prince became helpless, and the monarch now was ready to render him a final blow.

Yin-t'ang suffered the final imperial attack in early 1726 when he was found to have been in communication with his son through a code modified from the Latin alphabet he had learned from his

Portuguese fellow-prisoner.[56] The next day the emperor expelled him with Yin-ssu, Sunu, and another prince from the imperial clan, and three months later he was taken in irons from Kokonor to Pao-t'ing, Hopei, where he was put in confinement.[57] He was ordered to take a new name, *seshe* ("pig" in Manchu), and was charged with twenty-eight "crimes," involving heirdom struggle, factional activities, disobedience, and improper conduct.[58] He died in prison half a month earlier than Yin-ssu. Although the emperor was obliged to explain the cause of Yin-t'ang's death to the public, he was glad to have swept away another influential factional leader.[59]

Yin-t'i was another prince standing in Yung-cheng's way. With powerful armies he was the most potent threat to the new regime. The day after his accession to the throne the emperor ordered Yin-t'i to return to Peking under the supervision of a Manchu lieutenant-general, and sent another henchman, Yen-hsin, to the headquarters to control the troops.[60] This put double pressure on Yin-t'i, who at that time was already under the surveillance of Nien Keng-yao—then governor-general of Szechwan and Shensi—and whose armies were also supplied by the latter. In this circumstance Yin-t'i could do nothing but follow the order, although he resented it. It is said that after his arrival in the capital, he failed to pay homage to the new ruler.[61] In accordance with his strategy the emperor isolated the newcomer from his associates in Peking by sending him to an imperial resort north of the capital. Yin-t'i was publicly promoted to prince of the second degree without designation and was kept there under watch.[62]

The imperial attack centered on the personal conduct of Yin-t'i. Since he was once regarded by many of his contemporaries as a highly probable successor, the throne made an effort to disprove this by making a point of his misdeeds in the army and reprimanding him as a person of ignorance and arrogance.[63] Perhaps the emperor had taken into consideration the fact that he and Yin-t'i had the same mother. Therefore, the prince received a relatively lenient punishment in comparison with that rendered to Yin-ssu and Yin-t'ang. For instance, he was not forced to alter his name and, in the final verdict, was charged with only fourteen "crimes," such as disobedience, factional activities, corruption in the army, and so forth.[64] He was imprisoned in the capital until the death of the emperor and restored to the rank of prince of the second degree in 1748.

Yin-chih was the last of the princes removed by the Yung-cheng Emperor. Learned and peaceable, he was in personality different from the above-mentioned three princes. Furthermore, without a strong clique behind him he had not been a powerful contender in the succession struggle, and he presented a lesser threat to the new regime than did other rivals. This fact made the emperor deal differently with him, but did not exempt him from suppression. The ruler meant to remove any obstruction in the way of consolidation of his sovereign power.

In the suppression of Yin-chih the emperor relied largely on weakening his prestige as a learned prince. Early in 1723 he confiscated the *Ku-chin t'u-shu chi-ch'eng*, the book Yin-chih compiled, banished Ch'en Meng-lei, another editor, and finally removed all references to their connection with the work in its revised edition of 1726.[65] Yung-cheng did not have too many reasons to rebuke Yin-chih, but he found them in trivial matters dating from his childhood to middle age.[66] Though disgusted with the prince, the emperor used him against other princes. When he attacked Yin-ssu, he ordered Yin-chih to stand ahead of other courtiers to recommend a punishment for him.[67] In like manner, when he wanted to give Yin-t'ang a derisive name after excluding him from the imperial clan, he again asked Yin-chih with some other princes to suggest one for him.[68]

During the period 1723-1728 Yin-chih was comparatively unmolested. He led a private life. The year 1728 was, however, the beginning of his misfortune. After punishing other brothers, the emperor accused him of corruption and having flattered Lungkodo. A few months later he was degraded one degree in rank, expelled from the council of princes, and deprived of four companies of retainers for showing temper before the throne.[69] The worst misfortune came in 1730. The same year Yin-hsiang, the prince most trusted by the emperor, died. Since Yin-chih did not express due grief, the throne burst into wrath, reprimanded him, and asked the courtiers to discuss his case. He was accused of ten "crimes," of which his failure to grieve at Yin-hsiang's death was one.[70] He was then imprisoned where he died in 1732.

With the removal of Yin-chih, the emperor completed the suppression of the princely factions.

The rise and fall of Nien Keng-yao, a powerful factional leader during the first three years of the Yung-cheng period, manifested the ambivalent relations between ruler and bureaucrats. This case study begins with a brief survey of his relations with the emperor.[71] Nien Keng-yao and his family belonged to the Chinese Bordered Yellow Banner. After obtaining the *chin-shih* degree in 1700, he served in the Hanlin Academy for nine years, then was transferred to the Grand Secretariat as a subchancellor, and was made governor of Szechwan. About the same time the banner company to which the Nien family belonged was assigned to Yung-cheng, who had just been made Prince Yung. This initiated their relationship. According to the emperor's recollection, Nien Keng-yao was a man of good memory, literary skill, and straightforward character.[72] When the Eleuths under Tsewang Araptan (1643-1727) invaded Tibet, the province of Szechwan was destined to be an important center for military supplies and manpower for the Manchu armies. Nien Keng-yao actively supported the campaigns against the Eleuths and increased his prestige with time. During the short period 1718-1721 he was promoted to governor-general of Szechwan and Shensi provinces and became an important associate of Yin-t'i, who was commander-in chief of the Manchu armies on the northwestern frontier.

If Nien Keng-yao's part was important to the maintenance of frontier order, his role was more important to Yung-cheng's consolidation of power. With his rising influence he became a desirable ally sought after by the competitors for the throne. He was inclined to maintain friendly relations with all contenders in the competition. Because of his banner affiliation, he was naturally in Yung-cheng's camp, but he was on amicable terms with Yin-t'ang and Yin-chih.[73] Officially, he helped Yin-t'i direct the war against the Eleuths; his assistance proved to be a major factor in the defeat of the invaders. The multiplicity of his relationships provoked the emperor's suspicion, which is obvious in his decision, immediately after his enthronement, to send Yen-hsin instead of Nien Keng-yao to take over the command left vacant by Yin-t'i. This suspicion was a factor that later underlay the suppression of

Nien. Perhaps he cut off his relations with other princes only after hearing of Yung-cheng's succession. Surely his support was indispensable to consolidation of the sovereign power in the early Yung-cheng period. Although he did not directly contribute to the emperor's final victory in the struggle, his alliance insured the throne's success in removing Yin-t'i from the command. This seems to have been why Yin-t'i hated him.[74] He was also the man who watched Yin-t'ang for the new ruler. Besides, his importance lay in his ability to maintain order on the frontier, which increased the new ruler's ability to suppress the princes.

The years 1723-1724 saw the zenith of Nien Keng-yao's prosperity. The emperor had temporarily to put aside his suspicion of the governor-general for the sake of the political and military situation. In the capital the ruler decided to remove the powerful princes and their partisans, but he did not make much headway. When ordered to Kokonor by the throne about the beginning of 1723, Yin-t'ang, for instance, delayed departure until April 1723.[75] On the frontier, the Khoshotes, also a Mongol tribe, under Lobdzan Dandzin, were ready to take up arms in Kokonor. Evidently the emperor needed more substantial support. Although Lungkodo helped the throne with the police force, his service was limited to Peking. The support of Nien Keng-yao was in a sense even more important. Early in 1723 he was allowed to return to the capital for an audience.

Nien's relationship with the throne became closer after the audience of 1723. In subsequent months he received numerous honors and rewards, of which the post of commander-in-chief of the armies in the northwest was the most important. After this new appointment, he succeeded in quelling the Khoshotes in 1724. Undoubtedly, the military success on the frontier had repercussions in the capital. While Nien Keng-yao was given several favors and rewards, the emperor lost no time in transforming this military exploit into a political bonus for himself. He promoted closer friendship between Nien Keng-yao and Lungkodo, then two of his important supporters with military power. As early in 1723 he had told Nien Keng-yao that Lungkodo was the best and most loyal official of all.[76] Now he even ordered one of Nien Keng-yao's sons to be Lungkodo's foster son.[77] In the meantime, he began a relentless attack on the princes. His successful suppression of the princes was largely the result of the cooperation he got from these two men.

Nien Keng-yao depended on imperial favor more than on his military accomplishments, however. The height of his influence came with his close relationship to the throne, demonstrated by the frequency and intimacy of his correspondence with the emperor. A glance at the extant exchanges indicates their informality and flattery.[78] If this unusual imperial favor enhanced his influence, it also brought him to destruction. Power and prestige made him corrupt and arrogant. About his corruption, private sources provide quite a few stories, one of which claims that he had his cooks prepare menus for him one month in advance and each cook was responsible for just one dish.[79] Through illegal means he acquired a large amount of money, which he secretly deposited in various places.[80] Private works also supply accounts of his arrogance. It is said that when he returned to Peking for an audience, he made almost no response to high officials who greeted him and even gave little respect to the emperor.[81]

If the rise of Nien Keng-yao was a result of the conflict between the emperor and the princes, his downfall was the outcome of the strain between the throne and the bureaucrat. Students of modern Chinese history tend to interpret his tragedy as a result of the emperor's efforts to eliminate a person who had helped him ascend the throne and knew the truth about his illegal succession.[82] This is misleading. As mentioned earlier, Nien Keng-yao did not make any direct contribution to the emperor's victory in the succession struggle. His support became important only during the emperor's campaign to consolidate his position. Suppression of Nien Keng-yao was connected with the emperor's efforts at consolidation. He needed Nien as a power supporter, but not as a power intruder. An autocrat, especially while consolidating power, cannot tolerate encroachment by a bureaucrat, however important the latter's service. Han Fei provided the best explanation:

> The lord of men, when employing ministers, should not allow them, however wise and able they may be, to act contrary to the law and take all powers to themselves; should not allow them, however worthy and victorious

they may be, to claim any priority among the
men of merit and take precedence of the hard-
working people; and should not discard the
law and refrain from restricting them,
however loyal and faithful they may be. Such
a ruler is called an illustrator of the
law.[83]

After coming to prominence Nien Keng-yao led a faction. As governor-general and commander-in-chief he had administrative, fiscal, and military facilities and the capacity to place his followers in significant positions. Such facilities were greatly expanded by military necessity. When he led the army to fight the Khoshotes, he was given the authority to supervise all local officials and officers on the frontiers and in Yunnan, besides those originally under his jurisdiction.[84] He made numerous recommendations for dismissals, appointments, demotions, and promotions. He recruited followers not only from his friends but from the officials in the central government, including the imperial bodyguards.[85] A large number of bureaucrats in Szechwan and Shensi owed their appointments and promotions to his patronage, to which private sources and the emperor's actions to rebuild the bureaucratic structure in the two provinces attest.[86] Even after dismissal from the commandership, he still had an entourage of several hundred people.[87] From these three provinces—Shensi, Szechwan, and Yunnan—he obtained a base of popular support.

Although the Nien faction did not threaten the sovereign power outright, its interests conflicted with those of the ruler. Its members spread from the region that Nien Keng-yao administered to other provinces. While his sycophants in Szechwan constructed shrines to worship him as a living deity, officials elsewhere admired him as the greatest hero of the time, extended him salutations that were ordinarily intended for princes, or flattered him in other ways.[88] If these did not challenge the sovereign's power, they were certainly harmful to it.

Another area of conflict was Nien Keng-yao's abuse of authority, a point emphasized by Mailla, a Jesuit.[89] For instance, Nien is said in one case to have caused the death of several hundred innocent people in a district simply through carelessness, and the emperor redeemed this misdeed by remitting taxes of the people in that district for a year.[90] Nien is also presumed to have abused the imperial favor by claiming personal credit for promotions of high officials, even of those not in his area.[91] His domineering conduct was perhaps the most serious of his violations, in the emperor's judgment. It is said that Nien Keng-yao treated imperial bodyguards as personal retainers, that in official communications with top local administrators he wrote letters in the form of imperial decrees, and that he committed many other similar offenses.[92] It is understandable that an autocrat would consider these actions threatening and would be ready to take action as soon as the situation permitted.

The Nien clique fell even before that of the princes. The emperor started preparations to remove it by the end of 1724, when Nien Keng-yao had the last audience with him. On many occasions he privately told some officials that he could not tolerate the corrupt, arrogant, and domineering conduct of Nien and requested confidential information about his activities.[93] He finished his preparatory work in early 1725, and soon took open action when Nien inverted a phrase in a memorial.[94] It is not difficult to understand why he decided to remove Nien when he was devoting efforts to suppress the princes. By 1725 the emperor controlled the situation in the empire, reducing Nien's importance. Moreover, he could not afford to allow the rise of another faction while trying to remove the clique of princes. At the same time he had recruited new loyal supporters such as Chang T'ing-yü, Li Wei (1687?-1738), O-er-t'ai, and T'ien Wen-ching (1662-1732), and they were put in strategic positions, central and local. At the beginning of 1725 the emperor dispatched Tulisen (1667-1741) a Manchu bannerman, to control the financial administration in Shensi and to investigate the activities of Nien Keng-yao,[95] who was then under the surveillance of his associate, Yueh Chung-ch'i (1686-1754). This arrangement insured the emperor's successful removal of Nien Keng-yao.

In suppressing Nien the emperor also made efforts to acquire a general consensus among the officialdom. While pressing officials, especially those who had close connections with the Nien clique, to denounce their factional leader openly,[96] he issued decrees of reproach. Nien Keng-yao had perceived the ruler's intention immediately after his second audience and repeatedly submitted memorials, assuring the throne of his loyalty, expressing his gratitude, and asking for mercy.[97] However, mercy was not the consideration of an autocrat. To comply with the ruler's wish and also to keep themselves from being involved, many officials accused Nien of various misdeeds.[98] As the accusations mounted up, Nien was degraded from general to bannerman at large, and brought in irons to the capital in November 1725. There he was accused of ninety-two "crimes," among which were bribery, arrogance, abuse of authority, and treason. Being a general of military ability, he was allowed the privilege of taking his own life in early 1726. Punishment of his followers lasted until 1728.[99]

Lungkodo was another factional leader of considerable influence. He belonged to the Manchu Bordered Yellow Banner and through marriage relations was a cousin and brother-in-law of the K'ang-hsi Emperor.[100] He started his official career as an imperial bodyguard in 1688, but it was not until 1711 that he received a relatively important appointment as General Commandant of the Gendarmerie of Peking. It was this position that increased his importance in the eyes of the ambitious princes in their struggle for the heirdom. It was also this office that greatly helped the Yung-cheng Emperor, first in his accession to the throne and then in suppression of the princes.

The rise of Lungkodo also resulted from special imperial favor. During the first two years of the Yung-cheng period, the new ruler rewarded him with a shower of honors and offices. In addition to the commandership of the capital gendarmerie, he was concurrently made a member of the Council of Supervisors, president of the Board of Civil Appointments, president of the Board of Colonial Affairs, and director in charge of editing official works such as the *Veritable Records*, collected statutes for the K'ang-hsi period, and the *Ming History*.[101] These offices, old and new, made him a man second only to the ruler in Peking and provided him with the opportunity of attracting a following.

Many officials tried to approach him, and even the princes showed deference to him.[102] Men involved in his clique were scattered in the government, central and local. Cha Ssu-t'ing (1664-1727), for example, was vice-president of the Board of Rites, an appointment he owed to the patronage of

Lungkodo.[103] Some high provincial administrators such as Manbao (d.1725), governor-general of Chekiang and Fukien, and No-min (d.1734), governor of Shansi, are said to have been followers of Lungkodo, and a few of his men were from the imperial bodyguards and the Imperial Equipage Department (*luan-i wei*).[104] In comparison, his clique was not so powerful as that of Nien Keng-yao. The reason for this possibly lay in the fact that as a governor-general and commander-in-chief Nien Keng-yao had more opportunities to enlist followers.

In terms of functional characteristics the Lungkodo clique was not different from that of Nien or of the princes. Although they operated with different strengths, they developed at the cost of sovereign power. If power tends to corrupt, one can apply this analysis to the case of Lungkodo. Of the forty-one "charges" against him by Yung-cheng, more than one-third were corruption cases, which could not all have been forgeries.[105] Most important of all was his attempt to exercise his personal influence on the throne. He is said to have tried to move the emperor to execute Yin-ssu but interceded for others.[106] After allying with Nien Keng-yao through the throne's initiative, as previously mentioned, he acquired additional strength. They worked together to help the emperor to stabilize the situation in the early years of his reign, but at the same time they seem to have worked in concert for more personal interests. For instance, they had admirers in common and attacked, or covered up, the same people.[107] Even though these cases were not deliberately connected, they were easily interpreted by the throne as evidence of factionalism.

In discussing the elimination of Lungkodo one should not overemphasize the conventional interpretation that the emperor wished to remove the accomplice after the fact of his "illegal" succession. Such an explanation has no logical validity inasmuch as the legitimacy problem is an unsolvable puzzle. Moreover, if the emperor wanted to get rid of the accomplice, he would do better to sentence him to death. But he did not, and why? He punished Lungkodo simply in the interest of the suppression of factionalism, which he construed in its broader sense. As a Manchu noble and an influential official, Lungkodo was a center that some officials rallied around or tried to approach for personal considerations. Nien Keng-yao as well as Lungkodo contributed to the stability of sovereign power at the beginning of the Yung-cheng period, but with his emphasis on suppressing factionalism, the emperor made them an example to others. On one occasion he clearly pointed out that meritorious officials might be kept in office by three factors—imperial trust, self-discipline, and restraint of other officials from sycophancy.[108] While he regarded these three as indispensable, he stressed the last one, which, according to him, was the source of factionalism.

The Yung-cheng Emperor began his attack against Lungkodo under the same conditions and at the same time as he did against Nien Keng-yao. Early in 1725 he suspected both of them and warned officials to keep away from them.[109] By March of the same year, Lungkodo was released from the commandership of the gendarmerie of Peking and began to lose his offices one after another.[110] At the same time, he was assigned to the northwestern frontier, where he supervised construction of forts, cultivation of land, demarcation of boundaries between Mongolia and the Eleuths, and negotiation with Russia on a boundary dispute.[111] The assignment was no less than banishment.

In his suppression of Lungkodo, the emperor waited longer, perhaps because the clique was not so powerful as the two others. In 1727 Lungkodo was discovered to have obtained from Ablan—a supporter of Yin-t'i—a copy of the genealogy of the imperial family.[112] Since Yin-t'i was once believed in the court to be a potential candidate for the heirdom and Lungkodo recieved a copy of the imperial genealogy from the former's supporter, is it possible that the record included some hints about the succession issue? Without reliable sources no one can answer the question satisfactorily. Although Meng Sen gave an affirmative answer, his interpretation is not invulnerable in terms of adequate evidence.[113] Then there is the question about Lungkodo's motivation for keeping such a copy since he was not, according to the Manchu practice, entitled to have it. As Lungkodo was a close imperial affinal, he possibly kept a copy of the imperial genealogy for personal reasons, such as showing his descendants their connection with the ruling house. At any rate, if charisma was a requirement for the ruler's authority, the imperial genealogical record was a source of that quality. And Lungkodo's act naturally challenged it. The Yung-cheng emperor considered this the first instance of lese majesty, which was included in the forty-one "crimes" attributed to him. Lungkodo was eventually sentenced to life imprisonment in a specially built three-room enclosure outside the Pleasant Spring Villa,[114] where he had helped the emperor succeed to the throne.

PART THREE

Machineries for Autocracy

2. Yung-cheng is reading and thinking. He is one of the most studious and learned Ch'ing rulers.

V

The Weakening of the Censorial System

1. *Merging of the Censorate and the Offices of Scrutiny*

   The Yung-cheng period was the height of Ch'ing autocracy. Its strengths lay not only in the personal character and ideology of the emperor but in the political institutions of the period. A survey of Ch'ing history reveals that early Manchu rulers steadily increased their power through reorganization of the central government. The Yung-cheng Emperor followed this pattern as well. No sooner had he ascended the throne than he began to remodel the governmental structure, creating new instruments to meet his special needs. These instruments reflected his personality and ideology, implemented his decisions, and perpetuated imperial control over the officials. The institutions he introduced were the most workable tools of autocracy devised during the Ch'ing and lasted throughout the dynasty. To study the autocracy of the Yung-cheng period, therefore, an analysis of institutions is essential.

   The first institutional change was the diminishing of the censorial system. Charged with remonstrance and impeachment, the censorial system exercised a kind of check, though not a very effective one, on the imperial power and some political evils.[1] Autocratic monarchs or arbitrary officials had to weaken its power if they were to attain their goals. The rise of Chinese autocracy, then, caused the decline of the censorial system and gave rise to even greater imperial power.

The Ch'ing censorial system was copied from that of the Ming.[2] At the suggestion of some Chinese bannermen, the Censorate was founded by Hong-taiji in 1636, but not until the Shun-chih period was this office consolidated. It had two senior presidents (*tso tu-yü shih*) and four senior vice-presidents (*tso fu-tu-yü shih*). Appointments were given to the Chinese and Manchu in exactly equal numbers. In addition, there were fifty-six provincial censors (*yü-shih*), distributed over fifteen circuits.[3] The Six Offices of Scrutiny (*Liu-k'o chi-shih chung*), which might have been founded around 1636, were consolidated in the beginning years of the K'ang-hsi period. Staffed by supervising secretaries, the Six Offices were paired with the Six Boards. After some changes in the number of personnel, each of the Six Offices had two senior supervising secretaries and two supervising secretaries—half of whom were Manchus and half Chinese.[4]

The duties of the two organs—the Censorate and the Six Offices of Scrutiny—were originally very broad. The censors supervised the official and personal conduct of central and local government officials as well as provincial and metropolitan examinations and such leading activities of the day as the salt monopoly, grain tribute, and state granaries. They had a voice in court deliberations and a seat in the highest tribunal to review important cases. They monitored the attendance of general audiences, impeached those who were absent without excuses, and corrected officials whenever their behavior was improper. All municipal affairs, especially judicial, fell under their supervision. In short, they oversaw almost everything.

The supervising secretaries transmitted all decrees and endorsed memorials to the Six Boards, made a copy of each (except secret matters), and checked and reversed them if they were found impossible to carry out. They audited the accounts of the central and provincial governments, and they paid attention to government properties. As a whole, the censors and supervising secretaries, though without the power to enact, execute, annul, or amend laws, could inform the emperor about state affairs and urge action or inaction, as the case warranted.

They functioned as the "ears and eyes of the emperor" and exercised their power by remonstrance and impeachment.[5]

The censors and supervising secretaries were in theory given some privileges that other officials did not enjoy. For example, they had freedom of speech and the right to petition and were free from punishment for their performance of official duties. Their petitions and recommendations for impeachment could be made on hearsay. To avoid incurring the enmity of the impeached, the ruler usually kept the accuser's name secret, and exempted him from cross-examination and countercharges from the one to be impeached.

Because of intrinsic weaknesses the Chinese censorial system was destined to be powerless in the face of autocratic rulers. First, it was weakened by the gap between its conceptual foundation and the practical situation in which it fulfilled its major functions, remonstrance and impeachment. Based on Confucian doctrines, the system provided ethical and intellectual guidance for the ruler in the form of remonstrance, or moral suasion, with a view to attaining an enlightened rule.[6] Clearly, remonstrance functioned only within ethical limits that did not bind the ultimate power of the ruler. As a system also related to Legalism, the censorial institution exercised disciplinary surveillance over officials through impeachment, in the hope of maintaining justice (with the political and legal implications of the term). Without the ruler's sanction, such impeachment, even well substantiated, could not be carried out. As a matter of fact, neither censorial remonstrance nor impeachment was enforceable without imperial approval.

Second, the censorial system was defective because of the bureaucratic status of its personnel. In the bureaucratic structure, the difference between the censorial personnel and other officials was actually insignificant. Remonstrance and impeachment were the major responsibilities of the censors and supervising secretaries, but in the traditional Chinese state almost all scholar-officials could submit to the throne petitions of the same nature. Besides, the censorial personnel were recruited in the same manner as were other officials, and they were all subject to the same rules of transfer, dismissal, punishment, and promotion. The privileges that the censorial personnel enjoyed were far from guaranteed rights; they progressively faded into obscurity in the presence of autocratic masters.

The last defect concerned the personal conduct of the censors and supervising secretaries. Like other bureaucrats, they had personal failings or committed malpractice. Some accepted graft, oppressed the people, or curried favor with influential officials, while some criticized and impeached because of trivial matters or simply personal enmity. These shortcomings diminished their stature and also lent force to autocratic sovereigns who were looking for a chance to concentrate more power in their own hands. With these inherited weaknesses, the censorial institution had difficulty in fulfilling its missions although it functioned, to a certain extent, as a check on the abuse of power.

Adopted from the Ming, the Ch'ing censorial system not only shared the above defects,[7] but also suffered under more woeful predicaments than had its predecessor. The ethnic tension between Chinese and Manchu was detrimental. Chinese officials lived a life of humiliation under Manchu rulers, especially those of the early Ch'ing. Although Hong-taiji tried to ease this tension, Manchu nobles looked down upon the Chinese officials, who did not know the Manchu language and were given corporal punishment for minor faults.[8] During the K'ang-hsi period the Chinese officials controlled their tempers, kept silent in state meetings, never argued with their Manchu colleagues, and simply followed the latter's opinions.[9] This situation handicapped the operation of the censorial system.

The contempt and distrust of early Manchu rulers created another difficulty for the system. Like many rulers in Chinese dynastic history, the early Ch'ing monarchs paid lip service to the censorial institution, but in reality they did much to discourage censors and supervising secretaries. Conscious of their alien origin, the Manchu rulers' chief concern was to preserve their rule in China. They recruited equal numbers of Chinese and Manchu censors and supervising secretaries, and the ethnic tension prevailing elsewhere in the society also existed in the censorial system. The Manchu censors and supervising secretaries, many of whom could not write memorials,[10] obtained their appointments largely as spoils and could not fulfill the traditional missions of the institution. Their Chinese colleagues, who were recruited, as a rule, from among scholars with high academic degrees, were looked upon by the monarchs with suspicion and became the first victims of imperial attempts to check censorial functions. During the Shun-chih period, for example, the censors were deprived of their traditional privilege of making impeachments based on hearsay.[11] Many Chinese censors were reproached, dismissed, and forced to face countercharges by the impeached; some were even sentenced to death, while the supervising secretaries lost their traditional right to reverse imperial decrees (*feng-po*).[12] Suffice it to say that the censorial officials of the early Ch'ing could not perform their functions in such an unfavorable environment.

During the K'ang-hsi period, the circumstances under which the censorial system operated were even worse than before. Though generally known as a lenient ruler and a patron of scholarship, the K'ang-hsi Emperor was actually a despotic monarch, for, as contemporaries complained, he disregarded the censorial power.[13] In 1721 he banished thirteen censors who remonstrated with him to restore the deposed crown prince, and in his last years he empowered officials, central and local, with duties similar to those of censors.[14] The censorial offices were, then, deprived of their traditional status and functions and were at the mercy of the autocrat.

Combining the Censorate and the Six Offices of Scrutiny into one office in the Yung-cheng period was the most deadly blow that the censorial system had suffered in its long history. Although it is virtually impossible to provide details of this amalgamation, the two offices seem to have been combined by Yung-cheng in early 1723.[15] Perhaps the Censorate initiated a proposal with respect to the promotion and transfer of both censors and supervising secretaries, and the throne then gave it administrative authority over the Six Offices of Scrutiny.[16] However inadequate the information about their merger, it is apparent that from that time on the supervising secretaries lost their independent status and functional specialization.

Historically, although the two organs were independent of each other, their functions were closely related and, in documents, their staff members were frequently referred to by abbreviated collective designations such as *k'o-tao* (the Offices of Scrutiny and the Circuits) and *t'ai-chien* (the

Censorate and the Remonstration Office).[17] With their functional similarities, they could easily be regarded as a single homogeneous group, and their functional distinction had been reduced since the T'ang and Sung dynasties. Their final incorporation under the Ch'ing seems to have been a development relevant to this general trend.

The incorporation of the Six Offices of Scrutiny into the Censorate was intimately connected with political processes during the Yung-cheng period. Their amalgamation was an essential part of the emperor's campaign against factionalism. The partisanship of the censors and supervising secretaries in the late Ming dynasty is a well-known fact,[18] while some censorial officials of the late K'ang-hsi period were charged with factional practices and punished because they petitioned for the restoration of Yin-jeng after his second deposal. These facts could not but have had an effect on Yung-cheng who was devoted to the suppression of factions. Under the administration of a single office, the censors and supervising secretaries were not only prevented from developing rivalries between them, as had happened in Ming times, but were also kept under a centralized surveillance.

Moreover, the amalgamation of the two censorial institutions was a manifestation of Yung-cheng's efforts to consolidate power. If, theoretically, the censorial system did not restrict the ruler's ultimate authority, practically it exercised a check on the imperial power. This was particularly true of the supervising secretaries. For instance, they served as document inspectors who put "a kind of editorial veto" on state papers to and from the Six Boards, on memorials to the throne, and on decrees from the monarch.[19] Although they could not do the same with secret papers, they were allowed to register them according to the notation on their envelopes and subsequently to dispatch them to the related Boards. What they exercised in the process of their document inspection was a sort of procedural check of imperial orders. But autocratic rulers tolerate no checks, potential or actual, on their power. It is not surprising that the Yung-cheng Emperor found it necessary to incorporate the Six Offices of Scrutiny into the Censorate, and that he transferred three supervising secretaries to another office when they filed a protest against the amalgamation.[20]

The Six Offices were greatly weakened after their incorporation into the Censorate. They were not only deprived of their independent status but also charged with the functions of censors in addition to their own. Inasmuch as they busied themselves with both of these functions, they could fulfill neither.[21] The net result was the diminution of the Six Offices of Scrutiny. In the Shun-chih period, as a censor complained, secret decrees occasionally bypassed the regular channel, but the supervising secretaries could still read them some months later.[22] During the Yung-cheng period the secretaries were completely barred from scrutiny of secret papers and even suffered delay in their access to ordinary decrees through the Grand Secretariat, where they formerly checked and copied these papers.[23] They could only read them in the Peking Gazette about ten days after the Grand Secretariat had handled them. Thus, the secretaries lost their "editorial veto" on ordinary decrees and were no longer document inspectors.

2. *Enforcement of the Palace-Memorial System*

The palace-memorial system rendered a most serious blow to the Ch'ing censorial system. The incorporation of the Censorate and the Six Offices of Scrutiny took away the document-inspecting functions of the supervising secretaries; the palace-memorial system was designed to divide the authority of the censors. During the Yung-cheng period, palace memorials (*tsou-che*) took the form of personal secret reports. Selected by the ruler, the reporters were mainly provincial officials scattered across the country. Under imperial authorization, they could expose, criticize, and impeach officials for errors in personal conduct and administrative performance. In effect, they functioned as censors. Palace memorials went to the imperial desks through special channels composed of the Grand Secretaries, Grand Councillors, and a few other officials, while imperial orders, in the form of court letters or included in the vermilion-ink endorsements, were sent directly to the reporters. Like the censorial institution, the palace-memorial system during the Yung-cheng era was a network extending across the whole country.

The operation of the palace-memorial system is well known, but its origins have frequently eluded researchers. The system should be examined from a historical perspective and in light of the confidential official communication practices of the early Ch'ing. Because there are studies that have shed light on many aspects of the system,[24] the present discussion is intended to offer a few points that have escaped the attention of scholars, with emphasis on the Yung-cheng period.

The Ch'ing palace-memorial system resulted fundamentally from the rulers' efforts to achieve tight control over the bureaucracy, which traditionally was monocratically structured, with formal, impersonal rules serving the needs and goals of its imperial master and the polity itself. It is safe to say that the Chinese imperial system owed its centralized characteristics, in no small measure, to its bureaucratic structure. Yet, in their performance, the Chinese bureaucrats were inclined to reduce or undermine their organizational and functional distinctiveness, as originally required, by developing interests in the social, economic, and political spheres.[25] Since this tendency challenged imperial interests, curbing it was a perennial problem of rulers in Chinese history.

The palace-memorial system was a Chinese dynastic device for supervision of the bureaucrats. In Chinese dynastic history memorials of a secret nature are referred to as *feng-shih*, *feng-tsou*, *feng-chang*, and the like—all suggest the same meaning. In all likelihood, it was Emperor Hsüan of the Former Han dynasty who introduced the palace memorials, and the practice was followed by many later rulers, notably those of the Sung and Ming dynasties.[26] Although these memorials were not institutionalized before the Ch'ing, they were, at the very beginning, placed in black bags and, later, sealed in envelopes. In many cases they seem to have been opened in the presence of the ruler.[27] Due to their confidential nature they may be considered the predecessor of the Ch'ing palace memorials. It is not illogical to conclude that while copying the political institutions of the Ming, the Manchu rulers adopted the practice of confidential memorials.

The early Ch'ing practice of confidential official communication laid the foundation for the palace-memorial system in later years. As alien conquerors the Manchu monarchs were interested, more than previous dynastic rulers had been, in acquiring information through confidential memorials. Even before the Manchu conquest of China, Hong-taiji encouraged officials to submit confidential memorials and seems to have selected men of loyalty as his informers, who would be punished if they failed to perform their obligations.[28] Such memorials seem to have reached him first through the Literary Office (*Wen-kuan*) and then through the Three Inner Courts (*Nei san-yüan*). During the next reign the confidential memorials played an important role and operated according to certain rules. They were not only sealed in envelopes but also transmitted directly to the throne first by the Three Inner Courts and later by the Transmission Office (*t'ung-cheng-ssu*).[29] Unlike the regular memorials, the confidential ones could be sent to the ruler by the Transmission Office at any time, and were dealt with by the ruler himself, occasionally with the advice of a very few trusted officials.[30]

The K'ang-hsi period was crucial to the Ch'ing palace-memorial system. During his reign of more than half a century, especially after the Revolt of the Three Feudatories, the K'ang-hsi Emperor further developed the practice of confidential memorials. Through them he planned more fully to integrate elements of the traditional Chinese state with Ch'ing rule and to assert a more vigorous Manchu presence in the political tradition of China. This two-way project he energetically carried out in his maturity. While fighting against the Revolt of the Three Feudatories, basically a Chinese uprising, he adopted the Chinese system of imperial succession, selected the best Confucian scholars for compiling the *Ming History* and Confucian classics, and founded the Southern Imperial Study, staffed largely with Chinese scholars as his personal literary and political advisors. It is clear that he attempted to identify Manchu rule with the dynastic tradition of China through these programs. At the same time he emphasized confidential memorials.

Although little is known about the operation of the confidential memorials in the early years of the K'ang-hsi period, one may assume that as a Manchu ruler who knew more traditional Chinese governing practices than did his father or his grandfather, K'ang-hsi continued this dynastic political practice. At any rate, owing to the military necessity arising from the war to quell the Revolt of the Three Feudatories, commanders—banner and Green Standard—and related high provincial administrators frequently submitted confidential reports, while officials in the central government were likely to file secret memorials. During the war the throne appointed Wang Hsi (1628-1703), a trusted Chinese scholar, to take care of the confidential memorials on military matters.[31] After the suppression of the revolt in 1681 and the conquest of Taiwan two years later, all of China was unified under Manchu rule, which made effective imperial supervision important for the maintenance of peace and order within the Ch'ing empire. Therefore, confidential official communication acquired more importance with time. In the 1680s, for example, K'ang-hsi revealed before a governor-general that he was well informed of the personal and administrative conduct of all officials outside of the capital; he ordered that Grand Secretaries submit provincial weather data in small-lettered memorials attached to regular reports; and on another occasion he asked a new provincial governor to report all important matters concerning local affairs.[32] What he required in these cases was essentially palace memorials, although he did not specify the type of memorial.

Under the imperial auspices the palace-memorial system made rapid strides after the 1680s, so official records for the time, notably the palace memorials of Ts'ao Yin (1658-1712), Li Hsü (1655-1729), and Wang Hung-hsü (1645-1723), contain more information about its workings. K'ang-hsi received palace memorials from a wide variety of provincial officials and military officers, such as governors-general, governors, Tartar generals, commanders-in-chief (*t'i-tu*), brigade-generals (*tsung-ping*), and superintendents of the Imperial Manufactories (*chih-tsao*).[33] They actively submitted palace memorials after the 1680s, but in view of the long history of the Ch'ing confidential official communication and of the importance of local affairs to the maintenance of imperial order, they might have started filing such secret reports from the time of the Revolt of the Three Feudatories. High officials in the central government at first sent, or were required to send, palace memorials on occasion,[34] but the K'ang-hsi Emperor needed to have more from them when the struggle for heirdom became intense after the turn of the eighteenth century. In 1712 he bluntly advised that all high courtiers from the junior vice-president of the Censorate up to the Grand Secretaries, the banner commanders in the capital such as the lieutenant-general (*tu-t'ung*) and the deputy lieutenant-general (*fu tu-t'ung*), and the Chamberlain of the Imperial Bodyguard (*Ling shih-wei nei-ta-ch'en*) submit palace memorials.[35] Thus imperial informants were scattered throughout the empire, forming a network of palace memorials.

With the increasing use of palace memorials, there developed a set of rules for them. At times the K'ang-hsi Emperor told officials that he personally handled palace memorials, but the Imperial Diarists (*Ch'i-chü-chu küan*) were usually given access to them, and he sometimes asked advice of the Grand Secretaries on particularly important reports, such as those on confidential military matters.[36] Confidential memorialists were prohibited from leaking their reports, and with a few exceptions the throne kept their names secret.[37] In general, palace memorials did not bear official stamps, but the throne ordered in 1711 that the governor-general and the provincial governor mark such confidential reports with their official seals against unwarranted opening or manipulation in the course of delivery.[38] Palace memorials could be submitted alone or attached to regular, or routine, memorials (*t'i-pen, shu*, and so forth) or greeting memorials (*ch'ing-an che*).[39] Palace memorials from the provinces were usually delivered to the capital by the memorialist's personal couriers, perhaps with the exception of those on military matters and of some other special cases, and they finally reached the throne through the Chancery of Memorials (*Tsou-shih ch'u*), which might have been founded in the 1670s, or at the latest in the 1690s, for reception of the confidential reports.[40] Besides the Chancery of Memorials, officials in Peking might submit palace memorials to the throne in person at the audience or could present them to the Southern Imperial Study.[41] After reading the palace memorials, the emperor wrote his comments or instructions on them in vermilion ink and returned them in sealed envelopes to the memorialists.

With the above discussion in mind, one may conclude that the Ch'ing palace-memorial system was not an innovation or invention of the Manchu dynasty; nor was it an accidental development of the same period.[42] It was simply an extension of the earlier Chinese practice of close imperial supervision of bureaucrats. Perhaps no source has better analyzed this than the *Li-tai chih-kuan piao* (Tables of offices and officials of successive dynasties), an official Ch'ing compilation; its editors identified the palace-memorial system with the practice of confidential communication in the traditional Chinese state before the Manchu dynasty.[43] What the Ch'ing dynasty added to the confidential communication was the Manchu ruler's vigilance. In the long course of its development, this time-honored practice was finally systematized during the Yung-cheng period.

Reasons for the systematization of the palace memorial in the Yung-cheng period are understandable. After his succession to the throne Yung-cheng was confronted by administrative laxity and the factionalism of Manchu nobles and his former competitors for the throne. In the final analysis, both were unfavorable to the imperial authority; the former was probably even more detrimental because it threatened the regime as a whole. The problem of administrative laxity began midway through the K'ang-hsi period and became more disruptive toward the end of the era. In the years 1712-1726, for example, the state accounting list recorded deficits of more than 10 million taels of silver from tax arrears and official embezzlement in Kiangsu.[44] Clerks, runners, and servants of high officials in local governments became oppressors of the people, while public business was delayed at various levels in the central government.[45] Manchu officials and officers were the core of the Ch'ing regime, but they lapsed into corruption shortly after their conquest of China.[46] All this resulted in a general decline of the administration, central and local as well. Local administrators worried about riots and uprisings; the central government was concerned about security around the capital.[47] This adverse current had to be arrested, and Yung-cheng's determination to curb it was well attested to in the eleven decrees, issued shortly after his accession, in which he ordered officials, from prefect up to governor-general, to carry out imperial orders and do away with administrative evils.[48] The political climate and the imperial determination made necessary the systematization of the palace memorial.

During the Yung-cheng period palace memorials were personal and informal reports submitted secretly and directly by special individuals to the throne.[49] There was no official seal on them, and their authors were allowed to write in a cursive style. They were generally shorter than the memorials for official affairs (*t'i-pen*), and the number of words in them might vary from more than six thousand to only a few characters.[50] In general they bore the character *mi* (confidential), appearing somewhere on the document, but even those that did not bear it were nonetheless confidential.

Some of the palace memorials were written by officials serving in Peking and may be called metropolitan palace memorials. A large number were submitted by officials serving outside the capital; these were provincial palace memorials. Because the provincial memorials played a more important role than did their counterparts, they are the focus of the discussion in this section.

Palace memorials had the functional characteristics of the regular memorials and of the reports for personal matters (*tsou-pen*).[51] In principle the contents of palace memorials covered only important matters collected through observation or based on hearsay, but in practice they even included trivia about the memorialists themselves.[52] According to their contents, palace memorials of the Yung-cheng period may be divided into six types. The first type—informative memorials—provided general statements on local affairs such as the harvest, rainfall, customs, security, price of rice, and religious activity. The second type consisted of replies to secret inquiries from the throne, while the third exposed weaknesses in the personal behavior or administrative performances of certain officials. The fourth type included confidential suggestions by the reporters, and the fifth covered secret requests for imperial suggestions or approval of the memorialist's ideas. The sixth type—grateful and greeting memorials—expressed the memorialist's gratitude for imperial favors he had received and his respectful regard for the throne.

Reporters of palace memorials were individuals selected by the ruler from the bureaucrats. Most of them were chosen by written order with the exception of a few by spoken order.[53] In the Yung-cheng period memorialists were selected from a wider group of officials than in the K'ang-hsi era. In the central government, the Yung-cheng Emperor chose the members of the Hanlin Academy, department directors (*lang-chung*), chief ministers of the Nine Ministries, and even the secretaries of the various Boards, Ministries, and Courts (*t'ang-kuan*; *ssu-kuan*), in addition to those who were selected in the K'ang-hsi reign or were traditionally given the right of submitting confidential memorials.[54]

Besides the governors-general, governors, Tartar generals, provincial commanders-in-chief, and brigade generals—all of whom had been filing palace memorials since the K'ang-hsi period—Yung-cheng extended his selection to financial commissioners (*an-ch'a shih*) and judicial commissioners (*pu-cheng shih*) and many provincial directors of education, intendants, prefects, and even subprefects.[55] Some special officials such as the director-general of the Conservation of the Yellow River and the Grand Canal (*Ho-tao tsung-tu*), the director-general of Grain Transport (*Ts'ao-yün tsung-tu*), the salt controller of Liang-huai (*Liang-huai yen-yün shih*), and the three superintendents of the Imperial Manufactories at Nanking, Soochow, and Hangchow were also selected to submit palace memorials.[56] Deputy lieutenant-generals and colonels of the banners stationed in various places and colonels (*fu-chiang*) of the Green Standard were included in the list of such special memorialists.[57] Most of the memorialists were authorized by written imperial orders, but a few of them requested—and obtained—the right to file palace memorials.[58]

After being selected, the special memorialists had both obligations and privileges that other bureaucrats did not have. The most important obligation was to present the information honestly and in detail, and they would be warned or punished if they concealed the facts, performed their duties perfunctorily, or gave improper protection to their friends.[59] They were allowed not to make reports if nothing of importance happened. Secrecy was their severest discipline. They could not reveal the contents of their memorials, or those of imperial orders, or of endorsements; they could not leave the drafts of their reports unprotected or consult anybody about them in advance.[60] If they violated these rules, they would be fined or discharged from submitting palace memorials.[61] For the purpose of maintaining secrecy the memorialists had to write the palace memorials in their own handwriting. Although they could use clerks, they were held responsible for any leakage of the contents.[62] Their final obligation was to make reports not only while in office but during their leaves of absence and even after their retirement.[63]

In return, reporters of palace memorials, though laden with responsibilities, enjoyed some rights. Inclusion in the list of such reporters was considered an imperial favor: after they were chosen by the ruler, they had to thank him for his kindness.[64] The palace memorials were a means for the ruler to obtain information; they were also instruments through which reporters could expose and impeach other officials, or present their own opinions. If they were in embarrassing situations, they might ask for imperial help.[65] If they made worthy reports, they might have imperial commendation; some of them might be given promotions.[66] In sum, officials without the privilege of filing palace memorials were not powerful bureaucrats.

Reporters of palace memorials, no matter how low their rank, were permitted to send their reports directly to the monarch without going through ordinary official channels.[67] In 1723 Yung-cheng gave them special leather cases to keep their palace memorials safe and secret, and each case had attachments such as locks, keys, and wrapping cloths.[68] Each reporter kept only four cases, though sometimes he might be given more.[69] As the cases and their accessories were gifts from the ruler, the reporters were obliged to keep them; they could not duplicate a case or its attachments even if they lost the original.[70] The palace memorial was put in the case and delivered to Peking by private messengers. Except for matters of great importance, the memorialists were not allowed to use military post stations to dispatch the memorials. Lower officials usually sent ordinary palace memorials through their superiors or together with other officials' confidential reports.[71]

The palace memorials reached the ruler through two special channels operating according to the official ranks of the reporters. One of the channels was composed of two offices—the Outer Chancery of Memorials (*Wai tsou-shih ch'u*) and the Inner Chancery of Memorials (*Nei tsou-shih ch'u*). The Outer Chancery was situated outside the Ch'ien-ch'ing gate and staffed by secretaries and department directors for the reception of memorials from those officials serving in the central government and from governors-general, governors, and lower provincial reporters who sent their first palace memorials.[72] After receiving palace memorials this office had to transmit them to the Inner Chancery of Memorials, staffed with eunuchs and responsible for dispatching all memorials to the imperial desk.[73] Thus these two offices formed a channel of transmission and reduced the authority of the Transmission Office, which originally had been charged with this duty.

The other channel was formed by a few special individuals. They were usually chosen from the Grand Secretaries or other confidants of the Yung-cheng Emperor.[74] Each of them was held responsible for the reception of palace memorials from a certain number of reporters. Those provincial reporters below the rank of governor, when asked to send their first memorials to the Outer Chancery of Memorials, had to deliver their other palace memorials to one of the special individuals as ordered in the imperial endorsements. If they were promoted to the rank of governor, they could then send their reports directly through the Outer Chancery to the ruler, as did the governors-general and governors.[75] Although these special individuals received some palace memorials for the ruler, they were not the people who took the memorials to the throne personally. They transmitted them to the eunuchs of the Inner Chancery.[76] The reporters of palace memorials had to observe this procedure; otherwise they would meet with the ruler's rebuff. The diagram in Table 3 indicates the procedure for transmission of palace memorials.

Table 3*

Procedure for Transmission of Palace Memorials

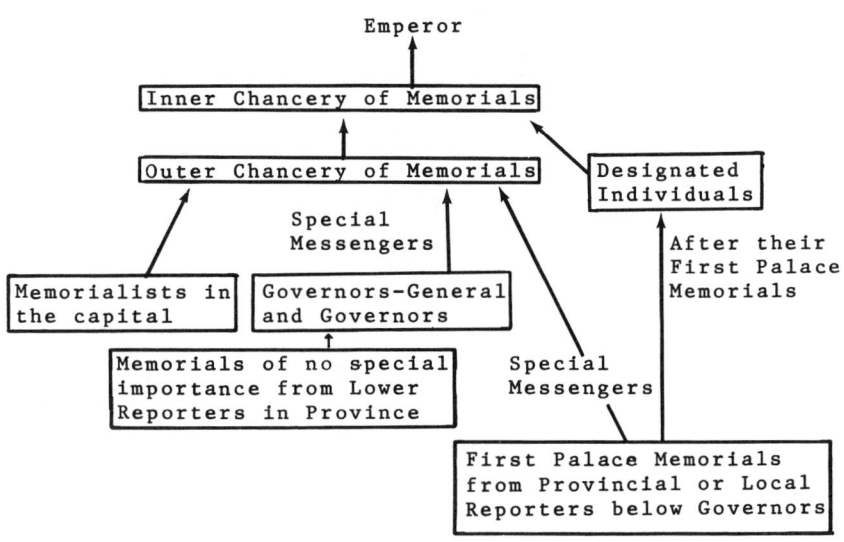

*Cf. the table in Wu, "The Memorial Systems," p.29.

The hard-working Yung-cheng Emperor dealt with these memorials personally. He read and checked them carefully and thoroughly, and sometimes even corrected graphic and grammatical errors in them, and wrote endorsements on them. As memorials arrived at the court daily, he had to work through the night.

A study of the endorsements he made on the palace memorials throws light on some of the principles by which he handled them. As they were only a source of information, he treated them simply as a consultative source. He never made a quick decision. He held an inquisitive attitude toward them, especially those reports that exposed the weaknesses of officials. He adopted a flexible policy for dealing with them. If they contained suggestions, he considered first their applicability, and then the proper Boards to put them into effect. If they were grateful memorials, he marked them with the characters "*lan*" (seen) or "*chih-tao liao*" (noted). If they were general reports—for example, of good harvests in certain places—he wrote endorsements of his delight and commendation. If a calamity was reported, he scolded the memorialists and asked them to improve their administrative and personal conduct because he believed in the interaction between Heaven and man.[77]

The emperor also used the palace memorials to compliment or chastise the memorialists, and his vermilion endorsements on the memorials were instructive as well. If a reporter conducted his office work satisfactorily, he encouraged him. If not, he warned him. He sought to maintain a harmonious relationship between the regular, or routine, memorials (such as the *t'i-pen* and *tsou pen*) and the palace memorials. While extending and strengthening the palace-memorial system, he tried to reinforce the traditional status of the regular, or routine, memorials. He allowed no one to abuse the system by submitting palace memorials when the regular ones sufficed. To maintain this rule, he would not permit memorialists of lower ranks to report, through palace memorials, provincial affairs for which the governors-general and governors had been given authority.[78]

After endorsing the palace memorials Yung-cheng returned them to their authors. As he did not keep any copies or abstracts of the palace memorials that he had received, the reporters had to send them back after they had read the endorsements.

3. *Political Significance of the Palace-Memorial System*

The most significant influence of the palace-memorial system was its contribution to China's autocracy. The claim can be supported on several counts. First, the system was the last and most important step toward undermining the traditional Chinese censorial institution, which was now reduced to a mere shadow of its former self. Since every reporter of palace memorials was given the privilege of impeachment and suggestion, he was no less than a censor. The palace-memorial system virtually fragmented the censorial institution's function of superintending the bureaucrats as a whole, while the amalgamation of the Censorate and the Six Offices of Scrutiny weakened its authority to supervise the central government. Under these combined attacks, the traditional Chinese censorial system lost almost all of its inherited functions; from then on, censors and supervising secretaries were but ordinary members of the bureaucracy. A few undaunted censors occasionally tried to fulfill their traditional obligation or right of remonstrance and impeachment, but they met with harsh punishment. In this regard, the Yung-cheng period marked a low point for the censorial system in the Ch'ing regime and in Chinese dynastic history as well.[79]

The deplorable censorial situation of the Yung-cheng period is well illustrated by the case of Hsieh Chi-shih (1689-1756), a Confucian scholar. A few days after his appointment as a censor in 1726, he impeached T'ien Wen-ching, then governor of Honan and one of the throne's favorite officials, for harsh, corrupt, and unjust administration.[80] The case involved a struggle between officials holding the *chin-shih* degree and those without that degree, but it was more correctly an attempt by the Confucian scholar to resume the traditional functions of the censorial system under an autocratic ruler who trusted his confidants rather than the censorial personnel. The impeachment of an imperial confidant was a challenge to the throne's authority, and the emperor considered it a great offense and took action to punish the offender. Instead of capital punishment, as recommended by many courtiers, he banished Hsieh to Mongolia. Hsieh was released from prison in 1730, but still served forced labor in exile until 1736, one year after the death of Yung-cheng. By its castigation of Hsieh, the throne clearly intended to make him an example to others. In other words, the throne wanted to frighten censors into submission. For fear of severe punishment, no censor dared to exercise the traditional censorial function. Like other bureaucrats, censorial officials were cowed into being obedient servants of the autocratic ruler.

Hsieh's case also indicated the emperor's distrust of criticism, a feature common to all autocratic systems. Remonstrance and impeachment in the traditional Chinese censorial system operated with the purpose of maintaining administrative efficiency. While focusing on bureaucratic conduct, censorial impeachment actually questioned the ruler's judgment, and remonstrance was an expression of disagreement with or opposition to the throne. In the final analysis, both impeachment and remonstrance were forms of criticism of the imperial administration, and their successful working depended on the cooperation of the ruler. Because autocratic rulers demand conformity, they allow no criticism whatsoever. This explains why Yung-cheng punished Hsieh so severely. In contrast, palace-memorial reporters were selected and obliged to follow the imperial will. They were at most the emperor's informants; their proposals were by nature different from censorial remonstrance or impeachment. If the censorial system was the custodian of the Confucian political tradition[81]—according to which not only the censorial personnel but also other bureaucrats were allowed to remonstrate and impeach— the palace-memorial system was the bulwark of the imperial interests, which tolerated no criticism.

A second way in which the palace-memorial system contributed to the strength of the autocracy was its function as an effective tool of imperial control over bureaucrats. This function had three aspects. For one thing, the ruler relied upon the palace-memorial system for preventive action against any usurper of the imperial prerogatives. After the censorial functions were extended to the reporters of palace memorials, the web of the palace-memorial system spread to every corner of the country. In the performance of their mission, such reporters, informing the ruler of everything that happened and exposing others' faults, were not only censors but also spies. With information from various localities, the ruler knew what was going on anywhere in the empire and could possibly take preventive measures vis-à-vis potential trouble. The emperor was so well-informed that his contemporaries believed that his spies were active everywhere.[82] Caught up in the network of the palace-memorial system, officials of the Yung-cheng period were constantly afraid of being impeached and dared not infringe upon the sovereign power. Moreover, they made efforts to follow the imperial will. It is not surprising that he could successfully nullify factions no matter how influential and powerful they were.

Another aspect is the introduction by the palace-memorial system of an atmosphere of mutual suspicion in the bureaucracy. Although the Yung-cheng Emperor frequently prohibited low-ranking reporters of palace-memorials from encroaching upon the authority of their superiors so as to maintain the centralizing characteristics of the bureaucratic structure, the palace-memorial system made each official suspect others. Within the web of the system, an official might be impeached by his colleagues in the same office, by those who were serving in the same area or in different places, or by his subordinates.[83] After being impeached, he had to submit to the final judgment of the ruler—the supreme arbiter, no matter whether the charge was true or not. As a result, the officialdom of the Yung-cheng period was divided by mutual suspicion, and a divided bureaucracy was unable to take concerted action against an autocratic ruler. Thus the palace-memorial system did away with bureaucratic checks on imperial power.

Further, the palace-memorial system was a tool for the terrorization which is characteristic of autocratic systems. As long as the palace-memorial system functioned, not only were the ordinary officials subject to its surveillance, but the memorialists were also targets of their fellow-reporters. In endorsing a palace memorial submitted by a provincial official, for instance, the Yung-cheng Emperor reminded him of his faults that other memorialists had reported.[84] Since the palace memorials were submitted and handled secretly, the impeached had no chance to defend himself before a formal cross-examination was held. The case of Ho Shih-chi (1666-1729), governor of Kweichow, may serve as a typical example. Because he rejected a personal request of an influential official, he was charged with a crime by the same official in a memorial. Although the charge was false, the throne removed Ho from office and summoned him to Peking for trial. He was released only after a cross-examination.[85] This practice instilled a fear in officials which was further increased by some memorialists who, despite the risk of betrayal of secrecy, used their privilege of submitting palace memorials to frighten other officials.[86] In this sense the palace-memorial system terrorized bureaucrats. When terror became internalized, officials conformed.[87] Even though such conformity was involuntary, it reinforced the imperial authority.

In a third way, the palace-memorial system contributed to China's autocracy in that it prevented the rise of regional power. Chinese dynastic records provide many cases which indicate that regional power was an important factor in the political processes of dynasties. If the weakening of the central government gave rise to regional power, the latter further enfeebled the former and finally dissolved it. Regional power developed at the cost of the ruler and therefore was a perennial problem of dynasties in Chinese history. Autocratic rulers always devise means of supervising local administrators. The establishment of circuit inspectors, for example, was largely for this purpose. In performing their duties, however, the circuit inspectors and, later, the censors, exercised only itinerant or periodic supervision, which naturally was not enough. For better results, Chinese dynastic rulers sometimes made such supervising officials permanent overseers with headquarters in strategic points. Yet, in the course of time, these supervisors became super-administrators above the supervised, gradually gathered more power, and aroused imperial suspicion which led to the emperors' placing them under the supervision of new overseers. What this cyclical development achieved was the increase of local administrative levels but not the solution of the problem itself. On the contrary, reporters of palace memorials were mostly administrators in different localities. Although they had no censorial status, they supervised local and provincial administrators more effectively and carried out the imperial orders more faithfully than regular censorial personnel. As they were responsible individually and directly to the ruler, they were the extension of imperial ears and eyes. In short, the palace-memorial system made the rise of regional power impossible and thus removed a potential threat to imperial power. Its successful working can be proved by the fact that after the Yung-cheng period the Manchu rulers were never threatened by regional power bases developing out of the provincial or local bureaucracy. No matter how powerful some governors-general were after the Taiping Rebellion (1850-1864), they did not attempt to challenge the imperial authority.

Lastly, the palace-memorial system facilitated the central decision-making process and enhanced administrative efficiency. The flow of palace memorials from various places to Peking carried all kinds of information vital to imperial decision-making. It is possible that some palace memorials might provide incomplete, conflicting, or distorted information. Nonetheless, when pieced together, such information enabled the Yung-cheng Emperor to reach a better understanding of a given situation, foresee potential problems, and decide on policy. Through the palace memorials, for example, he collected information about the conduct of candidates for important posts.[88] With a variety of information at his command he was able to scrutinize or reverse the decisions of provincial or local administrators and delineate policies for the entire empire; most important of all, he became the only effective decision maker.[89]

In the meantime, the palace-memorial system greatly expedited the administrative process of the Yung-cheng reign. Since palace memorials were transmitted, reviewed, and responded to in a special manner, their transaction was faster than the regular, or routine, memorials. For instance, from his residence in Paoting, about 110 miles south of Peking, the governor-general of the metropolitan area received an imperial reply only four days after he had dispatched his memorial.[90] In another case, the emperor sent out his response to a memorial that had been started on its way from Kaifeng, more than 400 miles from Peking, just six days before.[91] To be sure, the monopoly of decision-making and administrative efficiency made autocratic rule effective.

To sum up, the palace-memorial system was the last and highest stage of confidential official communication in the traditional Chinese state. It served the Manchu autocrats as an effective tool. Through it they successfully exercised personal rule; without their sanction nothing could be carried out. In contrast, within the same system all officials from top to bottom were caught up in a web of surveillance by censorial personnel and reporters of palace memorials; no one was able to challenge the imperial authority. The palace-memorial system thus thwarted bureaucratic ambition and consolidated the ruler's power.

It must be pointed out, however, that in the long run the system inevitably increased the inertia of the imperial administration of the Manchu dynasty. It is true that the administrative process of the traditional Chinese state had tended toward inertia, but the palace-memorial system made it even more unresponsive, as the events in the second half of the nineteenth century revealed.[92] In the web of the palace-memorial system, the imperial authority was overextended. Besides the regular, or routine, reports, palace memorials flowed to the imperial desk from everywhere in the empire; the dead weight of state administration centered on the ruler. Because none of the bureaucrats was given, or was willing to take up, full responsibility for any function, the ruler had to read and comment on all sorts of memorials that carried information, requests, and proposals—that is, state affairs. Nevertheless, the state was too large to allow for personal rule, while the administration was too complicated to be accomplished by a single man. He became more and more a memorial commentator rather than a policy maker, whereas the bureaucrats merely followed the instructions in edicts or in the imperial endorsements on their memorials. As a result, leadership was exhausted at the apex and frustrated below; both the ruler and the bureaucrats lost initiative.[93] Political innovation came neither from the top nor from the bottom. In this situation, imperial power was consolidated, but the state administration fell into inertia.

As far as the Yung-cheng reign is concerned, the operation of the palace-memorial system was effective, without the aforementioned side effects. This success resulted not only from the emperor's energy and devotion, but also from the service of his confidential assistants, who formed a small, informal, and efficient group around him. Their service, such as the upward and downward transmission of memorials, was of great importance. Their transmitting and secretarial duties were essential to the actual working of the system; their professional advice provided the ruler with alternative viewpoints indispensable to effective decision making. In due time, the emperor appointed Grand Councillors from among his confidential assistants and integrated their functions into the Grand Council.

VI

A New Instrument of Autocratic Rule— The Grand Council

1. *Formation of the Grand Council*

    The Grand Council contributed greatly to early Ch'ing autocracy: it took over the important functions of the Grand Secretariat, completed the changes in the Ch'ing censorial system, and carried out the imperial will. Students of Ch'ing history have tended to believe that the Council was founded mainly to prepare for the campaign against the Dzungars.[1] Nonetheless, military necessity was only one of the factors in its formation. For a better understanding of the full implications of its founding, its origin must be analyzed in connection with the administrative pattern of the traditional Chinese state, to which the Manchu dynasty was the last successor, and also in light of Ch'ing political practices prior to the organization of the Grand Council.

    Like the palace-memorial system, the Grand Council resulted from the administrative practices of the Chinese state before the Ch'ing. In Chinese dynastic history, since the time of Emperor Wu of the Former Han, autocratic rulers had frequently weakened the regular administrative organs by installing compact, personal units for the purpose of political centralization. During the Later Han, when the Outer

Court—the formally established administrative office under the premier or premiers—was overshadowed by the Inner Court consisting of the ruler and his confidants, the Masters of Documents (*Shang-shu*), originally lesser palace officials in charge of secretarial work, finally emerged as central figures second only to the monarch.[2] Throughout the chaotic years, from the fall of the Later Han to the rise of the Sui, the office of Imperial Secretaries (*Chung-shu*) and that of Imperial Aides (*Shih-chung*) developed, in that order, into power centers above the Outer Court under the chief Master of Documents.[3] After these three units merged and became the Outer Court in the seventh century, the T'ang rulers staffed their Inner Court first with imperial affinals and finally with eunuchs.[4] The Sung dynasty did not have a distinct Inner Court, perhaps because its rulers were able to dominate the regular administrative units in the central government. While the Mongol Inner Court included nobles, priests, and other special individuals, that of the Ming dynasty after 1380 was composed of eunuchs and a small group of selected scholars. The latter at last evolved into the Grand Secretariat, which was copied by the Manchus.

In sum, autocratic monarchs tried to rule the state personally with the assistance of their confidants, who formed compact and manageable units at various times. Whatever their differences in rank and nomenclature, members of these units worked for the autocratic cause. Because they enjoyed the imperial trust, they outweighed the regular chief administrators; they had constant access to the ruler, and were able to answer his call at any time. It was imperial confidence and easy access to the throne that made these units efficient and powerful. At first they operated behind the scenes, but, for functional reasons, they in due time became an Outer Court. As soon as this occurred, the ruler found it advisable to call into being another Inner Court. Thus, the Outer and Inner Courts, old and new, were taken over one after another to meet the autocrat's needs. When the Ming dynasty was conquered by the Manchus, the eunuchs who were for centuries staff members of the Inner Court were thrown out with the regime. When adopted by the Ch'ing, the Grand Secretariat, once functioning efficiently as part of the Inner Court of the Ming, was absorbed into the Outer Court and lost its efficiency. Beyond doubt it was incapable of meeting the requirements of the Manchu rulers who needed their own Inner Court to deal with the new situation.

To be sure, the Grand Council was closely related to the political practices of the early Manchu rulers, who became accustomed to the services of a small, informal, and carefully selected group of scholars.[5] Even before the rise of the Six Boards in 1631, Hong-taiji had founded the Literary Office,[6] a personal and informal unit directly under him. It recruited members from Manchus who had no military backing and especially from those Chinese scholars who surrendered themselves to, or were conquered by, the Manchus. Each was gifted with a specialized knowledge—linguistic, secretarial, political and so on. Among these men, for instance, were Dahai (d.1632), Fan Wen-ch'eng (1597-1666), Hife (d.1652), and Ning Wan-wo (d.1665)—all of whom enjoyed imperial trust, although they were not high officials.[7] They worked for the cause of Hong-taiji, who fought not only for the conquest of China but also for his supremacy over other Manchu princes. In 1636 the Literary Office developed into the Three Inner Courts, from which later came the Grand Secretariat, the center of Manchu administration before the formation of the Grand Council.

The Literary Office marked a milestone in Manchu evolution from a feudal group to a despotic polity. During the formative period of the Manchu dynasty, kinship was the first concern in choosing officials. Nurhaci made his sons and nephews princes who commanded banners—the earliest formal Manchu organization of political importance—and shared control of inter-banner matters, namely, state affairs. With their special kinship, the princes took care of civilian as well as military affairs; they had both military and political power. For example, the Five Councillors (*Li-cheng t'ing-sung wu ta-ch'en*) and the Ten Associates (*Shih Jargūci*) who were appointed to deal with civilian business were subordinate to the princes, or to all the princes collectively, rather than directly to the ruler.[8] In this situation Hong-taiji was merely *primus inter pares*, and he made efforts to break through the influence of the princes. The Literary Office was founded for this purpose.

The Literary Office served Hong-taiji in two ways. First, it was a major step toward an autocratic polity at the cost of aristocracy. Since the appointment of its staff members was based on expert ability, not on heredity, it was a nonaristocratic structure which Hong-taiji could make and unmake. Without military power behind them its members could not challenge their master. They were organized into a disciplined body of commissioned functionaries, depending on the ruler's favor and working for his interests. Within the bureaucratic framework, they were effective tools used by Hong-taiji to domesticate the aristocrats. Second, the Literary Office functioned as Hong-taiji's Inner Court. Because it was controlled exclusively by him, other princes had no authority over it. Its members served as his personal staff, drawing up imperial decrees, offering suggestions on military affairs, and carrying out special missions.[9] They were independent of the Six Boards, where the princes maintained their influence until 1641, and with the imperial trust they overshadowed these six offices. Once, during court deliberations, for instance, they were even ordered to suggest punishment for the improper conduct of Manggultai, one of the most powerful senior princes.[10] Apparently the Literary Office was an important tool in promoting Hong-taiji's absolute authority, and it became a model for later Manchu rulers, who organized units of the same nature when the situation required them.

The Shun-chih Emperor had an informal group of aides, including priests and eunuchs. The case of Father Adam Schall von Bell (1591-1666) was typical. In his various capacities he served the emperor as a very influential personal advisor. As Director of the Imperial Board of Astronomy (*Ch'in-t'ien chien cheng*), he was a moral interpreter of natural phenomena, which were a source of imperial authority within the Confucian order.[11] As a Catholic missionary with imperial favor, he was a spiritual advisor to the throne. Popular in the imperial house, he appeared as the emperor's close friend and "mafa," meaning grandfather in Manchu.[12] With these unusual relations the Father enjoyed special access to the emperor and gave the latter extensive advice on religious and political affairs. No wonder one source considers him the "actual regent of China" from 1651 to 1660.[13]

Shun-chih's entourage included a group of Buddhist monks. His interest in Ch'an Buddhism was not necessarily political, but some Buddhist priests—such as Hsing-ts'ung (1610-1666), T'ung-hsiu (1614-1675), Hsing-sen (1614-1677), and in particular

Tao-min (1596-1674)—became his trusted friends and informal, influential advisors.[14] It is said that Yu T'ung (1618-1704), a famous man of letters but an unsuccessful graduate student, owed his official appointment to Tao-min's recommendation.[15] Fundamentally, the service of these Buddhist monks was no different from that of Father Adam Schall von Bell. As a whole, they acquired influence at the cost of the bureaucrats who were the legitimate advisors to the ruler, and their services were basically the same as those performed by the Literary Office in the reign of Hong-taiji. In other words, these Jesuit and Buddhist advisors formed a sort of Inner Court to promote the sovereign power in one way or another.

Eunuchs were another group of imperial confidants in the Shun-chih period. They became influential after the death of Dorgon in 1651 and two years later were organized into the Thirteen Offices (*Shih-san ya-men*). Under their leader, Wu Liang-fu (d.1661), who helped the emperor eliminate Dorgon's henchmen from power, the eunuchs took charge of court affairs, served as intermediaries between bureaucrats and the throne, and even had an influence on state administration.[16] Their service was so useful to the promotion of the imperial authority that neither censorial remonstrance nor the admonition of the Manchu nobles could shake the throne's trust in them.[17] The bitterness of the Manchu aristocrats is evident from the fact that soon after the death of the emperor, they executed Wu Liang-fu and abolished the Thirteen Offices.[18]

The Southern Imperial Study was perhaps the most influential Inner Court of the Ch'ing before the organization of the Grand Council. Originally K'ang-hsi's reading place, it developed into an office for his personal advisors in 1677, a critical time during the campaign against the Three Feudatories.[19] Members of this office were literary men, most of whom were holders of the *chin-shih* degree from the Hanlin Academy and later also from the Grand Secretariat and the Supervisorate of Imperial Instruction (*Chan-shih fu*), but some were holders of the *chü-jen* degree, while a few were from a miscellaneous category of the licentiate, mathematicians, and military men.[20] As a whole, they were personally selected by the K'ang-hsi Emperor on the basis of their capacities as scholars, calligraphers, poets, or painters. Because the office was informal and personal, the size of its staff was not fixed. At first it had two members, Chang Ying and Kao Shih-ch'i (1645-1730), but it later expanded to include, besides a number of regular staff, temporary members who were selected from the Hanlin Academy, the Imperial University, and the Supervisorate of Imperial Instruction, and took turns attending the office.[21]

Members of the Southern Imperial Study acted upon the ruler's wishes, without regular functional differentiation. Although they originally served as imperial copyists, proofreaders, secretaries, and expositors of Chinese classics, mathematics, or astronomy, with the passing of time their work expanded to the political sphere. They drew up edicts for the throne, transmitted imperial orders to officials outside the capital, offered advice on state affairs, and even performed special assignments with Grand Secretaries.[22] Their service was so much appreciated by the ruler that they always found themselves among the imperial attendants on trips and frequently received special imperial favor. As a result, members of this office became very powerful men, who, if they did not outweigh the Grand Secretaries, at least shared the same prestige with them. After successful service in the office they were put in key positions. As a matter of fact, a large number of the Grand Councillors started their official careers as members of the Southern Imperial Study.

The Southern Imperial Study was important for several reasons. First, it became significant because of the prestige and talent of its staff, whose easy access to the ruler made their service more effective than that of regular administrative units. Second, as a compact and small unit, its staff took care of its own clerical work. Without clerks, it was free from clerical malfeasance, which was a major factor in administrative inefficiency in many other offices. Third, it was free from ethnic tension. Literary accomplishment was a basic requirement for its staff, and priority of appointment was given to Chinese scholars rather than to the Manchus, most of whom were trained to be warriors. Because it was an informal and personal group, the ruler could select men after his own heart, without considering the principle of numerical equality between Manchu and Chinese officials as required of the regular units in the central government. Due to the small size and personal nature of the office, it was possible to root out any potential ethnic conflict among the Manchu and Chinese members. As nonhereditary bureaucrats, the Chinese staff were more controllable than the Manchus who were, so to speak, hereditary members of the ruling class. Furthermore, because of their cultural orientation, the Chinese bureaucrats tended to favor political centralization, also a goal pursued by the Manchu rulers.

Fourth, the Southern Imperial Study benefited by its location inside the Ch'ien-ch'ing Gate, which was inaccessible to ordinary officials. Isolated from the Outer Court, it carried on its functions in a secret manner and protected important dealings from security leaks. For this reason, the emperor asked Wang Hung-hsü, one of the devoted reporters of palace memorials in the K'ang-hsi period, to submit his confidential reports to, and to take secret imperial instructions from, this office.[23] For the same reason, it later became the waiting room for Grand Councillors who were to receive assignments from the ruler, as well as the office of their secretaries (*chün-chi chang-ching*); the Study's eunuchs were assigned to serve in the Grand Council, a small building nearby.[24] Efficient and secret, it was the K'ang-hsi Emperor's Inner Court, prevailing over the Grand Secretariat after the middle of the K'ang-hsi period, and the immediate predecessor of the Grand Council.

Although the Southern Imperial Study lasted until the end of the Ch'ing dynasty, its influence waned substantially with the death of K'ang-hsi in 1722. The factors responsible for its decline accounted largely for the rise of the Grand Council. Of these factors, the personality of K'ang-hsi's successor was an important one. A political realist, Yung-cheng stressed practical matters rather than literary accomplishments. In a decree he advised members of the Hanlin Academy to write things of practical usefulness, not to indulge themselves in writing elegant and refined essays.[25] This is reflected in the fact that during the Yung-cheng period there were fewer literary and philosophical works published than in the era prior to it. The great encyclopedia, *Synthesis of Books and Illustrations of Ancient and Modern Times*, which was published in the Yung-cheng period, was in fact finished in the K'ang-hsi period. True, Yung-cheng's reign was too short for any major literary enterprise; nonetheless, his personality was mainly responsible for this. An office with a staff of literary fame, the Southern Imperial Study naturally lacked appeal to the new monarch.

A second factor which moved the Yung-cheng Emperor to disfavor the Southern Imperial Study was the succession struggle that engulfed almost the entire central political hierarchy, including the Southern Imperial Study. Ho Ch'o, for example, served as a member of the office and was deeply involved in the struggle on the side of Yin-ssu, the arch-opponent of the emperor. Chinese dynastic history has also well demonstrated that scholar-officials were prone to factional contention by virtue of philosophical attitudes, literary connections, geographical considerations, or personal interest. Whatever the reason for the struggle, factionalism ran counter to the imperial interest. As long as he was devoting himself to the removal of factions and his formal rivals he had little confidence in the officialdom which had been contaminated with the factionalism of the previous reign. Beyond question he needed a new Inner Court composed of his men.

The third factor was his desire for political centralization—his ultimate goal and a many-sided project including the suppression of his formal political rivals, the remodeling of the aristocracy, the eradication of factionalism, and the improvement of administrative efficiency. The project was so complicated that no single person or institution could push it through. Certainly the Southern Imperial Study was incapable of taking up this heavy duty, nor was the palace-memorial system alone sufficient to carry it out. The unsuitability of the Southern Imperial Study was clearly displayed by the fact that aside from its involvement in factionalism, it was incapable of completely taking over the vital functions of the Grand Secretariat, especially of the Office for Administrative Deliberations, which remained an aristocratic bastion. The inadequacy of the palace-memorial system lay in the fact that it operated largely in places outside the capital. Its members served mainly as imperial informers; they were too far away, and they were not all qualified, to render advisory and secretarial services whenever needed. The best solution seemed to be to select some loyal and able assistants organized into an institution at the top level so as to provide advisory and secretarial services. While all the above factors were working toward the formation of a new office, there arose the necessity for military preparations against the Dzungars, which added force to them. On the whole, the Grand Council was a logical development from the situation.

2. *Problems Concerning the Grand Council*

Studying the Grand Council presents some problems. The first and most controversial concerns the date of its establishment. Because neither official documents of the Ch'ing dynasty nor any private works of the Yung-cheng period give reliable information about the date of its establishment, a variety of scholarly opinion has arisen concerning this. These opinions may be divided into two broad categories. Until 1959 scholars suggested dates ranging from 1729 to 1732. A closer examination of the available sources shows that none of the dates is certain. In recent years the problem has invited new interest among scholars. Although they do not agree, many of them have considered a date before 1729 to be likely. The late Professor Li Tsung-t'ung of National Taiwan University was the first to trigger a revisionist gun in 1959; he believes that the office may have been established during the latter half of 1726. This date, again, is not definite, but, in light of the historical evidence, seems more logical than other interpretations.[26] One student of Ch'ing history, who in 1965 put the date at 1729, later tended to support Li's viewpoint; another well-known expert in Ch'ing history offered a new possibility for consideration, arguing that the year 1727 was the most likely date.[27] The problem is further complicated by another scholar who first preferred early 1731 and then 1730.[28] These interpretations generally overemphasize the military origin of the Grand Council, and they thus miss the point.

Military necessity was not the major consideration in the rise of the Grand Council. The case can be made that if it was founded simply for the campaign against the Dzungars, it had no reason to outlive the war. Yung-cheng, for example, appointed a special council to deal with the uprising of the Miao people, a minority group, in 1735.[29] but it ceased to operate as soon as the revolt was suppressed. He was known as a ruler who had little interest in military matters. As the Grand Council was not founded for the Dzungar campaign, the greatest foreign war in the Yung-cheng period, no other specific military reason could have accounted for its creation. Nor was there any general military purpose calling for its organization; if there had been any, the Council would have taken charge of all kinds of warfare, including the Miao revolt. The problem can be further scrutinized in terms of the functions of the Grand Council. After its formation it had political as well as military functions. Suffice it to say that the office was not established for military reasons, specific or general.

Because the Grand Council resulted primarily from political developments during the Yung-cheng period, the problem of its founding date should be reconsidered. As the censorial system underwent a change, the rudiments of a Grand Council took shape. Soon after his enthronement the Yung-cheng Emperor acquired the assistance of a special but informal group, which developed a set of practices not only related to the palace-memorial system but connected with the rise of the Grand Council. When palace memorials became the most frequent and important instruments of communication from officials to the throne, imperial orders were more often transmitted in the form of court letters, a practice beginning at least from the K'ang-hsi period.[30] Court letters came to the addressees through specific channels composed of a few special individuals who in most cases were the same officials charged with the duty of transmitting palace memorials to the throne.

The earliest court letters of the Yung-cheng period seem to have appeared in 1723.[31] They could be transmitted under the name of the Court, of some special individuals, or especially of the Grand Secretariat, which often transmitted imperial orders in the form of letters to provincial officials.[32] No doubt Grand Secretaries played a significant role, transmitting messages individually or jointly. Joint transmission went on in many ways. It might be done by two, three, or four people with their names indicated together in the letter, or with just one name mentioned in it.[33] Sometimes the court letters were transmitted jointly, by Grand Secretaries and Yin-hsiang, the most trusted of Yung-cheng's brothers.[34] Almost all Grand Secretaries had been transmitters individually or jointly; they were Chang T'ing-yü, Chu Shih (1665-1736), Chiang T'ing-hsi (1669-1732), Sunju (d.1733), Funinggan (d.1728), Jabina (d.1731), Marsai (d.1733), and O-er-t'ai.[35] Besides the Grand Secretaries, there was a long list of individuals who did the same work. Sometimes presidents of the Board of Revenue (*Hu-pu*), Chamberlains of the Imperial Bodyguard and their senior assistants, and the Commissioner of the Imperial Equipage Department (*Luan-i shih*), also took part in the transmission work.[36] In short, whatever their positions, they were largely imperial confidants who performed as concurrent assignments any specific service—such as the transmission of court letters—the emperor saw fit to give them. Those who enjoyed more imperial trust might receive more assignments and become more influential than others.

From the above discussion, one can see that the court letters were a form of confidential imperial communication directly to the addressees through special channels. Containing imperial instructions, inquiries, and answers, the court letters were the counterparts of palace memorials. Informed through palace memorials or through other sources or faced with certain unexpected situations, the emperor issued court letters. Having received instructions from court letters or comments from the endorsements on their memorials, or confronted with problems about their services, officials in places other than Peking submitted palace memorials as further reports or as replies.

As soon as the Yung-cheng Emperor ascended the throne, the issuing of court letters and the sending of palace memorials formed an unbroken chain of interaction, which operated through the same transmission system. The transmitters—imperial confidants with close access to the throne—became an informal group around the ruler and greatly contributed to the stabilization of the sovereign power in the beginning years of the Yung-cheng period. When the emperor started military preparations for the war against the Dzungars around 1726, he needed more services and suggestions.[37] Direct communication between him and various officials inevitably increased. To make the preparation work secret and efficient, he selected from this informal group a few individuals of high ability, credit, loyalty, and mastery of management of court letters and palace memorials as his special assistants or advisors—who ultimately came to be known as Grand Councillors. Therefore, the Grand Council developed out of the informal group and the date of its founding was blurred by secrecy, informality, and the fact that service in it was concurrent with service elsewhere. After appointment the

Grand Councillors continued to follow the same transmission practices that were actually borrowed by the Grand Council as its communication procedure. As it worked satisfactorily and its functions were originally nonmilitary, the office remained even after the campaign against the Dzungars.

The second problem with the Grand Council concerns the evolution of its name. Although scholars agreed that the *Chün-chi ch'u* was its final name, they have disputed its earlier name or names. Opinions fall into three categories. One holds that at the beginning the office appeared under the name, the "Office of Military Supplies" (*Chün-hsü fang*), then was referred to as the "Office of Military Strategy" (*Chün-chi fang*), and finally became the Grand Council. A second interpretation is that the earlier name of the Grand Council was the Office of Military Supplies. Scholars of the third category believe that the Office of Military Strategy was its original name. As each of the above points has its justification,[38] the problem is nearly as confusing as that of the date of establishment.

For a better understanding of the question, one may examine the clues provided by the Yung-cheng Emperor and two of his trusted officials. In many decrees the emperor used the terms *chün-hsü* (military supplies) and *chün-chi* (military strategy) almost interchangeably.[39] In their modern meanings, they suggest functions charged to different offices, but in eighteenth-century China they were handled by the same office. His liberal use of these two phrases as synonyms seems to have implied that the evolution of the name, "Grand Council," did not follow a course as strict as the first category of opinion suggests. Even after the words "*Chün-chi ch'u*" had appeared on the seal of the office by 1732, some contemporary high officials still cited it as the *Chün-chi fang* (Office of Military Strategy). Chang T'ing-yü, one of the first Grand Councillors, related around 1746 that in 1733 his son was made a secretary in the *Chün-chi fang*; a president of the Board of Revenue, Shih I-chih (1682-1736), also mentioned the Office by the same name in a memorial dated 1735.[40] These facts seem to suggest that the name *Chün-chi ch'u* might have been derived directly from it. Whatever the evolution of its name, at the early stage the office operated in secrecy and informality and was marked by its multifunctions and the concurrent service of its members—and these caused the above controversies.

The third problem concerning the Grand Council relates to its staff, especially the Grand Councillors. Like the Southern Imperial Study, the new office had no clerks; clerical duties were carried out by secretaries called the *chün-chi chang-ching*, also known colloquially as *hsiao chün-chi*. The secretaries were recruited from the lower ranks of the officials of the Grand Secretariat and the Six Boards and were appointed on the basis of recommendation.[41] They appeared later in the evolution of the office than did the Grand Councillors. At the beginning their number was not fixed and they functioned simply as clerks but, from the Ch'ien-lung period on, they were influential bureaucrats.

Without exception the Grand Councillors were the most favored and trusted confidants of the Yung-cheng Emperor. They had received palace memorials and transmitted court letters for the ruler before the formal establishment of the Grand Council and continued the same work after its formation. At first they were selected from courtiers in charge of civilian affairs—notably the three earliest Grand Councillors, Yin-hsiang, Chang T'ing-yü, and Chiang T'ing-hsi—but later some of them were military men.[42] Because their appointments to the Grand Council were concurrent, they retained their titles and the duties of the offices from which they were selected. The Grand Secretaries who worked in the Grand Council were sometimes informally referred to in some private sources as the "Inner Grand Secretaries" (*Nei chung-t'ang*), but they did not form a group officially different from other Grand Councillors in a nominal or functional sense.[43] Despite their previous backgrounds, all the Grand Councillors were the highest staff members of the Grand Council. Individually or jointly, they might receive any imperial assignment and carry it out and sign the papers in either of their official capacities according to the circumstances.[44]

Another difficulty concerns those Grand Secretaries who were busy transmitting court letters and receiving palace memorials for the Yung-cheng Emperor but who were not included in the list of Grand Councillors. The *Ch'ing-shih* (History of the Ch'ing dynasty) lists ten Grand Councillors for the Yung-cheng reign. An analysis of the positions that the ten Grand Councillors had held before their new service will show that four of them had been, and were still, Grand Secretaries.[45] Of the rest, two were Manchu princes, two had served either as Chamberlain of the Imperial Bodyguard or as Commissioner of the Imperial Equipage Department, one had been Subchancellor of the Grand Secretariat, and the last had served as provincial Commander-in-chief.[46] On the whole, in the Yung-cheng period the Grand Councillors were recruited largely from the ranks of Grand Secretaries and presidents and vice-presidents of the Six Boards, and five of them were still active in transmitting court letters and forwarding palace memorials for the emperor. Because all these transmitters were imperial confidants and the transmission work was an important reason for the rise of the Grand Council, those who performed this special transmission assignment but were omitted from the list of the Grand Councillors should be reconsidered here.

Of these transmitters worthy of reexamination, Chu Shih was the most important. He has been neglected by historians but was regarded by Liang Chang-chü (1775-1849) and some others as a Grand Councillor during the Ch'ien-lung period.[47] His addition to the list in that period was misleading because he died in 1736 and the Grand Council was abolished immediately after Ch'ien-lung's accession to the throne. Yet Chu Shih seems to have been a Grand Councillor during the Yung-cheng era. A scholar and favorite official of the emperor, he had served in the Southern Imperial Study early in 1723, and in 1725 obtained promotion from the presidency of the Board of Revenue to Grand Secretary. He was not only among the emperor's confidants who transmitted court letters and palace memorials but was an able and trusted assistant of Yin-hsiang. In this connection he was probably a Grand Councillor of the Yung-cheng, instead of the Ch'ien-lung, period.

The case of Jabina, a Manchu noble of the Plain Yellow Banner, was similar to that of Chu Shih. Although he had been involved in the succession struggle during the last years of the K'ang-hsi period, he was later pardoned and made president of the Board of War (*Ping-pu*), a position closely connected with the Grand Councillors in the work of military preparation. During his presidency he was also one of the individuals responsible for transmission of court letters,[48] and as soon as the campaign against the Dzungars was launched in 1729, he was sent to Kansu province to take charge of military supplies for the western route of troops. Inasmuch as his service was part of the work of the Grand Council, he might have been one of the Grand Councillors.

As for Sunju and Funinggan, it seems that their exclusion from the list of Grand Councillors is reasonable. For one thing, the former, though a Grand Secretary entrusted with transmitting court letters, was not so much in the imperial favor as were Chang T'ing-yü, Chiang T'ing-hsi, and Chu Shih. For another, the Grand Council, a compact and secret office, could not include so many people. Funinggan, a Manchu general given the rank of a Grand Secretary in 1723 and later a large sum of money for his nonalignment in the factional struggle of the K'ang-hsi period, had commanded armies on the northwestern frontier for many years.[49] That he was qualified for service in the Grand Council was also borne out by the fact that he was recalled to Peking from the Sinkiang front in late 1726, a time when military preparations against the Dzungars were underway. Judging by this fact, he might have been a choice as a Grand Councillor. But after a short stay in the capital he was sent to Sian as the Tartar General, was later humiliated, and finally died there in 1728.

The last problem concerns the organization and functions of the Grand Council. Since it developed out of informality and expediency, it was different from a regular office and, at its early stage, had no accessory unit. The Grand Councillors had to take care of all matters, including clerical services, designated to the Grand Council, and only at a later stage were secretaries appointed for the clerical work of the office. Most likely the Grand Council acquired two subordinate institutes, the Military Archives Office (*Fang-lüeh kuan*) and the Manchu-Chinese Translation Office (*Nei fan-shu fang*), during the Ch'ien-lung period. While the Ch'ien-lung Emperor was devoted to military exploits, Grand Councillors were busy drawing plans, forwarding court letters, and receiving memorials from commanders. He founded the Military Archives Office to keep documents of the Grand Council. As the Southern Imperial Study had long lost its importance, the new office also took charge of editing and publishing military and literary books. Its operations could be suspended after it had completed its work. At the same time he established the Manchu-Chinese Translation Office to translate state papers from Manchu to Chinese or vice versa. Since translation was a daily task this office became permanent.

Functions of the Grand Council were identified with the responsibilities of its staffs. The Grand Councillors were at first appointed on an equal footing and were responsible to the ruler individually, but gradually a chief Grand Councillor emerged from among the staff during the reign of Ch'ien-lung.[50] Because they had easy access to the throne, their obligations were almost all-inclusive. They were, for example, summoned to the imperial presence whenever the throne needed them, no matter where they were. Military affairs such as strategy, supplies, and the recruiting and training of troops were but part of their responsibilities; from the very beginning, their duties covered nonmilitary affairs, which were even more important than the military matters. When asked, they had to supply information and suggestions. As early as the Yung-cheng period, they took an active part in discussing Mongol, Tibetan, and other minority affairs.[51] Handling important judicial cases was also one of their functions. For example, in 1732 a Manchu general was punished in accordance with their suggestions. Making recommendations for rewards was another of their duties. When officials deserved commendation, the ruler often ordered the Grand Councillors to suggest a reward, and their suggestions were generally accepted without reservation.[52] As trusted officials of the ruler, they might suggest changes in official appointments.[53] Their last and most important function was drafting decrees and transmitting imperial orders and memorials. They were in all likelihood editors of books for the ruler as well. In short, their accessibility to the throne made all these responsibilities inevitable. They served the ruler as personal secretaries and as a sort of "brain trust."

3. *Political and Cultural Role of the Grand Council*

Its Political Role. The Grand Council played a significant political role from its very beginning to the end of the dynasty. It outweighed all other offices, and its chief members were at the head of the entire bureaucracy. Through its all-inclusive functions and special operating procedures, it did away with all checks, actual or potential, to the imperial power and facilitated autocratic rule. This can be understood from a survey of its influences on the aristocracy, Grand Secretariat, censorial organization, and palace-memorial system.

The political importance of the Grand Council lay in the fact that it removed the last influence of the Manchu aristocrats. Since the inception of the dynasty they had been handicapping the consolidation of imperial power. Their power was reduced with the de-emphasis of the banners;[54] toward the end of the K'ang-hsi period they were in fact members of the bureaucracy. What became their remaining stronghold was the Office for Administrative Deliberations, an office that took shape during the reign of Hong-taiji and consisted of princes and other banner dignitaries with some advisory and administrative responsibilities.[55] Early Manchu rulers from Hong-taiji onward attempted to manipulate it to weaken the hereditary power of princes, but it became a new power center as time went on. Its members were frequently ordered to discuss state policies and sometimes draw up edicts for the ruler.[56] It is clear that this office developed not only at the cost of the princes but also at the expense of the Grand Secretariat. After the formation of the Grand Council, the ruler relied on the service of the Grand Councillors instead of on that of the Office for Administrative Deliberations, and the office was finally abolished in 1791.[57] Without the title of Grand Councillor neither the princes nor the Manchu nobles had a voice in state affairs or shared state secrets with the ruler. Throughout the Ch'ing dynasty only nine princes and fifty-four other Manchu nobles were made Grand Councillors.[58] Thus, the great majority of Manchu aristocrats were precluded from service on the Council and were even prohibited from hearing and talking about its affairs. No matter whether they were Grand Councillors or not, they were bureaucrats obedient to the ruler.

The Grand Secretaries were also influenced by the Grand Council. As members of the Grand Secretariat, they were the highest-ranking functionaries in the Ch'ing political hierarchy. Their responsibilities were mainly to draw up edicts, register them, and send them to the Board of War for delivery to the recipients through the postal system. In addition, they were obliged to transmit, preserve, and review memorials, and they gave suggestions. From these functions the Grand Secretariat derived its influence. If the Southern Imperial Study undermined it, the Grand Council decisively devitalized it. Now important edicts and memorials bypassed it and were dealt with by the Grand Council. From then on the Grand Secretariat became an office for routine affairs, and, without the title of Grand Councillor, the Grand Secretaries were but ordinary bureaucrats.

The shift of major functions from the Grand Secretariat to the Grand Council resulted in two lasting effects on the Ch'ing central administration. First, the shift strengthened and systematized direct communication between sovereign and provincial officials. The Grand Councillors recorded important imperial orders in the form of court letters and passed them without registration in the Grand Secretariat to the Board of War, or sometimes to the Board of Revenue, for dispatch to the addressees by the postal system. Special deliveries were sent by express.[59] Through this direct communication officials outside Peking were brought under direct imperial supervision.

Second, the Grand Council caused the whole civil administration of the Manchu empire to function in a martial manner. As it dealt with imperial orders secretly and accurately and relayed them fast, the court letters were no less than military messages to the front. Like the commander-in-chief who, sitting in headquarters, commanded generals in the field, the ruler in Peking directed important affairs in the provinces through the Grand Council and commanded all other organs. This meant concentration of power in the hands of the ruler, who became virtually almighty in theory—and in practice.

The Grand Council overshadowed the Grand Secretariat, but did not replace it. The two existed concurrently and functioned at the highest level of the political structure. There was a delicate relationship between them that ensured the successful shift of major functions from the Grand Secretariat to the Grand Council and made their coexistence possible. The relationship generally resulted from concurrent service of officials, a practice fully exploited by the Ch'ing rulers for their own interests. Through this practice, the same men might concurrently work in several offices. With more imperial trust, a few officials were given more offices or more important assignments. On the other hand, with the shift of imperial confidence, some officials or offices might lose their importance, though nominally maintaining the same status. In like manner, many Grand Secretaries were made Grand Councillors and served in both offices—the Grand Secretariat and the Grand Council—at the same time. Their dual capacity reduced functional conflicts and contributed to the smooth relations between these two offices. During the years 1729-1911, the number of officials concurrently serving in both organs averaged 2.35 each year.[60] Because both groups of officials owed their appointments to imperial favor, they would gratefully work in either office.[61] They were both servants of the same master, the ruler. As a result, the Grand Councillors, even after being appointed, transmitted court letters for the ruler, sometimes still under the title of Grand Secretaries.[62]

During the last three years of the Yung-cheng period, a functional line developed between the Grand Council and the Grand Secretariat, providing another reason for avoidance of conflict between the two offices. Among its many assignments, the Grand Council focused on military affairs. To separate this function from those of the Grand Secretariat, the Grand Council stamped all its military documents with a special seal given to it in 1732.[63] When a particular matter concerned both institutions, they dealt with it in common. Therefore some decrees, though the same in content, were made public simultaneously under the name of Grand Secretaries and of Grand Councillors.[64] A strict division of labor was a later development.

The coexistence of the Grand Secretariat and the Grand Council reveals the techniques and objectives of Ch'ing autocracy. Dynastic rulers, who frequently couched their authority in terms of tradition, also carried on their autocratic rule in the name of tradition. Because the Grand Secretariat had been a ruling machine since the Ming dynasty, it became an institution of traditional importance related to imperial order and authority and it was worth retaining in the light of imperial tradition. The K'ang-hsi Emperor founded the Southern Imperial Study, but he kept the Grand Secretariat. Yung-cheng followed this precedent, retaining the Grand Secretariat and the Southern Imperial Study after the establishment of the Grand Council. Although the rise of new political machines led to the shift of weight from one office to another in the governmental structure, the shift was designed to facilitate autocratic rule within the tradition, not to break the existing order.

Another reason for the coexistence of the Grand Secretariat and the Grand Council was to maintain institutional balance. In the Chinese political tradition there were ideological and institutional balances. Confucianism was balanced by Legalism; the hereditary monarchy by the nonhereditary bureaucracy.[65] True, such balances moderated to some extent the oppressiveness of the dynastic government, but under skillful management they served the ruler as instruments to increase his power. For this reason, the ruler tried to maintain or create balances for his convenience. This practice was carried to a climax by Yung-cheng. For example, he struggled for an ideological balance by using Buddhism and Taoism, besides Legalism, to check Confucianism, and sought an institutional balance by creating new ruling machinery to outrank but not replace the old one. While the censorial offices and the palace-memorial system existed together, so did the Grand Secretariat, the Southern Imperial Study, and the Grand Council. The same officials were concurrently placed in several positions, and several offices shared the same functions. Some officials and offices might acquire more influence than others in performance of their obligations, but they were at the same time balanced by others. Thus none was able to attain an uncontrollable position against the ruler, who was the ultimate arbiter.

As a means of autocratic control, the Grand Council had a great effect on the Ch'ing censorial system. Theoretically after its change the Ch'ing censorial system functioned almost as before, but the Grand Council outranked it. In 1801 the Chia-ch'ing Emperor (Jen-tsung, r.1796-1820) assigned a censor to supervise the Grand Council to assure no leakage of information. In performing his duties the censor was not permitted by the emperor to set foot in the office, and in 1820 he was withdrawn.[66] The freedom of the office from any censorship seemed to mark the high tide of autocracy.

The Grand Council also overshadowed the palace-memorial system. During the Yung-cheng period the Grand Councillors were responsible for the transmission of the ruler's court letters and the reception of palace memorials from officials outside Peking. As the Grand Councillors were selected from imperial confidants, it is certain that Yung-cheng consulted with them about some of the palace memorials,[67] especially during the last years of his reign when his physical condition declined. Later, it seems, they were given the right to read those reports. During the Ch'ien-lung period the Manchu Grand Councillors were given the right to read the endorsed palace memorials in Manchu; from the Tao-kuang period (1821-1850) onward they even had the right to see those written in Chinese.[68] In the last decade of the eighteenth century Ho-shen (1750-1799), the most trusted imperial confidant and the most powerful Grand Councillor of his day, even had the reporters send to the Grand Council a copy of each of their palace memorials. Although this practice was stopped by Chia-ch'ing, the Grand Councillors later tended to be the ruler's personal assistants in his dealing with the palace memorials.[69] This development indicates that while free from censorial supervision, the Grand Council was given authority over the palace-memorial system. It also demonstrates that through the function of the palace-memorial system the ruler was placed above traditional censorial criticism; through the working of the Grand Council he was able to operate the palace-memorial system effectively. Suffice it to say that the formation of the Grand Council completed the de-emphasis of the censorial system undertaken during the Yung-cheng period.

In sum, then, because both the Grand Council and the palace-memorial system were designed specifically to enhance autocracy, they shared the same operational and functional characteristics. Members of these two institutions received assignments directly from the ruler and were responsible to him in the same way. They were required to carry out their tasks rapidly and secretly. Since the two institutions operated outside the regular administrative structure, the ruler was free from traditional bureaucratic procedures that could possibly check his authority. Their operational features were matched by their common functions. While the Grand Council worked at the center to provide the ruler with special assistance, the palace-memorial system functioned mainly outside the capital to supervise the bureaucrats and keep the throne informed of the situation in far-flung parts of the empire. They operated at different levels, but they both worked to serve the autocratic cause. As a whole, they formed a workable polity that discouraged intrigues and factional activities within and beyond the capital, and enforced the emperor's orders. If their operational characteristics enhanced administrative efficiency, their functional features increased political safety. Administrative efficiency and political safety were the primary concern of dynastic rulers,[70] especially of the Manchu emperors who appreciated the fact of their alien origin. Through the palace-memorial system and the Grand Council Yung-cheng achieved both.

    The palace-memorial system and the Grand Council also shared another operational feature which was important to Ch'ing autocracy. Both were completely under the control of the throne and carried out the will of the ruler, but they did not share his authority. In performance of their duties the staffs were prohibited from claiming personal credit. Chang T'ing-yü, for example, the most influential Grand Councillor of the Yung-cheng period, was simply an efficient imperial clerk. He owed his rise in importance, in no small measure, to his ability to memorize imperial oral orders and put them into written form.[71] Yin-hsiang was another example. During the Yung-cheng period no prince could match him in terms of imperial trust and favor, but he had to present to the ruler any letters or gifts he received from his subordinates.[72] When Yin-hsiang died in 1730, no official dared to mourn or to make sacrifices to the dead without imperial permission.[73] No matter how influential the reporters of palace memorials and the Grand Councillors were, they were no more than tools of the autocrat.

Its Cultural Role. The Grand Council played a cultural role, which also contributed to Yung-cheng autocracy. As conquerors the Manchus enjoyed political, financial, and legal privileges. Since the time of Hong-taiji, there had been an ethnic gulf between Manchu and Chinese officials, and a deep-seated animosity developed between them. During the K'ang-hsi period Chinese officials usually placed confidence in their Chinese subordinates and even covered up their faults, while Manchu officials did the same for their Manchu subordinates.[74] Since they were ill-disposed toward each other, the Manchu officials were impeached by their Chinese subordinates and vice versa.[75] Some extremist Manchus even suggested that promotion from lieutenant to lieutenant-colonel in the Green Standard in Peking should be withheld from Chinese, whereas some Chinese officials criticized their Manchu colleagues as useless people in memorials.[76]

Manchu-Chinese antagonism among the officials proved a ticklish problem to the Manchu rulers. Hongtaiji and his two successors—the Shun-chih and K'ang-hsi Emperors—did recruit mainly Chinese as their personal confidants, but they failed to take positive measures to improve the ethnic situation. Yung-cheng exerted himself to treat the Chinese and Manchus equally in an attempt to alleviate ethnic tension that was costly to sovereign power. He selected, rewarded, and punished officials without consideration of their ethnic origins. Princes Yinssu, Yin-t'ang, and Yin-t'i, who offended him, received harsh punishment; Chinese officials, Chang T'ing-yü, Chiang T'ing-hsi, and Li Wei, who worked diligently and loyally, received his favor.

During the years 1726-1729 Yung-cheng made an effort to put Manchu criminals under the same law as Chinese and permitted responsible local Chinese officials to punish Manchus found guilty.[77] He also did his best to make more openings available for Chinese. In 1727, for instance, he combined vacancies for the Chinese bannermen and those for the Chinese scholars into composite posts filled either by Chinese or by Chinese bannermen.[78] Although this new rule increased the chances for Chinese bannermen, the Chinese did not lose anything. He also opened to the Chinese the appointments in the Five Boards of Feng-t'ien (covering the former provinces of Liaoning and part of Jehol), originally open only to Manchus or Chinese bannermen; sometimes he put a Chinese in a job that was reserved for Manchus.[79] A recent study reveals that, of the early Ch'ing, the Yung-cheng period had the largest number of Chinese governors-general and Chinese governors.[80] Furthermore, according to practice, in audience all Manchu Grand Secretaries stood ahead of their Chinese counterparts. Yung-cheng decreed that, except for the senior Manchu Grand Secretary, the other Grand Secretaries, regardless of ethnicity, stood according to the dates on which they were appointed.[81]

Among the first Grand Councillors, there were two Chinese, Chang T'ing-yü and Chiang T'ing-hsi, and one Manchu, Yin-hsiang. Of the ten Grand Councillors listed in the *Ch'ing-shih* for the July 1729 to September 1735 period, only three were Chinese, but each of their names appeared several times. Thus, they must have held their position for longer periods, whereas the Manchu turnover was greater. A statistical table based on the number of names as they appeared and on their chronological distribution shows the proportion between Manchu and Chinese:

Table 4*

Proportion of Chinese and Manchu Grand Councillors during the Yung-cheng Period

Dates	1729		1730		1731		1732		1733		1734		1735	
C or M	C	M	C	M	C	M	C	M	C	M	C	M	C	M
Number of Names	2	1	2	2	2	1	3	1	1	5	1	3	2	8

*Source: *CS*, pp. 2486-87. Cf. Fu Tsung-mao, *Ch'ing-tai chün-chi ch'u tsu-chih...*, pp. 158 and 182.

C = Chinese; M = Manchu

During the first four years the Chinese and Manchu Grand Councillors were at a ratio of 9:5, although in the last three years of the same period the ratio was 4:16. Among the Grand Councillors of 1735 some were appointed after the death of Yung-cheng and should be counted as appointments of the next era.[82] If one adds Chu Shih to this table, the ratio will be more favorable to the Chinese Grand Councillors.[83] According to a recent study, during the years from its establishment to the end of the dynasty, there were 147 Grand Councillors—68 Manchus, 11 Mongols, 3 Chinese bannermen, and 65 Chinese.[84] If counted by individual reigns before 1862, the ratio tended to the advantage of the Manchus; after that date it turned definitely to the side of the Chinese.[85] Apparently the Grand Council broke through the tradition of numerical equality, and there the Chinese had better opportunities than in other offices in the central government. With the sovereign's trust they could achieve prominence comparable with that of their Manchu colleagues. In the Yung-cheng period no official other than O-er-t'ai could match Chang T'ing-yü, whose influence lasted until his retirement in 1750. Never before had a Chinese official enjoyed so much influence under a Manchu ruler. In other words, with the principle of numerical equality discarded in the Grand Council, the Manchu members had to compete for imperial favor as did their Chinese colleagues. When ethnic origin was given no political priority, ethnic tension lost its basis.

To summarize, the Grand Council originated primarily from the political requirements of the Yung-cheng Emperor and was mainly a political office. Since it developed informally and operated in secrecy, its founding date and early name remain open to question. As the most trusted personal assistants of the ruler, the Grand Councillors had frequent access to the throne and performed any task assigned by the emperor. With a staff of this nature, the Grand Council had charge of all important functions and became the most influential office of the Ch'ing dynasty. Its operation greatly reduced the influence of the Grand Secretariat and the Office for Administrative Deliberations, two important offices of the early Ch'ing—one was a dynastic institution of the Chinese state, the other a Manchu unit of aristocratic origin. As a matter of fact, it operated above the regular Ch'ing civilian and military structures that had functioned before its emergence.

The prestige of the Grand Council was derived from two major factors. First, the Grand Councillors enjoyed the greatest imperial confidence and access to the throne. Second, it operated according to its own procedures which differed from the regular administrative channels. The Grand Councillors transmitted imperial orders in the form of court letters directly to the addressees in provinces in peacetime and wartime alike, and they might receive or even deal with palace memorials when ordered to do so by the ruler. However important or unimportant, everything that they handled was kept secret and free from censorial surveillance. As a result, the Grand Councillorship was regarded by the bureaucrats as the most prestigious post, second only to the throne, and the Grand Council was looked upon with awe.

The factors accounting for the influence of the Grand Council were also the reasons for its workability. Overshadowing all other civilian and military structures and functioning under the ruler's

personal control, it created a new situation that
made institutional and bureaucratic checks on imperial power impossible. Whatever its function or
nature, no office within the empire could challenge
the imperial authority. Whatever their ethnic origin,
ranks, or duties, all officials, including the Grand
Councillors, worked as cogs in the autocratic
machinery. They functioned as directed and checked
one another—but not their operator, the ruler. The
failure of any of them to do so would be brought to
the imperial attention by the palace-memorial system.
In these circumstances, imperial authority became
absolute and universal throughout the empire. Like
the palace-memorial system, the Grand Council was
also liable to inertia because its successful working
depended upon the effective operation of the ruler.
When the operator lost his initiative, the Grand
Council became irresponsive—which is what it was in
the second half of the nineteenth century.

VII

Bureaucratization of the Banner System

1. *The Banner System under the Early Ch'ing*

    Of great significance to the autocracy of the Yung-cheng period was the bureaucratization of the banner system, the hard core of the Manchu regime. Since the reign of Hong-taiji, the banners had been undergoing changes, but during the Yung-cheng era they underwent the last and greatest change. The Manchu government was a system of bifurcation (as were some of the preceding alien dynasties in Chinese history), in which the conquerors and the conquered were ruled separately. While the Manchus together with a handful of trusted Chinese and Mongols were organized and governed under the banners, the majority of Chinese were under the dynastic governmental machinery. The palace-memorial system and the Grand Council reorganized the traditional Chinese governmental structure; the change in the banner system meant bureaucratization of the banners. Both of these strengthened the autocratic rule of the Yung-cheng Emperor. Given the detailed and thoughtful essay on the banner system by Meng Sen,[1] the following discussion will deal particularly with aspects of the Yung-cheng transformation of the banner system that he did not explore.

    The banner system included three detachments, Manchu, Mongol, and Chinese, each of which was composed of eight banners. The basic unit of the banners was a company (called *niru* in Manchu and later known as *tso-ling* in Chinese), theoretically of 300 men. It actually was far smaller than that. The size of the average Manchu company of the Yung-cheng period was between 200 and 80 men.[2] Functionally, there were two kinds of companies, regular (*ch'i-fen*) and household (*pao-i*, generally known as *boo-i*). The regular company consisted of free bannermen charged with ordinary duties such as fighting, while the household unit comprised bond servants serving princes as house workers, farm laborers, or personal retainers. Judging by the position of its leader, the company also fell into two categories—one was under a hereditary captain, the other under a captain chosen from meritorious bannermen. Officers above the company level were also appointed on the basis of personal merit, but they were largely from noble families.

The banners were not only military units but also political and social ones. They were the basic armed forces of the Manchu dynasty. All able bannermen were hereditary warriors. Although some of them were not in active service, they formed the military reservoir. As a political institution, the banners had civil administrative authority over all bannermen and their families. Military officers in banners identified themselves with banner civil officials. Socially, the banner system was rigidly stratified, composed of slaves, freemen, and nobles; personal status was largely determined by birth. The clan heads or elders exercised considerable influence on bannermen and their families.[3] The banner in which the individuals were born was usually the permanent place of their census registration. As a whole, the banner system combined bureaucratic, feudal, and clan elements, which made it a unique organization.

The banner system proved to be an effective military instrument for the Manchu regime in its early history. The regime expanded with the growth of the banner system, which started as a group of four Manchu banners in 1601. Fourteen years later they expanded to the eight Manchu banners, containing approximately 200 companies.[4] The next year, 1616, Nurhaci became ruler of a frontier state with the dynastic title of Later Chin (*Hou-chin*). By 1635 the banner system included eight Mongol banners, and Hong-taiji made himself emperor and changed the dynastic name to Ch'ing just one year later. After the eight Chinese banners were completed in 1642, the Manchu army greatly increased its strength. When the Manchus took Peking in 1644, they had an army of 563 companies, of which 278 were Manchu, 120 were Mongol, and 165 Chinese—a force totaling some 170,000 bannermen.[5] Naturally, it was this banner army that pacified the country and served as a main prop of the dynasty immediately after 1644. Within a short period of time, however, the banner system went into rapid decline.

Some Ch'ing historians tend to believe that the banner forces began to decline around 1800.[6] As a matter of fact, signs of their decay may be detected as early as the second half of the seventeenth century. If fighting techniques and spirit are used as measures of the military strength of troops, the banner army was not an effective war machine after the 1670s. When the Revolt of the Three Feudatories erupted in 1673, the Manchu government mobilized its entire banner force as well as Chinese provincial troops generally known as the Green Standard. It was not until 1681 that the revolt was defeated, the Green Standard under such Chinese commanders as Chang Yung (1616-1684) and Chao Liang-tung (1621-1697) probably having contributed more to its suppression than the banner forces.[7] Again, when the Khoshotes revolted in Kokonor in 1723, the Chinese soldiers under Yüeh Chung-ch'i, rather than the banner forces, deserved the primary credit for pacifying the area. In the campaign against the Dzungars (1729-1734), the Mongolian prince Tsereng (d.1750) won several decisive battles, while the bannermen suffered setbacks one after another.[8]

Although it is difficult to enumerate completely the reasons for the decline of the banners, an explanation, however imperfect, would be helpful in understanding the problems that the banner system presented to the Manchu dynasty and in understanding why Yung-cheng made efforts to bureaucratize the system. The banner decline was political in its manifestations but cultural in its roots. The Manchus, like other nomadic conquerors in Chinese history, were faced with cultural problems after their conquest of China. Long before they had attained the status of a frontier state, the Manchus had been affected by Chinese culture. The progress of their expansion was also the course of their adjustment to Chinese culture. The banner system, for example, resulted from such cultural adjustment.[9] In the course of adjustment, the Manchus moved into China.

The situation in China proper differed from that on the frontier, where the Chinese population was small and more or less influenced by Manchu cultural traits. In China proper the Manchus became a minority of conquerors and were entirely exposed to a strong Chinese socio-cultural configuration,[10] which required of the newcomers rapid and further adaptation.

Reactions to an environment vary with individuals. While some Manchus properly adapted themselves to their new surroundings, others adjusted poorly. At the same time the new generations who were born and brought up after the Manchu conquest found themselves different from their predecessors in many ways. Whatever the reasons, many bannermen were attracted to the luxuries and urbanity of Chinese life, a life far different from their traditional mode. Perhaps the most striking result of their new life was the degeneration of personal conduct, or discipline, and of group spirit. Although the degeneration of discipline and morale found expression in the behavior of individual Manchus, personal cases were an index of group tendencies. In decrees Manchu rulers frequently complained about the decline of banner discipline and morale. It is no wonder that the banner soldiers failed to serve the Manchu regime as an effective war machine in the campaign against the Three Feudatories.

The conflicting political requirements of the Manchu regime were another factor responsible for the decline of the banner forces. While a frontier state, the Manchu ruling group emphasized the clan and feudal elements,[11] but, with the conquest of China, the Manchu frontier state became an empire, requiring impersonal rules based on law, not on clan and feudal practices that were now even rebuffed by the ruler as the source of factionalism (as indicated in Chapter 4). Individual bannermen intimately identified themselves with the clan and feudal spirit. They fought not only for their group but for themselves; in frontier days, for instance, they received handsome spoils after each victorious battle. Under the empire system, they fought for the impersonal state, which only gave them limited reward. They were further confronted with other conflicting policies of their ruler. Though politically connected with China after 1644, they were socially isolated from the Chinese, for bannermen were prohibited from intermarriage with the Chinese, from speaking

Chinese, from wearing Chinese dress, and so on. On the one hand, they had to respond to impersonal rules; on the other, they had to act upon the imperial appeal for maintaining their cultural identity, which declined with time. Since the two requirements were incompatible, the bannermen found it difficult to comply with both at the same time. In short, either the problem of individual cultural adjustment or that of conflicting political requirements depreciated the old Manchu value system, a part of which was military spirit.

Yet another factor that led to the decline of the banner system was the privileged status of the bannermen. After the conquest of China the bannermen belonged to a privileged class. The government was responsible for their economic life and allowed them privileges before the law. When involved in judicial proceedings, they were subject to no Chinese authority even if it had jurisdiction over the case. For committing the same crime as their Chinese counterparts, the Manchu violators were punished more lightly. The nobles received hereditary titles and were placed in official positions according to a sort of spoils system. With their privileges the bannermen did not have to struggle for a good life. If the banner system grew through adversity before 1644, it declined through privileges after that date. Having lost their military skills, the bannermen became parasites of the Manchu dynasty.

During the Yung-cheng period there were various indications of the decline of the banners. The first sign was their lapse into a dissipated life. In a new environment many bannermen lost the spirit of frugality, which was a feature of their original life, and spent money for fine food and dress, alcohol, gambling, and the like. This mode of life obtained not only among the Manchus within China proper but among those on the frontier as well. Mukden, for instance, a Manchu center prior to the conquest, became a place of pleasure in the Yung-cheng period.[12] The new life-style affected the banner system in many ways. It first led to personal economic strain, which was intensified by population pressure and later also by the rise of commodity prices. Bannermen borrowed money at a high rate of interest, sold their land, and even mortgaged their armor.[13] As early as the K'ang-hsi period, the bannermen were poverty-stricken and depended upon special government appropriations for salvation.

K'ang-hsi, for example, appropriated more than ten million taels of silver as salvage. Personal financial strain easily paved the way for official corruption. When a bannerman was appointed a local administrator, he obtained money through illegal means for himself and also for his superior in the banner, as required by the old feudal practices.[14] Because many Manchu officials were involved in cases of graft or embezzlement, the Yung-cheng Emperor privately expressed his loss of confidence in bannermen.[15]

Besides the above economic effects, the dissipated life resulted in the decline of the bannermen's physical strength. They could not endure hard work or strict drill. Banner officers did not train their soldiers carefully, and the rank and file failed to practice archery and riding.[16] Few banner soldiers could use strong bows with ease; when required to use them, they had to take medicine for stimulation.[17] Both officers and soldiers failed to take care of their weapons, which were mortgaged, sold, or discarded, and the banner troops were consequently short of weapons.[18] After the bannermen lost their fighting spirit, the banner system became a bondage to them. Many young bannermen tried to stay away from their banners.[19] Suffice it to say that the banner forces were no longer the reliable cohorts of the Manchu dynasty.

If language, a cultural trait, holds a group of people together, the disintegration of the group is foretold when its members give up their native tongue. This was what happened with the Manchus. By the Yung-cheng period the great majority of the bannermen could not speak the Manchu language.[20] Instead, they used Chinese on both private and public occasions. This linguistic situation grew worse with time. In the Ch'ien-lung period even some members of the imperial clan did not know Manchu. These signs indicated the decline of the banner system and provided reasons for Yung-cheng's efforts to reform the banners.

Clan and feudal elements had a great impact on the banners and thus became another chief reason prompting the emperor to bureaucratize the banner system. Although these elements in former times had united the Manchus and their followers into a compact group, they served as a force for disunion as the dynasty wore on. From its very beginning, the banner system had no uniform rules; each banner operated according to practices that were developed by the commander. These practices were further strengthened by the clan and feudal elements. There were numerous clans in the banners, with the imperial clan at the top and others of varying strengths below it.[21] In many cases, clan heads were leaders of different levels in the banners, and therefore clan cohesion was an important cement for the whole banner system. Added to this were feudal practices, in which personal leadership and hereditary service were emphasized. The rank of company captain, for example, was largely a hereditary position, while under its commander each banner was a power unit of its own. Since Hong-taiji the Manchu rulers had tried to set uniform rules for the banners and to establish full authority over them. They achieved a certain success, but they failed to eliminate the clan and feudal influences.

When Yung-cheng succeeded to the throne, these old elements were still at work in the banners. In the Shun-chih period the princes had lost their traditional right to command the banners, but, as members of the imperial clan, they were granted a few companies each from the Five Inferior Banners as fiefs. They were the lords of their companies, and this relationship remained the same even after the companies were taken from them. Thus, the princes were able to organize strong cliques based on the banners. In like manner, the company captains and high officers in the banners exacted money, akin to feudal dues, from the bannermen under them.[22] At the same time, in the banners clan elders interfered with the administrative work.[23] Certainly these practices challenged the imperial requirements for uniformity and centralization.

2. *The Process of Bureaucratization*

The Yung-cheng Emperor reformed the banner system thoroughly. He changed its structure, administrative procedure, and basic spirit, and in the meantime he improved the material life of the bannermen. The changes were manifold, but all were oriented toward bureaucratization of the banner system. Since the clan and feudal forces were concentrated in the Five Inferior Banners, which were treated as fiefs for princes, they became the main object of the emperor's reform.

The most important change in the structure of the banner system was the transformation of the company, the basic unit of the banner. A distinctive feature of this change was the imperial decision to increase the number of public companies (*kung-chung tso-ling*), mostly carved out of the possessions of the princes. The public company functioned along the lines of the regular one that, as mentioned above, took charge of ordinary duties, but the major difference lay in the fact that the former was necessarily under an appointed captain and its soldiers were prohibited from assignment to hereditary units. The public company was formed from four categories of companies.[24] The first included companies of imperial clansmen or their collateral relatives. These companies were originally controlled by the princes, but Yung-cheng pointed out that only the sovereign was entitled to have authority over these special units, and in early 1725 he converted them to public companies. The second category consisted of companies removed from the princes by the lowest four degrees or from the imperial clansmen at large. By 1725 the emperor also transformed these into public companies. The third group comprised the Chinese bannermen and belonged to the princes below the first degree; these Chinese companies were transformed in 1730. The last category was made up of companies that were forfeited by their owners for punishment and of hereditary companies whose captains died without successors. No matter what their origins, after transformation the public companies were permanently separated from their old lords. Administratively they remained in their original banners, but functionally they were integrated with the Three Superior Banners—which were under the direct control of the ruler—or evenly distributed among the eight banners as regular companies.

    Changing the structure of the banner system served also to defeudalize it. Besides cutting down the number of companies that the princes possessed, the Yung-cheng Emperor worked to remove their other feudal privileges in the banners. At the beginning of his reign he decreed that they should neither maltreat their retainers—who were from the regular companies—nor select retainers from sons of high officials who happened to be under their command. There were limits to the number of bannermen a prince could have—from 40 to 200 according to his rank.[25] In analyzing the changes in the Five Inferior Banners, a scholar correctly pointed out:

With a masterful hand and unscrupulous methods he [Yung-cheng] undertook to reduce the power and influence of his ambitious brothers by taking the command of the five lower banners [Five Inferior Banners] out of their hands and placing it in his appointees.[26]

Another significant alteration affected high-ranking bannermen and clan heads—two influential groups in the banners. High-ranking bannermen always served as high officials in the central government; through inheritance or personal merit they sometimes concurrently served as captains of companies. This combination of services increased their influence, so the emperor permitted them to hold the captaincies only when no proper candidates were available.[27] Clan heads exercised personal influence on the bannermen through the clan relationship and had a strong voice in the affairs of the company, which was originally organized around the clan. Their status as clan head was traditionally registered in the company office and examined by the captain, who might be a junior member of the same clan or at the same time a high official in the central government. As a result, clan elements persisted in wielding power in the banner system and, together with feudal elements, they handicapped the extension of sovereign power. To eliminate their influence, the emperor severed the connection between captain and clan head—who was now selected according to personal merit and supervised by the banner commander or vice-commander.[28]

The last change in the banner structure also involved personnel, especially the captain. Between 1725 and 1732 Yung-cheng added one or two persons as administrative assistants to the chiefs at each level in the banners and even to the Chamberlains of the Imperial Bodyguard.[29] The difference between these new appointees and their chiefs was clear. The former were selected and appointed by the ruler personally and they owed their positions directly to him, whereas the latter's selection represented the feudal tradition of hereditary privilege and similar considerations. As a result, these assistants were obliged to carry out the imperial will in their units, and this proved a further blow to the clan and feudal practices of the banner system. For the same purpose, the emperor gradually appointed qualified persons to replace hereditary captains, and selected candidates from a whole banner rather than from a certain division of it.[30] During the first nine years of his reign, the emperor frequently appointed his trusted brothers, such as Yin-li and Yin-lu, to the commandership of the banners. If the change in the company was a reform from the bottom, these appointments to banner commandership may be considered a transformation from the top. It was through this double process that the emperor carried out his reforms in the banner system.

During the Yung-cheng period the banners began to operate according to uniform administrative rules. Because of the clan and feudal elements the banners had developed different procedures from the very beginning; before the Yung-cheng period, the Manchu rulers did not effectively standardize these diversified practices, although they tried. The banner commander, for instance, dealt with administrative work and deposited documents at his private home simply because he had no office.[31] Certainly the standardization of its administrative procedures and the change in its structure were equally important to the bureaucratization of the banner system, and Yung-cheng carried on both at the same time. Shortly after his accession to the throne, he assigned each banner an administrative building, which the commander and the vice-commander were required to occupy in managing daily banner affairs, later assisted by a considerable staff.[32] The importance of the banner administrative office lay in the fact that it separated official activity from private life and transferred authority from commander to ruler. However, this was only an initial step toward unifying banner administration.

Another step was the codification of administrative practices concerning banner affairs. The first set of codes was established in 1725. While basically it followed the rules and regulations issued by the Board of War, parts of it were based on the imperial decrees in connection with the banners.[33] Around 1732 these decrees were finally grouped with related memorials into three books entitled *Shang-yü pa-ch'i*, *Shang-yü ch'i-wu i-fu* (Imperial decrees and responding memorials governing banner affairs), and *Yü-hsing ch'i-wu tsou-i* (Memorials and related imperial comments concerning banner affairs), and later documents were added to the three works about 1735. The three compilations served both as imperial instructions and as a guide to banner administration. While the administrative building made the management of banner affairs an official business, the uniform rules laid down for the banners a central pattern of conduct. Toward the end of the Yung-cheng period the eight banners produced reports in the same form, carried out reward and punishment in the same way, trained soldiers by the same methods, and registered their documents in the same office; their commanders achieved coordination through conference when differences arose.[34]

The last step was the introduction of a system of supervision over the banners. After the commanders and vice-commanders had begun to carry on their administrative work in compliance with required rules in the assigned places, they were further put under a special supervision system. During the first six years the emperor several times dispatched censors and imperial bodyguards to oversee the banner administration and keep watch over the princes' activities in the banners.[35] Finally, each banner was subject to the supervision of six specially commissioned people; if these people did not perform their censorial duties as required, they were punished by the emperor. Besides these special individuals, the Censorate was also given the authority to supervise the banners.[36] Moreover, by imperial order each banner kept an eye on the other seven once every seven months.[37] Furthermore, the emperor had palace-memorial reporters among bannermen to inform him of the situation in the banners. This system of banner supervision was so thorough that it extended even to the bannermen-settlers who lived in the banner lands around Peking and frequently broke the law. The emperor sent itinerant censors to inspect those settlers, selected officials to function as their police chiefs, and introduced a community system modified from the pattern of Chinese village organization.[38] On the whole, like the Chinese bureaucrats, all the bannermen now were under strict imperial control.

Education was perhaps the most essential of the processes that contributed to the bureaucratization of the banner system. Prior to the Yung-cheng period the Manchu rulers, while trying to transform the banner system, failed to stress the education of the bannermen, whereas Yung-cheng put great emphasis on it and founded many schools for the young bannermen. Judging by its results, education was more important than any other means to the successful bureaucratization of the banner system. If political means were necessary to the introduction of changes into the banner system, as desired by the emperor, education was indispensable to their perpetuation. From an ideological position education inculcated in the bannermen the norms, mores, and values that were important to legitimize the imperial act and support the changes.

The banner schools of the Yung-cheng period were charged with two tasks, political and cultural. The political assignment was to maintain the Manchu people technically as the ruling group. For this purpose these schools offered courses in military skills. While all bannermen, even the old civil administrators, were required to practice archery and riding, a few bannermen might take Chinese courses. In any case, what they practiced and learned were ruling techniques. The cultural objective of these schools was to maintain the Manchus as a closely knit ethnic group aloof from the Chinese. Apart from military skills, the Manchu language was also a required subject for the young bannermen. This language program was supplemented by imperial decrees in which Yung-cheng repeatedly glorified the Manchu past, exaggerated traditional Manchu values, urged the Manchus to preserve them, and prohibited the Manchu bannermen from losing their identities among the Chinese.

In short, the banner schools were designed to facilitate imperial control of the bannermen. Since Yung-cheng emphasized banner education at a time when he was making efforts to concentrate powers in his hands, the banner schools were naturally directed toward the same goal. This can be further discerned from two other aspects of these schools. One was the emperor's emphasis on the importance of loyalty to the sovereign, the primary one of the five human relationships in the Confucian ethical canon. Although there is nowhere an indication that the banner schools taught this precise item, it was very likely a subject for inculcation because he explained it before the Manchu officials on many occasions. The other aspect was the nature of the staffs managing the schools. Not only sufficient academic or technical training but high moral qualifications were required of the school superintendents and the teaching staff. In other words, as the men approved by the emperor, they were entrusted to carry on their duties in conformity with his likes and dislikes.

Considering their curricula and management, these schools apparently were the instrument for transmitting the Manchu tradition and special imperial instructions to the students so as to maintain the Manchus as a ruling and ethnic group and also for training obedient servants.

The banner schools, founded by the Yung-cheng Emperor, fell into three broad categories. The first category, the school for the young noble bannermen, can be subdivided into two types—one for the boys of imperial clansmen (*tsung-shih*) and the other for those of the collateral relatives of the imperial house (*gioro*; *chiao-lo*). These two types of schools shared some common features in administration and organization. They were free of charge, and they were smaller than other banner schools. Their superintendents were selected from the imperial clan or its collateral relatives to match the special background of the students, while their instructors were rated according to the performance of the students, who received monthly stipends and were subject to strict discipline. The major difference between these two types of schools lay, besides the family background of their students, in their administration and curricula. The school for the young imperial clansmen began in the Shun-chih period, but it became a system only in 1724.[39] There were four campuses, grouped in two equal administrative units under two specially selected people. Brilliant students were given official appointments after studying for three years. The school for the young collateral relatives of the imperial house was established in 1729,[40] and operated in each banner as a two-section unit—one taught Chinese under a Chinese tutor, the other Manchu under a Manchu instructor. These two sections shared a coach for archery. Although the students, in general boys of 8 to 18 *sui*, were allowed to select a language, archery was common to both types of school.

The second category of banner schools was for the sons of the common bannermen. It too was subdivided into two types, which were also free of charge and gave students monthly stipends. The first type was under the Office of the Imperial Household and comprised two campuses recruiting students from the Three Superior Banners and named after their locations. One campus was known as the Coal Hill School (*Ching-shan kuan-hsüeh*), which began as early as 1685.[41] The other, founded in 1728 and referred to as the School of the Universal Peace Palace (*Hsien-an kung kuan-hsüeh*), had nine language teachers and nine archery coaches under two supervisors.[42] It enrolled ninety students, who were picked from among promising boys or from the students at the Coal Hill School. As a whole, students at these two schools might stay until they obtained official appointments.

The other type consisted of schools for the boys of bannermen at large. Also located in Peking, they were mainly the expansion of the old ones, appearing during the two years 1727-1728.[43] According to the treatment of their students, they can be classified into two kinds, one of which subsidized students, while the other provided free education but no stipends. The school with stipends had eight campuses, each taking from a particular banner one hundred boys—60 Manchus, 20 Mongols, and 20 Chinese. The school without stipends also had eight campuses to match the eight banners.

The last category of banner schools was set up in various places for special purposes and differed from the first two categories, which prepared the students for civil service examinations. Some emphasized both language and archery; others concentrated on either of these two subjects.[44] Schools of this category were administered according to a traditional Manchu policy aimed at keeping the Mongols a distinct ethnic group independent of the Manchus or Chinese. Whereas the Chinese bannermen had to learn the Manchu language, the Mongol bannermen studied their native tongue.

During the Yung-cheng period there were various informal educational projects for bannermen beyond school age. They were asked to learn the same subjects studied in the schools. For instance, all bannermen below the age of sixty *sui* had to speak Manchu and know military skills as a basis for promotion.[45] Obviously these projects were directed toward restoring the two traditional Manchu values—language and military skills—and preserving Manchu cultural identity. For this purpose, the emperor set rules to prevent the Manchus from separating from their own groups. Two of the rules, for example, provided that bannermen serving in places outside Peking had to return to their respective banners in the capital as soon as their tenure was over, and even that their remains could not be buried in the places where they had served.[46] Another rule stated that banner boys who left Peking with their parents for local administrative service had to return to the capital for study or military service when they came of age.[47]

Moral training was another important subject emphasized in the informal educational projects. Banner officers were required to read and explain before their men twice a month two imperial publications—"On Factions" and the *Sheng-yü kuang-hsün* (Amplified instructions on the Sacred Edict).[48] The first essay, as analyzed in Chapter 4, demanded the end of factionalism and conformity to the ruler's will; the second work included the sixteen maxims issued in the K'ang-hsi period and their commentaries written by Yung-cheng with emphasis on law, order, and orthodox ideology. They were also extensively read and taught among the Chinese. On the whole, these two publications covered bureaucratic behavior and personal conduct. Through the educational process, formal and informal, the Yung-cheng Emperor attempted to maintain the Manchus in a ruling position and transform them into a group of obedient servants for himself.

The decline of the banner system was closely connected with the deterioration of the bannermen's economic condition. The fundamental problem stemmed from the government policy that allowed no bannermen to do any productive work. Under this restriction they were bound to serve in the army or administrative branches of the government. Since the army and other official positions could not take all bannermen, those who had no official jobs or were not included in the active service list were not on the government payroll. During the Yung-cheng period, for example, more than half the bannermen were not on the official rolls.[49] This situation became worse with the increase of the banner population. After its subjugation of China the Manchu government allotted lands in the metropolitan area as enclosures for the bannermen. This banner land system was helpful to the bannermen's economic condition, but it soon found itself on the verge of collapse. If the bannermen's dissipated life was a factor in the decay of the banner land system, shortage of farming laborers was another reason for its decline.[50] Because the Manchus were not good farmers, they depended upon serfs and slaves for farm labor. After 1644 the flight of serfs and slaves diminished the labor force on the banner lands and thus further tapped the bannermen's economic resources. Up to the Yung-cheng period the bannermen were poverty-stricken, but when the Yung-cheng Emperor changed the banner system, he also improved the bannermen's economic condition.

In dealing with the bannermen's economic problem Yung-cheng differed from his father; their policies manifested their different ideologies and personalities. As the K'ang-hsi Emperor was lenient and more Confucian-oriented, his policy was placatory and it somewhat spoiled the bannermen. One of his important measures was to support them with a large amount of government aid. This did not solve the problem and, on the contrary, encouraged the bannermen's extravagant life.[51] By contrast, Yung-cheng was severe and Legalist; his policy was practical and rational. On various occasions he promoted a diligent and thrifty life, and made himself an example for the bannermen. He was perhaps the most frugal of early Ch'ing rulers. During his reign, for instance, he never made a tour or visit to his ancestral tombs.[52] Whatever the reason for his refraining from making a tour, which was usually expensive, it reflected the practicality and rationality which underlay his policy toward the bannermen's economic life. A good indication of his policy was the fact that while trying to help the bannermen in need, he collected liabilities from those Manchus who embezzled public funds.[53] Although he redeemed the lands mortgaged or sold by the bannermen and occasionally gave them additional money as an imperial favor,[54] under his reign government appropriations were no longer used as the major solution.

As soon as Yung-cheng succeeded to the throne, he took measures to relieve the economic strain of the bannermen including additional stipends, new openings, low interest loans, emergency aid, and reclamation. Early in 1723 he rationalized the distribution of extra stipends and gave them to high banner officers according to their ranks and later also to lower officers.[55] Banner boys were given more opportunity to study, and banner scholars were more likely to enter officialdom. Two new subjects, translation and military techniques, were added to the civil service examination for the Manchu and Mongol bannermen, and the number of licentiates in banners was also increased.[56]

Yung-cheng also created new openings for common bannermen. In the years 1724-1731 he expanded the active service list to cover about ten thousand bannermen—almost one-tenth of those who were originally excluded from it.[57] Since population increase exercised great economic pressure on the bannermen, especially on the Chinese bannermen, he permitted some young male Chinese bannermen to be civilians.[58] Among his other measures were programs of low-interest loans and emergency allowances. In 1723 he provided the banners with 900,000 taels of silver as an enterprise fund for trade or moneylending. If needed, bannermen could obtain loans from it at an interest of one percent, and the annual profits from this fund were used as subsidies for bannermen's weddings or funerals.[59]

His reclamation program was probably the most impressive of the measures the emperor took to improve the bannermen's economic situation. Although the reclamation program itself was not new, it represented his attempt to reconstruct the metropolitan banner lands and set a precedent for his successor. He organized three groups of settlers. The first group consisted of eight hundred landless banner soldiers, Manchu and Mongol. In 1723 they were sent to Jehol as military colonists and frontier garrison troops, of whom every fifty men formed a company under a captain and a lieutenant.[60] The second and third groups of settlers formed two particular units for a tentative program, which needs a little more elaboration.

The tentative programs were based on the well-field system as recorded in Confucian Classics. In Confucian tradition, it was described, and in some cases exaggerated, as a socio-economic system of the Chou dynasty (1122-256 B.C.), when society had feudal characteristics. Under this system farm land was divided into equal units, each consisting of nine equal portions. Eight portions were assigned to eight neighboring families as their private fields, and they cooperated to work the last, or central, portion as the public field. Inherent in the system are many problems, but it has attracted the attention of politicians and scholars.[61] Since Yung-cheng was politically opposed to feudal practices and ideologically not an orthodox Confucian, why did he resort to a system that had strong Confucian and feudal elements? The answer to the question need not be complicated. What attracted him was probably the relation between private and public interest that the system contained or was believed to have contained. After working their individual portions of land, for example, the eight families took care of the public land. Because the decline of the bannermen's public spirit was closely related to the deterioration of their economic situation, Yung-cheng attempted to improve their livelihood and, at the same time, to inspire their public-spiritedness through the well-field system. Moreover, when private and public portions were integrated into a unit, the well-field system might serve to reduce the possibility of the purchase and sale of the banner lands. With these goals in mind, he put it into effect in the years 1725-1729.

He carried out the well-field program in the metropolitan banner lands. The well-fields were scattered over four districts south of Peking, covering about 3,168 acres (more than 209 *ch'ing*).[62] Besides land, the government provided the banner tillers with houses and initial funds. The second and third groups of settlers, as mentioned above, were sent with their families to these well-fields in 1725 and 1727 respectively.[63] Members of the earlier group included 100 propertyless families—50 Manchu, 10 Mongol, and 40 Chinese—and later increased to 180 families. Members between 16 and 60 *sui* were given about 15.2 acres (100 *mou*) each for private use and 50 taels of silver for rations, seeds, plowing oxen, and necessary tools. Eight members worked in each unit, which included their private shares and the public land. The whole group was supervised by two officials. After harvest the tillers had to practice archery. The latter group was composed of convicts and dismissed officers. Their number was not indicated in official sources, but they were also assigned with their families. Each family received only about 4.5 acres (30 *mou*) and 15 taels of silver, and every five households shared three plowing oxen.

The well-field experiment was a failure. After 1727 no more bannermen were dispatched, so it seems, and at the beginning of his reign, Ch'ien-lung worked out the quartered-farm system (*t'un-chuang*) based on the well-field. The failure of the well-field system should not be attributed exclusively to the degeneration of the bannermen.[64] Other factors were inherent in the program itself. First, as the Yung-cheng Emperor indicated in his decree, the well-field was merely an experiment, carried on within an empire that actually did not permit the development of the system. Even though the well-field system had, as many people believe, really existed in the Chou, it did not survive after the rise of the imperial system. Second the banner well-fields were surrounded by Chinese villages. If the Chinese cultural environment had been a major reason for the decline of the banner system, it was also an important factor in the failure of the well-field tillers. Third, the well-fields included pieces of banner land that originally belonged to Manchu nobles; and under pressure from the dispossessed, some pieces of such land were privately carved out of the well-field system and returned to their former owners.[65] This illegal practice played a role in the collapse of the entire program. Finally, the well-field was designed for serious purposes, but it was carried on by a group of tillers and supervisors of low prestige. For instance, the second batch of tillers were law-breakers who could not carry out the program without proper supervision. However, the supervisors did not have high prestige either because they were, as the imperial edict indicated, demoted banner officers or officials. Although the emperor promised the tillers, and their supervisors alike, a better future, they were not the right men to undertake such a serious experiment.

3. *Political Importance of the Bureaucratization of the Banner System*

Bureaucratization of the banner system was the greatest and most comprehensive change that the system had undergone. The process of its bureaucratization denoted the course of conflict between monarch and aristocrat. It is a well-known fact that the banner system was an institution, feudal, aristocratic, and almost self-contained. Just as rulers drew force from it, princes too enlisted their following from it. The most influential princes were always the strongest factional leaders, who struggled among themselves or challenged the imperial authority. As their activity tapped the resources of sovereign power, it strained the relation between ruler and aristocrat. In dynastic history, rulers always allied themselves with bureaucrats to check the influence of aristocrats. Since Hong-taiji, the early Ch'ing rulers had followed this pattern. They constantly increased their power by making changes in the governmental structure—all the changes were related to the bureaucratization of the banner system. Nevertheless, it was not until the Yung-cheng period that these changes were completed.

A factor in the Yung-cheng Emperor's success in bureaucratizing the banner system was his personal character. He was a resolute and tactful ruler. His resoluteness largely resulted from his belief in the absolute power of the sovereign and also from his awareness of the role he played in connection with the Ch'ing empire and the Manchu people.[66] He worked tirelessly to stabilize his power and improve state administration. Although his grandfather and father had the same belief and awareness, they failed to put these into effect consistently. The Shun-chih Emperor was known as a monarch of "violent temper";[67] his policy lacked consistency. Yung-cheng's father lessened his efforts in the second half of the K'ang-hsi era; his relaxation resulted in his inability to settle authoritatively the succession issue in his last years. By comparison, the Yung-cheng Emperor unswervingly carried out any decisions he reached; in consolidation of power he spared no obstruction in his way.

Yung-cheng's tactfulness was linked with his philosophical training. If Confucianism was consensual in nature, Legalism was coercive. He depended on both of these and properly employed them to achieve centralization of his power. In his campaign against factionalism, for instance, he applied both consensual and coercive measures. In like manner, he appealed to the Manchu past and improved the bannermen's livelihood while forcibly introducing changes into the banners. It was through these tactful methods that he successfully bureaucratized the banner system.

Suppression of the powerful princes and their supporters was a second factor in Yung-cheng's success. Princes, together with their followers, were influential individuals whose strength came largely from the banners. When they were suppressed, the other bannermen were frightened into submission. In addition to these special individuals, the emperor dismissed many banner commanders and vice-commanders, replacing them with his loyal supporters. During the first three years of his reign, he dismissed 12 commanders and 17 vice-commanders and demoted one commander and one vice-commander. These 31 people represented 17 banners—5 Manchu, 6 Mongol, and 6 Chinese.[68] Some were dismissed because of factional activities, while others were dismissed or demoted for other reasons. At any rate, their dismissals loosened the obstruction to the bureaucratization of the banner system.

The last factor in the Yung-cheng Emperor's success can be attributed to the changes that had taken place prior to his reign. Since Hong-taiji, the Manchu rulers had imposed considerable changes on the banner system. Although they were not so comprehensive or systematic as those introduced by Yung-cheng, they considerably weakened the banner aristocrats. After their weakening, the emperor rendered the last and most fatal blow to the banner system.

Bureaucratization of the banner system was doubtlessly an important success for Yung-cheng. True, he failed to arrest the degeneration of the bannermen, physically or culturally, but he successfully transformed the banner system into a disciplined body operating according to prescribed procedures and subject to his will. One can judge his success from some aspects of the reformed system. First was the stability of imperial succession, which had brought powerful princes into the struggle in early Ch'ing history. As long as contenders established their strengths in the banners, removal of individual competitors was only a temporary measure. The best way to stop the competition for succession lay in fundamental change of the banner system, and its bureaucratization signified such a transformation. After bureaucratization the banner system lost its traditional influence and the princes were unable to contend for the heirdom. Both were at the mercy of the ruler. From the Yung-cheng period on, imperial succession became a family affair of the ruling house.

The second aspect was the weakening of the aristocracy that was entrenched in the banners. In terms of sovereign power, the Ch'ing dynasty may be divided into two stages with the Yung-cheng period as the demarcation line. Prior to it the ruler had to share his power with aristocrats; as a result he did not have final authority with which to settle vital disputes. On many occasions aristocrats had a strong voice not only in banner affairs but in state administration, and the succession struggle of the K'ang-hsi period was an illustration of this situation. After the advent of the Yung-cheng period, the ruler was able to make his word final in banner and state affairs. He became the supreme arbiter in name and reality. The main reason for this difference lay in the fact that with bureaucratization of the banner system the aristocrats were deprived of their sources of power. Without support from the banners, they were no longer powerful individuals able to obstruct the sovereign; they belonged to the banners, but not the reverse. What made them different from the common bannermen were their titles and the service of a limited number of retainers. This distinction was, however, by no means definite. Since these privileges were now considered an imperial favor instead of a feudal right, the sovereign could take them away at anytime he saw fit. To keep these privileges they had to accede to his will. In other words, they lost their traditional strengths after the banner system was bureaucratized. From that time, Ch'ing aristocracy was subordinate to the autocratic monarch.

    The last aspect was extension of imperial authority. Theoretically a ruler enjoyed supreme authority, but operationally his authority was not necessarily constant. With its clan and feudal elements at work, for example, the banner system frequently operated as an obstruction to imperial authority during the early years of the Ch'ing. If the establishment of the Grand Council and enforcement of the palace-memorial system facilitated the exercise of the sovereign's authority, bureaucratization of the banners had the same effect. After bureaucratization the banner system acquired uniform rules sanctioned by the monarch. Banner commanders and vice-commanders were the men to put these rules into effect. In the appointment of officials genealogical background gave way to personal ability; naturally, loyalty to the sovereign was another important criterion for selection. In short, they were a group of administrators who were subject to bureaucratic control and special surveillance. Those who carried out their duties in compliance with the imperial will received liberal rewards; those who failed to do so were punished relentlessly. It was through these faithful administrators that the ruler extended his authority into the banner system without deviation.

    In the final analysis, once Yung-cheng had bureaucratized the banner system, he had completed centralization of the Ch'ing empire. Since the banner system was a special institution, it was a structure more difficult than any other to transform. Through the process of bureaucratization, the emperor successfully changed it into a new ruling machine on the ruins of its clan and feudal elements. Although it still preserved some privileges, it was nearly equal to the other bureaucratic branch that ruled the

Chinese. Both of these branches were under his direct control. He used one to subjugate the other and welded both into a larger whole, that is, a centralized empire, which transcended all groups, regional or ethnic.[69] Over such an empire he exercised his absolute and universal rule.

PART FOUR

Effects of Autocratic Rule

3. A Life of Ease: The hard-working Yung-cheng is at ease.

VIII

The Literati

1. *Promotion of Orthodox Ideology*

Yung-cheng autocracy affected every status group within the Ch'ing empire. Its impact on the people varied in nature and depth according to their status. As intellectuals, the Chinese literati were more sensitive than others to autocratic rule. They found themselves greatly restricted in their intellectual activity. Whether they were bureaucrats or private individuals, they were subject to the same restrictions. In Chinese dynastic history, restraints on intellectual freedom reached their apogee under the Ch'ing, and the Yung-cheng period was a turning point toward that culmination. Prior to the Ch'ing, however autocratic a dynasty was, the Chinese literati had certain intellectual freedoms. For example, they could interpret Confucian doctrines in their own way, provided they did not use taboo words or show disrespect to the ruler or the dynasty. Furthermore, before the Ch'ing, scholar-officials submitted memorials for the rectification of the ruler when they deemed it necessary, but this rarely happened during the early Ch'ing. If restraint on intellectual freedom is a characteristic of autocracy, the Ch'ing regime, especially the reign of Yung-cheng, can be considered one of the high points of autocracy in the dynastic history of China.

Of great importance to the infringement of intellectual freedom in the Yung-cheng period was the enforcement of orthodox ideology. In the traditional Chinese state, the effort to maintain an orthodox ideology is too familiar to require any elaboration. What distinguished the Ch'ing regime, in particular the Yung-cheng era, from the previous dynasties was its extraordinary attempt to make the orthodox ideology not only the ideological pattern for the literati but also the political behavior of everyone within the empire. As a matter of fact, all the variant forms of intellectual restriction of the time were channeled toward the same end—the enforcement of orthodox ideology.[1]

Ch'ing orthodox ideology was formulated in the K'ang-hsi era and was based on the Neo-Confucian School of Principle or Reason, as was its Ming predecessor. Because the Ch'ing government made efforts in the Shun-chih period to suppress Chinese resistance to Manchu rule, it did not profess its commitment to any particular Confucian school—although it copied many Ming institutions relating to Confucianism and reaffirmed the historical role of Confucius.[2] With all of China except Taiwan pacified, the Ch'ing regime took firm action to install its orthodox ideology. In 1670, for instance, K'ang-hsi reestablished two Erudites of the Five Classics (*Wu-ching po-shih*) as hereditary titles for the descendants of the brothers Ch'eng Hao (1031-1085) and Ch'eng I (1032-1107), two great, pioneering Neo-Confucian philosophers, and issued the sixteen-maxim Sacred Edict—which exemplified the imperatives of the School of Principle.[3] A few years later he ordered the selection of outstanding scholars (*po-hsüeh hung-ju*) for high offices; they were largely students of the School.[4] In his reign many scholars of the same philosophical affiliation, such as Chang Po-hsing (1652-1725), Hsiung T'zu-li, Li Kuang-ti (1642-1718), and T'ang Pin, achieved prominence or were given important offices. Another imperial act was the compilation of several works that carried the same orthodox tenets; these were made standard references for schools and the civil service examination. The climax of such imperial acts was the emperor's conferring of an unusual posthumous honor on Chu Hsi (1130-1200), the greatest exponent of the School of Principle, in 1712, and publishing his works the next year.[5] Under imperial sponsorship the School of Principle, then, became Ch'ing orthodox ideology to be inculcated in the minds of the people.

For a better understanding of Ch'ing orthodoxy, it is necessary to know the factors responsible for the selection of the School of Principle, because they were related to the reasons for its vigorous enforcement. First, there were K'ang-hsi's personal intellectual interests. Of the Manchu rulers, he was a studious and inquisitive monarch who learned Chinese history and Confucian Classics in his boyhood and patronized artistic works and academic pursuits after his enthronement. Because the School of Principle commentaries on major Confucian works had been standard texts for students since the fourteenth century, he had come under their influence, which he acknowledged on occasion.[6] This influence moved him to adopt the School as the orthodox thought of the dynasty.

Second, the intellectual trends of the early Ch'ing favored the School.[7] After a short period of domination in the second half of the Ming dynasty, the School of the Mind declined. Its intuitionalist approach gradually became academic indolence and antagonized many assiduous scholars; its free speculation finally proved to be a pseudo-academic attempt to weaken the established scholastic order, which the political authority and the orthodox students deemed important. It was under these circumstances that the School of the Mind sank almost to obscurity in the last years of the Ming. Under the early Ch'ing the majority of scholars—private individuals as well as officials—had an ideological attachment to the credos of the Tung-lin movement, a political and philosophical crusade in the first three decades of the seventeenth century that struggled against the political evils of the time and reasserted the integral Confucian doctrines, with a tendency toward the School of Principle.[8] It is clear that the imperial sponsorship of this School fitted in with the intellectual climate of the time.

Third, of all the factors the political utility of the School was most important. That, despite its humanizing influence on the imperial system, Confucianism functioned generally as a servant of the traditional Chinese state is a well-known fact; Neo-Confucianism, especially the School of Principle, contributed even more to China's autocracy. Although Neo-Confucianism was largely a restatement of early Confucian tenets, it had something new. As two prominent scholars have recently pointed out, the School of Principle developed one-sided moral imperatives—such as the total subjection of women, the indisputable authority of fathers, and unquestionable loyalty to rulers—that were unknown to early Confucianism.⁹ With their broad scope and through school education that the Neo-Confucian scholars stressed, these imperatives were applied to all walks of life within the Chinese empire. Also because of the rigid and formalistic methodology that the School of Principle followed, its credenda became a compelling call to action. Most importantly, the School of Principle met the needs of autocratic rulers in traditional China and contributed greatly to the growth of the country's autocracy from the Sung dynasty onward. K'ang-hsi was fully aware of its political usefulness, frankly pointing out that its thesis was indispensable to state administration.¹⁰ It is primarily this political reason that enthroned the School as the Ch'ing orthodox ideology.

In the case of the Manchu dynasty, however, there is yet another political reason for the School as Ch'ing orthodoxy. As a regime of alien conquerors, the Manchus struggled for legitimacy so as to command the allegiance of the Chinese. For this purpose, even as early as 1644, the Manchu leaders took action, notably the state funeral granted the last Ming ruler immediately after they captured Peking.¹¹ What this measure, together with many others of the same nature, amounted to was the legitimization of the Manchu conquest. After China, with the exception of Taiwan, had been pacified through military operations in the Shun-chih period, political justification of the regime became more important in the next era. Because the School of Principle had been the orthodox ideology of the Ming dynasty and was still the major intellectual current of the early Ch'ing, the adoption of it by the conquerors as a state philosophy was intended to make the conquered ideologically subject to their authority and accept their takeover as legitimate. For the same reason the Manchu rulers made efforts to enforce this ideology.

Both Yung-cheng's personal character and the political circumstances of his reign led him to enforce ideological orthodoxy with more vigor than his father had. One of his important measures was the publication of orthodox books, with emphasis on the indoctrination of the great majority of the people. Of such publications, the earliest and most comprehensive was the *Amplified Instructions on the Sacred Edict*, consisting of the sixteen maxims issued by his father and commentaries on them which he himself wrote in 1724. Each maxim was composed of seven Chinese characters, standing for an important Confucian tenet. As a whole, the maxims covered all Confucian teachings—economic, intellectual, political, and social—expounded by successive Confucian scholars, especially those of the School of Principle. The sixteen maxims read as follows:[12]

1. Emphasize filial piety and brotherhood so as to exalt human relations.
2. Esteem kinship so as to display harmony and affection.
3. Cultivate peace in community so as to prevent quarrels and litigations.
4. Stress farming and sericulture so as to make food and clothing suffice.
5. Set store by economy so as to conserve money and goods.
6. Exalt schools so as to make proper the practice of scholars.
7. Renounce false doctrines so as to honor orthodox principles.
8. Explain the laws so as to caution the ignorant and obstinate.
9. Illustrate propriety and courtesy so as to cultivate good customs.
10. Attend to the fundamental vocation so as to make firm the will of the people.
11. Instruct sons and younger brothers so as to prevent them from doing evil.
12. Suppress false accusations so as to protect the innocent.
13. Warn those who harbor outlaws so as to avoid involvement.
14. Pay taxes fully so as to dispense with official urging.
15. Unite the tithing units so as to extirpate robbers and thieves.
16. Dissolve feuds so as to preserve lives.

A scrutiny of these maxims indicates that items 1-3, 9-11, and 15-16 were social in nature, items 8 and 12-14 covered relations between people and government, items 4-5 concerned economic activity, and the rest dealt with the intellectuals. The emphasis of these maxims was first on the general social sphere and then on the political realm, converging on the common people and soldiers; the commentaries followed the same pattern. The two

Manchu rulers were bent on reintroducing strict social order, which became increasingly rigid after the rise of Neo-Confucianism but almost disintegrated during the great political turmoil in the last years of the Ming dynasty. Certainly the Manchu effort was political in nature because social stability was essential for the authority and legitimacy that the dynasty required.

With great emphasis on the social sphere, these maxims and their commentaries extended the authority of the Ch'ing into every walk of life; never before in Chinese history had dynastic rule succeeded in reaching the broad masses of people. With the exception of the tax, labor service, and security units, the majority of the people below the county level were actually under the informal rule of families, clans, and the gentry, each being a Confucian-oriented social group.[13] Although these groups filled the gap between the government and the common people and, in a sense, helped to extend political control over the towns and villages, their activities were based on Confucian practices which sometimes ran counter to the imperial interest. Inasmuch as these groups maintained an informal rule over the masses of people, they intruded upon sovereign power. The maxims, especially items 8 and 13-14 and their commentaries, were Legalist in spirit but cloaked in Confucianism. They were designed and inculcated in an attempt to break the hold of families, clans, and the gentry on the common people and bring the imperial authority to the towns and villages.

Together with the commentaries written by Yung-cheng in 1724, the maxims became a requirement for every status group within the empire during his reign. In 1725 the throne ordered that in the district and prefectural examinations students should write from memory, without error, one of the maxims and its commentary.[14] Printed copies of the maxims were distributed among officials and schools, and, later, some scholar-officials rendered them into colloquial language for easy circulation. On the first and fifteenth of every month, government officials, military officers, students, soldiers, and common people in formal dress attended lectures on the maxims in public halls or Confucian temples.[15] Such lectures were also given in the rural areas with members of the gentry or students in government schools as speakers and magistrates supervising.[16] This practice continued throughout the rest of the

Ch'ing dynasty. It was through this intensive inculcation that the Confucian norms, mores, and values, as espoused by the School of Principle, were widely and deeply instilled in the broad masses of the Chinese people, and that the Chinese state and society under Manchu rule virtually became what Sinologists refer to as Confucian China.[17] It was through the same process that the sovereign's political directives reached the majority of the Chinese people.

The *Amplified Instructions on the Sacred Edict* also put pressure on the literati, who had to study it in school, in office, and on other occasions, such as the twice-a-month lectures. Of the sixteen maxims, two interrelated items (nos. 6-7) specifically concerned the literati. Maxim 6 exalted schools, public and private, not only as places of academic studies but as centers of moral training.[18] In other words, it encouraged the literati to cultivate proper behavior. In line with this theme, its commentary provided two working directives. It forbade students and scholars to struggle for fame or profit, engage in empty talk, learn false doctrines, or violate orthodox teachings. It encouraged them to read the right books, keep company with people of right conduct, and practice filial piety and brotherhood. If soldiers and common people did the same, the commentary went on, they were no less than students and scholars. Proper behavior was important, the Yung-cheng Emperor argued, because it underlay good scholarship and administration.

Maxim 7 and its commentary gave priority to orthodox doctrines but reiterated the importance of proper behavior. They started from the premise that orthodox doctrines lead to right thinking, which is in turn the basis of good public morals. For this reason, they required everyone to promote the orthodox doctrines. From the same reasoning, the maxim and its commentary concluded that their promotion depended on the extirpation of false teachings: books not written by sages, the principles not based on Confucian classics, and all records of appalling and strange ideas. In short, doctrines other than those of the School of Principle were regarded as fallacy or heterodoxy. However, in the maxim the terms "orthodoxy" and "heterodoxy" had strong political connotations;[19] neither suggested anything purely religious. Orthodoxy was promoted for its political usefulness, and heterodoxy was renounced because of its political disadvantage. For instance, the commentary on the maxim referred to some religious groups as heterodox on the ground that they distracted people's minds from their vocations, corrupted their personal conduct, and, most important of all, inspired the breaking of laws under the leadership of persons disposed to evil. In the final analysis, their activity ran counter to the authority of the sovereign and thus became the target of imperial attack.

These two maxims and their commentaries can be further explored from two different dimensions—philosophical reasoning and political application. In both cases they proved to be a relevant instrument for promotion of the orthodox ideology. In terms of philosophical reasoning, they faithfully reflect the two essential aspects—inner and outer—in Confucian tradition, particularly in Neo-Confucian thought.[20] The inner aspect concerned self-cultivation, according to which the literati, before serving society and the state, had first to cultivate their knowledge and virtue based on right doctrines. The outer aspect had to do with world pacification, the final ideal of Confucianism. Self-cultivation was thus the preparation for world pacification, which in turn consummated the former. Maxim 7 represented the inner aspect; Maxim 6, the outer. When orthodoxy becomes internalized, it externalizes a behavior. Such behavior was of paramount importance to the literati of the Yung-cheng period. Those having these inward and outward achievements were regarded by the ruler as commendable local leaders and, after passing the proper examinations, as desirable candidates for official or teaching positions.

In their political application, the two maxims and their commentaries stood distinct from the others, for they were specifically devised to discourage the self-seeking disposition of the literati as expressed in the historic tension between Confucianism and Legalism. Both philosophical schools assigned the common people to the same place in the social hierarchy and charged them with the same obligations. As members of the low social stratum, the common people had to support society by doing productive work, and the state by paying taxes and performing labor service. But the two schools developed different views toward the literati, views that provided the background for the conflict between monarch and bureaucrats.

The major difference between Confucianism and Legalism in relation to the literati was the issue of legal status. In the Legalist view, the literati might serve the ruler by their knowledge, but they had the same legal status as the common people. In Confucian tradition, the literati as private individuals were almost automatically at the top of the social ladder and were separate under the law from the rest of society. They owed their status to Confucianism, not to the ruler. While serving as officials, they were the ruler's administrative assistants. Either as bureaucrats or as private individuals, they tended to develop personal interests which conflicted with those of the ruler. Furthermore, from their philosophical orientation they frequently attempted to rectify the ruler's behavior, personal and official, to conform to Confucian doctrines; they therefore challenged the ruler's authority.

Through the two maxims and their commentaries, the Yung-cheng Emperor inculcated in the literati the approved ideology and required behavior. They had to think and behave in accordance with his likes and dislikes. If they failed to do so, he did not hesitate to enforce the orthodox ideology and required behavior with coercive means. As a result, he greatly reduced Confucian-Legalist tension and minimized monarch-bureaucrat conflict. His success was best proved by the fact that under his reign the literati were, as a whole, more compliant to the sovereign's wishes than in any other period of the Ch'ing dynasty.

During the Yung-cheng period another important Confucian classic, *Canon of Filial Piety*, received great emphasis, also for political purposes. The concept of filial piety has been an integral part of Chinese life for millennia. Because it was considered the cornerstone of all other virtues, the *Canon of Filial Piety* became required reading for students in the old days. The enforcement of filial piety had strong effects on the Chinese society and state and, on the whole, facilitated autocratic rule.

Filial piety was the foundation of the father-son relationship, the second of the five human relationships stressed by Confucianism and especially Neo-Confucianism. Of the many obligations that filial sons had to fulfill, unconditional obedience to the will of the parents was the most important. At no time should they forget or change the teachings of their parents whether the latter were alive or dead. Moreover, from this categorical submission of sons to parents developed the practice of subordination of younger to older in general. Family instructions and clan rules required the same obedience and started from the concept of filial piety. Clearly filial piety contributed to the stabilization of social order. It is no wonder that rulers strenuously encouraged filial piety because social stability was a factor necessary for imperial authority.

The political aspect of filial piety can be best explored in terms of loyalty, the first of the five human relationships. When a man was indoctrinated, during childhood, with the idea of unconditional submission to his parents, he developed, in manhood, an attitude of unqualified obedience to royal authority.[21] A Chinese proverb says that loyal ministers are from filial sons, and in historical sources, the characters *chün* (king or ruler) and *fu* (father), frequently appearing together, were almost used collectively as a term referring to the ruler. Obviously, political loyalty was the extension of filial piety. An official's obligation to the ruler was fundamentally the same as that of a son to his father. As the father had supreme authority over his son, so did the ruler over his officials. After serving a ruler, for instance, the person should devote himself to his official duties, advise his master even at the risk of severe punishment, and finally refuse to transfer his service to a new dynasty when the old one collapsed. Although there existed potential conflicts between filial piety and political loyalty,[22] the autocratic ruler was able to turn the balance to his favor. For example, in his essay "On Factions," Yung-cheng bluntly demanded that the official give himself to his ruler and no longer consider himself as belonging to his father and mother. In short, the doctrine of filial piety made a virtue of docility and this helped to achieve social and political stability. As long as autocratic rulers wanted to wield their power without obstruction, they made strenuous efforts to promote filial piety.

The Yung-cheng Emperor encouraged filial piety with more vigor than any other early Ch'ing ruler. On the day that he succeeded to the throne, he made it one of the qualifications for special recommendations. Those who were recommended received not only honorary titles but official appointments.[23] Every new Manchu ruler since that time did the same to promote filial piety. During the K'ang-hsi reign the *Canon of Filial Piety* was a subject for the provincial and metropolitan examinations but was dropped in 1702. Shortly after his accession Yung-cheng restored it to the list of requirements.[24] In 1728 he ordered publication of the *Canon of Filial Piety* in both Chinese and Manchu, and by the same year he had asked provincial administrators to report to him people of filial piety or chaste behavior.[25] Vigorously promoted by the emperor, the *Canon of Filial Piety* became increasingly a political instrument for his autocratic purposes. It is not accidental that of all the alien dynasties in Chinese history, the Manchu rule was the most effective and successful.

The Yung-cheng period saw the publication of two special books—the *Ta-i chüeh-mi lu* and the *Po Lü Liu-liang ssu-shu chiang-i* (A refutation of Lü Liu-liang's comments on the Four Books). Although they resulted from a literary inquisition, they were published for the furtherance of orthodox ideology. Inasmuch as they will be treated in detail in the next section, the following offers only a very brief discussion of their functions. In general, these two books reinforced the *Amplified Instructions on the Sacred Edict*. As explained in Chapter 3, the *Ta-i chüeh-mi lu* contained Yung-cheng's defense of his activities during the succession dispute and of his regime against Chinese anti-Manchu sentiment. During the Yung-cheng period it was read and explained, together with the sixteen maxims, before all the people, with the literati as its chief audience and reading public. Every school received a copy of it, and students were required to read it. The front pages of the book covered the emperor's order, according to which provincial and district educational directors should be severely punished if any schools under their supervision did not keep the book or failed to ask students to read it.[26] The other book, *Po Lü Liu-liang ssu-shu chiang-i*, contained philosophical arguments against free interpretations of the School of Principle. After its publication in early 1732, this work was also distributed to schools as a reference book.

Besides publishing these books, Yung-cheng worked out other measures for the enforcement of the orthodox ideology. One such measure was the appointment of special agents given the official title "Inspector of Morale" (*Kuan-feng cheng-su shih*). The first of these individuals was dispatched in 1726 to Chekiang province in connection with a literary inquisition, which will be treated in the next section.[27] During the years 1726-1730 the inspectors of morale established offices in Chekiang, Fukien, Hunan, Kwangtung, and Kwangsi provinces.[28] All these appointees were carefully selected from the imperial confidants. Since their chief work was to deal with the literati, they were largely the Chinese or Chinese bannermen with the highest degrees. Wang Kuo-tung (d. ca. 1735), for instance, the first of these appointees, was a Chinese bannerman who had obtained the *chin-shih*, or, roughly, doctoral degree.[29] After their appointment the inspectors of morale carried out special missions for the emperor.

The importance of the inspectors of morale lay in their comprehensive tasks.[30] Their first mission was to enforce the orthodoxy. In carrying out their duties they had to watch over the literati, keep an eye on students, and supervise educational and examination programs; they naturally transmitted imperial messages to the literati and took part in lecturing to the people on orthodox publications. Their second major function was the supervision of morals. Again, the literati were the chief objects of their supervision. They were prohibited from practicing factional activities or anything which was against examination rules, from interfering in local administration, and from publishing literary works of an immoral nature. The inspectors of morale were authorized to enforce these prohibitions.

A third function was a sort of police duty that entailed investigating and singling out those who disturbed the social and political order. For example, while serving as an inspector of morale in Hunan province, Li Hui examined the literati who were suspected of literary offense and anti-Manchu activity.[31] Besides investigating, the inspectors of morale had to keep under strict surveillance those who had been convicted as a result of literary inquisition. This can be seen in the case of Tseng Ching and his disciple. They were arrested in 1728 for their anti-Manchu agitation; after release from imprisonment they were put under constant surveillance and indoctrination by the inspector of morale in their native province.[32] Finally, the inspectors carried out missions of a less specific nature because they were special agents of the throne; they were given various ad hoc assignments as the ruler saw fit. When unexpected problems arose in the areas of their jurisdiction, they might be ordered to help the responsible administrators work out solutions, and they could administer the province as acting governors if the situation required.[33] In this sense they served as trouble-shooters. Whenever the situation in a particular place had improved, Yung-cheng recalled them one after another. The inspector of morale in Fukien province was the last to be recalled, in early 1734.

In every respect the inspectors of morale identified themselves as instruments of the autocracy. Because they were appointed by the throne, they were directly responsible to the ruler. To be sure, they were not provincial administrators, but they enjoyed unique status in the official hierarchy of the province. Each inspector had a regular office in the provincial capital. In the performance of their work, they made inspection tours, used local facilities to collect information, arrest, detain, and examine suspects, and discussed problems with governors.[34] In their formal communications with provincial authorities they stamped their documents with official seals provided by the throne.[35] Since they were the imperial confidants, they were allowed to submit palace memorials through which they reported their findings to the ruler. Instructions from him came through court letters or imperial comments on their memorials. Although they were only temporary commissioners and their activity did not cover the entire empire, they had the imperial confidence and special authorization and were thus effective enforcers of the orthodox ideology in certain crucial areas. Furthermore, they were succeeded by other special imperial appointees of the same nature.

During his reign the Yung-cheng Emperor frequently dispatched his confidants to promote proper mores. Even if they were not given the official title of inspector of morale, they carried out similar missions. For example, he believed that under the influence of Yin-t'i, Yin-t'ang, and Nien Keng-yao the people in Shensi and Kansu provinces criticized him and deviated from good morals. Therefore, in 1731, he sent a group of officials and scholars as commissioners charged with transmitting imperial messages to the people and giving lectures on the *Ta-i chüeh-mi lu*.[36] In view of their functions, these special appointees, including the inspectors of morale, did not differ from the reporters of palace memorials or the Grand Councillors. They functioned in different capacities and places, but they worked toward the same goal— increasing imperial power.

The provincial and local education administration underwent a great reform during the Yung-cheng period. Considering the situation of the time, this change was another measure to promote the orthodoxy, and it was perhaps more important than other means. The reason for its importance is apparent. The inspectors of morale were only temporary appointments; the provincial and local administrators were occupied by their regular duties, although they were obliged to enforce the orthodoxy. In contrast, the provincial and local education administrators were specifically to supervise scholastic activity and personal conduct of students; they were, then, more relevant to the work of enforcing the orthodox ideology than the inspectors. Surely, a reform of the provincial and local education administration was fundamental to the elevation of orthodox doctrines.

As was the case with many other institutions, the Ch'ing education administration followed the Ming system. In each province an education administrator assumed the highest authority over provincial education, and at each administrative level below him, there were an education official and several assistants. During the Shun-chih and K'ang-hsi periods, the provincial education administrator was always selected from scholar-officials who held the *chin-shih* degree and served in the central government. After selection he was given the official title, "Intendant of Education" (*Hsüeh-tao*), or "Director of Studies" (*Hsüeh-yüan*). Although he carried on his duties independently, he was at a relatively lower level in the provincial bureaucratic structure and was subordinate to the governor or governor-general.[37] When the Manchu rulers felt the importance of orthodox ideology, they changed the qualifications of the education administrators, with emphasis on the provincial director of studies. The change began in the K'ang-hsi period but was completed in the Yung-cheng era.[38]

Almost immediately after his succession to the throne the Yung-cheng Emperor took action to strengthen the provincial and local education administration. Of his eleven decrees to officials and officers, as already mentioned, one was specifically addressed to the provincial director of studies. In it, he reminded the director of the social and political significance of orthodox studies and advised him to promote them with devotion.[39] Before long he worked out a two-part reform program: one concerned the provincial director of studies,[40] and the other the sub-provincial education administrators.

The reform at the provincial level centered on the title and qualifications of its director of studies. Before the transformation, the title was based on the holders' qualifications.[41] They acquired the title *hsüeh-yüan* if they were selected from the scholars of the Hanlin Academy, from the censors, or from the supervising secretaries, all of whom were holders of the *chin-shih* degree. They were addressed as *hsüeh-tao* if they were chosen from other categories of bureaucrats who, in some cases, did not hold the highest academic degree. By comparison, the title *hsüeh-yüan* seems to have won more respect from students because they in general aspired to hold the same degree. In 1726 the emperor ordered that all provincial directors of studies take the same title, *hsüeh-cheng* (director of studies), a title sometimes interchangeable with the term *hsüeh-yüan*. This titular uniformity raised the prestige of the provincial education administrator and was helpful to his performance of official duties.

The change in title actually resulted from a change in the required qualifications. While regularizing their titles, the emperor ordered that the provincial education administrators be chosen from among the members of the Hanlin Academy. If they were selected from officials who had the *chin-shih* degree but served in other offices, they were given, besides *hsüeh-cheng*, additional titles taken from the Hanlin Academy. In other words, the *chin-shih* degree was the basic requirement for appointment of the provincial education administrators, and emphasis was also on membership in the Hanlin Academy. The importance of this change in qualifications lay in the fact that the *chin-shih* degree represented the highest academic achievement, and the Hanlin Academy the highest academic institute: each was held by students in great respect. Therefore, with such qualifications the provincial education administrators could effectively push forward their work. In later years the Yung-cheng Emperor recruited candidates through special examination.[42] Successful candidates were naturally those whose ideology was in conformity with orthodoxy. At any rate, these changes brought to the provincial directors of studies more prestige than their predecessors had had. Their official rank remained below that of the governors or governors-general, but they were functionally not the latter's direct subordinates. They communicated with the throne through palace memorials and were, in brief, the ruler's permanent agents to enforce the orthodox ideology in the provinces.

Below the provincial level the reform of the education administration focused on the personal qualifications of the education officials.[43] Prior to the Yung-cheng period, they were roughly from two sources, degree holder and office purchaser. In the second half of his reign, the K'ang-hsi Emperor occasionally made appointments from those holders of the *chü-jen* degree who failed in the metropolitan examination, but this did not become an established practice. During the years 1723-1727 Yung-cheng selected appointees by new rules that differed from the old ones in two ways. First, office purchasers were no longer eligible for the post of local education administrator, and even those office purchasers who were serving as education officials were transferred to other posts in 1723 on the ground that their academic training was inadequate.[44] Then he gradually made selections from those who had the *chü-jen* degree but failed in the metropolitan examination, and this became a rule in 1727.[45] He later supplemented the rule by transferring district magistrates—who held the *chin-shih* degree but did not satisfactorily perform their work—to education posts.[46] In summary, the *chü-jen* degree was made the basic requirement for such appointments.

Second, the new rules restricted the eligibility of senior licentiates (*kung-sheng*). Because the senior licentiates achieved their status usually after a long process, many of them were physically incapable of doing administrative work. According to the new regulation, only those senior licentiates in good health were made reserve candidates for the lowest education positions. Before receiving an appointment, these candidates had to present themselves to the governor and the provincial director of studies for physical inspection.[47] It seems that they were removed from the active list if their physical condition failed to meet the requirement.

The significance of Yung-cheng's reform in the provincial and local education administration is discernible in three respects. In the first place, it improved the quality of education administrators on whom he relied for the enforcement of the orthodoxy. In the second place, it provided enough personnel for the provincial and local education administration, which had been a weakness of the political structure under the early Ch'ing. Even in 1723, for example, there were no regular education officials in some places; thus, district magistrates were concurrently in charge of education.[48] Finally, the reform strengthened imperial control over students in government schools. They formed the vast bulk of the literati, and became potential bureaucrats after obtaining an advanced academic degree. No doubt their activity was the primary concern of rulers, in particular autocrats; effective control of them was important to the imperial authority. Since the provincial and local education administrators supervised the studies and personal conduct of these students, it was through the education administrators that the Yung-cheng Emperor extended his control, ideological and behavioral, over the vast body of literati.

Another major act for the enforcement of orthodox ideology was official support of private academies (*shu-yüan*). At least since the Sung dynasty they had played a significant role in traditional Chinese education.[49] The main distinction between private academies and state-supported schools was that the former followed their own methods, enjoyed a sort of intellectual freedom, and were not necessarily connected with the civil service examination system. As a result, the private academies were not only relatively free intellectually but also were places where political movements of potential challenge to the government were nurtured. The Tung-lin Academy of the late Ming dynasty was a notable example.

The early Ch'ing rulers responded differently to the private academies. To be sure, Shun-chih was aware of their potential danger. When he prohibited the literati from organizing literary associations, he also banned private academies.[50] However, if properly controlled by the government, the private academies might be useful tools of the ruler. This was obviously K'ang-hsi's opinion, for he relaxed the ban on private academies, while promoting the orthodox ideology. This relaxation allowed them to flourish in the beginning years of the eighteenth century. The Yung-cheng Emperor moved one step further. In 1733 he ordered that in the provinces public funds be approved to found a private academy in each provincial capital; this order finally resulted in twenty-one such schools.[51] Teachers and students received stipends from the government. Although sources are not adequate to make a thorough study, they provide enough material to examine the nature of the private academies under official support.

Under government support the private academies lost their traditional characteristics. Teachers and students were subject to government supervision. Their goals and curricula were greatly modified, with stress on the civil service examination rather than on free philosophical discourse.[52] Carefully supervised and strictly indoctrinated, students in government schools as well as in private academies strove for personal opportunities and competed to prove their loyalty to the Manchu ruler. Education, public and private, thus served the autocrat as a means of making all the educated think alike. This can be considered a great contribution of Yung-cheng to Ch'ing autocracy.

2. *Literary Inquisition*

Literary inquisition was another form of restriction on the Chinese literati during the Yung-cheng period. It was rigorously carried on, together with the measures to enforce ideological orthodoxy. Both of these were closely connected in a functional sense. When orthodox doctrines were promoted to achieve ideological conformity, literary inquisition was used to intimidate nonconformists. Both manifested the autocrat's passion for conformity and uniformity, which would enhance his political authority. However, one would be mistaken to consider them one and the same. Since the Han dynasty, Confucianism had adopted ideas from Taoism, Legalism, and, later, Buddhism. As long as Confucianism contained these non-Confucian ingredients, heterodox schools were in practice allowed to exist. They were persecuted mostly for political reasons. In the same light the Ch'ing literary inquisition was rarely carried out directly to support orthodox ideology;[53] its real motivation was also political. This was particularly applicable to the cases during the Yung-cheng period.

A careful examination of the literary inquisition in the Yung-cheng period reveals that it largely resulted from Confucian-Legalist tension, a long-standing problem between ruler and bureaucrats. As has frequently been mentioned, dynastic rulers recruited bureaucrats from Confucian scholars, but their relations were always ambivalent. During the Yung-cheng period that ambivalence was clearly manifested in many imperial decrees. On private and public occasions the emperor indicated his distrust of Confucian bureaucrats—which sprang mainly from his dissatisfaction with their bureaucratic behavior. According to him, in their official conduct Chinese bureaucrats followed evil practices that were opposed to his interest.[54] Such practices may be classified into four categories. One was self-seeking activity, such as corruption and graft. A second category covered the perfunctory nature of their performances, such as indolence and superficiality. In the third category were arrogant acts, such as disrespect to superiors and the ruler. The last category was their personal associations, such as relations between teacher and student, between fellow-degree holders (*t'ung-nien*), and so forth.

It is clear that what the emperor presented was a picture reflecting the conduct of the majority of bureaucrats of the traditional Chinese state. It is also clear that what he condemned was related to the Confucian pattern of personal and social conduct. As a group of individuals the Chinese bureaucrats were not different from the people of other occupations. Their self-seeking disposition was shared by other individuals but, in them, it was reinforced by the fact that under the Confucian influence, they had to support their large families however inadequate their salary—which in many cases was their major income and was usually far from enough to cover their personal and official expenses. Consequently there were cases of official graft. Besides, the Confucian value system played an equally important role in conditioning their conduct. For instance, they despised physical labor and looked up to an official career as their ultimate goal, but they were trained only as generalists, not as experts in the administrative work that they had to perform after their appointment.[55] In brief, the Confucian value system always ran counter to the practical requirements of administration.[56] Their bureaucratic conduct was further affected by the fact that they received official appointments from the ruler but acquired their high social status through the Confucian tradition. Even if they served as officials, they regarded themselves as bearers of Chinese culture. Whether or not they could justify their claim, such an assumption had repercussions on their official conduct and also on their relations with the ruler.

Of all these practices, the personal associations of bureaucrats perhaps commanded the most serious attention of the Yung-cheng Emperor. These associations, while personal, played a considerable part in bureaucratic conduct. The teacher-pupil relationship, for example, was one such association specified by the emperor. Unlike the affiliation between instructor and student in the school, this relationship was based on the civil service examination system. According to it, the teacher was the examiner who passed the student in his examination for his degree. Degree holders thus regarded their examiners as personal benefactors and respected the latter as teachers. In the Confucian moral norm, this was a lifetime relationship, and, if necessary, they were always ready to fulfill their obligations as students.

Fellow degree holders also had a strong relationship, another tie condemned by the emperor. This fellowship was based on the civil service examination system, too. The *chin-shih* holders who obtained their degrees in the same year had their names inscribed on a stone tablet set up in the yard of the Imperial University, while the names of the *chü-jen* holders of the same year appeared in yearbooks. With this relationship at work, fellow degree holders had to help each other out of trouble, personal or official. Both relationships, teacher-pupil and fellow degree holders, might be extended to the next generation of the individual concerned.[57] These associations, then, exercised a certain pressure on the scholar-officials in the performance of their official duties, developed at the cost of the ruler, and became a cause of Confucian-Legalist, or ruler-bureaucrat, tension.

Yung-cheng considered all these bureaucratic practices a great ill for state administration and scholastic work as well. There would be no justice, and scholastic dignity would trail in the dust, he contended, if these practices prevailed without check.[58] This perhaps explains why he always suspected bureaucrats and made them his targets. What he required in his essay "On Factions" and in the *Amplified Instructions on the Sacred Edict* was primarily concerned with bureaucratic behavior, and during his reign he constantly took measures to improve it.

These measures may be conveniently divided into two broad categories, positive and negative. The various actions that he took to enforce ideological orthodoxy were positively directed at the improvement of bureaucratic behavior. Another measure of the same nature was designed to improve the civil service system, through which most of the bureaucrats were recruited. This measure concerned not only students but examiners,[59] with emphasis on the provincial examination, a crucial stage in the whole system; after passing this stage, students obtained the *chü-jen* degree and were entitled to be low-level officials or to work for the highest degree. The same measure required the chief and associate examiners to take qualifying tests specifically designed for them before assuming their posts in the provincial examinations. While the candidates for chief examiners took the tests at the court, those for associate examiners took theirs from governors and governors-general of the related provinces. The successful candidates were of course the men whose academic accomplishments and personal conduct satisfied the emperor, and they were charged with selecting desirable bureaucrats for the throne.[60]

In a negative sense, Yung-cheng used office purchasers as a tool to check the scholar-officials. The sale of office had been a practice of long standing and usually served as a means of collecting money for the government in pressing need, but it was now given a political mission. The emperor argued that office purchasers had two advantages.[61] Because they were generally from rich families, they would not be so much concerned with fame and wealth as the scholar-officials. Also, office purchasers were not from the examination system, so it was hard for them to develop the personal relationships as did their counterparts. He further argued that without such relationships, they could be easily checked if found guilty.

It is obvious that the emperor's argument was short of sound reasoning. Office purchasers had their weak points. In general, they had less academic training than scholar-officials. Again, as they paid money for their appointments, they were possibly lured by the desire to make a profit from their investment. However unconvincing his argument, it sufficiently indexed his distrust of the scholar-officials. By 1727 he issued two orders regarding office purchasers.[62] They were selected to fill the local administrative vacancies from assistant district magistrate to subprefect. He even allowed them to serve in the Censorate and the Board of Civil Appointment, in which vacancies were traditionally reserved for the holders of the *chin-shih* degree. Although the appointment of office-purchasers did not replace the regular practice of bureaucratic recruitment, it affected the behavior of scholar-officials. Under pressure the latter had to compete with their rivals for the imperial confidence in terms of ideology and conduct.

The literary inquisition of the Yung-cheng period was also a negative measure to regulate bureaucratic behavior. It was carried out through punishment. In his prominent work a well-known Sinologist lists eight reasons for the censorship of the Ch'ien-lung period.[63] For that of the Yung-cheng era, the reasons fall into three categories: (1) cases of factionalism, actual or alleged; (2) cases of taboo words, criticism of the ruler or the dynasty, and insulting allusions to the monarch or the regime; and (3) anti-Manchu ideas and activity. Naturally, the ruler was the sole interpreter of these cases, and some accusations were based on suspicion. In a strict sense, there was no literary inquisition of heterodoxy at the time. The following pages present five case studies, most of which have been treated in two Western sources, *Eminent Chinese of the Ch'ing Period (1644-1912)* and *The Literary Inquisition of Ch'ien-lung*. Therefore, the discussion below will omit all but the most crucial points.

The category of factionalism includes two cases. One concerned Wang Ching-ch'i (1672-1726), a son of a scholar-official family in Chekiang.[64] He was gifted with writing ability, but fate seemed against him. His father, once a high official, was dismissed in 1706. His elder brother and cousin succeeded in obtaining the *chin-shih* degree, whereas he had never passed the metropolitan examination. In addition he was a man of self-complacency. These factors made his writing sarcastic, and this finally brought him trouble. In 1724 he made a long trip to seek his fortune in Shensi, where a friend was the provincial financial commissioner and a cousin served on the staff of Nien Keng-yao, then governor-general and commander-in-chief of the armies.[65] Through these relations he was acquainted with the powerful Nien. While Wang did not work with Nien, he became an ardent admirer of the general. Out of admiration he sent Nien a copy of his manuscript, *Tu-shu t'ang hsi-cheng sui-pi* (Jottings of a western journey), a collection of poems, notes, and essays. When Yung-cheng decided to remove Nien Keng-yao and his faction, this manuscript brought Wang Ching-ch'i under imperial attack.

Wang was regarded as fanatic and seditious because of his manuscript. In it he ridiculed some high officials as hypocrites, discussed some problems of the time, and included some notes that might be interpreted as disrespectful allusions to the Ch'ing rulers. For example, in one note he collected all Chinese dynastic year-periods composed of the character "*cheng*" and suggested that those reigns were destined to be bad. As this character was identical with the second word of Yung-cheng—the reign-title of the emperor in question—the note was considered lese majesty.[66] Besides this note, the emperor was angered by Wang's letter in praise of Nien Keng-yao, whom he later accused of ninety-two "crimes." In the letter the general was extolled as learned, incorrupt, filial, friendly, and heroic.[67] This high praise offended the emperor in at least two ways. For one thing, it gave Nien full credit for the military success on the frontier. However, since the establishment of the Chinese imperial system, the monarch had been the only person entitled to receive such credit. Therefore, in a sense, Wang's generous eulogy of Nien insulted the emperor. Furthermore, because such high admiration was given to a man under imperial attack, it served as a countervailing testimony to the action that the throne took. In other words, it indirectly raised the problem of justice, an important element in the ruler's authority and legitimacy.[68] This made a harsh penalty on Wang Ching-ch'i inevitable.

Wang's manuscript contained another note that was probably also greatly offensive to the throne. It pointed out that it is worthless to try to be a meritorious general.[69] Using examples from history, the author sarcastically speculated as to why dynastic rulers deposed successful generals as soon as the trouble was over. He approached the problem through the psychology of autocrats, concluding that rulers removed their meritorious generals because of suspicion, fear, anger, and disgust. This analysis foretold the fate of Nien Keng-yao and also exposed the emperor's thinking. It is no wonder that upon reading the manuscript Yung-cheng burst into anger. In this situation Wang Ching-ch'i became the first victim of the literary inquisition in the Yung-cheng period. He was decapitated, and his close relatives were banished to Manchuria as slaves in early 1726 (some of them were pardoned in 1736).[70]

A second case was that of Ch'ien Ming-shih, a native of Kiangsu.[71] As a renowned man of letters, he had been editing books in the Southern Imperial Study even before obtaining his *chin-shih* degree in 1703. In the last few years of the K'ang-hsi period he lost imperial favor probably because of factionalism, but a greater setback was in store for him in the next reign. His story epitomized the autocratic rule of Yung-cheng. As has been mentioned in chapter 4, at the beginning of the Yung-cheng era Nien Keng-yao was a very influential individual and an imperial favorite. When he returned to Peking from the frontier for an audience, Ch'ien Ming-shih sent him a poem in praise of his great contribution to the pacification of Tibet. It would be interesting to know exactly why he sent the general such a poem. The paucity of sources allows one only to suggest some possibilities. Perhaps he genuinely appreciated the general's military contribution to the dynasty. Also he might have been attempting to establish a fellow-degree-holder relationship with the general because they obtained their *chü-jen* degree in the same year, 1699.[72] Finally, he might have meant to show his compliance with the will of the emperor, who then frequently praised the general. In any case, after Nien Keng-yao was condemned by the throne, Ch'ien Ming-shih did not follow the imperial example and denounce the general. When, then, the emperor discovered the poem in 1726, he regarded it as evidence of factionalism and dismissed the author.

The emperor considered the matter of the poem such a grave one that he mobilized the whole court to condemn its author. Obviously, his true purpose was to reinforce what he required of the bureaucrats in "On Factions" and in the *Amplified Instructions on the Sacred Edict*; he disclosed his aim in the decrees issued for the case.[73] Under imperial orders every *chin-shih* holder serving in the central government wrote a poem to ridicule and condemn Ch'ien Ming-shih. These poems served the emperor in two ways: as a weapon against the victim and also as a tool to test the authors. The more poignant sarcasm the poem contained, the more it appealed to the throne. One author received imperial commendation, six were asked to rewrite their poems, and two received severe punishments.[74] However, this was not the close of the case. After the imperial examination all the poems were sent to Ch'ien Ming-shih for publication at his cost. According to the imperial will, the publication was entitled *Ming-chiao tsui-jen* (Offender against the orthodox doctrine) and included 385 poems and a preface by the emperor. Each government school was given a copy as a reference book, and the emperor had the four characters of the title inscribed on a tablet to hang outside the offender's house.[75] The poor scholar received no physical punishment, but he was made a lifetime example for other members of the literati.

The second category of literary inquisition involved two cases. The earlier case involved Cha Ssu-t'ing.[76] After obtaining the *chin-shih* degree in 1706, he served in the Southern Imperial Study and the Hanlin Academy. In the first three years of the Yung-cheng period, he seems to have enjoyed imperial favor, but his fortune was affected by two factors. One was the implication of factionalism. Possibly his scholarship attracted the attention of some high officials; he established friendly relations with two influential men, Lungkodo and Ts'ai T'ing. Under their patronage he first served as subchancellor of the Grand Secretariat and then as vice-president of the Board of Rites.[77] When his patron, Lungkodo, lost the imperial trust in early 1725 he was under suspicion. The other factor was connected with his assignment to conduct the provincial examination in Kiangsi in 1726. As the chief examiner he gave students topics for composition, and these topics became the source of his trouble.

Five such topics were considered by the emperor to contain disrespectful insinuations about him.[78] The first two topics were phrases taken from the *Analects* and the *Mencius*. Roughly, these two subjects stressed that a superior man should be open-minded, not blinded by personal likes and dislikes. The emperor suspected that they were implicit criticisms of his personnel policy. Two other subjects—two quotations from the *Book of Changes* and the *Book of Songs*—were interpreted by the emperor as even more affronting. From these quotations he picked two characters—*cheng*, a word identical with part of his reign-title, and *chih* (to end), a word which looks like the former but lacks a top stroke[79]—and came to conclude that selection of the two quotations was as seditious as Wang Ching-ch'i's inference from the year-periods. These two quotations thus became a key to the punishment of Cha Ssu-t'ing.

In discussing the castigation of Cha Ssu-t'ing some scholars insist that he had taken from the *Great Learning* a phrase, "*wei-min so-chih*" (where the people rest), which provoked the ruler to anger. This is actually misleading, because no reputable source has provided evidence of this.[80] The last of the five topics was also quoted from a Confucian classic. It explained the functional relations between ruler and officials to the effect that the latter served as a man's arms and legs, while the former his heart. The selection of the subject was interpreted as another great offense. According to the emperor, the ruler served as head of state, not merely as its heart.

Yung-cheng found further offense in Cha Ssu-t'ing's journals.[81] The original copies are not available, but some of their main points are retained in imperial decrees. Most of the affronts were criticisms of the state administration in the K'ang-hsi period. For instance, the author complained that some unqualified persons became holders of the *chin-shih* degree simply through imperial favors. A few statements were regarded as insulting allusions to the emperor himself, and some sentences were considered offensive to the dynasty as a whole.[82]

In terms of its effect, the case of Cha Ssu-t'ing was more important than others of the same period. It served the emperor's purpose in several ways. He removed the offender and punished many others. As a rule, the offender and his close relatives received harsh punishment.[83] Although Cha Ssu-t'ing died before the sentence was given, the dismembering of his remains was ordered. As he once owed his official appointment to the patronage of Lungkodo, his severe penalty marked the prelude to the latter's condemnation in 1727. Even at the beginning of the case, Lungkodo was questioned several times,[84] and his support of the scholar finally became one of the forty-one "crimes" charged against him. In short, the emperor regarded the case also as a form of factionalism.

Most important of all, Cha's case provided two incidents from which the emperor drew an excuse for tightening his control over the literati. One incidence was merely a coincidence; Cha and Wang Ching-ch'i, an earlier offender, happened to be natives of the same province, Chekiang. The other was that in Cha Ssu-t'ing's house were discovered some cribbed notes that had been used to cheat during the examinations.[85] With these incidents in mind, the emperor considered the case a manifestation of the undesirable scholastic atmosphere and behavior in the whole region. For rectification he appointed the first inspector of morale and prohibited the students of that province from taking provincial and metropolitan examinations.[86] Although the ban was soon lifted and did not substantially affect the literati of the province, it was a high-handed measure which frightened the scholars into submission.

A second case of the same category was that of Lu Sheng-nan, a scholar from Kwangsi.[87] It is said that he gave the throne a very poor impression in an audience before leaving for his new post as magistrate in Kiangsu. The throne thereupon canceled the appointment and reassigned him to a post in the central government so as to observe his conduct closely. Later he seems to have advised the ruler not to believe in Buddhism and Taoism. This advice so angered the emperor that he banished the outspoken scholar to forced labor in Uliasutai. In exile Lu Sheng-nan wrote seventeen essays on the *Mirror of History*, a famous historical work known as *Tzu-chih t'ung-chien* in Chinese. His essays had nothing to do with the Manchu ruler or dynasty directly, but after an imperial scrutiny they were construed as outrageous. Since the essays appeared in manuscript form and were unable to survive the literary inquisition, their gist is known only through the quotations and refutations in Yung-cheng's decrees.[88]

The main affront of Lu Sheng-nan seems to have been his antidespotic ideas. In political ideology, he was to a certain extent close to the two famous scholars, Ku Yen-wu (1613-1682) and Huang Tsung-hsi (1610-1695). Like the latter two, for example, he attacked the overcentralization of power in the hands of the ruler. He therefore recommended decentralization of power, advocating a return to the feudal system. He also deemed it necessary to distribute part of the imperial power to the prime minister on the ground that a wise ruler would not concentrate in himself responsibility for every aspect of state affairs. A sagacious monarch, he believed, would rather pay more attention to the selection of good officials, especially the prime minister. Because the ruler was always afraid of the usurpation of power by officials, Lu Sheng-nan tried to move the monarch by arguing from the viewpoint of personal security: the more power and authority the ruler possessed, the more precarious and dangerous his position was. What Lu discussed were probably his personal ideas, but unfortunately he presented his points in his exile and at a time when the emperor was devoted to concentrating all powers in his own hands. Lu became an easy victim under autocratic rule.

In his essays Lu Sheng-nan presented two other points that were also considered offensive. In discussing the militia system (fu-pin) of the T'ang dynasty, he complained about the large amount of money spent for standing armies after abrogation of that institution. From this the emperor inferred that the scholar was viciously alluding to the bannermen soldiers, who were at that time already incapable of fighting. The other point concerned the heir-apparent system. In the opinion of Lu Sheng-nan, a ruler should choose a successor in his lifetime because the designation of the heir apparent gave continuity and stability to the dynasty. However, he maintained that before succeeding to the throne, the crown prince should not interfere with state administration, thereby avoiding court struggle. The emperor associated this point with the power struggle from which he emerged to the throne, and considered it another grave offense. Because of these alleged offenses he accused the scholar of treason and ordered the latter executed in exile.[89]

A survey of Lu's case indicates a fact that has escaped many students of Ch'ing history. Apart from the literary offense, there were other reasons that resulted in his destruction. One may recall that while discussing bureaucratic behavior, Yung-cheng expressed his dissatisfaction with the arrogant acts of scholar-officials. Arrogance was also a factor in the punishment of Lu Sheng-nan, and this can be attested to by the emperor's testimony in his long decree concerning the victim. Imperial suspicion of factionalism was another reason for the scholar's persecution.[90] The suspicion came from the fact that he and Hsieh Chi-shih, another scholar under a cloud, happened both to be from Kwangsi. When the former advised the ruler to renounce Buddhism and Taoism, the latter recommended the removal of T'ien Wen-ching, governor of Honan and an official having imperial favor. Furthermore, they submitted their memorials at about the same time. Thus, the emperor believed that there was a sort of factional relationship between them and banished them to the same place. When the literary offense came to the front, the underlying factor was overshadowed and was neglected by many scholars of Ch'ing history. Finally, considered together with the punishment of Hsieh Chi-shih, the Lu case implied one more reason for his castigation. Both these men tried to rectify the emperor in compliance with the typical Confucian concept that scholars had the obligation to tutor the ruler. Their punishment suggests the imperial rejection of this traditional concept.

In brief, each of the above four cases was more or less related to factionalism, and it was so interpreted by the Yung-cheng Emperor. Factionalism differed from literary offenses, but both appeared at the expense of imperial authority. The emperor tolerated neither, and in every case he conveniently found justification for his actions.

The case of Tseng Ching belongs in a category of its own.[91] Because it involved an anti-Manchu movement and the last grave inquisition in the Yung-cheng period, it deserves a more detailed examination. Although the movement drew its ideological force from the orthodox doctrines, it had a special social and political background. Its chief proponent, Tseng Ching, was a scholar from an obscure family in Hunan. Since his youth, he had seen the social inequalities between rich and poor and suffered from the competitive examinations. Because of personal economic hardship he once planned to move to Szechwan province. What he experienced and suffered actually resulted from a condition of long standing,[92] but he tended to associate it with the Ch'ing administration. This social dissatisfaction was strengthened by political factors. It is said that in 1727 he happened to hear some stories, according to which the emperor murdered his father and brothers and, above all, was an illegitimate ruler.[93] These stories seem to have become the origin of others of a similar nature and were later proved to be slanders from the emperor's opponents, but they played a role in the scholar's anti-Manchu movement. To sum up, a combination of ideological, social, and political factors brought about Tseng Ching's movement in 1728.

If Tseng Ching was the organizer of the movement, Lü Liu-liang (1629-1683) was its ideological founder.[94] They were from different provinces and lived in different generations, but Tseng was influenced by Lü's ideology and soon became its exponent. After a chance reading of one of Lü's books, Tseng sent a disciple to obtain more books from the author's sons and students in Chekiang. From Lü's works Tseng drew heavily the material for his thought. Lü Liu-liang had won fame and respect from the Chekiang literati as a scholar and physician. During the Shun-chih period he took the local examinations for degrees, but from 1666 onward he withdrew from further examinations and became an ardent opponent of the Ch'ing regime. A study of his works shows that he ideologically belonged to the School of Principle, as promoted by the Manchu government. He relentlessly attacked the School of Intuition as a corrupter of morals and of the Chinese state.[95] From a belief that scholars should closely follow the School of Principle in order to arrest the adverse political and moral currents, he moved to the political field.

Like some scholars of the early Ch'ing, Lü Liu-liang preferred the feudal system, and he even made it a dividing line of Chinese social and political developments.[96] In his opinion, virtue was the dominant value of the feudal period. At that time, dynasties lasted longer than later ones, and their rise and fall were determined by virtue. When virtue prevailed, the ruler-minister relation was based on righteousness.[97] Scholars served the ruler as officials, provided this basic relation remained; they could quit office in the event the ruler acted in an unrighteous way. In other words, scholar-officials in feudal times were subject only to virtue, not to the ruler. Lü also believed that under the feudal system there was little distinction between ruler and people.[98] Although they functioned differently, they had to cultivate virtue and operated on the same moral basis. As virtue was the leading value, the ruler and officials worked for the common welfare of the state.

While discussing the situation of the feudal period, Lü Liu-liang attacked the political and social systems that replaced feudal institutions. According to him, the postfeudal situation was completely different because virtue was no more. Tricks and brute force took the reins. Dynasties were united and disunited by force and they became short-lived. With virtue gone, the ruler-minister relationship changed from one of righteousness to utilitarianism.[99] The ruler controlled officials by tricks and force and determined their appointment and dismissal, whereas officials tried to win the ruler's favor and forgot the welfare of the people. Lü therefore came to conclude that these clever officials were responsible for political upheavals. In addition, he bitterly criticized the holders of the *chin-shih* degree, especially their fellowship. To him the fellow degree-holder relationship caused factional struggle detrimental to state administration.[100] He also criticized rich people for their selfishness. For example, they had no sympathy with their poor relatives, but wasted money on Buddhist and Taoist practices for selfish reasons.[101] The above reproaches were evidently antidespotic.

Lü Liu-liang also drew his anti-Manchu ideas from the orthodox school. His anti-Manchu views appeared in various works, but were included mainly in his journals, which did not survive. He stressed that the distinction between Chinese and barbarians was the primary concern of Confucius and his followers; this distinction, he argued, was more important than the ruler-minister relation,[102] and he advised Chinese scholars not to serve the Ch'ing regime, which was of barbaric origin. It is said that he was pleased to hear of the Revolt of the Three Feudatories in expectation of its success.[103] He is also said to have regarded the Ch'ing dynasty as the worst time for Chinese to make a living. Since he acquired popularity in his native province, he spread his anti-Manchu ideas among the literati of Chekiang. Nevertheless, it was not until 1728 that Tseng Ching brought his anti-Manchu views to light.

In terms of ideology, Tseng Ching did not go beyond what Lü Liu-liang had expounded. The former included his political and social views in two manuscripts—*Chih-hsin lu* (Notes of new knowledge), a collection of notes on the Confucian classics, and *Chih-chi lu* (Record of miscellaneous instructions), another collection of notes for his disciple. Neither survived the inquisition, but their main points are quoted in the *Ta-i chüeh-mi lu*. In some places Tseng's ideology was even more positive than that of his predecessor. In discussing social inequalities, for instance, he stressed the well-field system as the only remedy.[104] With respect to the Ch'ing regime, he regarded the Manchus simply as a group of barbarians who stole China from the Chinese.[105] He accused the Manchu government of cruelty, labeled Yung-cheng a wicked ruler, and insisted that Chinese should not serve the Manchu regime at any cost. With this ideology added to the aforementioned social and political background, he expected and encouraged a Chinese revolt.

However, Tseng Ching was largely a political dreamer. Many Chinese scholars served in the Manchu government, and under the tight control of the Yung-cheng Emperor they competed for loyalty and conformed to the imperial will. Tseng's anti-Manchu ideas had some sympathizers among the literati, but no organized followers. What he had was a disciple, his sole follower, Chang Hsi (also known as Chang Cho, d.1736). After hearing some rumors, he considered Yüeh Chung-ch'i, then governor-general of Shensi, a possible collaborator; in 1728 he sent his disciple to urge the governor-general to lead an anti-Manchu revolt. But Yüeh Chung-ch'i turned informer,[106] and the movement failed. The planner, the courier, and many others were arrested.

The Tseng Ching case served the emperor's purpose in three ways. First, it brought to his attention the slanders about his succession. He immediately traced their origins and identified the defamers according to Tseng's testimony.[107] This case provided him with an opportunity to defend himself, and he put his defense in the *Ta-i chüeh-mi lu*, a work in four chapters that also contained Tseng's depositions. Because he understood that the slanders had circulated far and wide, he sent copies of the work to all public institutions within the empire. Under strict regulations, the book was read and explained, together with the *Amplified Instructions on the Sacred Edict*, before the people. The slanders were propaganda, to which the *Ta-i chüeh-mi lu* provided effective counterpropaganda.

Second, the anti-Manchu arguments of Lü Liu-liang appealed to a number of literati, but the Manchu government had never discovered before that they were circulated. Through the case of Tseng Ching, the emperor was informed of their contents. When he defended himself, he also defended the dynasty. His defense was based on Confucian doctrines and historical facts and is a classic of its kind. His argument presented three important points.[108] The first one emphasized virtue, instead of nationality, as the basic requirement for rulership—a point he shrewdly took from Confucian classics. In Confucian tradition, for example, there were two sage rulers, Shun and King Wen, the latter being a founder of the Chou dynasty. The former is said to have been from the eastern frontier of China; the latter from the western border. Both are believed to have won the state by virtue. In the same light, the emperor explained that although the Manchu ruling house was of barbarian origin, it possessed virtue. It was virtue, he insisted, that entitled the Manchu ruling house to receive the "Mandate of Heaven," a point never mentioned by his predecessors in defense of the Manchu conquest of China. A second point, an invention of the Shun-chih period, attempted to explain away the problem of the shift of power from Chinese to Manchus. It was not new, but eloquent. According to it, the Manchus took over China from the rebels who had destroyed the degenerate Ming regime. It further identified the Manchu conquest as the salvation of the Chinese. After its conquest of China, the emperor went on with more evidence, the Manchu regime reintroduced peace and order and, most important, added Mongolia to the empire. The point which concluded the debate stressed the importance of the ruler-minister relationship. Mankind, he contended, was distinguished from other animals by the five human relationships, of which the ruler-minister relationship was the first. Naturally he included in this point his threat to punish those who acted against the ruler. The above arguments are also retained in the *Ta-i chüeh-mi lu*.

A third way in which the case of Tseng Ching was useful to Yung-cheng was that it strengthened the process of ideological indoctrination that the emperor had been carrying on. This can be explored in light of the emperor's way of dealing with the case. Besides the above book, he published another, *Po Lü Liu-liang ssu-shu chiang-i*, a work of eight chapters following the order of the *Four Books*. It was compiled by Chu Shih and Wu Hsiang (1661-1735), two high officials in imperial favor. Fundamentally, their ideology was not different from that of Lü Liu-liang, but they interpreted the Confucian doctrines according to the ruler's will. After its publication the book was made a tool for ideological indoctrination. In line with his indoctrination purposes, the emperor treated the culprits differently. He harshly punished Lü Liu-liang, his descendants, and his disciples on the ground that they outrageously offended the late emperor. In other words, Yung-cheng meant to penalize them for the purpose of filial piety,[109] which he had promoted since the beginning of his reign. Before administering the punishments, he ordered that all students in government schools express their opinions about the case and its treatment.[110] The result was predictable. Although Lü and his eldest son had died long before, their corpses were dismembered.[111] Lü's close relatives and disciples were executed or banished in 1733. In this way, the emperor punished the offending literati, alive or dead, and indoctrinated the others.

Tseng Ching and Chang Hsi, the two plotters of the unsuccessful anti-Manchu movement, were treated very leniently. The emperor even denied the courtiers' petitions that they be executed, repeatedly declaring that they had been deluded by others, that they had shown repentance, and the like.[112] Tseng wrote an essay entitled "Kuei-jen shuo" (Return to humanity), which formed the last chapter of the *Ta-i chüeh mi-lu*. In it he expounded what the emperor had emphasized. In 1730 he was set free by the imperial grace, but he had to report to, and take assignments from, the inspector of morale—who had been appointed to Tseng's native province, Hunan, shortly after the case arose. Chang Hsi was dealt with separately but was given a similar duty. Under strict surveillance he was sent to Shensi with some imperial commissioners who took charge of ideological indoctrination there.[113] These two offenders, together with the two publications, seem to have served as imperial propaganda tools. This was perhaps a technique to counter propaganda with more propaganda, comparable to that used by modern totalitarian states. In this sense, the Yung-cheng Emperor was a tactful autocrat. However, his successor, Ch'ien-lung, did not adopt the same technique. Soon after his succession to the throne the new ruler reversed the case, imposing death sentences on the two offenders and ordering all copies of the *Ta-i chüeh-mi lu* destroyed.[114] Probably he meant to stop further circulation of the stories about his father known to the two culprits and included in the book, but this action may have invited more rumors.

3. Summary

The situation of the Chinese literati during the Yung-cheng period reflected the effectiveness of the autocratic rule of the time. The whole group was held tightly under imperial control through various means. The orthodox ideology was one such means. It was emphasized in maxims, imperial decrees, and special publications, and was expounded by the ruler, provincial and local officials, special commissioners, and others. Under strict governmental control, public and private schools served as important transmission channels for the orthodoxy. This process was one of systematic ideological indoctrination from Peking to the provinces and from scholar-officials to individual literati. Although in technique it was no match for modern totalitarian inculcation, in nature there is no difference between them.

If the orthodox ideology restrained the intellectual activity of the Chinese literati in the Yung-cheng period, the sale of office further checked their thought and behavior. Some office purchasers even achieved high and influential positions. Li Wei, for example, was a fortunate member of the purchase group. He was one of the governors-general most favored by the emperor. P'ei Shih-tu (d.1740), once governor of Kiangsi and later a senior president of the Censorate, also began his official career by purchase.

Tough provincial administrators provided another effective check to the literati. With the imperial confidence, they prohibited the intellectuals under their jurisdiction from carrying out activities against government interest. T'ien Wen-ching, a typical tough provincial administrator, was originally a student of the Imperial University, a status usually with little potential for official service.[115] In the early Yung-cheng period he was promoted to governor and later governor-general. His tough administration caused the students of local government schools in Honan to boycott the state examination and also moved the scholar-officials in the central government to impeach him.[116] While the students who actively led the boycott were given death sentences, his accusers, such as Hsieh Chi-shih and Li Fu, were harshly penalized by the emperor. It is obvious that these blows were designed to curb the influence of the Chinese literati, and in the final analysis, they facilitated ideological control.

Side by side with orthodox doctrines, the literary inquisition reinforced imperial control of the Chinese literati. The orthodox ideology set the imperial requirements for the literati as a whole, and the literary inquisition punished individuals as an example for others. The latter thus supported the former. Nonetheless, during the Yung-cheng period cases of literary inquisition had nothing to do with heterodox ideas. These cases sprang directly from Yung-cheng's political considerations. Of the five case studies presented in the previous section, the first four were more or less related to factionalism, while the last concerned anti-Manchu activity. In brief, through literary inquisition the emperor attempted to correct the undesirable behavior of bureaucrats and to defeat other activities against his person or the regime.

Both the orthodox ideology and the literary inquisition were aimed as an ideological control that might internalize a pattern of thought and externalize a standard of behavior according to the ruler's will. Consequently, ideological control was the key project of the Yung-cheng Emperor. During his reign all other considerations radiated from and returned to it. When he consolidated power, he removed his brothers and factional leaders. The main arguments for his actions, presented in many of his decrees and writings, notably the essay "On Factions," were unanimity or conformity to his will. For the same reasons, he degraded the traditional censorial institutions, strengthened the palace-memorial system, founded the Grand Council, and bureaucratized the banner system. In a broader sense, all these shared the same origin and purpose with the promotion of ideological orthodoxy and the literary inquisition. When combined, they tightened ideological control over the Chinese literati, an important group from which the scholar-officials and many local leaders were recruited.

Ideological control over the Chinese literati was implemented through consensual and coercive measures. For instance, orthodox doctrines were promoted in a consensual manner, but literary inquisition was carried out by coercive means. With the consensual method he persuaded the Chinese literati to follow his will; by coercion he frightened them into submission. Under these conditions no one dared to act against him or the regime. In other words, through these means he achieved ideological unanimity or conformity, the mainstay of an autocracy. Even if such conformity was only a facade, it still provided strength for his reign. In their discussion of totalitarian control, two well-known scholars state:

> Scattered opponents of the regime, if still undetected, become isolated and feel themselves cast out of society. This sense of loneliness, which is the fate of all but more especially of an opponent of the totalitarian regime, tends to paralyze resistance and make it much less appealing. It generates a universal longing to "escape" into the anonymity of the collective whole.[117]

Although Yung-cheng cannot be compared with any totalitarian dictator of this century, it is no exaggeration to say that he achieved to a great extent what the above quotation describes. This may be examined from many aspects. Chinese censorial officials, for example, were always anxious to rectify the ruler in the Confucian way, but during the Yung-cheng period they were rectified by the emperor in the Legalist manner. Moreover, private academies, which traditionally emphasized free philosophical discourse, began in the Yung-cheng era to shift their stress to preparation for state examinations. In their struggle for official service, students of private institutions were channeled from free philosophical studies to orthodox doctrines. As a result, the Chinese literati became less and less concerned with the foreign origin of the Ch'ing dynasty. Particularly after the case of Tseng Ching, few, if any, of the Chinese literati were interested in the anti-Manchu movement, which was taken over by secret societies with lower-class people as their members. After the Ch'ien-lung period the Chinese literati looked up to the Manchu dynasty as the bearer of Chinese tradition and identified their fate with that of the regime.

However, ideological orthodoxy was maintained at tremendous cost to the Ch'ing dynasty. First, it accelerated the Sinicization of the Manchus. For its maintenance, in addition to many other measures, the Manchu rulers had to adopt certain norms, mores, and values of Confucianism, which were the basis of such an ideology. For example, they paid homage to Confucius, participated in the exposition lectures of the Confucian classics, provided strict Confucian education for imperial princes, observed the three-year mourning ceremony, published orthodox works, encouraged loyalty and filial piety, and the like.[118] These practices made the Sinicization of the Manchus inevitable, even though they were not sincere Confucians at heart. True, the Manchus had begun to Sinicize before their conquest of China, and the process moved in strides after 1644. Nevertheless, their Sinicization was largely limited to the tangible elements of Chinese culture, and it was far from systematic. With the imperial insistence upon the orthodox ideology, many of the Confucian norms, mores, and values—the intangible traits of Chinese culture—were systematically inculcated in Manchu minds, and this inevitably hastened the course of their Sinicization. After the second half of the eighteenth century the process moved forward so fast and irresistibly that all imperial efforts to renew Manchu nativism were of no avail; by the mid-nineteenth century the Manchus had almost completely lost their cultural identity.

Second, the maintenance of orthodox ideology stifled new ideas. Because the orthodoxy provided an established ideological pattern that permitted no deviation, it was fundamentally a conservative force. This slugglish ideological force had been at work since Confucianism was made an orthodoxy, especially since the rise of Neo-Confucianism, but no dynasty in Chinese history had enforced it as seriously as had the Ch'ing.[119] Under intense pressure, scholars during the Ch'ing had to follow the beaten track carefully; even new interpretations within the accepted pattern of ideology were discouraged. In the Ch'ien-lung period, for example, Li Hui, once the inspector of morale of Hunan during the previous reign, and Hsieh Chi-shih—the same person who impeached T'ien Wen-ching—met with severe imperial censure when they attempted some new interpretations of the Confucian classics.[120] Because the imperial interpretation was final in all ideological cases, no fresh thoughts could be expressed without the approval of the ruler, who committed himself to defending the orthodox way. Thus intellectual innovation could be generated neither from the top nor from the bottom. This intellectual stagnancy was apparent in academic studies, state policies, and the administrative process. In fact, state and culture fell into a situation of almost complete unresponsiveness to the challenge from without—and this was the condition of the Ch'ing empire in the second half of the nineteenth century.

IX

The Populace of the Period

1. *Emancipation of the People of "Mean" Occupations*

The effect of Yung-cheng autocracy on the common people differed from its effect on the literati. While the upper classes endured more restrictions than had their predecessors, the populace enjoyed a better life than the broad masses of people in the Shun-chih or K'ang-hsi periods. After his enthronement the Yung-cheng Emperor took various measures to improve state administration. For example, he dismissed or reprimanded provincial administrators who maltreated the people. Pu-lan-t'ai, governor of Kiangsu, was dismissed for maladministration, and Hsü Jung (1686-1751), governor of Kansu, was reprimanded for the same reason.[1] Similarly, the self-seeking gentry who profited at the cost of the common people and at the expense of the imperial interests met with harsh punishment. These measures were directed toward promotion of the imperial authority, but at the same time they led to the improvement of the situation of the populace.

Emancipation of the people of "mean" occupations (*chien-min*) was the most striking feature of Yung-cheng autocracy. These people included members of a variety of social groups, such as the singing people (*yüeh-hu*), fallen people (*to-min*), hereditary servants (*shih-p'u*), the Tankas (*tan-min*), beggars (*kai-hu*), booth dwellers (*p'eng-min*), and perhaps banner slaves (*ch'i-nu*). All these groups were isolated from other members of society, held "mean" occupations, and were excluded from government service. They were special groups in a cultural, economic, and social sense.

Each group had a long history,[2] but in some cases their origins cannot be clearly traced. The singing people were scattered in many districts in Shansi and Shensi provinces. They are said to have originated from those officials loyal to Emperor Hui (1399-1402), the second ruler of the Ming dynasty. After he was defeated in a power struggle, his loyal followers were executed and their families were legally degraded to singers and music players by the victor. Since that time they had served as musicians at weddings, funerals, and other gatherings, and had belonged to the lower orders of the social hierarchy.

The fallen people were residents of the prefecture of Shao-hsing, Chekiang; according to one story, they were the descendants of the Mongol garrisons at Ningpo in the same province. After the collapse of the Mongol regime in China, they accepted low status in exchange for their lives.[3] Another story traces their origin to the Sung dynasty. Their ancestors are said to have followed Chiao Kuang-tsuan, a general of the Sung, in surrendering themselves to the Chin dynasty (1125-1234), but they were captured by the Sung government and given low status. Yet another story, while recognizing the relation between their ancestors and the general, contended that they were debased by the founder of the Ming dynasty.[4]

Of unknown class origin, the hereditary servants were natives of southern Anhwei. Neither ordinary domestic servants nor legal slaves, the hereditary servants were required to serve their masters at weddings and funerals.[5] They were traditionally treated as low-status people. Similar to them were beggars, who were scattered in Anhwei and Kiangsu and whose origins also were unclear. Some scholars see these two groups as identical, but actually they were not the same. Unlike the hereditary servants, the beggars were not tied to any particular masters. Furthermore, the beggars whom Yung-cheng emancipated were individuals from the prefecture of Soochow, Kiangsu.[6]

The Tankas were boatmen along the coast of Kwangtung, Kwangsi, Fukien, and Chekiang provinces. They probably belonged to an earlier native group from South China whose main occupations were fishing, gathering oysters, and collecting pearls. According to some sources, they worshipped snakes as their totem and their origins went at least as far back as the Ch'in dynasty.[7] Their legal status was the same as that of the common people, but they were treated as a legally degraded order and excluded from land residence. In contrast to them were the booth dwellers, who were simply poor individuals. Under personal economic pressure, they moved from their homes to the mountainous areas of the Kiangsi-Chekiang-Fukien border; hemp and indigo farming was their major occupation.[8] Poor and obscure, they were discriminated against as another group of low status.

Banner slaves were of Chinese origin. During their military conquest of China, the Manchus captured Chinese either in battles or in their homes and enslaved them. Some Chinese surrendered to the Manchus in the hope of getting protection. They and their descendants thus gave up their freedom to their Manchu captors or protectors, became legally degraded, and individually served their masters as domestic slaves or farming laborers. In the Shun-shih and early K'ang-hsi periods many of them became deserters and caused political and social problems. Whatever their origins, all these people were confined to the occupations despised by their fellow countrymen and became outcasts.

The first factor that moved the emperor to change the conditions of the outcast people was that of public order. As groups discriminated against by other Chinese, the outcasts formed a body of discontents in the society, providing the most likely recruits for revolts. Their very existence could threaten public order and finally affect the imperial authority. At the end of the Ming dynasty, for instance, domestic slaves in Kiangsu revolted. In 1723 booth dwellers in Kiangsi rose up under the leadership of an anti-Manchu Chinese. At a time when Yung-cheng felt concerned about his authority, he deemed it advisable to remove any possibly troublesome elements in the society.

The principles of justice and equality were the second factor impelling the emperor to emancipate the degraded people. As was pointed out in Chapter 2, he was a Legalist-oriented ruler who particularly emphasized justice and equality, which underlay the authority of law and were the major principles of Legalist philosophy. Such a consideration was manifested in his own testimony. In a decree of 1729, for example, he argued that the people of "mean" occupations, however disrespectable, fulfilled their obligations as did other subjects and had to be treated equally well.[9] Buddhism furnished him with further argument to the same effect. According to him, Buddhism tolerated no differentiation in personal status.[10] Whatever the source of his interpretation of justice and equality, Legalism or Buddhism, they were important to the maintenance of imperial authority and became the basic direction of his administration. Impelled by these two principles, he made efforts to suppress the self-seeking gentry and promote the well-being of the common people, including the outcasts. These were related actions, appearing in different forms but sharing the same purpose—justice and equality. Only with the suppression of the self-seeking gentry did the improvement of the situation of the common people became possible. By the same reasoning, the emancipation of the despised people was an indirect attack on the local self-seekers.

The last consideration in the emancipation of the degraded people was public morals. Since these people were isolated from other people in society, they had their special occupations, maintained their own way of living, and set their own moral standards. Obviously, their existence handicapped the emperor's efforts to promote public morality, which required uniform standards. For example, he prohibited practices such as gambling and cock-, quail-, and cricket-fighting as harmful to public morals.[11] In a broader sense, the *Amplified Instructions on the Sacred Edict*, the stress on filial piety, and the inspectors of morale may also be regarded as means of promoting public morals. The emancipation of the lower orders furthered the same cause. The chief reason for the emperor's elevation of public morals was to buttress imperial authority. If the people behaved in accordance with the ruler's definition of public morals, his rule would be made easier. More specifically, the ruler drew strength from public morals to justify and reinforce his authority.

Yung-cheng did not emancipate all of the outcast people. He liberated only the Tankas who were in Kwangtung. Emancipation of the banner slaves was also limited: he failed to liberate all of them or domestic slaves as a whole. Their status was even rigidified so as to maintain the regular social order; moreover, slavery was still a punishment for lawbreakers or political offenders. Nor did he emancipate all of the people of "mean" occupations at one time; they were liberated gradually. Of all the outcast groups, the singing people of Shansi and Shensi were the first emancipated. Through a petition of Nien Hsi (d.1724), the eldest son of Nien Keng-yao and then a censor, the emperor ordered their emancipation in early 1723.[12] A few months later, he acted upon the suggestion of Ko-er-t'ai, a salt inspector from Chekiang, to restore the fallen people of Shaohsing to their proper status.[13] In a decree of 1727 he freed the hereditary servants in southern Anhwei, and the next year enforced his order by supplementary acts.[14] The years 1729-1730 saw liberation of the Tankas in Kwangtung and the beggars in Soochow.[15] At the petition of high officials such as Chang T'ingyü, Jabina, and Pai Huang (d.1737), the booth dwellers were allowed to register along with other people in 1731.[16]

Yung-cheng was the first Manchu ruler to change the status of some banner slaves. Although his emancipation of the banner slaves was also, among other reasons, a measure to reduce the increasing population pressure in the banners, it was unprecedented in the early Ch'ing. Before 1723 banner slaves could get freedom only through the special favor of their masters, imperial grace, or desertion—which was prohibited by law. The first decree concerning the status of banner slaves (which appeared in 1725) stated that they might redeem themselves with the consent of their masters if they had become slaves after 1723 and were not given wives by the latter.[17] A second decree, as issued in 1728, had an even greater impact the first, permitting sons of banner slaves to become freemen.[18] A third decree, appearing in 1733, promised that all banner slaves who were recruited in the army and fought, with merit, against the Dzungars would be made freemen after the war.[19] These orders did not emancipate all banner slaves, but they did free a large number of them.

The emperor's effort to emancipate the degraded people proved, however, a failure. The singing people of Shansi and Shensi, for instance, remained active. According to a private record of the Yung-cheng period, their emancipation turned out to be but a prohibition of their open activities or, in some cases, a source of illegal income for corrupt officials. Nien Keng-yao is said to have received a great deal of money from a rich singer who wanted to be freed.[20] After emancipation, they and the beggars of Soochow were still not allowed to take civil service examinations until at least 1771; in like manner, the fallen people of Shao-hsing and the Tankas of Kwangtung did not substantially change their status.[21] The condition of the hereditary servants in southern Anhwei was no better than that of other degraded people. Some of their old masters claimed lordship over them as before and caused disputes in the first half of the nineteenth century.[22]

There were two major reasons for the failure of Yung-cheng's emancipation attempts. First, he relied too much on political, and not enough on economic, measures. While emancipating the outcasts, he did not make strenuous efforts to change the loathsome occupations that were closely associated with their status.[23] As long as they did the same jobs, they were still discriminated against even after their status had been legally changed. Secondly, after centuries of discrimination the degraded people became relatively indifferent to their lower status. Further, the gentry and other people were reluctant to accept them as regular members of society.[24] On the whole, they presented a combined force that defeated the imperial emancipation orders. One scholar complains that the emperor's efforts were destined to fail as long as slavery was a form of punishment.[25] Nevertheless, slavery as a punishment affected only a few individuals, whereas the emperor's emancipation orders influenced a wider range of outcasts. At any rate, these orders had a striking impact on Chinese social history, and laid the legal foundation for further emancipation decrees by subsequent Ch'ing rulers.

The suppression of the self-seeking gentry was a measure necessary to the advancement of the welfare of the common people. The self-seeking gentry are customarily referred to in documents as the bad gentry (*lieh-shen*). The term encompasses individual gentry from various backgrounds who engaged in unlawful activities for selfish ends, largely at the expense of the populace. Together with other members of the gentry, they belonged to the local elite, dominated public opinion, maintained intimate relations with one another, and had contacts with the local administration. Their legal privileges, such as exemption from labor service, immunity from the ordinary jurisdiction of local administrators, and the like, were a formal source of strength.[26] In addition, their status and the activities related to it provided them with informal influence in local affairs and opportunities for self-aggrandizement. Formally and informally, therefore, they were in a strategic position between the government and the common people. Their support was crucial to dynastic stability, but their activities (particularly those entailing abuse of their privileges) conflicted with the interest of the ruler in many ways. They tried to extend their privileges to relatives and friends, and for selfish ends some of them took advantage of their privileged position to cover up lawbreakers, profiteer from public enterprises, and act as judges of lawsuits. T'ien Wen-ching, a well-known tough provincial administrator of the Yung-cheng period, recorded many such cases.[27]

Of all the self-seeking activities, land-tax evasion probably exerted the greatest impact on the imperial authority. It resulted not only in the shift of their tax burden onto the common people but also in shortages in the state treasury. The K'ang-hsi period was generally known as a time of prosperity, but it actually saw a great deficit in the state accounts. During the years 1712-1726, for example, tax liabilities of the people of Kiangsu amounted to more than ten million taels of silver, about half of which was owed by corrupt officials and self-seeking gentry.[28] As a matter of fact, in Chinese dynastic history, the evasion of the land tax by the self-seeking gentry accounted at least in part for the collapse of many taxation systems and invited the introduction of new ones.[29]

Another self-seeking practice of the "bad gentry" that challenged the imperial interest was their intrusion into local administration. Their relations with local administrators were as ambivalent as those between them and the ruler.[30] As local leaders, they helped the local government by performing various community services which were semi-official activities in nature, and their support was vital to the official career of local administrators. In return, they needed the backing of the local administration for the maintenance of their prestige and influence. In particular, the self-seeking gentry and corrupt local administrators always helped each other. However, the semi-official activities that the bad gentry engaged in inevitably trespassed on the domain of local administrators. For their part, the local administrators unavoidably invited the antagonism of the self-seeking gentry when they tried to uphold justice and equality. Official and private sources furnish many cases of such antagonism. In his palace memorial, Li Wei, also a tough provincial administrator, revealed that under the instigation of self-seeking gentry, villagers in some counties of Kiangsu organized riots.[31] With a few exceptions, local administrators yielded to the influence of the self-seeking gentry for personal reasons. In this sense, the self-seeking gentry were the interlopers who contributed to the corruption of local governments and made justice and equality impossible.

The self-seeking gentry's activities had been a primary concern of dynastic rulers. In the Shun-chih period the Manchu monarch took harsh measures in an attempt to curb them. The Examination Case (*k'o-ch'ang an*) of 1654 and the Taxation Case (*Tsou-hsiao an*) of 1661 were manifestations of these measures.[32] Although many self-seeking gentry were punished or even destroyed, they found relief in the reign of the K'ang-hsi Emperor, who was considerably more lenient to them. Men like Kao Shih-ch'i, Hsü Ch'ien-hsüeh, and Wang Hung-hsü played dual roles—as high officials in the court and self-seeking gentry in their localities.

The Yung-cheng Emperor was the most determined of the early Ch'ing rulers; he persisted in his policy of holding the self-seeking gentry in check. His restrictions on the Chinese literati were also meant to discourage any unlawful activities of scholars. Besides, he issued special decrees to warn and threaten the selfish gentry. In one such decree in 1727 he prohibited them from oppressing tenants, and in 1731 he commanded them not to establish improper personal relations with local officials.[33] At the same time, he repeatedly ordered provincial bureaucrats to mete out tough measures to the gentry of bad repute. When officials were found accepting favors from, or associating with, the self-seeking gentry, they would be punished, or at least rebuked.[34] Under his rigorous prohibitions local administrators dared not deviate from the imperial requirements.

During the Yung-cheng period there were many tough provincial administrators who despite public criticism made the local government efficient, curbed the selfish gentry, and worked hard for the sovereign's interest. Of these provincial bureaucrats, T'ien Wen-ching, Li Wei, and O-er-t'ai were the three most famous governors-general, having won special imperial commendation.[35] For a better illustration of the emperor's effort to curb the self-seeking gentry, the administrative work of these three men deserves some elaboration.

T'ien Wen-ching started his official service as early as 1683, but until the end of the K'ang-hsi period he was only a reader in the Grand Secretariat, a post of about the same rank as prefect in the bureaucratic hierarchy. His ability and loyalty soon arrested Yung-cheng's attention; in 1724 he was promoted to the governorship of Honan and four years later he became governor-general of Honan and Shantung. During his tenure he honestly carried out imperial orders to punish incompetent and corrupt officials under him, suppress the self-seeking activities of the gentry and literati, and change infamous administrative practices. For example, as the provincial capital was the focus of the administration of the whole province, it was the center of activities of the local bureaucrats. For personal reasons magistrates and prefects frequently visited there or sent their confidants to live there in the hope of collecting administrative information and cultivating good relations with influential people in the provincial government. Because they proved a corrupting factor for local administration, during his governorship in Honan T'ien is said to have allowed no magistrates and prefects to linger in the provincial capital without official reason and expelled their personal aides.[36] His administration provoked not only the enmity of local self-seekers but the complaints of some officials in the central government. As was mentioned in Chapters 5 and 8, the student boycott of the Honan provincial examination in 1724 symbolized this local antagonism, while the impeachment of Li Fu and Hsieh Chi-shih represented the discontent of officials in the court. Although the emperor dealt with these incidents in favor of T'ien Wen-ching, the latter was portrayed as a notorious provincial administrator in many historical sources which followed the judgment of the literati.

Li Wei, another example of a strict administrator, was a man of pride, frankness, and resolution. He served as a low-ranking bureaucrat in the central government through office purchase in the last years of the K'ang-hsi period. He became prominent soon after Yung-cheng's accession to the throne, and within a short span (1723-1725) was appointed governor of Chekiang, an economic and cultural center. A little later his jurisdiction was extended to the southern part of Kiangsu, and he was given the special duty of administering the salt monopoly and suppressing desperados in the area. While punishing lawbreakers without mercy, he protected law-abiding people. By 1732 he was made governor-general of the metropolitan area, where he reported to the ruler corrupt officials no matter how influential they were. As his high-handedness checked the self-seeking gentry and corrupt bureaucrats, they worked hard to undermine the imperial trust in him. Despite their effort, the emperor had strong confidence in Li and this became his sole support. He is said to have fainted when told of his royal patron's death in 1735.[37]

In like manner, O-er-t'ai acquired importance in the early years of the Yung-cheng era. A man of courage and independence, he refused to flatter powerful officials or gentry and, during his service as financial commissioner of Kiangsu, he disciplined the self-seeking gentry. For this reason, he was known as a tough and upright administrator.[38] Since 1726 he had served as chief administrator of Yunnan, to which finally two more provinces, Kweichow and Kwangsi, were added. There he improved the welfare of the people by removing corrupt officials, suppressing selfish gentry, developing the irrigation system, and abolishing the hereditary chieftainship of the non-Han ethnic groups. The emperor trusted him so much that he was recalled to the court and made Grand Councillor, not too long after the death of Yin-hsiang, the ruler's most loyal brother. In the central government, none could match O-er-t'ai in terms of imperial favor, with the exception of Chang T'ing-yü.

These three governors-general were the toughest of provincial administrators who vigorously defended the imperial interest. Together with Grand Councillors and reporters of palace memorials, they were Yung-cheng's reliable supporters. The Grand Councillors were imperial confidants in the court; the tough provincial administrators and reporters of palace memorials served as royal agents in the provinces. Besides regular administrative relations, there were special channels for functional contacts between these three groups. As a rule, high provincial bureaucrats had the right to submit palace memorials to the ruler; tough provincial administrators usually made more such reports. They directly or indirectly supervised other officials in the province, some of whom also submitted palace memorials. Under the palace-memorial system strict provincial administrators were watched by other agents of the same system, and through palace memorials from different reporters the ruler had a clear picture of situations in various localities. His instructions reached directly to related provincial administrators through the palace-memorial system or court letters, in which the Grand Councillors played an important part. Tough provincial administrators naturally received more imperial instructions, and their official conduct became the model for local administration. For example, under imperial sponsorship T'ien Wen-ching and Li Wei in 1730 co-authored a book on district and department administration (*Ch'in-pan chou-hsien shih-i*), published again and again as an administrative guideline for magistrates throughout the empire. In consequence, local administrators of the Yung-cheng period followed a tough line, and tough administrators had the unswerving support of the ruler. One may find evidence in the *Chu-p'i yü-chih*, a voluminous collection of palace memorials selected by the Yung-cheng Emperor from those of more than two hundred reporters. The memorials of T'ien Wen-ching, Li Wei, and O-er-t'ai made up more than one-fifth of the reports in the collection. Obviously, these men were considered by the emperor to be model provincial administrators, and their memorials served as examples for other bureaucrats.

2. *Measures for the Welfare of the Common People*

In addition to the emancipation of the degraded people and the suppression of the self-seeking gentry, the Yung-cheng Emperor instituted river conservation programs and reclamation works. Also, like other dynasties in Chinese history, the Ch'ing regime emphasized hydraulic work. Yung-cheng was particularly persistent in this; thus his contribution to Ch'ing hydraulic work was in several respects much greater than either of his immediate predecessors. He accomplished this in four separate ways.

First, his hydraulic works were broader in scope. The Shun-chih Emperor was preoccupied with continuing warfare, and failed to pay sufficient attention to this work. The K'ang-hsi Emperor had emphasized the Yellow River and the Grand Canal only. Yung-cheng not only followed the pattern his imperial father had set, but went far beyond it by developing an irrigation system in the metropolitan area, southwestern and southeastern China, and the northwestern region.[39]

Second, the Yung-cheng Emperor reorganized the conservation administration so that it would function more effectively. In 1729 he appointed an additional director-general of conservation to take charge of the Yellow River and the Grand Canal, and the next year he created a third director-general responsible for work in the metropolitan area.[40] While strengthening the administration of river works, he increased the number of conservation troops (*ho-piao*) and every year selected two young officials from the central government to learn how to supervise such work.[41] As a result, he improved the administration of river works.

Third, he strengthened preventive work. In the years 1729-1731 he worked out precautionary measures, two of which were of great importance.[42] One was to ward off the collapse of dikes along the Yellow River and the Grand Canal. An imperial decree of 1729 required that these dikes be raised by half a Chinese foot every year. The other measure was to build small watch posts along these two rivers. Every two *li* (about 0.71 mile) there was a post manned by two guards, who inspected and repaired the section of dikes under their watch. This resulted in more than a thousand posts, which dotted the two rivers.

Fourth, the emperor improved coordination between officials of river works and provincial administrators. Because the lack of coordination had greatly handicapped river work in the K'ang-hsi period,[43] he made efforts to remove this weakness. In 1726 he ordered Ho Kuo-tsung (d.1766), then an imperial commissioner, Chi Tseng-yün (1671-1739), vice director-general of conservation work, and T'ien Wen-ching, governor of Honan, to discuss measures for dredging the section of the river in Honan.[44] The conservation and irrigation works of the metropolitan area largely resulted from cooperation of the river works officials and those of the provincial government. The irrigation works in northwestern China were an accomplishment of the cooperation between an imperial commissioner and the governor-general of Szechwan and Shensi.

Since the irrigation system of the Yung-cheng period was a very extensive and important project for human welfare, it deserves a detailed survey. It centered in three regions—southwestern and southeastern China, northwestern China, and the metropolitan area. The irrigation works in southwestern and southeastern China covered almost six provinces and were largely an accomplishment of O-er-t'ai, then governor-general of Yunnan-Kweichow-Kwangsi, in 1729-1730. In Yunnan he dredged the old watercourses and constructed new ones, both centered around Kunming.[45] Meanwhile, for military necessity and grain transportation, he developed the irrigation system in the southeastern Yunnan-Kwangsi border area and opened watercourses in Kweichow, especially along the southeastern Kweichow-Kwangsi border.[46] While working in Kiangsu, he improved the local irrigation system, which continued to develop after his tenure.[47] Provincial administrators in orther areas followed suit, and, with imperial support, they improved conservation work in Szechwan with Chengtu as the center, completed the Hunan-Kwangsi irrigation system by 1729, repaired a dike in Hsiang-yin, Hunan, in 1730, and started to construct a stone embankment along the Chekiang coast—the last of these undertakings being finished in the Ch'ien-lung era.[48]

The irrigation work in northwestern China included the Shensi-Kansu-Ninghsia area. Although earlier Manchu rulers had shown no interest in the project, Yung-cheng supported construction of two small rivers, Hui-nung ch'ü and Ch'ang-jün ch'ü, in 1726, and repaired three old irrigation courses—Ch'ing, Han, and T'ang—in the years 1730-1732.[49] These works were able to change a large pasture land in Ninghsia to farm land. Old watercourses in the province of Shensi were also improved in 1730.[50]

The most significant irrigation enterprise of the Yung-cheng period was the work in the metropolitan area. This project had been discussed even as early as the Sung dynasty and was again mentioned in the K'ang-hsi period, but it was dropped because many bureaucrats doubted its feasibility. However, after an inundation in that area in 1725, Yung-cheng decided to start the project at the suggestion of Yin-hsiang, who believed that a good irrigation system would prevent further flooding and make a rice crop possible.[51] Since rice was a part of the salary of bureaucrats, its production in the metropolitan area would supply, at least in part, the

demand in the capital. In 1726 Yin-hsiang was made
director of the Water-conserving and Field-cultivating Office (*Shui-li ying-t'ien fu*), which supervised four suboffices—Eastern Metropolitan Bureau
(*Ching-tung chü*), Western Metropolitan Bureau (*Ching-hsi chü*), Southern Metropolitan Bureau (*Ching-nan chü*), and Tientsin Area Bureau (*T'ien-chin chü*).[52]
The director had a special staff and was given the
authority to command all administrators in the metropolitan area, and each suboffice was under an intendant with the right to supervise the local officials
below him. As a whole, in cooperation with provincial authorities they took charge of both irrigation
and flood prevention in the area around Peking.

The irrigation works in the metropolitan area
were largely the contribution of Yin-hsiang, who was
able to construct dams, repair watercourses, and
introduce rice planting in a short period. There were
two factors responsible for his success: his own
character and ability and the encouragement of the
government.

Yin-hsiang was careful and clear-minded and was
an able financial administrator. In the first three
years of the Yung-cheng period, he successfully
improved the state financial administration by
stopping unnecessary expenditures, eliminating
corrupt practices, and thereby increasing the
deposits of the state treasury. Before taking charge
of the irrigation work in the metropolitan area, he
made an on-the-spot inspection and carefully worked
out a detailed program. His relationship with the
ruler was equally significant; as the most trusted
prince, he enjoyed full power in dealing with the
project—which of course facilitated his work.

The government invited experienced farmers from
South China to teach people in the area rice-planting
techniques and extended loans to poor farmers who
were interested in producing rice there. It asked
wealthy farmers to plant rice in the new fields,
promising them low taxes if they did so, and ruled
that rich persons convicted of crimes could have
their sentences commuted if they contributed to the
project.[53] According to one source, during the years
1726-1730 the project resulted in approximately
575,062 *mou*—roughly 85,601 acres—of newly converted
and reclaimed rice fields in the area.[54] Because of
technical and other problems, which will be discussed
below, this figure may be somewhat inaccurate, but
its relative importance is beyond question. For a

while the metropolitan area was regarded by the people as the "sub-Yangtze Valley" (*hsiao chiang-nan*).⁵⁵ Rice planters sold their products to the government for cash, and the rice production benefited not only the farmers but the central government.

However, irrigation work in the metropolitan area declined after the death of Yin-hsiang in 1730. At first the project was maintained under the direction of Chu Shih. Because he was no match for his predecessor in prestige and authority, it was hard for him to carry out the project as successfully as before. In early 1731 the project was divided into two parts: river work administered by a new director-general and irrigation under the governor-general of the metropolitan area.⁵⁶ Whatever the arrangement, it failed to facilitate the work, which was perhaps also affected by the campaign against the Dzungars in the northwestern frontier of China. Consequently, in the years 1731-1735, a span of the same length as the period 1726-1730, the same source recorded only a little more than one-fourth of the figure for the previous period, and about half the newly added acreage was transformed into dried fields in 1731.⁵⁷ After Yung-cheng's death the irrigation project and rice-planting experiments in the metropolitan area were dropped forever.

Reclamation was a long-range policy closely related to the river conservation projects of the early Ch'ing. As early as 1644 the Ch'ing government devised various measures to encourage reclamation of desert and uncultivated land for the purpose of economic recovery after the great political and social upheavals that had occurred immediately before and during the Manchu conquest of China. The Shun-chih and K'ang-hsi measures provided incentives for the prospective reclaimants and made reclamation a major duty of the provincial and local administrators. For example, poor reclaimants might borrow, or obtain without charge, plowing oxen and seeds from the local government; senior and junior licentiates, students of the Imperial Academy, and well-educated common people would receive lesser local administrative positions if they were able to reclaim 2,000-10,000 *mou* of land; and as a whole, newly cultivated land was in many cases owned by the reclaimants forever and was exempted from taxes for a five-year period, which was later extended to six years for rice paddies and ten years for dry fields.⁵⁸ On the other hand, local and provincial administrators were pressed to attract reclaimants; reclamation became one criterion of their service rating.[59]

During the Yung-cheng period, reclamation was carried on with new vigor. A perusal of the reclamation projects in the two previous reigns suggests that they centered on the desolate fields in provinces along the middle courses of the Yellow and Yangtze rivers.[60] Under the reign of the Yung-cheng Emperor, the projects not only focused on the same regions but radiated to the upper valleys of the two rivers and to frontier areas, such as Kweichow, Szechwan, Yunnan, and Manchuria, His new efforts seem to have been closely related to two problems of the time. One was population growth. As historical sources and recent studies indicate, the long peace and the various projects—notably river conservation—of the K'ang-hsi period after 1683 resulted in a steady growth of population.[61] Aware of this situation, the Yung-cheng Emperor made known to the public, shortly after his rise to power, that reclamation was the best way to meet the needs of the growing population.[62]

The concentration of land ownership was also a serious problem which concerned the Yung-cheng Emperor. Side by side with the population increase was the rise of great landlords, who reaped more benefits than common people from the period of long peace, and gradually acquired land from small farmers. Because of K'ang-hsi's leniency toward the upper class and the administrative laxity in the second half of his reign, the acquisition of land by rich people went nearly unchecked. There were signs of social unrest toward the beginning of the Yung-cheng period as landless farmers, notably the booth dwellers, moved around in search of wasteland; a few scholars, particularly Tseng Ching, seized upon this situation to promote an anti-Manchu movement; and some officials petitioned the throne to restrict landownership.[63] It was clear that, without mitigation, this situation would ultimately endanger imperial authority. When enforced with new strength in the Yung-cheng period, reclamation opened great possibilities for poor farmers to utilize and even own desert or uncultivated lands. It was indeed a timely method of relieving the land problem.

There is ample evidence of Yung-cheng's vigorous efforts to enforce reclamation. Some of his rules were more realistic than those of the two reigns prior to his. He required provincial and local administrators to carry on reclamation projects and prohibited them from exacting money from reclaimants; many provincial governors and governors-general concurrently were made directors-general of reclamation.[64] Every county or department could recommend a distinguished farmer, at first once a year but after 1729 once every three years, for the imperial honor of the eighth brevet rank, while poor peasants could apply for reclamation loans from local public funds.[65] The most remarkable of his efforts was the association of reclamation with some other projects. Irrigation works, especially those in the metropolitan area, made a large number of acres of land available for cultivation; the banner well-fields can be considered a project of the same nature. After emancipation the booth dwellers became legitimate reclaimants and the Tankas of Kwangtung were encouraged to engage in reclamation.[66] With the abolition of the tribal headman system among the Miao, Yao, and Lolo peoples, their areas were available for land-hunting Chinese farmers. In other words, all these projects formed a complicated whole, and it was in these circumstances that Yung-cheng reclamation was the climax of that carried out in the early Ch'ing.

No doubt reclamation in the Yung-cheng period was important to the state economy and public welfare. When it was energetically enforced, every provincial government released impressive statistics that appeared in official documents (such as the *Veritable Records*), local histories, and private works. But, for three reasons, the present discussion will not depend chiefly on these figures as a basis for evaluation. The most important of the reasons is the nature of the *mou*, which was not a unit of uniform size in customary land measurement. In many cases, local governments, for tax purposes, converted the *mou* in official registers to a unit that varied according to the productivity of land.[67] In short, by different local measurements the word *mou* lost its standard meaning; as a unit in land-tax payment it was no longer an actual *mou*.

Another reason for not relying on these figures as a basis for evaluation is the evidence of corrupt and unlawful practices relating to the reclamation projects. Since reclamation was an imperial decision and also a criterion for service rating, provincial and local administrators struggled for impressive figures in compliance with the throne's will. The officials who enjoyed imperial trust were the administrators who produced the larger figures. Some local administrators were dismissed for failing to enforce reclamation as required.[68] As a result, some made false returns through exaggeration or other means; some even pressed people to reclaim uncultivatable land. In the meantime, some reclaimants concealed newly reclaimed lands to evade taxation. Whatever the form of these practices, they brought about inaccurate reclamation figures.

Finally, a statistical analysis of the figures is beyond the scope and purpose of this study, although such a mathematical approach is helpful. In any case, reclamation figures, as released by provincial administrations, are unusually difficult to analyze. Actually, all official land returns from the Ming and Ch'ing share the same defects.

Despite its abuses and the unreliability of the figures concerning it, reclamation contributed greatly to rural rehabilitation in the early Ch'ing and laid an economic foundation for the Manchu regime. Toward the end of the seventeenth century, the Ch'ing government was able to achieve roughly the same land returns (701,397,628 *mou*) as the Wan-li period (1573-1615)—the land-tax rules and quotas of which were followed by the Manchu regime as a model—and the Yung-cheng period witnessed further progress.[69] Energetically and persistently enforced by the Yung-cheng Emperor, reclamation led to an increase in the number of small landowners. Through the assistance of government loans and free funds, many poor peasants were induced to reclaim land, and, in the end, they owned the land they reclaimed. In 1734, for example, about 200,000 people depended on their reclaimed fields in Honan; by the same year the provincial government of Kwangtung helped settle about 3,000 households plus 7,030 people.[70] Although these figures may also be inaccurate, they show that through reclamation a large number of poor peasants became small landowners, who formed the majority of providers of land levy and labor service in the traditional Chinese state.

Yung-cheng reclamation also accounted for a surge of population to frontier regions. During the early Ch'ing domestic migration from one province to another had begun in the K'ang-hsi era, and it has been well analyzed in a recent study.[71] What will be discussed below is a brief evaluation of the movement in the Yung-cheng reign, with emphasis on Szechwan, Yunnan, and Liaoning. Of these three frontier provinces, Szechwan was a typical example of this regional migration. Because of its mild temperature, fertile soil, large area, and sparse population resulting from the cruel slaughtering by Chang Hsien-chung (ca. 1605-1647)—a notorious rebel leader in the last years of the Ming dynasty—it had attracted a large influx of poor peasants from Kwangtung, Kwangsi, Hunan, Hupei, Kiangsi, and Fukien even prior to the Yung-cheng period. Under his reign the Yung-cheng Emperor promulgated more favorable rules, through which new settlers might obtain technical instruction from experienced reclaimants at government cost and receive emergency financial help from special appropriations of the central government.[72] Naturally these advantageous conditions attracted further waves of migrants. Among many reports, the memorials of Yüeh Chung-ch'i, a creditable governor-general, told of tens of thousands of households moving there in 1727.[73] With the increase of incoming peasants, Szechwan land returns shot up from 1,481,036 *mou* in 1671 to 22,323,137 *mou* in 1727; the latter registers were nearly doubled the next year.[74] Although the source of these figures did not analyze these returns and, as in other cases, they were subject to inaccuracies, generally speaking it may be inferred that the largest portion of the increased registers stemmed from reclamation.

Yunnan was another frontier region that received a large number of peasants from other provinces. Besides the factors common to all reclamation cases of the time, O-er-t'ai's contribution was of particular significance. During his governor-generalship (1725-1732) he improved the irrigation system and carried on campaigns against the non-Han ethnic minority groups in Yunnan. Many of his memorials presented the registers of land that he restored from concealment or that the people reclaimed.[75] According to the local history, the provincial land registers went up from 6,411,495 *mou* in 1724 to 7,973,272 *mou* in 1732, and 8,990,362 *mou* by 1736.[76] However defective and inadequate (because the source did not release much information on migrants), these figures indicate the rapid progress of reclamation achieved by farmers, many of whom can be reasonably considered settlers from other places. His work also contributed to reclamation in Kweichow, which will be dealt with in the last chapter.

Effects of Autocratic Rule

The prefecture of Feng-t'ien, roughly the province of Liaoning in later days, also received the influx of domestic migration. As early as the Shun-chih period the Ch'ing government attracted settlers by giving them food, land, and seeds.[77] In all likelihood, these reclaimants were poor people from Hopei and especially Shantung, and their number increased with time. In the years 1685-1724 Feng-t'ien's land returns and registers of *ting* (male adults of 16-60 *sui*) grew from 311,749 *mou* and 26,227 *ting* to 580,638 *mou* and 42,210 *ting* respectively, and reached 1,850,401 *mou* and 42,485 *ting* by 1734.[78] Admitting their inaccuracies, these figures suggest that Feng-t'ien developed almost into a regular province through the rapid influx of reclaimants during the Yung-cheng period.

All in all, Yung-cheng reclamation relocated many poor peasants, increased the number of small landowners, and enlarged the area of cultivated land. Since small landowners and cultivated land were taxable units, in the last analysis, both the state and the populace benefited from reclamation.

3. *Tax Reform*

Tax reform was another important measure taken for the welfare of the common people during the Yung-cheng period. Its significance will not be fully understood without reference to its political and social implications. In China, as in many other countries, the tax system had persistently interacted with the fluctuation of political power.[79] When taxation replaced feudal tributes, the ruler was able to wrest power from his vassals, and the state developed toward centralization. In consequence, dynastic rulers struggled desperately to maintain a sound tax system which underlay their power and the dynastic glories; when the dynasty lost its strength, its tax system became deficient, and this quickened the decline or collapse of the dynasty. In Chinese dynastic history tax systems declined and finally collapsed one after another, roughly for two fundamental reasons: technical and administrative.

The Chinese tax system frequently suffered from poor techniques, as reflected in land measurement and classification and in population census. The dynastic government never worked out a scientific method to measure or classify the land, so land measurement and classification were subject to regional differences. Nor did it develop satisfactory demographical skills for gathering population data. Although it tried to keep land and population records up to date by periodic surveys, new registers were still the outcome of the same defective techniques. At the same time, the Chinese tax system was plagued by mismanagement. For personal interests, runners, clerks, secretaries, and sometimes even administrators of the local government, who had charge of tax assessment and collection, developed various corrupt practices.[80] Either defective techniques or mismanagement handicapped effective and fair taxation and was therefore responsible for the decline and collapse of successive Chinese tax systems.

The combined effect of poor techniques and maladministration was responsible for two major tax evils. The first was tax evasion, widespread among the self-seeking gentry and big landlords. As a rule, the gentry legally enjoyed limited exemption from the land tax and full immunity from labor-service levy, but many of its members abused the privilege and tried to cover their families, relatives, or others simply for personal reasons. Because of their wealth, big landlords were influential individuals in their communities, and in many cases they were virtually identical to the gentry. For this reason they had close connections with the local government and the self-seeking members of their group evaded obligations, although their legal status was the same as the commoners'.

The second evil was the shift of the tax burden onto the common people. This often happened because the local government had to make up the tax evaded by the gentry or big landlords at the cost of the common people in accordance with the assigned tax quota for the locality under its jurisdiction. This extra charge was unjust, but without power or influence the common people were forced to bear it or evade it by desertion. Both of these evils were closely related and operated at the expense of the imperial treasury and common people.

The early Ch'ing tax system was no less faulty than its predecessors. Specifically, it had three flaws. First, its land and *ting* registers lacked accuracy. At first, the Manchu dynasty taxed the people exactly according to the rules, rates, and amount indicated in the records of the Wan-li period, which were no doubt out of date. Although it compiled its own registers, with some adjustments, in 1657,[81] inaccuracies remained. Second, the early Ch'ing tax structure was complicated with multifarious names and items. Of the four categories of tax—land and labor-service levies, the *gabelle*, merchandise dues, and miscellaneous charges, such as imposts on tea, mining, licenses, and so forth—each had confusing classifications and methods of conversion varying with local situations. True, the complexity of the tax structure was not necessarily a flaw. However, it became a defect and provided opportunities for corrupt officials when it was handled without proper techniques and experience. Third, surcharges were a serious flaw of the early Ch'ing tax system. Despite repeated imperial prohibition, the local government overtaxed the people, especially the small taxpayers, on various pretexts, and the surcharges were even higher than the regular levies.

The effects of these flaws on the early Ch'ing tax system are apparent. They were exemplified by the Taxation Case, the *cause célèbre* of 1661, in which many members of the Kiangsu gentry were involved and severely punished for their tax delinquency. Because the case resulted not only from the self-seeking disposition of the gentry members but also from the intrinsic flaws of the tax system, no punishment could effectively stop the cases of tax evasion or delinquency that were rampant throughout the K'ang-hsi period. It is therefore clear that the tax reform of the Yung-cheng period was a timely action.

The tax reform was the most complicated and salient of all the measures enforced by the Yung-cheng Emperor for the public welfare. Tax evasion or delinquency ran counter to the law, and in either case the self-seeking gentry and big landlords were the major offenders. As in the case of the emancipation of the outcast people, and in that of the self-seeking gentry, the basic issues were again justice and equality, which are the basis of the law. Under the tax reform, the gentry and big landlords were held responsible for the taxes levied on them, while the local government was prohibited from shifting taxes onto the common people. Like the conservation and reclamation projects, tax reform was a positive measure to improve the welfare of the common people. It reduced the tax burden on small taxpayers, relieved the landless peasants of the labor-service levy, and strengthened the local granary system (which will be discussed below). At the same time, because it reduced the cases of tax evasion, delinquency, and other related evils, it led to an increase in the number of taxpayers and thus contributed to the state income.

In general, the tax reform of the Yung-cheng period (1) reduced and legalized the meltage fee (*huo-hao*) and some customary gratuities (*kuei-fei*), and (2) merged the labor-service levy with the land tax. These two aspects were carried on side by side in the first half of the era.

For better comprehension of the problem a technical explanation of some special terms is in order. The meltage fee might have begun, as the term suggests, when silver became the chief currency of the state budget and income. Some scholars traced its origin back to the Ming dynasty or even earlier.[82] At any rate, the rise of the meltage fee was at first demanded by necessity. In the course of payment, taxpayers were allowed to hand in copper coins or fragmentary pieces of silver, but the local government had to send large pieces of silver, in ingots or shoes, to the provincial administration and, by order, to the imperial treasury. As a result, it was necessary to exchange copper coins for silver, and finally, melt all silver fragments into large pieces. Since a certain percentage of silver was lost in the melting process, this wastage was referred to as *huo-hao*. Because loss of this sort was not officially deductible from the required tax quotas, the local government collected extra charges, together with the land and labor-service tax, to meet this loss. Extra charges for this purpose were commonly called *huo-hao*, *huo-hao yin* (silver for meltage), *chia-hao yin* (extra charge for meltage), or sometimes *hao-hsien*—which originally meant a surplus from the meltage fee.[83]

The term *hao-mi* (rice wastage) was similarly derived. Because the tax in kind, such as the grain tribute, was also subject to a sort of wastage from transit or storage, the local government collected from it the rice wastage. The surplus from the rice wastage was called *hsien-mi*, but it occasionally appeared in private and official accounts as identical with *hao-mi*. Apparently, the term *huo-hao* was broad enough to cover various forms of extra charges, and so was *hao-hsien*.

The customary "gratuities," in the guise of gifts or auxiliary funds, were required by almost all offices, central and local, for personal or budgetary use. They passed not only from private individuals to certain special offices, but also from subordinate to superior offices. Gifts of money were variously designated as birthday gifts (*shou-li*), festival gifts (*chieh-li*), or seasonal gifts (*chi-kuei*), all presented by individuals in subordinate positions to their superiors. In like manner, a superior office obtained from offices subordinate to it auxiliary funds variously called: money for scale balance (*p'ing-kuei* or *k'u-p'ing yin*), salt gratuity (*yen-kuei*), gratuity of grain tribute (*ts'ao-kuei*), customs gratuity (*shui-kuei*), among others. Actually there was no definite distinction between gifts and auxiliary funds, both of which were loosely referred to in private and official records as *kuei-fei* or *kuei-li*. Tips were another category of customary gratuities required by the personal secretaries, clerks, runners, and servants in provincial and local governments.[84] They seem to have been popular among the unclassified personnel and more personal than the above-mentioned customary gratuities. However, in a broad sense, there was no fundamental difference between tips and customary gratuities, both being generally known as vile practices (*lou-kuei*).

In operation, the process of sending and accepting customary gratuities began in the administrative units—such as district, department, or subprefecture governments, salt offices, customs houses, offices of river intendants, and grain tribute offices—that directly administered the land and labor-service taxes, salt distribution, customs duties, river works, and grain tribute. Since magistrates of the district, department, and subprefecture governments collected the land and labor-service taxes that made up the principal revenues of dynasties, they played the most important role in this process. They sent gifts and auxiliary funds to their direct superior, prefect or subprefect, who in turn did the same with regard to his superior. Thus the local phase of this process finally stopped in the office of the provincial governor or governor-general.

In the operation of the customary gratuities the provincial administration connected the local and central phases. After receiving the customary gifts or auxiliary funds from its subordinate units, the provincial government sent the board fee (*pu-fei*) or the food cost (*fan-shih yin*) to the related boards or some other offices in the central government, such as the Censorate. Owing to their special functions, the superintendent of customs and the intendants of salt, river, and grain also sent the customary money to the central government. In short, almost every office had its share of customary gratuities. Even the provincial director of studies, the Tartar general, the provincial commander-in-chief, and the brigadier-general each had a share.[86] Thus the customary gratuities connected and supplied the whole bureaucratic structure, central and local, and in effect became an operational force behind the ruling machinery.

The meltage fee and the customary gratuities were closely interrelated. From the meltage fee that he collected, the magistrate paid the customary gratuities. Nevertheless, it would be a mistake to identify them as one and the same because the meltage fee generally covered only a large part of the required customary gratuities, a certain amount of which was from other sources. For example, some small districts or departments were assigned almost negligible tax quotas; the meltage fee that they might collect was necessarily small, even less than 100 taels of silver,[87] not nearly enough to pay off the customary gratuities to their superior offices. They therefore had to depend generally on two additional sources. In one case, they charged all the taxpayers with the customary gratuities in addition to the meltage fee, or they collected these charges from mercantile ships, fishing boats, pawnshops, salt merchants, and others.[88] In the other case, they made up the customary gratuities by means of gifts or contributions from salt merchants, deduction of salaries and wages from bureaucrats and unclassified personnel, or even embezzlement from official funds. In the final analysis, the meltage fee and the customary gratuities were similar in function and source. Both were charged to the people and were a sort of official corruption.

The meltage fee and the customary gratuities proved to be heavy burdens to the people. Their rates varied according to locality and were conditioned by two factors:
(1) The local tax quota formed an inverse ratio to their rates. Southern Kiangsu, for instance, was far richer and had a larger tax quota than its northern counterpart; its meltage fee reached 8-10 percent of the regular tax, in contrast to a rate of 15.6-17.8 percent in northern Kiangsu.[89] The local governments

in Shansi and Shensi collected a meltage fee of as much as 20-30 percent because these two provinces were noted for their poverty and were charged with small tax quotas.[90]
(2) The more avaricious officials could raise rates in spite of factors such as the tax quota, precedents, and so on. Yingte, an average district in Kwangtung, was subject to an extremely high meltage fee at a rate of 80-90 percent during the K'ang-hsi period.[91] Although the meltage fee and the customary gratuities were collected irregularly, even when their rates were low they were the financial plague of the people.

In spite of the repeated prohibitions of the Manchu government prior to the Yung-cheng period, the local administrators persistently collected the fee and required the gratuities. An examination of the problem suggests that, besides the bureaucratic conduct and the weak points of the tax system, two other factors made these extra charges inevitable. Overcentralization of the traditional Chinese bureaucratic structure seems to have contributed greatly to this situation. Overcentralization meant that the most qualified bureaucrats and the largest portion of tax flowed to the central government. Without sufficient money and staff, the local governments were reduced to being mere agents of the central administration and were destined to have trouble. To keep the administrative machinery working, they needed more funds and personnel than had been officially allowed to them; to smooth out the administrative process, they found gifts and auxiliary funds necessary. In this situation, the meltage fee and the customary gratuities became indispensable.

Poor pay for officials during the early Ch'ing was also a factor that perpetuated the fee and the gratuities. During the founding of the dynasty, the banner troops depended upon plunder and the banner lands. Although the regime introduced a pay system after its conquest of China, official salaries were inadequate and the system was insignificant. Bannermen still drew their incomes largely from the banner land and from occasional pillages in their campaigns against Chinese resistance. Chinese bureaucrats received even lower pay than their Manchu colleagues. To make matters worse, the Manchu government reduced and postponed payment of official salaries when its treasury was almost exhausted by military operations in the years 1644-1683. From 1675 on, for instance, it did not pay official salaries for five years.[92] No doubt, low pay, reduction of salaries, or arrears in payment drove officials to collect the meltage fee and the customary gratuities. This can be well proved by two reputable officials of the time. Lu Lung-ch'i (1630-1693), famed for his impartiality and incorruptibility, collected the meltage fee at a rate of 4 percent of the regular tax when he was a magistrate in Kiangsu; Shen Chinssu (1671-1728), a high official opposed to the legalization of the meltage fee, confessed his collection of it at a lower rate when he was a local administrator.[93] In short, these extra charges were so deeply related to practical problems that no bans could be effective. Obviously, there had to be a rational solution, and the Yung-cheng Emperor's approach was just that.

He moved step by step to solve the problem of the meltage fee and the customary gratuities. His first act was to end the state deficit and tax delinquency by founding the Office of Audit (*Hui-k'ao fu*) that approved or rejected provincial financial reports and checked the expenditures of the central government.[94] At the same time he reformed the customs offices, which were notorious for their corruption and had long been the source of spoils for the Manchus of the Imperial Household. Since the K'ang-hsi period these offices had gradually been taken over by the provincial government; by early 1723 most of them were under provincial governors, and shortly afterwards each office was ordered to make public its tax schedule, which had been kept secret and therefore manipulated by collectors.[95] Because all these changes involved financial administration and tax collection, they strengthened the Yung-cheng Emperor's determination to deal with the meltage fee and the customary gratuities. For example, the emperor prohibited provincial officials and officers from sending gratuities to the related boards in the central government, after establishing the Office of Audit, which operated, in addition to its other functions, as an incorruptible model for the imperial administration.[96]

As Yung-cheng resolutely pushed through his financial reform, some state and provincial administrators responded enthusiastically to the imperial action. Yang Tsung-jen (1659-1725), governor-general of Hunan and Hupei, permitted the magistrates to collect the meltage fee at a rate of 10 percent, but prohibited all gratuities or other extra charges.[97] Among other early respondents to the imperial reform were Shih I-chih, a high official in the central government, and Shih Wen-ch'o (d.1735), governor of Honan. While the former petitioned the throne for the legalization of all kinds of meltage fees and gratuities in the provinces, the latter made receipt of gratuities punishable and set 13 percent as the rate of the meltage fee, which was used to make up the provincial deficit and cover other public expenses.[98] Soon high administrators in Hopei and Yunnan, such as Li Wei-chün (d. ca. 1727), Li Wei, and Yang Ming-shih, followed suit. They all worked toward legalizing the meltage fee and reducing the extra charges that small taxpayers had to bear, but they did not grasp the major point of the problem. Because they failed to understand the functional relationship between the meltage fee and the customary gratuities, they let the local government keep the meltage fee it had collected. As long as the local administrators held this fee, they had to send gratuities to their superior officials, who had no opportunity to collect extra charges directly from the people and thus needed gifts and auxiliary funds from subordinates. Where the local government sent gifts and auxiliary funds to their superiors, there the people paid more extra charges. Beyond question this was not the point of the Yung-cheng Emperor's reform.

Of all provincial administrators, No-min, governor of Shansi, made the greatest contribution towards finally solving the problem of the meltage fee and the customary gratuities. Owing to the shortage of reputable documents, only an outline of his program can be drawn for discussion.[99] Unlike many other officials, he seems to have perceived the interrelation between the meltage fee and the customary gratuities, and looked for a double-edged knife to cut the complicated knot. Finally he found it in his effort to make up the Shansi provincial deficit by requiring the magistrates and the related administrators to hand over the meltage fee which they collected to the provincial treasury for centralized management under his supervision. Because this measure was adoped by the throne, it needs some elaboration.

The serviceability of No-min's measure lay in the fact that it separated management from collection of the meltage fee. Without management of it, the magistrates and other collectors gained no direct profit from overloading the people with the fee; nor did they have resources for use as gifts and auxiliary funds for their superior administrators, as they had through their free management of the fee. In other words, gifts and auxiliary funds no longer were a sufficient excuse for increasing the meltage fee.

Another advantage of No-min's approach was his stress on centralized management. Through it the governor was able to use the meltage fee more effectively by having a complete scheme based on public and personal needs in the province; with the support of his associate, Kao Ch'eng-ling (d. ca. 1752), he succeeded in making up the provincial deficit and assigning the remainder of the meltage fee as fringe benefits for officials throughout the province. When superior officials had benefits from the meltage fee in this way, they had no excuse for requiring gifts or auxiliary funds from their subordinates, who received their share through the same management. Considering all its advantages, No-min's measure represented a rational approach to the problem. Although it did not remove all extra charges from the people, it did reduce them.

The problem of the meltage fee and the customary gratuities became a state issue in early 1724. Because the program that No-min carried on in Shansi had invited both opposition and support,[100] it became the subject of a special court meeting. According to the various opinions, the discussants fell into four groups:[101] (1) courtiers who preferred to have the meltage fee collected at a uniform rate; (2) those who proposed that the district and departmental governments keep what they needed from the meltage fee and hand over only the remainder to the provincial treasury; (3) some cautious officials, who believed that before extending it to the whole country, the project should be tried only in Shansi; and (4) some discussants who doubted the possibility of making it a permanent policy. An analysis of the arguments indicates that the controversy actually represented the long-term tension between Confucianism and Legalism. Opponents of the project were more likely to be those scholar-officials who had little insight into the problem, were dogmatically attached to the Confucian principle, or were concerned with personal interests. Shen Chin-ssu, for instance, raised objection to the project for the sake of the Confucian political ideal. Supporters of this program were men such as T'ien Wen-ching, Li Wei, and No-min, to mention a few, who followed the imperial interest and worked hard to solve the problem. It was through the insistence of the emperor that the approach of No-min and Kao Ch'eng-ling was adopted as a principle for handling the meltage fee. This adoption virtually legalized the meltage fee.

Legalization of the meltage fee was completed throughout the empire during the years 1723-1729. In general, there developed two types of management, complete and partial.[102] With complete management some provincial governments followed exactly the approach of No-min, in which all the meltage fee was taken from its collecting offices and sent to the provincial treasury. The provincial administration, which preferred partial management, allowed its magistrates or other collecting offices to keep a part of the fee according to their needs. Table 5 shows the chronological order of the change in various places.

Table 5*

Dates for Legalization of
the Meltage Fee

Beginning Date	Names of Province
1723	Shansi
1724	Chekiang (?), Honan, Hopei (?), Shantung
1725	Kansu, Kweichow
1726	Shensi, Szechwan (?)
1727	Kiangsi, Yunnan
1728	Hunan (?), Hupei (?), Kiangsu, Kwangsi (?), Kwangtung
1729	Anhwei, Feng-t'ien (?), Fukien,

*Sources: based on the *CYPC*; for the case of Shensi, see *KCT*, the joint memorial of Shih I-chih and Sose, p. 2, May 8, 1734. This table is somewhat different from those in Abe Takeo, "Kōsen teikai no kenkyū," p. 228, and Wang Yeh-chien, "Ch'ing Yung-cheng shih-ch'i (1723-1735) ti ts'ai-cheng kai-ke," pp. 65-66. However, in some dates Abe and Wang differ from each other.

After its legalization, a meltage fee of 10-30 percent of the regular taxes was generally collected. The new rates were lower than the old ones; this can be seen in Table 6.

Table 6*

Percentage of the Meltage Fee before and after Its Legalization

	Meltage Fee Collected as Percentage of the Regular Taxes		
	Old Rate	New Rate**	
Name of Province		Nominal	Actual
Anhwei	?	10%	10+% (?)
Chekiang	5-8%	5-10%	8-14%
Chihli (Hopei)	7-15%	7-12%	7-12%
Fukien	10-17%	10%	14%
Honan	18-20%	14-15%	11-17%
Hunan	?	10%	10+%
Hupei	?	10%	14-15%
Kansu	?	10-20%	17+-22+%
Kiangsi	10%	10%	10% (?)
Kiangsu	6-10+%	10%	10+%
Kwangsi	?	?	10-10.5%
Kwangtung	20+%	10%	20%
Kweichow	20-50%	20%	10-20%
Shansi	30-40%	13%	13-20%
Shantung	20-30%	16-18%	16%
Shensi	?	20%	20% (?)
Szechwan	30-50%	30%	30%
Yunnan	?	10%	10+%

*Sources: *CPYC*. Cf. Abe Takeo, "Kōsen teikai no kenkyū," p. 228; Wang Yeh-chien, "Ch'ing Yung-cheng shih-ch'i (1723-1735) ti ts'ai-cheng kai-ke," pp. 65-66; *Ch'in-ting ta-Ch'ing hui-tien*, "Shih-li," ch. 139, pp. 9-15. For comparison, one may see the latest, and perhaps the most detailed, study in Saeki Tomi, "Shindai Yosei chō ni okeru yōrengin no kenkyū—chihō zaisei no seiritsu o megutte" ('A study on the yang-lian-yin at the Yong-zheng period, Qing dynasty'), *Tōyōshi kenkyū* 30. 4:55-58 (March 1972).

**This new rate should be divided into two categories, nominal and actual. The nominal rate was set by the provincial government after legalization of the meltage fee, but with only a few exceptions it was, in actual collection, higher than what was officially regulated.

Since data were insufficient and the rates of the meltage fee varied from place to place even in the same province, the above table is a general indication of the reduction of the meltage fee. The general tendency in the table was verified by Ch'ien Ch'en-ch'ün (1686-1744), then a junior vice-president of the Board of Punishments, when the problem of the meltage fee again became an issue in 1742.[103]

With the legalization of the meltage fee the customary gratuities were reduced. Provincial governments developed various practices to deal with these extra charges: (1) renunciation of all customary gratuities, (2) renunciation of most items that belonged to customary gratuities, and (3) reduction of the customary gratuities rate or its partial legalization together with the meltage fee.[104] Between 1724 and 1729 almost all provincial governments made an effort to reduce or stop the customary gratuities. Perhaps some figures will be helpful for explanation of this development. Table 7 includes the amount of customary gratuities annually received by some high provincial administrators before legalization of the meltage fee.

Table 7*

Annual Customary Gratuities Received
by Some High Provincial Officials

Name of Province	Official Title	Amount of annual gratuities in taels of silver
Kiangsi, Kiangsu and Anhwei	Governor-general	43,700
Honan	Governor	200,000
Kiangsi	Lieutenant-governor (Financial commissioner)	40,000
Chekiang	Judicial Commissioner	26,677

*Source: *CPYC*, v. 1, Memorials of Fan Shih-i, p. 25, April 25, 1728; v. 29, Memorials of T'ien Wen-ching, p. 61, March 8, 1725; v. 48, Memorials of Shih Ch'eng-o, p. 45; v. 18, Kan Kuo-k'uei, p. 100, Jan. 8, 1725.

Among its many functions the legalized meltage fee provided regular extra stipends for provincial administrators, who were now strictly prohibited from accepting any customary gratuities from their subordinates.[105] It is true that, despite imperial orders, some bureaucrats still collected the gratuities, but these gratuities were reduced to a reasonable extent, as a high official of the time testified.[106]

The legalization of the meltage fee was an administrative and financial reform of great help to local affairs, state finance, officials of provincial and local governments, as well as to the common people. Because the meltage fee was collected from particular localities, the emperor insisted that the provincial government should use it for the good of the people instead of wasting it or sending it to the imperial treasury. This encouraged local public projects. For instance, in the province of Shensi the legalized meltage fee financed the construction of more than 400 community granaries; in Honan, it helped build 7,127 storerooms to keep public grain for the local people.[107]

The legalized meltage fee also relieved the provincial government's financial difficulties. With centralized management of the meltage fee, the provincial government was able to make a fund pool to meet the financial needs of administration such as the deficit, additional expenditure, emergency funds, and the like. Considering its financial significance to the provincial administration, it is no exaggeration to say that the legalized meltage fee functioned to a certain extent as a countervailing force to overcentralization, which tended to draw off financial resources and talented people from the provincial government. In like manner, the legalized fee greatly helped stabilize state finance, which relied upon the provincial coffers. Any deficits in the provincial account (frequent in the K'ang-hsi period) drained funds from the tax quotas required by the central government. The legalized meltage fee provided funds to make up provincial deficits, and this consolidated state income.

The legalized meltage fee supplied the funds for the supplementary salary for officials, known as *yang-lien yin*, literally, "extra stipends for the cultivation of incorruptibility." From 1723 onward, provinces one after another appropriated a large part of the legalized meltage fee as extra stipends to provincial officials, and this practice became well established in the whole country after 1728. They received their additional pay according to their ranks, positions, and localities where they served. In general, the extra stipends were several times their regular salaries. The maximum amount for a governor-general, for instance, might reach 30,000 taels of silver or more; the minimum amount was something under 10,000 taels.[108] The supplementary salary for magistrates was in the range of 500-2,000 taels. Yung-cheng even appropriated funds from regular taxes to cover the extra stipends for those places where the meltage fee was negligible.[109]

The system of extra stipends operated not only to relieve the provincial and local bureaucrats from their personal financial difficulties but to help them solve their financial problems with private assistants including personal secretaries (*mu-k'e* or *mu-pin*), clerks (*shu-li*), runners (*ya-i*), and servants (*ch'ang-sui*).[110] Their number varied with the individual locality. A magistrate of a busy district needed about ten personal secretaries and several hundred clerks, while that of a remote and small county had only two or three secretaries and a few score of clerks. Their service was indispensable to the various levels of administration in the province, but they were also a source of trouble to provincial and local governments in two ways. First, many of them were corrupt and oppressive, and they were largely responsible for many evils in local administration. Second, they were not on the government payroll, so, theoretically, they depended upon the administrators whom they served. In fact, however, they obtained incomes through various illegal means, of which the meltage fee and gratuities were the most important. Because the problem that they presented was related to the whole dynastic administrative structure, no simple imperial order would be effective enough to solve it.

The legalized meltage fee was perhaps the most effective of the measures that Yung-cheng had adopted to solve the problem. For instance, he ordered that personal assistants be carefully selected and properly employed, forbade their unlawful activities, and even allowed provincial governors and governors-general to recommend their meritorious personal secretaries for official appointment.[111] Nevertheless, none of these measures was as effective as the legalized meltage fee, which touched the crux of the problem—the financial aspect. Through the extra stipends the legalized meltage fee enabled important provincial and local administrators to pay their personal staff. In some cases the fund pool resulting from the legalized meltage fee directly furnished salaries for the personal assistants.[112]

In a different way, the extra stipends helped the provincial military officers, who were under the same financial pressure and needed private assistants as did the civilians. As soon as the meltage fee was legalized, the Yung-cheng Emperor granted these provincial military commanders the privilege of keeping some soldier vacancies in the army for their personal assistants. Table 8 indicates the number of soldier vacancies assigned to the officer of each level.

Table 8*

Extra Stipends for Officers in the Provincial Army

Military rank	Number of vacancies
Commander	80
Brigade-General	60
Colonel	30
Lt. Colonel	20
Major	15
First Captain (*Tu-ssu*)	10
Second Captain (*Shou-pei*)	8
Lieutenant	5
Sub-Lieutenant (*Pa-tsung*)	4

*Sources: Wang Ch'ing-yün, *Hsi-ch'ao chi-chêng* or *Shih-chü yü-chi* (A record of our prosperous dynasty), (1898 ed.), ch.2, p. 29.

At first all these vacancies were counted as infantrymen whose rations were less than those of the cavalrymen. After 1730 they were counted as half-infantrymen and half-cavalrymen.[113] Although these vacancies had no relationship to the legalized meltage fee, their operation doubtlessly ensured successful application of the system of extra stipends, which was devised to eliminate official corruption and facilitate provincial administration.

Finally, the system of extra stipends was extended to cover the officials of the central government who had unexpected expenses and occasionally needed the service of personal secretaries. They were also underpaid, and never before 1725 had they been fully paid. For example, the Chinese official was given, besides regular pay, bushels (hu) of rice corresponding to the number of taels of silver he received as salary. But, in practice, if his salary was 180 taels of silver, he received only 24, instead of 180, bushels of rice. These facts explain why many officials in the central government required, with various excuses, gifts and auxiliary funds from provincial administrators. By 1725 the emperor gave the Chinese officials the actual numbers of bushels of rice their salary warranted and even doubled the pay for some busy presidents and vice-presidents of the Six Boards.[114] Later on he appropriated funds from the state treasury as extra stipends to officials in the central government. Their extra stipends were in general smaller than those for provincial administrators, but they rounded out the supplementary salary system from Peking to the provinces. While the extra stipends and soldier vacancies in provinces were meant to stop maladministration from the bottom, the supplementary salary for officials in the central government was designed to ward off corruption from the top.

The legalization of the meltage fee was a reform unprecedented in the early Ch'ing. Because it was important to both the people and the state, the emperor made an effort to keep it going, although his final goal was to do away with all sorts of extra levies on the people. Close supervision was one of his many measures. For example, the provincial authorities had to send to the Board of Revenue detailed reports about the management of the meltage fee. To make the system work, he decreed in 1729 that on no account would the meltage fee be exempted, even when the regular taxes were remitted, and by 1735 he introduced a kind of audit system to check provincial management of the legalized meltage fee.[115] Nevertheless, all his efforts ended with his death. A few years after his death the meltage fee problem caused another great debate in the court; roughly after the mid-eighteenth century, local bureaucrats gradually collected new extra charges in addition to the legalized meltage fee, despite imperial prohibition.

There were at least three reasons why it was difficult to halt the meltage fee and gratuities. First, self-seeking officials preferred free collection of extra charges to the legalized meltage fee. Even in the Yung-cheng period, a few provincial officials still accepted gratuities at their own risk, and some provincial governors lavishly spent the legalized meltage fee for private purposes.[116] This tendency was more marked in the Ch'ien-lung period. Second, the problem of extra charges manifested the Legalist-Confucian tension, or the monarchical-bureaucratic conflict, and it required of the ruler energetic and persistent efforts to carry out his decision. At first the Ch'ien-lung Emperor followed his father's policy toward the extra charges, then he turned his attention to military exploits, and finally he became lax in his surveillance over provincial and local administrators, who collected extra charges as they saw fit.

Third, political overcentralization was an important factor in accounting for the difficulty of eliminating the meltage fee and customary gratuities. Although the legalized meltage fee helped improve the financial situation and facilitated the working of provincial administration, it did not change the power relations between central and provincial governments. In other words, the basic structure and process of provincial administration remained the same, and, without a sufficient budget, the provincial administrators needed the meltage fee and the customary gratuities. Under strong central guidance, they reduced the extra charges as required; as soon as supervision from the top loosened, they returned to free collection of the meltage fee, gifts, and auxiliary funds.

The merger of the labor-service levy ($ting$ tax) with the land tax was no less important to the people than the legalization of the meltage fee. They were carried on in the same situation and for the same purpose. The labor-service impost was closely associated with the land tax; both shared the same internal weaknesses. The labor-service impost was based on the male adults of 16-60 sui, who were necessary for farm labor. Thus, it was unfavorably viewed by peasants—who formed the majority of the country's population and for productive purposes liked to increase the number of male adults in families—more than any other status group. When combined with tax and administrative evils, it became a dead load on peasants, especially the landless who had to pay the same impost. The labor-service levy was also a problem to the government. Because it was based on the *ting* returns, which were more liable to change or abuses than were the land registers, it presented more administrative difficulty to the government than did the land tax.

The merger of the *ting* tax with the land levy first appeared as a reform to equalize the labor-service impost on a local scale early in the K'ang-hsi period.[117] This reform relieved peasants of an unfair burden and in the long run increased state income, but it failed to elicit a nationwide response. An important stage came in 1712 when the K'ang-hsi Emperor set the *ting* returns of 1711—the fiftieth anniversary of his reign—as the permanent basis for computing the labor-service tax, without consideration of any later increase.[118] Although K'ang-hsi's act was commended in many contemporary and later works as a great imperial benefaction, it was actually a realistic political move. Because of poor demographic techniques and taxation and administrative evils, the Manchu government was unable to achieve accurate registers of the male adults, some of whom ran away in order to evade the labor-service tax. With the *ting* returns fixed on a permanent basis, the male adults could be consolidated into the regular labor army to help rural rehabilitation—an important imperial project. Whatever motivated the emperor's decision, it gave rise to two problems which made necessary the merger of the labor-service levy with the land tax. First, after the registers of male adults had been fixed, the labor-service tax lost its traditional importance as a separate levy. Second, there was a technical problem. In 1711 *ting* returns were permanently fixed as far as state and provincial accounts were concerned, but the number of male adults in a household, a village, or a district fluctuated for various reasons. In cases where a household or district had fewer male adults than its 1711 register, the difference had to be made up by the family or place that happened to have more than the original number assigned to it that same year. Because this frequently caused difficulty and abuses, in 1716 a censor petitioned the throne to include the labor-service levy in the land tax.[119] Although the proposal did not meet with the imperial sanction, Kwangtung and Szechwan provincial authorities happened to carry out what it suggested. This zone usually had one or more clerks (*li-shu* or *t'u-shu*), who helped the head prepare assessment, introduced the long process that ended in merger of the land and labor-service taxes.

In the Yung-cheng period Huang Ping, governor of Shantung, was the first provincial administrator who cried for the merger of these two taxes. He made the request to the throne in July 1723, and was followed by Li Wei-chün, then governor of Hopei, one month later.[120] Sensible and forceful, Li's petition invited more imperial attention and finally caused a debate in a court meeting in which Yung-cheng's determination won the day. With imperial sponsorship, province after province combined these two levies during the years 1723-1729. Because the economic situation and taxation practices differed from place to place and even in the same province, the merger was enforced largely on the district level. Shansi, for example, started in 1724, but a few of its districts did not complete the change until 1837. Kansu did not change at all because the amount of land and labor-service taxes was too small. Table 9 indicates the starting dates for the merger in various provinces.

Table 9*

Starting Dates of the Merger of the
Land and Labor-Service Taxes

Date of beginning	Name of province
1716-1722	Kwangtung, Szechwan
1723	Chihli, Shantung
1724	Shansi
1725	Yunnan
1726	Chekiang, Fukien
1727	Honan, Kansu, Kiangsi, Shensi
1728	Anhwei, Kiangsu, Kwangsi
1729	Hunan, Hupei

*Sources: *SYNK*, v. 10, p. 9, Aug. 10, 1726; *CSL*, YC, chs. 11, 24, 29, 51, 54, 64 and 79; Wang Ch'ing-yün, *Hsi-ch'ao chi-cheng*, ch. 3, pp. 24-28. Since Wang's book followed the traditional Chinese calendar, in many cases its dates differed from those supplied by *CSL*, YC. Cf. Ch'ü, *Local Government in China*, p. 286, n. 23.

On the whole, toward the end of the Yung-cheng period the great majority of districts had completed the merger in three ways:[121] (1) apportionment of the labor-service levy to the land tax on the per tael of silver basis; (2) apportionment of it to the land tax on the per *mou* basis; and (3) apportionment of it on the basis of per picul of grain as collected from the land tax, which was a practice followed by only a few districts in Szechwan, Hunan, and other provinces. Although the labor-service levy was converted to the land tax at various rates according to the local situation, the rates were generally in the range of from 1 percent to 30 percent of the land tax. After this merger, the landless peasants were free from the labor-service levy, which was consolidated with the land tax forever.

In addition to the above-mentioned changes, the tax reform of the Yung-cheng period also reduced the unfair tax quotas of the prefectures of Soochow and Sungkiang in Kiangsu and of Chia-hsing and Huchow in Chekiang. For centuries, inhabitants of these four places had paid an extremely high tax. According to a popular version, the high tax quotas were imposed on these inhabitants by the founder of the Ming dynasty as a form of punishment for their support of his opponent, Chang Shih-ch'eng (1352-1367), in the struggle for supremacy. Nevertheless, the high productivity of these prefectures was possibly a contributing factor to their high tax quotas. In the early Ch'ing period the people there repeatedly petitioned the throne for a reduction, but their appeals were unrewarded until the reign of Yung-cheng. In 1725 he reduced the quotas of Soochow and Sungkiang to a certain extent and those in Chekiang two years later.[122]

The tax reform enforced by the Yung-cheng Emperor also attempted to improve the organization of the units from which land and labor-service taxes were collected. In rural areas, these units appeared in two forms—the tithe (*chia*) including ten households under a head (*chia-chang* or *chia-shou*) and the zone (*li* or *t'u*), composed of 110 households also under a head (*chia-chang* or *chia-shou*) and the zone (*li* or *t'u*), composed of 110 households also under a head (*li-chang*). The heads served as government agents responsible for various aspects of the land tax and labor-service levy. As a large unit, the records, and many other things related to taxes in his zone. There were many cases in which he and his superior oppressed small taxpayers and profited through unlawful means. Because the clerks who prepared and kept tax records for their zones contributed even more to corrupt practices, many were unseated in 1734 by Yung-cheng.[123]

The emperor also tried to reorganize the zonal structure in accordance with the actual households in the villages so as to eliminate false registers.[124] It is difficult to make a full evaluation of this zonal reorganization owing to the lack of sources and also to the fact that these two categories of units officially ceased to perform tax registration after 1772.[125] But it is clear that such a change attempted to eliminate inaccurate land records and their implications.

4. *Summary*

How, then, does one evaluate the importance of the above measures? On the whole, they completed the course of economic rehabilitation that started in the K'ang-hsi era, consolidated its achievements, and led to the economic prosperity of the Yung-cheng period. The life of the populace and domestic commerce indicated the thriving economy of the period.

The common people in the Yung-cheng era had a better life than in preceding reigns. In other words, they reaped the fruit of autocratic rule because they and the ruler had, as in many other eras, worries in common. While the ruler was concerned about the political and social order under him, the common people were interested in a better life. But both were confronted by the self-seeking activities of corrupt officials, greedy gentry, and other lawbreaking individuals. Yung-cheng reforms aimed at stopping these activities; they represented not only the interest of the ruler but that of the common people. For example, emancipation of the degraded people, suppression of the self-seeking gentry, and punishment of corrupt officials were beneficial to the populace. The honors given to exceptional farmers were encouragement to the common people. Needless to say, the river works improved agricultural conditions, with which the common people were more concerned than were other social classes. Regardless of abuses inflicted by corrupt officials, reclamation projects increased opportunities for poor peasants.

The most remarkable of all the measures was perhaps the tax reform. The legalization of the meltage fee reduced the extra charges the people had to bear and made possible the supplementary stipends for bureaucrats so as to diminish cases of official corruption. Furthermore, the legalized meltage fee financed many public projects, notably the community, public, and ever-normal granaries (*she-ts'ang*, *i-ts'ang*, and *ch'ang-p'ing ts'ang*, respectively). As a result granaries, especially community ones, were found everywhere in the country, including Manchuria, Mongolia, Sinkiang, and Tibet.[126] Although individual donations and regular government budgets were important to the granary system, many community and public granaries owed their existence to the legalized meltage fee, those in Shensi and Honan, for example.[127] No matter how these granaries were financed, they served the welfare of the common people. Their importance may be considered together with the river projects; both were preventive measures. The river works helped reduce the danger of floods and droughts; the granaries functioned to provide for the emergency needs of the common people and to stabilize grain prices. These preventive projects might have been a reason for the fact that the period was almost free from serious natural calamities.

At the same time, the integration of the labor-service levy with the land tax freed the landless people from the labor-service tax and gave them more personal freedom. Free of that tax, they were no longer tied down to their native places, needed no more protection from local influential people, and were able to move from place to place seeking new opportunities.[128] Some scholars complain that the merger of these two taxes led to the neglect of a regular population census.[129] This complaint is far from justified because before the merger the regular population survey had never achieved accurate figures for reasons previously stated.

To sum up, the common people of the Yung-cheng period had fewer taxes to bear, were given more opportunities, and were aided by more public welfare measures than before. They probably became more law-abiding than the people under the two previous Manchu reigns. As a matter of fact, the Yung-cheng period did not see a serious peasant revolt, which well attests to the improvement in the common people's lives.

A discussion of the price of some major commodities of the Yung-cheng period will throw light on the common people's life. In general, prices of various commodities remained relatively stable throughout the Yung-cheng period. The price of rice was kept lower than in the K'ang-hsi period.[130] In most localities two bushels of rice cost less than one tael of silver; only in a few places did they occasionally reach a little more than two taels during the Yung-cheng era. In Shansi, for example, two bushels of rice did not go beyond two and a half taels and sometimes even dropped to below two taels, whereas under the K'ang-hsi reign their price always reached more than two taels and once a famine brought it up to four.[131] Various memorials in the *Chu-p'i yü-chih* indicated that in the Yung-cheng reign prices of wheat and millet did not suffer much fluctuation.

The relatively low cost of staples—rice and wheat—was of great benefit to the populace because the general cost of living remained low. Salt, for instance, stayed at a reasonable price level.[132] In Taiwan sugar makers sold their product at two and a half taels of silver for 100 catties in regular times, while in Hangchow, Chekiang, one ounce of raw silk cost less than one-tenth of a tael of silver.[133] The price of land kept pace with the costs of other commodities. In Kiangsu, for example, where the land usually cost little more than in other places, a farmer purchased one *mou* of fertile land for only two or three taels of silver—an amount much less than in the K'ang-hsi or Ch'ien-lung periods.[134] By contrast, labor was not too cheap. A skilled worker in Honan might obtain about two taels of silver for a month's labor; an ordinary laborer made half that amount.[135] In short, commodity prices of the Yung-cheng period appear to be a reliable index of the life of the populace of the time.

The remission and reduction of the land and labor-service taxes in the reign of the Yung-cheng Emperor also shed light on the life of the common people. Prior to the Yung-cheng period, the Manchu rulers frequently remitted or reduced these taxes from localities or provinces for three reasons: (1) poor harvest; (2) natural or human calamities; and (3) special imperial considerations. In contrast, the tax remission and reduction of the Yung-cheng period were distinguished by a new provision under which the provincial government might fill in, for its people, the regular tax quotas with the surplus from the legalized meltage fee. The emperor argued that because the surplus was derived from their previous tax payments, all the taxpayers of the place should have a share in it by paying less current levies. For this reason, in 1733 the provincial governments of Honan and Shantung paid part of their citizens' regular taxes with the surplus from the legalized meltage fee.[136]

All in all, under Yung-cheng the common people achieved better living conditions. Some of his measures received applause not only from his contemporaries, such as Ch'ien Ch'en-ch'ün, but from later generations. With favorable living conditions people enjoyed a longer life span. By 1726, for example, the people who were between seventy and a hundred years of age numbered as many as 1,421,652.[137] And this figure might have grown larger toward the end of the period. Their life was much better than that of their contemporaries in France under the reigns of Louis XIV and Louis XV, in Russia, or in Tokugawa Japan, and it could not have been worse than that of the poor in pre-Speenhamland England.[138]

Domestic commerce was another indicator of the economic prosperity of the Yung-cheng period. Like many other dynastic rulers in Chinese history, the emperor gave importance to agriculture, but many of his policies directly or indirectly encouraged domestic commerce. When he made efforts to improve the life of the peasants, he also took action to protect small merchants and traders. The latter's status was comparable to that of the former, who formed the majority of the population. Both fell easy prey to corrupt officials, the self-seeking gentry, and other influential people, and their conditions shared the same political and social implications for the imperial interest. Improvement of the life of the common people stimulated domestic commerce and trade.

Some factors were particularly important to the flourishing of domestic commerce. Peace and order, the most important of these factors, were the first concern of the Yung-cheng Emperor. The campaigns that he carried out against the Khoshotes and Dzungars in the northwest of China and the Miao tribes in the southwest were fundamentally short, small-scale wars which did not significantly interrupt the peace and order of the country. Furthermore, they were fought primarily to maintain the frontier peace and interior order. What he stressed throughout his reign was domestic peace and order, not military exploits. Compared with other eras of the Ch'ing dynasty, his reign was characterized by peace and order, which were indispensable not only to the improvement of the life of the peasants but to the activities of domestic commerce.

The second factor was his suppression of the self-seeking gentry and other influential people. Under tough provincial administrators and special commissioners, such as the inspector of morale and tax expediters, they had to perform their obligations as the law required and to conduct themselves as imperial orders suggested. In this situation they found less profit from their landed property, and some of them practically suffered bankruptcy.[139] The net result of this was to lower the price of land. For example, a native scholar of Kiangsu testified in the early Ch'ien-lung period that some descendants of the gentry and landlords in his district gave up their dream of an official career via the regular route and became merchants or hard-working farmers.[140] After the tax reform the landless people were exempted from the labor-service impost and had more freedom than before; some became small merchants and traders.[141] Whatever the reason, merchants and traders increased in number, and this led to more domestic commerce and trade.

The third factor was the various direct imperial measures for the protection of small merchants and traders. The administrative reform in the customs offices, as mentioned before, was one such measure. In the years 1733-1734 the emperor further prohibited malpractices in awarding licenses that affected small merchants throughout the country and removed duplicate taxation of marketers in Kweichow.[142] These measures helped not only small merchants and traders but peasants who formed the great majority of consumers. Another measure also favorable to domestic commerce was the increase of copper coins, which were more vital than silver to the daily life of the people. A shortage of copper coins had been a problem during the early Ch'ing. Yung-cheng prohibited counterfeiting and melting of copper coins, lowered the percentage of copper in coins, purchased copper utensils, and increased minting,[143] all contributing to mitigation of the copper currency problem. Although he did not entirely solve the problem, his measures improved the currency situation, stabilized commodity prices, and therefore enhanced commercial activities.

The emperor's office-purchasing policy served indirectly to encourage domestic commerce. As discussed in the preceding chapter, he made lower-level offices available to purchasers, originally as a check on scholar-officials. This induced some members of the gentry and landlords to engage in commerce or trade (when landed property yielded meager profits) so as to obtain money—which offered an access to official service. All these factors provided a favorable background for domestic commerce and trade of the time.

During the Yung-cheng period there was a variety of commercial activities. Merchants and traders traveled everywhere in the country. Their major activities might differ from region to region, but cotton and cotton cloth seem to have played a very important interregional role, with South China as the center. In Kiangsu, for example, farmers planted various kinds of cotton, and cotton culture became a major source of their incomes.[144] Merchants purchased cotton from one place, exchanged it for cloth in another, and sold the textile everywhere.[145] Hunan and Hupei were among other centers of cotton cloth, which was sold as far away as among the Miao tribes in the high mountains of Kweichow.[146] In all likelihood, Kwangtung was also a center of cotton industry of the time and its fabric trade became very prosperous in the Ch'ien-lung period; cotton merchants were equally active in some northern provinces.[147]

Brewing, which had been a prosperous business in the early Ch'ing, had become even more so by the Yung-cheng era. It was nationwide but centered in North China. In 1725 Yung-cheng revealed that there were about a thousand liquor stores in Mukden, and on various occasions he complained of the drunk and disorderly conduct of the Manchus.[148] The metropolitan area, where many Manchu bannermen were crowded, was probably another center of the prosperous brewing trade.

Because commerce prospered, farmers in some places, notably Wu-hsi, changed their subsistence crops to cash crops.[149] Copper mining in Yunnan attracted public and private attention at the time, and there the officials' memorials contained a great deal of information on the activities of miners.[150] True, the miners were simply poor people, not modern industrialists. Nonetheless, mining was a trade related to the entire economic situation. In brief, merchants and traders of the Yung-cheng period carried their goods from north to south, from west to east, and *vice-versa*, with Chinkiang in Kiangsu becoming a banking center and Hankow in Hupei a transportation center, where many boats waited for patrons.[151]

Two other facts illustrate the economic prosperity of the Yung-cheng period. (1) There were significant changes in the local administrative structure in interior and border provinces. Many local administrative units were raised from a lower level to an upper level; most commanderies (*wei*) and military posts (*so*) were abolished. Although a number of these transpositions took place for the sake of administrative convenience, some of them were undeniably adjustments to economic and population growth.[152] (2) State finances provided further evidence of economic prosperity. The state treasury had had only 17 million taels of silver at the end of the K'ang-hsi period; this amount rose to 50 million by 1727.[153] Personal frugality on the part of the Yung-cheng Emperor and his administrative efficiency resulted in this large deposit of silver; certainly the general economic growth in his reign contributed more to it. As a matter of fact, the glories of the Ch'ien-lung period were built on this economic foundation.

In short, Yung-cheng consolidated his power, improved state finance, and enhanced the common people's well-being. His rule was benevolent as well as autocratic.

X

Non-Han Ethnic Minorities: The Miao, Yao, and Lolo Tribes

1. *The Tribes and Their Geographic Distribution*

During the Yung-cheng period the non-Han ethnic groups did not escape the attention of the emperor. Their lives underwent great changes when the majority, Han Chinese and Manchus, were affected by his autocratic rule. Transformation of the lives of the non-Han ethnic minorities was another example of the imperial effort to achieve universal rule over all ethnic and regional groupings within the empire. Thus, a discussion of changes in the non-Han ethnic groups during the Yung-cheng era will help explore the dimensions of the autocracy of the time. China's borders have contained many non-Han ethnic groups, such as Mongols, Tibetans, Uighurs, and others, but this chapter considers only the Miao, Yao, and Lolo tribes, for they experienced the most significant changes.

In discussing the Miao, Yao, and Lolo peoples, one is confronted with ethnological problems. Since these problems are not the theme of this study, they will not be examined in great detail. What is presented in the following pages is a brief survey necessary for an understanding of the changes in these tribes.

Scholars differ over their ethnic origins. Although ancient Chinese sources failed to distinguish one group from another, they considered them different from the Han Chinese and recognized them as natives in China. This information later became the major source of local histories and special studies.[1] When the Chinese central government moved to Southwest China during the Sino-Japanese War (1937-1945), the local tribes, once neglected, became the favorite topics of many Chinese anthropologists. They applied modern scholarship to their work, published the results of their investigations, and encouraged later studies.[2] Almost all of these works tended to suggest that the tribesmen belong to a broad ethnological family not different from that of the majority of the Chinese people.[3] Of the Japanese scholars, Torii Ryūzō was the most famous pioneer on the subject. After field study in China he classified the Miao people in the Mongoloid family, especially its South Asian branch.[4] Western, in particular French, scholars described these tribes as early as the eighteenth century.[5] Some of their recent works analyze these non-Han ethnic groups on the basis of language instead of ethnic composition. One such work, for example, puts the Miao people in the Mon-Khmer group, the Yao in the Austronesians, and the Lolo in the Tibeto-Burman family.[6] After examining the above works, one may tentatively conclude that the Miao, Yao, and Lolo peoples are not migrants of foreign origin. In all likelihood, they and the Han Chinese are physically derived from the same broad ethnological family—the Mongoloid. The difference between them and the Han Chinese is cultural rather than racial.

With reference to the relations between the three groups and the Han Chinese, scholars also have reached no agreement. For lack of reliable evidence, it is generally impossible to decide when these non-Han ethnic minorities appeared in China. With the exception of two authors, most sources believe that they have inhabited China as long as the Han Chinese have. One of the former assigned seniority to the Han Chinese; the other argued that the Miao and Yao groups were earlier inhabitants of China.[7] Inasmuch as neither provides substantial evidence, their points of view are debatable. As to the earliest locations of the Miao, Yao, and Lolo tribes, almost all scholars regard the latter two groups as natives of South China, but their interpretations of the Miao people fall into two different categories. Ruey Yih-fu, a leading anthropologist, insists that the Miao moved to the south from North China, whereas others challenge that position and hold that they were from the beginning a people of South China.[8] Because these interpretations derived from painstaking studies based on written sources available today, unless there is archaeological evidence in the future, one will be unable to take issue with either side. However, all agree that the present geographic distribution of the three groups resulted from the constant pressure of the Han Chinese.

The intertribal relations of the Miao, Yao, and Lolo are also important to an understanding of the changes in their lives during the Yung-cheng period. With a few exceptions,[9] many sources, through historical, mythological, and cultural approaches, treat the Miao and Yao as two cognate groups with only regional differences. One account gives more detailed information about the Yao; according to it, they were Miao people who moved to Kwangtung and Kwangsi.[10] If this interpretation is valid, the Yao acquired their name from their locality rather than from their ethnic origin. In fact, these two tribes had many cultural characteristics in common.

In regard to their relations with the Lolo, there are two entirely different explanations. Traditional Chinese records tended to designate all non-Han ethnic groups in South China by terms such as barbarians (*man* or *man-i*), southern barbarians (*nan-man*), or Miao on different occasions, and consequently the three tribes appear as one and the same.[11] This has caused students a great deal of difficulty distinguishing the Miao and Yao from the Lolo people. Fortunately, recent works separate the former two from the latter, but this ethnic separation does not deny their intertribal relations. In some localities those two broad groups had a kind of cultural contact, which will be discussed below.

Since each of the Miao, Yao, and Lolo peoples appeared in many subgroups with different names, the intratribal relations are as confusing as other problems about them. For instance, one may obtain from various sources more than a hundred names for the Miao, several scores of names for the Yao, and more than ninety names for the Lolo.[12] The long list of names puzzles researchers, but it should be noted that all the subgroups and their designations within each tribe are regional and cultural, instead of ethnic. As two anthropologists point out, these ethnic groups have lived in less accessible mountainous areas, and within each of the three tribes there developed some special cultural traits.[13] This betrayed outside observers into considering them different groups and designating them in accordance with their dress, professions, areas of residence, and special customs. Although most of these traditional designations convey little academic meaning, some of them are of cultural significance.

In some recent works the Miao people are given only five names—"red," "blue," "white," "black," and "flowery," according to the colors of their clothes; more accounts mention the Yao with two general names, "indigenous" (*chen*) and "non-indigenous" (*chia*, the Han-Chinese adherent to Yao culture); and the Lolo are frequently referred to as "black," or original, and "white," or adherent.[14] These designations are simple and practical enough to describe relations within each tribe, but they indicate little connection between them and the majority of the Chinese. In terms of Chinese cultural influence, each of the three tribes may be classified as "unassimilated" (*sheng*) or "assimilated" (*shu*). In view of their political relations with the Han Chinese, they may be divided into "uncontrolled" and "controlled" subgroups. The uncontrolled always identified themselves with the unassimilated, while the controlled with the assimilated. As in many other eras, the unassimilated groups were the central object of imperial concern during the Yung-cheng period.

In a broad cultural context, the Miao, Yao, and Lolo peoples shared some common traits that marked them as distinct from the majority of the Chinese people.[15] Most of these people were mountaineers, chiefly dependent upon primitive farming followed by pasturing and hunting. They carried on barter trade in fairs. Inasmuch as they were confined to mountains and hills, their settlements were small and scattered. This situation thwarted the attempts of many dynasties in Chinese history to bring them under effective control; it also handicapped the people themselves in their attempts to establish any kind of formal political organization on a permanent basis. On the contrary, they made the patrilineal clan an important social unit, whose leadership stressed personal ability more than other qualifications. Their religious beliefs were primitive. Even today they still worship various spirits, and wizards became influential individuals in their communities.

To a certain extent, these three tribes shared some common cultural traits. Because of the general geographic conditions, contacts between different tribes were likely to be difficult to maintain to any large extent. Intertribal relations were limited largely to the regions where different tribes were interspersed. Since the Miao and Yao were cognates, there were more contacts between them. Many traditional accounts and recent studies, for example, confirm that a number of Miao and Yao groups shared the practice of shifting cultivation.[16] The torch festival, a harvest celebration marked by singing, dancing, feasting, sacrifice-offering, and torch-lighting, was popular among many tribal communities in southwest China.[17] This festival might not have originated in any of these communities, but it undoubtedly took root among them through intertribal contacts. Buddhism, practiced by some tribesmen including the Lolo and Miao, may serve as more evidence of these relations.[18]

Of the three tribes, the Lolo were perhaps the most advanced culturally. They possessed a written language of long history and used the scripts for religious purposes and emotional expression.[19] They also had a sort of semi-political organization of hereditary and socioeconomic nature. Like the Miao and Yao peoples, the Lolo were organized into clans. Unlike the former two tribes, they had long clung to a strict three-level class system.[20] Their nobility consisted of the Black Bones (*He-i*, *Wu-man*, etc.), the commoners were the White Bones (*Po-i*, *Po-man*, and so forth), who rose from the originally conquered or kidnapped individuals, Han Chinese or others. At the bottom of this class hierarchy were slaves made up of the conquered or the kidnapped. Individuals of the lowest class might be admitted to the next group after generations of slavery, whereas the line between commoners and nobility could not be crossed. As nobles, the Black Bones were owners of land and slaves, and they maintained their genetic purity by clan exogamy within the same class. With this socioeconomic strength the Black Bones were a hereditary leading class.

The Black Bones were also politically dominant over the other two groups. Although the Lolo did not develop any large-scale political organization, their settlements were headed by individual Black Bones according to their personal ability and status within the class. Further, they were, as a whole, landlords and protectors of the other two classes. In time of emergency, the Black Bones supplied commanders for a temporarily organized army.[21] As long as they were necessarily the leaders in peacetime and wartime, they formed a hereditary ruling class. Thus the class system of the Lolo was more or less an informal political organization.

During the Yung-cheng period the Miao, Yao, and Lolo groups were scattered over a wide area loosely referred to as the Miao region (*Miao-chiang*) in some Chinese sources. This area roughly covered seven provinces: Hunan, Hupei, Kwangsi, Kwangtung, Kweichow, Szechwan, and Yunnan. Wherever they came from, they had been settled in these provinces for centuries. Their settling was largely determined by the geographic situation of this region, which is characterized by physical barriers such as hills and plateaus. Hunan and Hupei are noted for fertile plains, but they are also covered in great part by the central mountain belt. Kwangsi and Kwangtung are cut by intersecting mountain ranges. Yunnan and Kweichow form a plateau in southwest China, while Szechwan is the upper valley of the Yangtze River. In their long struggle with the Han Chinese, these ethnic minorities consistently retreated toward the less accessible mountainous regions, which were the only protection they could rely on.

It is very difficult to pinpoint the location of each minority subgroup since, in traditional Chinese accounts, there were too many subgroups under inconsistent names, and some of the groups changed their locations after the military campaigns during the Yung-cheng and Ch'ien-lung periods. In view of these difficulties, their geographic distribution will be discussed on a tribal basis. The Miao people had been crowded into the western part of Hunan and east and north Kweichow—on the whole, a hilly and densely forested interior that was identical, in a strict sense, with the Miao region of the Yung-cheng period. In addition to this center, small Miao groups appeared in southwestern Hupei and were also scattered along the Kwangsi-Kweichow border. The Yao people inhabited the mountainous land in northwestern Kwangtung and the great part of Kwangsi; some of their subgroups went across the provincial border and founded new settlements among the Miao in central Kweichow.[22]

The Lolo population was the largest of the three non-Han ethnic groups. Their settlements covered the widest area of the Yunnan-Kweichow plateau. In western Kweichow they became neighbors of the Miao groups; their fellow-tribesmen in Mt. Liang (*Liang-shan*) crossed the border of southern Szechwan to establish habitations in part of Sikang. They appeared almost everywhere in Yunnan and even lived in places close to various other ethnic groups, including those from across the national boundaries. Of this wide realm the Yung-cheng Emperor emphasized western Kweichow, eastern Yunnan, and southern Szechwan, thereby identifying what must have been the center of the Lolo people in the Yung-cheng period. The accompanying map indicates the distribution of the three tribes.

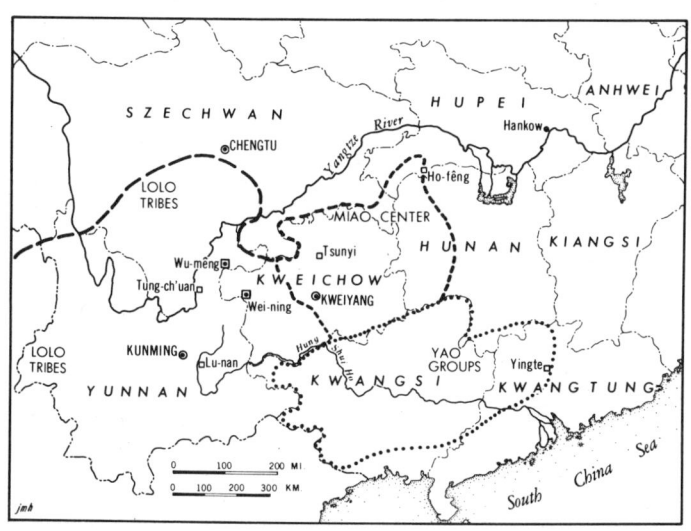

Distribution of the Miao, Yao, and Lolo
Tribes in Southwest China

------ Center of Miao tribes
_._._. Region of the Lolos
...... Sketchy boundary of Yao groups

· City
⊙ Provincial capital
□ District or department
⊡ Prefecture

2. *The Tribal Headman System*

The non-Han ethnic minorities in South China have played a considerable role in Chinese dynastic history. Almost every dynastic account has recorded their uprisings, some of which were of national significance. As the Han Chinese were forced to march steadily southward for political or economic reasons, they had more contact as well as conflict with the ethnic minorities. Control of these groups became a perennial problem for successive dynasties: many means for this purpose were devised but none worked effectively. After long evolution the tribal headman system was institutionalized during the Ming dynasty, and it was closely followed by the first two Manchu rulers. Inasmuch as various studies have thoroughly treated the organizational and functional aspects of the system,[23] the following few pages will analyze those facts that have not received due emphasis.

The tribal headman system was the most elaborate institution that China had developed for administering the non-Han ethnic groups in South China prior to the Yung-cheng period. Its elaborateness found expression in several respects. First, the system combined Confucian principle and utilitarian purposes. Because Confucianism distinguished Chinese from barbarians on the basis of culture, its early followers applied the same yardstick to divide China into five parts (*wu-fu*)—the remoter the part from the center of Chinese civilization, the lower the cultural level of the inhabitants. From this cultural viewpoint, early Confucian works referred to far-flung inhabitants as barbarians and allowed them autonomous status under Chinese suzerainty.[24] Therefore, these ideas recognized the difference in cultural levels between the Han Chinese and the non-Han ethnic groups and separated them by different administrative systems. These attitudes underlay dynastic governments' policies toward the non-Han ethnic minorities in South China. Provided these groups did not threaten the peace within the empire, they were permitted to go their traditional ways undisturbed and were exempted from obligations such as the land and labor-service taxes. The tribal headman system was the final expression of such ideas.

The tribal headmen system was elaborate also in its practical aspects.[25] Inasmuch as most of those non-Han ethnic regions in South China were hilly,

forested, humid, less productive, and difficult to
approach, their penetration by the regular Chinese
political system was hindered and dynastic rulers
were discouraged from bringing the regions under
their direct control. For the same reason scholar-
officials frequently tried to avoid accepting assignment to such regions even when the regular administrative system was introduced there. Furthermore, a
regular administrative establishment in a less
productive region did not always pay the cost of its
maintenance, to say nothing of providing the central
government with income. All these factors, then,
justified the tribal headman system, in which the
headmen, selected largely from the non-Han ethnic
groups, were entrusted with the administration of
their fellow-tribesmen and the maintenance of peace
in their domains. Evidently, this was the policy of
administering the barbarian through the barbarian, a
principle also applied by China to Westerners when
they came in the nineteenth century.

The selection and classification of headmen
revealed another aspect of the elaborateness of the
tribal administrative system. The headmen were chosen
primarily from the chiefs of the non-Han ethnic
groups, with emphasis on their personal conduct and
influence. Occasionally, headmen were selected from
those Chinese who had been living among, or close to,
ethnic groups, or whose ancestors had served as local
officials or officers to maintain peace and order in
the ethnic areas. The local administration made
preliminary selections, and the central government
gave the final approval. The headmen were classified, according to Chinese bureaucratic structure,
into three categories—civil, military, and
unclassed—and given titles and ranks suited to their
original status.[26]

Despite their official titles and ranks, the
headmen stood apart from regular bureaucrats. As
administrators of special ethnic groups, they generally were not allowed to serve in the regular administrative system, local or central.[27] Nor were they
permitted to have official ranks above the third
level in the bureaucratic hierarchy, however meritorious they were; whatever their official ranks,
they were subordinate to the authority of regular
local administrators. They were neither given salaries nor allowed to take the civil service examinations at the provincial level.[28] Nevertheless, they
enjoyed some privileges that were not available to

regular bureaucrats. Because they were not on the payroll, for example, they were not subject to salary forfeiture or reduction, a form of penalty applied to all regular officials. Furthermore, the office of headman was hereditary. Once appointed, he enjoyed the right to select any relative, male or female, as his successor and even if he were removed from office for punishment, his family still had the right to succession. With these inheritable privileges, the headmen became overlords of those under them. In short, the headman system was a special institution within a bureaucratic empire.

For dynastic rulers, the serviceability of the tribal headman system depended upon the means of control over the headmen. There were four means of control through the system itself, but they were relatively ineffective (see below). First, a control device operated through the regular bureaucratic channels. Because each of the ethnic regions in South China was under a local administrative unit—prefecture, subprefecture, district, or the like—and since a band of the provincial army usually guarded a strategic point within, or near, that area, the civil administrator or the garrison commander had jurisdiction over the headman. If the above represented a check from outside, there was also one inside. Under the headman there was a subprefect ($t'ung$-$p'an$) or police chief (li-mu), who served as a nonhereditary assistant after the bureaucratic model. The nonhereditary appointment was doubtlessly devised as a check on the headman from within.[29] Moreover, any member of the non-Han ethnic groups was permitted to report abuses committed by their headmen to the relevant office of the local government. Although this office was almost empty, it was established as a means of control over the headman and occasionally the common tribesmen did appeal to the local administration for justice.[30]

Second, the central government directly supervised the headman through a ritualized process. As a rule, the headman had to send tributes every three years and pay periodic visits to the imperial court. These requirements were ceremonial, but they were designed to enable the ruler to exert his personal influence on the headman and lend additional strength to other devices of control over them. Third, dynastic rulers applied the strategy of divide and rule to control the headmen. For this reason, the non-Han ethnic regions were divided into independent units in a variety of sizes and levels according to the titles and ranks of their headmen. Because headmen were prohibited from expanding their territory through alliance or conquest, these independent units became fragmentary forces to check each other and facilitate imperial control. Fourth, the various restrictions on official titles and ranks and activities of the headman were imperial control mechanisms.

The tribal headman system was far from effective. Since its institutionalization in the Ming dynasty, tribal revolts had remained a problem. For instance, the revolt (1599-1600) in Po-chou, Szechwan, by Yang Ying-lung—whose family had been headmen of the same area for more than seven centuries—was a notable case in the Ming dynasty.[31] In the K'ang-hsi period the Manchu government mobilized troops from several provinces to fight the Yao in Kwangtung and the Miao in Hunan.[32] Although private and official sources tended to attribute these rebellions to the evil nature of the ethnic minorities, the true reasons lay in the weaknesses of the tribal headman system.

The tribal headman system was fundamentally an institution for maintaining peace and order through the tribal chiefs, not for the welfare of the common tribesmen. In the name of peace and order the chiefs strengthened their traditional influence among the tribesmen and maintained the status quo in the tribal communities by keeping away outside influences. Obviously, the tribal headman system did not improve the economic or social life of the tribesmen, although tribal well-being was vital to the maintenance of peace and order. In discussing the Yao people, for instance, one author regards economic factors, such as land and exchange of goods, as a reason for their revolts.[33] In view of the fact that these economic conditions were common to all non-Han ethnic groups, the same reason probably accounted for other revolts of tribesmen in South China.

Another weakness that affected the successful working of the tribal headman system was the lack of effective control over the headmen. Because the system was based on typical Confucian ethical and political doctrines, all the means of control were ritual rather than practical. This may be explained in terms of the headman's appointment, obligations, and relations to the regular local administrators. The process of regular bureaucratic appointment gave the ruler a means of control over the officials, but the selection of headmen was largely a ceremony of investiture. The periodic tributes and visits that the headmen were required to perform had little impact on their administrative conduct and failed to bring the headmen under administrative control. Nor did the local government have the effective whip-hand. For geographic and cultural reasons the regular local bureaucrats always had difficulty achieving a decisive supervisory role over the headmen under their jurisdiction; nor could the nonhereditary assistants to the headmen satisfactorily supervise their masters, whose hereditary office overshadowed their own.

To sum up, the tribal headman system did not provide effective political control over the headmen. After receiving appointment from the imperial court, they had full responsibility for maintaining peace and order in their realms. As long as they did not directly challenge the imperial authority, the ruler was usually reluctant to take action against them, and so were the bureaucrats below him. In fact, the tribal system resembled the tributary system, through which the ruler aimed at ritual satisfaction of his universal authority, but not actual control.

In some ways the local government acted to handicap the successful functioning of the tribal headman system. Extortion was an almost common practice of local administrators in dealing with the headmen and proved to be an important cause of many non-Han ethnic uprisings.[34] Injustice was an even more important cause of their revolts. As a system operating beside the regular Han Chinese political establishment, the tribal headman institution was a structure based on discrimination. Whenever quarrels about land and trade arose between Han Chinese and non-Han ethnic people, local administrators were almost invariably on the side of the Han Chinese disputants. One local history pointed out that prejudice caused a serious non-Han ethnic revolt in the Tao-kuang period.[35]

Maltreatment of the assimilated or controlled tribesmen by the local government always played a significant part in non-Han ethnic discontent. Because, in addition to regular obligations of the common people, these tribesmen performed special roles such as interpreters and guards in peacetime and informers, guides, and vanguards of the provincial army in emergencies, the workability of the headman system depended greatly on their cooperation.

Nonetheless, they were looked down upon by the Han Chinese, overworked by local officials, and victimized by corrupt army officials.[36] Thus were the assimilated tribesmen alienated, and their estrangement contributed directly or indirectly to ethnic revolts.

During the first two reigns of the Ch'ing dynasty, the tribal headman system underwent no fundamental change. After the collapse of the Ming dynasty, with a few exceptions tribal chiefs in South China switched their allegiance to the Manchus and were in return awarded the same titles and offices as they had had before. The Revolt of the Three Feudatories led to the formation of a Ch'ing policy toward the Miao, Yao, and Lolo groups. In their revolt, leaders of the Three Feudatories recruited support from some of the chiefs of these tribal groups; after their suppression, the Ch'ing court reexamined its policy toward headmen by dispatching in 1683 a commissioner to scrutinize the situation in tribal regions in Kweichow and Yunnan.

As a result of this special commission, the throne took firmer action, deciding that the non-Han ethnic realms, once changed to regular administrative units, should remain forever in the bureaucratic system.[37] Once the ruler's stand was firm, local administrators moved further. They brought several tribal regions under their direct control. According to the local history of Kweichow, the province had a total of ninety-four different tribal units, sixteen of which were incorporated into the regular administrative structure during the years 1684-1720.[38] Because the throne refrained from disturbing peace and order in the provinces,[39] the traditional tribal headman system did not undergo any great changes until the Yung-cheng period.

3. *Bureaucratization of the Tribal Headman System*

The Yung-cheng period distinguished itself by adopting a positive minority policy, which transformed many Miao, Yao, and Lolo regions into regular administrative units. Since the policy was implemented at a time when the emperor was devoting himself to autocracy, it should be discussed in terms of this general background. The factors that called for changes in various areas of his administration were also the reasons for his positive stand toward the tribal regions. Like the banner aristocrats, bureaucratic factions, corrupt officials, and self-seeking gentry, all of whom challenged sovereign power, the tribal headman system operated in certain respects against the imperial interest. When the emperor cleared the way for consolidation of his power, the tribal headman system surely had to fall under his axe. The contradictions between this institution and the imperial interest are worth elaborating.

The ambivalent relations between the monarchy and the tribal headman system provided the background for their conflict. Philosophically, the system depended upon the virtue of the ruler and the voluntary loyalty of the headman, clearly a Confucian assumption. In political reality this Confucian assumption was applicable to neither ruler nor headman; both pursued courses they deemed serviceable to their best interests. The relations between them were no less ambivalent than those between monarch and bureaucrat; in that ambivalence existed their conflicts, which were fundamentally a manifestation of the strain between Legalism and Confucianism. Like his suppression of factional activity, corrupt officials, and self-seeking gentry, Yung-cheng's efforts to change the tribal headman system were aimed at removal of this ambivalence.

The various weaknesses of the tribal headman system worked against the interests of the ruler: because of them, the system failed to keep peace and order among the non-Han ethnic groups. Since the consequence of its ineffectiveness was always political, the system was a detriment to imperial control. Under Yung-cheng's reign, many changes in government, notably the reorganization of the Censorate and the founding of the Grand Council, were designed to improve administrative efficiency, which was important to the imperial interest. For Yung-cheng, then, the ineffectiveness of the tribal headman system was a reason for changing it.

Reforms in the tribal headman system exemplified the emperor's unswerving determination to remove feudal elements from the imperial administrative structure. In terms of its structure and working, the tribal headman system was feudal. Selected largely from the tribal chiefs, given ranks and titles according to their original status, and granted the privilege of hereditary office, the headmen were assigned through the practice of investiture, not the regular process of bureaucratic appointment. Their official duties, such as periodic tributes to the imperial court, regular visits to the throne, and guardianship of the tribesmen, were in reality feudal obligations. The headmen were fiefholders outside the regular bureaucratic system, and the non-Han ethnic regions became special territorial units within the empire.

The feudal character of the tribal headman system was irreconcilable with the basic requirement for autocracy—absolute and universal rule—that the Yung-cheng Emperor persisted in pursuing. With feudal privileges, the headmen concentrated in their own hands the political and economic power within their realms. The common tribesmen were their subjects and also their tenants; their staff served as their administrative assistants and concurrently as private managers of their lands.[40] With the combination of political and economic power, the headmen were absolute rulers of their areas. For example, they administered their realms with private codes and collected rent, special contributions, and labor service from the tribesmen as they pleased. According to one source, they were so tyrannical that when a person was punished and put to death by the headman, the victim's family had to pay dearly for his execution.[41]

Obviously, the tyrannical rule of headmen intruded upon imperial authority, which claimed supremacy over all local groups. This point is best reflected in an imperial decree of 1728. In it Yung-cheng bluntly stated that he could not allow Han Chinese to suffer from insecurity caused by the tribesmen, nor could he bear to see the common tribesmen under the tyrannical rule of the headmen.[42] Under his rule, everyone, whatever his ethnic or social background, was subject to, and protected by, the imperial law, but not by any other code.

The conflict between the monarchy and the tribal headman system grew also out of the fact that under hereditary headmen the tribal regions became self-contained. This special situation resulted not only from the headman but from conditions in the region itself. Because the headmen were selected largely from the tribal chiefs and were given hereditary privileges, they owed their offices to their own status more than to the investiture, and they made their realms feudal domains. Besides the feudal aspect, the tribal regions were further distinguished by their geography and cultural traditions. In combination, these factors created a barrier against the absolute and universal norms, mores, and values that dynastic rulers in Chinese history always tried to apply to the entire empire. In short, the tribal regions were within the empire but not directly subject to imperial authority. They formed centers of power that presented a potential threat to absolute and universal rule.

Moreover, the potential threat of the tribal regions under hereditary headmen could become an actual challenge, when opportunity permitted. T'ien Min-ju (d.1734), for example, was made headman of Jung-mei, a tribal region known later as Ho-feng in present-day Hupei. Since he administered a realm of 3,000 households or so, a number much larger than an average tribal region, he became very powerful. Out of personal ambition he expanded his influence over neighboring regions and even assumed royal privileges of a kind, such as construction of a palace modeled after the imperial court, appointment of a group of special advisors, and selection of eunuchs from young tribesmen.[43] The emperor found this intolerable. It is not surprising that upon reading a report on the headman's presumptuousness, he wrote on it: "The law of the state allows no delay for action to correct T'ien."[44]

In light of the headman's challenge, potential or actual, to the ruler, reform of the tribal headman system was imperative to the consolidation of sovereign power. The importance of changing the headman system can be seen from the emperor's esteem for the man who carried it out. During the Yung-cheng period O-er-t'ai was an influential official of the throne, comparable with any other imperial confidant such as Chang T'ing-yü, T'ien Wen-ching, Li Wei, or the like, who faithfully put through the emperor's programs for the consolidation of power in the central government or disciplined the self-seeking gentry in the provinces. Of the reasons for the rise of O-er-t'ai, his effort to transform the tribal headman system in Kweichow, Kwangsi, and Yunnan was the most important.

Economic considerations seem to have played a role in the decision to alter the headman institution. Despite the Yung-cheng Emperor's denial of economic interest in the abolition of the headman system,[45] there were some positive clues to such a connection. In view of his emphasis on reclamation, reform of the tribal headman system seems to have been designed, at least in part, to increase the acreage of cultivated land. This point was supported by an imperial decree of 1733, which ordered provincial and local governments in southwest China to induce settlers to reclaim land in the hills and forests of the tribal regions.[46]

The action of provincial authorities also indicated a close relationship between economic interest and changes in the tribal headman system. When river works, irrigation construction, and reclamation projects were promoted by the throne, provincial and local officials competed for imperial favor by showing larger and larger growth figures. Beyond doubt, the tribal regions provided enthusiastic bureaucrats with a great opportunity to better their records. In a memorial, for example, O-er-t'ai recommended reclamation plans for the uncultivated lands around the tribal regions in Yunnan and Kweichow, including pacification of the tribesmen.[47] What he actually was suggesting was the transformation of the tribal headman system, which would be essential to fruitful reclamation.

The urgent need for copper seems also to have played a part in the desire to reform the headman system.[48] The claim can be made that in its first century the Manchu regime was constantly under the pressure of copper shortage. The shortage led to a rise in the price of copper, illegal casting of copper coins, melting of coins for utensils, and, most important of all, weakening the position of copper coins, the chief currency in the daily life of the people. To ensure dynastic stability, early Manchu rulers tried every means to solve the copper problem by increasing the copper supply, changing the denomination of coins, prohibiting forgery and the melting of copper coins, and importing copper from Vietnam and Japan.[49] Because the copper trade had caused diplomatic tension between China and Japan since the last years of the K'ang-hsi era, copper mines in Yunnan acquired more and more importance with time, especially under the governorship of O-er-t'ai.

There are two other indications of the close relationship between the problem of copper supply and changes in the tribal headman system—the location of the copper mines and the administration of O-er-t'ai. The copper mines were scattered throughout the provinces of Kweichow and Yunnan, but the prosperous ones were located within or near the tribal regions. In Kweichow, for example, a large quantity of copper ore came from the department of Chen-hsiung and, in particular, the prefecture of Wei-ning, where a mint was located:[50] both were Lolo regions. In several of his memorials, O-er-t'ai reported that the department of Lu-nan and the prefecture of Tung-ch'uan, also Lolo regions, had Yunnan's largest copper mines. By 1726, miners in Lu-nan obtained more than half a million catties of copper ore.[51] Copper mines were also found in tribal regions in Szechwan, southern Hunan, and on the southern Kweichow-Kwangsi border. The provinces of Kweichow and Yunnan were also rich in lead deposits;[52] copper and lead were the two necessary components of coins.

The appointment of O-er-t'ai as governor-general of Yunnan and Kweichow occurred in 1726, when the copper supply was critical. On different occasions, he revealed that the major goal of his administration was threefold: pacification of tribesmen, reclamation, and mining. According to him, the pacification of tribesmen was the foundation of reclamation, which was in turn the groundwork for mining because miners needed food supplies.[53] Thus, these three projects were combined into one enterprise, which O-er-t'ai carried out with imperial support. Under him Yunnan provided, under normal conditions, more than four million catties of copper ore annually, and Kweichow, about three million catties of lead annually.[54]

The importance of copper and lead ores from Yunnan and Kweichow was apparent, for their supplies were not only enough for local mints but sufficient to provide copper for many other provinces. True, copper mining in Kweichow and Yunnan did not completely solve the currency problem, but it greatly reduced its seriousness. This can be proved by the number of Chinese ships that anchored in Nagasaki for copper purchase. There, Japanese merchants found forty-two Chinese ships in 1726, and the same number the next year,[55] these being the first two years of O-er-t'ai's governor-generalship. After 1727 the number of Chinese ships generally decreased. The same conclusion can be verified by the coin-minting situation. After 1728 many provincial governments purchased copper from Yunnan and began to mint their own coins to meet the public need. With the increase in the circulation of copper coins, the emperor was able to stabilize currency, ease the daily life of the people, encourage domestic trade, and, most important of all, maintain political and social order. Small wonder that O-er-t'ai received the high commendation of the emperor.

Yung-cheng devised his new policy toward the non-Han ethnic groups around 1726. Before that date, because he paid more attention to factional activities among the princes and powerful officials, he followed a traditional policy that emphasized fragmentation of the headmen's realms through investiture of their sons.[56] After he had removed the influential factions from the central government, he turned to the non-Han ethnic problem. In the formation of his new policy, he was greatly influenced by a few provincial administrators, notably O-er-t'ai, who mapped out, with the help of his staff, a positive program toward the tribal regions under his jurisdiction as soon as he took over the governorship of Yunnan. Because his program was the basis of the ethnic policy of the Yung-cheng period, it is necessary to discuss it further.

The major focus of O-er-t'ai's policy dealt with the relationship between the headmen's economic base and their political strength. Accordingly, it insisted that only with their economic strength weakened could they be put under effective supervision. Control of the headmen, it went on, would facilitate the pacification of the common tribesmen, which would finally lead to peace and order in the tribal regions.[57] But the ultimate goal of O-er-t'ai's program was to reorganize the tribal communities after the regular administrative pattern and introduce Chinese culture to the tribesmen. With this general motive, he removed lawbreaking headmen, inaugurated census registration and tithing units (*pao-chia*), set tax quotas based on a land survey, shaved and braided the tribesmen in accordance with the required hair style, and charged them with mutual responsibility for peace and order on the household and village level.[58] In later years he devised more measures to change the tribal headman system. With imperial approval his programs were also carried on among the Miao, Yao, and Lolo groups outside Yunnan and Kweichow.

The emperor also contributed significantly to the new policy. Without his determination, it would not have been formulated because provincial administrators were not uniformly in favor of the new policy. In general, men who preferred a "get tough" policy toward the headmen were largely bannermen and army officers. For example, O-er-t'ai, Mai-chu (1670-

1738), governor-general of Hupei and Hunan, Shih Li-ha, then acting governor of Kweichow, Ma Hui-po (d.1736), acting provincial commander-in-chief of the same province, and Chang Kuang-ssu (d.1749), a man promoted from prefect to many high posts, all worked hard to promote the imperial interest. Those who favored an appeasement attitude were Yang Ming-shih, once governor of Yunnan, Ho Shih-chi, governor of Kweichow (1726-1727) and Chin Kung (also known as Kuo Kung, 1679-1741), governor of Kwangsi.[59] They were ardent Confucian scholar-officials, and on various occasions they were reprimanded or punished by the emperor for their failure to act in conformity with the imperial requirements. The difference between these two groups was yet another example of Confucian-Legalist tension. The emperor naturally responded favorably to those who had the sovereign interest in mind. No doubt the new policy owed its formation to his determination to brook no threat to the imperial prerogative.

During the years 1726-1735, the new policy was put into effect, focusing on the non-Han ethnic regions in the interior rather than on those at the national borders in southwest China. The inner areas in Yunnan and Kweichow became the starting point of the new policy: from there it was extended to the provinces of Hunan, Hupei, Kwangsi, and Szechwan. Men like O-er-t'ai, Mai-chu, and a few others who helped in the formation of the policy were also the ones who executed it. In a technical sense, the administrators of these provinces carried out the policy in various ways. For instance, some headmen gave up their hereditary office when they encountered dissension from their counterparts in the neighborhood, or they did this simply at the persuasion of local administrators.[60] The hereditary office might also be abolished when a headman had no heir or when he was punished for a crime.[61] No matter what course was adopted, it led to the same result, that is, abolition of the headman.

Armed interference was the most important method of introducing the new policy. Although military campaigns started in 1724, large-scale operations did not get underway until O-er-t'ai took charge of the administration of Yunnan and Kweichow two years later. With the support of the emperor and the assistance of Chang Kuang-ssu and Ha Yuan-sheng (d.1738), a man rising from low military rank, he successfully pacified many tribal regions. The frequent troubles

of the tribesmen led him to take high-handed
measures, and his armed interference stirred up more
unrest among them. In turn, disorders in tribal
regions moved him to take an even firmer stand. His
first blow fell on the Miao group of Kuang-shun,
southwest of Kweiyang, Kweichow, because it had
frequently threatened the local peace since the
K'ang-hsi period. After a few months he suppressed
the revolt.[62] In the years 1726-1730, he carried on
many campaigns, of which two were most significant.

One operation occurred in 1728, with the Miao
group in the border area of Kweichow, Hunan, and
Kwangsi as the chief target. With their geographic
advantage, the Miao tribes imposed a few setbacks on
the campaigners commanded by Chang Kuang-ssu. Thanks
to both military and political means, most of this
area was pacified after two years of operations and
was guarded by garrison posts.[63] Since almost no
dynastic ruler in Chinese history had successfully
extended the imperial authority to this Miao center,
Yung-cheng expressed great satisfaction with its
pacification and liberally rewarded those who
contributed to it. However, in view of later events,
the success proved temporary.[64]

The other significant campaign that O-er-t'ai
directed during his governor-generalship was aimed
at the Lolo people in Wu-meng, a place in Yunnan
covering the present-day country of Yung-shan and
its vicinity. With the cooperation of Yüeh Chung-
ch'i, governor-general of Szechwan and Shensi, he
pacified the Lolo tribes in 1726 and later garrisoned
the place with a brigade. Owing to the oppressive
military rule of the brigade general, peace was shat-
tered when the tribesmen rebelled in 1730, with
support from their kinsmen around Wu-meng. The situation was so serious that the garrisons and the local
administration in the area were wiped out.[65] It was
suppressed by a large punitive army of about 10,000
men, who under the command of O-er-t'ai penetrated
into the insurrection center from three directions in
the same year.[66] Defeat of this Lolo uprising brought
to an end O-er-t'ai's important military campaigns in
Southwest China, and also marked the height of the
success of the new policy.

In the short span of five years (1726-1730)
O-er-t'ai transformed many non-Han ethnic regions
into regular prefectures and districts. This can be
counted as his greatest accomplishment, which in
turn signified the success of the new ethnic policy.

For a better explanation of the bureaucratization of the tribal regions, it is necessary to analyze the factors responsible for this accomplishment. The strategy and personality of O-er-t'ai was a major factor. Since he was an experienced and practical administrator of Manchu origin, he had less commitment to Confucian tradition than the Confucian-oriented scholar-official. Thus, he approached the ethnic minority problem realistically and was able to grasp its importance. Readers of his memorials on tribal affairs cannot fail to detect his practical approach to the problem. The same approach can also be seen in the fact that in formation of his strategy he took advice from experts in ethnic minority affairs.

One such specialist in ethnic problems was Fang Hsien, a native of Hunan, which contained tribal regions. This environment provided him with information about the ethnic minorities, and he acquired further knowledge through service in Kweichow as a local official. He submitted to O-er-t'ai a sixteen-point program, including introduction of Chinese culture, organization of tithing units, and construction of military posts and transportation lines, all realistic goals.[67] O-er-t'ai adopted these suggestions, and opened watercourses in the Yunnan-Kwangsi, Kweichow-Kwangsi, and Kweichow-Hunan border areas.[68] These watercourses served both economic and military purposes. Chang Kuang-ssu was another expert in the Miao region and a brave army commander in campaigns against the tribesmen. He and Fang Hsien played an important role in formation and realization of the strategy that was attributed to their superior, O-er-t'ai. With devotion and determination, O-er-t'ai put it through.

Another factor in O-er-t'ai's achievement was imperial support. He was one of the few governors-general who won and retained the imperial confidence. Both his loyalty and his practical approach to problems appealed to the throne and helped his rise to power. In memorials, for example, he always gave detailed information, analyzed problems, and suggested an approach. Unlike many Confucian-oriented bureaucrats, he rarely colored his reports with impractical conventionalities. As a consequence, he won high commendation from Yung-cheng who was a political realist by nature. Imperial favor greatly facilitated his work.

Finally, the achievement of O-er-t'ai was due in part to interprovincial cooperation. He enjoyed both the support of the throne and the cooperation of the highest administrators in the neighboring provinces. All these administrators were men of ability and activity, enthusiastic about the new policy and responsive to the imperial decision. When O-er-t'ai carried it out in Yunnan and Kweichow, they responded in their provinces. Yüeh Chung-ch'i, for example, tried to remove some Lolo and Tibetan tribal headmen in Szechwan province; his cooperation helped suppress the Lolo people along the borders of Yunnan and Szechwan.[69] At the same time Mai-chu vigorously supported O-er-t'ai's work. In carrying out the new policy in Hunan and Hupei, he adopted a kind of guerrilla warfare against the restless Miao and removed many headmen from office.[70] The provincial government of Kwangsi did not enthusiastically take action, but in late 1728 the throne put it under the supervision of O-er-t'ai, who thus administered Yunnan, Kweichow, and Kwangsi. With the three provinces under his jurisdiction he was able to combine their resources to expedite his work, and this resulted in the pacification of some strong Miao and Yao groups in Kwangsi.[71]

The new policy was carried out in a systematic manner. Tribal headmen lost their hereditary offices one after another, and after their displacement, they were further subject to the rewards and punishments in accordance with their previous conduct. Headmen who voluntarily filed petitions to give up their offices were rewarded with money and title, whereas those who were removed by force were punished.[72] Although the degree of punishment varied with individuals, in all cases punishment seems to have been limited to the headman. Even if his penalty fitted into the category of banishment or death, his family was well treated. T'ien Min-ju, for instance, a headman who offended the throne by assuming royal prerogatives, committed suicide under pressure from the provincial authorities, but his family was allowed to keep his property without receiving a penalty, as in ordinary cases.[73]

Because tradition served the tribal headmen as a major source of their strength, the success of the new policy depended on the removal not only of the headmen but also of their traditional influence. Almost without exception, those headmen who received less than capital punishment were transferred to places far from the tribesmen. No matter what punishment they were given, their families were always relocated. In short, they were forced to live in other provinces where the local administrators took care of them and by the throne's order kept strict watch over them.[74] In one of his memorials, for instance, a provincial governor revealed that every ten of such families were given five rooms and about seven and a half acres of land.[75] Obviously, their standard of living declined. Without political support and economic strength, the dislocated headmen and their families were completely under bureaucratic control. By comparison, small headmen and lower officers received better treatment. After removal from office, in most cases they were given titles, nominal or actual, stipends, or even assigned to the garrison troops in the provinces in which they had been active.[76] After the chiefs, lower officers, and their families were removed, the tribal regions were open to a new administrative system.

During the last half of the Yung-cheng period, many tribal regions were changed to regular prefectures or districts defended by the provincial troops and administered by bureaucrats. In other words, they became new units within the ordinary administrative hierarchy. Through the process of bureaucratization imperial authority was extended directly into the tribal regions and the emperor carried out the process with care, requiring administrators in those areas to do the same. What he particularly stressed, besides effective administration and active supervision, was justice. He argued that after the abolition of the headman system, the Han Chinese and the non-Han ethnic groups should be treated alike, without discrimination.[77] Posts in the newly bureaucratized regions were generally referred to as vacancies in the Miao area (*Miao-chiang ch'üeh*), but fundamentally they were the same as those in other places. Like bureaucrats everywhere within the empire, administrators in the new units carried on work assigned by the throne, and, like the majority of people in China, the non-Han ethnic groups were subject to the same imperial law.

The process of bureaucratization affected the traditional way of life of the common tribesmen. At the beginning administrators in the newly pacified areas had even more work than their colleagues in other regions. In general, their work included land

and census registration, compilation of tax quotas, organization of tithing units, collection of weapons from the tribesmen, and prohibition of the Han Chinese from entering the tribal regions without official permission. In certain cases provincial authorities developed individual programs that differed slightly from place to place. For example, the administrators in Hunan, Hupei, and Szechwan selected some young tribesmen as local police, while the provincial authority in Kwangtung organized the Yao people into fifty-household units under a salaried chief selected from among them and appointed by the government.[78] In the final analysis, all these programs centered on two points, tax payment and police control, both of which were the foundation of imperial authority. At the same time, provincial administrators developed other projects such as issuance of landownership certificates, emancipation of tribal bondservants from their Chinese masters, and periodic fairs at the borders of the newly created units.[79] On the whole, these programs, either imposing obligations on the tribesmen or taking care of their well-being, changed the political, social, and economic structures of their traditional communities.

Chinese culture was introduced into the tribal regions after the transformation of their administrative structure. For instance, O-er-t'ai introduced Chinese dress, hair style, and family names into the pacified tribal areas in Yunnan and Kweichow; Yüeh Chung-ch'i forced the tribesmen under his jurisdiction to shave and braid their heads and wear Chinese clothing.[80] Intermarriage between Han Chinese and non-Han ethnic groups had always been prohibited by dynastic rulers prior to the Yung-cheng era but, with the approval of the emperor, it was encouraged by the provincial administrators in Hunan and Hupei.[81] Although the introduction of these customs failed to have a lasting impact, they were an attempt to eliminate cultural barriers between Han and non-Han ethnic groups so as to facilitate imperial rule.

Education was perhaps the most significant of the changes that were imposed on the tribal regions after their headmen were removed. It started even in the beginning years of the K'ang-hsi period, but it was mainly limited to the sons of tribal chiefs.[82] This situation changed in the Yung-cheng period when provincial authorities made education a special program for the newly pacified ethnic regions. This special program appeared generally in the form of charity schools (*i-hsüeh*) for tribal boys,[83] supervised by the education administrators in the local government. Besides the basic texts, the *Amplified Instructions on the Sacred Edict* seems to have been taught to tribal pupils and also explained to adult tribesmen.[84] Apparently, these charity schools functioned, as did other local schools, to enforce the orthodox ideology and promote the imperial authority. Promising pupils were sent to the government schools and allowed to take the regular state examination.[85] Their examination papers at first seem to have been rated separately according to a standard which favored them, but later they were put on the same level as their Chinese counterparts.[86]

The new policy suffered setbacks, however. While the changes were being instituted, uprisings occurred and recurred in the former tribal regions. The Lolo people of Wu-meng rose in 1730; the Miao in southeastern Kweichow revolted in 1733 and again in 1735. The factors contributing to these uprisings were the traditional ones, but the revolts themselves indicated a great setback for the new tribal policy introduced by the Yung-cheng Emperor. The Miao rebellion of 1735 was so serious that it almost destroyed the entire bureaucratic establishment in the whole area and attracted the armed forces from several neighboring provinces.[87] The Yung-cheng Emperor appointed a temporary commission of thirteen people, including three princes, to take charge of Miao pacification, and he is said to have even attempted to abandon the new policy.[88] Owing to the unfavorable geographic situation and the lack of cooperation between commanders, the warfare ended in 1736, one year after the death of the emperor.

The new policy was perhaps the most aggressive enterprise undertaken by the Yung-cheng Emperor, who devoted his reign to peace and order rather than to military exploits. In view of the Miao revolt of 1735 and the great uprisings in later periods, one is inclined to regard his new ethnic minority policy as a failure. True, in a cultural sense it did not successfully transform the tribal ways of life into the Chinese mode. Nevertheless, it should be noted that any changes of such a nature inevitably take time. The Miao revolts were unnecessarily taken to mean a defeat for the new policy. In fact tribesmen had frequently risen in rebellion before the introduction of the regular administrative system, and even Chinese who were used to the bureaucratic government organized revolts. What the Miao uprisings in and after 1735 suggested was simply the problems that were intrinsic to dynastic administration in Chinese history.

From an overall viewpoint, the new ethnic policy was an important contribution from Yung-cheng to the Ch'ing dynasty and China as well. Three aspects of that contribution may be noted. First, the policy increased the lead and copper supplies, which were the foundation of copper currency. In the K'ang-hsi period the Ch'ing government heavily depended on Japanese copper and sent merchants to Japan to purchase it. In addition to the hardship and uncertainty of the voyages, Chinese copper merchants were subject to various restrictions and exactions by the Japanese sellers. The net result of this situation was to push up the price of copper, degrade its quality, and strain relations between China and Japan. It also became a reason for the transfer of the customs administration in Kiangsu and Chekiang from the Manchus of the Imperial Household to the provincial governors who were charged with purchasing copper.[89] This change, however, did not increase the supply of copper. It was not until the enforcement of the new ethnic minority policy that the copper and lead mines in Yunnan and Kweichow were exploited to a greater extent. The increase in their output significantly reduced Chinese dependency on Japanese copper. From that time on, Ch'ing mints depended mainly on the supplies of these two provinces. In short, Yung-cheng's minority policy stabilized not only Ch'ing currency but also the dynasty itself.

Second, the new ethnic policy laid the foundation of Ch'ing strategy toward the tribesmen in southwest China. After Yung-cheng, subsequent Manchu rulers followed it by removing headmen and introducing the regular bureaucratic structure whenever the opportunity arose. Therefore, in the interior of Yunnan, Kweichow, and Szechwan, the strong headmen gradually disappeared;[90] what remained was small tribal regions and those on the outlying borders.

The new ethnic policy also encouraged military colonization, a tactic for frontier defense at various times in Chinese history. Although the Yung-cheng Emperor did not directly take action to encourage it, with his approval the provincial administrators of Yunnan, Kweichow, Szechwan, Hunan, and Hupei carried out some measures toward that end.

After pacifying the Lolo people in Wu-meng, for example, O-er-t'ai divided up the uncultivated lands among the garrison soldiers and the extra-quota men in their families; each received about five acres (30 *mou*) and initial funds for reclamation.[91] The document fails to denote whether these troops were Han Chinese or assimilated tribal soldiers, but one may reasonably interpret this practice as military colonization. Later on, the provincial governor of Kwangsi gave about three acres of land to each of the non-Han ethnic garrisons in some Yao regions.[92] When combined with the militia system and castle construction, military colonization became an effective means of pacifying Miao rebellions during the early nineteenth century.[93]

Third, the most significant and enduring effect of the new ethnic policy was development of southwest China. Because most of the area had been populated by various less advanced tribal groups before the enforcement of the new policy, the whole region, including southwestern Hunan, western Hupei, Kwangsi, a great part of Szechwan, and especially Yunnan and Kweichow, was a backward area. It was largely inhabited by miserable farmers, poor migrants, adventurers, and convicted exiles in addition to the tribesmen. This situation encouraged bureaucrats to evade acceptance of assignments to these provinces; for the same reason those officials who served there tried to find a way out as soon as possible. The shortage of qualified administrators was a serious factor in the backwardness of these places. This situation gradually improved after the enforcement of the new ethnic policy.

The new policy also helped the development of southwest China by prompting the adjustment of provincial boundaries. Among many factors responsible for the problems of the area, the lack of reasonable physical divisions was one. For example, southern Kweichow was geographically separated from northern Kwangsi by a river, the Hung-shui Ho, which failed to serve as the natural boundary line of the two provinces. At Chengtu, capital of Szechwan, the provincial government had jurisdiction over the prefecture of Tsunyi more than 400 miles to the north, only about 100 miles away from Kweiyang, where the provincial governor of Kweichow was stationed. Both the personnel and boundary problems affected administrative work and handicapped the development of these provinces. While putting through his new ethnic policy, the Yung-cheng emperor made a series of boundary adjustments based on administrative necessity. It was through these adjustments that these provinces, especially Kweichow, acquired their present-day shapes.

Transformation of the tribal regions into regular administrative units was the most important factor in the development of southwest China. Although the new ethnic policy did not bring all the tribal communities under direct bureaucratic control, during the years 1727-1735 it raised two places to the prefectural level and created six prefectures, twenty districts, and five departments.[94] After 1735 more new units were added. The whole course of transformation was the process of bureaucratization and Sinicization. When peace and order prevailed in the new administrative units, they naturally attracted an endless flow of farmers from other provinces; at the time of ethnic revolts, the Manchu government ruthlessly suppressed the rebels by force. As every campaign invariably reduced the tribal population and forced it into the deep interior, more opportunities were therefore made available to the land-hunting Han Chinese. With energy, patience, and skill these immigrants tried new and old crops on the wasteland and hilly slopes and even cut down virgin forests,[95] colonizing and developing southwest China.

The development of southwest China, which originated mainly in the Yung-cheng Emperor's new ethnic minority policy, contributed to the extension of the imperial authority and consolidation of the southwestern interior frontiers of China. The contribution was important not only to the Manchu regime but also to China. As one renowned scholar has noted: "Without the extension and consolidation of the southwestern internal frontiers, it is doubtful that the southwest could have served so well as China's last territorial base of operation against Japan during the critical years from 1937 to 1945."[96]

XI

Conclusion

The Yung-cheng Emperor died in October 1735, without seeing the end of the Miao revolt. Beyond a doubt he was the most efficient of the Manchu monarchs, and one of the most successful autocratic rulers in the traditional Chinese state, essentially because of his ability to reshape all the political forces inimical to the imperial interest. His reign, though short, had a lasting influence. The Ch'ing empire thereafter was a polity quite different from what it had been before.

The emperor's task had been a large one, affecting both the nobility and the bureaucracy.[1] They had acted chiefly in their own interests. Time and again they abused their privileges, circumvented imperial directives, and engaged in feuds. They had a strong influence on the early Ch'ing political process, and notably on the succession struggle in the late K'ang-hsi period. Because of their special status and great political influence, the nobles were the first to fall under the Yung-cheng Emperor's axe.[2] His severe punishment of the powerful imperial clansmen paralyzed the old aristocratic factions; the imprisonment of Lungkodo, once his henchman, thwarted the formation of any new clique. Through bureaucratization the emperor removed the last feudal vestiges from the banner system,[3] which was an aristocratic stronghold. To obtain obedience and loyalty he also used imperial publications—decrees, essays, and books.

As a result the Ch'ing aristocracy changed in shape and spirit. The aristocrats gave up their personal differences and self-seeking activities. Although they retained some privileges, their traditional status, as well as their political influence, was leveled to fit the bureaucratic framework. Lineage was no longer the determining factor in the ups and downs of their careers, which now depended on the irresistible imperial will. Within the bureaucratic structure they became subject to the uniform service code, supervised by the ruler or his agents, committed to efficiency, and working to further the monarch's interest.

The transformation of the aristocracy was not only a great success of Yung-cheng's rule but a permanent victory for Ch'ing autocracy. Although Ch'ing rulers since Hong-taiji had striven to transform the aristocrats, the task was not carried out until the Yung-cheng period. The effect of this transformation was obvious. It straightened out the relations between monarchy and aristocracy. With the threat of the aristocracy removed, Ch'ing emperors throughout the rest of the dynasty could freely exercise their will. The Yung-cheng Emperor also organized the Grand Council, largely at the expense of the aristocrats. Its successful operation and durability became possible only with the weakening of the aristocracy.

The transformation of the bureaucracy was another prominent aspect of Yung-cheng's rule, centering on the creation of a new service attitude. Using both coercive and persuasive methods, he prohibited bureaucratic conduct that was undesirable to him and introduced patterns of behavior that he considered desirable.[4] He was strongly against factionalism because it diverted officials' loyalty from him. He looked upon all close personal contacts among bureaucrats as partisanship and severely punished them. He prohibited perfunctory, indiscreet, reckless, and corrupt behavior. He desired legalist-oriented conduct—loyal, active, righteous, impersonal. Bureaucrats whose conduct met imperial standards were showered with rewards. To discourage any deviation he preferred office purchasers to scholar-officials; in his opinon, the latter were prone to partisanship. His reforms in provincial and local education and his reorientation of private academies can be regarded as efforts to introduce the new service attitude. One may also consider his promotion of orthodoxy among the literati as directed to the same purpose.

The Ch'ing bureaucracy of the Yung-cheng period stood distinct from its predecessor. It became unitary. Since factionalism was forbidden, the bureaucrats gave up their divergent loyalties. Moreover, inasmuch as the aristocracy and the bureaucracy were transformed by Yung-cheng for the same autocratic purposes, the Chinese-Manchu dichotomy was nearly eliminated. Whatever their differences of rank or origin, both Chinese and Manchu officials became workers for the same master, pursuing his interest under the same rules, within the same framework.

The new service attitude inspired high morale among the bureaucrats. They were active, accountable, and hard-working. Li Wei and T'ien Wen-ching, officials in key positions, exemplified this new attitude; because of their high morale they were promoted from obscurity, and they in turn stimulated their subordinates. The bureaucracy of the time was noted for its efficiency.

After its transformation the bureaucracy submitted itself without question to the imperial will and so became more serviceable to the emperor. Guided by a capable ruler, it could perform its duties, such as attending to the livelihood of the people, maintaining peace and order, and preserving the imperial system. With any weakening of imperial leadership the bureaucracy might have been relaxed, less responsive, incapable of enforcing imperial orders. In no case would it challenge imperial authority. The bureaucracy made no decisions and took no initiative because all decisions and initiatives were the prerogatives of the monarch, whatever the quality of his rulership. How fortunate, then, that the Yung-cheng Emperor was a strong ruler.

The successful changes in the aristocracy and the bureaucracy were perpetuated in part by the palace-memorial system.[5] This system operated as a means of checking on the bureaucracy. It was composed of reporters, selected largely from among provincial bureaucrats by the ruler, to whom they were responsible directly and individually. Besides their regular administrative duties the reporters as members of the system had to keep an eye out for other bureaucrats and report their observations confidentially to the throne through palace memorials. No official—aristocrat or bureaucrat—including the reporter himself could be outside the system's vigilant network. By means of palace memorials Yung-cheng was able to find out whether his will was executed, circumvented, ignored, or distorted, and to take necessary action. The system enforced the new service attitude among the bureaucrats.

The palace-memorial system formed a web of communication circuits which also helped keep the bureaucrats in conformity with the new service attitude. Palace memorials reached the imperial desk directly from reporters all over the empire; after reading the reports the monarch returned them with his instructions to their authors. Incoming and outgoing memorials provided channels of direct communication between ruler and bureaucrat. From the memorials the ruler received a variety of information vital to imperial authority, on the basis of which he could take care of urgent problems, make decisions, effect what he desired, and ward off any challenge to his authority. Through the returned memorials reporters obtained messages that invariably reminded them of the ruler's will. All in all, when fully operated either as a supervision web or as a means of communication, the palace-memorial system facilitated the monarch's personal rule.

In a different way the Grand Council reinforced imperial control over the aristocracy and the bureaucracy. Its serviceability derived from the effectiveness of its chief staff, the Grand Councillors, and from its operational procedures. Appointment of Grand Councillors was based on the same qualifications required of the bureaucrats—ability, loyalty, and accountability—with no regard to the question of ethnic numerical equality, which had assured the Manchus of offices in the central government. With the imperial confidence, and easy access to the throne, the Grand Councillors became a small, efficient group of personal assistants to the ruler, and in time the highest and most influential officials in the bureaucracy. Although their regular work was the drafting and conveying of imperial decrees and the transmission of palace memorials, they took charge of any task assigned by the emperor. They assumed many assignments previously performed by the Grand Secretariat, originally the highest office in the bureaucratic structure, and by the Office for Administrative Deliberations, which had been a traditional domain of the Manchu nobles.

The Grand Council developed its own procedures. The office veiled itself from outsiders; it transacted all affairs with extreme secrecy, not allowing censorial supervision. The Grand Councillors set down the ruler's oral messages in the form of court letters and dispatched them through the postal system directly to addressees. Important imperial orders were recorded even after normal office hours and sent out by express. It is clear that secrecy protected the office's business from leaks and from outside influence, and direct and fast transactions speeded up the administrative process. These secret, direct, speedy operations provided political security and executive efficiency, indispensable to imperial control.

One may conclude that the Grand Council was independent of aristocratic influence and bureaucratic machinery and worked for the autocratic cause. It was the ideal "inner court" dreamed of by early Ch'ing rulers, and its members—the Grand Councillors—were the ideal secretaries. Because it was answerable to the ruler, efficient, and easily controlled, it enjoyed strong imperial favor. It had much in common with the palace-memorial system. Both institutions worked to bring the aristocracy and the bureaucracy under personal control of the ruler. The result was the longevity of Ch'ing autocracy.

During the Yung-cheng period the local elite, which encompassed mainly the private literati with academic degrees, was also reshaped.[6] The importance of individual members might differ with their background, but as a group exercising an informal power they were a political force which filled the vacuum in imperial administration below the district level. In their various roles they came to be actual rulers of local communities. Yung-cheng disciplined the local elite through ideological indoctrination, tough administration, and literary inquisition. Ideological indoctrination was the chief responsibility of local education administrators, especially inspectors of morale. Besides having to read orthodox works—such as the *Amplified Instructions on the Sacred Edict*—the local elite were required to attend periodic lectures on these books. With the throne's encouragement provincial and local officials sternly checked the victimization of the common people and tax evasion; the Yung-cheng Emperor rigorously carried on his literary inquisition against such offending writers as Wang Ching-ch'i and Tseng Ching. These disciplinary actions developed in the local elite of the Yung-cheng period a new frame of mind to accord with the imperial ideal.

Yung-cheng's attitude toward the local elite was important. Early discipline of the local elite was essential to transformation of the bureaucracy, the members of which were usually drawn from its ranks. The literati, so disciplined, would likely conduct themselves in a manner approved by the throne. Despite their constructive role in community offices, the local elite had tended to profit at the expense of the common people. Tax evasion, common among the self-seeking literati, increased the common people's burden; the alliance of corrupt gentry and corrupt local officials was another tribulation. Suppression of the local elite contributed to peace, order, and prosperity.[7]

Imperial authority reached towns, villages, every corner of the empire, after the elite were forced into line. Whatever their roles, the local elite had intruded upon the ruler's prerogatives. As holders of academic degrees they owed their prestige and importance to Confucian tradition, not to the monarch's favor. In the name of Confucian values they had assumed leadership in local affairs which lay legally in the realm of imperial authority. In their personal interest they could become oppressors of the people and manipulate the power of government. The conflict was basically a Confucian-Legalist confrontation. Yung-cheng's power now penetrated all the activities of the local elite.

The Yung-cheng Emperor was a true autocrat—indomitable, persistent, efficient. Regimentation marked his reign. All political and social forces were bent to his will. He transformed the aristocrats from participants in power struggles into a group of docile individuals who retained some privileges but no political power. They could be made and unmade by the ruler. Fear of punishment and hope of reward reduced the bureaucrats to tax collectors, law enforcers, and transmitters of imperial messages; they were everything except political initiators or decision makers. Their watchwords were loyalty and obedience.

The local elite also submitted to the imperial purposes. Unlike their predecessors, they no longer considered Manchu rule foreign. They disseminated Confucian teachings, together with the norms of the state, and praised the imperial grace to the common people. Their personal fate, Confucian tradition, and the Ch'ing empire were three in one. All the common subjects, even outcasts, found in the Yung-cheng Emperor a great benefactor because he improved their lives. They became diligent farmers, taxpayers—above all a silent, obedient majority. After military campaigns against non-Han minority groups,[8] as a result of which the emperor removed hereditary headmen from office, Yung-cheng systematically introduced the customs, schools, tithing units, and regular administrative structure indispensable to imperial authority. No group of people in China was left beyond his control. His rule was absolute, and—for China—universal.[9]

Yung-cheng's reign was short but his legacy was great. He consolidated power and established a new political and social foundation for the remainder of the Ch'ing era. Although his methods of autocracy were traditional, he perfected the imperial system of the traditional Chinese state. Under him the Ch'ing period was marked by vigor and efficiency and, most important, by effective paternalistic despotism. Ruler and empire were identical. State and culture were one and the same. A true Confucian China had come into being.

Notes

I: Aspects of Autocracy in the Yung-cheng Period

1. Carl J. Friedrich and Zbigniew K. Brzezinski, *Totalitarian Dictatorship and Autocracy* (Cambridge, Mass., 1965), p.5.
2. For a revealing discussion, see Ping-ti Ho, "Salient Aspects of China's Heritage," in Ping-ti Ho and Tang Tsou, eds., *China in Crisis*, vol. 1: *China's Heritage and the Communist Political System* (Chicago, 1968), I, 9-25.
3. Hsiao Kung-ch'üan, "Chung-kuo cheng-chih ssu-hsiang chung chih cheng-yüan lun" (Theories on the origins of political power in Chinese political thought), *Tsing Hua Journal* 9.3:535-48 (July 1934).
4. Miao Chuan-chi, "K'ung-tzu chün-ch'en cheng-i" ('Confucian theory on the "Monarch and His Courtiers"'), *Chung-shan hsüeh-shu wen-hua chi-k'an* (Bulletin of the Sun Yat-sen Cultural Foundation), 1:43-45 (March 1968).
5. Ho, "Salient Aspects of China's Heritage," p.14.
6. Ch'ien Mu, *Chung-kuo li-tai cheng-chih te-shih* (The Merits and Demerits of the Chinese Governmental System during Various Dynasties), 2nd ed. (Hong Kong, 1956), pp.7-11.
7. Lao Kan, "Lun Han-tai ti nei-ch'ao yü wai-ch'ao" ('On the "Inner Cabinet" and "Outer Cabinet" of the Han Dynasty'), *Bulletin of the Institute of History and Philology, Academia Sinica* 13:227-67 (1948); also Pan Ku, *History of the Former Han Dynasty*, tr. by Homer H. Dubs (Baltimore, 1944), II,

8-11; also Wang Yü-ch'üan, "An Outline of the Central Government of the Former Han Dynasty," *Harvard Journal of Asiatic Studies* 12:166-73 (1949).

8. Ch'ien Mu, *Chung-kuo li-tai cheng-chih*, pp. 69-71.

9. Charles O. Hucker, *The Censorial System of Ming China* (Stanford, 1966), pp.273-86 and Table 23 (p.318).

10. Lao Kan, *Ch'in-han shih* (History of Ch'in and Han dynasties), (Taipei, 1952), pp.131-33.

11. Ch'en Yin-k'o, *Sui-T'ang chih-tu yüan-yüan lüeh-lun kao* (Studies of the origins of Sui and T'ang institutions), (Peking, 1963), pp.85-87.

12. Ch'ien Mu, *Chung-kuo li-tai cheng-chih*, pp. 99-101.

13. Edward A. Kracke, Jr., "The Chinese and the Art of Government," in Raymond Dawson, ed., *The Legacy of China* (Oxford, 1964), p.333; also Ch'ien Mu, *Chung-kuo li-tai cheng-chih*, pp.16-17.

14. For their legal and social privileges, see T'ung-tsu Ch'ü, *Law and Society in Traditional China* (Paris, 1961), pp. 177-85.

15. Ho, "Salient Aspects of China's Heritage," p.10.

16. For a well-analyzed discussion of the Sui, see Arthur F. Wright, "The Formation of Sui Ideology, 581-604," in John K. Fairbank, ed., *Chinese Thought and Institutions* (Chicago, 1957), pp.71-104.

17. Fu Lo-ch'eng, *Sui-T'ang wu-tai shih* (History of Sui, T'ang, and the Five Dynasties), (Taipei, 1957), p.99; for a discussion of the T'ang ruling class, see Ch'en Yin-k'o, *T'ang-tai cheng-chih shih shu-lun kao* (A Study of the political history of the T'ang dynasty), (Chungking, 1943), pp.1-38.

18. Ch'ien Mu, *Kuo-shih ta-kang* (Outline of Chinese history), (Taipei, 1967), II, 454-73.

19. Charles O. Hucker, *The Traditional Chinese State in Ming Times (1368-1644)* (Tucson, 1961), pp. 46-48; for a critical article on Ming autocracy, see Frederick W. Mote, "The Growth of Chinese Despotism," *Oriens Extremus* 8.1:18-31 (August 1961). For an informative and highly analytical article, see Ssu-yü Teng, "Ming T'ai-tsu's Destructive and Constructive Work," *Chinese Culture* 8.3:14-38 (September 1967).

20. Ch'ien Mu, *Kuo-shih ta-kang*, II, 476-79, 485; for a detailed account of the Ming secret services, see Ting I, *Ming-tai t'e-wu cheng-chih* (Government by secret services during the Ming

period), (Peking, 1951); also Mote, "The Growth of Chinese Despotism," pp.27-31; and especially Teng, "Ming T'ai-tsu's Destructive and Constructive Work," pp.20-23.

21. Carl J. Friedrich, *Man and His Government: An Empirical Theory of Politics* (New York, 1963), pp.617-18.

22. Hucker, *The Traditional Chinese State in Ming Times*, p. 63.

23. Friedrich and Brzezinski, *Totalitarian Dictatorship and Autocracy*, pp.11-12.

24. For a general discussion of Ch'ing intra-elite conflict, see Chao Kuang-hsien, "Ch'ing-ch'u chu-wang cheng-kuo chi" ('Fight for the succession to the throne in the beginning of the Manchu dynasty'), *Fu-jen hsüeh-chih* 12.1-2:181-99 (December 1943); also Li Tsung-t'ung, "Ch'ing-tai chung-yang cheng-ch'üan hsing-t'ai ti yen-pien" ('Changes in the pattern of central political power of the Ch'ing dynasty'), *Bulletin of the Institute of History and Philology, Academia Sinica*, 37, part 1 (1967), pp. 84-134.

25. There were too many cases of political corruption in the local government. For example, see *CSL*, KH, pp.12-14, Sept. 2, 1717.

26. Friedrich and Brzezinski, *Totalitarian Dictatorship and Autocracy*, p.11.

27. *CPYC*, v.19, Memorials of Wang Shih-chün, pp. 87-88, Oct. 30, 1732.

28. *ECCP*, I, 264-265; II, 756-57, 759, 917.

29. The quote is translated from *Lettres édifiantes et curieuses: écrites des missions étrangères, mémoires de la Chine*, nouvelle édition (Toulouse, 1811), v.20, p.299.

30. Like the term personal memorial which I used in my previous writing, the words palace memorial cannot fully cover all aspects of the system. However, I adopt the term palace memorial because in a certain sense it implies the fact that the system bypassed the regular procedure of communication. For these two terms, see Pei Huang, "Aspects of Ch'ing Autocracy: An Institutional Study, 1644-1735," *Tsing Hua Journal of Chinese Studies*, new series 6.1-2:109-16 (December 1967); Silas Hsiu-liang Wu, "The Memorial Systems of the Ch'ing Dynasty (1644-1911)," *Harvard Journal of Asiatic Studies* 27:25-37 (1967).

31. Charles O. Hucker, "Confucianism and the Chinese Censorial System" in Arthur F. Wright, ed.,

Confucianism and Chinese Civilization (New York, 1964), p.55.

32. Max Weber, *The Theory of Social and Economic Organization*, tr. by A. M. Henderson and Talcott Parsons (Glencoe, Ill., 1947), p.376.

33. For a detailed discussion, see Ch.7.

34. See Arthur F. Wright, "Comments by Arthur Frederick Wright," in Ho and Tsou, *China in Crisis*, vol. 1, I, p.39.

35. Joseph R. Levenson, *Confucian China and Its Modern Fate*, vol. 2: *The Problem of Monarchical Decay* (Berkeley, 1964), p. 43.

36. Jean Baptiste du Halde, *The General History of China*, tr. by Richard Brookes (London, 1741), II, 9. Capitalization and punctuation in the quotation follow the original.

37. Cf. Karl A. Wittfogel, *Oriental Despotism: A Comparative Study of Total Power* (New Haven, 1964), p.126. For critical comments on Wittfogel's general thesis, see Mote, "The Growth of Chinese Despotism," pp.1-41

II: *The Person of the Yung-cheng Emperor*

1. The new baby's mother, Empress Hsiao-kung, the Benevolent (1660-1723), was the daughter of Wei-wu, a Manchu lieutenant colonel. She was a careful and quiet woman who was made a secondary consort of the K'ang-hsi Emperor before giving birth to Yung-cheng. In 1679 she was promoted to the fourth rank with the title of the Virtuous Concubine (Te-pin); three years later she was elevated to the third rank. It was not until 1723, when her son became ruler of the country, that she was made Empress Dowager. Fortune played a trick on her, for she died the same year. She was also the mother of Yin-t'i (1688-1755), a competitor with Yung-cheng for succession.

For her biography, see T'ang Pang-chih, *Ch'ing-huang-shih ssu-p'u* (Four genealogies of the Ch'ing imperial family), (Shanghai, 1923), ch. 2, pp.11-12; *CS*, p.3495; *ECCP*, I, 302. Hope Danby considers Hsiao-kung to have been originally the wife of a man named Wei, who was the father of Yung-cheng. However, she does not support this statement with evidence. See Danby's *The Garden of Perfect Brightness: The History of the Yüan Ming Yüan and of the Emperors Who Lived There* (London, 1950), p.23.

2. The K'ang-hsi Emperor had thirty-five sons,

fifteen of whom died before the age of eleven. For reference see Ai-hsin Chüeh-lo Hsiu-p'u Ch'u, *Hsin-yüan chi-ch'ing* (A genealogy of the Manchu ruling family) in the same compiler's *Ai-hsin chüeh-lo tsung-p'u* (A genealogy of the Ai-hsin Gioro clan), (Mukden, 1938), pp.49-54; T'ang Pang-chih, *Ch'ing huang-shih*, ch.3, pp.12-20. He had twenty daughters, only eight of whom reached maturity (see *ibid.*, ch.4, pp.11-15).

3. *CSL*, KH, ch.235, pp.24-25, Dec. 27, 1708.

4. In English accounts his name always appears as Yin-t'i (for instance, see *ECCP*, II, 929-30). However, in Manchu documents it appears as 𠃊𠃍 which are pronounced Yin-shih. See the Manchu version of *SYPC*, v.4, p.105. For the Jesuit's appraisal of him, see Jesuits, *Travels of the Jesuits into Various Parts of the World: Particularly China and the East Indies*, tr. by John Lockman, 2nd ed. (London, 1743), II, 113-50 and 417.

5. *ECCP*, II, 922-23.

6. For a comprehensive treatment of this subject, see Harold L. Kahn, *Monarchy in the Emperor's Eyes: Image and Reality in the Ch'ien-lung Reign* (Cambridge, Mass., 1971), ch.7. Although Kahn's discussion centers on the education of the Ch'ien-lung Emperor, it can be well applied to that of the Yung-cheng Emperor.

7. For qualification of tutors, see Ch'ing-kuei et al., *Ch'ing kung-shih hsü-pien* (Supplement to the history of Ch'ing palaces), (Peiping, 1932), ch.6, p.7, July 31, 1805.

8. For his work with Gubadai, see *CS*, p.3926; for his study with Father Pedrini, see Alphonse Favier, *Péking: Histoire et description* (Peking, 1897), p.199; for his work with Hsü, see *ECCP*, II, 695; *YHL*, p.295.

9. Chao-lien, *Hsiao-t'ing tsa-lu* (A miscellaneous record of Hsiao-t'ing), (Shanghai, 1901), "Supplement," ch.1, p.12.

10. Joachim Bouvet, *History of Cang-Hy: The Present Emperor of China* (London, 1699), p.91.

11. For the pupil-teacher relationship, see Yü Min-chung et al., *Kuo-ch'ao kung-shih* (History of Ch'ing palaces), (Tientsin, 1925), ch.3, p.2, Feb. 21, 1723; for their attendance, see Ch'ing-kuei, *Ch'ing kung-shih*, ch.1, pp.5 and 7, May 31, 1770, and Jan. 18, 1771. For disciplinary practices, see Ch'ing-kuei, *Ch'ing kung-shih*, ch.1, p.7, Jan. 18, 1771; ch.3, pp.4-5, April 2, 1789.

12. Friedrich, *Man and His Government*, pp.129-130.
13. Miyazaki Ichisada, *Yōsei-tei, Chūgoku no dokusai kunshu* ('The Yung-cheng Emperor—China's autocratic ruler'), (Tokyo, 1950), p.164.
14. *CSL*, KH, ch.236, pp.24-25, April 7, 1709.
15. *CPYC*, v.34, Memorials of Wang Shao-hsü, p.23, Mar. 31, 1727.
16. *Ibid.*
17. Antonio Sisto Rosso, *Apostolic Legations to China of the Eighteenth Century* (South Pasadena, Calif., 1948), p.212.
18. For his charge of military affairs, see *ECCP*, II, 922. For his assignment of literary work, see n.5 above.
19. For Yin-chih's princedom, see *ECCP*, II, 922. For Yung-cheng's, see *ibid.*, 916, and T'ang Pang-chih, *Ch'ing huang-shih*, ch.1, p.8.
20. *CSL*, KH, ch.235, pp.19-20, Dec. 25, 1708.
21. For Yin-t'i's appointment, see *ECCP*, II, 930.
22. Ch'ing Shih-tsung, *Yü-hsüan yü-lu* (A collection of selected Buddhist and Taoist sayings), (Palace ed., 1733), ch.12, p.28; Edmund Trelawny Backhouse and John Otway Percy Bland, *Annals and Memoirs of the Court of Peking* (London, 1914), pp. 291-92.
23. His decrees provided many clues. For instance, see *SYNK*, v.4, pp.2-4, April 29, 1724; v.5, pp.8-12, Oct. 8, 1724.
24. *CPYC*, v.8, Memorials of Li Fu, p.97, Dec. 18, 1726.
25. For a detailed discussion of them, see Ch.4.
26. *YHL*, p.267; Miyazaki Ichisada, *Yōsei-tei*, p.27.
27. Yin-hsiang, *I-hsien ch'in-wang shu-ch'ao* (A collection of Prince I's memorials), (1823 ed.), p.3.
28. *CPYC*, v.1, Memorials of Fan Shih-i, p.20, Nov. 30, 1727; v.8, Memorials of Ho T'ien-p'ei, p.16, July 9, 1724.
29. *Ibid.*, v.48, Memorials of A-k'e-tun, p.66, Jan. 24, 1727.
30. *SYNK*, v.15, pp.1-2, June 22, 1727.
31. Chang T'ing-yü, *Ch'eng-huai yüan-yü* (Sayings at the Ch'eng-huai Garden), in *Hsiao-yüan ts'ung-shu*, ch.1, p.15.
32. *SYNK*, v.11, p.17, Nov. 6, 1726; v.23, p.1, Oct. 22, 1729.

33. According to *CS*, the number of imperial consorts of Manchu rulers from Nurhaci to the Kuang-hsü Emperor were, in order, 16, 15, 18, 31, 7 (Yung-cheng), 17, 11, 16, 15, 5, and 3. For reference, see *ibid.*, pp.3490-503. In another source the figures are respectively 15, 15, 19, 40, 9 (Yung-cheng), 28, 15, 20, 16, 5, and 3 (T'ang Pang-chih, *Ch'ing huang-shih*, ch.2, pp.2-39).

34. *CSL*, YC, ch.3, pp.1-26, Feb. 5, 1723.

35. *CPYC*, v.7, Memorials of Huang Kuo-ts'ai, p. 111, Nov. 30, 1724. For a very sketchy description of Yung-cheng's daily schedule, see Silas Hsiu-liang Wu, "Emperors at Work: The Daily Schedules of the K'ang-hsi and Yung-cheng Emperors 1661-1735," *Tsing Hua Journal of Chinese Studies*, new series, 8.1-2:220-21 (August 1970).

36. Miyazaki Ichisada, *Yōsei tei*, pp.163-64.

37. For discussion of Chinese nationalist feeling, see Ch.8.

38. For his relationship with the Mongol Lama, see Ch'ing Shih-tsung, *Yü-hsüan yü-lu*, ch.18, p.1. For his contacts with other Ch'an monks, see *ibid.*, p.3.

39. Perhaps this sense has a "charismatic" implication. See Weber, *Theory of Social and Economic Organization*, pp.358-373; for criticism of his discussion, see Friedrich, *Man and His Government*, pp.114-15, and 172-75.

40. Max Weber, *The Religion of China: Confucianism and Taoism*, tr. and ed. by Hans H. Gerth (Glencoe, Ill., 1951), p.143.

41. Ch'ing Shih-tsung, *Yü-hsien yü-lu*, ch.18, p.1.

42. *Ibid.*, ch.19, pp.1-3.

43. Du Halde, *The General History of China*, II, 9.

44. *Ibid.*, I, 505. In the above quotation spelling, capitalization, and punctuation follow the original.

45. For his addition of Confucian scholars to the Confucian temple, see *CSL*, YC, ch.18, p.24, May 21, 1724; ch.20, pp.18-20, July 9, 1724; for his repair of the Confucian temple, see *ibid.*, ch.23, pp.23-24, Oct. 10, 1724.

46. *Ibid.*, ch.7, p.18, June 23, 1723; ch.64, pp. 3-4, Jan. 13, 1728.

47. A detailed discussion of the Sacred Edict and its expansion will be presented in Ch.8.

48. For example, see Ch'ing Shih-tsung, *Yü-hsüan yü-lu*, v.1, p.7 (preface).

49. Weber, *The Religion of China*, pp.169-70.

50. Perhaps the remarks of Emperor Hsüan (r. 73-49 B.C.), whose reign marked the height of Chinese power and civilization under the Former Han, are the most candid confession of such a deviation. After hearing the remonstrance of his Confucian-minded heir apparent that a lenient state policy be followed and that more Confucian scholars be put in high office, Emperor Hsüan said:

> The Han dynasty has its own laws and institutes, which embody and blend the principles of realistic statecraft as well as those of ancient sage-kings. How could I rely entirely on moral instruction which [is alleged to have] guided the government of the Chou dynasty [1122-256 B.C.]? Moreover, the ordinary Confucians seldom understand the needs of changing times. They love to praise the ancient and to decry the present, thus making people confused about ideals and realities and incapable of knowing what to abide by. How could the Confucians be entrusted with the vital responsibilities of the state?

Emperor Hsüan's words well explain the case of the Yung-cheng Emperor. For the quote, see Pan Ku, *History of the Former Han Dynasty*, II, 301. Its translation is based on Ho, "Salient Aspects of China's Heritage," pp.12-13.

51. Hsiao I-shan, *Ch'ing-tai t'ung-shih* (A general history of the Ch'ing dynasty), (Taipei, 1963), I, 940-41.

52. Charles O. Hucker, "The Tung-lin Movement of the Last Ming Period," in Fairbank, *Chinese Thought and Institutions*, pp. 132-63; Heinrich Busch, "The Tung-lin Academy and Its Political and Philosophical Significance," *Monumenta Serica* 14:1-163 (1949-1955).

53. Besides the above two articles, also useful is Ch'ien Mu, *Chung-kuo chin san-pai nien hsüeh-shu shih* (Chinese intellectual history of the last three hundred years), (Taipei, 1957), I, 14.

54. Levenson, *Confucian China and Its Modern Fate*, II, 28 and 38ff.

55. A detailed discussion of the aristocratic factions and succession struggle will be presented in Chs.3-4.

56. *CPYC*, v.13, Memorials of Li Fu, pp.41-42, July 19, 1723; for analysis of the religious activity in support of the political order, see C. K. Yang, *Religion in Chinese Society* (Berkeley, 1967), pp.110-12, 136-43.
57. *CPYC*, v.27, Memorials of O-er-t'ai, p.51, June 14, 1729.
58. *Ibid.*, v.44, Memorials of Chi Tseng-yün, pp. 29-30, Aug. 27, 1726.
59. *Ibid.*, v.3, Memorials of K'ung Yü-hsün, p.38, March 15, 1726.
60. *Ibid.*, v.47, Memorials of Sun Wen-ch'eng, p.102, May 21, 1727; v.44, Memorials of Chi Tseng-yün, p.35, Dec. 8, 1726.
61. *CSL*, YC, ch.31, p.9, May 22, 1725; *CPYC*, v.53, Memorials of Hsü Jung, p.30, Nov. 5, 1724.
62. *SYNK*, v.24, p.25, Feb. 8, 1730.
63. For a discussion of justice and the ruler's authority and legitimacy, see Friedrich, *Man and His Government*, pp.254, 259; for political equality, see *ibid.*, ch.16.
64. *CPYC*, v.18, Memorials of Tung Yung-wen, pp. 54-55.
65. *Ibid.*, v.13, Memorials of Ho Shih-chi, p.12, May 9, 1726.
66. *Ibid.*, v.2, Memorials of Yang Ming-shih, p.8, Oct. 22, 1724; v.22, Memorials of Jen Kuo-jung, p.31, Oct. 10, 1729.
67. Ch'ing Shih-tsung, *Ch'in-ting chih-chung ch'eng-hsien* (Historical examples of the mean), (Palace ed., 1733), ch.1, pp.1-6.
68. *Shang-yü ch'i-wu i-fu* (Imperial decrees and responding memorials governing banner affairs), (Yung-cheng ed.), v.3, p.24, entries of 1725.
69. *CPYC*, v.18, Memorials of Tung Yung-wen, p.54; *CSL*, YC, ch.50, pp.6-7, Dec. 4, 1726.
70. *CSL*, YC, ch.136, p.11, Nov. 25, 1733; Ch'ing Shih-tsung, *Ch'in-ting chih-chung ch'eng-hsien*, ch.1, p.5.
71. Han Fei, *The Complete Works of Han Fei Tzu: A Classic of Chinese Legalism*, tr. by W. K. Liao (London, 1939), I, 282; Niccolò Machiavelli, *The Prince*, tr. by George Bull (Baltimore, 1961), p.95.
72. For example, Chu Hung-hsü, one of the commissioners sent to check the liabilities of the people in Kiangsu, carried out his mission by very harsh means. Accordingly, he was impeached for excessive harshness by some officials, but the Emperor pardoned him because he meant to maintain the

authority of law. For reference, see *CPYC*, v.50, Memorials of Kao Pin, p.73, Nov. 1, 1729.

73. *CSL*, YC, ch.136, p.10, Nov. 25, 1733.

74. Inoue Ichii, "Shinchō kyūtei shaman kyō shiden ni tsuite" ('The Shamanistic sanctuaries in the Peking Palace'), in *Haneda Hakushi Shō jukinenū Tōyōshi ronsō* ('Asiatic Studies in Honor of Toru Haneda on the Occasion of His Sixtieth Birthday'), (Kyoto, 1950), pp.75-94.

75. For the Manchu patronage of Lamaism, see Kenneth K. S. Ch'en, *Buddhism in China: A Historical Survey* (Princeton, 1964), pp.449-50. For activities of the Ch'an monks, see *ECCP*, I, 257.

76. Ch'ü Hsüan-ying, *Chung-kuo she-hui shih-liao ts'ung-ch'ao* (A collection of materials concerning Chinese social history), (Shanghai, 1938), p.233.

77. Ch'en, *Buddhism in China*, p.439.

78. Ch'ing Shih-tsung, *Yüeh-hsing chi* (A collection for mental amusement), Ts'ung-shu chi-ch'eng ch'u-pien ed., preface, p.1; Ch'ing Shih-tsung, *Yü-hsüan yü-lu*, ch.7, preface, p.13. For his view of Confucianism, Buddhism, and Taoism as a single unity, see Tsukamoto Shunkō, "Yōsei tei no ju-butsu-do sankyō ittaikan" ('The Yung-cheng Emperor's view of Confucianism, Buddhism, and Taoism as a single unity'), *Tōyōshi Kenkyū* (Journal of Oriental researches), 18.3:124-41 (December 1959).

79. Ch'ing Shih-tsung, *Yü-hsüan yü-lu*, ch.12, preface, p.1; Ch'ing Shih-tsung, *Yüeh-hsing chi*, preface, p.1.

80. Ch'ing Shih-tsung, *Yü-hsüan yü-lu*, ch.12, pp.33, 38, 43.

81. For his repair and construction of Buddhist temples and Taoist shrines, see Ch'ing Shih-tsung, *Shih-tsung hsien huang-ti yü-chih wen-chi* (Collection of Emperor Shih-tsung's essays), (Palace ed., 1897), ch.14, p.17; ch.16, pp.14, 22-26, and ch.17, pp.4-6, 10-16, 22-25.

82. Ch'ing Shih-tsung, *Yü-hsien yü-lu*, v.1, preface, p.2; ch.18, preface, p.2.

83. Ch'en, *Buddhism in China*, pp.445-47.

84. Ch'ing Shih-tsung, *Yü-hsien yü-lu*, ch.12, p. 64; Ch'ing Shih-tsung, *Chien-mou pien-i lu* (Criticisms of Buddhist heresies), (Palace ed., 1733), v.1, p.1; Tsukamoto Shunkō, "Yōsei tei no bukkyō kyōdan e no kundai" ('Emperor Yung-cheng's admonition against the Buddhist order'), *Indogaku bukkyōgaku kenkyū* (Journal of Indian and Buddhist Studies) 9.1:323-26 (January 1961). For the Ch'an sects attacked by him,

see Fujii Sosen, "Shintei to bukkyō—koto ni rinsai shu" (The Ch'ing court and Buddhism, especially the Lin-chi sect of Ch'an), *Ōtani Gakuhō* (Journal of Buddhism and Cultural Science) 16.3:158-61 (October 1935).

85. For a list of such publications, see *ECCP*, II, 918.

86. See Ch'ing Shih-tsung, *Yü-hsüan yü-lü*, v.1, general preface, p.9.

87. Ch'ing Shih-tsung, *Chien-mu pien-i lu*, v.1, edicts, p.15.

88. *YHL*, p.358.

89. For the fifteen members, see Fujii Sosen, "Shintei to bukkyō" 167. Actually there were a few more Taoist priests who served at the court but not included in this group (see *CSL*, CL, ch.1, p.20, Oct. 10, 1735).

90. *YHL*, p.358.

91. For a useful study, see S. N. Eisenstadt, "Religious Organizations and Political Process in Centralized Empires," *Journal of Asian Studies* 21.3: 271-94 (May 1962). In this section the analysis of the relationship between political and religious systems is based on this article. For another useful analysis, see S. N. Eisenstadt, *The Political Systems of Empires* (London, 1963), ch.4 and pp.140-43.

92. Hans Kelsen, "Centralization and Decentralization," in Harvard Tercentenary Conference of Arts and Sciences, ed., *Authority and the Individual* (Cambridge, Mass., 1937), pp.227-28.

93. For the magical means the Taoist priest applied, see *CSL*, YC, ch.98, p.15, Nov. 5, 1730; for his sentence, see *ibid.*, ch.99, p.1, Nov. 11, 1730; *YHL*, p.380.

94. Ch'ing Shih-tsung, *Yü-hsüan yü-lu*, ch.14, pp.6-7.

95. *SYNK*, v.21, p.3, May 4, 1729; v.26, pp.1-2, June 20, 1730.

96. *Ibid*, v. 21, pp.3-4, May 4, 1729; v.21, pp. 1-2, June 20, 1730.

97. *Ibid.*, v.14, p.14, May 28, 1727; *CPYC*, v.3, Memorials of K'ung Yü-hsün, p.28, Dec. 14, 1724.

98. *Han ming-ch'en chuan* (Biographies of eminent Chinese officials) in *Man-han ming-ch'en chuan* (Biographies of eminent Manchu and Chinese officials), ed. by Ch'ing-shih Kuan (Chin-hsiang ed.), ch.16, p.42.

99. For instance, J. A. M. de Mailla, *Histoire générale de la Chine* (Paris, 1777-85), v.11, pp.379-

500; Paschal M. d'Elia, *The Catholic Missions in China* (Shanghai, 1934), pp.50-55; Joseph Brucker, "La Mission de Chine de 1722 à 1735," *Revue des questions historiques* 29:491-532 (1881); *Lettres édifiantes et curieuses*, v.20, pp.241-270; Matteo Ripa, *Memoirs of Father Ripa during Thirteen Years' Residence at the Court of Peking in the Service of the Emperor of China*, tr. by Fortunato Prandi (London, 1855), ch.23; Rosso, *Apostolic Legations*, chs. 4,6,10; Arnold H. Rowbotham, *Missionary and Mandarin: The Jesuits at the Court of China* (Berkeley, 1942), chs.9-14; and A. Thomas, *Histoire de la mission de Pékin* (Paris, 1923), I, 135-404. For a brief article, see C. R. Boxer, "Jesuits at the Court of Peking, 1601-1775," *History Today* 7.9:580-89 (September 1957).

100. Rowbotham, *Missionary and Mandarin*, p.225; Thomas, *Histoire de la mission de Pékin*, p.316.

101. For Father Mourão's relation with Yin-t'ang, see *Wen-hsien ts'ung-pien* (Collectanea from the Historical Records Office), (Peiping, 1930-1943), v.1, "Yün-ssu Yün-t'ang an," pp.1-4; For the priest's confession and his sentence to death, see Rosso, *Apostolic Legations*, pp.407-18.

102. For Sunu's biography, see *ECCP*, II, 692-94.

103. For Yung-cheng's conversation with the priests, see Mailla, *Histoire générale de la Chine*, v.11, pp.400-403. For some points of his letter to the Pope, see Rowbotham, *Missionary and Mandarin*, pp.173-74. For his public decree, its translation, and a discussion of it, see *SYNK*, v.14, p.14, May 28, 1727; Paul A. Cohen, *China and Christianity: The Missionary Movement and the Growth of Chinese Antiforeignism, 1860-1870* (Cambridge, Mass., 1963), pp. 13-15.

104. Brucker, "La mission de Chine de 1722 à 1735," p.505; Rosso, *Apostolic Legations*, p.213.

105. For instance, see Cohen, *China and Christianity*, pp.3-34; For a recent study of the anti-Christian movement from a broad cultural basis, see George H. C. Wong, "The Anti-Christian Movement in China: Late Ming and Early Ch'ing," *Tsing Hua Journal of Chinese Studies*, new series, 3.1:187-222 (May 1962).

106. Fang Hao, *Fang Hao Wen-lu* (Collected essays of Fang Hao), (Peiping, 1948), pp.47-65.

107. For a detailed study of the topic, see Rowbotham, *Missionary and Mandarin*, chs.9-12.

108. *Ibid.*, p.195; Mailla, *Histoire générale de*

la Chine, v.11, pp.330-31; *CSL*, KH, ch.272, p.8, May 24, 1717.
　　109. *CPYC*, v.3, Memorials of K'ung Yü-hsün, p.27, Dec. 14, 1724.
　　110. *Ibid.*, v.57, Memorials of Chao Hung-en, p.12, Dec. 26, 1729.
　　111. *Ibid.*, v.7, Memorials of Fei Chin-wu, p.49, Dec. 26, 1729.

　　　　　III: The Road to the Throne

　　1. For the three stories, see Ch'ing Shih-tsung, *Ta-i chüeh-mi lu* (A record of great tenor for the deluded), (Palace ed., 1730), ch.3, pp.33-35; Antonio S. Rosso seems to have adopted the second story. See Rosso, *Apostolic Legations*, p.212. For the third story, see Danby, *The Garden of Perfect Brightness*, p.16.
　　2. For discussion of Tseng's case, see ch.8. For discussion of him and the *Ta-i chüeh-mi lu*, see Onogawa Hidemi, "Yōsei tei to Taigi kakumei-roku" ('Emperor Yung-cheng and *Ta-i chüeh-mi lu*'), *Tōyōshi Kenkyū* 16.4:95-107 (March 1958).
　　3. For some works in Chinese, see Meng Sen, *Ch'ing-tai shih* (History of the Ch'ing dynasty), (Taipei, 1960), pp.477-510; Wang Chung-han, *Ch'ing-shih tsa-k'ao* (Miscellanea on the history of the Ch'ing dynasty), (Peking, 1957), pp.147-93. For some works in English, see Rosso, *Apostolic Legations*, p. 212; especially *ECCP*, II, 916.
　　4. Meng Sen, *Ch'ing-tai shih*, pp.477-510.
　　5. *Ibid.*, pp.487-99; *ECCP*, I, 552-54, 587-90.
　　6. Wang Chung-han, *Ch'ing-shih tsa-k'ao*, pp. 194-207; *ECCP*, II, 930-31.
　　7. *ECCP*, II, 917.
　　8. *CSL*, KH, ch.266, p.5, Dec. 3, 1715.
　　9. In the 1690s K'ang-hsi gave this post to a brother, Fu-ch'üan (1653-1703), and to Fiyanggu (1645-1701), a Manchu general, on the basis of qualifications. See *ECCP*, I, 248, 251.
　　10. Jesuits, *Travels of the Jesuits*, II, 418.
　　11. For a detailed discussion, see the next section.
　　12. For the case of Yin-t'i, see section 3.
　　13. Ripa, *Memoirs of Father Ripa*, p.83.
　　14. For a critical discussion, see Lien-shang Yang, "The Organization of Chinese Official Historiography," in W. G. Beasley and E. G. Pulleyblank, ed.,

Historians of China and Japan (London, 1961), pp.50-52; also see Harold L. Kahn, "Some Mid-Ch'ing Views of the Monarchy," *Journal of Asian Studies* 24.2:229-43, especially 229-35 (February 1965).

15. Ch'ing Shih-tsung, *Yü-chih lu* (Record of imperial edicts of the Yung-cheng period), ed. by Yüeh Chung-ch'i (Sian, 1728), ch.1, p.10; *SYNK*, v.1, p.8, Jan. 13, 1723; *CSL*, YC, ch.2, p.12, Jan. 13, 1723. For other examples, see Pei Huang, "Five Major Sources for the Yung-cheng Period, 1723-1735," *Journal of Asian Studies* 27.4:849, 854 (August 1968).

16. See the Manchu names in *CSL*, YC, ch.14, pp. 1-2, Dec. 27, 1723, and *SYPC*, v.1, p.22, Dec. 27, 1723.

17. See *SYPC*, v.8, pp.12-15, June 23, 1730; for comparison between these two sources, see Huang, "Five Major Sources," p.855.

18. Meng Sen, *Ch'ing-tai shih*, p.479.

19. For a detailed analysis and comparison of some major official works, see Huang, "Five Major Sources", pp.848-57.

20. *SYNK*, v.24, p.20, Dec. 5, 1729.

21. Wang Hsien-ch'ien, *Tung-hua lu* (Tung-hua records), (Changsha, 1884-90), YC, ch.14, pp.46-47, June 27, 1729; ch.15, pp.43-50, Nov. 27, 1729.

22. Cf. *ibid.*, with Ch'ing Shih-tsung, *Ta-i chüeh-mi lu*, ch.3, pp.31-33, 43-59.

23. For example, *ECCP*, II, 749.

24. Huang, "Five Major Sources", pp.848-55.

25. For instance, see Jesuits, *Travels of the Jesuits*, II, 417-20; Meng Sen, *Ch'ing-tai shih*, p. 186.

26. See n.24 in Ch.1. In a recent article based on the old Manchu archival source, Li Hsüeh-chih argues that Nurhaci did make his eldest son heir apparent. See his "Ch'ing T'ai-tsu shih-ch'i chien-ch'u wen-t'i ti fen-hsi". ('An analysis of the designation of heir apparent in the time of Nurhaci'), *Ssu yü yen* (Thought and word) 8.2:1-9 (July 1970).

27. For the nine articles, see Chu Chih-jen, *Pen-ch'ao cheng-chih ch'üan-shu* (Complete works on the political administration of the Ch'ing dynasty), (Ch'eng-en T'ang ed.), v.25, p.37; O-hai, *Liu-pu tse-li ch'üan-shu* (Statutes and precedents of the Six Boards), (1716 ed.), v.30, p.37.

28. For information about his teachers, see *CSL*, KH, ch.234, p.11, Oct. 29, 1708; *ECCP*, II, 710.

29. For example, see *CSL*, KH, ch.234, p.11, Oct. 29, 1708; Hsü Ch'ien-hsüeh, *Tan-yüan ch'üan-chi* (The

complete collection of Tan-yüan), (1883 ed.), ch.12, pp.2-3; Sung Lao, *Hsi-p'o lei-kao* (A collection of classified writings of Hsi-p'o), (1917 ed.), ch.25, pp.3, 8; Bouvet, *History of Cang-Hy*, pp.91-93; Jesuits, *Travels of the Jesuits*, II, 116.

30. *CSL*, KH, ch.210, pp.2 and 6, Nov. 23 and Dec. 9, 1702.

31. For the two cases that made the throne unhappy, see *ibid.*, ch.147, p.24, Aug. 28, 1690; ch. 171, p.20, March 30, 1696. For his receipt of the imperial paternal love, see *ECCP*, I, 330; II, 924.

32. For Yin-shih's recall, see *CSL*, KH, ch.148, pp.6-7, Sept. 15, 1690; for his second appointment, see *ibid.*, ch.172, p.12, May 18, 1696.

33. For example, see *ibid.*, ch.236, pp.8, 23-27, March 3 and April 7, 1709.

34. For Yin-shih's strength in the five banners, see *ibid.*, ch.237, p.14, May 24, 1709.

35. *SYNK*, v.5, p.13, Oct. 8, 1724.

36. For Yin-shih's scheme to remove Yin-jeng, see *CSL*, KH, ch.234, pp.20-21, Nov. 7, 1708; for Yin-shih's dream of the designation, see Jesuits, *Travels of the Jesuits*, II, 417.

37. *CSL*, KH, ch.234, p.21, Nov. 7, 1708; ch.235, pp.3-4, Nov. 13, 1708.

38. For Yin-ssu's punishment, see *ibid.*, ch.235, p.5, Nov. 13, 1708; for Yin-shih's resort to magic means, see *ibid.*, p.12, Nov. 26, 1708; Jesuits, *Travels of the Jesuits*, II, 418.

39. For Yin-jeng's confinement, see Jesuits, *Travels of the Jesuits*, II, 417-18; *CSL*, KH, ch.234, pp.2-5, Oct. 17, 1708; for his dismissal, see *ibid.*, pp.16-20, Oct. 31 and Nov. 6, 1708; for the gracious proclamation, see Chu Chih-jen, *Pen-ch'ao cheng-chih*, v.25, pp.60-64.

40. *ECCP*, II, 925; for the original texts, see *CSL*, KH, ch.234, pp.2-5, 18-20, Oct. 17 and Nov. 6, 1708. A Korean source records him as a cruel and immoral man. See *Chosŏn wangjo sillok* (The veritable records of the Yi dynasty), (Seoul, 1955-1958), Sukchong's reign, ch.47, p.20, May 2, 1709.

41. *CSL*, KH, ch.235, pp.23-26, Dec. 27, 1708; ch.237, pp.2-3, April 18, 1709.

42. *Ibid.*, ch.251, pp.7-12, Oct. 29-30, 1712; ch.252, pp.5-6, Dec. 13, 1712. For an English account of this case, see Ripa, *Memoirs of Father Ripa*, p.83.

43. For instance, see Hsiao I-shan, *Ch'ing-tai t'ung-shih*, I, 817-820. A recent book accepts the official interpretation of Yin-jeng's "crimes" and

even exaggerates them. See Silas H. L. Wu, *Communication and Imperial Control in China: Evolution of the Palace Memorial System, 1693-1735* (Cambridge, Mass., 1970), ch.6.

44. For example, see Meng Sen, *Ch'ing-tai shih*, pp.175-86.

45. For example, Kahn, "Some Mid-Ch'ing Views," p.231. He adopted the point from Miyazaki Ichisada, *Yōsei-tei*, pp.4-5.

46. *CSL*, KH, ch.234, pp.7 and 9, Oct. 22 and 24, 1708.

47. For information about K'ang-hsi's private life, see Ripa, *Memoirs of Father Ripa*, pp.115-16; *Chosŏn wangjo sillok*, Hyonjong's reign, ch.18, p.47, April 14, 1668; Sukchong's reign, ch.13, part 1, p.18, April 24, 1682, and ch.14, part 1, p.29, April 3, 1683. For a story about Ch'ien-lung's immoral life, see the discussion in Kahn, "Some Mid-Ch'ing Views", pp.238-39.

48. For general information about this matter, see *YHL*, p.30. For Wang's memorial, see *CSL*, KH, ch. 291, pp.25-28, April 11, 1721. For Chu's petition, see *ibid.*, ch.277, pp.6-7, Feb. 19, 1718.

49. *CSL*, KH, ch.237, p.16, May 28, 1709; *SYPC*, v.2, p.29, Dec. 13, 1724. According to a Korean source, K'ang-hsi even regretted his redismissal of Yin-jeng. See *Chosŏn wangjo sillok*, Sukchong's reign,, section of Corrigenda, ch.15, p.1, Feb. 16, 1714.

50. *CSL*, KH, ch.253, p.8, Feb. 26, 1713.

51. For information about his supporters, see *ibid.*, ch.248, pp.15-18, Dec. 6, 1711; ch.250, pp. 6-7, May 17, 1712; and ch.253, p.10, Feb. 27, 1713. For the minister of the Imperial Household, see *ibid.*, ch.257, pp.13-14, Feb. 2, 1714; ch.261, p.10, Jan. 2, 1715. For their plan to release Yin-jeng, see *ibid.*, ch.277, p.20, March 7, 1718.

52. *Ibid.*, ch.235, p.23, Dec. 27, 1708.

53. *Ibid.*, p.6, Nov. 13, 1708.

54. Jesuits, *Travels of the Jesuits*, II, 417.

55. *YHL*, p.205.

56. *SYNK*, v.4, p.3, April 29, 1724.

57. *ECCP*, I, 284; II, p.927; *YHL*, p.35; *CSL*, KH, ch.266, p.7, Dec. 6, 1715; *Wen-hsien ts'ung-pien*, v.1, "Yün-ssu Yün-t'ang an," pp.4-8.

58. *CSL*, YC, ch.44, p.26, June 16, 1726; *ibid.*, KH, ch.234, p.24, Nov. 11, 1708; ch.235, p.25, Dec. 27, 1708; *SYNK*, v.10, p.7, June 8, 1726.

59. *CSL*, KH, ch.235, pp.19-20, Dec. 25, 1708; Jesuits, *Travels of the Jesuits*, II, 419.

60. *CSL*, KH, ch.235, p.2, Nov. 12, 1708.
61. For Yin-ssu's attempt to assassinate the crown prince, see n.37 above. For the contributions of Alingga, K'uei-hsü and Mawu to Yin-jeng's deposal, see *YHL*, p.324; *SYPC*, v.2, pp.29-30, Dec. 13, 1724.
62. For their punishments, see the first entry, n.38 above; *CSL*, KH, ch.237, p.15, May 24, 1709; Jesuits, *Travels of the Jesuits*, II, 420. For the emperor's decrees about Yin-shih and Yin-ssu, see *CSL*, KH, ch.234, pp.4-5, Oct. 17, 1708; ch.236, pp. 4-7, March 2, 1709.
63. For information about Yin-ssu's special assignments, see *CSL*, KH, ch.236, pp.17, 23, March 8 and April 5, 1709. For the case of Maci, see *ECCP*, I, 561.
64. *CSL*, KH, ch.261, p.10, Jan. 2, 1715.
65. For Yin-jeng's cooperation with the police chief, see *ibid.*, ch.250, pp.6-7, May 17, 1712. For his despatch of agents to watch others, see *ibid.*, ch.251, p.9, Oct. 30, 1712.
66. They invited the emperor to feast in their gardens. For information, see *ibid.*, ch.250, pp.3, 24, May 7 and Aug. 8, 1712.
67. Ripa, *Memoirs of Father Ripa*, p.83.
68. *CSL*, KH, ch.266, p.5, Dec. 3, 1715; *ECCP*, II, 925.
69. *CSL*, KH, ch.253, pp.8-10, Feb. 26, 1713.
70. *Ibid.*, ch.275, pp.19-20, Dec. 28, 1717. For the contents of their memorials, see *Wen-hsien ts'ung-pien*, v.4, "K'ang-hsi chien-ch'uan", pp.1-8.
71. See the first two references, n.48 above. For the case about the twelve censors, see *CSL*, KH, ch.291, p.25, April 9, 1721. For the twelve censors, compare *ECCP*, II, 830.
72. *CSL*, KH, ch.291, pp.28-30, April 11 and 21, 1721.
73. See the last reference of n.48 above; du Halde, *The General History of China*, I, 499.
74. For the throne's anger, see Chao-lien, *Hsiao-t'ing tsa-lu*, ch.5, p.4. For examination of the petitioner and related individuals, see *CSL*, KH, ch.277, pp.6-7, 9, Feb. 19-20, 1718; for their punishment, see *ibid.*, pp.30-31, March 27, 1718. Cf. du Halde, *The General History of China*, I, p.499.
75. *CSL*, KH, ch.277, pp.8-9, 25-26, Feb. 20 and March 13, 1718.
76. *Ibid.*, ch.195, p.2, Nov. 2, 1699; *ECCP*, II, 922.
77. *CSL*, KH, ch.236, p.8, March 3, 1709.

78. For his compilation of two encyclopedias, see *ibid.*, ch.255, p.13, July 23, 1713; ch.256, p.8, Nov. 7, 1713; ch.258, p.3, March 2, 1714; ch.261, p.6, Dec. 23, 1714; ECCP, II, 922.
79. For his support of Yin-jeng, see CSL, KH, ch.234, p.6, Oct. 20, 1708; for his report of Yin-shih's conduct, see the last two references, n.38 above.
80. CSL, KH, ch.253, p.9, Feb. 26, 1713.
81. *Ibid.*, ch.248, p.18, Dec. 6, 1711.
82. ECCP, II, 922.
83. YHL, p.83; Lo Chen-yü, ed. *Shih-liao ts'ung-pien* (Miscellaneous historical materials), (Port Arthur, 1935), v.2, "Yung-cheng shang-yü tang," ch.2, p.25.
84. CSL, KH, ch.231, p.16, Dec. 13, 1707; ch. 250, p.3, May 7, 1712. The last feast was given in 1722. For reference, see *ibid.*, ch.297, p.19, July 1, 1722.
85. *Ibid.*, ch.270, p.25, Jan. 28, 1717; ch.280, p.11, Sept. 1, 1718.
86. For information about Ch'en Meng-lei, see ECCP, I, 94; II, 922. For his relation with Wang Mou-hung, see Wang Mou-hung, *Pai-t'ien ts'ao-t'ang ts'un-kao* (Writings of the Pai-t'ien Studio), (Ko-t'ang ed., 1752), ch.10, p.1.
87. For his approach to Lungkodo, see SYPC, v.6, p.4, March 15, 1728. For his approach to Nien Keng-yao, see *Chang-ku ts'ung-pien* (Collected historical documents), compiled and published by the Palace Museum (Peiping, 1928-1930), v.5, "Nien Keng-yao tsou-che," pp.8-9, June 28, 1717.
88. For information about Yin-ssu's reaction, see CSL, YC, ch.45, p.12, July 2, 1726. For Yin-t'ang's response, see SYNK, v.9, p.5, Feb. 5, 1726.
89. YHL, p.55
90. CSL, KH, ch.235, p.27, Dec. 29, 1708; ch. 237, p.5, April 19, 1709.
91. *Ibid.*, ch.231, p.14, Dec. 4, 1707.
92. *Ibid.*, ch.297, pp.3-4, April 27 and May 10, 1722; YHL, p.20.
93. CSL, KH, ch.247, p.5, Sept. 8, 1711; ch.250, p.24, July 25, 1712; ch.268, p.25, July 4, 1716; ch.288, pp.17-18, Aug. 29, 1720.
94. YHL, p.20.
95. CSL, KH, ch.235, pp.27-28, Dec. 30, 1708.
96. See Chang Mu, *Yen Ch'ien-ch'iu hsien-sheng nien-p'u* (A chronological biography of Yen Jo-chü), (Shou-yang, 1847), v.4, pp.101-2; Teng Chih-ch'eng,

Ku-tung so-chi ch'üan-pien (Miscellanea of historical materials), (Peking, 1955), pp.612-13. However, another source maintains that the Yung-cheng Emperor did not invite Yen. For reference, see Chao-lien, *Hsiao-t'ing tsa-lu*, ch.5, p.36.

97. See Chang Mu, *Yen Ch'ien-ch'iu*, v.4, pp.105-7; Hang Shih-chün, *Tao-ku t'ang ch'üan-chi* (The complete works of the Tao-ku Studio), (Chen-ch'i T'ang ed., 1888), ch.29, pp.16-18.

98. Ch'üan Tsu-wang, *Chi-chi t'ing chi* (The complete works of Chi-chi t'ing), (Ssu-pu ts'ung-k'an ed.), "Wen-chi," ch.17, p.9.

99. For Mawu's relationship with the Yung-cheng Emperor, see *YHL*, pp.323-24. For English biographies of Lungkodo, Maci, Nien and T'ung, see *ECCP*, I, 552-54, 560-61, 587-590; II, 795-96 respectively.

100. *CSL*, YC, ch.87, pp.6-7, Nov. 26, 1729.

101. For their commission, see *ibid.*, KH, ch.299, p.12, Nov. 17, 1722. For Yen-hsin's English biography, see *ECCP*, II, 907-8.

102. *SYNK*, v.26, p.5, June 23, 1730.

103. *CSL*, KH, ch.281, pp.22-23, Dec. 17, 1718; Wang Chung-han, *Ch'ing-shih tsa-k'ao*, pp.194-95.

104. *CSL*, KH, ch.282, pp.10-11, Jan. 31, 1719; *ECCP*, II, 930.

105. For Yin-t'i's belief in this interpretation, see *SYNK*, v.5, pp.11-12, Oct. 8, 1724. For the conjecture of the general public, see Mailla, *Histoire générale de la Chine*, v.11, p.371.

106. *ECCP*, II, 928 and 930.

107. *SYPC*, v.4, p.45, July 2, 1726.

108. For their relations with Yin-t'i, see *YHL*, pp.336-38, 389; *ECCP*, I, 305; II, 795.

109. *SYNK*, v.6, p.18, April 11, 1725.

110. For Yin-t'i's invitation of Li Kung, see Feng Ch'en, *Li Ssu-ku hsien-sheng nien-p'u* (A chronological biography of Li Kung), (Li Kao ed., 1836) ch.5, pp.25-26, 29. For Yin-chih's attempt to invite Li Kung, see *ibid.*, ch.4, p.12.

111. For his frugality, see Chang P'eng-ko, *Chang Wen-tuan kung ch'üan-chi* (The complete works of Chang P'eng-ko), (1882 ed.), ch.7, p.49. For his monument, see *SYNK*, v.4, p.8, June 5, 1724.

112. For his request, see *CSL*, KH, ch.295, p.6, Nov. 27, 1721. Cf. *ECCP*, II, 930.

113. *SYPC*, v.4, p.44, July 2, 1726.

114. See n.101 above.

115. Meng Sen, *Ch'ing-tai shih*, pp.494-95; *ECCP*, II, 916, 928, 930; cf. *ECCP*, I, 588.

116. *CSL*, KH, ch.300, p.6, Dec. 17-19, 1722.
117. *Ibid.*, pp.6-7, Dec. 20, 1722; cf. *YHL*, p.49 and Meng Sen, *Ch'ing-tai shih*, pp.477-510. For some English works in support of the Yung-cheng Emperor's legitimate designation, see, for example, Herbert A. Giles, *China and the Manchus* (Cambridge, 1912), p.51; John Ross, *The Manchus, or the Reigning Dynasty of China* (Paisley, 1880), p.545. A Korean record also supports Yung-cheng's claim (*Chŏson wangjo sillok*, Kyongjong's reign, ch.10, p.37, Jan. 23, 1723),
118. Ripa, *Memoirs of Father Ripa*, p.119.

IV: *Consolidation of Power*

1. For an analytic discussion of their interrelations, see Levenson, *Confucian China and Its Modern Fate*, II, ch.3; Eisenstadt, *The Political Systems*, chs.7-8.
2. Kelsen, "Centralization and Decentralization," pp.227-28.
3. The discussion of universal rulership is based on the points suggested in *ibid.*, pp.212, 226-28 and in Friedrich, *Man and His Government*, chs.14-15.
4. Discussion of legitimacy is based on Friedrich, *Man and His Government*, ch.13, especially pp.239-41.
5. For their biographies in English, see *ECCP*, I, pp.1-3, 8-9, 214-15, 562-63. For a detailed Chinese article on their struggle, see Chao Kuang-hsien, "Ch'ing-ch'u chu-wang," pp.181-199. For a Japanese article, see Oshibuchi Hajime, "Shinsho ni okeru Shin shitsu nai fun ni kansuru kenkyū—tokuni Taisō o chūshin toshite" ('The internal strife of the Ch'ing ruling house in the early years of the Ch'ing dynasty, with special reference to Emperor T'ai-tsung'), in *Ishihama Sensei kanreki kinen rombun shū* ('Asiatic studies in honor of Juntaro Ishihama on the occasion of his sixtieth birthday'), (Osaka, 1958), pp.1-24. Also see Li Tsung-t'ung, "Ching-tai chung-yang," pp.84-125.
6. *ECCP*, I, 215-19.
7. *Ibid.*, pp.397-98.
8. *Ibid.*, pp.599-600.
9. *Ibid.*, pp.310-12.
10. For information about the Songgotu faction, see Hsiao I-shan, *Ch'ing-tai t'ung-shi*, I, 802-4.
11. *ECCP*, I, 588.

12. For the eight maxims, see *Ch'ing-ch'ao wen-hsien t'ung-kao* (Encyclopedia of the Ch'ing dynasty), compiled under the imperial auspices of Ch'ing Kao-tsung (Shih-t'ung ed.), I, 5486. However, the *Veritable Records* give only six maxims. For reference, see *CSL*, Shun-chih, ch.63, p.3, March 17, 1652. According to another source, there were only seven maxims. For information, see Shang Yen-liu, *Ch'ing-tai k'o-chü k'ao-shih shu-lu* (A brief record of the examination system of the Ch'ing dynasty), (Peking, 1958), n.13 in ch.1.

13. Ch'ing Shih-tsu, *Yü-chih jen-ch'en ching-hsin lu* (Imperial admonitions on the conduct of officials and subjects), (Palace ed., 1655), pp.1-5.

14. *CSL*, KH, ch.68, pp.12-13, Aug. 27, 1677; ch. 103, p.22, Aug. 30, 1682; ch.212, pp.13-14, July 1, 1703.

15. See the cases of Hsü Ch'ien-hsüeh and Kao Shih-ch'i, *ECCP*, I, 310-12, 413-14.

16. For points in the decree, see *CSL*, YC, ch.6, pp.17-19, May 22, 1723. For discussion of this decree, see David S. Nivison, "Ho-shen and His Accusers: Ideology and Political Behavior in the Eighteenth Century," in David S. Nivison and Arthur F. Wright, eds., *Confucianism in Action* (Stanford, 1959), pp. 224-25.

17. *CSL*, YC, ch.20, p.21-22, July 10, 1724.

18. For text of the essay, see *ibid.*, ch.22, pp. 14-19, Sept. 3, 1724. For discussion of the essay, see Nivison, "Ho-shen and His Accusers," pp.225-28; Levenson, *Confucian China and Its Modern Fate*, II, 69-70.

19. For the original text, see *CSL*, YC, ch.22, p.15, Sept. 3, 1724. An English translation of the emperor's essay "On Factions" appears in part in Nivison, "Ho-shen and His Accusers," p.226.

20. For an English translation of his essay, see Wm. Theodore de Bary *et al.*, eds., *Sources of Chinese Tradition* (New York, 1960), pp.446-48.

21. Friedrich, *Man and His Government*, pp.240-41.

22. For instance, see *CPYC*, v.13, Memorials of Ho Shih-chi, p.12, May 9, 1726.

23. *CSL*, YC, ch.22, p.18, Sept. 3, 1724.

24. For a systematic discussion of the subject, see C. K. Yang, "Some Characteristics of Chinese Bureaucratic Behavior" in Nivison and Wright, *Confucianism in Action*, pp.134-64.

25. For example, he forced Li Wei-chün, a member of the Nien clique, to denounce his factional leader. For information, see *CPYC*, v.5, Memorials of Li Wei-chün, pp.53-54, June 11, 1725. He ordered Yin-ssu to consider a punishment for Yin-e. For reference, see *SYNK*, v.4, pp.6-7, April 30, 1724.

26. Levenson, *Confucian China and Its Modern Fate*, II, 69-70.

27. See Giles, *China and the Manchus*, p.52; Ross, *The Manchus*, p.549.

28. In 1778. See *ECCP*, II, 927, 929.

29. For Yin-hsiang's charge of the Board of Revenue, see *CSL*, YC, ch.6, p.6, May 11, 1723; for Yin-lu's official duties, see *ibid.*, ch.1, p.12, Dec. 22, 1722; ch.8, p.2, July 4, 1723; for Yin-li's appointments, see *ibid.*, ch.9, pp.4, 26, Aug. 6 and 27, 1723.

30. See *ibid.*, ch.10, pp.15-17, Sept. 16, 1723.

31. For these appointments, see *ibid*, ch.1, pp. 8-9, Dec. 21, 1722; ch.2, p.26, Jan. 19, 1723. For his promotion, see *ibid.*, ch.2, p.17, Jan. 17, 1723.

32. *Ibid.*, ch.30, pp.34-35, May 9, 1725.

33. *SYNK*, v.4, p.8, June 5, 1724; v.5, p.16, Dec. 11, 1724.

34. *YHL*, p.54.

35. *CSL*, YC, ch.3, p.39, Feb. 20, 1723.

36. *YHL*, p.70; Thomas, *Histoire de la mission de Pékin*, p.311.

37. For instance, see *SYNK*, v.3, p.9, Dec. 26, 1723; v.4, pp.2-4, April 29, 1724; *ECCP*, II, 927.

38. *SYNK*, v.4, pp.6-9, April 30, 1724.

39. For example, Arsungga and Olondai were first banished to Mukden in 1725 and then executed there in 1726. For information, see *ibid.*, v.6, pp.19-22, April 11, 1725.

40. For the Emperor's actions, see respectively *ibid.*, v.8, p.12, Jan. 24, 1726; *YHL*, p.268; *SYNK*, v.9, p.13, Feb. 6, 1726.

41. For petition of the courtiers, see *SYNK*, v.9, pp.2-3, March 10, 1726. For Yin-ssu's imprisonment, see *CSL*, YC, ch.41, pp.8-9, March 13, 1726; for punishment of the official, see *SYNK*, v.9, p.4, March 13, 1726.

42. *CSL*, YC, ch.42, p.11, April 13, 1726. Cf. *SYNK*, v.9, p.4, March 13, 1726.

43. *CSL*, YC, ch.45, pp.7-16, July 2, 1726; *ECCP*, II, 927.

44. For example, Wang Chung-han, *Ch'ing-shih tsa-k'ao*, pp.156-57; *ECCP*, II, 927.

45. *Wên-hsien ts'ung-pien*, v.1, "Yün-ssu Yün-t'ang an," p.3; du Halde, *The General History of China*, I, 501-2.
46. For example, see *YHL*, pp.63, 129, 207.
47. For a few Jesuits' records, see *Lettres édifiantes et curieuses*, v.20, pp.20-21, 47-52ff; Mailla, *Histoire générale de la Chine*, v.11, pp.375-78, 403-8ff.
48. Thomas, *Histoire de la mission de Pékin*, p.351. For a general discussion of Sunu and his family, see Yazawa Toshihiko, "Sodo ikka ni tsuite" ('Reconstruction of the family of Sunnu'), in *Wada Hakushi koki kinen Tōyōshi ronsō* ('Oriental studies presented to Sei Kiyoshi Wada'), (Tokyo, 1960), pp. 981-991.
49. *Wen-hsien ts'ung-pien*, v.1, "Yün-ssu Yün-t'ang an," pp.1-4.
50. Ripa, *Memoirs of Father Ripa*, p.121.
51. The above discussion of Mourão is based on *ibid.*, pp.121-123; Rosso, *Apostolic Legations*, pp. 407-415; Thomas, *Histoire de la mission de Pékin*, pp. 310-315.
52. *Chang-ku ts'ung-pien*, v.10, "Yung-cheng chu-p'i Nien Keng-yao tsou-che," p.76, Aug. 26, 1723.
53. *Ibid.*, v.9, p.4; *KCT*, Memorials of Nien Keng-yao, p.1, undated (No. 19967); and *Nien Keng-yao tsou-che chuan-ch'i* (A Special Collection of the Memorials of Nien Keng-yao), comp. by National Palace Museum (Taipei, 1971), I, 7 (June 13, 1723).
54. *Wen-hsien ts'ung-pien*, v.1, "Yün-ssu Yün-t'ang an," pp.2-4.
55. *SYNK*, v.6, p.16, April 11, 1725.
56. *Ibid.*, v.9, pp.3-4, Feb. 5, 1726; *YHL*, pp. 258, 274.
57. For his expulsion from the imperial clan, see the last reference of n.40 above. For his transfer to Paoting, see *YSL*, pp.275, 299-300.
58. For his change in name, see *CSL*, YC, ch.44, p.23, June 13, 1726. For his accusation, see *ibid.*, ch.45, pp.16-21, July 2, 1726.
59. For Yin-t'ang's death, see *SYNK*, v.10, p.19, Sept. 23, 1726. For the emperor's defense, see *ibid.*, v.24, pp.6-7, Nov. 26, 1729; *ECCP*, I, 456; II, 929.
60. *CSL*, YC, ch.1, pp.9-10, Dec. 21, 1722.
61. *SYPC*, v.4, pp.49-50, July 2, 1726.
62. For surveillance on him, see *SYNK*, v.1, pp. 13-14, Dec. 31, 1722. For his promotion, see *CSL*, YC, ch.7, p.23, June 25, 1723.

63. *SYNK*, v.6, p.18, April 11, 1725; *CSL*, YC, ch.7, p.23, June 25, 1723.
64. *CSL*, YC, ch.45, pp.21-24, July 2, 1726.
65. *Ibid.*, ch.2, pp.20-21, Jan. 18, 1723; *ECCP*, I, 94; II, 922.
66. For example, see Lo Chen-yü, *Shih-liao ts'ung-pien*, v.2, "Yung-cheng shang-yü tang," ch.2, pp.25-27; *SYPC*, v.6, pp.2-4, March 14-15, 1728.
67. *SYPC*, v.4, pp.2-8, March 8, 1726.
68. *CSL*, YC, ch.44, p.23, June 23, 1726.
69. For the emperor's accusation, see *SYPC*, v.6, pp.2-4, March 14-15, 1728. For punishment of him, see *CSL*, YC, ch.70, pp.12-13, July 26, 1728.
70. *CSL*, YC, ch.94, pp.19-22, July 8, 1730; *Shang-yü ch'i-wu i-fu*, v.8, pp.6-16, July 8, 1730. Cf. *ECCP*, II, 922.
71. For a good English biography of Nien, see *ECCP*, I, 587-590. For a Chinese article, see Huang Pei, "Ch'ing Shih-tsung yü Nien Keng-yao chih kuan-hsi" (The relationship between Emperor Shih-tsung of the Ch'ing dynasty and Nien Keng-yao), *Ta-lu tsa-chih* (The Continent Magazine) 16.4:112-13 (February 1958); 16.5:151-58 (March 1958).
72. *SYPC*, v.2., p.41, Dec. 30, 1724.
73. For his relation with Yin-t'ang, see n.49 above; for his relation with Yin-chih, see the last reference of n.87, ch.3.
74. *SYPC*, v.2, pp.40-41, Dec. 30, 1724.
75. T'ang Pang-chih, *Ch'ing huang-shih*, ch.3, p.14; Rosso, *Apostolic Legations*, p.214.
76. *Chang-ku ts'ung-pien*, v.10, "Nien Keng-yao tsou-che," p.70.
77. *Wen-hsien ts'ung-pien*, v.6, "Nien Keng-yao tsou-che," p.10, Aug. 3, 1724; *ECCP*, I, 588.
78. See *Chang-ku ts'ung-pien*, v.10, "Nien Keng-yao tsou-che," pp.70-79; *Wen-hsien ts'ung-pien*, vols. 5-6, "Nien Keng-yao tsou-che," pp.1-7, 8-17, respectively; *KCT*, Memorials of Nien Keng-yao, p.1, undated (no. 19980).
79. Liang Chang-chü, *Kuei-t'ien so-chi* (Miscellaneous notes after retirement), in the same author's *Liang Chang-chü pi-chi* (A collection of Liang Chang-chü's notes), (Shanghai, 1918), ch.7, p.12.
80. *YHL*, pp.180, 186, 194; *CPYC*, v.5, Memorials of Li Wei-chün p.60, Aug.26, 1725; v.21, Memorials of Ts'ai T'ing, pp.67-68.
81. Chao-lien, *Hsiao-t'ing tsa-lu*, ch.5, p.12; Ch'ien I-chi, *Pei-chuan chi* (A collection of epitaphs

and biographies), (1893 ed.), ch.25, p.15.

82. For instance, see Meng Sen, *Ch'ing-tai shih*, p.487; Wang Chung-han, *Ch'ing-shih tsa-k'ao*, p.158; *ECCP*, I, 589.

83. Han Fei, *Complete Works of Han Fei Tzu*, I, p.151.

84. *YHL*, p.120.

85. *CSL*, YC, ch.28, p.7, March 8, 1725; ch.32, pp.15-16, June 29, 1725.

86. For the private source, see *YHL*, pp.188-89ff. For the rebuilding of the bureaucratic structure, see *ibid.*, pp.205-6, 210, 225; *SYNK*, v.7, pp. 1, 6, Aug. 8 and 19, 1725.

87. *CPYC*, v.10, Memorials of Fu-min, p.2, Oct. 5, 1725.

88. For his shrines, see *ibid.*, v.10, Memorials of Wang Ching-hao, p.107, Sept. 14, 1725. For poems of admiration, see Wang Ching-ch'i, *Tu-shu t'ang hsi-cheng sui-pi* (Jottings of a western journey), (Peiping, 1928), pp.20-22, 56-57; *CPYC*, v.8, Memorials of T'ung Chi-t'u, p.42, July 29, 1725. For improper salutations, see *YHL*, p.182.

89. Mailla, *Histoire générale de la Chine*, v.11, p.432.

90. *YHL*, p.236.

91. *Ibid.*, pp.184-85.

92. *Ibid.*, pp.182, 186-87; *KCT*, Memorials of Li Wei, pp.4-6, June 16, 1725.

93. For example, see *CPYC*, v.10, Memorials of Wang Ching-hao, p.98, Dec. 17, 1724; v.5, Memorials of Li Wei-chün, pp.41-42, Dec. 28, 1724; v.2, Memorials of Yang Tsung-jen, p.51, Dec. 30, 1724.

94. For information about his finishing preparation, see *ibid.*, v.5, Memorials of Li Wei-chün, p.47, March 14, 1725. For his open action against Nien, see *SYNK*, v.6, pp.17-18, May 5, 1725.

95. *ECCP*, I, 589; II, 786, 958.

96. For example, see *CPYC*, v.5, Memorials of Li Wei-chün, pp.53-54, 58, June 11, July 10, and Aug. 5, 1725.

97. For instance, see *Wen-hsien ts'ung-pien*, v.6, "Nien Keng-yao tsou-che," pp.16-17, Jan. 24, 1725.

98. For the ninety-two "crimes," see *CSL*, YC, ch.39, pp.6-14, Jan. 13, 1726.

99. Ch'ien I-chi, *Pei-chuan chi*, ch.25, pp.15-16; *YHL*, p.382.

100. For his English biography, see *ECCP*, I, 552-54.

101. For his honors and offices, see *Man ming-ch'en chuan* (Biographies of eminent Manchu officials) in *Man-han ming-ch'en ch'uan*, ch.21, pp.5-6.
102. *SYPC*, v.3, p.21, July 2, 1725.
103. *YHL*, p.304; *ECCP*, I, 22.
104. For information about Manbao, see *Man ming-ch'en chuan*, ch.22, p.33. For No-min, see *SYPC*, v.3, p.40, Nov. 21, 1725. For his other followers, see *YHL*, p.295; *Man ming-ch'en chuan*, ch.38, p.44. Cf. Yuan Mei, *Hsiao-ts'ang shan fang wen-chi* (Works of the Hsiao-ts'ang Studio), in the same author's *Sui-yüan ch'üan-chi* (Complete Works of Sui-yüan), (Shanghai, 1918), ch.2, p.4.
105. For the forty-one charges, see *CSL*, YC, ch.62, pp.6-9, Nov. 17, 1727. For a few individual corrupt cases, see *YHL*, pp.259-60; *Man ming-ch'en chuan*, ch.21, p.8.
106. *YHL*, p.191.
107. For their common admirers, see *ibid.*, pp. 187-88, 359. For their common targets, see T'ien Wen-ching, *Fu-yü hsüan-hua lu* (Record of the administrative work in Honan), (c.1728 ed.), v.2, ch.1, p.103; for the case they covered up in common, see *SYNK*, v.10, p.23, Sept. 25, 1726.
108. *CPYC*, v.10, Memorials of Wang Ching-hao, pp.100-101, Feb. 3, 1725.
109. *Ibid.*, v.1, Memorials of Ch'i-su-le, p.72, Jan. 26, 1725; v.10, Memorials of Wang Ching-hao, p.100, Feb. 3, 1725.
110. *CSL*, YC, ch.28, p.7, March 8, 1725; for other information, see *ECCP*, I, 553.
111. *CSL*, YC, ch.34, p.14, Aug. 19, 1725; ch.40, pp.25-26, Feb. 22, 1726.
112. *Ibid.*, ch.55, p.36, May 15, 1727.
113. Meng Sen, *Ch'ing-tai shih*, p.492; *ECCP*, I, 554.
114. *CSL*, YC, ch.62, p.10, Nov. 17, 1727.

V: *The Weakening of the Censorial System*

1. This chapter is largely based on Huang, "Aspects of Ch'ing Autocracy," pp.105-49. Section 2 in particular deals with many points covered in my article, "Yung-cheng shih-tai ti mi-tsou chih-tu" (The secret-report system during the Yung-cheng period, 1723-1735), *Tsing Hua Journal of Chinese Studies*, new series 3.1:17-52 (May 1962). There are many other works and articles on the censorial

system. For a short but general work, see Kao I-han, *Chung-kuo yü-shih chih-tu ti yen-ke* (A history of the Chinese censorial system), (Shanghai, 1934). For a critical article in English, see Hucker, "Confucianism and the Chinese Censorial System," pp.50-76.

2. For an English treatment of the Ming censorial system, see Charles O. Hucker, "Governmental Organization of the Ming Dynasty," *Harvard Journal of Asiatic Studies* 21:48-55 (December 1958), and his *The Censorial System of Ming China*, pp.30-65.

3. For the staff members of the Censorate, see *Li-tai chih-kuan piao* (Tables of offices and officials of successive dynasties), compiled by Chi Yün *et al*. (Ssu-pu pei-yao ed.), ch.18, pp.4-6. The number of censors was fixed in the Ch'ien-lung period. A recent scholar prepared a chart to indicate the organization of the Ch'ing censorial system. See Richard L. Walker, "The Control System of the Chinese Government," *Far Eastern Quarterly*, 7.1:13 (November 1947). For another useful article, see T'ang Chi-ho, "Ch'ing-tai k'o-tao tsu-chih yen-ke" (Evolution of the Ch'ing censorial system), *Hsin shehui k'o-hsüeh chi-k'an* (Quarterly Journal of New Social Sciences), 1.1:67-74 (February 1934).

4. In 1665 each of the six offices had only two supervising secretaries. For information, see *CSL*, KH, ch.14, pp.5-6, Feb. 26 and March 2, 1665. By the next year two senior supervising secretaries, one Manchu and one Chinese, were added to each section. For reference, see *ibid.*, ch.19, p.9, July 11, 1666.

5. For all these functions, see *Ch'ing-chao wenhsien t'ung-k'ao*, I, 5603-5. For a detailed article, see T'ang Chi-ho, "Ch'ing-tai k'o-tao chih chihchang" (The functions of the censors and supervising secretaries of the Ch'ing dynasty), *Tung-fang tsachih* (Eastern miscellany) 33.1:343-51 (January 1936). For an English work, see Hsieh Pao-chao, *The Government of China (1644-1911)* (Baltimore, 1925), pp.90-92.

6. For the ideological basis of the censorial system, see Hucker, "Confucianism and the Chinese Censorial System," pp.57-64.

7. For some evil cases of the Ch'ing censors and supervising secretaries, see *CSL*, Shun-chih, ch.97, pp.8-9, Feb. 13, 1656; ch.103, pp.12-13, Oct. 6, 1656; KH, ch.14, p.5, Feb. 26, 1665. Cf. Walker, "The Control System of the Chinese Government," pp.12-15.

8. For example, see *CSL*, T'ai-tsung, ch.10, pp. 35-36, Feb. 13, 1632.

9. *Ibid.*, KH, ch.127, pp.21-22, Nov. 3, 1686.

10. Li Yüeh-jui, *Ch'un-ping shih yeh-ch'eng* (Private historical notes of the Ch'un-ping Studio), (Taipei, 1967), ch.3, p.18

11. *CSL*, KH, ch.1, pp.12, 15, Feb. 18 and 25, 1661; ch.2, p.20, May 21, 1661. This prohibition was removed in 1700 (*ibid.*, ch.201, pp.23-24, Nov. 18, 1700).

12. For cases about the censors, see *Chang-ku ts'ung-pien*, v.3, Memorials of Chuang Hsien-tsu, pp. 3-5; Memorials of Li Shen-hsien, pp.11-13; v.4, Memorials of Wu Ta, pp.10-11; Memorials of Tu Li-te, p. 15; *CS*, p.3785; Wei Hsiang-shu, *Han-sung t'ang-chi* (Works of the Winter-pine Studio), (Ts'ung-shu chi-ch'eng ch'u-pien ed.), ch.2, pp.25-26, 29-31. Cf. Hsieh, *The Government of China*, p.95. For the case of the supervising secretaries, see Ch'in-ch'üan Chü-shih, ed., *Huang-Ch'ing tsou-i* (Collection of memorials of eminent Ch'ing officials) (Tu-ch'eng kuo-shih kuan ed.), ch.14, pp.15-16.

13. *SYNK*, v.1, p.11, March 22, 1723.

14. For the thirteen censors, see *CSL*, KH, ch.291, pp.28-30, April 11 and 21, 1721; *Wen-hsien ts'ung-pien*, v.4, "K'ang-hsi chien-ch'u an," pp.7-8. Cf. *ECCP*, II, 830. For his fragmentation of censors' duties, see the discussion in the next section.

15. There were two different dates. The following sources put the date in 1723: *YHL*, p.166; *Li-tai chih-kuan piao*, ch.18, p.4; *Ch'ing-ch'ao wen-hsien t'ung-k'ao*, I, 5605; Ts'ao I-shih, *Ssu-yen chai ch'üan-chi* (Works of Ssu-yen Studio), (Hsüan-t'ung ed.), "tsou-shu," ch.2, p.13; Tai Lu and Wang Chia-hsiang, *Kuo-ch'ao liu-k'o Han chi-shih chung t'i-ming lu* (A list of the Chinese supervising secretaries in the Ch'ing dynasty), (Kuang-hsü ed.), p.23; and so forth. The following sources give the year 1724 as the date of the amalgamation: *Ch'in-ting ta-Ch'ing hui-tien* (Collected statutes of the Ch'ing dynasty), compiled under the imperial auspices of Ch'ing Jen-tsung (1818 ed.), "Shih-li," ch.754, p.11; Huang Yü-pu et al., *Kuo-ch'ao yü-shih t'i-ming lu* (List of censors in the Ch'ing dynasty), (Ching-chi Tao ed.), v.1, YC, p.2; and so forth.

16. The only evidence is found in *CSL*, YC, ch.4, pp.13-14, March 19, 1723.

17. Hucker, *The Censorial System of Ming China*, p.55.

18. *Ibid.*, Table 23 on p.318. T'ang Chi-ho also believes that the Yung-cheng Emperor combined these

two organs in an attempt to prevent their partisanship. For reference, see his "Ch'ing-tai k'o-tao tsu-chih yen-ke," p.67.

19. Hucker, "Confucianism and the Chinese Censorial System," p.55. For a case study of documental control by the Ming censorial system, see Hucker, *The Censorial System of Ming China*, pp.100-107.

20. *YHL*, p.166.

21. Ts'ao I-shih, *Ssu-yen chai ch'üan-chi*, ch.2, p.14.

22. Ch'in-ch'uan Chü-shih, *Huang-Ch'ing tsou-i*, ch.14, p.16.

23. See n.21 above.

24. The pioneering study of Ch'ing memorials is by John K. Fairbank and Ssu-yü Teng, *Ch'ing Administration: Three Studies* (Cambridge, Mass., 1961), pp. 36-106. For three recent studies, see Wu, *Communication and Imperial Control in China*, chs.5 and 7; Jonathan D. Spence, *Ts'ao Yin and the K'ang-hsi Emperor: Bondservant and Master* (New Haven, 1966), ch.6; and Huang Pei, "Yung-cheng shih-tai ti mi-tsou chih-tu," pp.17-52.

25. For a general, theoretical analysis of this self-seeking orientation, see Eisenstadt, *The Political Systems*, pp.157-72, 279-80, 286-87. For a specific analysis of the Chinese bureaucrats, see Yang, "Some Characteristics of Chinese Bureaucratic Behavior," pp.146-56.

26. Pan Ku, *History of the Former Han Dynasty*, II, 218; also *Li-tai chih-kuan piao*, ch.21, pp.6, 7, 15, and 17.

27. *Li-tai chih-kuan piao*, ch.21, pp.7, 17.

28. Lo Chen-yü, ed., *Shih-liao ts'ung-k'an ch'u-pien* (Miscellaneous historical materials, first series), (Tung-fang Hsüeh-hui, 1924), "T'ien-ts'ung ch'ao ch'en-kung tsou'i," Part 1, p.29; *Man ming-ch'en chuan*, ch.3, pp.1-2.

29. *Ch'in-ting ta'Ch'ing hui-tien*, "Shih-li," ch.10, pp.2-3.

30. *CSL*, Shun-chih, ch.135, p.9, June 25, 1660; Ch'ien I-chi, *Pei-chuan chi*, ch.7, p.7 and ch.12, p.14.

31. *ECCP*, II, 819; Ch'ien I-chi, *Pei-chuan chi*, ch.12, p.5.

32. *CSL*, KH, ch.113, p.1, Dec. 18, 1683; ch.125, p.3, March 26, 1686; ch.133, p.13, Feb. 24, 1688.

33. For a general description, see Wu, "The Memorial Systems," pp.38-44 and his *Communication and Imperial Control in China*, ch.5. Because Wu based his

research on a very limited number of sources, his generalization is far from invulnerable.

34. For example, Wei Hsiang-shu (1617-1687) submitted a confidential memorial when he was President of the Censorate in 1679. For reference, see *CSL*, KH, ch.224, p.21, April 20, 1706. In 1711 the throne ordered that the Grand Secretaries, presidents of the Six Boards, and a few others send him palace memorials (*ibid*., ch.246, p.11, June 23, 1711).

35. *Ibid*., ch.249, pp.5-6, March 5, 1712.

36. For his personal handling of palace memorials, see *ibid*., ch.216, p.19, Aug. 17, 1704; ch.221, p.19, Sept. 12, 1705. For cases of the Imperial Diarists and the Grand Secretaries, see *ibid*., ch.225, p.17, July 14, 1706; ch.232, p.23, July 3, 1708.

37. For exceptions, see *ibid*., ch.225, p.17, July 14, 1706; ch.271, p.17, April 16, 1717.

38. *Ibid*., ch.247, p.5, Sept. 5, 1711.

39. For cases of their attachment to the routine or greeting memorials, see *ibid*., ch.125, p.3, March 26, 1686; ch.249, p.6, March 5, 1712; for their attachment to the greeting memorials, see Li Hsü's memorials in *Wen-hsien ts'ung-pien*, vols. 29-45.

40. *CSL*, KH, ch.255, p.3, May 27, 1713; ch.259, p.14, Aug. 21, 1714; Spence, *Ts'ao Yin*, pp.216-17. For the Chancery of Memorials, see the biography of Lai-pao in *Man ming-ch'en chuan*, ch.38, p.45.

41. For their personal delivery of palace memorials to the throne, see *CSL*, KH, ch.225, p.17, July 14, 1706. For the case of the Southern Imperial Study, see *Wen-hsien ts'ung-pien*, v.3, "Wang Hung-hsü mi-shan hsiao-che," p.36.

42. Cf. Wu, "The Memorial Systems," pp.8,39 and his *Communication and Imperial Control in China*, pp. 36-46. For critical comments on Wu's book, see my review essay in *Harvard Journal of Asiatic Studies* 31:323-32 (1971), See also Spence, *Ts'ao Yin*, p.225.

43. *Li-tai chih-kuan piao*, ch.21, p.7.

44. *CSL*, YC, ch.115, pp.3-4, Feb. 27, 1732. For an article in Japanese, see Iwami Hiroshi, "Yōsei nenkan no minketsu ni tsuite" ('On the policies to clean up the tax-arrears [mien-chien] for the Yung-cheng period'), *Tōyōshi kenkyū*, 18.3:61-84 (December 1959).

45. For the abuses of clerks and servants, see *SYNK*, v.1, pp.10, 13, March 22, 1723. For relaxation of the central administration, see *ibid*., v.2, p.5, April 18, 1723.

46. *Ibid.*, v.30, p.1, Oct. 27, 1733.
47. *Han ming-ch'en chuan*, ch.13, pp.59-60; ch.14, pp.42-43; Teng Chih-ch'eng, *Ku-tung so-chi*, ch.2, p.331.
48. *CSL*, YC, ch.3, pp.1-26, Feb.5, 1723.
49. For their physical aspects, see Huang Pei, "Yung-cheng shih-tai ti mi-tsou chih-tu," pp.24-25.
50. For the shortest ones, see *CPYC*, v.23, Memorials of Wei Ching-kuo, p.72, April 24, 1723.
51. For the functional distinctions of the *t'i-pen* and *tsou-pen*, see *Ta-Ch'ing hui-tien* (Collected statutes of the Ch'ing dynasty), compiled under the imperial auspices of Ch'ing Sheng-tsu (1690 ed.), ch.50, p.29. For two early Chinese articles, see Teng Shih-hsi, "Ch'ing-tai pen-chang chih-tu chih kai-t'i wei tsou k'ao" ('The change from t'i-pen to tsou-pen in the Manchurian government'), *Shih-hsüeh chi-k'an* (Historical Journal), 3:322 (April 1937); Shan Shih-k'uei, "Ch'ing-tai t'i-pen chih-tu k'ao" (The system of memorials for official affairs of the Ch'ing dynasty) in Ku-kung Po-wu Yüan, comp., *Wen-hsien lun-ts'ung* (Collected articles from the Historical Records Office), (Peiping, 1936), p.179. For a recent publication, see Chuang Chi-fa, "Ts'ung Ku-kung Po-wu Yüan hsien-ts'ang kung-chung tang-an t'an Ch'ing-tai ti tsou-che" ('A discussion of Ch'ing memorials based on the National Palace Museum collection of Ch'ing documents'), *Ku-kung wen-hsien* (Ch'ing Documents at National Palace Museum), 1.2:43-53 (March 1970).
52. *SYNK*, v.6, p.2, March 21, 1725. Cf.*CPYC*, v. 48, Memorials of O-ch'ang, p.87, July 13, 1729; v.47, Memorials of Hsing-kuei, p.2, Sept. 5, 1728.
53. For the case of oral selection, see *CPYC*, v.47, Memorials of Hsing-kuei, p.2, Sept. 5, 1728.
54. For those selected in the Yung-cheng period, see *SYNK*, v.6, pp.12-13, April 28, 1725; v.17, p.5, Jan. 16, 1728. For those selected in the K'ang-hsi period, see n.35 above. Those who were traditionally given the right of submitting confidential memorials included imperial commissioners and censorial officials.
55. For cases of financial and judicial commissioners, see *CPYC*, v.38, Memorials of Chao Ch'eng, p.100, Nov. 12, 1728. But some of these commissioners had not been given this right (see *SYNK*, v.16, p.5, May 19, 1728). For cases of provincial directors of education, intendants, prefects, and subprefects, see *CPYC*, v.47, Memorials of Wu Kuan-chieh, p.98ff.;

v.52, Memorials of Ch'eng Yüan-chang, p.49ff.; v.48, Memorials of Liao K'un, p.50ff.

56. For cases of the first three, see *CPYC*, v.1, Memorials of Ch'i-su-le, p.61ff.; v.16, Memorials of Chang Ta-yu, p.50ff.; v.15, Memorials of Chang T'an-lin, p.69ff. For cases of the superintendents of the Imperial Manufactories, see *ibid.*, v.47, Memorials of Li Ping-chung, p.37ff.

57. For these banner officers, see *CSL*, YC, ch. 64, pp.6-7, Jan. 16, 1738. For colonels of the Green Standard, see *CPYC*, v.23, Memorials of Yang P'eng, p.24ff.

58. For those who filed palace memorials through their own requests, see *CPYC*, v.35, Memorials of K'ung Yü-p'o, p.33, Oct. 31, 1727.

59. For cases of warning, see *ibid.*, v.14, Memorials of I Chao-hsiung, p.92, Sept. 21, 1727. For case of punishment, see *SYNK*, v.16, pp.8-9, Oct. 26, 1727; *CPYC*, v.53, Memorials of Hsü Jung, p.10, Aug. 2, 1727.

60. *SYNK*, v.23, pp.13-14, Sept. 10, 1729; Chu Chih-jen, *Pen-ch'ao cheng-chih*, v.21, pp.60-61.

61. For the case of pecuniary penalty, see *SYNK*, v.23, pp.13-14, Sept. 10, 1729. For the case of discharge, see *Han ming-ch'en chuan*, ch.17, pp.14-15.

62. For their obligation to write memorials by their own hands, see *CPYC*, v.24, Memorials of Chi Ch'eng-pin, p.87, March 14, 1725. For their responsibility for any leakage of secret, see *ibid.*, v.51, Memorials of Chao Kuo-lin, p.6, Oct. 17, 1730.

63. The case of Yang T'ien-tsung may serve as an example (see *ibid.*, v.20, Memorials of Yang T'ien-tsung, p.20, Jan. 14, 1732). For submitting palace memorials during their leaves of absence, see *KCT*, Memorials of Chu Shih, p.1, May 21, 1726, and p.1, Aug. 17, 1726; Memorials of Chang T'ing-yü, pp.2-3, Dec. 17, 1733.

64. *CYPC*, v.23, Memorials of Yang Ch'ang-ch'un, p.90, July 11, 1723.

65. Ch'i-su-le's case may serve as a good example (see *ibid.*, v.1, Memorials of Ch'i-su-le, p.71, Dec. 6, 1724).

66. For rewards for worthy reports, see *ibid.*, v.24, Memorials of Yen Kuang-wu, p.28, May 26, 1728. Sun Chi-tsung, one of such reporters, exposed the mistake made by an official. As his report was regarded as valuable, he was promoted. See *ibid.*, v.24, Memorials of Sun Chi-tsung, pp.18-19, Sept. 9, 1725.

67. According to the regulations, only governors-general, governors, Tartar generals, and lieutenant-generals had the right to submit memorials directly to the ruler. Other officials below these ranks such as financial commissioners, judicial commissioners, intendants in provinces, and lower officials of the central government were to ask their superiors to forward their memorials to the throne.

68. For these leather cases, see Chiang Liang-chi, *Tung-hua lu* (Tung-hua records), (n.p., n.d.), ch.26, p.12, Dec. 1724-Jan.1725. Before receiving such cases, reporters might use substitutes (see *CPYC*, v.57, Memorials of Chao Hung-en, p.59, July 10, 1734). For attachments to the case, see *CPYC*, v.47, Memorials of Chao Hsiang-k'uei, p.82.

69. *CPYC*, v.24, Memorials of Chang Yao-tsu, p.84, Feb. 9, 1731. For discussion about the reason why they kept just four boxes, see Huang Pei, "Yung-cheng shih-tai ti mi-tsou chih-tu," p.37.

70. Ch'ang-lai, governor of Kwangtung, made locks and keys by himself because he lost them. He was pardoned by the ruler from the death sentence only because of his special family background (see *Man ming-ch'en chuan*, ch.29, p.23).

71. For regulations of delivery through military post stations, see *CPYC*, v.49, Memorials of Kuo Kung, p.61, Dec. 10, 1728. For delivery of ordinary palace reports, see *ibid.*, v.35, Memorials of Sun Kuo-hsi, p.61, May 8, 1729.

72. For information about this office, see Chao-lien, *Hsiao-t'ing tsa-lu*, ch.1, p.8. For the department directors, see *KCT*, Memorials of Li Wei, p.4, March 18, 1735. For its location, see *CSL*, Chia-ch'ing period, ch.315, pp.4-6, Feb. 4, 1816. For its reception of the memorials from the officials serving in Peking, see *Ch'in-ting ta-Ch'ing hui-tien*, "Shih-li," ch.10, p.3. For its reception of memorials from governors-general and governors, see *CPYC*, v.13, Memorials of Ch'ang-lai, p.66, Oct. 16, 1727. For its reception of the reports from the lower provincial officials, see *CPYC*, v.18, Memorials of Chang Yüan-huai, p.39, Oct. 17, 1728.

73. For its transmission of memorials to the imperial desk, see Chen-chün, *T'ien-chih ngou-wen* (Overheard at court), (Kan-t'ang chuan-she ed.), ch.1, p.3.

74. These individuals were Chang T'ing-yü, Chiang T'ing-hsi, Yin-hsiang, and Lungkodo and a few others. For discussion, see section 2, the next

chapter. In addition to them, Se-er-t'u was also charged with this duty (see *CPYC*, v.34, Memorials of Hsien-te, p.65, July 7, 1726).

75. For transmission of the palace memorials from the provinces, see *ibid.*, v.18, Memorials of Chang Yüan-huai, p.39, Oct. 17, 1728; v.52, Memorials of Yang Yung-pin, p.6, April 25, 1732.

76. In an endorsement the Yung-cheng Emperor told a memorialist that Se-er-t'u, though ordered to receive the palace memorials for him, was not the person to take them personally to the imperial desk (see *ibid.*, v.34, Memorials of Hsien-te, p.65, July 7, 1726). In this regard it is safe to say that these special individuals were to forward the secret reports to the eunuchs.

77. For the emperor's principles for handling personal memorials, see Huang Pei, "Yung-cheng shih-tai ti mi-tsou chih-tu," pp.41-42.

78. For the emperor's third and fourth principles, see *ibid.*, pp.42-43.

79. As one scholar points out, the Ch'ing censorial officials before the Yung-cheng period were quite active. See Shih-liang, *Yeh-t'ang hsüan wen-chi* (A Collection of essays of the Yeh-t'ang Studio), (Peiping, 1929), "chih-yen," ch.2, pp.1-2.

80. For this case, see *ECCP*, I, 306-7.

81. Hucker, *The Censorial System of Ming China*, p.296.

82. Chao-lien, *Hsiao-t'ing tsa-lu*, ch.1, pp.4-5; *Lettres édifiantes et curieuses*, v.20, "Du Père Parrenin," p.9.

83. For impeachment by subordinates, see *SYPC*, v.6, p.36, Sept. 12, 1728.

84. *CPYC*, v.48, Memorials of Liu T'ing-ch'en, p.46, May 20, 1724.

85. Chang T'ing-yü, *Ch'eng-huai yüan wen-ts'un* (An anthology of the Ch'eng-huai Studio), (1891 ed.), ch.11, pp.18-19.

86. *CPYC*, v.18, Memorials of Ts'ai Shih-shan, pp.69-70, May 22, 1730; v.19, Memorials of Wang Shih-chün, p.47, May 27, 1730.

87. Friedrich and Brzezinski, *Totalitarian Dictatorship and Autocracy*, p.170.

88. *KCT*, Memorials of Li Wei, pp.1-2, Feb. 16, 1733.

89. For example, Wang Jou, an intendant in Hunan, worked out plans to change the traditional headman system of the Miao tribes to the regular administrative structure. After reading his memorials

the emperor ordered Yin-hsiang and a few others to deliberate the plans and with their advice he finally reversed Wang's policy. See *ibid.*, "Wang ta-jen mi-i tsou-p'ien," the memorial (under Yin-hsiang) concerning Wang Jou, no. 13894. The emperor's taxation reform was based on the information from many palace memorials (see section 2, Ch.9).

90. On July 7, 1934, Li Wei received the emperor's response to his memorial of July 3, 1734 (*KCT*, Memorials of Li Wei, p.1, July 10, 1734).

91. *Ibid.*, Memorials of Wang Shih-chün, pp.1-2, Aug. 17, 1733, and the imperial reply dated Aug. 23, 1733, and written by Chang T'ing-yü and O-er-tai.

92. For a revealing analysis of the inertia of the Ch'ing administration, see John K. Fairbank *et al.*, *East Asia: The Modern Transformation* (Boston, 1965), pp.99-108.

93. *Ibid.*, p.103.

VI: A New Instrument of Autocratic Rule— The Grand Council

1. For instance, Wang Ch'ang, *Ch'un-jung t'ang-chi* (Works of the Ch'un-jung Studio), (Shu-nan Shu-she, 1892), ch.47, p.1; Chao I, *Yen-pao tsa-chi* (Miscellaneous notes), in the same author's *Ou-pei ch'üan-chi* (Complete works of Chao I), (1877 ed.), ch.1, p.1; *CS*, p.2486; Hsiao I-shan, *Ch'ing-tai t'ung-shih*, I, 501-2; Tu Lienche, *Kuan-yü chün-chi ch'u ti chien-chih* ('On the establishment of the Ch'ün-chi ch'u'), (Canberra, 1963), pp.1, 24; *ECCP*, I, 55; II, 917-18; and Fairbank and Teng, *Ch'ing Administration*, p.55.

2. Pan Ku, *History of the Former Han Dynasty*, II, 10-11; Ho, "Salient Aspects of China's Heritage," pp.19-20; and Lao Kan, "Lun Hai-tai ti nei-ch'ao yü wai-ch'ao," pp.227-67.

3. *Li-tai chih-kuan piao*, ch.2, pp.12, 15; Fu Lo-ch'eng, *Sui-T'ang wu-tai shih*, pp.12-13.

4. Ho, "Salient Aspects of China's Heritage," pp.20-21.

5. Fairbank and Teng, *Ch'ing Administration*, p.56. Miyazaki Ichisada, a well-known Japanese scholar, provided a thorough discussion of these practices in terms of the Manchu language in his "Shinchō ni okeru kokugo mondai no ichimen" ('A view of the problem of national language in the Ch'ing dynasty') in the same author's *Ajia-shi kenyū* (A

study of Asian history), (Kyoto, 1963), III, 333-93.

6. For the establishment of this office, see *CSL*, T'ai-tsung, ch.5, pp.11-12, April 23, 1629. According to a recent study, it took shape even during the reign of Nurhaci. See Kanda Nobuo, "Shinsho no bunkan ni tsuite" ('Wenkuan [Archives] in the early years of Ch'ing'), *Tōyōshi kenkyū*, 19.3: 350-66 (December 1960).

7. For their English biographies, see *ECCP*, I, 213, 231-32, and 592-93; II, 663.

8. For the appointments and functions of these officials, see *CSL*, T'ai-tsu, ch.4, p.21, Dec. 20, 1615. For an English article on the subject, see Piero Corradini, "Civil Administration at the Beginning of the Manchu Dynasty: A Note on the Establishment of the Six Ministries (liu-pu)," *Oriens Extremus* 9.2:134 (December 1962).

9. *CS*, pp.3661-62, 3666; Lo Chen-yü, *Shih-liao ts'ung-k'an ch'u-pien*, v.2, Memorials of Kao Shih-chün, pp.6-7, 23-24; Memorials of Wang Wen-k'uei, pp. 18-21, 24-26; v.3, Memorials of Ma Kuo-chu, pp.1-4 and *passim*.

10. Fu Tsung-mao, "Ch'ing-ch'u i-cheng t'i-chih chih yen-chiu" ('A study on the deliberative body in early Ch'ing'), *The National Chengchi University Journal* 11:271 (May 1965).

11. For the political function of the Board, see Wolfram Eberhard, "The Political Function of Astronomy and Astronomers in Han China," in Fairbank, *Chinese Thought and Institutions*, pp.33-70.

12. Alfons Väth, S. J., *Johann Adam Schall von Bell, S. J.*, trans. into Chinese by Yang Ping-ch'en (Taipei, 1960), II, 295-325; Ch'en Yüan, "T'ang Jo-wang yü Mu-ch'en min" ('Father John A. Schall von Bell and the bonze Mu-ch'en Wen'), *Fu-jen hsüeh-chih* 7.1 and 2:1-27, especially 15-25 (December 1938); *ECCP*, I, 256.

13. Väth, *Johann Adam Schall von Bell*, II, 294.

14. *ECCP*, I, 257; Ch'en Yüan, "T'ang Jo-wang," pp.3-4.

15. Tao-min, "Tsou-tui chi-yüan" (Replies made at the imperial service), in Chang Ch'ao, ed., *Chao-tai ts'ung-shu i-chi* (The Chao-tai collected works, Series B),(Sao-yeh Shan-fang ed.), ch.19, pp.14-15.

16. For establishment of the Thirteen Offices, see *CSL*, Shun-chih, ch.76, pp.16-17, July 11, 1653; for their influence, see *ibid.*, ch.77, pp.2-3, Aug. 26, 1653; KH, ch.1, pp.21-22, March 15, 1661. For Wu's contribution, see *ECCP*, I, 256.

17. For the censorial remonstrance, see *CSL*, Shun-chih, ch.77, pp.2-3, Aug. 26, 1653. For the admonition of the Manchu nobles, see Ch'ien I-chi, *Pei-chuan chi*, ch.1, part 1, pp. 14-15.

18. *CSL*, KH, ch.1, p.22, March 15, 1661.

19. Chang Ying, *Chang Wen-tuan kung ch'üan-shu* (Complete works of Chang Ying), (T'ung-ch'eng, The Chang Family ed., 1897), "Tu-su t'ang wen-chi," ch.5, p.4; *ECCP*, I, 64.

20. For the holder of the *chü-jen* degree, see the biography of Ho Ch'o in *ECCP*, I, 284. For men of the miscellaneous category, see Chang T'ang-jung, *Ch'ing-kung shu-wen* (Miscellaneous accounts about the Ch'ing court), (Palace Museum, 1941), ch.4, p.24; *ECCP*, I, 491.

21. Chiang Liang-chi, *Tung-hua lu*, ch.16, p.12.

22. For their political functions, see Chao-lien, *Hsiao-t'ing tsa-lu*, "supplement," ch.1, p.12; *CSL*, KH, ch.254, p.6, April 5, 1713; ch.260, p.18, Nov. 27, 1714.

23. *Wen-hsien ts'ung-pien*, v.2, preface to "Wang Hung-hsü mi-shan hsiao-che," pp.1-2; v.3, "Wang Hung-hsü mi-shan hsiao-che," p.36.

24. Chi-ch'ang, *Hsing-su chai tsa-chi* (Miscellaneous notes of the Hsing-su Studio), (1901 ed.), ch.1, p.8; Ch'ing-kuei, *Ch'ing kung-shih hsü-pien*, ch.6, p.1, Feb. 13, 1799; Ch'ü Hung-chi, *Pao-chih chi-lüeh* (Brief notes of an official on duty), (1920 ed.), pp.16,20.

25. Ch'ing Shih-tsung, *Shih-tsung hsien huang-ti yü-chih wen-chi*, ch.3, pp.23-24.

26. For Li's argument, see his "Pan-li chün-chi ch'u lüeh-k'ao (A brief study of the Chün-chi ch'u), *Yu-shih hsüeh-pao* (The Youth Journal) 1.2:1-19 (1959). The same argument also appears in his "Ch'ing-tai chung yang," pp.144-48. I supported Professor Li's argument with more evidence included in my theses of 1959 and 1963. For my 1959 thesis, see Huang Pei, "Yung-cheng shih-tai chung-yang t'ung-chih t'i-hsi ti kai-pien" (Reorganization of the central governmental system during the Yung-cheng period), M. A. Thesis, National Taiwan University (Taipei, 1959), pp.224-28. The problems concerning the Grand Council are also discussed in Chapter IV of my Ph. D. thesis, "A Study of the Yung-cheng Period, 1723-1735: A Political Phase," Indiana University (Bloomington, 1963).

27. The argument for 1729 is in Fu Tsung-mao, "Ch'ing-tai chün-chi ch'u she-chih chih yen-chiu"

('The study on the establishment of the Council of State in Ch'ing dynasty'), *The National Chengchi University Journal* 12:246 (December 1965). For his revised point, see his *Ch'ing-tai chun-chi ch'u tsu-chih chi chih-chang chih yen-chiu* (A study of the organization and function of the Grand Council of the Ch'ing dynasty), (Taipei, 1967), pp.120-26, 136-37. The approach, sources, and conclusion of Fu's article, as cited above, are almost a duplicate of my "Yung-cheng shih-tai chung-yang t'ung-chih," pp. 224-28. For my review of Fu's book, see *Harvard Journal of Asiatic Studies* 30:248-56 (1970). For the argument for 1727, see Tu Lienche, *Kuan-yü chün-chi ch'u*, pp.1, 11, and 23.

28. Wu, *Communication and Imperial Control in China*, pp.91-92. In another article, the same author changed the date to 1730. See Wu Hsiu-liang, "Ch'ing-tai chün-chi ch'u chien-chih ti tsai chien-t'ou" ('A reappraisal of the establishment of the Grand Council under the Ch'ing'), *Ku-kung wen-hsien* (Ch'ing Documents at the National Palace Museum), 2.4:27-32 (September 1971).

29. For the creation of this council, see *CSL*, YC, ch.156, p.15, July 15, 1735. For a general review and some arguments, see Piero Corradini, "Riforme nell'amministrazione centrale cinese durante il periodo Yung-cheng (1723-1736)," *Rivista degli Studi Orientali* 36:141-45 (1961).

30. A photo-copy of this imperial order dated Oct. 31, 1716 appears in Rosso, *Apostolic Legations*, p.308.

31. On November 30, 1723, Yin-hsiang and Lungkodo transmitted a decree through the Board of War to a provincial official. For reference, see *CPYC*, v.45, Memorials of Kao Ch'i-cho, p.11, Jan. 15, 1724.

32. For reference to the transmission under name of the Court, see *ibid.*, v.40, Memorials of Li Wei, p.40, Nov. 18, 1726. For the transmission done by the Grand Secretariat, see *ibid.*, v.16, Memorials of Chang Ta-yu, p.76, June 10, 1727; v.14, Memorials of I Chao-hsiung, p.79, May 24, 1727.

33. For the transmission done individually, see *ibid.*, v.10, Memorials of Fu-t'ai, p.94, June 12, 1730. For joint transmission by two people, see *ibid.*, v.34, Memorials of Sung K'o-chin, p.62, Aug. 8, 1732. For joint transmission by three people, see *ibid.*, v.32, Memorials of T'ien Wen-ching, p.42, July 29, 1729. For joint transmission by four people, see

ibid., v.5, Memorials of Ch'en Shih-hsia, p.105, Jan. 5, 1728. For joint transmission but under one name, see *ibid.*, v.15, Memorials of Shen T'ing-cheng, p.43, Jan. 25, 1729.

34. This type of transmission was carried out in many ways. For the joint transmission by Yin-hsiang and one Grand Secretary, see *ibid.*, v.13, Memorials of Ch'ang-lai, p.72, Jan. 3, 1728. For his transmission with two or three Grand Secretaries, see *ibid.*, v.58, Memorials of Shih-lin, p.29, Oct. 8, 1728.

35. For the transmission done by Chang, Chiang, Sunju, Funinggan, Jabina, and Marsai, check notes 32-34 above. Chu Shih's name appeared very seldom in the court letters. For reference, see *ibid.*, v.58, Memorials of Shih-lin, p.18, March 2, 1728. After his appointment as Grand Secretary in 1732, O-er-t'ai became one of the transmitters (see the second reference of n.33 above).

36. Even as a president of the Board of Revenue, Chiang T'ing-hsi transmitted court letters (see *CPYC*, v.38, Memorials of T'ien Wen-ching, p.52, March 13, 1728). Feng-sheng-e had this duty when he was Chamberlain of the Imperial Bodyguard and Senior Assistant Chamberlain of the Imperial Bodyguard. For reference, see *ibid.*, v.34, Memorials of Sung K'o-chin, p.62, Dec. 29, 1731; v.58, Memorials of Shih-lin, p.67, April 30, 1732. For the case of the Commissioner of the Imperial Equipage Department, see *ibid.*, v.54, Memorials of Mai-chu, p.95, Dec. 28, 1734.

37. For the beginning of the preparation, see *SYNK*, v.28, p.5, May 13, 1731. For the emperor's demand for more services and suggestions, see *CPYC*, v.12, Memorials of Chu Kang, p.86.

38. These three categories are analyzed in Huang Pei, "Yung-cheng shih-tai chung-yang t'ung-chih," pp.228-31. For another discussion similar to mine, see Fu Tsung-mao, *Ch'ing-tai chün-chi ch'u tsu-chih*, pp.126-128, and his "Ch'ing-tai chün-chi ch'u," pp. 247-48. Silas Wu seems to accept the first category. See his *Communication and Imperial Control in China*, pp.88-89. For an article which supports the last category, see Shan Shih-yüan, "Ku-kung chün-chi ch'u chih-fang" (The quarters of the Grand Council), *Wen-wu* (Cultural relics) 6.1:41 (January 1960).

39. Huang Pei, "Yung-cheng shih-tai chung-yang t'ung-chih," pp.228-31; also Fu Tsung-mao, *Ch'ing-tai chün-chi ch'u tsu-chih*, pp.127-28.

40. Chang T'ing-yü, *Ch'eng-huan yüan wen-ts'un*, ch.15, p.31; *KCT*, Shih I-chih, p.1, April 4, 1735.

41. Chao-lien, *Hsiao-t'ing tsa-lu*, ch.2, p.4. From 1813 on they were chosen first through recommendation and then by examination (see *CSL*, Chia-ch'ing, ch.271, pp.16-17, Aug. 5, 1813).

42. According to the list in *CS*, pp.2486-2487, there were ten Grand Councillors. Besides these three, the seven others were Marsai, O-er-t'ai, Ha Yüan-sheng (d.1738), Marantai (only two months), Fu-p'eng (Prince P'ing), No-ch'in (d.1749), and Bandi (d.1755). Most of these seven men had received military training.

43. For instance, Yeh Feng-mao, *Nei-ko hsiao-chih* (A brief account of the Grand Secretariat), in Shen Yün-lung, ed. *Ming-Ch'ing shih-liao hui-pien*, I (Collection of Ming and Ch'ing historical materials, I), (Taipei, 1967), v.6, pp.2 and 9-10. In his *Communication and Imperial Control in China*, pp.86 and 174 n.29, Silas Wu separates the "Inner Grand Secretaries" nominally and functionally from the Grand Councillors.

44. For a detailed discussion of the "Inner Grand Secretaries," see my review of Silas Wu's book in *Harvard Journal of Asiatic Studies*, 31:329-331 (1971), The case of Chiang T'ing-hsi seems against my interpretation. In a decree of 1731, the emperor mentioned Chiang as a Grand Secretary, independent of the Grand Councillors, whom he spoke of at the same time (see *Shang-yü ch'i-wu i-fu*, v.6, p.8, Sept. 21, 1731). It can be reasonably inferred that Chiang received the assignment in his capacity as a Grand Secretary because the matter also concerned the Grand Secretariat.

45. Not until 1728 was Chiang made a Grand Secretary. If the Grand Council was created in 1726, he should not be included in these four. For his English biography, see *ECCP*, I, 142-43.

46. This analysis is made according to the notes afforded in the *Chün-chi ta-ch'en nien-piao* (see *CS*, pp.2486-87). The Chia-ch'ing Emperor said that since the creation of the office no princes had been made Grand Councillors. For reference, see *CSL*, Chia-ch'ing, ch.53, p.22, Nov. 19, 1799; Liang Chang-chü, *Shu-yüan chi lüeh* (Brief notes on the Grand Council), (1875 ed.), ch.2, p.10. Cf. Fu Tsung-mao, *Ch'ing-tai chün-chi ch'u tsu-chih*, pp. 148-50, 529-35.

47. For example, see Liang Chang-chü, *Shu-yüan*

chi-lüeh, ch.15, p.5; Hsiao I-shan, *Ch'ing-tai t'ung-shih*, V, pp.76-77.

48. For his humiliation, see *YHL*, pp.279-80. For his service in the presidency, see *CS*, p.4105. For his transmission of court letters, see the first part of n.35 above and *CPYC*, v.34, Memorials of Wang Shao-hsü, p.26, Aug. 14, 1727.

49. For his English biography, see *ECCP*, I, 263-64.

50. This chief Grand Councillor appeared during the early years of the Ch'ien-lung period when No-ch'in served in the Grand Council. In 1771 there were even two chief Grand Councillors, one Chinese and one Manchu. For reference, see Liang Chang-chü, *Shu-yüan chi-lüeh*, ch.27, p.6 and ch.13, p.13, respectively.

51. For example see *CSL*, YC, ch.122, pp.12-13, Oct. 4, 1732; ch.131, pp.8-9, July 3, 1733; ch.155, p.4, May 29, 1735. But another expert believes that during the Yung-cheng period its daily functions were limited to the military campaigns in the northwest. For reference, see Tu Lienche, *Kuan-yü chün-chi ch'u*, p.17. For a detailed discussion about their duties, see Fu Tsung-mao, *Ch'ing-tai chün-chi ch'u tsu-chih*, chs.6-7.

52. For their suggestions about punishment and reward, see *CSL*, YC, ch.120, pp.11-12, 15, Aug. 6 and 16, 1732.

53. *Ibid*., ch.150, p.4, Dec. 28, 1734.

54. For a detailed discussion, see Meng Sen, *Ch'ing-tai shih*, pp.20-100.

55. *CSL*, T'ai-tsung, ch.34, pp.23-24, May 22, 1637. Cf. Fu Tsung-mao, *Ch'ing-tai chün-chi ch'u tsu-chih*, pp.52-58.

56. *CSL*, KH, ch.99, pp.4-5, Jan. 17, 1682; Lo Chen-yü, *Shih-liao ts'ung-pien*, v.1, "Sheng-tsu ch'in-cheng shuo-mo jih-lu," p.20, Nov. 13, 1696; Fu Tsung-mao, *Ch'ing-tai chün-chi ch'u tsu-chih*, pp.58-59. The best study of the topic is Kanda Nobuo, "Shinsho no gisei daijin ni tsuite" ('The I-cheng Ta-ch'en in the earlier Ch'ing dynasty'), in *Wada hakushi kanreki kinen Tōyōshi Ronsō* ('Oriental Studies presented to Sei [Kiyoshi] Wada in celebration of his sixtieth birthday'), (Tokyo, 1951), pp.171-72, 182-85.

57. *CSL*, CL, ch.1389, pp.26-27, Nov. 19, 1791.

58. The nine princes were Yin-hsiang, Fu-p'eng, Yung-hsin, I-hsin, I-k'uang, Shih-to, Tsai-feng, Tsai-i, and Yü-lang (see *CS*, pp.2486-97, 2504-8, 2510-12). For the fifty-four nobles, see Fu Tsung-mao, *Ch'ing-tai chün-chi ch'u tsu-chih*, pp.182-83.

59. For information about this communication through the Board of Revenue, see *CPYC*, v.44, Memorials of Chi Tseng-yün, p.36, Jan. 16, 1732. For express court letters, see *ibid.*, v.14, Memorials of Liu Shih-ming, p.38, July 18, 1731.

60. According to John K. Fairbank and Ssu-yü Teng, during these years there were approximately 1140 names of Grand Councillors and 1310 names of Grand Secretaries (see Fairbank and Teng, *Ch'ing Administration*, p.57). For the average cited, see *ibid.*, p.58.

61. Hsieh, *The Government of China*, p.80.

62. See *CPYC*, v.10, Memorials of Fu-t'ai, p.94, June 12, 1730; v.32, Memorials of T'ien Wen-ching, p.42, July 29, 1729.

63. *SYPC*, v.9, p.5, May 17, 1732.

64. For example, two imperial orders appear in the *CSL* as decrees made public through Grand Secretaries (see *ibid.*, YC, ch.109, p.24, Sept. 25, 1731; ch.112, pp.6-7, Dec. 4, 1731). But they appear in the *SYNK* as orders made public by Grand Councillors (see *ibid.*, v.28, p.6, Sept. 24, 1731; p.1, Dec. 4, 1731). There was another decree published through the Grand Councillors in *CSL*, YC, ch.120, pp.11-12, Aug. 6, 1732, but through the Grand Secretaries in *SYNK*, v.29, p.2, on the same day.

65. Raymond Dawson, "The Value of the Study of Chinese Civilization," in Dawson, *The Legacy of China*, p.365.

66. For his appointment of the censor, see *CSL*, Chia-ch'ing, ch.76, pp.21-22, Jan. 2, 1801. For his withdrawal of the censor, see Liang Chang-chü, *Shu-yüan chi-lüeh*, ch.14, p.10.

67. These were generally the palace memorials which needed the expert advice. Some examples have been dealt with in Wu, *Communication and Imperial Control in China*, pp.93-100.

68. For the Ch'ien-lung period, see Liang Chang-chü, *Shu-yüan chi-lüeh*, ch.13, pp.2-3; for the Tao-kuang era, see *ibid.*, p.3.

69. For Ho-shen's case, see *CSL*, Chia-ch'ing, ch.38, p.9, Feb. 23, 1799. For discussion on the case of Ho-shen, see Nivison, "Ho-shen and His Accusers," pp.209-43. For later developments, see Liang Chang-chü, *Shu-yüan chi-lüeh*, ch.13, pp.14-15.

70. For an analytic discussion about these two objectives of the Manchu rulers, see Levenson, *Confucian China and Its Modern Fate*, II, 59.

71. *CSL*, YC, ch.87, p.26, Dec. 14, 1729.

72. *SYPC*, v.8, pp.26-28, July 30, 1730.
73. *Ibid.*, p.18, June 25, 1730.
74. *SYNK*, v.10, p.1, May 31; p.3, June 1, 1726.
75. *CSL*, KH, ch.251, p.16, Nov. 4, 1712.
76. For the extreme Manchu suggestion see *SYNK*, v.20, pp.3-4, Nov. 7, 1728; for the Chinese criticism, see *CSL*, Shun-chih, ch.72, pp.10-11, March 17, 1653.
77. *SYNK*, v.11, p.31, Nov. 12, 1726; v.21, p.5, March 6, 1729; *CPYC*, v.57, Memorials of Chao Hung-en, p.76, Dec. 1, 1734; *SYPC*, v.6, p.9, April 11, 1728.
78. *Pa-ch'i t'ung-chih ch'u-chi* (General history of the eight banners, first series), compiled under the imperial auspices of Ch'ing Kao-tsung (Palace ed., 1739), ch.144, "Chih-kuan chih," part 2, pp.5, 10-11, and 19.
79. For the first case, see *YHL*, p.10; for the second case, see Chao-lien, *Hsiao-t'ing tsa-lu*, ch.5, p.11.
80. Lawrence D. Kessler, "Ethnic Composition of Provincial Leadership during the Ch'ing Dynasty," *Journal of Asian Studies* 28.3:497-98, 500 (May 1969).
81. *CSL*, YC, ch.61, p.23, Nov. 5, 1727.
82. According to Fu Tsung-mao, *Ch'ing-tai chün-chi ch'u tsu-chih*, pp.149-50 and 535, of the ten Grand Councillors in 1735, four were appointed in the Ch'ien-lung period, while two were not given the same title and served only as secretaries.
83. For the case of Chu Shih, see the discussion in section 2 of this chapter.
84. Narakino Shimesu, "Shindai jūyō shokukan Man-Kan hiritsu no hendō, (Changes in the ratio of important Manchu and Chinese officials during the Ch'ing dynasty), *Gunma Daigaku kiyō* (Bulletin of Gunma University) 17:52 (1967). However, different scholars provide different figures. For example, Fu Tsung-mao states that there were 139 Grand Councillors—63 Manchus, 66 Chinese, and 10 Mongols (see his *Ch'ing-tai chün-chi ch'u tsu-chih*, pp.182-83. One author gives 145 Grand Councillors—72 Manchus, 64 Chinese, 6 Mongols, and 3 Chinese bannermen. See Alfred Kuo-liang Ho, "The Grand Council in the Ch'ing dynasty," *Far Eastern Quarterly* 11.2:175 (February 1952). In his *The Government of China*, p.81, Hsieh relates that during the years 1730-1875 there were 115 Grand Councillors—59 Manchus, 47 Chinese, and 9 Mongols.
85. Fu Tsung-mao, *Ch'ing-tai chün-chu ch'u tsu-chih*, pp.182-83. For a more detailed comparison, see

ibid., pp.158-65. Cf. Ho, "The Grand Council in the Ch'ing Dynasty," p.175.

VII: Bureaucratization of the Banner System

1. For the essay, see Meng Sen, *Ch'ing-tai shih*, pp.20-100.
2. *SYNK*, v.16, p.16, Oct. 11, 1727.
3. See Franz Michael, *The Origin of Manchu Rule in China: Frontier and Bureaucracy as Interacting Forces in the Chinese Empire* (New York, 1965), pp.62-79.
4. For expansion to the eight Manchu Banners, see *CSL*, T'ai-tsu, ch.4, p.20, Dec. 20, 1615. The number of companies about 1615 is based on two authoritative articles: Chaoying Fang, "A Technique for Estimating the Numerical Strength of the Early Manchu Military Forces," *Harvard Journal of Asiatic Studies* 13:193 and 211 (1950), and Abe Takeo, "Hakki Manshū niru no kenkyū" ('On the Manchu niru system of the eight banners'), *Tōa jimbun gakuho* 2.2:37-41 (July 1942). For a different opinion, see Meng Sen, *Ch'ing-tai shih*, pp.21-22.
5. For growth of the companies, see Fang, "A Technique for Estimating the Numerical Strength," pp.202-3, 208. The figure 170,000 is based on the assumption that each company had 300 men. Very possibly before 1644 each company comprised 300 men, although after that date the size of the company generally became smaller (see *ibid.*, p.204).
6. Edwin O. Reischauer and John K. Fairbank, *East Asia: The Great Tradition* (Boston, 1960), p.390.
7. *ECCP*, I, 66-67, 77-78.
8. See biographies of Tsereng and Furdan in *ibid.*, I, 264-65; II, 756-57. For a story about the decline of Manchu military valor, see Chao-lien, *Hsiao-t'ing tsa-lu*, ch.5, p.13.
9. See n.3 above; Owen Lattimore, *Inner Asian Frontiers of China* (Boston, 1962), pp.130-33.
10. For discussion about the culture and minority of the Manchus, see Sano Manabu, *Kokka to shakai* (State and society), in the same author's *Shinchō shakai shi* (Social history of the Ch'ing dynasty), (Tokyo, 1947), part 1, v.1, pp.75-76, 82.
11. For discussion about the clan elements in the banners, see Michael, *The Origin of Manchu Rule in China*, pp.80-98.
12. *SYNK*, v.6, p.5, May 23, 1725.

13. For loans at high interest, see *Yü-hsing ch'i-wu tsou-i* (Memorials and related imperial comments concerning banner affairs), compiled by Yin-lu et al. (Palace ed.), v.1, pp.8-9, Jan. 15, 1724. For selling of banner lands, see *SYNK*, v.25, p.8, May 27, 1730. For mortgage of armors, see *ibid.*, v.4, p.9, May 5, 1725.

14. *SYPC*, v.1, p.8, July 30, 1723.

15. *CPYC*, v.38, Memorials of Ko Shen, p.11, Sept. 30, 1725; v.54, Memorials of Mai-chu, p.73, July 3, 1733.

16. *SYPC*, v.1, p.6, May 22, 1723; *CSL*, YC, ch.12, p.8, Nov. 3, 1723.

17. *SYPC*, v.5, p.7, April 16, 1727.

18. *SYNK*, v.3, Oct. 9, 1723.

19. *Yü-hsing ch'i-wu tsou-i*, v.5, pp.22-23, 38, Oct. 5, 1734, and Jan. 14, 1735.

20. *SYPC*, v.6, p.2, March 9, 1728; v.10, p.10, Feb. 2, 1734. For a thoughtful discussion of the Manchu language problem, see Miyazaki Ichisada, "Shinchō ni okeru kokugo mondai no ichimen," pp.386-93.

21. For an argument about the clans in the banner system, see Michael, *The Origin of Manchu Rule in China*, pp.80-81.

22. *SYPC*, v.1, p.8, July 30, 1723; *SYNK*, v.30, pp.1-2, Oct. 27, 1733.

23. *Shang-yü ch'i-wu i-fu*, v.1, p.19, Feb. 3, 1725.

24. See *ibid.*, pp.20-22, Feb. 3, 1725; v.5, p.27, Jan. 22, 1731. The discussion of these four categories are based on the above pages.

25. For limitations to their feudal privileges, see *SYNK*, v.1, p.10, Dec. 24, 1722; v.3, pp.10-11, Aug. 16, 1723. For the number of bannermen, see *Shang-yü ch'i-wu i'fu*, v.1, pp.10-12, Sept. 24, 1724.

26. Hsieh, *The Government of China*, p.51.

27. *SYPC*, v.10, p.3, April 20, 1734.

28. *Yü-hsing ch'i-wu tsou-i*, v.1, pp.9-10, Sept. 1, 1725.

29. *SYNK*, v.3, p.1, Jan. 1, 1724; v.16, pp.17-18, Oct. 11, 1727; v.29, p.9, July 19, 1732; *CSL*, YC, ch.18, p.4, April 26, 1724; ch.30, pp.19-20, April 26, 1725.

30. *Shang-yü ch'i-wu i-fu*, v.2, pp.6-8, March 31, 1726; v.4, pp.14-15, Oct. 11, 1729; v.5, p.30, Jan. 24, 1731.

31. *CSL*, YC, ch.32, pp.18-19, July 1, 1725.

32. For assignment of the office, see *Pa-ch'i t'ung-chih ch'u-chi*, ch.23, p.6. For requirement on the commander and the vice commander, see Lai-pao *et al.*, ed., *Ch'in-ting pa-ch'i tse-li* (Statutes for the eight banners), (Palace ed., 1764), ch.2, p.7, For new staff members, see *Shang-yü ch'i-wu i-fu*, v.1, pp.26-27, Jan. 7, 1724; *CSL*, YC, ch.85, p.2, Sept. 25, 1729; *SYNK*, v.29, p.9, June 20, 1732.

33. *CSL*, YC, ch.30, p.6, April 17, 1725; *SYPC*, v.3, pp.42-43, Jan. 22, 1726; v.9, p.5, July 15, 1731.

34. For information about these items, see respectively *SYPC*, v.1, p.13, Oct. 12, 1723; v.3, pp. 42-43, Jan. 22, 1726; *Shang-yü ch'i-wu i-fu*, v.2, pp. 27-29, Oct. 8, 1725; *CSL*, YC, ch.117, pp.16-17, May 23, 1732; ch.65, pp.11-12, March 7, 1728; *Shang-yü ch'i-wu i-fu*, v.5, p.25, Nov. 18, 1730.

35. *SYPC*, v.1, p.10, Aug. 16, 1723; *CSL*, YC, ch.70, pp.14-15, Aug. 1, 1728; *SYNK*, v.21, p.7, Feb. 19, 1729.

36. *SYPC*, v.4, p.14, May 26, 1726.

37. *Ibid.*, v.8, pp.5-6, April 20, 1730.

38. *SYNK*, v.11, pp.15-16, Nov. 4, 1726; *Shang-yü ch'i-wu i-fu*, v.5, pp.16-21, Sept. 20, 1730.

39. For details about the school, see *Pa-ch'i t'ung-chih ch'u-chi*, ch.25, "ying-chien chih," part 3, p.8; Chao-lien, *Hsiao-t'ing tsa-lu*, ch.2, p.4.

40. For details, see *Shang-yü ch'i-wu i-fu*, v.4, pp.18-20, Feb. 6, 1729.

41. Chang T'ang-jung, *Ch'ing-kung shu-wen*, ch.3, p.35.

42. *Ibid.*, Chao-lien, *Hsiao-t'ing tsa-lu*, ch.2, p.4; *CSL*, YC, ch.75, p.8, Dec. 10, 1728.

43. For details, see *Pa-ch'i t'ung-chih ch'u-chi*, ch.25, "Ying-chien chih," part 3, pp.18, 20-21; *Yü-hsing ch'i-wu tsou-i*, v.2, pp.6-8, Nov. 25, 1727; Chao-lien, *Hsiao t'ing tsa-lu*, ch.2, pp.4-5.

44. For schools with emphasis on both, see *CSL*, YC, ch.124, p.8, Nov. 26, 1732; *SYPC*, v.9, pp.1-2, March 29, 1731. For schools with emphasis only on the language, see *CPYC*, v.39, Memorials of Po Chih-fan, p.19, Oct. 18, 1733.

45. *SYNK*, v.10, pp.8-9, Oct. 10, 1726; v.30, pp. 6-7, Jan. 17, 1734; *SYPC*, v.7, pp.21-22, Sept. 17, 1729.

46. *Yü-hsing ch'i-wu tsou-i*, v.5, pp.22-23, Oct. 5, 1734; *CSL*, YC, ch.121, p.2, Aug. 20, 1732.

47. *SYNK*, v.30, pp.6-7, Dec. 29, 1733.

48. *Yü-hsing ch'i-wu tsou-i*, v.1, p.5, June 3, 1725. The second essay will be discussed in detail in the next chapter.

49. Li Fu, *Mu-t'ang ch'u-kao* (Works of Li Fu, First Series) (1831 ed.), ch.40, p.37.

50. For a detailed discussion of the banner land system, see Ishibashi Hideo, "Shinchō no Kiho kichi seisaku" ('On the policies on banner lands in ch'i-fu at the middle age of Ch'ing dynasty'), *Tōyō gakuhō* (Reports of the Oriental Society) 39.2:23-72, especially 24-28 (September 1956); 39.3:67-98 (December 1956). The most detailed treatment of the subject is Liu Chia-chü, *Ch'ing-ch'ao ch'u-ch'i ti pa-ch'i ch'üan-ti* ('The allotted land policy for the eight banners in the early Ch'ing dynasty'), (Taipei, 1964), chs.1-4.

51. SYPC, v.5, pp.18-19, June 2, 1727.

52. Sonoda Kazuki, *Zen Shin rekidai kōtei no tōjun* (Eastern trips of early Ch'ing emperors), (Mukden, 1930), pp.66-68.

53. SYPC, v.2, p.4, April 11, 1724.

54. Ibid., v.5, p.19, June 2, 1727; SYNK, v.25, pp.8-9, May 27, 1730.

55. CSL, YC, ch.10, p.22, Sept. 19, 1723; ch.30, pp.15-16, April 23, 1725; ch.41, pp.19-20, March 23, 1726.

56. SYNK, v.1, p.7, Feb. 20, 1723; *Ch'ing-ch'ao wen-hsien t'ung-k'ao*, I, 5445.

57. SYNK, v.4, pp.7-8, Feb. 20, 1724; *Yü-hsing ch'i-wu tsou-i*, v.2, pp.7-8, Nov. 25, 1727; *Shang-yü ch'i-wu i-fu*, v.5, p.28, Jan. 22, 1731; SYPC, v.9, p.3, April 6, 1731; CSL, YC, p.27, Aug. 24, 1731.

58. *Shang-yü ch'i-wu i-fu*, v.3, pp.7-9, April 7, 1728.

59. Ibid., v.1, pp.5-6, June 2, 1723.

60. Ibid., pp.15-16, July 15, 1723.

61. There is a great deal of literature on the well-field system. For a thorough treatment, see Joseph R. Levenson, "Ill Wind in the Well-field: The Erosion of the Confucian Ground of Controversy," in Arthur F. Wright, ed., *The Confucian Persuasion* (Stanford, 1960), pp.268-87.

62. For details, see *Pa-ch'i t'ung-chih ch'u-chi*, ch.22, "t'u-t'ien chih," part 5, pp.1-2; Ishibashi Hideo, "Shinchō no kiho," (39.3:)68-73.

63. For composition and treatment of these two groups, see *Shang-yü ch'i-wu i-fu*, v.1, pp.8-10, Aug. 11, 1724; v.5, pp.13-14, Sept. 9, 1727; *Pa-ch'i*

t'ung-chih ch'u-chi, ch.18, "t'u-t'ien chih," part 1, pp.41-46; Ishibashi Hideo, "Shinchō no kiho," (39.3:) 68-73.

64. For instance, see Wei Chien-yu, "Ch'ing Yung-cheng ch'ao shih-hsing ching-t'ien chih ti k'ao-ch'a" ('A study on the experiment of the "Tsing-t'ien" system in the reign of Yung-cheng'), *Shih-hsüeh nien-pao* 1.5:113-26 (August 1933).

65. *Han ming-ch'en chuan*, ch.26, p.20.

66. Miyazaki Ichisada, *Yōsei-tei*, p.165.

67. *ECCP*, I, 257.

68. For these dismissals and degradations, see *CSL*, YC, chs. 1-39.

69. For analysis of the nature of the empire, see Friedrich, *Man and His Government*, ch.31, especially pp.567-74.

VIII: The Literati

1. For a general discussion of early Ch'ing intellectual restrictions, see Ono Kazuko, "Shin sho no shiso tōsei o megutte" ('On the regulation of thoughts for the early Ch'ing'), *Tōyōshi kenkyū* 18.3: 99-123 (December 1959).

2. For instance, see *CSL*, Shun-chih, ch.107, pp. 16-17, March 30, 1657.

3. For the hereditary titles, see *ibid.*, KH, ch. 32, p.2, Jan. 28, 1670; for the sixteen maxims, see *ibid.*, ch.34, pp.10-11, Nov. 21, 1670. It was decided to publish these maxims as imperatives for all the people in 1671 (*ibid.*, p.21, Jan. 6, 1671).

4. For selection of these scholars, see *ibid.*, ch.71, pp.11-12, Feb. 14, 1678; ch.80, pp.1 and 14, April 11 and May 9, 1679. For an English article, see Hellmut Wilhelm, "The Po-hsüeh hung-ju Examination of 1679," *Journal of the American Oriental Society* 71: 60-66 (1951). For an inspiring article on the early Ch'ing policy toward the Chinese scholars, see Lawrence D. Kessler, "Chinese Scholars and the Early Manchu State," *Harvard Journal of Asiatic Studies* 31: 179-200 (1971).

5. For the posthumous honor, see *CSL*, KH, ch.249, pp.7-8, March 10, 1712; for publication of his works, see *ibid.*, ch.256, p.9, Nov. 13, 1713.

6. *Ibid.*, ch.117, p.19, Dec. 9, 1684; ch.249, pp.7-8, March 10, 1712.

7. Cf. the brief discussion in section 3, Ch.2.

8. Ch'ien Mu, *Chung-kuo chin san-pai nien hsüeh-shu shih*, I, 11-12, 14, 20-21, and *passim*. For the

Tung-lin movement, see Hucker, "The Tung-lin Movement of the Last Ming Period," pp.132-63; Busch, "The Tung-lin Academy and Its Political and Philosophical Significance," pp.1-163.

9. Ho, "Salient Aspects of China's Heritage," p.14; Wright, "Comments by Arthur Frederick Wright," p.39.

10. *Ch'ing-ch'ao wen-hsien t'ung-k'ao*, I, 6876.

11. *CSL*, Shun-chih, ch.5, pp.3-4, June 8, 1644.

12. For the Chinese text, see Ch'ing Shih-tsung, *Sheng-yü kuang-hsün* (Amplified instructions on the Sacred Edict), (Palace ed., 1724), pp.1-48. For their English translation, see William Milne, trans., *The Sacred Edict* (London, 1817), pp.29, 49, 64ff.; F. W. Baller, trans., *The Sacred Edict* (Shanghai, 1907), pp.1, 19, 29, 42ff. The translation is an adaption of Kung-chuan Hsiao, *Rural China: Imperial Control in the Nineteenth Century* (Seattle, 1960), pp.187-88. Cf. T'ung-tsu Ch'ü, *Local Government in China under the Ch'ing* (Cambridge, Mass., 1962), n.161, pp.309-10.

13. Ch'ü, *Local Government in China*, pp.1-3.

14. *CSL*, YC, ch.31, p.32, June 7, 1725.

15. *Ho-nan t'ung-chih* (Gazetteer of Honan province), ed. by T'ien Wen-ching and Wang Shih-chün (Honan Chiao-yü Ssu ed.), ch.10, p.4.

16. Chü, *Local Government in China*, pp.162-63.

17. Ping-ti Ho, "The Significance of the Ch'ing Period in Chinese History," *Journal of Asian Studies* 26.2:192-93 (February 1967).

18. For these two maxims and their comments see Ch'ing Shih-tsung, *Sheng-yü kuang-hsün*, pp.16-21. For a detailed analysis of Maxim 7, see Cohen, *China and Christianity*, pp.10-13.

19. For the contrast between orthodoxy and heterodoxy, see Weber, *The Religion of China*, ch.7, especially pp.205-18.

20. For a detailed discussion about these two aspects, see Benjamin Schwartz, "Some Polarities in Confucian Thought," in Nivison and Wright, *Confucianism in Action*, pp.54-58; Levenson, *Confucian China and Its Modern Fate*, II, 51-52.

21. Weber, *The Religion of China*, pp.158, 305.

22. For discussion of these potential conflicts, see Levenson, *Confucian China and Its Modern Fate*, II, 61-62, and his article entitled: "The Suggestiveness of Vestige: Confucianism and Monarchy at the Last" in Nivison and Wright, *Confucianism in Action*, p.254.

23. *YHL*, pp.54, 105, 141.
24. *Ibid.*, pp.118-19.
25. For its publication, see *CSL*, YC, ch.64, pp.3-4, Jan. 13, 1728. For his inquiry concerning filial piety and chaste behavior, see *SYNK*, v.20, pp. 16-17, Dec. 28, 1728.
26. Ch'ing Shih-tsung, *Ta-i chüeh-mi lu*, ch.1, p.13.
27. For appointment of the first inspector of morale, see *YHL*, p.310.
28. Yokoyama Hiroo, "Kampū seizoku shih kō" ('On the Kuan-feng cheng-su shih or inspector-general of morale'), *Tōyōshi kenkyū* 22.3:94-110 (December 1963).
29. For instance, the *Ch'ing-shih* (pp.4056-58) lists six people—Chiao Ch'i-nien, Hsü Jung, Li Hui, Liu Shih-shu, Ts'ai Shih-shan, and Wang Kuo-tung— all of whom served as inspectors of morale. Except for Hsü and Ts'ai the rest were holders of the *chin-shih* degree.
30. *YHL*, pp.310, 325-26; *CPYC*, v.17, Memorials of Wang Kuo-tung, pp.50-57.
31. *CPYC*, v.17, Memorials of Wang Kuo-tung, pp. 99-100.
32. Lo Chen-yü, *Shih-liao ts'ung-pien*, v.3, "Yung-cheng shang-yü tang," part 3, pp.10-11, Sept. 2, 1730.
33. *CSL*, YC, ch.89, pp.15-16, Jan. 26, 1730; ch. 79, p.26, April 19, 1729.
34. *CPYC*, v.17, Memorials of Wang Kuo-tung, pp. 99-100. This is also reflected in the case of Ts'ai Shih-shan, inspector of morale in Chekiang. During his term he arrested and examined extortioners in the government, local bullies, and racketeering gentry. See *KCT*, Memorials of Ts'ai Shih-shan pp.1-3, Aug. 19, 1729; p.1, May 22, 1730.
35. *CSL*, YC, ch.49, p.7, Oct. 30, 1726.
36. *SYNK*, v.28, pp.7-8, May 13, 1731.
37. For a case of his subordination to the governor or governor-general, see Ts'ai Shih-yüan, *Erh-hsi t'ang wen-chi* (Works of the Erh-hsi Studio), (1735 ed.), ch.4, p.6.
38. For discussion of changes in provincial and local education administration, see Araki Toshikazu, "Yōsei jidai ni okeru gakushinsei no kaikaku" ('Government school inspectors in the Yung-cheng period'), *Tōyōshi kenkyū* 18.3:27-43 (December 1959).
39. *CSL*, YC, ch.3, pp.8-9, Feb. 5, 1723.
40. Araki Toshikazu, "Yōsei jidai ni okeru gakushinsei," pp.31-39. In this section discussion

of the change in the provincial education administration is based on Araki's article.

41. *Li-tai chih-kuan piao*, ch.51, p.3.

42. Chang T'ing-yü, *Ch'eng-huai yüan wen-ts'un*, ch.12, p.13.

43. For a detailed study, see Araki Toshikazu, "Choku-shō kyōgaku no sei o tsūjite mitaru Yōsei chika no bunkyō seisaku" ('Emperor Yung-cheng's educational reform'), *Tōyōshi kenkyū* 16.4:70-78 and 84-87 (March 1958).

44. *YHL*, p.91.

45. *Ibid.*, p.173; *CSL*, YC, ch.56, pp.5-6, May 23, 1727.

46. Araki Toshikazu, "Choku-shō kyōgaku no," p.87.

47. A discussion of the classification and qualifications for the senior licentiates is in Ping-ti Ho, *The Ladder of Success in Imperial China: Aspects of Social Mobility, 1368-1911* (New York, 1962), pp.28-32. For physical inspection, see *YHL*, p.239.

48. *YHL*, p.144.

49. For a brief but analytic discussion of Chinese private academies, see Ho, *The Ladder of Success in Imperial China*, pp.197-203.

50. Shang Yen-liu, *Ch'ing-tai k'o-chü k'ao-shih shu-lüeh*, p.222.

51. *Ibid.*, p.223; *CSL*, YC, ch.127, pp.7-8, Feb. 23, 1733; Hsiao, *Rural China*, p.235-36.

52. Ho, *The Ladder of Success in Imperial China*, p.200.

53. Wm. Theodore de Bary, "Some Common Tendencies in Neo-Confucianism," in Nivison and Wright, *Confucianism in Action*, p.29.

54. For the emperor's comments on the undesirable official conduct, see *SYNK*, v.15, pp.18-19, Aug. 1, 1727; pp.11-12, Oct. 29, 1727; *CYPC*, v.52, Memorials of Ch'eng Yüan-chang, p.51; *CSL*, YC, ch.87, pp. 28-33, Dec. 14, 1729; For analysis of political struggles between ruler and bureaucrats, see Eisenstadt, *The Political Systems*, pp.159-62.

55. For an analytic discussion, see Yang, "Some Characteristics of Chinese," pp.136-46.

56. Ch'ü, *Law and Society in Traditional China*, ch.6.

57. Ch'ü, *Local Government in China*, pp.176-78.

58. *CSL*, YC, ch.87, p.30, Dec. 14, 1729; *CPYC*, v.5, Memorials of Ch'en Shih-hsia, p.74, Feb. 18, 1727.

59. For discussion about the examiners, see Araki Toshikazu, "Yōsei chika ni okeru kosahō no seiritsu" ('The appointment of examiners and associate examiners for provincial examinations'), *Tōyōshi kenkyū* 22.3:56-72 (December 1963).
60. Yü Cheng-hsieh, *Kuei-ssu ts'un-kao* (Selected Works of Yü Cheng-hsieh), (Ts'ung-shu chi-ch'eng ed.), ch.12, p.375.
61. *SYNK*, v.15, pp.18-19, Aug. 1, 1727. For an article on the office-purchasing practice under the Ch'ing, see Hsü Ta-ling, *Ch'ing-tai chuan-nai chih-tu* ('The system of purchasing offices by contributions during the Ch'ing period, 1644-1911'),(Peking, 1950), pp.1-97.
62. *SYNK*, v.15, pp.18-19, Aug. 1, 1727; v.17, pp.6-7, Nov. 18, 1727.
63. Luther Carrington Goodrich, *The Literary Inquisition of Ch'ien-lung*, 2nd ed. (New York, 1966), pp.44-53.
64. For his biographical data, see *ibid.*, p.83; *ECCP*, II, 812-13; *YHL*, pp.256-57.
65. For information about his friend and cousin, see *YHL*, pp.256-57.
66. *SYNK*, v.11, pp.17-18, Oct. 21, 1726.
67. Wang Ching-ch'i, *Tu-shu t'ang hsi-cheng sui-pi*, pp.20-23 and 56-57.
68. Friedrich, *Man and His Government*, p.254.
69. Wang Ching-ch'i, *Tu-shu t'ang hsi-cheng sui-pi*, pp.54-55.
70. *CSL*, YC, ch.39, pp.21-22, Jan. 20, 1726; *ibid.*, CL, ch.14, pp.7-8, April 16, 1736.
71. For his biographical data, see Goddrich, *Literary Inquisition* pp.21-22; *ECCP*, I, 590; *YHL*, pp.273-74; Wang Shih-chen, *Hsiang-tsu pi-chi* (Miscellaneous notes of Wang Shih-chen), (n.p., n.d.), ch.1, p.20.
72. *YHL*, p.274.
73. *CSL*, YC, ch.42, pp.20-21, May 1, 1726; Ch'ing Shih-tsung, *Ming-chiao tsui-jen* (Offender against the orthodox doctrine), (Peiping, 1930), p.1 (preface).
74. *YHL*, p.274; *SYNK*, v.9, p.9, May 22, 1726.
75. *CSL*, YC, ch.44, p.16, June 8, 1726.
76. For his biographical data, see *ECCP*, I, 22; Goodrich, *Literary Inquisition*, pp.80-81; *YHL*, p.149.
77. *SYNK*, v.11, p.17, Oct. 21, 1726.
78. For the five topics, see *YHL*, pp.304-5.
79. One quotation is "*Cheng-ta erh t'ien-ti chih ch'ing k'o-chien i*" (If uprightness prevails, the

universal principle will be perceptible). The other reads, "*Po-shih ying-chih, fu-tzu ning-chih*" (Those hundred houses being full, the wives and children have a feeling of repose). For an English translation of the second quotation, see James Legge, trans., *The Chinese Classics* (Hong Kong, 1960), IV, 605.

80. *ECCP*, I, 22. Cf. Shang Yen-liu, *Ch'ing-tai k'o-chü k'ao-shih shu-lüeh*, pp.327-28.
81. *SYNK*, v.11, p.19, Oct. 21, 1726.
82. *YHL*, p.411.
83. *CSL*, YC, ch.57, pp.6-7, June 25, 1727. His sons and nephews were pardoned in 1736 (*ibid.*, CL, ch.14, p.8, April 16, 1736).
84. *Man ming-ch'en chuan*, ch.21, p.9.
85. *YHL*, p.321.
86. *CSL*, YC, ch.50, p.19, Dec. 20, 1726. Cf. *ECCP*, I, 22.
87. For his biographical data, see Goodrich, *Literary Inquisition*, p.82; *SYNK*, v.22, pp.24-26, July 21, 1729.
88. For the main points of his essays, see *SYNK*, v.22, pp.26-38, July 21, 1729.
89. *Ibid.*, pp.24-25.
90. *Ibid.*, p.26.
91. For his biographical data, see *ECCP*, II, 747-49; Goodrich, *Literary Inquisition*, pp.84-85; Ch'ing Shih-tsung, *Ta-i chüeh-mi lu*, ch.1, p.73; ch.2, pp.2-3.
92. Miyazaki Ichisada, *Yōsei-tei*, pp.155-56.
93. Ch'ing Shih-tsung, *Ta-i chüeh-mi lu*, ch.1, pp.15-29; ch.2, p.58; ch.3, pp.10-11, 33-42, and 54-55.
94. For Lü's biographical data, see *ECCP*, I, 551-52. For a general analysis of his ideology, see Hsiao Kung-ch'üan, *Chung-kuo cheng-chih ssu-hsiang shih* (A history of Chinese political thought), (Shanghai, 1947), II, 292-97; Jung Chao-tsu, "Lü Liu-liang chi ch'i ssu-hsiang" ('De philosopho Lü Liu-liang [1629-1683], a dynastia Ch'ing postmortem proscripto'), *Fu-jen hsüeh-chih* 5.1-2:1-86 (December 1936). For a Japanese article, see Yuasa Yukihiko, "Ryo Banson no chasaku to sono seiji" ('On the works and political ideas of Lo-wan-sun'), *Geirin* (The Journal of Cultural Sciences) 4.1:66-74 (February 1953).
95. Lü Liu-liang, *Lü Wan-ts'un hsien-sheng wen-chi* (Works of Lü Liu-liang), (1689 ed.), ch.1, pp. 9-10, 23-24.

96. For his emphasis on the feudal system, see Lü Liu-liang, *Lü Wan-ts'un hsien-sheng ssu-shu chiang-i* (Comments of Lü Liu-liang on the Four Books), ed. by Ch'en Tsung (1686 ed.), ch.34, p.40ff; Chu Shih and Wu Hsiang, *Po Lü Liu-liang ssu-shu chiang-i* (A refutation of Lü Liu-liang's comments on the Four Books), (Palace ed., 1732), v.6, p.6; v.7, p.22.
97. Lü Liu-liang, *Lü Wan-ts'un hsien-sheng ssu-shu chiang-i*, ch.27, pp.9-10.
98. Chu Shih and Wu Hsiang, *Po Lü Liu-liang*, v.1, pp.10-11; v.3, p.25.
99. For their relationship in the post-feudal period, see Lü Liu-liang, *Lü Wan-ts'un hsien-sheng ssu-shu chiang-i*, ch.27, pp.9-10; ch.33, p.3; ch.41, p.7.
100. Lü Liu-liang, *Lü Wan-ts'un hsien-sheng wen-chi*, ch.7, p.1.
101. Lü Liu-liang, *Lü Wan-ts'un hsien-sheng ssu-shu chiang-i*, ch.4, p.7.
102. *Ibid.*, ch.17, pp.8-9.
103. For the anti-Manchu points in his journals, see *CSL*, YC, ch.81, p.27, June 17, 1729.
104. For instance, see Ch'ing Shih-tsung, *Ta-i chüeh-mi lu*, ch.1, p.1.
105. For some of his anti-Manchu points, see *ibid.*, ch.1, pp.39, 49, 68; ch.2, p.10.
106. See *Ch'ing-tai wen-tzu yü tang* (Documents about the literary inquisition during the Ch'ing dynasty), (Peiping, 1934), v.9, pp.1-9.
107. For instance, see *CPYC*, v.21, Memorials of Yüeh Ch'ao-lung, pp.13-14, Feb. 2, 1730; v.54, Memorials of Mai-chu, pp.30-31, Nov. 7, 1729.
108. For his arguments, see *CSL*, YC, ch.86, pp. 8-18, Nov. 2, 1729. For a general discussion of his arguments, see Onogawa Hidemi, "Yōsei tei to Taigi kakumei-roku," pp.95-107.
109. *ECCP*, II, 748.
110. *SYNK*, v.27, p.4, Jan. 26, 1731.
111. For punishment of Lü Liu-liang and his family and disciples, see *CSL*, YC, ch.126, pp.8-9, 14-15, Jan. 27 and Feb. 1, 1733; *ECCP*, I, 551.
112. *SYNK*, v.24, pp.4-5, 20, Nov. 26 and Dec. 5, 1729; *ECCP*, II, 749.
113. *CPYC*, v.51, Memorials of Shih I-chih, pp. 62-63, Feb. 28, 1732.
114. *Ch'ing-tai wen-tzu yü t'ang*, v.9, p.52.
115. Ho, *The Ladder of Success in Imperial China*, p.34.

116. For the student boycott, see Araki Toshikazu, "Yōsei ninen no rakō jikan to Den Bunkyō" ('T'ien Wen-ching and boycott for state examination'), *Tōyōshi kenkyū* 15.4:100-119 (March 1957).
117. Friedrich and Brzezinski, *Totalitarian Dictatorship and Autocracy*, p.170.
118. Some of these practices are ably analyzed in Ho, "The Significance of the Ch'ing Period in Chinese History," pp.192-93.
119. *Ibid.*, p.192.
120. For Hsieh's case, see *Ch'ing-tai wen-tzu yü tang*, v.1, pp.1-2; for Li's case, see *CSL*, CL, ch.13, p.2, March 27, 1736.

IX: *The Populace of the Period*

1. *CSL*, YC, ch.75, pp.15-16, Dec. 22, 1728; ch. 94, pp.14-15, June 29, 1730.
2. For a Japanese article on these people as a whole, see Terada Takanobu, "Yōsei tei no semmin kaihō rei ni tsuite" ('On the emancipation of the lower orders by the Yung-cheng Emperor'), *Tōyōshi kenkyū* 18.3:124-41 (December 1959). For a Chinese treatment, see Ch'ü, *Law and Society in Traditional China*, pp.129-32. For a French treatment, see Pierre Hoang, *Mélanges sur l'administration* (Shanghai, 1902), pp.120-24.
3. This group is translated as the "lazy people" and identified with the beggars in Ch'ü, *Law and Society in Traditional China*, p.130. For the story about their origin, see *Che-chiang hsin-chih* (A new gazetteer of Chekiang), ed. by Chiang Ch'ing-yün et al. (Hangchow, 1936), ch.7, p.18.
4. *CPYC*, v.39, Memorials of Ko-er-t'ai, p.90, Aug. 11, 1723; *Shao-hsing fu-chih* (Gazetteer of Shao-hsing prefecture), ed. by P'ing Shu nd Li Heng-t'e (1792 ed.), ch.18, p.41. For the variant study, see *Ting-hai hsien-chih* (Gazetteer of Ting-hai district), ed. by Ch'en T'ien-yin (1924 ed.), ch.16, p.52.
5. For the nature of their service, see *CSL*, YC, ch.56, p.27, June 16, 1927. Cf. Ch'ü, *Law and Society in Traditional China*, pp.131-32; Terada Takanobu, "Yōsei tei no semmin," p.133.
6. *CSL*, YC, ch.94, p.17, July 3, 1730.
7. *Hsing-ning hsien-chih* (Gazetteer of Hsing-ning district), ed. by Chang Huo-ling (1929 ed.), ch.12, p.91.
8. Chang T'ing-yü, *Ch'eng-huai yüan wen-ts'un*, ch.4; *Man Ming-ch'en chuan*, ch.19, p.25.

9. *CSL*, YC, ch.81, p.38, June 24, 1729.
10. Ch'ing Shih-tsung, *Yü-hsüan yü-lu*, ch.12, p.38.
11. *YHL*, pp.307, 361; *CSL*, YC, ch.82, p.23, July 18, 1729; ch.107, pp.12-13, July 14, 1731; ch. 132, pp.12-13, Aug. 1, 1733.
12. *YHL*, pp.102-3; *CSL*, YC, ch.6, p.23, May 23, 1723.
13. *CPYC*, v.39, Memorials of Ko-er-t'ai, p.90, Aug. 11, 1723; *CSL*, YC, ch.11, p.27, Oct. 18, 1723.
14. *Ibid.*, ch.56, pp.27-28, June 16, 1727; *YHL*, p.396; *CPYC*, v.18, Memorials of Liu Nan, pp.17-18.
15. *CSL*, YC, ch.81, pp.38-39, June 24, 1729; ch.94, p.17, July 3, 1730.
16. *Ibid.*, ch.103, p.6, March 16, 1731. For the petitions of officials, see Chang T'ing-yü, *Ch'eng-huai yüan wen-ts'un*, ch.4, pp.4-5; *Man ming-ch'en chuan*, ch.19, p.25; ch.22, p.30.
17. Ch'ing Shih-tsung, *Yü-chih lu*, ch.2, pp.99-100; *Yü-hsing ch'i-wu tsou-i*, v.1, pp.2-3, April 6, 1725.
18. *CSL*, YC, ch.64, p.27, Feb. 2, 1728.
19. *Ibid.*, YC, ch.103, p.33, April 6, 1731; ch. 130, p.24, June 11, 1733.
20. Wang Ching-ch'i, *Tu-shu t'ang hsi-cheng sui-pi*, pp.6-7, 19-20; *YHL*, p.251.
21. For the cases of singers and beggars, see *Ch'in-ting hsüeh-cheng ch'üan-shu* (A guide to the education administration), (1812 ed.), ch.43, pp.4-5; for the case of Tankas, see *Che-chiang hsin-chih*, ch. 7, p.18.
22. Pao Shu-yün, *Hsing-an hui-lan* (A collection of judicial cases), (1834 ed.), ch.39, pp.10-16.
23. Ts'ai Ch'eng, *Ch'ing-tai shih-lun* (Historical comments on the Ch'ing), (Shanghai, 1920), ch.6, p.7.
24. Hoang, *Mélanges sur l'administration*, pp. 133-34.
25. Ts'ai Ch'eng, *Ch'ing-tai shih-lun*, pp.133-34.
26. For a short description of the term *lieh-shen*, see Ch'ü, *Local Government in China*, p.190. For the gentry's informal influences and legal privileges, see *ibid.*, pp.173-85, and Ch'ü, *Law and Society in Traditional China*, pp.178-85.
27. T'ien Wen-ching, *Fu-yü hsüan-hua lu*, ch.1, p.98; ch.4, p.120. A Japanese article supplies other cases. For reference, see Miyazaki Ichisada, "Yōsei jidai chihō seiji no jitsujō" ('The real state of

the local administration in the Yung-cheng period'),
Tōyōshi kenkyū 18.3:1-26 (December 1959). For a
general discussion of their various malpractices,
see Hsiao, *Rural China*, pp.132-37 and *passim*.

28. *CSL*, YC, ch.115, p.4, Feb. 27, 1732. For a
Japanese article on the tax-arrears of the Yung-cheng
period, see Iwami Hiroshi, "Yōsei nenkan no minketsu
ni tsuite," pp.61-84.

29. For further discussion, see section 3 below.

30. For discussion of the ambivalent relationship between gentry and local administrators, see
Ch'ü, *Local Government in China*, pp.190-92.

31. *CPYC*, v.42, Memorials of Li Wei, p.68, July
20, 1730. For another similar case, see *ibid.*, v.39,
Memorials of Po Chih-fan, p.14, Jan. 17, 1730.

32. For a detailed study of these two cases, see
Meng Sen, *Ming-Ch'ing shih lun-chu chi-k'an*
(Collected essays on the history of the Ming and the
Ch'ing), (Taipei, 1961), pp.391-452. Further discussion of the taxation case will be given in the last
section of this chapter.

33. *CSL*, YC, ch.61, p.26, Nov. 8, 1727; Wang
Shih-chün, *Ho-tung ts'ung-cheng lu* (Record of administrative work in Honan and Shantung), (1735 ed.),
ch.9, p.46.

34. *CYPC*, v.55, Memorials of Ho Yü-lin, p.64,
Nov. 21, 1731; v.14, Memorials of I Chao-hsiung, p.
85, July 27, 1727; *YHL*, pp.356, 420.

35. For T'ien's biography, see *ECCP*, II, 719-21.
For Li's biography, see *ibid.*, pp.720-21. For O-er-
t'ai's biography, see *ibid.*, I, 601-3; see also Kent
C. Smith, "O-erh-t'ai and the Yung-cheng Emperor,"
Ch'ing-shih wen-t'i (Bulletin of the Society for
Ch'ing Studies) 1.8:10-15 (May 1968). For their
contributions to the local administration, see
Miyazaki Ichisada, *Yōsei-tei*, pp.105-20.

36. Ch'ien Yung, *Li-yüan ts'ung-hua* (Collected
notes of Ch'ien Yung), (1870 ed.), ch.1, p.27. For
his requirements of magistrates, see T'ien Wen-ching
and Li Wei, *Ch'in-pan chou-hsien shih-i* (Guide to
the district and department administration), (1868
ed.), pp.1-30.

37. Yüan Mei, *Hsiao-ts'ang shan-fang wen-chi*,
ch.6, p.3.

38. *Ibid.*, ch.8, p.1.

39. For the hydraulic work of the Shun-chih
period, see Chou Fu, *Chou Ch'üeh-shen kung ch'üan-chi*
(The complete collection of Chou Fu's works), (Ch'iu-
p'u, The Chou family ed., 1922), v.27, "Chih-shui

shu-yao," ch.4, pp.1-6. For the hydraulic work of the K'ang-hsi period, see *Shih-ch'ao sheng-hsün* (Sacred instructions of the Ten Emperors), (Kuang-hsü ed.), KH, chs. 33-35. For the irrigation system in the Yung-cheng period, see *CSL*, YC, ch.53, pp.22-23, March 8, 1727; ch.92, pp.8-9, April 28, 1730; and ch.114, pp.9-10, Feb. 16, 1732; P'an Hsi-en, *Chi-fu shui-li ssu-an* (Four conservation enterprises in the metropolitan area), (Tao-kuang ed.), v.1; *CPYC*, v.27, Memorials of O-er-t'ai, pp.40-41, 58-60, March 23 and July 13, 1729; v.28, pp.6-7, 18-19, 26-27, March 1, May 12, and June 5, 1730.

40. For appointments of these two additional directors-general, see *CSL*, YC, ch.78, pp.6-7, March 4, 1729; ch.101, pp.2, 7, Jan. 12 and 26, 1731.

41. For increase of the conservation troops, see *ibid.*, ch.53, pp.10-11, Feb. 26, 1727; ch.65, pp.1-2, Feb. 11, 1728. For addition of two young officials, see *ibid.*, ch.137, pp.8-9, Dec. 27, 1733.

42. For these two measures, see *ibid.*, ch.83, pp.23-24, Aug. 2, 1729; K'ang Chi-t'ien, *Ho-ch'ü chi-wen* (A record of river works), (1936 ed.), ch.18, p.39.

43. For instance, see *ECCP*, I, 161-63.

44. *Shih-ch'ao sheng-hsün*, YC, ch.27, p.2, Aug. 11, 1726.

45. *CPYC*, v.27, Memorials of O-er-t'ai, pp.40-41, March 23, 1729; v.28, pp.6-7, 18-19, 30-31, March 1, May 12, and July 10, 1730.

46. For the irrigation system in the Yunnan-Kwangsi border, see *ibid.*, v.27, Memorials of O-er-t'ai, pp.40-41, 59-60, March 23 and July 13, 1729; v.28, p.7, March 1, 1730. This work was continued after his transfer to Peking in late 1731. Consequently, a river of more than 281 miles was completed under Yin Chi-shan (1696-1771) in 1734 (see *ibid.*, v.60, Memorials of Yin Chi-shan, p.53, Aug. 21, 1734). For the watercourse in the Kweichow-Kwangsi border, see *ibid.*, v.28, Memorials of O-er-t'ai, p. 23, May 12, 1730.

47. *Ibid.*, v.25, Memorials of O-er-t'ai, pp. 98-99, Sept. 24, 1727; *YHL*, pp.366-67, 392, 397-98, 408, 409-10.

48. For the work in Szechwan, see K'ang Chi-t'ien, *Ho-ch'ü chi-wen*, ch.19, pp.53, 65; for the work in Hunan, see *ibid.*, ch.18, pp.108-10; ch.19, p.24; for the stone embankment, see *YHL*, pp.400, 412; Chu Shih, *Chu Wen-tuan kung wen-chi* (Works of Chu

Shih), (Ku-huan chai ed.), "Pu-pien," ch.1, pp.8-10; Ku I, "Ch'ing-ch'ao ch'ien-ch'i tui Che-chiang hai-t'ang ti hsiu-chu" (Early Ch'ing constructions of the sea wall in Chekiang province), *Shixue Yuekan* (Shih-hsüeh yüeh-k'an), 10:25-26 (October 1958).

49. K'ang Chi-t'ien, *Ho-ch'ü chi-wen*, ch.18, pp. 42-44; ch.19, pp.17-18; *Shih-ch'ao sheng-hsün*, YC, ch.27, p.5, April 28, 1730.

50. K'ang Chi-t'ien, *Ho-ch'ü chi-wen*, ch.18, pp. 64, 86-88.

51. P'an Hsi-en, *Chi-fu shui-li ssu-an*, v.1, pp. 6-8, 13-16.

52. *Ibid.*, pp.9-11.

53. *Ibid.*, pp.7-8; *YHL*, pp.332-33.

54. According to P'an Hsi-en, *Chi-fu shui-li ssu-an*, v.1, pp.55-82, there were about 575,062 *mou* of new rice fields. In standard conversion 6.6 *mou* equal one acre.

55. *Ibid.*, p.81.

56. *Ibid.*, pp.52, 54-55.

57. By standard conversion, the newly reclaimed lands equaled about 18,984 acres, of which 8,015 acres were made dried fields (see *ibid.*, pp.59-82).

58. *Ch'ing-ch'ao wen-hsien t'ung-k'ao*, I, 4858, 4865, 4867; Otake Fumio, "Shindai no kōchi kaikon—kōchi zouka ni tsukite" (Reclamation works of the Ch'ing dynasty—the increase of the cultivated land), *Shina Kenkyū* 24:67-87 (December 1930).

59. *Ch'ing-ch'ao wen-hsien t'ung-k'ao*, I, 4858 and 4863.

60. For example, see *ibid.*, p.4863; for a general evaluation, see Otake Fumio, "Shindai no kōchi kaikon," pp.87-95.

61. Ping-ti Ho, *Studies on the Population of China, 1368-1953* (Cambridge, Mass. 1959), ch.2; Chuan Han-sheng and Wang Yeh-chien, "Ch'ing-tai ti jen-k'ou pien-tung" ('Population changes in China during the Ch'ing dynasty'), *Bulletin of the Institute of History and Philology, Academia Sinica* 32:139-80, especially 143-49 (July 1961).

62. *CSL*, YC, ch.6, p.25, May 30, 1723.

63. For proposal of landowning restriction and its counterproposal, see *SYNK*, v.21, pp.4-5, April 1, 1729; Chang T'ing-yü, *Cheng-huai yüan wen-ts'un*, ch.3, pp.39-41.

64. For his requirement and prohibition, see *CSL*, YC, ch.6, p.25, May 30, 1723; for his concurrent appointment, see Wang Shih-chün, *Li-chih hsüeh-ku*

p'ien (A record of administration after ancient principles), (Chung-cheng T'ang ed.), ch.1, pp.3-6.

65. For commendation of distinctive farmers, see *CSL*, YC, ch.16, pp.25-26, March 14, 1724; for change in the recommendation period, see *ibid.*, ch.81, p.10, June 3, 1729. Each county or department in Honan province recommended two farmers after 1729 (*ibid.*, ch.79, p.3, March 30, 1729). For reclamation loans, see *ibid.*, ch.80, p.14, May 11, 1729.

66. For the Tankas, see *ibid.*, ch.81, p.38, June 24, 1729.

67. For a thorough discussion, see Ho, *Studies on the Population of China*, pp.102-23.

68. Yüan Mei, *Hsiao-ts'ang shan-fang wen-chi*, ch.5, p.2.

69. For evaluation of early Ch'ing reclamation, see Otake Fumio, "Shindai no kōchi kaikon," pp.66-95; for the Wan-li returns, see *Ta-Ming hui-tien* (Collected statutes of the Ming dynasty), comp. by Li Tung-yang and Shen Ming-hsing [*sic.*, Shen Shih-hsing] (Taipei, 1964), ch.17, pp.8-12.

70. For the case of Honan, see Wang Shih-chün, *Ho-tung ts'ung-cheng lu*, ch.7, pp.11-12; for the case of Kwangtung, see *CPYC*, v.56, Memorials of Omida, pp. 65, 70, June 5, 1734 and Feb. 18, 1735.

71. Ho, *Studies on the Population of China*, pp. 138-53.

72. *Ch'ing-ch'ao wen-hsien t'ung-k'ao*, I, 4877; *CSL*, YC, ch.61, p.29, Nov. 9, 1727.

73. *CSL*, YC, ch.61, p.29, Nov. 9, 1727.

74. *Ssu-ch'uan t'ung-chih* (Gazetteer of Szechwan province), comp. by Jalangga and Kao Wei-hsin (1733-1736 ed.), ch.5, p.3.

75. *CPYC*, v.25, Memorials of O-er-t'ai, pp.100-101, Sept. 24, 1727; v.26, p.54, June 28, 1728; v.27, p.40, March 23, 1729.

76. *Yün-nan t'ung-chih* (Gazetteer of Yunnan), ed. by Ts'en Yü-ying (1894 ed.), ch.57, pp.26, 32; ch.58, p.2.

77. *Sheng-ching t'ung-chih* (Gazetteer of Liaoning), comp. by Lü Yao-tseng and Wei Shu (1779 ed.), ch.23, p.1.

78. For the *ting* returns, see *ibid.*, pp.8, 11-13; for the land registers, see *ibid.*, ch.24, pp. 8, 14-17.

79. Wang Yü-ch'üan, "The Rise of Land Tax and the Fall of Dynasties in Chinese History," *Pacific Affairs* 9:201-20 (1936). The thesis of this article has been recently challenged by a highly analytical

case study. See Yeh-chien Wang, "The Fiscal Importance of the Land Tax during the Ch'ing Period," *Journal of Asian Studies* 30.4:829-42 (August 1971).
   80. Ch'ü, *Local Government in China*, pp.51-52, 67, 133 ff.
   81. *CSL*, Shun-chih, ch.112, pp.7-8, Nov. 12, 1657.
   82. For instance, see Hsiao I-shan, *Ch'ing-tai t'ung-shih*, II, 389; Ch'ien Ch'en-ch'ün, *Hsiang-shu chai ch'üan-chi* (Complete works of the Hsiang-shu Studio), (1885 ed.), "Wen-chi," ch.4, p.15. The shortest and yet best article on the subject is Ko Han-feng, "Ch'ing-tai t'ien-fu chung chih hao-hsien" (Hao-hsien in the Ch'ing land and labor-service tax), *Nung-hsüeh* (Agricultural science) 1.5:45-46 (May 1939).
   83. E-tu Zen Sun, ed. and trans., *Ch'ing Administrative Terms* (Cambridge, Mass., 1961), p.89; Abe Takeo, "Kōsen teikai no kenkyū—Yōsei shi no isshō toshite mita" ('On hao-hsien'), *Tōyōshi kenkyū* 16.4: 126 (March 1958). Cf. Ch'ü, *Local Government in China*, p.132.
   84. For the fees required by the unclassified personnel, see Ch'ü, *Local Government in China*, pp. 25-26, 50-51, 89-90.
   85. For the case of the Censorate, see *CPYC*, v. 56, Memorials of Omida, p.30, Aug. 21, 1732.
   86. For example, see *ibid.*, v.36, Memorials of Sung Yün, p.4, Oct. 15, 1728; v.24, Memorials of Tsu Ping-heng, p.14, Dec. 28, 1728; v.39, Memorials of Po Chih-fan, pp.4-5, May 14, 1728; v.23, Memorials of Chao Kuo-ying, p.103.
   87. *Ibid.*, v.22, Memorials of Hsü Ting, p.45, April 5, 1729.
   88. *Ibid.*, v.35, Memorials of Ch'iao Shih-ch'en, p.4, Jan. 4, 1732; v.21, Memorials of Pien Shih-wei, p.38, Aug. 10, 1735; v.40, Memorials of Li Wei, pp.2 and 4, July 20, 1723.
   89. T'ang Pin, *T'ang-tzu i-shu* (Works of T'ang Pin) (1703 ed.), ch.9, pp.1-2.
   90. *CSL*, KH, ch.183, pp.22-23, July 5, 1697.
   91. Lo Chen-yü, *Shih-liao ts'ung-pien*, "erh-chi," v.2, "Biography of T'ien Ts'ung-tien," p.6.
   92. For these cases, see Ch'in-ch'uan Chü-shih, *Huang-Ch'ing tsou-i*, ch.21, "Memorials of Chin Shih-chien," p.10; *CSL*, Shun-chih, ch.144, p.4, Feb. 5, 1661; KH, ch.240, p.4, Dec. 10, 1709. For a general discussion of the topic, see Wang Shih, "Po-feng yü lou-kuei" (Poor payment and customary gratuities)

Wen-shih tsa-chih (Journal of literature and history) 3.1-2:53-72 (January 1944).

93. For Lu, see Ch'ien Ch'en-ch'ün, *Hsiang-shu chai ch'üan-chi*, "Wen-chi," ch.4, p.16; for Shen, see Ch'ien I-chi, *Pei-chuan chi*, ch.23, "Biography of Shen Chin-ssu," p.5.

94. For a detailed survey of his various measures, see Wang Yeh-chien, "Ch'ing Yung-cheng shih-ch'i (1723-1735) ti ts'ai-cheng kai-ke" ('Financial reforms during the Yung-cheng period [1723-1735]'), *Bulletin of the Institute of History and Philology, Academia Sinica* 32:56-62 (July 1961); Iwami Hiroshi, "Yōsei nenkan no minketsu ni tsuite," pp.62-79.

95. *YHL*, pp.82-83, 125; *CSL*, YC, ch.26, p.3, Dec. 19, 1724.

96. *YHL*, p.102; Saeki Tomi, "Shindai ni okeru sōshō seido" ('The tsou-hsiao system of the Ch'ing dynasty') *Tōyōshi kenkyū* 3:25-55 (December 1963).

97. *CYPC*, v.2, Memorials of Yang Tsung-jen, p. 25, Jan. 17, 1723; cf. Abe Takeo, "Kōsen teikai no kenkyū," pp.187-88.

98. For Shih I-chih, see *KCT*, his memorial, pp. 2-4, Sept. 7, 1723; for Shih Wen-ch'o, see *Man ming-ch'en chuan*, ch.31, pp.38-39. Cf. Abe Takeo, "Kōsen teikai no kenkyū," p.193; *CPYC*, v.11, Memorials of Shih Wen-ch'o, pp.60-61, Sept. 26, 1723; p.66, Feb. 16, 1724.

99. The outline of his points is based on *SYNK*, v.16, pp.13-15, Oct. 29, 1727; v.18, p.13, May 30, 1728; *CYPC*, v.13, Memorials of Kao Ch'eng-ling, pp. 79-80, July 27, 1724; *Man ming-ch'en chuan*, v.30, pp.61-62; Abe Takeo, "Kōsen teikai no kenkyū," p.195; Iwami Hiroshi, "Yōsei jidai no kohi ni kansuru ichi kosatsu" ('Public expenditure in the reign of Emperor Yung-cheng'), *Tōyōshi kenkyū* 15.4:87-92 (March 1957). For a general discussion, see Meng Sen, *Ch'ing-tai shih*, pp.196-206.

100. For example, the lieutenant governor of Shansi supported him. See *CPYC*, v.13, Memorials of Kao Ch'eng-ling, pp.79-80, July 27, 1724.

101. For points of these four groups, see *CSL*, YC, ch.22, pp.3-5, Aug. 24, 1724; Wang Yeh-chien, "Ch'ing Yung-cheng shih-ch'i (1723-1735) ti ts'ai-cheng kai-ke," pp.63-65. Cf. Abe Takeo, "Kōsen teikai no kenkyū," pp.236-46.

102. Abe Takeo, "Kōsen teikai no kenkyū," pp. 216-23; Iwami Hiroshi, "Yōrengin seido no sōsetsu ni tsuite" ('On the Yang-lien-yin system'), *Tōyōshi*

kenkyū 22.3:118-40 (December 1963).

103. Ch'ien Ch'en-ch'ün, *Hsiang-shu chai ch'üan-chi*, "Wen-chi," ch.4, p.16.

104. *CPYC*, v.16, Memorials of Ch'ang Te-shou, p.101, May 14, 1725; v.6, Pu-lan-t'ai, p.17, Dec. 15, 1726; *ibid.*, v.6, Memorials of Mao Wen-ch'üan, p.59, Dec. 23, 1725; v.17, Memorials of Chang Pao, p.10, Jan. 7, 1727.

105. *Ibid.*, v.19, Memorials of Wang Shih-chün, p.64, Jan. 3, 1732. For the beginning and distribution of the extra stipends, see Saeki Tomi, "Shindai Yōsei chō ni okeru yōrengin no kenkyū" 29.1:41-59 (June 1970).

106. Ch'ien Ch'en-ch'ün, *Hsiang-shu chai ch'üan-chi*, "Wen-chi," ch.4, p.15.

107. *SYNK*, v.22, pp.38-39, July 21, 1729; *Ho-nan t'ung-chih*, ch.41, p.1.

108. For the scale of extra stipends, see Saeki Tomi, "Shindai Yōsei chō ni okeru yōrengin no kenkyū," 30.4:63-66 (March 1972); *Ch'ing-ch'ao wen-hsien t'ung-k'ao*, I, 5245-47. Cf. Wang Shih, "Po-feng yü lou-kuei," p.60. For a list of extra stipends in Honan, Hunan, and Kweichow, see Wang Yeh-chien, "Ch'ing Yung-cheng shih-ch'i (1723-1735) ti ts'ai-cheng kai-ke," pp.66-67. According to a document dated 1729, the extra stipends for the governor-general of Fukien were only 7,000 taels. See *KCT*, Memorials of Shih I-chih, p.3, Sept. 24, 1729. For supplementary salary of magistrates, see Ch'ü, *Local Government in China*, p.23.

109. For instance, see *SYNK*, v.17, pp.27-28, Dec. 9, 1727; v.30, p.1, April 17, 1733.

110. For a detailed analysis of these private assistants, see Ch'ü, *Local Government in China*, chs. 3-6; Miyazaki Ichisada, "Shindai no shori to bakuyu, toku ni Yōsei chō o chūshin toshite" ('The clerk and private secretary in the Ch'ing dynasty'), *Tōyōshi kenkyū* 16.3:1-28 (November 1957). For discussion about their historical development, see Kenneth E. Folsom, *Friends, Guests, and Colleagues: The Mu-fu System in the Late Ch'ing Period* (Berkeley, 1968), ch.2.

111. For his prohibitions, see *CSL*, YC, ch.3, pp.5, 9, Feb. 5, 1723; ch.4, pp.19-20, March 22, 1723; *YHL*, p.128. For his permission to appoint the meritorious personal secretaries, see *YHL*, p.95.

112. For instance, see *CPYC*, v.17, Memorials of Chang Pao, p.10, Jan. 7, 1727; v.57, Memorials of Chao Hung-en, p.4.

113. *Ibid.*, v.32, Memorials of T'ien Wen-ching, pp.103-4, March 19, 1730.

114. *YHL*, p.231. The Manchu officials in the central government had already received sufficient rice from the national granaries.

115. For his decree, see *CSL*, YC, ch.82, pp.8-10, July 7, 1729; for the audit system, see *ibid.*, ch.157, pp.6-7, July 26, 1735.

116. *CPYC*, v.35, Memorials of Ch'iao Shin-ch'en, pp.3-4, Jan. 4, 1732; *SYNK*, v.16, p.15, Oct. 29, 1727.

117. *Su-chou fu-chih* (Gazetteer of Soochow), ed. by Feng Kuei-fen and Li Ming-huan (1883 ed.), ch.13, pp.25-26.

118. *CSL*, KH, ch.249, pp.14-16, April 4, 1712. For a recent interpretation of this decision, see T'ang Ti, "Lüeh-lun Ch'ing-tai ti ti-ting chih-tu" (A brief survey of the land-ting tax system of the Ch'ing), *Li-shih chiao-hsüeh* 1:32 (January 1955).

119. *Sung-chiang fu-chih* (Gazetteer of Sungkiang prefecture), ed. by Sun Hsing-yen and Sung Ju-lin (1819 ed.), ch.21, pp.26-27.

120. *CPYC*, v.9, Memorials of Huang Ping, pp.10-11, July 9, 1723; v.5, Memorials of Li Wei-chün, p.8, Aug. 12, 1723. But at first the emperor did not enthusiastically support Li's petition (*KCT*, Memorials of Li Wei-chün, p.3, Aug. 3, 1725). For a general discussion, see Meng Sen, *Ch'ing-tai shih*, pp.192-96.

121. Wang Ch'ing-yün, *Hsi-ch'ao chi-cheng*, ch.3, pp.24-28.

122. The reductions for Soochow and Sungkiang were 300,000 taels and 150,000 taels, respectively (see *CSL*, YC, ch.30, pp.29-30, May 1, 1725). By 1727 the emperor reduced ten percent from the quotas of the two places in Chekiang (*ibid.*, ch.62, pp.25-28, Dec. 9, 1727).

123. For corruption of the zone office, see Hsiao, *Rural China*, pp.104-5; *KCT*, Memorials of Chu Shih, pp.1-2 (undated). For abolition of the post for the clerk, see *Su-chou fu-chih*, ch.13, p.27. Due to the insufficiency of sources, it is not certain whether this abolition was nationwide or regional.

124. Wang Ch'ing-yün, *Hsi-ch'ao chi-cheng*, ch.3, p.19. This new zonal structure did not last long (*ibid.*).

125. Hsiao, *Rural China*, p.93.

126. *YHL*, pp.259 and 317; Lien-tching Lu, *Les greniers publics de prévoyance sous la dynastie de*

T'sing (Paris, 1932), pp.155-56, 161-65. Cf. Ch'ü, *Local Government of China*, p.159.

127. See n.107.

128. Shang Hung-k'uei, "Lüeh-lun Ch'ing-ch'u ching-chi hui-fu ho kung-ku ti ku-ch'eng chi ch'i ch'eng-chiu" ('Economic recovery and stabilization in the earlier Ch'ing period, 1681-1735'), *Pei-ching Ta-hsüeh Hsüeh-pao: Jen-wen k'o-hsüeh* (Journal of Peking University, Humanity science) 2:126 (May 1957). Cf. Mo Tung-yin, "Ti-ting ch'ien-liang k'ao" (A critical study of the land and labor-service tax of the Ch'ing), *Chung-ho yü-k'an* (Chung-ho Monthly) 4.1: 41-42 (January 1943).

129. Ts'ai Ch'eng, *Ch'ing-tai shih-lun*, ch.6, p.6.

130. Chuan Han-sheng and Wang Yeh-chien, "Ch'ing Yung-cheng nien-chien (1723-1735) ti mi-chia" ('The price of rice of China during the Yung-cheng period [1723-1735] of the Ch'ing dynasty'), *Bulletin of the Institute of History and Philology, Academia Sinica* 30, part 1:158-85 (October 1959).

131. *CPYC*, v.47, Memorials of Liu Yü-i, p.54, June 29, 1724; p.56, June 19, 1725. For the K'ang-hsi period, see Chu Shih, *Kao-an Chu Wen-tuan kung yao-ch'e lu kuang-hui p'ien* (A record to the memory of Chu Shih), (1782 ed.), part 1, pp.6, 24.

132. *CPYC*, v.57, Memorials of Chao Hung-en, p. 38, Aug. 11, 1733; p.83, Jan. 13, 1735. Cf. Saeki Tomi, *Shindai ensei no kenkyū* ('A study on the salt administration under the Ch'ing dynasty'), (Kyoto, 1956), p.272.

133. *CPYC*, v.51, Memorials of Chao Kuo-lin, p.2, April 25, 1731; v.47, Memorials of Sun Wen-ch'eng, p.100, Sept. 26, 1726. For raw silk prices in the period 1712-1726, see Spence, *Ts'ao Yin*, p.295.

134. Ch'ien Yung, *Li-yüan ts'ung-hua*, ch.1, p.30.

135. *CPYC*, v.44, Memorials of Chi Tseng-yün, pp. 66-67.

136. *SYNK*, v.30, pp.1-2, July 20, 1733; p.1, Sept. 13, 1733.

137. Ho, *Studies on the Population of China*, p. 214.

138. *Ibid.*, p.213.

139. Huang Ang, *Hsi-chin shih-hsiao lu* (Miscellaneous notes about Wu-hsi district), (1896 ed.), ch.1, pp.13-15, 18.

140. *Ibid.*, ch.4, p.11.

141. Shang Hung-k'uei, "Lüeh-lun Ch'ing-ch'u ching-chi," p.126.
142. *SYNK*, v.30, p.2, Nov. 2, 1733; v.31, p.3, July 26, 1734.
143. Saeki Tomi, "Shindai Yōsei chō ni okeru tsūka mondai" ('The currency problem in the Yung-cheng period'), *Tōyōshi kenkyū* 18.3:142-211 (December 1959).
144. *Chiang-nan t'ung-chih* (Gazetteer of Kiangnan), ed. by Huang Chih-sui and Yin Chi-shan (1735 ed.), ch.96, p.9; Huang Ang, *Hsi-chin shih-hsiao lu*, ch.1, pp.6-7. For discussion of commercialized farming, see Ho, *Studies on the Population of China*, pp.200, 202-4.
145. Ch'ien Yung, *Li-yüan ts'ung-hua*, ch.23, pp. 24-25; Huang Ang, *Hsi-chin shih-hsiao lu*, ch.1, pp. 6-7.
146. Li Tsung-fang, *Ch'ien-chi* (Records about Kweichow), (Ts'ung-shu chi-ch'eng ch'u-pien ed.), ch.2, p.7.
147. For the case of Kwangtung, see Li T'iao-yüan, *Nan-yüeh pi-chi* (Miscellaneous notes about Kwangtung), (Ts'ung-shu chi-ch'eng ch'u-pien ed.), ch.5, p.78-79; for cotton merchants in North China, see *SYPC*, v.6, p.27, Aug. 10, 1728; *KCT*, Memorials of Wang Shih-chün, p.3, Sept. 18, 1734.
148. *SYNK*, v.6, p.5, May 23, 1735. For a general discussion of the brewing trade in Manchuria, see Kawakubo Teirō, "Shindai Manshū ni okeru shōka no zokusei ni tsuite" ('On the prosperity of shao-kuo in Manchuria during the Ch'ing period'), in *Wada Hakushi koki kinen Tōyōshi ronsō* ('Oriental studies presented to Sei Kiyoshi Wada'), (Tokyo, 1960), pp.303-13.
149. Huang Ang, *Hsi-chin shih-hsiao lu*, ch.1, p.5.
150. Yen Chung-p'ing, *Ch'ing-tai Yun-nan t'ung-cheng k'ao* ('A study of the copper administration in Yunnan under the Ch'ing'), (Peking, 1957), pp.8-9. For discussion on various aspects of the Ch'ing miners, see E-tu Zen Sun, "Mining Labor in the Ch'ing Period," in Albert Feuerwerker *et al.*, ed., *Approaches to Modern Chinese History* (Berkeley, 1967), pp.45-67.
151. Huang Ang, *Hsi-chin shih-hsiao lu*, ch.1, p.6.
152. Shang Hung-k'uei, "Lüeh-lun Ch'ing-ch'u ching-chi," pp.123-24; *Man ming-ch'en chuan*, ch.32, p.17; *Nien Keng-yao tsou-che chuan-ch'i*, I, pp.29-31 (Nov. 28, 1724).

153. *Chang-ku ts'ung-pien*, v.4, "Memorials of O-er-t'ai," p.15.

X. *Non-Han Ethnic Minorities:*
The Miao, Yao, and Lolo Tribes

1. For instance, see the *Kuang-tung t'ung-chih* (Gazetteer of Kwangtung) ed. by Chiang Fan and Juan Yüan (1864 ed.), ch.330, p.1; *Feng-huang t'ing-chih* (Gazetteer of Feng-huang subprefecture), ed. by Sun Chün-ch'üan and Huang Ying-p'ei (1824 ed.), ch.11, pp.1-3; *Ch'ien-nan chih-fang chi-lüeh* (Gazetteer of southern Kweichow), ed. by Lo Jao-tien (1847 ed.), ch.9, pp.1-3; Liu Hsi-fan, *Ling-piao chi-man* (Records of the barbarian groups in Kwangtung and Kwangsi), (Shanghai, 1934), pp.1-10.
2. Of these wartime and postwar publications the most prominent are Lin Yao-hua, *Liang-shan i-chia* (The Lolo people of Mt. Liang), (Shanghai, 1947), also see its English version, *The Lolo of Liang Shan*, trans. by Ju-shu Pan and ed. by Wu-chi Liu (New Haven, Conn., Human Relations Area File, 1961); Ling Ch'un-sheng and Ruey Yih-fu, *Hsiang-hsi Miao-tsu t'iao-ch'a pao-kao* (Reports on the Miao people in western Hunan), (Shanghai, 1947); She I-tse, *Chung-kuo t'u-ssu chih-tu* (The tribal headman system of China), (Chungking, 1944); Wu Tse-lin and Ch'en Kuo-chün, *Kuei-chou miao-i she-hui yen-chiu* (A study of the Miao and Lolo peoples in Kweichow), (Kweiyang, 1942).
3. For examples, see Lin Yao-hua, *Liang-shan i-chia*, p.71; Ling Ch'un-sheng and Ruey Yih-fu, *Hsiang-hsi Miao-tsu*, pp.7-11.
4. Torii Ryūzō, *Miao-tsu t'iao-ch'a pao-kao* (Reports on the Miao people), trans. into Chinese by the Chinese National Institute of Compilation and Translation (Shanghai, 1936), pp.58, 62, 64, 348-49.
5. For comments on some of these publications, see *ibid.*, pp.8-15; Yang Ch'eng-chih, "Chung-kuo hsi-nan min-tsu chung-ti lo-lo tsu" (The Lolos among the ethnic groups in Southwest China), *Ti-hsüeh tsa-chih* (Journal of geography) 1:10-20 (1934).
6. Harold J. Wiens, *China's March toward the Tropics* (Hamden, Conn., 1954), pp.38, 40, 77.
7. Chang Ping-lin, *Chang-shih ts'ung-shu* (Collected works of Chang Ping-lin), (Shanghai, 1915), "Pieh-lu," part I, pp.13-20; Liu Hsi-fan, *Ling-piao*, pp.2, 4, 6.

8. Ling Ch'un-sheng and Ruey Yih-fu, *Hsiang-hsi Miao-tsu*, p.9; Ruey Yih-fu, "The Miao: Their Origin and Southward Migration" in International Association of Historians of Asia, Second Biennial Conference, Taipei, 1962, *Proceedings* (Taipei, 1963?), pp. 185-86; Chiang Ying-liang, *Hsi-nan pien-chiang min-tsu lun-ts'ung* (Collected papers on the minority groups in Southwest China), (Canton, 1948), pp.45-55; Wiens, *China's March*, p.36.

9. For instance, Liu Hsi-fan, *Ling-piao*, pp.4-6, 9; Wiens, *China's March*, p.36.

10. Chiang Ying-liang, *Hsi-nan pien-chiang*, pp. 74-77, 148-155.

11. For a critical discussion of these terms, see Ruey, "The Miao," pp.179-183; Ling Ch'un-sheng and Ruey Yih-fu, *Hsiang-hsi Miao-tsu*, pp.7-11; Torii Ryūzō, *Miao-tsu t'iao-ch'a pao-kao*, p.376; Wiens, *China's March*, pp.67-70. For cases of confusion, see *Ch'ien-nan chih-fang chi-lüeh*, ch.9, pp.1-2.

12. For list of names for the Miao and Lolo, see Ch'en Kuo-chün, "Kuei-chou miao-i she-hui kai-k'uang" (A general survey of the Miao and Lolo groups in Kweichow) in Wu Tse-lin and Ch'en Kuo-chün, *Kuei-chou Miao-i*, pp. 3-4; Yang Ch'eng-chih, "Chung-kuo hsi-nan," pp.4-5.

13. Ch'en Kuo-chün, "Kuei-chou," pp.3-4; Yang Ch'eng-chih, "Chung-kuo hsi-nan," pp.5-6.

14. For the five Miao names, see Ch'en Kuo-chün, "Kuei-chou," p.4; Torii Ryūzō, *Miao-tsu t'iao-ch'a pao-kao*, pp.45-47. For the two Yao divisions, see Li T'iao-yüan, *Nan-yüeh pi-chi*, p.101; etc. For the two general Lolo divisions, see Lin Yao-hua, *Liang-shan i-chia*, p.71; Tseng Chao-lun, *Ta-liang shan i-ch'ü k'ao-ch'a chi* (A field study of the Lolo tribes in Mt. Liang), (Kunming, 1945), p.95.

15. For these common traits, see *Kuei-chou t'ung-chih* (Gazetteer of Kweichow), ed. by Ching Tao-mu and O-er-t'ai (1741 ed.), ch.7, pp.14-16, 24; Ch'en Kuo-chün, "Kuei-chou," pp.12-13; *T'ien-hsi* (Gazetteer of Yunnan), by Shih Fan (1887 ed.), v.37, section 10, part 2, pp.4-7.

16. *Feng-huang t'ing-chih*, ch.11, p.59; Hsü I-t'ang, "Kuang-hsi hsiang-p'ing chien Yao-min chih chu-wu" ('The dwellings of the Yao tribes in Hsiang-ping, Kwangsi'), *Chin-ling hsüeh-pao* (Nanking journal) 10.1-2:25 (May-November 1940).

17. Wei-pang Chao, "A Lolo Legend Concerning the Origin of the Torch Festival," *Studia serica* 9, part 2:95-104 (1950).

18. Chiang Ying-liang, *Hsi-nan pien-chiang*, pp. 246, 250; *CPYC*, v.36, Memorials of Wang Jou, p.99.
19. K'o Hsiang-feng, "Lo-lo wen-tzu chih ch'u-pu yen-chiu" (A preliminary study of the written language of the Lolos), *Chin-ling hsüeh-pao* 8.1-2:23-38 (May-November 1938). Wen Yu, "Lo-lo i-yü k'ao" ('On Lolo i yü—Lolo-Chinese vocabularies'), *Studia serica* 1, part 1:77-97 (September 1940). Wen Yu, "Ch'uan-tien-ch'ien lo-wen chih pi-chiao" ('A comparison of three varieties of the Lolo characters in Szechwan, Yunnan, and Kweichow'), *Chung-kuo wen-hua yen-chiu hui-k'an* (Bulletin of Chinese studies) 7:245-49 (September 1947).
20. Lin Yao-hua, *Liang-shan i-chia* p.71; Hu Ch'ing-chün, "Chiai-fang ch'ien liang-shan i-tsu she-hui hsing-chih yen-chiu shu-p'ing" (A critical study of the nature of the Lolo society in Mt. Liang before 1949), *Lishi Yanjiu* (Li-shih yen-chiu) 2:135-52 (April 1963).
21. For these points, see Hsü I-t'ang, "Liang-shan lo-min chih lei cheng-chih ti tsu-chih" ('The government-like organization of the Lolo people at Liang-shan'), *Chung-kuo wen-hua yen-chiu hui-k'an* 3:368-80 (September 1943).
22. *Kuei-chou t'ung-chih*, ch.5, p.24.
23. For an elaborate study, see She I-tse, *Chung-kuo t'u-ssu*, pp.1-222, especially 18-43; Wiens, *China's March*, pp.214-32. For a general article on the system, see Hu Nai-an, "Ming-Ch'ing liang-tai t'u-ssu" (The tribal headman system of the Ming and Ch'ing dynasties), in Ta-lu tsa-chih pien-chi wei-yüan hui, ed., *Ch'ing-shih chi chin-tai shih yen-chiu lun-chi* (Collected papers on Ch'ing and modern Chinese history), (Taipei, 1960), pp.110-17. For the case of the Ming, see Huang Kai-hua, "Ming-tai t'u-ssu chih-tu she-shih yü hsi-nan k'ai-fa" ('The institution of tribal authorities and the development of Southwest China during the Ming dynasty'), *Hsin-ya hsüeh-pao* (New Asia journal) 6.1-2:285-365, 397-495 (February and August 1964).
24. Legge, *Chinese Classics*, III, part I, "Tribute of Yu," pp.142-50.
25. She I-tse, *Chung-kuo t'u-ssu*, pp.13-14.
26. For a detailed description of their titles and ranks, see *ibid*., pp.1, 21-22, 38-39; Cf. Wiens, *China's March*, p.214.
27. For exceptions, see She I-tse, *Chung-kuo t'u-ssu*, p.41.

28. *CSL*, KH, ch.41, pp.16-17, April 28, 1673; cf. She I-tse, *Chung-kuo t'u-ssu*, p.41. For prohibition from taking examination, see *CSL*, YC, ch.157, p.11, Aug. 4, 1735.

29. She I-tse, *Chung-kuo t'u-ssu*, pp.32, 78; *YHL*, p.136.

30. For example, see *CSL*, YC, ch.74, pp.14-15, Nov. 15, 1728.

31. For a detailed account of the revolt, see Li Hua-lung, *P'ing-po ch'üan-shu* (An account of the campaign in Po-chou), (Ts'ung-shu chi-ch'eng ch'u-pien ed.).

32. For these two campaigns, see *CSL*, KH, ch. 206, pp.24-25, Jan. 17, 1702; ch.213, p.12, Nov. 5, 1703.

33. Chiang Ying-liang, *Hsi-nan pien-chiang*, pp. 164-66.

34. *CSL*, KH, ch.124, pp.4-5, Feb. 11, 1686; *CPYC*, v.49, Memorials of Kuo Kung, p.50, April 27, 1728.

35. *Kuei-yang chih-li chou-chih* (Gazetteer of Kweiyang independent department), ed. by Wang K'ai-yün and Wang Hsiao-hao (1868 ed.), ch.23, pp.8-9.

36. Yang Ming-shih, *Yang-shih ch'üan-shu* (Complete works of Yang Ming-shih), (1909 ed.), "Wen-chi," part 2, ch.18, p.23.

37. For appointment of this commissioner, see *CSL*, KH, ch.108, p.11, April 12, 1683; for the joint request, see *ibid.*, ch.113, p.17, Jan. 27, 1684.

38. *Kuei-chou t'ung-chih*, ch.21, pp.12-27, especially 25-27.

39. *CSL*, KH, ch.124, pp.16-17, March 9, 1686.

40. Li Fu, *Mu-t'ang ch'u-kao*, ch.42, p.15.

41. For these tyrannical practices, see Lan Ting-yüan, *Lan Lu-chou ch'üan-chi* (Complete works of Lan Ting-yüan), (1880 ed.), "Lu-chou ch'u-chi," ch.1, p.25.

42. *CSL*, YC, ch.75, pp.24-26, Dec. 29, 1728.

43. *CPYC*, v.54, Memorials of Mai-chu, p.41, June 9, 1730.

44. *Ibid.*

45. *CSL*, YC, ch.159, pp.2-4, Sept. 18, 1735.

46. *Ch'ing-ch'ao wen-hsien t'ung-k'ao*, I, 4877.

47. *CPYC*, v.25, Memorials of O-er-t'ai, p.39, Dec. 8, 1726.

48. This point was kindly supplied by Professor Chaoying Fang of Columbia University.

49. Wang Ch'ing-yün, *Hsi-ch'ao chi-cheng*, ch.5, pp.16-17; Li Fu, *Mu-t'ang ch'u-kao*, ch.40, p.32;

SYNK, v.10, pp.1-2, Oct. 2, 1726; v.30, pp.1-2, Dec. 21, 1733; John Hall, "Notes on Early Ch'ing Copper Trade with Japan," *Harvard Journal of Asiatic Studies* 14:444-61 (1949); Saeki Tomi, "Shindai Yōsei chō ni okeru tsūka mondai," pp.142-211.

50. *CPYC*, v.26, Memorials of O-er-t'ai, p.9, Nov. 20, 1727.
51. *Ibid.*, v.25, pp.35-36, Oct. 14, 1726.
52. *Ibid.*, v.27, pp.95-96, Dec. 26, 1729.
53. *Ibid.*, v.25, p.55, Feb. 15, 1727.
54. For the annual production of copper, see *ibid.*, v.26, p.60, June 28, 1728; v.27, p.97, Dec. 26, 1729; for the annual yield of lead, see *ibid.*, pp.95-96, Dec. 26, 1729.
55. Saeki Tomi, "Shindai Yōsei chō ni okeru tsūka mondai," p.181.
56. *CPYC*, v.2, Memorials of Yang Tsung-jen, p.23, May 9, 1723.
57. *Ibid.*, v.25, Memorials of O-er-t'ai, p.10, March 27, 1726.
58. *Ibid.*, v.25, pp.33-34, Oct. 14, 1726.
59. *CSL*, ch.46, pp.20-21, Aug. 14, 1726; Yüan Mei, *Hsiao-ts'ang shan-fang wen-chi*, ch.3, p.6; Yang Ming-shih, *Yang-shih ch'üan-shu*, ch.18, p.25.
60. For the first case, see *CSL*, YC, ch.81, pp. 19-20, June 12, 1729; ch.143, pp.14-15, June 30, 1734; for the second case, see *ibid.*, ch.74, pp.14-15, Nov. 15, 1728; ch.144, pp.1-2, July 3, 1734.
61. For the first case, see *ibid.*, ch.115, p.6, Feb. 27, 1732; for the second case, see *Kuei-chou t'ung-chih*, ch.21, p.26.
62. Kano Naosada, "Chin chao myao no heitei o megutte" (On the suppression of Ch'ing-chia Miao), *Tōyōshi kenkyū* 18.3:85-98 (December 1959).
63. *CPYC*, v.26, Memorials of O-er-t'ai, pp.20-22, Jan. 23, 1728; v.48, Memorials of Chang Kuang-ssu, p.1, Nov. 23, 1728; pp.8-10, Jan. 24, 1729; for a special book, see Fang Hsien, *P'ing-Miao chi-lüeh* (A brief account of the pacification of the Miao people), (1873 ed.), pp.4-15.
64. A discussion of this will be given below.
65. *CPYC*, v.28, Memorials of O-er-t'ai, pp.44-45, Oct. 25, 1730; *CSL*, YC, ch.99, pp.12-13, Nov. 23, 1730.
66. *CSL*, YC, ch.99, pp.17-18, Nov. 26, 1730; *CPYC*, v.28, Memorials of O-er-t'ai, pp.45-48, Nov. 26, 1730.
67. Fang Hsien, *P'ing-Miao chi-lüeh*, pp.2-5.

68. For openings of watercourses, see *CPYC*, v. 27, Memorials of O-er-t'ai, pp.40-41, 59-60, March 23 and July 13, 1729; v.28, pp.7 and 23, March 1 and May 12, 1730; *Ch'ien-nan shih-lüeh* (A brief gazetteer of South Kweichow), comp. by Ai-pi-ta (1847 ed.), ch.8, pp.1-2.

69. *CSL*, YC, ch.55, pp.15-16, May 7, 1727.

70. *CPYC*, v.53, Memorials of Mai-chu, pp.84-85, 87-88, April 27 and May 28, 1728; v.54, pp.6 and 25, Jan. 1 and Aug. 21, 1729.

71. For example, see *CSL*, YC, ch.106, pp.21-22, June 30, 1731.

72. *Ibid.*, ch.81, pp.18-20, June 12, 1729; ch. 150, p.15, Jan. 14, 1735.

73. For imperial ordinance about headmen's families, see *ibid.*, ch.62, p.2, Nov. 14, 1727; for T'ien's family, see *ibid.*, ch.150, p.15, Jan. 14, 1735.

74. For a few exceptions to his, see *ibid.*, ch. 60, pp.3 and 20, Sept. 15 and Oct. 4, 1727. For their removal and subjection to strict watch of local officials, see *ibid.*, ch.62, p.2, Nov. 14, 1727; and *SYNK*, v.16, p.13, Oct. 8, 1727; *KCT*, Memorials of Yin Chi-shan, pp.1-3, May 8, 1735.

75. *CPYC*, v.37, Memorials of Hsü Pen, p.18.

76. *CSL*, YC, ch.144, pp.1-2, July 3, 1734; ch. 150, p.15, Jan. 14, 1735; ch.158, p.23, Sept. 9, 1735.

77. *Ibid.*, ch.64, pp.21-22, Jan. 28, 1728.

78. *Ibid.*, ch.83, p.31, Aug. 18, 1729; *CPYC*, v. 56, Memorials of Omida, pp.14-15, Oct. 6, 1731.

79. *CSL*, YC, ch.66, p.3, March 11, 1728; ch.83, p.31, Aug. 18, 1729.

80. *KCT*, "Wang ta-jen mi-i tsou-p'ien," (under O-er-t'ai), No.19879, p.3, Aug. 24, 1729; *CPYC*, v.25, Memorials of O-er-t'ai, pp.33-34, Oct. 14, 1726; v.25, p.65, April 3, 1727; *CSL*, YC, ch.60, p.11, Sept. 26, 1727; for change in their names, see *ibid.*, ch.54, p.31, April 18, 1727; ch.63, p.18, Dec. 28, 1727.

81. *CSL*, YC, ch.123, p.14, Oct. 30, 1732; *CPYC*, v.36, Memorials of Wang Jou, p.99; v.54, Memorials of Mai-chu, pp.47-48, April 27, 1731.

82. *CSL*, KH, ch.20, pp.6-7, Nov. 5, 1666; ch. 113, pp.4-5, Dec. 23, 1683. There were some schools opened for the tribal boys in Hunan by 1714. For example, see *ibid.*, ch.218, p.17, Jan. 15, 1705; ch. 258, p.22, June 10, 1714.

83. *Ibid.*, YC, ch.60, p.11, Sept. 26, 1727; ch.

96, p.21, Aug. 31, 1730; ch.123, p.14, Oct. 30, 1732.
 84. For a general discussion, see Hsiao, *Rural China*, pp.240-41; for a special reference, see *CPYC*, v.56, Memorials of Omida, p.15, Oct. 6, 1731
 85. *CSL*, YC, ch.124, p.3, Nov. 21, 1732; ch.141, p.10, April 23, 1734.
 86. *Ibid.*, ch.120, p.1, July 22, 1732; ch.154, p.5, April 27, 1735.
 87. *Ibid.*, ch.156, pp.9-10, 13, July 8 and 11, 1735; ch.157, pp.22-24, Aug. 16, 1735; *ECCP*, I, 272.
 88. *CSL*, YC, ch.156, p.15, July 15, 1735; *ibid.*, CL, ch.2, p.27, Oct. 24, 1735.
 89. For the situation of copper purchase, see Li Fu, *Mu-t'ang ch'u-kao*, ch.40, pp.32-33; for discussion of the Chinese copper merchants, see Fu I-ling, *Ming-ch'ing shih-tai shang-jen chi shang-yeh tzu-pen* (The Ming and Ch'ing merchants and their capitals), (Peking, 1956), pp.176-97; for the change in the customs administration, see Li Fu, *Mu-t'ang ch'u-kao*, ch.28, p.19.
 90. She I-tse, *Chung-kuo t'u-ssu*, p.165.
 91. *CSL*, YC, ch.96, p.21, Aug. 31, 1730.
 92. *Ibid.*, ch.120, p.17, Aug. 19, 1732.
 93. Meng Sen, *Ch'ing-tai shih*, pp.295-299.
 94. These figures are based on *CSL*, YC, chs.54-158.
 95. For discussion concerning the use of new crops and the development of Szechwan and the Yangtze highlands, see Ho, *Studies on the Population of China*, pp.139-48, 169-95.
 96. Ho, "The Significance of the Ch'ing Period in Chinese History," p.191.

CONCLUSION

 1. Two works, each of which deals with a European country, have sharpened my perception of the problems of aristocracy and bureaucracy in China. They are Hans Rosenberg, *Bureaucracy, Aristocracy, and Autocracy: The Prussian Experience, 1660-1815* (Boston, Beacon Press, 1966, paperback); and Charles Harold Williams, *The Making of the Tudor Despotism* (London: Thomas Nelson, 1935).
 2. See Ch.4.
 3. See Ch.7.
 4. For details, see Chs.5-6 and 8 and the last part of section 1, Ch.9.
 5. For details, consult Chs.5-6.

6. See Ch.8 and the last part of section 1, Ch. 9. Here the term "elite" is used to suggest without value judgment the persons who exercised the major influence in society.

7. See Ch.9.

8. See Ch.10.

9. Although in his lifetime he did not thoroughly carry out his projects to change the non-Han ethnic minority groups in southern China, he laid a sound foundation for his successors to follow.

List of Chinese Characters

This list includes the names and terms which appear in transliteration in the text and the footnotes. They are in alphabetical order of first syllables, without consideration of aspirate marks and umlauts. Names of individual provinces are excluded. The Chinese characters for authors, titles, and publishers of works can be found in the bibliography.

The page numbers indicate the first appearance of the item. Frequently appearing items are included in the index also.

A-k'e-tun 阿克敦
   314n.29
Abahai (Hong-taiji; Emperor T'ai-tsung) 皇太極(太宗)
   60
Ablan 阿布蘭
   109
acina 阿其那
   98
Alingga 阿靈阿
   68
Amin 阿敏
   84
an-ch'a shih 按察使
   126
Arsungga 阿爾松阿
   330n.39
Bandi 班第
   348n.42
boo-i (pao-i) 包衣
   163
Cha Ssu-t'ing 查嗣庭
   107
Ch'an 禪
   33
Chan-shih fu 詹事府
   140
Chang Chao 張照
   45
Chang Cho (Chang Hsi) 張倬(張熙)
   218
Ch'ang-ch'un Yüan 暢春園
   69
Chang Hsi (Chang Cho) 張熙(張倬)
   218

Chang Hsien-chung 忠瀅泗倉行誠有麟壽玉祖懷奎恩肯麟瑛棟喬雷
244
Ch'ang-jün ch'ü
238
Chang Kuang-ssu
292
Ch'ang-lai
341n.70
Chang Pao
371n.104
Ch'ang-p'ing ts'ang
267
Chang Po-hsing
188
Chang Shih-ch'eng
265
ch'ang-sui
259
Chang Ta-yu
340n.56
Chang T'an-lin
340n.56
Ch'ang Te-shou
371n.104
Chang T'ing-yü
28
Chang Yao-tsu
341n.69
Chang Ying
60
Chang Yüan-huai
341n.72
Chang Yung
164
Chao Ch'eng
339n.55
Chao Hsiang-k'uei
341n.68
Chao Hung-en
321n.110
Chao K'uang-yin
9
Chao Kuo-lin
340n.62
Chao Kuo-ying
369n.86
Chao Liang-tung
164
Chao Shen-ch'iao
70
chen
276
Chen-hsiung
290
Ch'en Meng-lei
74

List of Chinese Characters

Ch'en Shih-hsia 陳時夏
 347n.33
cheng 正
 209
ch'eng 誠
 39
Cheng Ch'eng kung 鄭成功
 11
Ch'eng-Chu li-hsüeh 程朱理學
 5
Ch'eng Hao 程顥
 188
Ch'eng I 程頤
 188
cheng-ta erh t'ien-ti chih ch'ing k'o chien i
 正大而天地之情可見矣
 360n.79
Ch'eng Yüan-chang 程元章
 340n.55
Chengtu 成都
 238
Chi Ch'eng-pin 紀成斌
 340n.62
Ch'i-chü-chu kuan 起居注官
 123
ch'i-fen 旗分
 163
chi-kuei 季規
 249
ch'i-nu 旗奴
 226
Ch'i-shih 七十
 98
chi-shih chung 給事中
 6
Ch'i-su-le 齊蘇勒
 334n.109
Chi Tseng-yün 嵇曾筠
 237
chia 甲；假
 265,276
chia-chang 甲長
 265
Chia-ch'ing (Emperor Jen-tsung) 嘉慶 (仁宗)
 155
chia-hao yin 加耗銀
 248
Chia-hsing 嘉興
 265
chia-shou 甲首
 265
Chiang Liang-chi 蔣良騏
 57
Chiang T'ing-hsi 蔣廷錫
 145

Chiao Ch'i-nien 焦祈年
　358n.29
Chiao Kuang-tsuan 焦光瓚
　227
Ch'iao Shih-ch'en 喬世臣
　369n.88
chieh-li 節禮
　249
Ch'ien Ch'en-ch'ün 錢陳群
　257
Ch'ien-ch'ing 乾清
　142
Ch'ien-lung (Emperor Kao-tsung) 乾隆（高宗）
　12
chien-min 賤民
　226
Ch'ien Ming-shih 錢名世
　210
Chien-mu pien-i lu 揀魔辨異錄
　33
chih 止
　212
Chih-chi lu 知幾錄
　217
Chih-hsin lu 知新錄
　217
chih-kuo p'ing t'ien-hsia 治國平天下
　8
Chih-kuan chih 職官志
　351n.78
Chih-shui shu-yao 治水述要
　365n.39
chih-tao liao 知道了
　129
chih-tsao 織造
　122
Chihli 直隸
　31
Chin 金
　227
ch'in 秦
　8
Chin Kung (Kuo Kung) 金鉷（郭鉷）
　292
Ch'in-pan chou-hsien shih-i 欽頒州縣事宜
　236
chin-shih 進士
　102
Chin Shih-chien 金世鑑
　369n.92
Ch'in Tao-jan 秦道然
　67
Ch'in-t'ien chien cheng 欽天監正
　139

List of Chinese Characters

Ch'in-ting chih-chung ch'eng-hsien
    41   欽定執中成憲
ch'ing
    179   頃
Ch'ing (dynasty)
    4   清（朝）
ch'ing-an che
    123   請安摺
Ching-hsi chü
    239   京西局
Ching-nan chü
    239   京南局
Ching-shan kuan-hsüeh
    174   景山官學
Ch'ing-shih
    148   清史
ching-t'ien
    18   井田
Ching-tung chü
    239   京東局
Chinkiang
    272   鎮江
chiu-ch'ing
    6   九卿
Chou
    178   周
Chu Hsi
    188   朱熹
Chu-hung
    43   袾宏
Chu Hung-hsü
    317n.72   朱鴻緒
chü-jen
    140   舉人
Chu Kang
    347n.37   朱綱
Chu-p'i yü-chih
    236   硃批諭旨
Chu Shih
    145   朱軾
Chu T'ien-pao
    65   朱天保
Chu Yüan-chang (Emperor T'ai-tsu, Ming)
    5   朱元璋（明太祖）
chüan
    58   卷
Chuang Hsien-tsu
    336n.12   莊憲祖
Ch'üeh-li
    36   闕里
Chüeh-lo (gioro)
    174   覺羅

chün 君
  6, 196
chün-chi 軍機
  147
Chün-chi chang-ching 軍機章京
  142
Chün-chi ch'u 軍機處
  14
Chün-chi fang 軍機房
  147
Chün-chi ta-ch'en 軍機大臣
  15
Chün-chi ta-ch'en nien-piao 軍機大臣年表
  348n.46
chün-hsü 軍需
  147
chün-hsü fang 軍需房
  147
chün-shou 郡守
  6
chung 中
  40
chung-shu 中書
  137
Cuyen 褚英; 褚燕
  98
Dahai 達海
  138
Daisan 代善
  84
Dorgon 多爾袞
  11
Dzungar 準噶爾
  12
Eleuth 厄魯特
  31
Fa-tsang 法藏
  44
Fahai 法海
  78
Fan Shih-i 范時繹
  257n
fan-shih yin 飯食銀
  249
Fan Wen-ch'eng 范文程
  138
Fang Hsien 方顯
  294
Fang-lüeh kuan 方略館
  150
Fang, Maurus (Hao Fang) 方豪
  49
Fei Chin-wu 費金吾
  321n.111

List of Chinese Characters

feng-chang 封章
120
feng-po 封駁
117
Feng-sheng-e 豐盛額
347n.36
feng-shih 封事
120
Feng-t'ien 奉天
245
feng-tsou 封奏
120
Fiyanggu 費揚古
321n.9
fu 父
196
fu-chiang 副將
126
Fu-ch'üan 福全
61
Fu-min 福敏
333n.87
Fu-p'eng (Prince P'ing) 福彭（平郡王）
45
fu-pin 府兵
214
Fu-t'ai 傅泰
346n.33
fu tu-t'ung 副都統
123
Fu-yüan ta chiang-chün 撫遠大將軍
52
Funinggan 富寧安
145
Furdan 傅爾丹
352n.8
gioro 覺羅
174
Gubadai 顧八代
28
Ha Yüan-sheng 哈元生
292
Han 漢
4
Han Fei 韓非
41
Hangchow 杭州
126
Hankow 漢口
272
Hao Fang (Fang, Maurus) 方豪
49
hao-hsien 耗羨
248
hao-mi 耗米
248

He-i 黑夷
  277
Hife 希福
  138
Ho Ch'o 何焯
  67
Ho-feng 鶴峯
  288
Ho Kuo-tsung 何國宗
  237
ho-piao 河標
  237
Ho-shen 和珅
  156
Ho Shih-chi 何世璂
  132
Ho-tao tsung-tu 河道總督
  126
Ho T'ien-p'ei 何天培
  314n.28
Ho Yü-lin 郝玉麟
  365n.34
Hong-taiji (Abahai; Emperor Tai-tsung) 皇太極 (太宗)
  60
Hou-chin 後金
  163
Hsia wu-ch'i 下五旗
  62
Hsiang-yin 湘陰
  238
Hsiao-ch'eng, Empress 孝誠 (仁) 皇后
  60
hsiao chiang-nan 小江南
  240
Hsiao-ching 孝經
  36
Hsiao chün-chi 小軍機
  148
Hsiao-kung, Empress 孝恭 (仁) 皇后
  75
Hsiao Yung-tsao 蕭永藻
  78
Hsieh Chi-shih 謝濟世
  130
Hsien-an kung kuan-hsüeh 咸安宮官學
  175
hsien-mi 羨米
  248
Hsien-te 憲德
  342n.76
Hsin-hsüeh 心學
  5

List of Chinese Characters

Hsing-kuei
    339n.52
Hsing-sen
    139
Hsing-ts'ung
    139
Hsiung Tz'u-li
    60
Hsü Ch'ien-hsüeh
    85
Hsü Jung
    226
Hsü Pen
    380n.75
Hsü Ting
    369n.87
Hsü Yüan-meng
    28
Hsüan, Emperor
    120
Hsüeh-cheng
    201
Hsüeh-tao
    200
Hsüeh-yüan
    200
hu
    261
Huchow
    265
Hu-pu
    146
Huang-ching
    45
Huang Kuo-ts'ai
    315n.35
Huang Ping
    264
Huang Tsung-hsi
    213
Hui, Emperor
    227
Hui-k'ao fu
    252
Hui-nung ch'ü
    238
Hung-chou
    45
Hung-jen
    44
Hung-li
    45
Hung-shui Ho
    300
huo-hao
    248

huo-hao yin 火耗銀
    248
i 義
    40
I Chao-hsiung 宜兆熊
    340n.59
I-cheng ch'u 議政處
    16
I-hsin 奕訢
    349n.58
i-hsüeh 義學
    298
I-k'uang 奕劻
    349n.58
i-ts'ang 義倉
    267
Jabina 查郎納
    145
jen 仁
    38
Jen Kuo-jung 任國榮
    155
Jen-tsung, Emperor (Chia-ch'ing) 仁宗（嘉慶）
    155
Jirgalang 濟爾哈朗
    84
Jung-mei 容美
    288
kai-hu 開戶
    226
Kan Kuo-k'uei 甘國奎
    257n
K'ang-hsi (Emperor Sheng-tsu) 康熙（聖祖）
    11
K'ang-hsi chien-ch'u an 康熙建儲案
    325n.70
Kao Ch'eng-ling 高成齡
    254
Kao Ch'i-cho 高其倬
    346n.31
Kao Pin 高斌
    318n.72
Kao Shih-ch'i 高士奇
    141
Kao Shih-chün 高士俊
    344n.9
Kao-tsung, Emperor (Ch'ien-lung) 高宗（乾隆）
    12
Ko-er-t'ai 鄂爾泰
    230

List of Chinese Characters

Ko-shen
    353n.15
k'o-ch'ang an
    233
k'o-tao
    117
Khoshote
    103
Ku-chin t'u-shu chi-ch'eng
    28
k'u-p'ing yin
    249
Ku Yen-wu
    213
Kuan-feng cheng-su shih
    197
Kuang-hsü
    315n.33
Kuang-shun
    293
kuei-fei
    248
K'uei-hsü
    68
Kuei-jen shuo
    220
kuei-li
    249
kung
    40
kung-chung tso-ling
    169
kung-sheng
    202
K'ung Yü-hsün
    317n.59
K'ung Yü-p'o
    340n.58
Kunming
    238
Kuo Kung (Chin Kung)
    292
Kweiyang
    293
lan
    129
Lang-chung
    125
li
    237
li-chang
    265
li-cheng t'ing-sung wu ta-ch'en
    138

葛森
科場案
科道
和碩特
古今圖書集成
庫平銀
顧炎武
觀風整俗使
光緒
廣順
規費
揆敘
歸仁說
規禮
公
公中佐領
貢生
孔毓珣
孔毓璞
昆明
郭鉷（金共鉷）
貴陽
覽
郎中
里
里長
理政聽訟五大臣

Li Fu (1675-1750) 31	李紱
Li Fu 314n.24	李馥
Li Hsü 122	李煦
Li Hui 198	李徽
Li Kuang-ti 188	李光地
Li Kung 78	李塨
li-mu 282	吏目
Li Ping-chung 340n.56	李秉中
Li Shen-hsien 336n.12	李森先
li-shu 265	里書
Li-tai chih-kuan piao 123	歷代職官表
Li Tsung-t'ung 144	李宗侗
Li Wei 106	李衛
Li Wei-chün 264	李維鈞
Liang Chang-chü 149	梁章鉅
Liang-huai 126	兩淮
Liang-huai yen-yün shih 126	兩淮鹽運使
Liang-shan 279	梁山
Liao K'un 340n.55	廖坤
lieh-shen 231	劣紳
Lin-chi 45	臨濟
Ling shih-wei nei ta-ch'en 123	領侍衛內大臣
Liu-k'o chi-shih chung 15	六科給事中
Liu Nan 364n.14	劉枏
Liu-pu 28	六部
Liu Shih-ming 350n.59	劉世明
Liu Shih-shu 358n.29	劉師恕

List of Chinese Characters

Liu T'ing-ch'en
  342n.84
Liu Yü-i
  373n.131
Lobdzan Dandzin
  103
Lolo
  20
lou-kuei
  249
Lu-chou ch'u-chi
  378n.41
Lü-li yüan-yüan
  28
Lü Liu-liang
  216
Lu Lung-ch'i
  252
Lu-nan
  290
Lu Sheng-nan
  213
Luan-i shih
  146
Luan-i wei
  108
Lungkodo
  32
Ma Hui-po
  292
Ma Kuo-chu
  344n.9
Maci
  62
Mai-chu
  291
man
  275
man-i
  275
Manbao
  108
Manggultai
  84
Mao Wen-ch'üan
  371n.104
Marantai
  348n.42
Marsai
  145
Mawu
  68
Meng Sen
  52
mi
  125

Miao 苗
    20
Miao-chiang 苗疆
    278
Miao-chiang ch'üeh 苗疆缺
    296
Ming 明
    5
Ming-chiao tsui-jen 名教罪人
    211
mou 畝
    242
mu-k'e 幕客
    259
mu-pin 幕賓
    259
nan-man 南蠻
    275
Nan Shu-fang 南書房
    38
Nei chung-t'ang 內中堂
    148
Nei fan-shu fang 內繙書房
    150
Nei-ko 內閣
    16
Nei san-yüan 內三院
    121
Nei tsou-shih ch'u 內奏事處
    127
Nei-wu fu 內務府
    62
Nien Hsi 年熙
    230
Nien Keng-yao 年羹堯
    32
Nien Keng-yao tsou-che 年羹堯奏摺
    332n.76
Ning Wan-wo 寧完我
    138
Ningpo 寧波
    227
niru 牛彔
    163
No-ch'in 訥親
    348n.42
No-min 諾敏
    108
Nurhaci (T'ai-tsu) 努爾哈赤（太祖）
    59
O-ch'ang 鄂昌
    339n.52
O-er-t'ai 鄂爾泰
    38
Oboi 鰲拜
    11

List of Chinese Characters

Olondai 62 鄂倫岱

Omida 368n.70 鄂彌達

Ou-yang Hsiu 92 歐陽修

pa-tsung 260 把總

Pai Huang 230 白潢

pao-chia 291 保甲

pao-i (boo-i) 163 包衣

Paoting 100 保定

P'ei Shih-tu 221 裴律度

P'eng-min 226 棚民

P'eng-tang lun 90 朋黨論

Pieh-lu 375n.7 別錄

Pien Shih-wei 369n.88 邊士偉

p'ing 40 平

P'ing, Prince (Fu-p'eng) 45 平郡王 (福彭)

p'ing-kuei 249 平規

ping-pu 149 兵部

Po Chih-fan 354n.44 柏之蕃

Po-chou 283 播州

Po-hsüeh hung-ju 188 博學鴻儒

Po-i 277 白夷

Po Lü Liu-liang ssu-shu chiang-i 197 駁呂留良四書講義

Po-man 277 白蠻

Po-shih ying-chih, fu-tzu ning-chih 361n.79 百室盈止, 婦子寧止

pu-cheng shih 126 布政使

pu-chün t'ung-ling 51 步軍統領

pu-fei 部費
249
Pu-lan-t'ai 布蘭泰
226
Pu-pien 楷編
367n.48
Ruey Yih-fu 芮逸夫
274
San-fan 三藩
11
Se-er-t'u 塞爾圖
342n.74
seshe 塞思黑
100
Shang san-ch'i 上三旗
61
Shang-shu 尚書
137
Shang shu-fang 上書房
28
Shang-yü ch'i-wu i-fu 上諭旗務議覆
171
Shang-yü nei-ko 上諭內閣
52
Shang-yü pa-ch'i 上諭八旗
52
Shao-hsing 紹興
227
she-ts'ang 社倉
267
Shen Chin-ssu 沈近思
252
Shen T'ing-cheng 沈廷正
347n.33
sheng 生
276
Sheng-tsu, Emperor (K'ang-hsi) 聖祖（康熙）
11
Sheng-tsu ch'in-cheng shuo-mo jih-lu 聖祖親征朔漠日錄
349n.56
Sheng-yü 聖諭
36
Sheng-yü kuang-hsün 聖諭廣訓
176
Shih Ch'eng-o 石成峨
257n
Shih-chung 侍中
137
Shih I-chih 史貽直
147

List of Chinese Characters

Shih Jarguchi 十札爾固齊
  138
Shih Li-ha 石禮哈
  292
Shih-lin 石麟
  347n.34
Shih-lu 實錄
  28
shih-p'u 世僕
  226
shih-san ya-men 十三衙門
  140
Shih-t'o 世鐸
  349n.58
Shih-tsu, Emperor (Shun-chih) 世祖(順治)
  11
Shih-tsung, Emperor (Yin-chen; Yung-cheng) 世宗(胤禛;雍正)
  11
Shih Wen-ch'o 石文焯
  253
shou-li 壽禮
  249
shou-pei 守備
  260
shu 熟;疏
  123,276
shu-li 書吏
  259
shu-yüan 書院
  203
shui-kuei 稅規
  249
Shui-li ying-t'ien fu 水利營田府
  239
Shun 舜
  41
Shun-chih (Emperor Shih-tsu) 順治(世祖)
  11
so 所
  272
Songgotu 索額圖
  60
Soochow 蘇州
  126
Sose 碩色
  255n
ssu-kuan 司官
  125
sui 歲
  179
Sui (dynasty) 隋(朝)
  9

List of Chinese Characters

Sun Chi-tsung 340n.66 孫繼宗
Sun Kuo-hsi 341n.71 孫國璽
Sun Wen-ch'eng 317n.60 孫文成
Sung 4 宋
Sung K'o-chin 346n.33 宋可進
Sung Yün 369n.86 宋筠
Sunggayan 62 舜安顏；順安顏
Sungkiang 265 松江
Sunju 145 孫柱 (遜柱)
Sunu 48 蘇努
Ta-Ch'ing li-ch'ao shih-lu 52 大清歷朝實錄
Ta-i chüeh-mi lu 52 大義覺迷錄
t'ai-chien 117 台諫
T'ai-shou 6 太守
T'ai-tsu, Emperor (Ming) (Chu Yüan-chang) 5 (明) 太祖 (朱元章)
T'ai-tsu (Nurhaci) 322n.26 太祖 (努爾哈赤)
T'ai-tsung, Emperor (Hong-taiji; Abahai) 344n.6 太宗 (皇太極)
tan-min 226 蛋民
T'ang 8 唐
t'ang-kuan 125 堂官
T'ang Pin 60 湯斌
Tao-kuang 156 道光
Tao-min 140 道民
Te-pin 312n.1 德嬪

List of Chinese Characters

t'i-pen
  123
t'i-tu
  122
T'ien Min-ju
  288
T'ien-tsin chü
  239
T'ien Ts'ung-tien
  369n.91
T'ien Wen-ching
  106
ting
  245
t'ing-chi
  15
to-min
  226
Tsai-feng
  349n.58
tsai-hsiang chih-tu
  5
Tsai-i
  349n.58
Ts'ai Shih-shan
  342n.86
Ts'ai T'ing
  76
ts'ao-kuei
  249
Ts'ao-tung
  45
Ts'ao Yin
  122
Ts'ao-yün tsung-tu
  126
Tseng Ching
  52
Tseng Ts'an
  36
Tsereng
  164
Tsewang Araptan
  102
Tso fu-tu-yü shih
  114
Tso-ling
  163
Tso tu-yü shih
  114
tsou-che
  119

tsou-che chih-tu 14	奏摺制度
Tsou-hsiao an 233	奏銷案
tsou-pen 125	奏本
tsou-shih ch'u 123	奏事處
tsou-shu 336n.15	奏疏
Tsu Ping-heng 369n.86	祖秉衡
Tsung-ching lu 44	宗鏡錄
Tsung-ching lu ta-kang 44	宗鏡錄大綱
Tsung-li shih-wu wang ta-ch'en 95	總理事務王大臣
Tsung-ping 122	總兵
tsung-shih 174	宗室
Tsunyi 300	遵義
t'u 265	圖
Tu-ch'a yüan 15	都察院
Tu Li-te 336n.12	杜立德
t'u-shu 265	圖書
Tu-shu t'ang hsi-cheng sui-pi 209	讀書堂西征隨筆
tu-ssu 260	都司
t'u-ssu 20	土司
Tu-su t'ang wen-chi 314n.19	篤素堂文集
t'u-t'ien chih 355n.62	土田志
tu-t'ung 122	都統
Tulisen 106	圖理琛
t'un-chuang 179	屯莊
t'ung-cheng ssu 121	通政司
T'ung Chi-t'u 333n.88	佟吉圖

List of Chinese Characters

T'ung-chih 22 同
Tung-ch'uan 290 東
T'ung-hsiu 139 通
Tung-hua lu 52 東華錄
T'ung Kuo-kang 78 佟國綱
T'ung Kuo-wei 62 佟國維
Tung-lin 37 東林
t'ung-nien 205 同年
t'ung-p'an 282 通判
Tung Yung-wen 317n.64 董永治
Tzu-chih t'ung-chien 213 資治通鑑
Tz'u-shih 6 刺史
Uliasutai 213 烏里雅蘇台
Wai tsou-shih ch'u 127 外奏事處
Wan-li 243 萬曆
Wang Ching-ch'i 208 汪景祺
Wang Ching-hao 333n.88 王景瀬
Wang Chung-han 52 王鍾翰
Wang Hsi 122 王熙
Wang Hsien-ch'ien 57 王先謙
Wang Hung-hsü 122 王鴻緒
Wang Hung-hsü mi-shan hsiao-che 345n.23 王鴻緒密繕小摺
Wang Jou 342n.89 王柔
Wang Kuo-tung 198 王國棟
Wang Mou-hung 74 王懋竑
Wang Shan 65 王掞
Wang Shao-hsü 314n.15 王紹緒

Wang Shih-chün 王士俊
  311n.27
Wang Shou-jen (Wang Yang-
  ming) 王守仁（王陽明）
  37
Wang Wen-k'uei 王文奎
  344n.9
Wang Yang-ming (Wang Shou-
  jen) 王陽明（王守仁）
  37
wei 衛
  272
Wei Ching-kuo 魏經國
  339n.50
Wei Hsiang-shu 魏象樞
  338n.34
wei-min so-chih 維民所止
  212
Wei-ning 威寧
  290
Wei-wu 衛武（威武）
  312n.1
Wen, King 文王
  219
Wen-chi 文集
  327n.98
Wen-chüeh 文覺
  45
Wen-kuan 文館
  121
Wu, Emperor 武帝
  4
wu-ching po-shih 五經博士
  188
wu-fu 五服
  280
Wu Hsiang 吳襄
  219
Wu Kuan-chieh 吳闗杰、輔
  339n.55
Wu Liang-fu 吳良
  140
Wu-man 烏蠻
  277
Wu-meng 烏蒙
  293
Wu San-kuei 吳三桂
  27
Wu-hsi 無錫
  271
Wu Ta 吳達
  336n.12
ya-i 衙役
  259

List of Chinese Characters

Yang Ch'ang-ch'un 楊長春
340n.64
yang-lien 養廉
18
yang-lien yin 養廉銀
258
Yang Ming-shih 楊名時
38
Yang P'eng 楊鵬
340n.56
Yang T'ien-tsung 楊天縱
340n.63
Yang Tsung-jen 楊宗仁
252
Yang Ying-lung 楊應龍
283
Yang Yung-pin 楊永斌
342n.75
Yao 傜猺
20
Yao 堯
41
Yen-hsin 延信
76
Yen Hui 顏回
36
Yen Jo-chü 閻若璩
76
Yen Kuang-wu 顏光昨
340n.66
yen-kuei 鹽規
249
Yen-shou 延壽
43
Yin-chen (Emperor Shih-
  tsung; Yung-cheng) 胤禛（世宗；雍正）
  27
Yin-ch'i 胤（允）祺
72
Yin Chi-shan 尹繼善
366n.46
Yin-chiai 胤（允）衸
63
Yin-chih 胤（允）祉
28
Yin-e 胤（允）䄉
67
Yin-hsi 胤（允）禧
72
Yin-hsiang (Prince I) 胤（允）祥（怡親王）
31
Yin-hu 胤（允）祜
72
Yin-i 胤（允）禕
72

List of Chinese Characters

Yin-jeng 27 — 胤（允）礽
Yin-li (Prince Kuo) 31 — 胤（允）禮（果親王）
Yin-lu 31 — 胤（允）祿
Yin-shih 27 — 胤（允）禔
Yin-ssu 30 — 胤（允）禩
Yin-t'ang 31 — 胤（允）禟
Yin-t'ao 72 — 胤（允）祹
Yin-t'i 30 — 胤（允）禵
Yin-wu 72 — 胤（允）禑
Yin-yu 72 — 胤（允）祐
ying-chien chih 354n.39 — 營建志
Yingte 251 — 英德
Yü-chih jen-ch'en ching-hsin lu 89 — 御製人臣儆心錄
Yü-chih lu 55 — 諭旨錄
Yü-hsing ch'i-wu tsou-i 171 — 諭行旗務奏議
Yü-hsüan yü-lu 33 — 御選語錄
Yü-lang 349n.58 — 毓朗
yü-shih 114 — 御史
yü-shih chih-tu 5 — 御史制度
Yu T'ung 140 — 尤侗
Yüan 9 — 元
Yüan-hsin 45 — 元信
Yüeh Ch'ao-lung 362n.107 — 岳超龍
Yüeh Chung-ch'i 106 — 岳鍾琪
yüeh-hu 226 — 樂戶
Yün-ssu Yün-t'ang an 320n.101 — 允禩允禟案
Yung, Prince 71 — 雍親王

List of Chinese Characters

Yung-cheng (Yin-chen; Emperor Shih-tsung)
    11
    雍正（胤禎；世宗）

Yung-cheng chu-p'i Nien Keng-yao tsou-che
    331n.52
    雍正硃批年羹堯奏摺

Yung-cheng shang-yü tang
    326n.83
    雍正上諭檔

Yung-hsin
    45
    永瑆

Yung-shan
    293
    永善

Bibliography

For the sake of convenience, this bibliography lists all works in alphabetical order, ignoring the practice of ordinary classifications such as primary, secondary, and periodical sources. It divides into two broader parts.

Part I contains only books and articles cited in the footnotes. They are subdivided by languages: Chinese, Japanese and Korean, and European. While most of these works are arranged by authors or compilers, others, for instance, local gazetteers, government publications, books known usually by their titles, and those whose authors or compilers cannot be identified, are listed by titles. Works referred to in abbreviated form in the footnotes appear in the bibliography as cited, followed by the titles in full. Chinese works are in alphabetical arrangement of first syllables, without consideration of aspirate marks and umlauts. They also include translations from other languages into Chinese. Since some Chinese authors romanized their names by different practices, the bibliography follows their original forms instead of the Wade-Giles system. While the Chinese character *chüan* (卷), roughly meaning chapter, is abbreviated as ch., the word "volume" in its shortened form (v.) stands for *ts'e* (冊) in Chinese. In some cases, traditional Chinese books contain chapters as additions to the regular ones. The bibliography indicates both of these according to the cataloging practice, e.g., 80+2 ch.

Part II covers works consulted by the writer but not cited by him in the footnotes. These works are listed together without distinction of languages in which they are written.

All translations not enclosed in single quotation marks are the work of the author.

I. *Works Cited in the Footnotes*

A. *Chinese*

Ai-hsin Chüeh-lo Hsiu-p'u Ch'u 愛新覺羅修譜處, *Hsin-yüan chi-ch'ing* 星源集慶 (A Genealogy of the Manchu Ruling Family), in the same compiler's *Ai-hsin chüeh-lo tsung-p'u* 愛新覺羅宗譜 (A Genealogy of the Aisin Gioro Clan), Mukden, 1938, 8 v.

Chang-ku ts'ung-pien 掌故叢編 (Collected Historical Documents), compiled and published by the Palace Museum, Peiping, 1928-1930, 10 v.

Chang Mu 張穆, *Yen Ch'ien-ch'iu hsien-sheng nien-p'u* 閻潛邱先生年譜 (A Chronological Biography of Yen Jo-chü), Shou-yang, The Ch'i Family ed. 壽陽祁氏刊本, 1847, 4 v.

Chang P'eng-ko 張鵬翮, *Chang Wen-tuan kung ch'üan-chi* 張文端公全集 (The Complete Works of Chang P'eng-ko), 1882 ed., 7+1 ch., 8 v.

Chang Ping-lin 章炳麟, *Chang-shih ts'ung-shu* 章氏叢書 (Collected Works of Chang Ping-lin), Shanghai, Yu-wen She 右文社, 1915, 22 v.

Chang T'ang-jung 章唐容, *Ch'ing-kung shu-wen* 清宮述聞 (Miscellaneous Accounts about the Ch'ing Court), Peiping, Palace Museum, 1941 ed., 6 ch., 3 v.

Chang T'ing-yü 張廷玉, *Ch'eng-huai yüan wen-ts'un* 澄懷園文存 (An Anthology of the Ch'eng-huai Studio), 1891 ed., 15 ch., 8 v.

―――, *Ch'eng-huai yüan yü* 澄懷園語 (Sayings at the Ch'eng-huai Garden) in *Hsiao-yüan ts'ung-shu* 嘯園叢書, 4 ch.

Chang Ying 張英, *Chang Wen-tuan kung ch'üan-shu* 張文端公全書 (Complete Works of Chang Ying), T'ung-ch'eng, The Chang Family ed. 桐城張氏刊本, 1897, 58 ch., 20 v.

Chao I 趙翼, *Yen-pao tsa-chi* 簷曝雜記 (Miscellaneous Notes), in the same author's *Ou-pei ch'üan-chi* 甌北全集 (Complete Works of Chao I), Yün-nan, The T'ang Family ed., 雲南,唐氏刊本, 1877, 7 ch., 2 v.

Chao Kuang-hsien 趙光賢, "Ch'ing-ch'u chu-wang cheng-kuo chi" 清初諸王爭國記 ('Fight for the succession to the throne in the beginning of the Manchu dynasty'), *Fu-jen hsüeh-chih* 輔仁學誌, 12.1-2:181-99 (Dec. 1943).

Chao-lien 昭槤, *Hsiao-t'ing tsa-lu* 嘯亭雜錄 (A Miscellaneous Record of Hsiao-t'ing), Shanghai, Wen-pao Shu-chü 文寶書局, 1901, 8 ch., 4 v.; supplement, 2 ch., 2 v.

Che-chiang hsin-chih 浙江新志 (A New Gazetteer of Chekiang), ed. by Chiang Ch'ing-yün 姜卿雲 et al., Hangchow, Cheng-chung Shu-chü 正中書局, 1936, 86 ch., 2 v.

Chen-chün 震鈞, *T'ien-chih ngou-wen* 天咫偶聞 (Overheard at Court), Kan-t'ang Chuan-she ed.

甘棠轉舍列本 1907, 10 ch., 8 v.

Ch'en Kuo-chün 陳國鈞, "Kuei-chou miao-i she-hui kai-k'uang" 貴州苗夷社會概況 (A general survey of the Miao and Lolo groups in Kweichow), in Wu Tse-lin 吳澤霖 and Ch'en Kuo-chün 陳國鈞, ed., *Kuei-chou miao-i she-hui yen chiu* 貴州苗夷社會研究 (A Study of the Miao and Lolo Peoples in Kweichow), Kweiyang, Wen-t'ung Shu-chü 文通書局, 1942, pp.1-14.

Ch'en Yin-k'o 陳寅恪, *Sui-T'ang chih-tu yüan-yüan lüeh-lun kao* 隋唐制度淵源略論稿 (Studies of the Origins of Sui and T'ang Institutions), Peking, Chung-hua shu-chü 中華書局, 1963, 158 p.

―――, *T'ang-tai cheng-chih shih shu-lun kao* 唐代政治史述論稿 (A Study of the Political History of the T'ang Dynasty), Chungking, Commercial Press, 1943, 116 p.

Ch'en Yüan 陳垣, "T'ang Jo-wang yü Mu-ch'en min" 湯若望與木陳忞 ('Father John A. Schall von Bell and the Bonze Mu-ch'en wen'), *Fu-jen hsüeh-chih* 輔仁學誌 7.1-2:1-27 (Dec. 1938).

Chi-ch'ang 繼昌, *Hsing-su chai tsa-chi* 行素齋雜記 (Miscellaneous Notes of the Hsing-su Studio), Hunan, Nieh-shu 湖南臬司列本, 1901, 2 ch., 2 v.

Chiang Liang-chi 蔣良騏, *Tung-hua lu* 東華錄

(Tung-hua Records), n.p., n.d., 32 ch., 16 v.

Chiang-nan t'ung-chih 江南通志 (Gazetteer of Kiangnan), ed. by Huang Chih-sui 黃之雋 and Yin Chi-shan 尹繼善, 1735 ed., 200+5 ch., 42 v.

Chiang Ying-liang 江應樑, *Hsi-nan pien-chiang min-tsu lun-ts'ung* 西南邊疆民族論叢 (Collected Papers on the Minority Groups in Southwest China), Canton, Chu-hai Ta-hsüeh 珠海大學, 1948, 288 p.

Ch'ien Ch'en-ch'ün 錢陳群, *Hsiang-shu chai ch'üan-chi* 香樹齋全集 (Complete Works of the Hsiang-shu Studio), 1885 ed., 87 ch., 22 v.

Ch'ien I-chi 錢儀吉, *Pei-chuan chi* 碑傳集 (A Collection of Epitaphs and Biographies), 1893 ed., 160 ch., 60 v.

Ch'ien Mu 錢穆, *Chung-kuo chin san-pai nien hsüeh-shu shih* 中國近三百年學術史 (Chinese Intellectual History of the Last Three Hundred Years), Taipei, Commercial Press, 1957, 2 v.

―――, *Chung-kuo li-tai cheng-chih te-shih* 中國歷代政治得失 (The Merits and Demerits of the Chinese Governmental System during Various Dynasties), 2nd ed., Hong Kong, n.p., 1956, 146 p.

―――, *Kuo-shih ta-kang* 國史大綱 (Outline of Chinese History), Taipei, Kuo-li Pien-i Kuan 國立編譯館, 1967, 2 v.

Ch'ien-nan chih-fang chi-lüeh 黔南職方紀略 (Gazetteer of Southern Kweichow), ed. by Lo Jao-tien 羅繞典, n.p., 1847 ed., 9 ch., 2 v.

Ch'ien-nan shih lüeh 黔南識略 (A Brief Gazetteer of South Kweichow), by Ai-pi-ta 愛必達, n.p., 1847 ed., 32 ch., 4 v.

Ch'ien Yung 錢詠, *Li-yüan ts'ung-hua* 履園叢話 (Collected Notes of Ch'ien Yung), Ch'ien Hsieh-ching T'ang 錢寫經堂版, 1870, 24 ch., 8 v.

Ch'in-ch'uan Chü-shih 琴川居士, *Huang-Ch'ing tsou-i* 皇清奏議 or *Huang-Ch'ing ming-ch'en tsou-i* 皇清名臣奏議 (A Collection of Memorials of the Eminent Officials during the Ch'ing Dynasty), Peiping, Tu-ch'eng Kuo-shih Kuan 都城國史館本, n.d., 68 ch., 48 v.

Ch'in-ting hsüeh-cheng ch'üan-shu 欽定學政全書 (A Guide to the Education Administration), n.p., 1812 ed., 86 ch., 16 v.

Ch'in-ting ta-Ch'ing hui-tien 欽定大清會典 (Collected Statutes of the Ch'ing Dynasty), compiled under the imperial auspices of Ch'ing Jen-tsung, 1818 ed., 80 ch.; *t'u* 圖 (Illustrations), 132 ch.; *shih-li* 事例 (Precedents), 920 ch., 240 v.

Ch'ing-ch'ao wen-hsien t'ung-k'ao 清朝文獻通考 (Encyclopedia of the Ch'ing Dynasty), compiled under the imperial auspices of Ch'ing

Bibliography

Kao-tsung, in *Shih-t'ung* 十通, 300 ch., 2 v.

Ch'ing-kuei 慶桂 et al., *Ch'ing kung-shih hsü-pien* 清宮史續編 (Supplement to the History of Ch'ing Palaces), Peiping, Palace Museum, 1932, 100 ch., 12 v.

Ch'ing-shih Pien-tsuan Wei-yüan Hui, see *CS*.

Ch'ing Shih-tsu 清世祖, *Yü-chih jen-ch'en ching-hsin lu* 御製人臣儆心錄 (Imperial Admonitions on the Conduct of Officials and Subjects), Palace ed. 殿本, 1655, 32 leaves.

Ch'ing Shih-tsung 清世宗, *Chien-mou pien-i lu* 揀魔辨異錄 (Criticisms of Buddhist Heresies), Palace ed. 殿本, 1733, 8 ch., 4 v.

―――, *Ch'in-ting chih-chung ch'eng-hsien* 欽定執中成憲 (Historical Examples of the Mean), Palace ed. 殿本 1733, 8 ch., 4 v.

―――, *Ming-chiao tsui-jen* 名教罪人 (Offender Against the Orthodox Doctrine), Peiping, Palace Museum, 1930.

―――, *Sheng-yü kuang-hsün* 聖諭廣訓 (Amplified Instructions on the Sacred Edict), Palace ed. 殿本, 1724.

―――, *Shih-tsung hsien huang-ti yü-chih wen-chi* 世宗憲皇帝御製文集 (Collection of Emperor Shih-tsung's Essays), Palace ed. 殿本, 1897, 30 ch., 16 v.

―――, *Ta-i chüeh-mi lu* 大義覺迷錄 (A Record of Great Tenor for the Deluded), Palace ed.

殿本, 1730, 4 ch., 4 v.

―――――, [Yung-cheng] *Yü-chih lu* 〔雍正〕諭旨錄 (Record of Imperial Edicts of the Yung-cheng Period), ed. by Yüeh Chung-ch'i 岳鍾琪, Sian 西安, 1728, 10 ch., 10 v.

―――――, *Yü-hsüan yü-lu* 御選語錄 (A Collection of Selected Buddhist and Taoist Sayings), Palace ed. 殿本, 1733, 19 ch., 14 v.

―――――, *Yüeh-hsing chi* 悅心集 (A Collection for Mental Amusement), Ts'ung-shu chi-ch'eng ch'u-pien 叢書集成初編 ed., 108 p.

Ch'ing-tai ti-hou hsiang 清代帝后像 (Portraits of Ch'ing Emperors and Imperial Consorts), compiled and published by the Palace Museum, 2nd ed., Peiping, 1934-1935, 4 v.

Ch'ing-tai wen-tzu yü tang 清代文字獄檔 (Documents about the Literary Inquisition during the Ch'ing Dynasty), compiled and published by the Palace Museum 故宮博物院, Peiping, 1931-1934, 12 v.

Chou Fu 周馥, *Chou Ch'üeh-shen kung ch'üan-chi* 周慤慎公全集 (The Complete Collection of Chou Fu's Works), Ch'iu-p'u, The Chou Family ed. 秋浦周氏刊本, 1922, 44 ch., 36 v.

Chu Chih-jen 朱植仁, *Pen-ch'ao cheng-chih ch'üan-shu* 本朝政治全書 (The Complete Work on the Political Administration of the Ch'ing Dynasty), Ch'eng-en T'ang ed. 承恩堂刊本,

Bibliography

Yung-cheng 雍正年間, 31 v.

Ch'ü Hsüan-ying 瞿宣穎, *Chung-kuo she-hui shih-liao ts'ung-ch'ao* 中國社會史料叢鈔 (A Collection of Materials concerning Chinese Social History), Shanghai, Commercial Press, 1938, 3 v.

Ch'ü Hung-chi 瞿鴻磯, *Pao-chih chi-lüeh* 儤直紀略 (Brief Notes of an Official on Duty), incorporated with *Sheng-te chi-lüeh* 聖德紀略 (Brief Notes on Imperial Virtues), *En-yü chi-lüeh* 恩遇紀略 (Brief Notes on the Imperial Grace), and *Chiu-wen chi-lüeh* 舊聞紀略 (Miscellaneous Notes), Photolithographic ed., n.p., 1920. (unpaginated).

Chu-p'i yü-chih, see *CPYC*.

Chu Shih 朱軾, *Chu Wen-tuan kung wen-chi* 朱文端公文集 (Works of Chu Shih), *Wen-chi* 文集, 4 ch., 4 v.; *Pu-pien* 補編, 4 ch., 4 v.; *Nien-p'u* 年譜 is attached. Ku-t'ang, The Chu Family ed. 古唐朱氏, Ku-huan Chai 古懽齋 刊本, 1873.

―――, *Kao-an Chu Wen-tuan kung yao-ch'e lu kuang-hui p'ien* 高安朱文端公軺車錄廣惠篇 (A Record to the Memory of Chu Shih), Shan-yü T'ang 善餘堂 ed., 1782.

―――, and Wu Hsiang 吳襄, *Po Lü Liu-liang ssu-shu chiang-i* 駁呂留良四書講義 (A Refutation of Lü Liu-liang's Comments on the

Four Books), Palace ed. 殿本, 1732, 8 ch., 8 v.

Chuan Han-sheng 全漢昇 and Wang Yeh-chien 王業鍵 "Ch'ing-tai ti jen-k'ou pien-tung" 清代的人口變動 ('Population changes in China during the Ch'ing Dynasty'), *Bulletin of the Institute of History and Philology, Academia Sinica* 32:139-80 (July 1961).

―――――, "Ch'ing Yung-cheng nien-chien (1723-1735) ti mi-chia" 清雍正年間 (1723-1735) 的米價 ('The Price of rice of China during the Yung-cheng period [1723-1735] of the Ch'ing dynasty'), *ibid.* 30, part 1:157-85 (Oct. 1959).

Ch'üan Tsu-wang 全祖望, *Chi-chi t'ing-chi* 鮚埼亭集 (The Complete Works of Chi-chi t'ing), Ssu-pu ts'ung-k'an Ch'u-pien, Chi-pu 四部叢刊初編, 集部, 108 ch., 35 v.

Chuang Chi-fa 莊吉發, "Ts'ung Ku-kung Po-wu Yüan hsien-ts'ang kung-chung tang-an t'an Ch'ing-tai ti tsou-che" 從故宮博物院現藏宮中檔案談清代的奏摺 ('A discussion of Ch'ing memorials based on the National Palace Museum Collection of Ch'ing documents'), *Ku-kung wen-hsien* 故宮文獻 (Ch'ing Documents at National Palace Museum) 1.2:43-53 (March 1970).

CPYC: *Chu-p'i yü-chih* 硃批諭旨 (Vermilion Endorsements and Edicts), n.p., n.d., 60 v.

CS: Ch'ing-shih Pien-tsuan Wei-yüan Hui 清史

Bibliography

編纂委員會 Ch'ing-shih 清史 (History of the Ch'ing Dynasty), Taipei, Kuo-fang Yen-chiu Yüan 國防研究院, 1961, 550 ch., 8 v.

CSL: Ta-Ch'ing li-ch'ao shih-lu 大清歷朝實錄 (Veritable Records of Successive Reigns of the Ch'ing Dynasty), Tokyo, Ōkura Shuppan Kabushiki Kaisha 大藏出版株式會社, 1937-1938, 4485 ch. Reigns from T'ai-tsu to Jen-tsung.

Fang Hao 方豪, Fang Hao wen-lu 方豪文錄 (Collected Essays of Fang Hao), Peiping, Shang-chih I-shu Kuan 上智譯書館, 1948, 346 p.

Fang Hsien 方顯, P'ing Miao chi-lüeh 平苗紀略 (A Brief Account of the Pacification of the Miao People), Wuchang 武昌刊本, 1873.

Feng Ch'en 馮辰, Li Ssu-ku hsien-sheng nien-p'u 李恕谷先生年譜 (A Chronological Biography of Li Kung), Li Kao 李誥 ed., 1836, 5 ch., 4 v.

Feng-huang t'ing-chih 鳳凰廳志 (Gazetteer of Feng-huang Subprefecture), ed. by Sun Chün-ch'üan 孫均銓 and Huang Ying-p'ei 黃應培, 1824, 20+1 ch., 10 v.

Fu I-ling 傅衣凌, Ming-ch'ing shih-tai shang-jen chi shang-yeh tzu-pen 明清時代商人及商業資本 (The Ming and Ch'ing Merchants and Their Capitals), Peking, Jen-min Ch'u-pan She 人民出版社, 1956, 216 p.

Fu Lo-ch'eng 傅樂成, Sui-T'ang wu-tai shih

隋唐五代史 (History of Sui, T'ang, and the Five Dynasties), Taipei, Chung-hua Wen-hua ch'u-pan Shih-yeh Wei-yüan Hui 中華文化出版事業委員會, 1957, 194 p.

Fu Tsung-mao 傅宗懋, "Ch'ing-ch'u i-cheng t'i-chih chih yen-chiu" 清初議政體制之研究 ('A study on the deliberative body in early Ch'ing'), *The National Chengchi University Journal* 11:245-94 (May 1965).

―――, "Ch'ing-tai chün-chi ch'u she-chih chih yen-ch'iu" 清代軍機處設置之研究 ('The study on the establishment of the Council of State in Ch'ing dynasty'), *ibid.* 12:229-263 (Dec. 1965).

―――, *Ch'ing-tai chün-chi ch'u tsu-chih chi chih-chang chih yen-chiu* 清代軍機處組織及職掌之研究 (A Study of the Organization and Function of the Grand Council of the Ch'ing Dynasty), Taipei, Chia-hsin Shui-ni Kung-ssu Wen-hua Chi-chin Hui 嘉新水泥公司文化基金會, 1967, 694 p.

Han ming-ch'en chuan 漢名臣傳 (Biographies of Eminent Chinese Officials) in *Man-han ming-ch'en chuan* 滿漢名臣傳 (Biographies of Eminent Manchu and Chinese Officials) ed. by Ch'ing

Shih-kuan 清史館, Chü-hua shu-shih 菊花書室, Chin-hsiang ed.

Hang Shih-chün 杭世駿, *Tao-ku t'ang ch'üan-chi* 道古堂全集 (The Complete Works of the Tao-ku Studio), Chen-ch'i T'ang 振綺堂 ed., 1888, *Wen-chi* 文集, 48 ch.; *Shih-chi* 詩集, 26 ch.; with supplement, 2 ch., 16 v.

Ho-nan t'ung-chih 河南通志 (Gazetteer of Honan Province), ed. by T'ien Wen-ching 田文鏡 and Wang Shih-chün 王士俊, Ho-nan Chiao-yü Ssu 河南教育司, n.d., 80 ch., 40 v.

Hsiao I-shan 蕭一山, *Ch'ing-tai t'ung-shih* 清代通史 (A General History of the Ch'ing Dynasty), Taipei, Commercial Press, 1963, 5 v.

Hsiao Kung-ch'üan 蕭公權, "Chung-kuo cheng-chih ssu-hsiang chung chih cheng-yüan lun" 中國政治思想中之政原論 (Theories on the origins of political powers in Chinese political thought), *Tsing Hua Journal* 清華學報 9.3: 535-48 (July 1934).

―――, *Chung-kuo cheng-chih ssu-hsiang shih* 中國政治思想史 (A History of Chinese Political Thought), Shanghai, Commercial Press, 1947, 2 v.

Hsiao Shih, see *YHL*.

Hsing-ning hsien-chih 興寧縣志 (Gazetter of

Hsing-ning District), ed. by Chang Huo-ling 張鶴齡, Hsing-ning Shu-tien 興寧書店, 1929, 12 ch., 4 v.

Hsü Ch'ien-hsüeh 徐乾學, Tan-yüan ch'üan-chi 憺園文存 (The Complete Collection of Tan-yüan), ed. by Chin Wu-lan 金吳瀾, 1883, 36 ch., 12 v.

Hsü I-t'ang 徐益棠, "Kuang-hsi hsiang-p'ing chien yao-min chih chu-wu" 廣西象平間傜民之住屋 ('The dwellings of the Yao tribes in Hsiang-ping, Kwangsi'), Chin-ling hsüeh-pao 金陵學報 (Nanking Journal) 10.1-2:19-30 (May-Nov. 1940).

———, "Liang-shan lo-min chih lei cheng-chih ti tsu-chih" 涼山倮民之類政治組織 ('The government-like organization of the Lolo people at Liang-shan'). Chung-kuo wen-hua yen-chiu hui-k'an 中國文化研究彙刊 (Bulletin of Chinese Studies) 3:365-86 (Sept. 1943).

Hsü Ta-ling 許大齡, Ch'ing-tai chuan-nai chih-tu 清代捐納制度 ('The System of Purchasing Offices by Contributions during the Ch'ing Period, 1644-1911'), Peking, Harvard-Yenching Institute, 1950, 97 p.

Hu Ch'ing-chün 胡慶鈞, "Chiai-fang ch'ien liang-shan i-tsu she-hui hsing-chih yen-chiu shu-p'ing" 解放前涼山彝族社會性質研究述評 (A critical study on the nature of the Lolo society in Mt. Liang before 1949), *Lishi Yanjiu* [Li-shi Yen-chiu] 歷史研究 (Journal of Historical Studies) 2:135-52 (April 1963).

Hu Nai-an 胡耐安, "Ming-Ch'ing liang-tai t'u-ssu" 明清兩代土司 (The tribal headman system of the Ming and Ch'ing dynasties), in Ta-lu Tsa-chih Pien-chi Wei-yüan Hui 大陸雜誌編輯委員會, ed., *Ch'ing-shih chi chin-tai shih yen-chiu lun-chi* 清史及近代史研究論集 (Collected Papers on Ch'ing and Modern Chinese History), Taipei, Ta-lu Tsa-chih She 大陸雜誌社 1960, pp.110-17.

Huang Ang 黃卬, *Hsi-chin shih-hsiao lu* 錫金識小錄 (Miscellaneous Notes about Wu-hsi District), 1896 ed., 12 ch., 6 v.

Huang Kai-hua 黃開華, "Ming-tai t'u-ssu chih-tu she-shih yü hsi-nan k'ai-fa" 明代土司制度設施與西南開發 ('The institution of tribal authorities and the development of southwest China during the Ming dynasty'), *Hsin-ya Hsüeh-pao* 新亞學報 (New Asia Journal) 6.1:285-365 (Feb. 1964); 6.2: 397-495 (Aug. 1964).

Huang Pei 黃培, "Ch'ing Shih-tsung yü Nien Keng-yao chih kuan-hsi" 清世宗與年羹堯之關係 (The relationship between Emperor Shih-tsung of the Ch'ing and Nien Keng-yao), *Ta-lu*

Tsa-chih 大陸雜誌 (The Continent Magazine) 16.4:112-13 (Feb. 1958); 16.5:151-58 (March 1958).

⎯⎯⎯, "Yung-cheng shih-tai chung-yang t'ung-chih t'i-hsi ti kai-pien" 雍正時代中央統治體系的改變 (Reorganization of the Central Governmental System during the Yung-cheng Period), unpublished M.A. thesis, National Taiwan University, Taipei, Taiwan, 1959, 292 p.

⎯⎯⎯, "Yung-cheng shih-tai ti mi-tsou chih-tu— Ch'ing shih-tsung chih-shu ti i-tuan" 雍正時代的密奏制度—清世宗治術的一端 ('The secret-report system during the Yung-cheng period, 1723-1735: A political practice of Emperor Shih-tsung'), *Tsing Hua Journal of Chinese Studies*, new series 3.1:17-52 (May 1962).

Huang Yü-pu 黃玉圃 et al., *Kuo-ch'ao yü-shih t'i-ming lu* 國朝御史題名錄 (List of Censors in the Ch'ing Dynasty), Ching-chi Tao 京畿道 ed., ca.1904, 3 v.

Jung Chao-tsu 容肇祖, "Lü Liu-liang chi ch'i ssu-hsiang" 呂留良及其思想 ('De philosopho Lü Liu-liang [1629-1683], a dynastia Ch'ing postmortem proscripto'). *Fu-jen Hsüeh-chih* 輔仁學誌, 5.1-2:1-86 (Dec. 1936).

K'ang Chi-t'ien 康基田, *Ho-ch'ü chi-wen* 河渠紀聞 (A Record of River Works), Chung-kuo

Bibliography

    Shui-li Kung-ch'eng Hsüeh-hui 中國水利工程學會, 1936, 31 ch.

Kao I-han 高一涵, *Chung-kuo yü-shih chih-tu ti yen-ke* 中國御史制度的沿革 (A History of the Chinese Censorial System), Shanghai, Commercial Press, 1934, 77 p.

KCT: *Kung-chung tang-an* 宮中檔案 (Ch'ing Palace Archives), which cover largely the palace memorials of the K'ang-hsi and Yung-cheng reigns, housed in the National Palace Museum, Taipei, Taiwan. Many memorials of the K'ang-hsi era have been published in the *Ku-kung wen-hsien* 故宮文獻 (Ch'ing Documents at National Palace Museum) since December 1969. I selected and microfilmed many memorials of the Yung-cheng period, including the *Wang ta-jen mi-i tsou-p'ien* 王大人密議奏片 (Short Memorials Containing Secret Deliberations by Yin-hsiang and Other High Officials), which are uncatalogued.

Ko Han-feng 葛寒峯, "Ch'ing-tai t'ien-fu chung chih hao-hsien" 清代田賦中之耗羨 (Hao-hsien in the Ch'ing land and labor-service tax), *Nung-hsüeh* 農學 (Agricultural Science) 1.5: 45-54 (May 1939).

K'o Hsiang-feng 柯象峯, "Lo-lo wen-tzu chih ch'u-pu yen-chiu" 玀玀文字之初步研究 ('A preliminary study of the written language of the

Lolos'), *Chin-ling hsüeh-pao* 金陵學報 (Nanking Journal) 8.1-2:23-38 (May-Nov. 1938).

Ku I 谷依, "Ch'ing-ch'ao ch'ien-ch'i tui Che-chiang hai-t'ang ti hsiu-chu" 清朝前期對浙江海塘的修築 (Early Ch'ing constructions of the sea wall in Chekiang province), *'Shixue Yuekan'* [Shih-hsüeh yüeh-k'an] 史學月刊, 10:23-28 (Oct. 1958).

Ku-kung Po-wu Yüan 故宮博物院, comp. *Wen-hsien lun-ts'ung* 文獻論叢 (Collected Articles from the Historical Records Office), Peiping, Palace Museum, 1936, 80+214+70 p.

Kuang-tung t'ung-chih 廣東通志 (Gazetteer of Kwangtung), ed. by Chiang Fan 江藩 and Juan Yüan 阮元, 1864 ed., 334+1 ch., 120 v.

Kuei-chou t'ung-chih 貴州通志 (Gazetteer of Kweichow), ed. by Ching Tao-mu 靖道謨 and O-er-t'ai 鄂爾泰, 1741 ed., 46+1 ch., 32 v.

Kuei-yang chih-li chou chih 桂陽直隸州志 (Gazetteer of Kweiyang Independent Department), ed. by Wang K'ai-yün 王闓運 and Wang Hsiao-hao 汪㲄灝, 1868 ed., 27 ch., 13 v.

Lai-pao 來保 et al., eds., *Ch'in-ting pa-ch'i tse-li* 欽定八旗則例 (Statutes for the Eight Banners), Palace ed. 殿本, 1764, 12 ch., 4 v.

Lan Ting-yüan 藍鼎元, *Lan Lu-chou ch'üan-chi* 藍鹿洲全集 (Complete Works of Lan Ting-yüan), 1880 ed., 43 ch., 24 v.

Lao Kan 勞榦, *Ch'in-han shih* 秦漢史 (History of Ch'in and Han Dynasties), Taipei, Chung-hua Wen-hua Ch'u-pan Shih-yeh Wei-yüan Hui 中華文化出版事業委員會, 1952, 155 p.

———, "Lun Han-tai ti nei-ch'ao yü wai-ch'ao" 論漢代的內朝與外朝 ('On the "Inner Cabinet" and "Outer Cabinet" of the Han Dynasty'), *Bulletin of the Institute of History and Philology, Academia Sinica* 13:227-67 (1948).

Li Fu 李紱, *Mu-t'ang ch'u-kao* 穆堂初稿 (Works of Li Fu, First Series) Shan-ch'eng Fu-ch'i T'ang 珊城阜祺堂 ed., 1831, 50 ch., 16 v.

Li Hsüeh-chih 李學智, "Ch'ing T'ai-tsu shih-ch'i chien-ch'u wen-ti ti fen-hsi" 清太祖時期建儲問題的分析 ('An analysis of the designation of heir apparent in the time of Nurhaci'), *Ssu yü yen* 思與言 (Thought and Word) 8.2:1-9 (July 1970).

Li Hua-lung 李化龍, *P'ing-po ch'üan-shu* 平播全書 (An Account of the Campaign in Po-chou), Ts'ung-shu chi-ch'eng ch'u-pien 叢書集成初編 ed., 15 ch., 7 v.

Li-tai chih-kuan piao 歷代職官表 (Tables of Offices and Officials of Successive Dynasties), compiled by Chi Yün 紀昀 et al., Ssu-pu pei-yao 四部備要 ed., 72 ch., 20 v.

Li T'iao-yüan 李調元, *Nan-yüeh pi-chi* 南越筆記 (Miscellaneous Notes about Kwangtung), *Ts'ung-shu chi-ch'eng ch'u-pien* 叢書集成初編 ed., 16 ch., 3 v.

Li Tsung-fang 李宗昉, *Ch'ien-chi* 黔記 (Records about Kweichow), *Ts'ung-shu chi-ch'eng ch'u-pien* 叢書集成初編 ed., 43 p.

Li Tsung-t'ung 李宗侗, "Ch'ing-tai chung-yang cheng-ch'üan hsing-t'ai ti yen-pien" 清代中央政權形態的演變 ('Changes in the pattern of central political powers of the Ch'ing dynasty'), *Bulletin of the Institute of History and Philology, Academia Sinica* 37, part 1:79-158 (1967).

―――, "Pan-li chün-chi ch'u lüeh-k'ao" 辦理軍機處略考 (A brief study of the Chün-chi ch'u), *Yu-shih hsüeh-pao* 幼獅學報 (The Youth Journal) 1.2:1-19 (1959).

Li Yüeh-jui 李岳瑞, *Ch'un-ping shih yeh-ch'eng* 春冰室野乘 (Private Historical Notes of the Ch'un-ping Studio), Taipei, Wen-hai Ch'u-pan She 文海出版社, 1967, 410 p.

Liang Chang-chü 梁章鉅, *Kuei-t'ien so-chi* 歸田瑣記 (Miscellaneous Notes after Retirement), in the same author's *Liang Chang-chü pi-chi* 梁章鉅筆記 (A Collection of Liang Chang-chü's Notes), Sao-yeh Shan-fang 掃葉山房 ed., Shanghai, 1918, 8 ch., 2 v.

————, *Shu-yüan chi-lüeh* 樞垣紀略 (Brief Notes on the Grand Council), 1875, 28 ch., 6 v.

Lin Yao-hua 林耀華, *Liang-shan i-chia* 涼山夷家 (The Lolo People of Mt. Liang), Shanghai, Commercial Press, 1947, 133 p. Its English translation is entitled *The Lolo of Liang Shan*, trans. by Ju-shu Pan and ed. by Wu-chi Liu, New Haven, Conn., Human Relations Area Files, 1961, 159 p.

Ling Ch'un-sheng 凌純聲 and Ruey Yih-fu 芮逸夫, *Hsiang-hsi Miao-tsu t'iao-ch'a pao-kao* 湘西苗族調查報告 (Reports on the Miao People in Western Hunan), Shanghai, Commercial Press, 1947, 477 p.

Liu, Chia-chü 劉家駒, *Ch'ing-ch'ao ch'u-ch'i ti pa-ch'i ch'üan-ti* 清朝初期的八旗圈地 ('The Allotted Land Policy for the Eight-Banners in the Early Ch'ing Dynasty'), Taipei, College of Arts, National Taiwan University, 1964, 218 p.

Liu Hsi-fan 劉錫蕃, *Ling-piao chi-man* 嶺表紀蠻 (Records of the Barbarian Groups in Kwangtung and Kwangsi), Shanghai, Commercial Press, 1934, 307 p.

Lo Chen-yü 羅振玉, ed., *Shih-liao ts'ung-k'an ch'u-pien* 史料叢刊初編 (Miscellaneous Historical Materials, First Series), Tung-fang Hsüeh-hui 東方學會, 1924, 10 v.

———, *Shih-liao ts'ung-pien* 史料叢編 (Miscellaneous Historical Materials), Port Arthur, 1935, 12 v., and *erh-chi* 二集, 6 v.

Lü Liu-liang 呂留良, *Lü Wan-ts'un hsien-sheng ssu-shu chiang-i* 呂晚村先生四書講義 (Comments of Lü Liu-liang on the Four Books), ed. by Ch'en Tsung 陳縱, 1686, 43 ch., 8 v.

———, *Lü Wan-ts'un hsien-sheng wen-chi* 呂晚村先生文集 (Works of Lü Liu-liang), 1689 ed., 8 ch., 4 v.

Man-han ming-ch'en chuan 滿漢名臣傳 (Biographies of Eminent Manchu and Chinese Officials), ed. by Ch'ing Shih-kuan 清史館, Chü-hua shu-shih 菊花書室, Chin-hsiang ed. 巾箱本, 90 ch., 96 v.

Man ming-ch'en chuan 滿名臣傳 (Biographies of Eminent Manchu Officials), in *ibid*.

Meng Sen 孟森, *Ch'ing-tai shih* 清代史 (History of the Ch'ing Dynasty), Taipei, Cheng-chung shu-chü 正中書局, 1960, 546 p.

———, *Ming-Ch'ing shih lun-chu chi-k'an* 明清史論著集刊 (Collected Essays on the History of the Ming and the Ch'ing), Taipei, World Book Co., 1961, 634 p.

Miao Chuan-chi 繆全吉, "K'ung-tzu chün-ch'en cheng-i" 孔子君臣正義 ('Confucian theory on the "monarch and his courtiers"'), *Chung-shan hsüeh-shu wen-hua chi-k'an* 中山學術文化

集刊(Bulletin of the Sun Yat-sen Cultural Foundation) 1:41-80 (March 1968).

Mo Tung-yin 莫東寅,"Ti-ting ch'ien-liang k'ao" 地丁錢糧考(A critical study of the land and labor-service tax of the Ch'ing), *Chung-ho yüeh-k'an* 中和月刊 (Chung-ho Monthly) 4.1:27-64 (Jan. 1943).

Nien Keng-yao tsou-che chuan-ch'i 年羹堯奏摺專輯 (A Special Collection of the Memorials of Nien Keng-yao), comp. by National Palace Museum, Taipei, National Palace Museum, 1971, 3 v.

O-hai 鄂海, *Liu-pu tse-li ch'üan-shu* 六部則例全書 (Statutes and Precedents of the Six Boards), n.p., prefaced in 1716, 40 v.

Pa-ch'i t'ung-chih ch'u-chi 八旗通志初集 (General History of the Eight Banners, First Series), compiled under the imperial auspices of Ch'ing Kao-tsung, Palace ed., 1739, 253 ch., 60 v.

P'an Hsi-en 潘錫恩, *Chi-fu shui-li ssu-an* 畿輔水利四案(Four Conservation Enterprises in the Metropolitan Area), n.p., Tao-kuang 道光 ed., 4 v.

Pao Shu-yün 鮑書芸, ed., *Hsing-an hui-lan* 刑案滙覽(A Collection of Judicial Cases), T'ang-yüeh Shen-ssu t'ang 棠樾慎思堂 ed., 1834, 60+2 ch., 64 v.

Shan Shih-k'uei 單士魁, "Ch'ing-tai t'i-pen chih-tu k'ao" 清代題本制度考 (The system of memorials for official affairs of the Ch'ing dynasty) in Ku-kung Po-wu Yüan 故宮博物院 comp., Wen-hsien lun-ts'ung 文獻論叢 (Collected Articles from the Historical Records Office), Peiping, Palace Museum, 1936, pp.177-89.

Shan Shih-yüan 單士元, "Ku-kung chün-chi ch'u chih-fang" 故宮軍機處值房 (The quarters of the Grand Council), Wen-wu 文物 (Cultural Relics) 60.1:41-43 (Jan. 1960).

Shang Hung-k'uei 商鴻逵, "Lüeh-lun Ch'ing-ch'u ching-chi hui-fu ho kung-ku ti ku-ch'eng chi ch'i ch'eng-chiu" 略論清初經濟恢復和鞏固的過程及其成就 ('Economic recovery and stabilization in the earlier Ch'ing period, 1681-1735'), Pei-ching Ta-hsüeh Hsüeh-pao: Jen-wen k'o-hsüeh 北京大學學報一人文科學 (Journal of Peking University, Humanity Science) 2:113-30 (May 1957).

Shang Yen-liu 商衍鎏, Ch'ing-tai k'o-chü k'ao-shih shu-lu 清代科舉攷試述錄 (A Brief Record of the Examination System of the Ch'ing Dynasty), Peking, San-lien Shu-tien 三聯書店, 1958, 350 p.

Shang-yü ch'i-wu i-fu 上諭旗務議覆 (Imperial Decrees and Responding Memorials Governing Banner Affairs), Yung-cheng 雍正 ed., 8 v.

Shang-yü nei-ko, see *SYNK*.

Shang-yü pa-ch'i, see *SYPC*.

Shao-hsing fu-chih 紹興府志 (Gazetteer of Shao-hsing prefecture), ed. by P'ing Shu 平恕 and Li Heng-t'e 李亨特, Shao-hsing Fu-ya 紹興府衙 ed., 1792, 80+1 ch., 46 v.

She I-tse 佘貽澤, *Chung-kuo t'u-ssu chih-tu* 中國土司制度 (The Tribal Headman System of China), Chungking, Cheng-chung Shu-chü 正中書局, 1944, 222 p.

Shen Yün-lung 沈雲龍, ed., *Ming-Ch'ing shih-liao hui-pien, I* 明清史料彙編第一集 (Collection of Ming and Ch'ing Historical Materials, I), Taipei, Wen-hai ch'u-pan She 文海出版社 1967, v.6.

Sheng-ching t'ung-chih 盛京通志 (Gazetteer of Liaoning) comp. by Lü Yao-tseng 呂耀曾 and Wei Shu 魏樞, 1779 ed., 48 ch., 24 v.

Shih-ch'ao sheng-hsün 十朝聖訓 (Sacred Instructions of the Ten Emperors), Kuang-hsü ed. 光緒刊本, 922 ch., 100 v.

Shih-liang 奭良, *Yeh-t'ang hsüan wen-chi* 野棠軒文集 (A Collection of Essays of the Yeh-t'ang Studio), 5 ch.; *Shih-chi* 詩集 (A Collection of Poems), 4 ch.; *Tz'u-chi* 詞集 (A Collection of Metric Poems), 4 ch.; *Shih-t'ing shih-hsiao lu* 史亭識小錄 (Trifling

Notes on History), 1 ch.; *Hsien-ch'ou chi* 獻酬集 (Writings as Presents), 1 ch.; *Yu-hsi chi* 遊戲集 (Burlesques), 1 ch.; *Yeh-t'ang hsüan chih-yen* 野棠軒摭言 (Miscellaneous Notes), 8 ch., Peiping, The Shih Family ed. 麯氏刊本, 1929, 6 v.

Ssu-ch'uan t'ung-chih 四川通志 (Gazetteer of Szechwan Province), comp. by Jalangga 查郎阿 and Kao Wei-hsin 高維新, 1733-1736 ed., 47+1 ch., 80 v.

Su-chou fu-chih 蘇州府志 (Gazetteer of Soochow), ed. by Feng Kuei-fen 馮桂芬 and Li Ming-huan 李銘皖, Chiang-su Shu-chü 江蘇書局 ed., 1883, 150+3 ch., 46 v.

Sung-chiang fu-chih 松江府志 (Gazetteer of Sungkiang Prefecture), ed. by Sun Hsing-yen 孫星衍 and Sung Ju-lin 宋如林, 1819 ed., 84+3 ch., 40 v.

Sung Lao 宋犖, *Hsi-p'o lei-kao* 西陂類稿 (A Collection of Classified Writings of Hsi-p'o), 1917, 50+1 ch., 20 v.

SYNK: *Shang-yü nei-ko* 上諭內閣 (Edicts and Decrees to the Grand Secretariat), Palace ed. 殿本, 1741, 159 ch., 30 v.

SYPC: *Shang-yü pa-ch'i* 上諭八旗 (Edicts and Decrees for the Eight Banners), Palace ed. 殿本, ca.1735, 10 v.; also its Manchu edition.

Bibliography

Ta-Ch'ing hui-tien 大清會典 (Collected Statutes of the Ch'ing Dynasty), comp. under the imperial auspices of Ch'ing Sheng-tsu, 1690 ed., 162 ch., 64 v.

Ta-Ch'ing li-ch'ao shih-lu, see *CSL*.

Ta-Ming hui-tien 大明會典 (Collected Statutes of the Ming Dynasty), comp. by Li Tung-yang 李東陽 and Shen Ming-hsing [Shen Shih-hsing] 申明行 [申時行], Taipei, Tung-nan Shu-pao She 東南書報社, 1964, 228 ch., 5 v.

Tai Lu 戴璐 and Wang Chia-hsiang 王家相, *Kuo-ch'ao liu-k'o han chi-shih chung t'i-ming lu* 國朝六科漢給事中題名錄 (A List of the Chinese Supervising Secretaries in the Ch'ing Dynasty), Kuang-hsü 光緒 ed.

T'ang Chi-ho 湯吉禾, "Ch'ing-tai k'o-tao chih chih-chang" 清代科道之職掌 (The functions of the censors and supervising secretaries of the Ch'ing dynasty), *Tung-fang Tsa-chih* 東方雜誌 (Eastern Miscellany) 33.1:343-351 (Jan. 1936).

———, "Ch'ing-tai k'o-tao tsu-chih yen-ke" 清代科道組織沿革 (Evolution of the Ch'ing censorial system), *Hsin she-hui k'o-hsüeh chi-k'an* 新社會科學季刊 (Quarterly Journal of the New Social Sciences) 1.1:67-74 (Feb. 1934).

T'ang Pang-chih 唐邦治, *Ch'ing huang-shih ssu-*

p'u 清皇室四譜 (Four Genealogies of the Ch'ing Imperial Family), Shanghai, Chi-chen Fang-sung Yin-shu Chü 聚珍仿宋印書局, 1923, 2 v.

T'ang Pin 湯斌, *T'ang-tzu i-shu* 湯子遺書 (Works of T'ang Pin), Ai-jih T'ang 愛日堂 ed., 1703, 10+1 ch., 4 v.

T'ang Ti 唐棣, "Lüeh-lun Ch'ing-tai ti ti-ting chih-tu" 略論清代的地丁制度 (A brief survey of the land-ting tax system of the Ch'ing), *Li-shih chiao-hsüeh* 歷史教學, 1:30-33 (Jan. 1955).

Tao-min 道忞, "Tsou-tui chi-yüan" 奏對機緣 (Replies made at the imperial service), in Chang Ch'ao 張潮, ed., *Chao-tai ts'ung-shu i-chi* 昭代叢書乙集 (The Chao-tai Collected Works, Series B), Sao-yeh Shan-fang 掃葉山房 ed., ch.19, pp.14-15.

Teng Chih-ch'eng 鄧之誠, *Ku-tung so-chi ch'üan-pien* 骨董瑣記全編 (Miscellanea of Historical Materials), Peking, San-lien Shu-tien 三聯書店, 1955, 656 p.

Teng Shih-hsi 鄧詩熙, "Ch'ing-tai pen-chang chih-tu chih kai t'i wei tsou k'ao" 清代本章制度之改題為奏考 ('The change from t'i-pen 題本 to tsou-pen 奏本 in the Manchurian government'), *Shih-hsüeh chi-k'an* 史學集刊 (Historical Journal) 3:321-27 (April

1937).

T'ien-hsi 滇繫 (Gazetteer of Yunnan), by Shih Fan 師範 Yün-nan T'ung-chih Chü 雲南通志局, 1887 ed., 40 v.

T'ien Wen-ching 田文鏡, *Fu-yü hsüan-hua lu* 撫豫宣化錄 (Record of the Administrative Work in Honan), n.p., ca.1728 ed., 4 ch., 8 v.

———, and Li Wei 李衛, *Ch'in-pan chou-hsien shih-i* 欽頒州縣事宜 (Guide to the District and Department Administration), Chiang-su Shu-chü 江蘇書局, ed., 1868.

T'ing-hai hsien-chih 定海縣志 (Gazetteer of Ting-hai District), ed. by Ch'en T'ien-yin 陳天嬰, 1924 ed., 16 ch., 6 v.

Ting I 丁易, *Ming-tai t'e-wu cheng-chih* 明代特務政治 (Government by Secret Services during the Ming Period), Peking, Chung-wai Ch'u-pan She 中外出版社, 1951, 616 p.

Torii Ryūzō 鳥居龍藏, *Miao-tsu t'iao-ch'a pao-kao* 苗族調查報告 (Reports on the Miao People), trans. into Chinese by Chinese National Institute of Compilation and Translation, Shanghai, National Institute of Compilation and Translation, 1936, 507 p.

Ts'ai Ch'eng 蔡郕, *Ch'ing-tai shih-lun* 清代史論 (Historical Comments on the Ch'ing), Shanghai, Hui-wen T'ang 會文堂, 1920, 16 ch., 8 v.

Ts'ai Shih-yüan 蔡世遠, *Erh-hsi t'ang wen-chi 二希堂文集* (Works of the Erh-hsi Studio), 1735, 11+1 ch., 4 v.

Ts'ao I-shih 曹一士, *Ssu-yen chai ch'üan-chi 四焉齋全集* (Works of the Ssu-yen Studio), Hsüan-t'ung 宣統 ed., 14 ch., 6 v.

Tseng Chao-lun 曾昭掄, *Ta-liang shan i-ch'ü k'ao-ch'a chi 大涼山夷區考察記* (A Field Study of the Lolo Tribes in Mt. Liang), Kunming, Ch'iu-chen Ch'u-pan She 求真出版社, 1945, 316 p.

Tu Lienche 杜聯喆, *Kuan-yü chün-chi ch'u ti chien-chih 關於軍機處的建置* ('On the Establishment of the Chün-chi ch'u'), Canberra, The Australian National University, Center of Oriental Studies, Occasional Paper No. 2, 1963, 30 p.

Väth Alfons, *Johann Adam Schall von Bell, S. J.*, trans. into Chinese by Yang Ping-ch'en 楊丙辰, under the title *T'ang Jo-wang chuan 湯若望傳* (Biography of Johann Adam Schall von Bell), Taipei, Commercial Press, 1960, 2 v. in one.

Wang Ch'ang 王昶, *Ch'un-jung t'ang chi 春融堂集* (Works of the Ch'un-jung Studio), Shu-nan Shu-she 塾南書舍 ed., 1892, 68 ch., 20 v.

Wang Ching-ch'i 汪景祺, *Tu-shu t'ang hsi-cheng sui-pi 讀書堂西行隨筆* (Jottings of a

Western Journey), Peiping, Palace Museum, 1928, 57 leaves.

Wang Ch'ing-yün 王慶雲, *Hsi-ch'ao chi-cheng* 熙朝紀政 or *Shih-chü yü-chi* 石渠餘記 (A Record of Our Prosperous Dynasty), Changsha, The Lung Family ed. 龍氏刊本, 1898, 6 ch., 6 v.

Wang Chung-han 王鍾翰, *Ch'ing-shih tsa-k'ao* 清史雜考 (Miscellanea on the History of the Ch'ing Dynasty), Peking, Jen-min Ch'u-pan She 人民出版社, 1957, 323 p.

Wang Hsien-ch'ien 王先謙, *Tung-hua lu* 東華錄 (Tung-hua Records), Changsha, The Wang Family ed. 王氏刊本, 1884-1890, 525 ch. Reigns from T'ai-tsu to Kao-tsung.

Wang Mou-hung 王懋竑, *Pai-t'ien ts'ao-t'ang ts'un-kao* 白田草堂存稿 (Writings of the Pai-t'ien Studio), Ko-t'ang 葛堂本 ed., 1752, 24 ch., 8 v.

Wang Shih 王栻, "Po-feng yü lou-kuei" 薄俸與陋規 (Poor payment and customary gratuities), *Wen-shih Tsa-chih* 文史雜誌 (Journal of Literature and History) 3.1-2:53-72 (Jan. 1944).

Wang Shih-chen 王士禛, *Hsiang-tsu pi-chi* 香祖筆記 (Miscellaneous Notes of Wang Shih-chen), n.p., n.d., 12 ch., 4 v.

Wang Shih-chün 王世俊, *Ho-tung ts'ung-cheng lu* 河東從政錄 (Record of Administrative

Work in Honan and Shantung), 1735, 14 ch., 10 v.

———, *Li-chih hsüeh-ku p'ien* 吏治學古篇 (A Record of Administration after Ancient Principles), Chung-cheng T'ang 中正堂 ed., 1733-1734, 2 ch., 2 v.

Wang Yeh-chien 王業鍵, "Ch'ing Yung-cheng shih-ch'i (1723-1735) ti ts'ai-cheng kai-ke" 清雍正時期(1723-1735)的財政改革 ('Financial reforms during the Yung-cheng [雍正] period [1723-1735]'), *Bulletin of the Institute of History and Philology, Academia Sinica* 32:47-75 (July 1961).

Wei Chien-yu 魏建猷, "Ch'ing Yung-cheng ch'ao shih-hsing ching-t'ien chih ti k'ao-ch'a" 清雍正朝試行井田制的考察 ('A study on the experiment of the "Tsing-t'ien" system in the reign of Yung-cheng'), *Shih-hsüeh nien-pao* 史學年報 (Historical Annual) 1.5:113-26 (1933).

Wei Hsiang-shu 魏象樞, *Han-sung t'ang chi* 寒松堂集 (Works of the Winter-pine Studio), Ts'ung-shu chi-ch'eng ch'u-pien 叢書集成初編 ed., 10 ch., 6 v.

Wen-hsien ts'ung-pien 文獻叢編 (Collectanea from the Historical Records Office), compiled and published by the Palace Museum, Peiping, 1930-1943, 46 v.

Wen Yu 聞宥, "Ch'uan-tien-ch'ien lo-wen chih pi-chiao" 川滇間儺文之比較 ('A comparison of three varieties of the Lolo characters in Szechwan, Yunnan, and Kweichow'), *Chung-kuo wen-hua yen-chiu hui-k'an* 中國文化研究彙刊 (Bulletin of Chinese Studies) 7:245-49 (Sept. 1947).

―――――, "Lo-lo i-yü k'ao" 倮儸譯語考 ('On Lolo i-yü—Lolo-Chinese vocabularies'), *Studia Serica* 1, part 1:77-97 (Sept. 1940).

Wu Hsiu-liang 吳秀良, "Ch'ing-tai chün-chi ch'u chien-chih ti tsai chien-t'ao 清代軍機處建置的再檢討 ('A reappraisal of the establishment of the Grand Council under the Ch'ing'), *Ku-kung wen-hsien* 故宮文獻 (Ch'ing Documents at the National Palace Museum), 2.4:21-45 (Sept. 1971).

Wu Tse-lin 吳澤霖 and Ch'en Kuo-chün 陳國鈞, ed., *Kuei-chou miao-i she-hui yen-chiu* 貴州苗夷社會研究 (A Study of the Miao and Lolo Peoples in Kweichow), Kweiyang, Wen-t'ung Shu-chü 文通書局, 1942, 378+6 p.

Yang Ch'eng-chih 楊成志, "Chung-kuo hsi-nan min-tsu chung-ti lo-lo tsu" 中國西南民族中的羅羅族 (The Lolos among the ethnic groups in southwest China), *Ti-hsüeh tsa-chih* 地學雜誌 (Journal of Geography) 1:1-45 (1934).

Yang Ming-shih 楊名時, *Yang-shih ch'üan-shu* 楊氏全書 (Complete Works of Yang Ming-shih),

Chiang-yin Nan-ching Kao-teng Hsüeh-t'ang 江陰南菁高等學堂 ed., 1909, 36+1 ch., 10 v.

Yeh Feng-mao 葉鳳毛, *Nei-ko hsiao-chih* 內閣小志 (A Brief Account of the Grand Secretariat), in Shen Yün-lung 沈雲龍, ed., *Ming Ch'ing shih-liao hui-pien*, I, 明清史料彙編第一集 (Collection of Ming and Ch'ing Historical Materials, I), Taipei, Wen-hai Ch'u-pan She 文海出版社 1967, v. 6.

Yen Chung-p'ing 嚴中平, *Ch'ing-tai Yün-nan t'ung-cheng k'ao* 清代雲南銅政考 ('A Study of the Copper Administration in Yunnan under the Ch'ing,), Peking, Chung-hua Shu-chü 中華書局, 1957, 100 p.

YHL: Hsiao Shih 蕭奭, *Yung-hsien lu* 永憲錄 (A Record for Permanent Illustration), Peking, Chung-hua Shu-chü 中華書局, 1959, 4 ch., with a supplement, 424 p.

Yin-hsiang 胤祥, *I-hsien ch'ing-wang shu-ch'ao* 怡賢親王疏鈔 (A Collection of Prince I's Memorials), ed. by Wu Pang-ch'ing 吳邦慶, 1823 ed.

Yü Cheng-hsieh 俞正燮, *Kuei-ssu ts'un-kao* 癸巳存稿 (Selected Works of Yü Cheng-hsieh), Ts'ung-shu chi-ch'eng ch'u-pien 叢書集成初編 ed., 15 ch., 5 v.

Yü-hsing ch'i-wu tsou-i 諭行旗務奏議 (Memorials and Related Imperial Comments concerning Banner Affairs), compiled by Yin-lu 胤祿 et al. under the imperial auspices of Ch'ing Shih-tsung 清世宗, Palace ed. 5 v.

Yü Min-chung 于敏中 et al., *Kuo-ch'ao kung-shih* 國朝宮史 (History of Ch'ing Palaces), Tientsin, Tung-fang hsüeh-hui 東方學會, 1925, 36 ch., 8 v.

Yüan Mei 袁枚, *Hsiao-ts'ang shan-fang wen-chi* 小倉山房文集 (Works of the Hsiao-ts'ang Studio), in the same author's *Sui-yüan ch'üan-chi* 隨園文集 (Complete Works of Sui-yüan), Shanghai, Wen-ming Shu-chü 文明書局, 1918, 35 ch., 35 v.

Yün-nan t'ung-chih 雲南通志 (Gazetteer of Yunnan), ed. by Ts'en Yü-ying 岑毓英, 1894 ed., 242+41+10 ch., 220 v.

Yung-cheng Emperor. See Ch'ing shih-tsung.

B. Japanese and Korean

Abe Takeo 安部健夫, "Hakki Manshū niru no kenkyū" 八旗滿洲ニルの研究, II, ('On the Manchu niru system of the Eight Banners') *Tōa jimbun gakuhō* 東亞人文學報 (Journal of Chinese Humanities Studies) 2.2:26-90 (July 1942).

―――, "Kōsen teikai no kenkyū—Yōsei shi no isshō toshite mita" 耗羨提解の研究—雍正史の一章としてみた ('On hao-hsien'),

Tōyōshi Kenkyū 東洋史研究 (The Journal of Oriental Researches) 16.4:108-126 (March 1958).

Araki Toshikazu 荒木敏一, "Choku-shō kyōgaku no sei o tsūjite mitaru Yōsei chika no bunkyō seisaku" 直省教學の制を通じて觀たる雍正治下の文教政策 ('Emperor Yung-cheng's 雍正 educational reform'), *ibid.* 70-94.

_____, "Yōsei chika ni okeru kosahō no seiritsu" 雍正治下に於ける考差法の成立 ('The appointment of examiners and associate examiners for provincial examinations'), *ibid.* 22.3:56-72 (Dec. 1963).

_____, "Yōsei jidai ni okeru gakushinsei no kaikaku—shu toshite sono nin yōhō o chūshin to shite 雍正時代に於ける學臣制の改革—主として其任用法を中心として ('Government school inspectors 學政 in the Yung-cheng period'), *ibid.* 18.3:27-43 (Dec. 1959).

_____, "Yōsei ninen no rakō jikan to Den Bunkyō" 雍正二年の罷考事件と田文鏡 (T'ien Wen-ching 田文鏡 and boycott for state examination'), *ibid.* 15.4:100-119 (March 1957).

Chosŏn wangjo sillok 朝鮮王朝實錄 (The Veritable Records of the Yi Dynasty), Comp. by Kuksa P'yŏnch'an Wiwonhoe 國史編纂委員

會, Seoul, T'aeback-san ed., 1955-58, 48 v. Reigns of Hyŏnjong-Kyŏngjong (1660-1724).

Fujii Sosen 藤井草宣, "Shintei to bukkyō—koto ni rinsai shu" 清廷と佛教・殊に臨濟宗 (The Ch'ing court and Buddhism, especially the Lin-chi sect of Ch'an), *Ōtani Gakuhō* 大谷學報 (Journal of Buddhism and Cultural Science) 16.3:150-72 (Oct. 1935).

Haneda Hakushi Shō jukinenū Tōyōshi ronsō 羽田博士頌壽紀念東洋史論叢 ('Asiatic Studies in Honor of Toru Haneda on the Occasion of His Sixtieth Birthday'), Kyoto, Kyoto University, Tōyōshi Kenkyūkai 東洋史研究會, 1950, 1051 p.

Inoue Ichii 井上以智為, "Shinchō kyūtei shaman kyō shiden ni tsuite" 清朝宮廷薩滿教祠殿に就いて ('The Shamanistic sanctuaries in the Peking Palace'), in *ibid.*, pp.75-94.

Ishibashi Hideo 石橋秀雄, "Shinchō no Kiho kichi seisaku—Tokuni Yōsei Kenryū nenkan no seido jō ni ara wareta kichi hōkai no bōshi to kijin no kyūsai ni kansuru seisaku o chū shin toshite" 清朝の畿輔旗地政策—特に雍正乾隆年間の制度上にあらわれた旗地崩壞の防止と旗人の救濟に関する政策を中心として ('On the policies on Banner lands 旗地 in ch'i-fu

畿輔 at the middle age of Ch'ing dynasty—Particularly on the policies seen in the system in Yung-cheng 雍正 and Ch'ien-lung 乾隆 periods to prevent the ruin of Banner lands and to relieve the banner-men 旗人'), *Tōyō Gakuhō* 東洋學報 (Reports of the Oriental Society) 39.2:23-72 (Sept. 1956); 39.3:67-98 (Dec. 1956).

Ishihama Sensei kanreki kinen rombun shū 石濱先生還曆紀念論文集 ('Asiatic Studies in Honor of Juntaro Ishihama on the Occasion of His Sixtieth Birthday'), Osaka, Kansai University Institute of Oriental and Occidental Studies, 1958, v.2.

Iwami Hiroshi 岩見宏, "Yōsei jidai no kohi ni kansuru ichi kosatsu" 雍正時代の公費に関する一考察 ('Public expenditure in the reign of Emperor Yung-cheng'), *Tōyōshi Kenkyū* 東洋史研究 (The Journal of Oriental Researches) 15.4:65-99 (March 1957).

―――, "Yōsei nenkan no minketsu ni tsuite" 雍正年間の民欠について ('On the policies to clean up the tax arrears [mien-chien 民欠] for the Yung-cheng period'), *ibid.* 18.3:61-84 (Dec. 1959).

―――, "Yōrengin seido no sōsetsu ni tsuite" 養廉

銀制度の創設について ('On the Yang-lien-yin 養廉銀 system'), *ibid* 22.3:113-40 (Dec. 1963).

Kanda Nobuo 神田信夫, "Shinsho no bunkan ni tsuite" 清初の文館について ('Wenkuan [Archives] 文館 in the early years of Ch'ing 清'), *ibid*. 19.3:350-66 (Dec. 1960).

———, "Shinsho no gisei daijin ni tsuite" 清初の議政大臣について ('The I-cheng Ta-ch'en 議政大臣 in the earlier Ch'ing dynasty') in *Wada hakushi kanreki kinen Tōyōshi Ronsō* 和田博士還暦紀念東洋史論叢 ('Oriental Studies Presented to Sei [Kiyoshi] Wada in Celebration of His Sixtieth Birthday'), Tokyo, Kōdansha 講談社, 1951, pp.171-89.

Kano Naosada 狩野直禎, "Chin chao myao no heitei o megutte" 狆家苗の平定をめぐいて (On the suppression of Ch'ing-chia Miao), *Tōyōshi Kenkyū* 東洋史研究 (The Journal of Oriental Researches) 18.3:85-98 (Dec. 1959).

Kawakubo Teirō 川久保悌郎, "Shindai Manshū ni okeru shōka no zokusei ni tsuite" 清代満洲における燒堝の簇生について ('On the prosperity of shao-kuo 燒鍋 in Manchuria during the Ch'ing period') in *Wada Hakushi koki kinen Tōyōshi ronsō* 和田博士古稀紀念東洋史論叢 ('Oriental Studies Presented to

Sei Kiyoshi Wada'), Tokyo, Kōdansha 講談社, 1960, pp.303-13.

Miyazaki Ichisada 宮崎市定, *Ajia-shi kenkyū* アジア史研究 (A Study of Asian History), Kyoto, Kyoto University, Tōyōshi Kenkyūkai 東洋史研究會, 1963, v.3, 426 p.

―――, "Shinchō ni okeru kokugo mondai no ichimen" 清朝に於ける國語問題の一面 ('A view of the problem of national language in the Ch'ing dynasty') in *ibid.*, pp.333-93.

―――, "Shindai no shori to bakuyu—toku ni Yōsei chō o chūshin toshite" 清代の胥吏と幕友—特に雍正朝を中心として ('The clerk and the private secretary in the Ch'ing dynasty'), *Tōyōshi Kenkyū* 東洋史研究 (The Journal of Oriental Researches) 16.3:1-28 (Nov. 1957).

―――, "Yōsei jidai chihō seiji no jitsujō—Shuhi Yushi to Kashū kōan" 雍正時代地方政治實狀—硃批諭旨と鹿洲公案 ('The real state of the local administration in the Yung-cheng 雍正 period'), *ibid.* 18.3:1-26 (Dec. 1959).

―――, *Yōsei-tei, Chūgoku no dokusai kunshu* 雍正帝，中國の獨裁君主. ('The Yung-cheng Emperor—China's Autocratic Ruler'), Tokyo, Iwanami Shoten 岩波書店, 1950, 168 p.

Narakino Shimesu 楢木野宣, "Shindai jūyō shokukan Man-Kan hiritsu no hendō" 清代重要職官満漢比率の變動 (Changes in the ratio of important Manchu and Chinese officials during the Ch'ing dynasty), *Gunma Daigaku kiyō* 群馬大學紀要 (Bulletin of Gunma University) 17:47-70 (1967).

Ono Kazuko 小野和子, "Shin sho no shiso tōsei o megutte" 清初の思想統制をめぐいて ('On the regulation of thoughts for the early Ch'ing'), *Tōyōshi Kenkyū* 東洋史研究 (The Journal of Oriental Researches) 18.3:99-123 (Dec. 1959).

Onogawa Hidemi 小野川秀美, "Yōsei tei to Taigi kakumei-roku" 雍正帝と大義覺迷錄 ('Emperor Yung-cheng and *Ta-i Chüeh-mi Lu*'), *ibid.* 16.4:95-107 (March 1958).

Oshibuchi Hajime 鴛淵一, "Shinsho ni okeru Shin shitsu nai fun ni kansuru kenkyū—Tokuni Taisō o chūshin toshite" 清初に於る清室内紛に関する研究—特に太宗を中心として ('The internal strife of the Ch'ing ruling house in the early years of the Ch'ing dynasty, with special reference to Emperor T'ai-tsung'), in *Ishihama Sensei kanreki kinen rombun shū* 石濱先生還曆紀念論文集 ('Asiatic Studies in Honor of Juntaro Ishihama on the Occasion of

His Sixtieth Birthday'), Osaka, 1958, v.2, pp. 1-24.

Otake Fumio 小竹文夫, "Shindai no kōchi kaikon—kōchi zouka ni tsukite" 清代の荒地開墾—耕地増加に就きて (Reclamation works of the Ch'ing dynasty—the increase of the cultivated land), *Shina Kenkyū* 支那研究 24:65-131 (Dec. 1930).

Saeki Tomi 佐伯富, *Shindai ensei no kenkyū* 清代塩政の研究 ('A Study on the Salt Administration under the Ch'ing Dynasty'), Kyoto, Tōyōshi Kenkyūkai 東洋史研究會, 1956, 400 p.

―――, "Shindai ni okeru sōshō seido" 清代における奏銷制度 ('The tsou-hsiao 奏銷 system of the Ch'ing dynasty'), *Tōyōshi Kenkyū* 東洋史研究 (The Journal of Oriental Researches) 22.3:25-55 (Dec. 1963).

―――, "Shindai Yōsei chō ni okeru tsūka mondai" 清代雍正朝における通貨問題 ('The currency problem in the Yung-cheng 雍正 period'), *ibid*. 18.3:142-211 (Dec. 1959).

―――, "Shindai Yōsei chō ni okeru yōrengin no kenkyū—chihō zaisei no seiritsu o megutte" 清代雍正朝における養廉銀の研究—地方財政の成立をめぐって ('A study on the yang-lian yin 養廉銀 at the Yong-zheng 雍正

period, Qing dynasty—concerning the organization of local finance'), *Tōyōshi Kenkyū* 東洋史研究 (The Journal of Oriental Researches) 29.1:30-60 (June 1970); 29.2 and 3:56-117 (Dec. 1970); 30.4:55-92 (March 1972).

Sano Manabu 佐野學, *Kokka to shakai* 國家と社會 (State and Society), in the same author's *Shinchō shakai shi* 清朝社會史 (Social History of the Ch'ing Dynasty), Tokyo, Bunkyūdō 文求堂, 1947, Part 1, v.1.

Sonoda Kazuki 園田一龜, *Zen Shin rekidai kōtei no tōjun* 前清歷代皇帝之東巡 (Eastern Trips of Early Ch'ing Emperors), Mukden 奉天, Seikyo Jihōsha 盛京時報社, 1930, 178 p.

Terada Takanobu 寺田隆信, "Yōsei tei no semmin kaihō rei ni tsuite" 雍正帝の賤民開放令について('On the emancipation of the lower orders by the Yung-cheng emperor'), *Tōyōshi Kenkyū* 東洋史研究 (The Journal of Oriental Researches) 18.3:124-41 (Dec. 1959).

Tsukamoto Shunkō 塚本俊孝, "Yōsei tei no bukkyō kyōdan e no kunkai" 雍正帝の佛教團への訓誨 ('Emperor Yung-cheng's admonition against the Buddhist Order'), *Indogaku bukkyōgaku Kenkyū* 印度學佛教學研究 (Journal of

Indian and Buddhist Studies) 9.1:323-26 (Jan. 1961).

───, "Yōsei tei no ju-butsu-do sankyō ittaikan" 雍正帝の儒佛道三教一體觀 ('The Yung-cheng Emperor's view of Confucianism, Buddhism, and Taoism as a single unity'), *Tōyōshi Kenkyū* 東洋史研究 (The Journal of Oriental Researches) 18.3:44-60 (Dec. 1959).

Wada Hakushi kanreki kinen Tōyōshi ronsō 和田博士還曆紀念東洋史論叢 ('Oriental Studies Presented to Sei [Kiyoshi] Wada in Celebration of His Sixtieth Birthday'), Tokyo, Kōdansha 講談社, 1951, 806+71 p.

Wada Hakushi koki kinen Tōyōshi ronsō 和田博士古稀紀念東洋史論叢 ('Oriental Studies Presented to Sei Kiyoshi Wada'), Tokyo, Kōdansha 講談社, 1960, 1076+54 p.

Yazawa Toshihiko 矢澤利彦, "Sodo ikka ni tsuite" 蘇努一家について ('Reconstruction of the family of Sunu'), in *ibid.*, pp. 981-91.

Yokoyama Hiroo 橫山裕男, "Kampū seizoku shih kō" 觀風整俗使攷 ('On the Kuan-feng cheng-su shih 觀風整俗使 or Inspector-General of Morale') *Tōyōshi Kenkyū* 東洋史研究 (The Journal of Oriental Researches) 22.3:94-112 (Dec. 1963).

Yuasa Yukihiko 湯淺幸孫, "Ryo Banson no chosaku to sono seiji" 呂晚村の著作とその政治 ('On the works and political ideas of Lo-wan-sun'), *Geirin* 藝林 (The Journal of Cultural Sciences) 4.1:62-74 (Feb. 1953).

C. *European*

Backhouse, Sir Edmund Trelawny, and Bland, John Otway Percy, *Annals and Memoirs of the Court of Peking (From the 16th to the 20th Century)*, London, William Heinemann, 1914, 531 p.

Baller, F.W., trans., *The Sacred Edict*, 2nd ed., Shanghai, American Presbyterian Mission Press, 1907, 216 p.

Beasley, W.G., and Pulleyblank, E.G., ed., *Historians of China and Japan*, London, Oxford University Press, 1961, 351 p.

Bouvet, Père Joachim, *History of Cang-Hy: The Present Emperor of China*, London, 1699, 111 p.

Boxer, C.R., "Jesuits at the court of Peking, 1601-1775," *History Today* 7.9:580-89 (Sept. 1957).

Brucker, Joseph, "La mission de Chine de 1722 à 1735," *Revue des questions historiques* 29:491-532 (1881).

Busch, Heinrich, "The Tung-lin academy and its political and philosophical significance," *Monumenta Serica* 14:1-163 (1949-1955).

Chao, Wei-pang, "A Lolo legend concerning the origin

of the torch festival," *Studia Serica* 9, part 2: 95-104 (1950).

Ch'en, Kenneth K.S., *Buddhism in China: A Historical Survey*, Princeton, Princeton University Press, 1964, 560 p.

Ch'ü, T'ung-tsu, *Law and Society in Traditional China*, Paris, Mouton, 1961, 304 p.

———, *Local Government in China under the Ch'ing*, Cambridge, Harvard University Press, 1962, 360 p.

Cohen, Paul A., *China and Christianity: The Missionary Movement and the Growth of Chinese Antiforeignism, 1860-1870*, Cambridge, Harvard University Press, 1963, 392 p.

Corradini, Piero, "Civil administration at the beginning of the Manchu dynasty: A note on the establishment of the six ministries (liu-pu)," *Oriens Extremus* 9.2:133-38 (Dec. 1962).

———, "Riforme nell'amministrazione centrale cinese durante il periodo Yung-cheng (1723-1736): Note sull'istituzione del Chün-chi-ch'u (軍機處)," *Rivista degli Studi Orientali* 36:135-45 (1961).

Danby, Hope, *The Garden of Perfect Brightness: The History of the Yüan Ming Yüan and of the Emperors Who Lived There*, London, Williams and Norgate Ltd., 1950, 239 p.

Dawson, Raymond, ed., *The Legacy of China*, Oxford, England, The Clarendon Press, 1964, 392 p.

_____, "The value of the study of Chinese civilization," in *ibid.*, pp.363-80.

de Bary, Wm. Theodore, "Some common tendencies in Neo-Confucianism," in David S. Nivison and Arthur F. Wright, ed., *Confucianism in Action*, Stanford, Stanford University Press, 1959, pp. 25-49.

_____, Chan, Wing-tsit, and Watson, Burton, ed., *Sources of Chinese Tradition*, New York, Columbia University Press, 1960, 976 p.

Du Halde, Jean Baptiste, *The General History of China*, trans. by Richard Brookes, 3rd ed., London, J. Watts, 1741, 4 v.

Eberhard, Wolfram, "The political function of astronomy and astronomers in Han China," in John King Fairbank, ed., *Chinese Thought and Institutions*, Chicago, University of Chicago Press, 1957, pp.33-70.

ECCP: Hummel, Arthur W., ed., *Eminent Chinese of the Ch'ing Period (1644-1912)*, Washington, D.C., United States Government Printing Office, 1943-1944, 2 v.

Eisenstadt, S.N., *The Political Systems of Empires*, London, The Free Press of Glencoe, Collier-Macmillan Ltd., 1963, 524 p.

_____, "Religious organizations and political process in centralized empires," *Journal of Asian Studies* 21.3:271-94 (May 1962).

Elia, Paschal M. de, S.J., *The Catholic Missions in China: A Short Sketch of the History of the Catholic Church in China from the Earliest Records to Our Own Days*, Shanghai, Commercial Press, 1934, 122 p.

Fairbank, John King, ed., *Chinese Thought and Institutions*, Chicago, University of Chicago Press, 1957, 438 p.

_____, Reischauer, Edwin O., and Craig, Albert M., *East Asia: The Modern Transformation*, Boston, Houghton Mifflin, 1965, 955 p.

_____, and Teng, Ssu-yü, *Ch'ing Administration: Three Studies*, Cambridge, Harvard University Press, 1960, 218 p.

Fang, Chaoying, "A technique for estimating the numerical strength of the early Manchu military forces," *Harvard Journal of Asiatic Studies* 13: 192-215 (1950).

Favier, Alphonse, *Péking: Histoire et description*, Peking, 1897, 562 p.

Feuerwerker, Albert, Murphey, Rhoads, and Wright, Mary C., ed., *Approaches to Modern Chinese History*, Berkeley, University of California Press, 1967, 356 p.

Folsom, Kenneth E., *Friends, Guests, and Colleagues:*

The Mu-fu System in the Late Ch'ing Period, Berkeley, University of California Press, 1968, 234 p.

Friedrich, Carl J., *Man and His Government: An Empirical Theory of Politics*, New York, McGraw-Hill, 1963, 737 p.

———, and Brzezinski, Zbigniew K., *Totalitarian Dictatorship and Autocracy*, 2nd ed., Cambridge, Harvard University Press, 1965, 439 p.

Giles, Herbert A., *China and the Manchus*, Cambridge, Cambridge University Press, 1912, 148 p.

Goodrich, Luther Carrington, *The Literary Inquisition of Ch'ien-lung*, 2nd ed., New York, Paragon Book Reprint Corp., 1966, 275 p.

Hall, John, "Notes on early Ch'ing copper trade with Japan," *Harvard Journal of Asiatic Studies* 14: 444-61 (1949).

Han, Fei, *The Complete Works of Han Fei Tzu: A Classic of Chinese Legalism*, trans. into English by W.K. Liao, London, Arthur Probsthain, 1939, 2 v.

Harvard Tercentenary Conference of Arts and Sciences, ed., *Authority and the Individual*, Cambridge, Harvard University Press, 1937, 371 p.

Ho, Alfred Kuo-liang, "The Grand Council in the Ch'ing dynasty," *Far Eastern Quarterly* 11.2:167-82 (Feb. 1952).

Ho, Ping-ti, *The Ladder of Success in Imperial China:*

Aspects of Social Mobility, 1368-1911, New York, Columbia University Press, 1962, 385 p.

―――――, "Salient aspects of China's heritage" in Ping-ti Ho and Tang Tsou, ed., *China in Crisis*: vol. I, *China's Heritage and the Communist Political System*, I, Chicago, University of Chicago Press, 1968, pp. 1-37.

―――――, "The significance of the Ch'ing period in Chinese history," *Journal of Asian Studies* 26.2: 189-95 (Feb. 1967).

―――――, *Studies on the Population of China, 1368-1953*, Cambridge, Harvard University Press, 1959, 341 p.

―――――, and Tsou, Tang, ed., *China in Crisis*: vol. 1, *China's Heritage and the Communist Political System*, I, Chicago, University of Chicago Press, 1968, 447 p.

Hoang, Pierre, *Mélanges sur l'administration*, Shanghai, Imprimerie de la Mission Catholique, 1902, 233 p.

Hsiao, Kung-chuan, *Rural China: Imperial Control in the Nineteenth Century*, Seattle, University of Washington Press, 1960, paperback, 783 p.

Hsieh, Pao-chao, *The Government of China (1644-1911)*, Baltimore, Johns Hopkins University Press, 1925, 414 p.

Huang, Pei, "Aspects of Ch'ing autocracy: An institutional study, 1644-1735," *Tsing Hua Journal of*

Chinese Studies, new series 6.1-2:105-49 (Dec. 1967).

———, "A Study of the Yung-cheng Period, 1723-1735: A Political Phase," Ph.D. thesis, Indiana University, Bloomington, Indiana, 1963.

———, "Five major sources for the Yung-cheng period, 1723-1735," *Journal of Asian Studies* 27.4:847-57 (Aug. 1968).

———, "[A Review of] Ch'ing-tai Chün-chi ch'u tsu-chih chi chih-chang chih yen-chiu" (A Study of the Organization and Function of the Grand Council of the Ch'ing Dynasty) by Fu Tsung-mao, *Harvard Journal of Asiatic Studies* 30:248-256 (1970).

———, "[A Review of] Communication and Imperial Control in China: Evolution of the Palace Memorial System, 1693-1735, by Silas H.L. Wu," *Harvard Journal of Asiatic Studies* 31:323-332 (1971).

Hucker, Charles O., *The Censorial System of Ming China*, Stanford, Stanford University Press, 1966, 406 p.

———, "Confucianism and the Chinese censorial system," in Arthur F. Wright, ed., *Confucianism and Chinese Civilization*, New York, Atheneum, 1964, pp.50-76.

———, "Governmental organization of the Ming dynasty," *Harvard Journal of Asiatic Studies*

21:1-66 (Dec. 1958).

———, *The Traditional Chinese State in Ming Times (1368-1644)*, Tucson, University of Arizona Press, 1961, 85 p.

———, "The Tung-lin movement of the late Ming period," in John K. Fairbank, ed., *Chinese Thought and Institutions*, Chicago, University of Chicago Press, 1957, pp.132-163.

Hummel, W. Arthur, ed., see *ECCP*.

International Association of Historians of Asia, Second Biennial Conference, Taipei, 1962, *Proceedings*, Taipei, 1963(?), 826 p. + 252 p.

Jesuits, *Travels of the Jesuits into Various Parts of the World: Particularly China and the East-Indies*, trans. into English by John Lockman, 2nd ed., London, 1743, 2 v.

Kahn, Harold L., *Monarchy in the Emperor's Eyes: Image and Reality in the Ch'ien-lung Reign*, Cambridge, Harvard University Press, 1971, 314 p.

———, "Some mid-Ch'ing views of the monarchy," *Journal of Asian Studies* 24.2:229-43 (Feb. 1965).

Kelsen, Hans, "Centralization and decentralization," in Harvard Tercentenary Conference of Arts and Sciences, ed., *Authority and the Individual*,

Cambridge, Harvard University Press, 1937, pp. 210-39.

Kessler, Lawrence D., "Chinese scholars and the early Manchu state," *Harvard Journal of Asiatic Studies* 31:179-200 (1971).

———, "Ethnic composition of provincial leadership during the Ch'ing dynasty," *Journal of Asian Studies* 28.3:489-511 (May 1969).

Kracke, Edward A., Jr., "The Chinese and the art of government" in Raymond Dawson, ed., *The Legacy of China*, Oxford, The Clarendon Press, 1964, pp. 309-39.

Lattimore, Owen, *Inner Asian Frontiers of China*, Boston, Beacon Press, 1962, paperback, 585 p.

Legge, James, trans., *Chinese Classics*, Hong Kong, University of Hong Kong Press, 1960, vols.3-4.

Lettres édifiantes et curieuses: écrites des missions étrangères, mémoires de la Chine, nouvelle édition, Toulouse, 1811, vols. 19-24.

Levenson, Joseph R., *Confucian China and Its Modern Fate*: vol.2, *The Problem of Monarchical Decay*; vol.3, *The Problem of Historical Significance*, Berkeley, University of California Press, 1964-1965.

———, "Ill wind in the well-field: The erosion of the Confucian ground of controversy," in Arthur

F. Wright, ed., *The Confucian Persuasion*, Stanford, Stanford University Press, 1960, pp. 268-87.

_____, "The suggestiveness of vestige: Confucianism and monarchy at the last" in David S. Nivison and Arthur F. Wright, ed., *Confucianism in Action*, Stanford, Stanford University Press, 1959, pp.244-67.

Lu, Lien-tching, *Les greniers publics de prévoyance sous la dynastie de Ts'ing*, Paris, Jouve & Cie, 1932, 212 p.

Machiavelli, Niccolò, *The Prince*, trans. into English by George Bull, Baltimore, Penguin Books Inc., 1961, 153 p.

Mailla, Joseph Anne Marie Moyria de, *Histoire générale de la Chine, ou annales de cet empire*, Paris, R.D. Pierres, 1777-1785, v.11, 610 p.

Michael, Franz, *The Origin of Manchu Rule in China: Frontier and Bureaucracy as Interacting Forces in the Chinese Empire*, New York, Octagon Books Inc., 1965, 127 p.

Milne, William, trans., *The Sacred Edict, Containing Sixteen Maxims of the Emperor Kang-he, Amplified by His Son, The Emperor Yoong-ching; Together with a Paraphrase on the Whole, by a Mandarin*, London, Black, Kingsbury, Parbury, & Allen, 1817, 299 p.

Mote, Frederick W., "The growth of Chinese despotism:

A critique of Wittfogel's theory of oriental despotism as applied to China," *Oriens Extremus* 8.1:1-41 (Aug. 1961).

Nivison, David S., "Ho-shen and his accusers: Ideology and political behavior in the eighteenth century" in David S. Nivison and Arthur F. Wright, eds., *Confucianism in Action*, Stanford, Stanford University Press, 1959, pp. 209-243.

————, and Wright, Arthur F., eds., *Confucianism in Action*, Stanford, Stanford University Press, 1959, 390 p.

Pan Ku, *History of the Former Han Dynasty*, trans. by Homer H. Dubs, Baltimore, Waverly Press, 1944, vol.2, 426 p.

Reischauer, Edwin O. and Fairbank, John King, *East Asia: The Great Tradition*, Boston, Houghton Mifflin, 1960, 739 p.

Ripa, Matteo, *Memoirs of Father Ripa during Thirteen Years' Residence at the Court of Peking in the Service of the Emperor of China*, trans. into English by Fortunato Prandi, new ed., London, John Murray, 1855, 160 p.

Rosenberg, Hans, *Bureaucracy, Aristocracy, and Autocracy: The Prussian Experience, 1660-1815*, Boston, Beacon Press, paperback, 1966, 237 p.

Ross, Rev. John, *The Manchus, or the Reigning Dynasty of China: Their Rise and Progress*, Paisley,

Scotland, J. & R. Parlane, 1880, 751 p.

Rosso, Antonio Sisto, *Apostolic Legations to China of the Eighteenth Century*, South Pasadena, Calif., P.D. and Ione Perkins, 1948, 502 p.

Rowbotham, Arnold H., *Missionary and Mandarin: The Jesuits at the Court of China*, Berkeley, University of California Press, 1942, 374 p.

Ruey, Yih-fu, "The Miao: Their origin and southward migration," in International Association of Historians of Asia, Second Biennial Conference, Taipei, 1962, *Proceedings*, Taipei, 1963(?), pp.179-90.

Schwartz, Benjamin, "Some polarities in Confucian thought," in David S. Nivison and Arthur F. Wright, ed., *Confucianism in Action*, Stanford, Stanford University Press, 1959, pp.50-62.

Smith, Kent C., "O-erh-t'ai and the Yung-cheng Emperor," *Ch'ing-shih wen-t'i* (Bulletin of the Society for Ch'ing Studies) 1.8:10-15 (May 1968).

Spence, Jonathan D., *Ts'ao Yin and the K'ang-hsi Emperor, Bondservant and Master*, New Haven, Yale University Press, 1966, 329 p.

Sun, E-tu (Zen), ed. and trans., *Ch'ing Administrative Terms*, Cambridge, Harvard University Press, 1961, 421 p.

_____, "Mining labor in the Ch'ing period" in Albert Feuerwerker *et al.*, ed., *Approaches to*

Modern Chinese History, Berkeley, University of California Press, 1967, pp.45-67.

Teng, Ssu-yu, "Ming T'ai-tsu's destructive and constructive work," *Chinese Culture* 8.3:14-38 (Sept. 1967).

Thomas, A., *Histoire de la mission de Pékin: Depuis les origines jusqu'à l'arrivée des lazaristes*, Paris, Imprimerie de la Presse Française, 1923, 463 p.

Walker, Richard L., "The control system of the Chinese government," *Far Eastern Quarterly* 7.1: 2-21 (Nov. 1947).

Wang, Yeh-chien, "The fiscal importance of the land tax during the Ch'ing period," *Journal of Asian Studies* 30.4:829-42 (Aug. 1971).

Wang Yü-ch'üan, "An outline of the central government of the Former Han dynasty," *Harvard Journal of Asiatic Studies* 12:134-87 (1949).

———, "The rise of land tax and the fall of dynasties in Chinese history," *Pacific Affairs* 9:201-20 (1936).

Weber, Max, *The Religion of China: Confucianism and Taoism*, trans. into English and ed. by Hans H. Gerth, Glencoe, Ill., Free Press, 1951, 308 p.

———, *The Theory of Social and Economic Organization*, trans. by A.M. Henderson and Talcott Parsons, Glencoe, Ill., Free Press, 1947, 436 p.

Wiens, Harold J., *China's March toward the Tropics*,

Hamden, Conn., Shoe String Press, 1954, 441 p.

Wilhelm, Hellmut, "The po-hsüeh hung-ju examination of 1679," *Journal of the American Oriental Society* 71:60-66 (1951).

Williams, Charles Harold, *The Making of the Tudor Despotism*, London, Thomas Nelson, 1935, 280 p.

Wittfogel, Karl A., *Oriental Despotism: A Comparative Study of Total Power*, New Haven, Yale University Press, 1964, paperback, 556 p.

Wong, George H.C., "The anti-Christian movement in China: Late Ming and early Ch'ing," *Tsing Hua Journal of Chinese Studies*, new series 3.1:187-222 (May 1962).

Wright, Arthur F., *The Confucian Persuasion*, Stanford, Stanford University Press, 1960, 390 p.

———, "Comments by Arthur Frederick Wright," in Ping-ti Ho and Tang Tsou, ed., *China in Crisis:* vol. I, *China's Heritage and the Communist Political System*, I, Chicago, University of Chicago Press, 1968, pp.38-41.

———, *Confucianism and Chinese Civilization*, New York, Atheneum, 1964, 362 p.

———, "The formation of Sui ideology, 581-604," in John K. Fairbank, ed., *Chinese Thought and Institutions*, Chicago, University of Chicago Press, 1957, pp.71-104.

Wu, Silas H.L., *Communication and Imperial Control in China: Evolution of the Palace Memorial System, 1693-1735*, Cambridge, Harvard University Press, 1970, 204 p.

———, "Emperors at work: the daily schedules of the K'ang-hsi and Yung-cheng Emperors 1661-1735," *Tsing Hua Journal of Chinese Studies*, new series 8.1-2:210-26 (Aug. 1970).

———, "The memorial systems of the Ch'ing dynasty (1644-1911)," *Harvard Journal of Asiatic Studies* 27:7-75 (1967).

Yang, C.K., *Religion in Chinese Society: A Study of Contemporary Social Functions of Religion and Some of Their Historical Factors*, Berkeley, University of California Press, 1967, paperback, 473 p.

———, "Some characteristics of Chinese bureaucratic behavior," in David S. Nivison and Arthur F. Wright, ed., *Confucianism in Action*, Stanford, Stanford University Press, 1959, pp. 134-164.

Yang, Lien-sheng, "The organization of Chinese official historiography: Principles and methods of the standard histories from the T'ang through the Ming dynasty," in W.G. Beasley and E.G. Pulleyblank, ed., *Historians of China and Japan*, London, Oxford University Press, 1961, pp.44-59.

II. *Works Consulted but Not Cited in the Footnotes*

Bodde, Derk and Morris, Clarence, trans. and comp., *Law in Imperial China: Exemplified by 190 Ch'ing Dynasty Cases*, Cambridge, Harvard University Press, 1967, 615 p.

Brandt, J. Van den, *Les lazaristes en Chine, 1697-1935: Notes biographiques recueillies et mises à jour*, Peiping, Imprimerie des lazaristes, 1936, 321 p.

Brunnert, H.S. and Hagelstron, V.V., *Present Day Political Organization of China*, rev. by N. Th Kolessoff and trans. by A. Beltchenko and E.E. Moran, Taipei, 1960(?), 572 p.

Chang, Chung-li, *The Chinese Gentry: Studies on Their Role in Nineteenth-Century Chinese Society*, Seattle, University of Washington Press, 1955, 250 p.

Chang, Po-ch'üan 張博泉, "Kuan-i ching-t'ien chih-tu wen-t'i ti t'an-t'ao" 關於井田制度問題的探討 (A discussion about the problem of the ching-t'ien system), *Wen Shi Zhe* [Wen-shih-che] 文史哲, 7:1-13 (July 1957).

Chang Te-tse 張德澤, "Chün-chi ch'u chi ch'i tang-an" 軍機處及其檔案 (The Grand Council and its archives), in Ku-kung Po-wu Yüan 故宮博物院, comp., *Wen-hsien lun-ts'ung* 文獻論叢 (Collected Articles from the Historical Records Office), Peiping, Palace

Museum, 1936, pp.57-84.

Ch'en Chieh-hsien 陳捷先, "K'ang-hsi ch'ao tsou-che yü chu-p'i yen-chiu" 康熙朝奏摺與硃批研究 ('Vermilion endorsement in K'ang-hsi period'), *Chung-kuo li-shih hsüeh-hui shih-hsüeh chi-k'an* 中國歷史學會史學集刊 (Bulletin of Chinese Historical Association) 3:127-41 (May 1971).

―――, "Lüeh-lun Ch'ing Shih-tsung chih hsing-ke" 略論清世宗之性格 (A brief discussion of the character of Emperor Shih-tsung of the Ch'ing dynasty), *Yu-shih hsüeh-chih* 幼獅學誌 (The Youth Quarterly) 9.3:1-22 (Sept. 1970).

―――, "A study of the succession to the throne in the Ch'ing dynasty," presented to the International Association of Historians of Asia, 3rd Biennial Conference, Hong Kong, 1964. Paper no. 16, mimeographed, 8 p.

Ch'en Fu-lin 陳福霖, "Pa-ch'i ping-chih k'ao-lüeh" 八旗兵制攷略 (A brief study of the military system of the Eight Banners), *Hsiang-kang ta-hsüeh li-shih hsüeh-hui nien-pao* 香港大學歷史學會年報 (History Society Annual, University of Hong Kong) 1:17-24 (1960).

Ch'en Hsü-ching 陳序經, *Tan-min ti yen-chiu* 蛋民的研究 (Studies on the Tankas), Shanghai, Commercial Press, 1936, 212 p.

Chen, Shao-kuan, *The System of Taxation on China in the Tsing Dynasty, 1644-1911*, New York, Columbia University Press, 1914, 225 p.

Ch'en Teng-yüan 陳登原, *Chung-kuo t'ien-fu shih* 中國田賦史 (History of Land Taxes in China), Shanghai, Commercial Press, 1936, 268 p.

Ch'en Wen-shih 陳文石, "Man-chou pa-ch'i niu-lu ti kou-ch'eng" 滿洲八旗牛彔的構成 (Formation of the Manchu niru), *Ta-lu tsa-chih* 大陸雜誌 (The Continent Magazine) 31.9: 14-18 (Nov. 15, 1965); 31.10:26-30 (Nov. 30, 1965).

Ch'en Yüan 陳垣, "Yung-ch'ien chien feng t'ien-chu chiao chih tsung-shih" 雍乾間奉天主教之宗室 ('De Sunu Tehp'ei duobus membris catholicis familiae imperatoris saeculi decimi octavi'), *Fu-jen hsüeh-chih* 輔仁學誌, 3.2:1-36 (July 1932).

Cheng T'ien-t'ing 鄭天挺, "Ch'ing ju-kuan chien Man-chou tsu ti she-hui hsing-chih" 清入關前滿洲族的社會性質 ('Nature of the society of the Manchus before the Ch'ing conquest'). *Lishi Yanjiu* [Li-shih yen-chiu] 歷史研究 (Journal of Historical Studies) 6:87-96 (Dec. 1962).

———, *Ch'ing-shih t'an-wei* 清史探微 (Some Critical Notes on the History of the Ch'ing),

Bibliography

    Tu-li Ch'u-pan She 獨立出版社, 1946, 134 p.

Chien Po-tsan 翦伯贊, Li-shih wen-ti lun-ts'ung 歷史問題論叢 (Collected Papers on Historical Problems), Peking, San-lien Shu-tien 三聯書店, 1956, 196 p.

―――――, "Lun shih-pa shih-chi shang-pan ch'i chung-kuo she-hui ching-chi ti hsing-chih..." 論十八世紀上半期中國社會經濟的性質... ('The social-economical character of China in the first half of eighteenth century...'), Pe-ching ta-hsüeh hsüeh-pao: Jen-wen k'o-hsüeh 北京大學學報：人文科學 (Journal of Peking University: Humanity Science) 2:79-124 (Nov. 1955).

Ch'in-ting li-pu ch'u-feng tse-li 欽定吏部處分則例 (Regulations about the Board of Civil Appointment), Yung-cheng ed. 雍正刊本, 57 ch., 26 v.

Ch'in-ting ta-Ch'ing hui-tien 欽定大清會典 (Collected Statutes of the Ch'ing Dynasty), compiled under the imperial auspices of Ch'ing Kao-tsung, 1764 ed., 100 ch., 120 v.

Ch'in-ting tsung-shih wang-kung kung-chi piao-chuan 欽定宗室王公功績表傳 (Tables and Biographies of the Nobles of the Imperial Clan), Peking, 1781, 13 ch., 8 v.

Ch'ing-ju lieh-chuan 清儒列傳 (Biographies of

Ch'ing Scholars), manuscript, n.d., unpaginated, 12 v.

Ch'ing-shih kao 清史稿 (Draft History of the Ch'ing Dynasty), comp. by Chao Erh-sun 趙爾巽 *et al.*, Peking, 1928, 534 ch., 132 v.

Ch'ing-shih lieh-chuan 清史列傳 (Biographical Series of the Ch'ing Dynasty), Shanghai, Chung-hua Shu-chü 中華書局, 1928, 80 ch., 80 v.

Ch'ing Shih-tsung 清世宗, *Ching-hai i-ti* 經海一滴 (Extracts of Buddhist Sutras), Palace ed. 殿本, 1735, 6 ch., 6 v.

_____, "Ch'ing Shih-tsung kuan-i fo-hsüeh chih yü-chih" 清世宗關於佛學之諭旨 (The Yung-cheng Emperor's Decrees on Buddhism), *Wen-hsien ts'ung-pien* 文獻叢編 (Collectanea from the Historical Records Office), no. 3 (May 1930); no. 4 (June 1930). With individual pagination.

_____, *Tsung-ching lu ta-kang* 宗鏡錄大綱 (An Outline of the Mirror for Ch'an Buddhists), Palace ed. 殿本, 1735, 20 ch., 4 v.

Chuan Han-sheng 全漢昇 and Wang Yeh-chien 王業鍵, "Ch'ing chung-yeh i-ch'ien chiang-che mi-chia ti pien-tung ch'ü-shih" 清中葉以前江浙米價的變動趨勢 ('Fluctuation trends of the rice price in Kiangsu and Chekiang before the middle of the Ch'ing dynasty'), *Bulletin of the Institute of History and Philology, Academia Sinica*, extra 4.1:351-358 (July 1960).

Chuang Chi-fa 莊吉發, "Ch'ing-ch'u tsou-che chih-tu ch'i-yüan k'ao" 清初奏摺制度起源考 ('The origin of the memorial system in the Ch'ing dynasty'), *Shih-huo yüeh-k'an* 食貨月刊 (Shih-huo Monthly) 4.1-2:13-22 (May 1974).

Commeaux, Charles, *De K'ang Hi à K'ien Long; L'âge d'or des Ts'ing (1662-1796)*, Paris, Les Belles Lettres, 1957, 181 p.

Eberhard, Wolfram, *The Local Cultures of South and East China*, Leiden, E.J. Brill, 1968, 520 p.

Eisenstadt, S.N., "Political struggle in bureaucratic societies," *World Politics* 9.1:15-36 (Oct. 1956).

Fang, Chaoying, *The Asami Library: A Descriptive Catalogue*, edited by Elizabeth Huff, Berkeley, University of California Press, 1969, 424 p.

Fang Chaoying 房兆楹, "Ch'ing-ch'u Man-chou chia-t'ing li ti fen-chia tzu ho wei fen-chia tzu" 清初滿洲家庭裡的分家子和未分家子 ('The practice of ultimogeniture in early Manchu dynasty'), in Pei-ta Wen-hsüeh Yüan 北大文學院 ed., *Pei-ching ta-hsüeh wu-shih chou-nien chi-nien lun-wen chi* 北京大學五十週年紀念論文集 ('Fiftieth Anniversary Papers of the National Peking

University'), Peiping, Pei-ta Wen-hsüeh Yüan 北大文學院, 1948, no.3, pp.1-16.

_____, and Tu Lienche 杜聯喆, *Tseng-chiao Ch'ing-ch'ao chin-shih t'i-ming pei-lu* 增校清朝進士題名碑錄 (A Critical List of the Holders of the Chin-shih Degree under the Ch'ing Dynasty), Harvard-Yenching Institute Sinological Index Series, Supplement no. 19, Peiping, Harvard-Yenching Institute 燕京學社, 1941, 434 p.

Fang Kuan-ch'eng 方觀承 et al., *Liang-che hai-t'ang t'ung-chih* 兩浙海塘通志 (Gazetteer of the Coast of Chekiang Province), 1750 ed., 20 ch., 6 v.

Fei, Hsiao-t'ung, "Peasantry and gentry: An interpretation of Chinese social structure and its changes," *American Journal of Sociology* 52:1-17 (1946-1947).

Feng, Han-yi and Shryock, J.K., "The historic origins of the Lolo," *Harvard Journal of Asiatic Studies* 3:103-27 (1938).

Feng Yu-lan 馮友蘭, *Chung-kuo che-hsüeh shih* 中國哲學史 (History of Chinese Philosophy), Chungking, Commercial Press, 1944, 2 v.

Freemen, Mansfield, "The Ch'ing dynasty criticism of Sung political-philosophy," *Journal of the North*

China Branch, Royal Asiatic Society 59:78-110 (1928).

Fu Jen-kan 傅任敢, "Yung-cheng nien-chien I-ta-li ti Chung-kuo hsüeh-yüan 雍正年間意大利的中國學院 (The Chinese academy in Italy during the Yung-cheng period), *Chung-hua Chiao-yü Chieh* 中華教育界 (Journal of Chinese Education) 23.9:61-64. (March 1, 1936).

Fujiwara Sadamu 藤原定, "Shindai ni okeru hōken shisō to hōkensei no zanson" 清代に於ける封建思想と封建制度の残存 ('Remnants of feudal thought and the feudal system in the Ch'ing period'), *Mantetsu chōsa geppō* 満鉄調査月報 (Bulletin of the Research Bureau of the South Manchuria Railway) 20.4:1-61 (April 1940).

Hattori Unokichi 服部宇之吉, *Shinkoku tsūkō* 清國通考 (A General Account of the Ch'ing Government), Tokyo, Sanseidō 三省堂, 1905, 2 v.

Herson, Lawrence J.R., "China's imperial bureaucracy: Its direction and control," *Public Administration Review* 17.1:44-53 (Winter, 1957).

Hibbert, Eloise Talcott, *Kang-hsi, Emperor of China*, London, Kegan Paul, 1940, 298 p.

Ho Ch'o 何焯, *I-men hsien-sheng chi* 義門先生集 (Works of Ho Ch'o), Chung-hua T'u-shu Kuan 中華圖書館, 1911, 12 ch., 4 v.

Ho Ping-sung 何炳松, *Che-tung hsüeh-p'ai su-yüan* 浙東學派溯源 (Origins of the Eastern Chekiang School), Shanghai, Commercial Press, 1932, 205 p.

Ho, Ping-ti, "The salt merchants of Yang-chou: A study of commercial capitalism in eighteenth-century China," *Harvard Journal of Asiatic Studies* 17.1-2:130-168 (June 1954).

Hsi Wu-ao 席吳鰲, *Nei-ko chih* 內閣志 (An Account of the Grand Secretariat), Ts'ung-shu Chi-ch'eng ch'u-pien 叢書集成初編 ed., 9 p.

Hsia Chin 夏靳, "Yen Ch'ien-ch'iu hsien-sheng nien-p'u pu-cheng" 閻潛邱先生年譜補正 ('Supplements and corrections to the Yen Ch'ien-ch'iu nien-p'u'), *Yu-shih Hsüeh-pao* 幼獅學報 (The Youth Journal) 1.2:1-9 (April 1957).

Hsiao-heng-hsiang Shih Chu-jen 小橫香室主人, ed., *Ch'ing-ch'ao yen-shih ta-kuan* 清朝野史大觀 (Collection of Unorthodox Historical Notes on the Ch'ing Dynasty), Taipei, 1959, 5 v.

Hsiao I-shan 蕭一山, *Ch'ing-tai chün-chi ta-ch'en piao* 清代軍機大臣表 (A Chronological Table of Grand Councillors under the Ch'ing), n.p., n.d., 124 p.

Hsiao, Kung-ch'üan, "Rural control in nineteenth

century China," *Far Eastern Quarterly*, 12:173-181 (1952-1953).

Hsieh Chi-shih 謝瀡世, *Mei-chuang tsa-chu* 梅莊雜著 (Miscellaneous Writings of Mei-chuang), Chi-sheng Ts'ao-t'ang 寄生草堂刊本, 1884, 12 ch., 4 v.

Hsieh Kuo-chen 謝國楨, *Ming-Ch'ing chih-chi t'ang-she yün-tung k'ao* 明清之際黨社運動考 (A Study of Political Cliques and Literary Clubs during the Ming and the Ch'ing Dynasty), Shanghai, Commercial Press, 1934, 328 p.

Hsü Chi-ying 許霽英, "Ch'ing-shih tsa-k'ao" 清史雜考 (Miscellaneous notes on Ch'ing history), *Jen-wen yüeh k'an* 人文月刊 (Journal of Humanities) 7.10:1-3 (Dec. 1936).

Hsü Chung-shu 徐中舒, "Ching-t'ien chih-tu t'an-yüan" 井田制度探原 ('A study on the ching-t'ien system'), *Chung-kuo wen-hua yen-chiu hui-k'an* 中國文化研究彙刊 (Bulletin of Chinese Studies) 4, part 1:121-156 (Sept. 1944).

Hsü, Immanuel C.Y., *The Rise of Modern China*, New York, Oxford University Press, 1970, 830 p.

Hu, Ch'ang-tu, "The Yellow River administration in the Ch'ing dynasty," *Far Eastern Quarterly* 14.4: 505-13 (Aug. 1955).

Hu-nan t'ung-chih 湖南通志 (Gazetteer of Hunan), ed. by Tseng Kuo-ch'üan 曾國荃 and Li Han-chang 李翰章, Tsun-ching Ko 尊經閣

ed., 1885, 288+27 ch., 160 v.

I-shih 一士, "Ch'ing-ch'u wen-tzu yü yü Shen Chin-ssu" 清初文字獄與沈近思 (The literary inquisition of the early Ch'ing dynasty and Shen Chin-ssu), *Yüeh-feng* 越風, 13:27-28 (May 1936).

———, "Nei-ko t'an" 內閣談 (On the Grand Secretariat), *Chung-ho yüeh-k'an* 中和月刊 (Chung-ho Monthly) 1.6:25-42 (June 1940).

Inaba Kunsan 稻葉君山, *Shinchō Zenshi* 清朝全史 (A Complete History of the Ch'ing Dynasty), trans. into Chinese by Tan Tao 但燾, Shanghai, 1924, 2 v.

Jen-yün 忍云, "Ch'ing-tai kuan-yüan feng-mi kao-feng k'ao" 清代官員俸米誥封攷 (A study of the salaries and title-bestowal of the officials under the Ch'ing), *Pei-p'ing Ch'en-pao* 北平晨報 (Peiping Morning News), (Oct. 12, 1934), p.8.

Jenkins, Robert C., *The Jesuits in China and the Legation of Cardinal de Tournon: An Examination of Conflicting Evidence and Attempt at an Impartial Judgment*, London, David Nutt, 1894, 165 p.

Kahn, Harold L., "The education of a prince: The emperor learns his roles" in Albert Feuerwerker, Rhoads Murphey, and Mary C. Wright, ed., *Approaches to Modern Chinese History*, Berkeley,

University of California Press, 1967, pp.15-44.

Kan Ju-lai 甘汝來, *Kan Chuang-k'o kung ch'üan-chi* 甘莊恪公全集 (Complete Works of Kan Ju-lai), 1791 ed., 16 ch., 8 v.

Kanda Nobuo 神田信夫, "Shinsho no bai-roku ni tsuite" 清初の貝勒について ('On the beile of the early Ch'ing dynasty'), *Tōyō Gakuhō* 東洋學報 (Reports of the Oriental Society) 40.4:1-23 (March 1958).

―――, Matsumura Jun 松村潤, and Okada Hidehiro 岡田英弘, *Hakki tsūshi retsuden sakuin* 八旗通志列傳索引 ('Index to the Biographical Sections of Pa Ch'i T'ung Chih'), Tōyō Bunko Mambun rōtō kenkyūkai 東洋文庫滿文老檔研究會 (Seminar on Manchu History, Tōyō Bunko), Tokyo, 1964, 206 p.

Kondo Hideki 近藤秀樹, "Shindai no sensen―Gaiho sei no seiritsu" 清初の銓選―外補制の成立 ('The installation system under the Ch'ing dynasty') *Tōyōshi Kenkyū* 東洋史研究 (The Journal of Oriental Researches) 17.2:34-55 (Sept. 1958).

Kuang-hsi t'ung-chih 廣西通志 (Gazetteer of Kwangsi), ed. by Hsieh Ch'i-k'un 謝啟昆, Kwei-yüan Shu-chü 桂垣書局, 1891, 279+1 ch., 80 v.

Kuo-shih lieh-chuan 國史列傳 (National Biographical Series of the Ch'ing), n.p., n.d., 60 ch., 60 v.

Lei Hai-tsung 雷海宗, "Huang-ti chih-tu chih ch'eng-li" 皇帝制度之成立 ('Establishment of the imperial system'), *Tsing Hua Journal* 清華學報, 9.4:853-871 (Oct. 1934).

Li Chow, Chung-cheng, *L'examen provincial en Chine (hiang che) sous la dynastie des Ts'ing (de 1644 à 1911)*, Paris, Jouve et cie, 1935, 137 p.

Li, Hsiung-fei, *Les censeurs sous la dynastie Manchoue (1616-1911) en Chine*, Paris, Les Presses Modernes, 1936, 144 p.

Li Hua 李華, "Shih lun Ch'ing-tai ch'ien-ch'i ti shih-min tou-cheng" 試論清代前期的市民鬥爭 (On the struggle of the townspeople during the early Ch'ing dynasty), *Wen Shi Zhe* [Wen-shih-che] 文史哲 10:54-62 (Oct. 1957).

Li Kuang-ti 李光地, *Jung-ts'un yü-lu hsü-chi* 榕村語錄續集 (Supplement to the Collected Notes of Li Kuang-ti), 1894 ed., 20 ch., 6 v.

Li Shu 黎澍, *Chin-tai shih lun-ts'ung* 近代史論叢 (Collected Essays of Modern Chinese History), Peking, Hsüeh-hsi Tsa-chih She 學習雜誌社, 1956, 136 p.

Li Yüan-tu 李元度, *Kuo-ch'ao hsien-cheng shih-*

lüeh 國朝先正事略 (Short Biographies of the Late Worthies of the Imperial Dynasty), Hsün-kai Ts'ao-t'ang 循陔草堂 ed., 1866, 60 ch., 24 v.

Liang, Ch'i-ch'ao, *Intellectual Trends in the Ch'ing Period*, trans. into English by Immanuel C.Y. Hsü, Cambridge, Harvard University Press, 1959, 147 p.

Liang, Fang-chung, *The Single-Whip Method of Taxation in China*, trans. into English by Wang Yü-ch'üan. Cambridge, Harvard University Press, 1956, 71 p.

Lin Hui-hsiang 林惠祥, *Chung-kuo min-tsu shih* 中國民族史 (An Ethnological History of China), Shanghai, Commercial Press, 1937, 2 v.

Lin Yüeh-hwa, "The Miao-man peoples of Kweichow," *Harvard Journal of Asiatic Studies* 5:261-345 (1940).

Liu Chia-chü 劉家駒, "Ch'ing-ch'u Han-chün pa-chi ti chao-chien" 清初漢軍八旗的肇建 (Formation of the Eight Chinese Banners during the early Ch'ing), *Ta-lu tsa-chih* 大陸雜誌 (The Continent Magazine) 34.11:13-18 (June 15, 1967); 34.12:17-19 (June 30, 1967).

Liu Hsüan-min 劉選民, "Ch'ing-tai Tung-san sheng i-min yü k'ai-k'en" 清代東三省移民與開墾 (The colonization of the three eastern provinces during the Ch'ing period), *Shih-hsüeh nien-pao*

史學年報 (Historical Annual) 2.5:67-120 (Dec. 1938).

Liu Ts'ui-jung 劉翠溶, "Ch'ing-ch'u Shun-chih K'ang-hsi nien-chien chien-mien fu-shui ti ku-ch'eng" 清初順治康熙年間減免賦稅的過程 ('Land-toll tax reduction and exemption during the reigns of Shun-chih and K'ang-hsi'), *Bulletin of the Institute of History and Philology, Academia Sinica* 37, part 3:757-777 (1967).

Lo Hsiang-lin 羅香林, *Pai-yüeh yüan-liu yü wen-hua* 百越源流與文化 (The Origin of the Yüeh People and Their Culture), Taipei, Chung-hua Ts'ung-shu Wei-yüan Hui 中華叢書委員會, 1955, 312 p.

Lü Liu-liang 呂留良, *T'ien-kai lou ou-p'ing* 天蓋樓偶評 (Commentary on a Collection of Essays), 1672 ed., 36 v.

———, *T'ien-kai lou ssu-shu yü-lu* 天蓋樓四書語錄 (Notes on the Four Books Made in the T'ien-kai Studio), ed. by Chou Tsai-yen 周在延, Nanking, Ta-yeh T'ang 大業堂 ed., prefaced in 1684, 46 ch., 14 v.

Lui, Adam, "The education of the Manchus, China's ruling race (1644-1911)," *Journal of Asian and African Studies* 6.2:126-133 (April 1971).

Ma Ch'i-hua 馬起華, "Ch'ing Shih-tsung chi ch'i chih-shu" 清世宗及其治術 (Emperor

Shih-tsung of the Ch'ing dynasty and his administrative practices), *Tung-fang tsa-chih* 東方雜誌 (Eastern Miscellany) 1.7:82-91 (Jan. 1, 1968).

Ma Feng-ch'en 馬奉琛, "Ch'ing-ch'u Man-han she-hui chin chi ch'ung-t'u chih i-pan" 清初滿漢社會經濟衝突之一班 (Manchu-Chinese social and economic conflicts in early Ch'ing), *Shih-huo Pan-yüeh K'an* 食貨半月刊 4.6:32-39 (Aug. 16, 1936); 4.8:27-34 (Sept. 16, 1936); 4.9:16-34 (Oct. 1, 1936). For an English translation of the article, see E-tu Zen Sun and John de Francis, trans., *Chinese Social History*, Washington, D.C., American Council of Learned Societies, 1956, pp.333-351.

Marsh, Robert M., "Bureaucratic constraints on nepotism in the Ch'ing period," *Journal of Asian Studies*, 19.2:117-133 (Feb. 1960).

Matsui Yoshio 松井義夫, "Shinchō keihi no kenkyū" 清朝經費の研究 ('A study of the expenditures of the Ch'ing dynasty'), *Mantetsu Chōsa Geppō* 滿鐵調查月報 (Bulletin of the Research Bureau of the South Manchuria Railway) 14.11:1-39 (Nov. 1934); 14.12:29-61 (Dec. 1934); 15.1:41-82 (Jan. 1935).

Mayers, William Frederick, *The Chinese Government: A Manual of Chinese Titles Categorically Arranged* and Explained, 3rd and rev. ed., Shanghai, Kelly and Walsh, 1897, 196 p.

Meng Sen 孟森, Ch'ing-ch'u san-ta i-an k'ao-shih 清初三大疑案考釋 (A Critical Study of the Three Disputed Cases during the Early Ch'ing), Peiping, National Peking University, 1934.

―――――, Ch'ing-shih chiang-i 清史講義 (Lectures on the Ch'ing Dynasty), Shanghai, Chung-kuo wen-hua Fu-wu She 中國文化服務社, 1947, 629 p.

Metzger, Thomas A., *The Internal Organization of Ch'ing Bureaucracy: Legal, Normative, and Communication Aspects*, Cambridge, Harvard University Press, 1973, 469 p.

Mitamura Taisuke 三田村泰助, Shinchō zenshi no kenkyū 清朝前史の研究 ('A Study of the Ch'ing Dynasty in the Manchu Period'), Kyoto, Tōyōshi Kenkyūkai 東洋史研究會, 1965, 492 p.

Miyazaki Ichisada 宮崎市定, "Yōsei shuhi yushi kaidai" 雍正硃批諭旨解題 ('Notes on Emperor Yung-cheng's Instructions in Red'), *Tōyōshi Kenkyū* 東洋史研究 (The Journal of Oriental Researches) 15.4:1-32 (March 1957).

―――――, "Yōsei tei ni yoru hōkogin kōan no teishi ni tsuite" 雍正帝による捧工銀捐の傅止について ('On Emperor Yung-cheng's financial reforms'), *ibid.* 22.3:1-24 (Dec. 1963).

Mo Tung-yin 莫東寅, *Man-tsu shih lung-ts'ung* 滿族史論叢 (Collected Essays on the Manchus), Peking, Jen-min Ch'u-pan She 人民出版社, 1958, 205 p.

Naitō Torajirō 内藤虎次郎, *Dokushi sōroku* 讀史叢錄 (Collected Notes on History), Kyoto, Kōbundō 弘文堂, 1929, 531 p.

———, *Shinchō shi tsūron* 清朝史通論 (A Survey of the History of the Ch'ing Dynasty), Kōbundō 弘文堂, 1944, 423 p.

Nakayama Hachirō 中山八郎, "Shinshō Nuruhachi Ōkoku no tōchi kikō" 清初ヌル八チ王國の統治機構 (The ruling machinery of the early Manchu state under Nurhachi), *Hitotsubashi Ronsō* 一橋論叢 (Journal of Hitotsubashi University) 14.2:15-32 (Aug. 1944).

Nishi Junzō 西順藏, "Ryo Banson" 呂晚村 ('Lü Wan-ts'un'), *ibid.* 49.4:1-17 (April 1963).

Otake Fumio 小竹文夫, "Shinchō jidai ni okeru ginsen hika no hendō ni tsukite" 清朝時代に於ける銀錢比價の變動に就きて (Fluctuations of the exchange rates between silver and copper coins under the Ch'ing), *Shina Kenkyū* 支那研究, 22: 283-339 (May 1930).

Ping-heng Chü-shih 秉衡居士, "Ho-hsiang Kuan so-yen" 荷香館瑣言 (Miscellaneous Notes of the Ho-hsiang Studio), *Jen-wen yü-k'an* 人文月刊 (Monthly of Humanities) 1.6:37-45 (March 1931).

Rinji Taiwan Kyūkan Chōsakai 臨時台灣舊慣調查會, *Shinkoku gyōseihō* 清國行政法 (Administrative Laws of the Ch'ing Dynasty), Tōkyō, 1910-1914, 6 kan in 7 v.

Saeki Tomi 佐伯富, "Kōki Yōsei nendai ni okeru Nisshin bōeki" 康熙雍正年代に於ける日清貿易 ('Sino-Japanese trade during the reigns of Emperors K'ang-hsi [康熙] and Yung-cheng [雍正]'), *Tōyōshi Kenkyū* 東洋史研究 (The Journal of Oriental Researches) 16.4:29-69 (March 1958).

―――, "Shindai no jiei ni tsuite—kunshu dokusai ken kenkyū no hitokoma" 清代の侍衛について―君主獨裁權研究の一齣 ('On Shi-wei 侍衛 in Qing dynasty—A study of the despotic power of monarch'), *ibid*. 27.2:38-58.

Sakai Tadao 酒井忠夫, "Kyōshin ni tsuite" 鄉紳について ('Hsiang-shen, the Chinese gentry in the society of Ming and Ch'ing periods'), *Shichō* 史潮 (The Journal of History) 47:1-18 (Dec. 1952).

Shan Shih-k'uei 單士魁, "Ch'ing-tai chün-chi ch'u ti yen-ke, chih-chang, ho chu-yao tang-an" 清代軍機處的沿革, 職掌, 和主要檔案 (Evolution, function, and major archives of the

Grand Council of the Ch'ing dynasty), *Kuang-ming jih-pao* 光明日報 (Kuang-ming Daily News) (July 18, 1957), p.3.

Shan-yin hsien-chih 山陰縣志 (Gazetteer of Shan-yin District), ed. by Chu Wen-han 朱文翰 et al., Shao-hsing Hsien Hsiu-chih Wei-yüan Hui 紹興縣修志委員會, 1936, 30+1 ch., 7 v.

Shen Jen-yüan 沈任遠, "Ch'ing-ch'ao ti Chün-chi ch'u" 清朝的軍機處 (The Grand Council of the Ch'ing), *Chung-yang jih-pao* 中央日報 (Central Daily News), "Hsüeh-jen chou-k'an" 學人週刊, No. 135 (Taipei, Taiwan, Sept. 15, 1959), p.3.

Shih-liao hsün-k'an 史料旬刊 (Historical Materials Published Every Ten Days), compiled and published by the Palace Museum, Peiping, 1930-1931, 40 v.

Shih-sheng 柿生, "Nien Keng-yao tsou-che chih chu-p'i chi ch'i-t'a" 年羹堯奏摺之硃批及其他 (The vermilion endorsement on the memorials of Nien Keng-yao and others concerned), *I-ching* 逸經 (Magazine of Anecdotes) 34:26-28 (July 1937).

Shimizu Morimitsu 清水盛光, "Kyū Shina ni okeru sensei kenryoku no kiso" 舊支那に於ける專制權力の基礎 (The foundation of autocratic power in traditional China), *Mantetsu*

Chōsa Geppō 滿鉄調査月報 (Bulletin of the Research Bureau of the South Manchuria Railway) 17.2:1-60 (Feb. 1937).

Spence, Jonathan D., *Emperor of China: Self-Portrait of K'ang-hsi*, New York, Knopf, 1974, 217 p.

Sprenkel, Sybille van der, *Legal Institutions in Manchu China: A Sociological Analysis*, London, University of London, The Athlone Press, 1962, 178 p.

Sudō Yoshiyuki 周藤吉之, *Shindai Manshū tochi seisaku no Kenkyū—tokuni kichi seisaku o chūshin toshite* 清代滿洲土地政策の研究,特に旗地政策を中心として (A Study of Manchu Land Policy under the Ch'ing Dynasty, with Special Attention to the Policy concerning Banner Lands), Kwawade Shobō 河出書房, 1944, 495 p.

Ta-Ch'ing hui-tien 大清會典 (Collected Statutes of the Ch'ing Dynasty), compiled under the imperial auspices of Ch'ing Shih-tsung 清世宗, 1732 ed., 250 ch., 100 v.

Ta-Ch'ing kuo-shih kung-ch'en lieh-chuan 大清國史功臣列傳 (Biographical Series of Meritorious Officials of the Ch'ing Dynasty), n.p., n.d., 19 v.

Teng, Ssu-yü, *Japanese Studies on Japan and the Far*

Bibliography

  East, Hong Kong, Hong Kong University Press, 1961, 485 p.

_____, and Biggerstaff, Knight, *An Annotated Bibliography of Selected Chinese Reference Works*, Cambridge, Harvard University Press, 1950, 326 p.

T'ien Wen-ching 田文鏡, *Tsung-tu Ho-nan Shan-tung ho-tao hsüan-hua lu* 總督河南山東河道宣化錄 (Experience of Conservancy Administration of the Yellow River and the Canal), Pen-ya ed. 本衙藏版, n.d., 3 ch., 2 v.

_____, *Tsung-tu liang-ho hsüan-hua lu* 總督兩河宣化錄 (Experience of Conservancy Administration of the Yellow River and the Canal), Pen-ya ed. 本衙藏版, n.d., 4 ch., 5 v.

Ting Yen-kung 丁燕公 et al., *Mo-tai huang-ch'ao i-shih* 末代皇朝軼事 (Anecdotes of the Manchu Dynasty), Taipei, Ch'un-ch'iu ch'u-pan She 春秋出版社, 1967, 167 p.

Tsukamoto Shunkō 塚本俊孝, "Yōsei tei no bukkyō kyōdan hihan" 雍正帝の佛教團批判 ('Emperor Yung-cheng's Criticism of Buddhist order'), *Indogaku Bukkyōgaku kenkyū* 印度學佛教學研究 (Journal of Indian and Buddhist Studies) 7.1:158-159 (Dec. 1958).

Tze Yun-peng 左雲鵬, "Lun Ch'ing-tai ch'i-ti ti

hsing-ch'eng, yen-pien chi ch'i hsing-chih" 論清代旗地的形成,演變及其性質 ('The enclosure movement of the Manchus in the Ch'ing dynasty—Its rise, development, and characteristics'), *Lishi Yanjiu* [Li-shih Yen-chiu] 歷史研究 (Journal of Historical Studies) 1: 46-63 (Oct. 1961).

Wang Sung-ju 王嵩儒, *Chang-ku ling-shih* 掌故零拾 (Miscellaneous Notes of Historical Records), Changchun 長春, I-pao Chai Yin-shu Chu 藝寶齋印書局, 1936, 4 ch., 4 v.

Wei Yüan 魏源, *Sheng-wu chi* 聖武記 (Record of the Imperial Military Exploits), Ssu-pu pei-yao 四部備要 ed., 14 ch., 6 v.

Wiens, Herald J., "Some of China's thirty-five million non-Chinese," *Journal of the Hong Kong Branch of the Royal Asiatic Society* 2:54-74 (Aug. 1962).

Wu Ch'ang-shou 吳昌綬, *Ch'ing ti-hsi hou-fei huang-tzu huang-nü ssu-k'ao* 清帝系后妃皇子皇女四考 (Four Studies of the Emperors, Empresses, Concubines, Princes, and Princesses of the Manchu Imperial Family), n.p., 1917, 48 leaves.

Wu-chih 五知, "Hsi-cheng sui-pi chung ti Ch'ing-ch'u shih-liao" 西征隨筆中的清初史料 (Historical information on the early Ch'ing, as seen in the Jottings of a Western

Journey), *I-ching* 逸經 (Magazine of Anecdotes) 21:8-11 (Jan. 1937).

Wu Hsiao-ming 吳孝銘, *Shu-yüan t'i-ming* 樞垣題名 (A List of Grand Councillors), rev. ed., 1884.

Wu, Silas Hsiu-liang 吳秀良, "Nan shu-fang chih chien-chih chi ch'i ch'ien-ch'i chih fa-chan" 南書房之建置及其前期之發展 ('The founding of Nan-shu-fang and its early development'), *Ssu yü yen* 思與言 (Thought and Word) 5.6:6-12 (March 1968).

————, "A note on the proper use of documents for historical studies: A rejoinder," *Harvard Journal of Asiatic Studies*, 32:230-239 (1972).

Wu Yü-nien 吳玉年, "Fu-yüan ta chiang-chün tsou-i po" 撫遠大將軍奏議跋 (A colophon on the memorials of the generalissimo for the pacification of distant lands), *Yü-kung* 禹貢 (The Chinese Historical Geography, Semimonthly Magazine) 6.12:73-74 (Feb. 1937).

Yang Hsüeh-ch'en 楊學琛, "Ch'ing-tai ch'i-ti ti hsing-chih chi ch'i pien-hua" 清代旗地的性質及其變化 (The nature and transformation of Ch'ing banner lands), *Lishi Yanjiu* [Li-shih Yen-chiu] 歷史研究 (Journal of Historical Studies) 3:175-194 (1963).

Yin-hsiang 胤祥, *Chiao-hui yüan i-kao* 交暉園遺稿 (A Work of the Chiao-hui Garden),

Palace ed. 殿本, 1738, 1 ch., 1 v.

Yin Shang-ch'ing 尹尚卿, "Ming-Ch'ing liang-tai ho-fang k'ao-lüeh" 明清兩代河防考略 (The river conservancy work of the Ming and Ch'ing dynasties), *Shih-hsüeh chi-k'an* 史學集刊 (Historical Journal) 1.97-122 (April 1936).

Yonhaengnok sonjip 燕行錄選集 (Selective Notes on China Trips), Seoul, Sung Kyun Kwan University 成均館大學 1960-1962, 2 v.

Yü-t'ang 諭堂, "Ta-i chüeh-mi lu" 大義覺迷錄 (On A Record of Great Tenor for the Deluded), *Jen Chien Shih* 人間世 (The World of Mortals) 30:33-36 (1935).

Yüeh-san 月三, "Ch'ing-tai tsou-che ti hsin kuan-nien" 清代奏摺的新觀念 (New light on the Ch'ing memorials), *Chung-yang jih-pao* 中央日報 (Central Daily News) (Taipei, Taiwan, International Edition, Jan. 11, 1970), p.4.

Index

Abahai. *See* Hong-taiji
academies, private, 203-4, 223, 303
Alingga, 68, 71
Amplified Instructions on the Sacred Edict (*Sheng-yü kuang-hsün*): 197, 207, 210, 218, 229, 298, 306; explained, 190-95
anti-Manchu activities: 11, 92, 197, 198, 208, 223, 228; of Tseng Ching, 215-18, 220, 241
aristocracy: 81, 138-39, 140, 143, 152; in the banners, 11, 14, 16-17, 182-83; factionalism, 82-87, 95-102
Army of the Green Standard, 164
autocracy: defined, 3-4, 82, 94

balance, in Chinese political tradition, 20-21, 155. *See also* Legalism, Manchu-Chinese tension
banner slaves, 226, 229, 230
banner system; 61-62, 84, 86-87, 88-89; aristocracy, 11, 14, 16-17, 182-83; feudalism, 14, 16, 87, 302. *See also* Chap.VII
Board of Civil Appointment, 107, 208
Board of Revenue, 153, 261

Board of War, 152, 153
boundaries, provincial, 300-1
Bouvet, Joachim, Father, 29
Buddhism: Yung-cheng and, 12, 13, 21, 38, 42-48, 155, 229. *See also* Ch'an Buddhism
bureaucracy: and imperial power, 7-8, 155, 215, 304-5; factionalism, 86-88; and Censorate, 115-16; and palace memorial system, 131-32, 135, 305; and Grand Council, 156, 305-6; in the banners, 162, 180-84; criticized by Yung-cheng, 205-6; in non-Han tribes, 285, 294, 296-97

Censorate (*Tu-ch'a yüan*): 130, 172, 208; and palace memorial system, 14, 119-20, 130; powers and duties, 15, 113-19, 130, 172; and Grand Council, 155-56. *See also* Six Offices of Scrutiny, Chap.V
censorial system (*Yü-shih chih-tu*): pre-Ch'ing, 5-6, 9, 114. *See also* Censorate; Six Offices of Scrutiny, Chap.V
censorship, 208. *See also* literary inquisition

493

Cha Ssu-t'ing, 107, 211-13
Ch'an Buddhism: Yung-cheng and, 33-34, 36, 42-45; Shun-chih and, 139-40
Chang Hsi, 218, 220
Chang Kuang-ssu, 292-94
Chang T'ing-yü, 28, 45, 145, 148, 157, 158, 160, 230, 341n.74
Chang Ying, 60, 141
Chao Shen-ch'iao, 70
Ch'en Meng-lei, 74, 101
Ch'eng-Chü li-hsüeh. See School of Principle or Reason
Chia-ch'ing (Emperor Jen-tsung), 155, 348n.46
Chiang Liang-chi, 57-58
Chiang T'ing-hsi, 145, 148, 158, 341n.74, 347n.36, 348n.45
Ch'ien Ch'en-chün, 257, 269
Ch'ien-lung (Emperor Kao-tsung, 12, 45, 57, 95, 156, 179, 220
Ch'ien Ming-shih, 210-11
Chien-mu pien-i lu (Criticism of Buddhist Heresies), 33, 44
chin-shih degree, 130, 192, 200-2, 206, 212, 217
Ch'in-ting chih-chung ch'eng-hsien (Historical Examples of the Mean), 41, 43
Chinese language, 28, 166, 167, 173, 174
Chinese-Manchu tension. See Manchu-Chinese tension
Ch'ing-shih (History of the Ch'ing Dynasty), 148, 158
Christianity, in China, 48-50
Chu Hsi, 188
Chu-p'i yü-chih (Vermilion Endorsements and Edicts), 13, 236, 268

Chu Shih, 145, 149, 219, 240, 347n.35
Chu T'ien-pao, 65, 70-71
Chu Yüan-chang, 5, 10
chü-jen degree, 140, 202, 206, 207
Chün-chi ch'u. See Grand Council
circuit inspectors, 133
civil service examinations, 9, 114, 206, 207, 211
clan system, in the banners, 167-68, 170
cliques: explained, 81-82. See also factionalism
colonization, military, 299-300
commerce, domestic, 269-72
common people: improved status, 19, 22, 266-69; tax burden, 246, 250, 251, 263
Confucianism: 204, 280, 283; an orthodox philosophy, 4-5, 7-8, 20-21, 36-39, 92-93, 187-97; in Yung-cheng's ideology, 13, 33, 36-43, 45-48, 155; tension with Legalism, 115, 194-95, 205-6, 254, 262, 286, 292. See also Neo-Confucianism
Constancin, Father: quoted, 13
copper, 289-90, 299
corruption, official, 18, 116, 124, 205, 242-43, 246-47, 250, 259-60
court letters (*t'ing-chi*), 15-16, 145-46, 148, 155
customary gratuities (*kuei-fei*), 248-54, 257-58, 261-62
customs offices, 252

Dorgon, 11, 64, 84
du Halde, Jean Baptiste: quoted, 34-35

Index

Dzungars: war against, 12-13, 144, 146, 149-50, 269

economic conditions, 266, 268-72
education: 10, 20; of Manchu princes, 28-29; reform of, 200-3, 303. See also schools.
Eleuths, 31, 53, 61, 102
elites, 81-82, 306-7. See also aristocracy, bureaucracy, gentry
equality (*p'ing*): Legalist view of, 40-41, 228-29
ethnic minorities, 20, 273. See also Lolo people, Miao people, Yao people
eunuchs, 10, 37, 127-28, 137, 139-40
examinations, civil service, 9, 114, 206, 207, 211

factionalism: and autocracy, 81-82, 88, 93-94; early Ch'ing, 84-85, 89-90; Yung-cheng's opposition, 82-84, 85-88, 90-92, 118, 302-4; of bureaucrats, 208, 214. See also On Factions
Fang, Maurus, 49
father, authority of, 189, 195
fees, meltage (*huo-hao*), 248, 250-62, 267
feudalism: in the banners, 14, 16, 87, 163, 167-68, 169-70, 302; in non-Han tribes, 286-87
Filial Piety Canon (*Hsiao-ching*), 36, 195-97, 220
flood control, 19, 236-37, 239
Friedrich, Carl J., 3, 29
Fu-ch'üan, 61, 321n.9
Fu-p'eng, 45, 349n.42

Funinggan, 145, 150

gentry, 18, 21, 231-35, 246, 247, 270, 307
Giles, Herbert A., 95
granaries, public, 258, 267
Grand Council (*Chün-chi ch'u*): 14, 15-16, 21, 136, 158-60; origin, 144-47; staff and functions, 148-51; and Grand Secretariat, 152-55; and Censorate, 155-56; and palace memorials, 155-57; ethnic balance in, 158-60
Grand Secretariat (*Nei-ko*), 16, 52, 116, 137-38, 145; and Grand Council, 21, 148, 152-55, 160
gratuities, customary (*kuei-fei*), 248-54, 257-58, 261-62
Green Standard, Army of the, 164

Ha Yuan-sheng, 292, 348n.42
Han Fei: 41; quoted, 104-5
headmen, tribal (*t'u-ssu*), 20, 21, 280-87, 295-96
Ho Ch'o, 67, 76, 143
Ho Kuo-tsung, 237
Ho-shen, 156
Ho Shih-chi, 132, 292
Hong-taiji (Emperor Tai-tsung), 60, 84, 85, 89, 114, 116, 120-21, 138-39, 152, 158
Hsiao-ching (Filial Piety Canon), 36, 195-97, 220
Hsiao-kung, Empress: 312n.1; quoted, 75
Hsieh Chi-shih, 130-31; 214-15, 221, 224
Hsin-hsüeh. See School of the Mind or Intuition
Hsiung Tz'ü-li, 60, 188

Hsü Ch'ien-hsüeh, 85, 233
Hsü Jung, 226, 358n.29
Hsüan, Emperor: 120; quoted, 316n.50
Huang Ping, 264
huo-hao. *See* meltage fees

I-cheng ch'u. *See* Office for Administrative Deliberations
inertia, in Chinese government, 135, 161
Inner Court, 137-43
inspectors: circuit, 133; of morale (*kuan-feng chang-su shih*), 197-99, 213
irrigation, 19, 237-40, 242

Jabina, 145, 149-50
Jen-tsung. *See* Chia-ch'ing
Jesuits, 27, 48-50, 59, 67, 99, 139-40
justice (*kung*), Legalist view of, 40-41, 228-29

K'ang-hsi (Emperor Sheng-tsu): 11, 15, 17, 18, 27, 29, 49-50, 58, 60, 61, 72-73, 74-75, 78-80, 124, 188-89; choice of successor, 51, 53-54, 64-66, 70-73; and Manchu-Chinese tension, 116-17, 157-58; orthodoxy, 188-89; Sacred Edict, 190-95
Kao Shih-ch'i, 141, 233
Kao-tsung. *See* Ch'ien-lung
Khoshotes: war against, 103, 105, 164, 269
Ku-chin t'u-shu chi-ch'eng (Synthesis of Books and Illustrations of Ancient and Modern Times), 28, 74, 101, 142
Kuan-feng chang-su shih. *See* inspectors of morale
kuei-fei. *See* gratuities

labor service levy, 19, 247, 248, 262, 263-66, 267
land: reclamation, 178-80, 236, 240-44, 288; ownership, 241, 243; taxation, 247, 262-65, 267
law, Legalist view of, 40-41
Legalism: 4; in Yung-cheng's ideology, 33, 36, 39-42, 91-93; and tension with Confucianism, 115, 194-95, 205-6, 254, 262, 286, 292
legitimacy: 190; and Yung-cheng, 40, 51-60, 83, 92-93, 190
Li Fu, 31-32, 221
Li Hui, 198, 224, 358n.29
Li Tsung-t'ung, 144
Li Wei, 106, 221, 233-36, 253, 304
Li Wei-chün, 253, 264, 330n.25
literary inquisition, 18-20, 198, 204-20, 222
Literary Office, 138-39
literati: imperial control, 18, 193-95, 198, 203, 204, 221, 306. *See also* bureaucracy, gentry, Chap. VIII
Liu-k'o chi-shih chung. *See* Six Offices of Scrutiny
local administration, 6-7, 192
Lolo people: 20; culture, 273-78; location, 278-79; administration, 280-88; imperial policy, 285, 291-300; sinicization, 291, 297; uprisings, 293, 298
loyalty, 189, 196, 273
Lu Sheng-nan, 213-15
Lü Liu-liang, 216-17, 218, 219-20
Lu Lung-chi, 252

Index

Lungkodo: 52, 62, 95, 97, 103; supported Yung-cheng, 76, 79, 90; faction of, 86, 87-88, 107-8; degraded, 108-10

Maci, 62, 68, 76, 97
Mai-chu, 291, 292, 295
Mailla (Jesuit): quoted, 77, 105
Manchu-Chinese tension: 141-42, 304; in Censorate, 15, 114, 116-17; in Grand Council, 16, 157-60; and the banners, 165-66. See also anti-Manchu activities
Manchu language, 28, 167, 174-75
Manchus: sinicization of, 164-65, 223-24
Mandate of Heaven, 4, 219
Manggultai, 84, 139
Marsai, 145, 348n.42
mean (*chung*), principle of, 40, 41
meltage fees (*huo-hao*), 248, 250-62, 267
memorials, 124, 125, 129. See also palace memorials
Meng Sen, 52, 56, 109
Miao people: 20; uprisings, 144, 269, 293, 298-99, survey, 273-77; location, 278-79; administration, 280-88; imperial policy, 285-91; sinicization, 291, 297
migration of population, 243-45
military colonization, 299-300
Ming dynasty, 5, 6, 7, 8, 10, 107, 120, 121, 137, 188, 189
missionaries, 48-50
Mongols, 162, 163, 164, 175. See also Dzungars
mou, 239, 242, 367n.54

Mourão, João, Father, 48, 50, 98-99

Nan Shu-fang. See Southern Imperial Study
Nei-ko. See Grand Secretariat
Neo-Confucianism, 5, 10, 13, 18, 36-37, 188-97. See also Confucianism
Nien Keng-yao: 52, 99, 230; supported Yung-cheng, 76-77, 79, 99; faction of, 86-88, 102-6, 108-9; degraded, 94, 106-7
No-ch'in, 348n.42, 349n.50
No-min, 108, 253-55
Nurhaci, 59, 85, 138, 163, 322n.26

O-er-t'ai: 38, 45, 106, 145, 238; influence of, 160, 235-36; land reclamation, 244, 300; and non-Han tribes, 289-95
Oboi, 11, 85, 89
office, sale of, 18, 21, 207-8, 271
Office for Administrative Deliberations (*I-cheng ch'u*), 16, 143, 152, 160, 305
Office of Audit, 252
Office of Military Strategy (*Chün-chi fang*), 147
Offices of Scrutiny. See Six Offices of Scrutiny
Olandai, 62, 86, 94, 330 n.39
On Factions (*P'eng-tang lun*), 90-92, 176, 207, 210, 222
orthodoxy, 4-5, 7-8, 20-21, 36-39, 92-93, 187-97. See also Confucianism, Neo-Confucianism

Ou-yang Hsiu, 92
outcasts, 20, 21, 226-31, 242
Outer Court, 136-37

palace memorials (*tsou-che*): defined, 119, 124, 125, 311n.30; endorsements, 119, 129; early history, 119-24; and control of bureaucracy, 120, 123, 131-32, 134-35; transmission, 123, 127-29, 134; reporters, 125-27; and autocracy, 130-35; and censorial system, 130-31; and Grand Council, 155-57
Pedrini, Theodore, Father, 28
P'eng-tang lun. See On Factions
"people of mean occupations," 19-20, 21, 226-31
Po Lü Liu-liang ssu-shu chiang (A Refutation of Lü Liu-liang's Comments on the Four Books), 197, 219-20
population: growth, 241; migration, 243-45; data, 246-47
premiership (*tsai-hsiang chih-tu*), 5, 9, 10
prices, commodity, 268
provincial government, 258-60, 262

reclamation of land, 178-80, 236, 240-44, 288
regionalism, 133-34
religions, 42-43, 45-46, 48-50
Revolt of the Three Feudatories, 11, 121-22, 164, 285
Ripa, Matteo, Father: quoted, 69, 80
Rites Controversy, 49
river conservation, 19, 236-37
Rosso, Antonio S., 30

Sacred Edict (*Sheng-yü*): 36, 188; quoted, 190-91
salaries of officials, 251-52, 258-61
sale of office, 18, 21, 207-8, 271
San-fan. See Revolt of the Three Feudatories
Schall von Bell, Adam, Father, 139
School of Principle or Reason (*Ch'eng-Chü li-hsüeh*), 5, 13, 18, 37, 188-90, 193, 197
School of the Mind or Intuition (*Hsin-hsüeh*), 5, 18, 37, 43-44
schools: 17, 28-29, 223, 298; textbooks for, 19, 172-75, 188, 192-93; government support and control, 203-4, 221, 223, 303
secret societies, 46, 223
Shang-yü nei-ko (Edicts and Decrees to the Grand Secretariat), 52, 56-57
Shang-yü pa-ch'i (Edicts and Decrees for the Eight Banners), 52, 56-57, 171
Shen Chin-ssu, 252, 254
Sheng-tsu. See K'ang-hsi
Sheng-yü. See Sacred Edict
Sheng-yü kuang-hsün. See Amplified Instructions on the Sacred Edict
Shih I-chih, 147, 253
Shih-lu. See Veritable Records of Successive Reigns of the Ch'ing Dynasty
Shih-tsu. See Shun-chih
Shih-tsung. See Yung-cheng
Shih Wen-ch'o, 253
shu-yüan. See academies
Shun-chih (Emperor Shih-tsu): 11, 15, 17, 18, 158; advisers, 42,

139-40; and factions, 84, 89
sinicization: of Manchus, 164-65, 223-24; of non-Han tribes, 291, 297
Six Offices of Scrutiny (*Liu-k'o chi-shih chung*), 15, 114-19. See also Censorate
slavery, 229-31, 266
Songgotu, 60, 61, 65, 86, 89
Southern Imperial Study (*Nan Shu-fang*), 38, 123, 140-43, 150, 154
succession, imperial: 60, 96, 182; contest over; K'ang-hsi period, 60-75; Yung-cheng's policy, 95-96
Sunju, 145, 150
Sunu, 48-49, 98

Ta-Ch'ing li-ch'ao shih-lu. See Veritable Records of Successive Reigns of the Ch'ing Dynasty
Ta-i chüeh-mi lu (A Record of Great Tenor for the Deluded), 57-58, 197, 199, 217-20
taboo words, 208, 211-12
T'ai-tsung. See Hong-taiji
tan-min. See Tanka people
T'ang Pin, 60, 188
Tanka people, 226, 227-28, 229, 230, 242
Taoism, 12, 13, 21, 33, 36, 42-43, 45-48, 155
Taxation Case of 1661, 233, 247
taxes: reform, 19, 245, 247-48, 252-56, 263-65, 267; evasion, 232, 243, 246-48; remission, 240, 268-69; defects, 245-52
Thomas, A., 48, 99
Three Feudatories, Revolt of, 11, 89, 121-22, 164, 285

T'ien Min-ju, 288, 295
T'ien Wen-ching, 106, 130, 221, 232, 236, 237, 254, 304
ting, 245, 246, 262-63
t'ing-chi. See court letters
totalitarianism, 221, 223
tsai-hsiang chih-tu. See premiership
Ts'ai Shih-shan, 358n.29, 358n.34
Ts'ai T'ing, 76, 211
Tseng Ching, 52, 215-20, 241
tsou-che. See palace memorials
tsou-che chih-tu. See palace memorials
Tsung-ching lu ta-kang (An Annotated Outline of the Mirror for Ch'an Buddhism), 44
Tu-ch'a yüan. See Censorate
t'u ssu. See headmen
Tung-hua lu (Tung-hua Records), 52, 57-58
T'ung Kuo-wei, 62, 86
Tung-lin movement, 37, 189

Veritable Records of Successive Reigns of the Ch'ing Dynasty, 28, 52-53, 55-59, 107

Wang Ching-ch'i, 208-10
Wang Hsien-ch'ien, 57-58
Wang Hung-hsü, 122, 142, 203
Wang Kuo-tung, 198, 358, n.29
Wang Shan, 65, 70
Wang Yang-ming, 37
Weber, Max, 16
well-field system (*ching-t'ien*), 18, 178-80, 218, 242
Wen-chüeh, 45
women, position of, 189
Wu, Emperor, 4, 5, 6, 8-9
Wu Hsiang, 219
Wu Liang-fu, 140

Yang Ming-shih, 38-39, 253
Yang Tsung-jen, 252-53
Yao people: 20; survey, 273-78; location, 278-79; government, 280-300
Yen-hsin, 76-77, 100, 102
Yen-shou, 43, 44
Yin-chen. *See* Yung-cheng
Yin-chih: 28, 30-31; in struggle for throne, 68, 71-75, 76, 79; his faction, 85, 95; degraded, 101
Yin-e, 67, 72, 97
Yin-hsiang: 31, 72-73, 95, 101, 157, 341n.74; in Grand Council, 97, 145, 148; irrigation projects, 238-39
Yin-jeng: 89; heir apparent, 27, 53, 54, 59-70, 72-73
Yin-li, 31, 45, 56, 72-73, 95, 171
Yin-lu, 31, 45, 72-73, 95, 171
Yin-shih: 27-28, 30, 89; in struggle for throne, 61, 63, 65, 67-68, 72-73
Yin-ssu: 30; in struggle for throne, 31, 62, 63, 65, 67-69, 72-73, 75, 77-78; his faction, 82, 85, 95, 96; degraded, 97-98
Yin-t'ang: 31; and Jesuits, 48-49, 98-99; in struggle for throne, 67-68, 72-73, 79; faction of, 82, 85, 95, 97; degraded, 98-100
Yin-t'i: 30, 31, 102, 103, 312n.1; in struggle for throne, 51, 53-54, 67, 68, 71, 72-73, 77-79; faction of, 82, 85, 95, 97; degraded, 100-1
Yü-hsuen yü-lu (A Collection of Selected Buddhist and Taoist Sayings), 33, 43, 44, 45
Yü-shih chih-tu. *See* censorial system
Yueh Chung-ch'i, 106, 164, 218, 244, 293, 297
Yung-cheng (Emperor Shih-tsung): publications, 13, 33, 41, 43, 44, 45, 52, 171, 190-7, 236; education, 28-29; quoted, 32, 38, 91; religious beliefs, 42-50. *See also* balance, Buddhism, bureaucracy, Ch'an Buddhism, Confucianism, factionalism, Legalism, legitimacy, orthodoxy, palace memorials, succession

Zen. *See* Ch'an Buddhism